Listing the Law

Medieval Law and Its Practice

Edited by

John Hudson (*University of St Andrews*)

VOLUME 46

The titles published in this series are listed at *brill.com/mlip*

Listing the Law

The Legal Glossary of Dubhaltach Mac Fhirbhisigh

By

Charlene M. Eska

BRILL

LEIDEN | BOSTON

Cover illustration: Page 5 of Dubhaltach Mac Fhirbisigh's seventeenth-century legal glossary, Trinity College, Dublin MS 1401, *olim* H.5.30. The image is reproduced by permission of The Board of Trinity College Dublin.

The Library of Congress Cataloging-in-Publication Data is available online at https://catalog.loc.gov
LC record available at https://lccn.loc.gov/2026935213

Typeface for the Latin, Greek, and Cyrillic scripts: "Brill". See and download: brill.com/brill-typeface.

ISSN 1873-8176
ISBN 978-90-04-54144-3 (hardback)
ISBN 978-90-04-75567-3 (e-book)
DOI 10.1163/9789004755673

This book is printed on acid-free paper and produced in a sustainable manner.

For Nick, yet again

Contents

Preface

How I came to be working with this text is a story unto itself. In October 2017, while I was working on parts of my last two books in the old manuscripts reading room at Trinity College, Dublin, I had called up the paper manuscript TCD MS 1401 [H.5.30] on a whim so I would have something to look at while waiting for the humidity to be at the appropriate level so that I could examine the vellum manuscripts that I had ordered. I took one look at the rough and worn pages and I was fascinated, hoping to be able to return to it at a later date.

Over the course of the next several years, I worked on parts of the manuscript in between other projects. It was not until I was generously awarded a Dean's Faculty Fellowship by the College of Liberal Arts and Human Sciences at Virginia Tech for spring 2021 that I was able to begin work on the text in earnest.

Editing any text is not an easy task, especially when said text is a legal glossary which used several sources which are no longer extant and some sources which do not yet have modern editions or translations. Those factors, combined with the fact that many of the words in the glossary are not to be found in *eDIL*, make the task even more challenging. As the field moves forward, it is inevitable that future scholars will refine the translations, find more sources, create separate studies, etc. As more critical editions of texts are created, it is hoped that this glossary will instigate a two-way dialogue between Dubhaltach and modern editors. This is especially true of the *Bretha Nemed Dédenach* material because, as it is argued herein, Dubhaltach had access to a glossed version of the text which is no longer extant (Breatnach 2016: 130). It is hoped that this small contribution to wider scholarship will help generate future studies concerning the early Irish laws, history, and lexicography.

Acknowledgments

It is the rare person who writes a book in isolation. I am grateful not to be one of them. This project has benefited from the support of many people and institutions.

Portions of this book have been read by Joseph F. Eska and Paul Russell. Their comments and suggestions have greatly improved the content and presentation of this book. I should also like to offer my sincerest thanks to the two anonymous readers, both of whom generously offered many detailed suggestions for improvements. I am very grateful for the time and care they took reading an earlier draft of this manuscript. Any errors are, of course, my own.

This project has benefited enormously from the support of a Guggenheim Fellowship in academic year 2022–2023. This prestigious fellowship awarded me the resources necessary to be able to devote a full year to working on the glossary, and I am very grateful for their generous support of this project. A Niles Research Grant and Dean's Faculty Fellowship from the College of Liberal Arts and Human Sciences and resources from the Department of English at Virginia Polytechnic Institute & State University provided me funding and the time away from teaching and service obligations to devote myself to research and writing.

I am grateful to the Department of Anglo-Saxon, Norse and Celtic at the University of Cambridge for status as an Honorary Research Associate for parts of 2022 through 2024. They provided a warm, welcoming, and intellectually stimulating home during my time in Cambridge.

A special note of thanks is due to Alice Taylor-Griffiths for correcting my primitive Excel spreadsheet of Eugene O'Curry's transcription and turning it into a professional spreadsheet. Special thanks are also due to Laura Jensen for editorial assistance. The schematic diagrams of the manuscript pages were drawn by Paul Russell; I am very grateful for his willingness to take on this task.

I should also like to thank Deborah Hayden for providing assistance with the section concerning women's health. The book has benefited tremendously from her expertise in medieval Irish medicine.

I am grateful to the staff at the National Library of Scotland, Weston Library, Oxford, the University of Cambridge Library, The British Library, and Trinity College, Dublin for allowing me access to manuscripts and research materials. In particular, I should like to thank Aisling Lockhart, Reading Room Services Executive, at Trinity College, Dublin for her patient assistance during my many visits to consult manuscripts.

Parts of this book are based on papers given at: the Department of Anglo-Saxon, Norse and Celtic, University of Cambridge (2023); the IONA conference, King's College (2024); the Harvard Celtic Colloquium (2025), the Modern Language Association (2026), and the Celtic Studies Association of North America (2022, 2025).

Throughout this process Marcella Mulder and John Hudson have guided the book from proposal to publication. A book of this nature relies on expert typesetting, and I wish to thank Marlou Meems for their expertise.

On a personal note, I should like to thank Sharon Paice MacLeod, Dorothy Africa, Sneha Rajan, and Cinder. My mother, stepfather, and brother have been unwavering in their support. My family has put up with more monologues about Dubhaltach than I am certain they really wanted to hear; I thank them for their patience and understanding. By the end of this project, I suspect that even my two cats had become tired of hearing about it. The largest debt of gratitude, however, is owed to my son, Nicholas Morgan Shipman; thank you for everything.

CME
Blacksburg, VA

Abbreviations

AL	*Ancient Laws and Institutes of Ireland*, 6 vols., eds. W.N. Hancock et al. (Dublin, 1865–1901).
BL	British Library
CCIH	Liam Breatmach, *A Companion to the Corpus Iuris Hibernici* (Dublin, 2005).
CGH	*Corpus genealogiarum Hiberniae*, ed. M.A. O'Brien (Dublin, 1962).
CIH	*Corpus Iuris Hibernici*, 6 vols., ed. D.A. Binchy (Baile Átha Cliath, 1978).
Comm.	Commentary
DDC	*Dúil Dromma Cetta* https://www.asnc.cam.ac.uk/irishglossaries/
DG	Dubhaltach's Glossary
eDIL	*eDIL 2019: An Electronic Dictionary of the Irish Language*, based on the *Contributions to a Dictionary of the Irish Language* (Dublin, 1913–1976) (www.dil.ie 2019.)
EMI	Early Modern Irish (c. 1200–1600)
Fél.	*Félire Óengusso Céli Dé: The Martyrology of Oengus the Culdee*, ed. Whitley Stokes (London, 1905).
GEIL	Fergus Kelly, *A Guide to Early Irish Law* (Dublin, 1988) (2009 reprint with updated bibliography).
GOI	Rudolf Thurneysen, *A Grammar of Old Irish*, rev. ed. and trans. D.A. Binchy and Osborn Bergin (Dublin, 1946).
Ir. Gl.	*Irish Glosses: A mediaeval tract on Latin declension, with examples explained in Irish, to which are added The Lorica of Gildas with the gloss thereon, and a selection of glosses from the Book of Armagh*, ed. Whitley Stokes (Dublin, 1860).
Lec. Gl.	*The Lecan Glossary*, ed. Whitley Stokes, *Archiv für celtische Lexikographie* 1 (Halle, 1900), pp. 50–100.
LEIA	*Lexique étymologique de l'irlandais ancien*, ed. J. Vendryes, E. Bachellery, and P.-Y. Lambert (Dublin, 1959–).
ME	Middle English (c. 1100–1500)
Met. Dind.	*The Metrical Dindsenchas*, ed. and trans. E.J. Gwynn (Dublin, 1903–1935).
Metr. Gl.	*On the Metrical Glossaries of the Mediaeval Irish*, ed. Whitley Stokes, *Beiträge zur Kunde der indogermanischen Sprachen* 29 (1893): 1–120.
MG	*A Medieval Glossary*, ed. A.I. Pearson, *Ériu* 13 (1942): 61–87.
MI	Middle Irish (c. 900–1200)
Mod. Ir.	Modern Irish (c. 1600–present)
NLI	National Library of Ireland
O'Cl	*O'Clery's Glossary*, ed. Arthur W.K. Miller, *Revue celtique* 4 (1879–1880): 349–428, 479–480, and 5 (1881–1883): 1–69.

O'Dav *O'Davoren's Glossary*, ed. Whitley Stokes, *Archiv für celtische Lexikographie* 2 (Halle, 1904), pp. 197–504.

O'Don. Suppl. "Supplement to O'Reilly's Irish-English Dictionary", ed. John O'Donovan. In: Edward O'Reilly, *An Irish-English Dictionary*, rev. ed. (Dublin, 1864), pp. 557–725.

OI Old Irish (c. 600–900)

OM *O'Mulconry's Glossary*, ed. Pádraic Moran. In *De Origine Scoticae Linguae (O'Mulconry's Glossary)* (Turnhout, 2019).

SC *Sanas Cormaic* https://www.asnc.cam.ac.uk/irishglossaries/

SM *Senchas Már*

Stowe Gl. *Stowe Glossaries*, ed. Whitely Stokes, *Archiv für celtische Lexikographie* 3 (Halle, 1907), pp. 268–289.

TC *Tecosca Cormaic*, ed. and trans. Kuno Meyer. In *The Instructions of King Cormac Mac Airt* (Dublin, 1909).

TCD Trinity College, Dublin

Grammatical Abbreviations

acc. accusative
act. active
adj. adjective
art. article
dat. dative
f. feminine
fut. future
gen. genitive
impf. imperfect
impv. imperative
ind. indicative
indep. independent
juss. jussive
m. masculine
n. neuter
nom. nominative
part. participle
pass. passive
poss. possessive
pl. plural
pres. present

pret.	preterite
pron.	pronoun
rel.	relative
sg.	singular
subj.	subjunctive
vn.	verbal noun

Irish Legal Texts Cited in This Volume

For those not familiar with the medieval Irish legal corpus, what follows is a list of the Irish law texts referenced herein, whether in the introductory material, as part of the edited Irish legal material itself, or within the textual notes. Not all of the texts below have been critically edited. For those that have, the full reference for each text can be found in the Printed and Digital Sources section of the Bibliography. Both *GEIL* 264–286 and *CCIH* 160–321 contain more detailed descriptions and bibliographic information for these and other early Irish legal texts. Both of these sources and *Córus Bésgnai* 326–327 have been used to provide the translations of the titles below. Texts which are from the *Senchas Már* 'Great Tradition' collection of legal texts are listed with a number reflecting their textual order within the collection; see *CCIH* 268–314; and Breatnach 1996b.

Old Irish Title	English Meaning	Main Content
Aidbred	'Claiming'	A tract concerning the recovery of lost or stolen property, primarily livestock.
Anfuigell	'Wrong Judgement'	A tract concerning a range of legal scenarios difficult to judge or where judgement is hindered by a lack of evidence.
Ántéchtae (*Breth*)	'Splendid Propriety (of Judgements)'	A tract concerning a wide range of topics, including satire, procedure, and arson.
Bechbretha (*SM* 21)	'Bee-Judgements'	A tract concerning bee-keeping.
Bretha Cairdi (*SM* 31)	'Treaty Judgements'	A fragmentary text concerning treaties.
Bretha Crólige (*SM* 33)	'Judgements on Blood-Lyings'	A tract concerning sick-maintenance.
Bretha Comaithchesa (*SM* 10)	'Judgements of Neighborhood'	A tract concerning neighborhood responsibilities, mainly in respect to land management and livestock offenses.
Bretha Déin Chécht (*SM* 34)	'The Judgements of Dían Cécht'	A tract concerning personal injury and the payments due to physicians.
Bretha Éitgid	'Judgements of Inadvertence'	A tract concerning accidental injury and death.

(*cont.*)

Old Irish Title	English Meaning	Main Content
Bretha for Catṡlechtaib (SM 29)	'Judgements on Categories of Cats'	A fragmentary tract concerning cats.
Bretha for Conṡlechtaib (SM 30)	'Judgements on Categories of Dogs'	A fragmentary tract concerning dogs.
Bretha for Macṡlechtaib (SM 28)	'Judgements on Categories of Sons'	A fragmentary tract concerning 'children, inheritance and paternity'[1]
Bretha im Ḟuillemu Gell	'Judgements Concerning Pledge-Interests'	A tract on pledges.
Bretha Nemed Dédenach	'The Last *Bretha Nemed*'[2]	A tract on the privileges of poets.
Bretha Nemed Toísech	'The First *Bretha Nemed*'	A tract concerning the church.
Cáin Aicillne (SM 6)	'The Law of Base Clientship'	A tract concerning base clientship.
Cáin Domnaig	'The Law of Sunday'	A tract concerning activities which are not allowed to be performed on Sundays.
Cáin Ḟuithirbe	'The Law of Fuithirbe'	A fragmentary text concerning offenses.
Cáin Íarraith (SM 4)	'The Law of Fosterage-Fee'	A fragmentary text concerning the regulation of fosterage.
Cáin Lánamna (SM 7)	'The Law of Couples'	A tract concerning the number of legally recognized unions and the division of household goods in the event of divorce.
Cáin Ṡóerraith (SM 5)	'The Law of Noble Fief'	A tract concerning free clientship.
Cethairṡlicht Athgabálae (SM 2)	'The Four Divisions of Distraint'	A tract concerning distraint.
Coibnes Uisci Thairidne (SM 22)	'Kinship of Conducted Water'	A tract concerning the regulations for conducting water over private property to power a mill.
Cóic Conara Fugill	'The Five Paths of Judgement'	A tract concerning legal procedure.
Córus Aithni (SM 45)	'The Ordering of Depositing'	A fragmentary text on deposits.
Córus Bésgnai (SM 8)	'The Arrangement of Discipline'	A tract concerning the obligations of the church and the laity to each other.
Córus Fine	'The Regulation of Kindred'	A tract concerning the kin-group.

1 *CCIH* 300.

2 The phrase *bretha nemed* means 'judgements of privileged persons'.

(*cont.*)

Old Irish Title	English Meaning	Main Content
Córus Íubaile	'The Ordering of Limitation Periods'	A fragmentary tract concerning contracts.
Críth Gablach	'Branched Purchase'	A legal text concerning status.
Di Astud Chirt 7 Dligid (*SM* 14)	'On the Establishing of Right and Entitlement'	A tract concerning a wide variety of topics, including the establishment of lawful ownership, inheritance, kingship, ordeals, and legal entry.
Di Astud Chor	'On the Securing of Contracts'	A tract concerning contract law.
Di Brethaib Gaire (*SM* 42)	'Concerning Judgements on Maintenance'	A fragmentary tract on the care of those physically or mentally impaired.
Di Choimét Dligthech (*SM* 2a)	'On Lawful Impounding'	A fragmentary tract on impounding property.
Di Gnímaib Gíall (*SM* 3)	'On the Functions of Hostages'	A fragmentary tract on hostages.
Din Techtugud (*SM* 11)	'On Taking Possession'	A tract concerning legal entry.
Díre-tract (*SM* 19)	'On Compensation'	A fragmentary tract on compensation or offenses against family members and dependents.
Dúil	'Book, Collection?'	The text itself is not extant, but several sources refer to the text by name.
Dúilchinni (*SM* 43)	'Renumerations for Manufactured Articles'	A fragmentary text concerning payments for manufactured items.
Dúil Roscadach	'Book of Aphorisms'	The text itself is not extant, but several sources refer to the text by name.
Fidbretha (*SM* 41)	'Tree-Judgements'	A fragmentary text on damage to trees and bushes.
Findṡruth Fíthail	'The Fair Stream of Fíthal'	A wisdom text.
Fuidir-tract (*SM* 16)	'Tract on the Semi-freeman'	A text on the rights and obligations of the semi-free.
Gúbretha Caratniad	'The False Judgements of Caratnia'	A "collection of exceptions to general rules."[3]

3 *CCIH* 262.

(*cont.*)

Old Irish Title	English Meaning	Main Content
Midbae Breth	'The Middle Way of Judgements'	Nothing is known about this tract.
Muirbretha (*SM* 38)	'Sea-Judgements'	A tract on maritime law.
Osbretha	'Deer-Judgements'	Fragments concerning deer.
Pseudo-Historical Prologue to the Senchas Már[4]		A text concerning the origins of how the law was transmitted.
Recholl Breth (*SM* 13)	'Shroud of Judgements'	A tract on contractual faults.
Róda, cis lir-side?	'Roads, how many are there?'	A tract on the different categories of roads.
Sechtae (*SM* 9)	'Heptads'	A text containing legal material on a wide range of topics arranged in groups of seven.
Slicht Othrusa (*SM* 32)	'Regulation of Sick-Maintenance'	A text on sick-maintenance.
Status-tract (*SM* 26)[5]		A fragmentary text on non-ecclesiastical social grades.
Tecosca Cormaic	'The Instructions of Cormac'	A wisdom text on the duties and characteristics of a good king.
Tosach Bésgnai	'The Beginnings of Discipline'	A text in *roscad* concerned with "the distrubution of a woman's estate."[6]
Tract on Marriage and Divorce (*SM* 40)[7]		A fragmentary text on marriage and divorce law.
Uraicecht Becc	'Small Primer'	A text on status.
Uraicecht Cóel	'Slender Primer'	A fragmentary text covering a variety of topics such as theft, arson, defective goods, and absconding from the law.
Uraicecht na Ríar	'The Primer of the Stipulations'	A text primarily concerned with the seven grades of poets.

4 The text does not have a known title in Irish.
5 The text does not have a known title in Irish.
6 *CCIH* 293.
7 The text does not have a known title in Irish.

Plates

Page 1 of Dubhaltach Mac Fhirbisigh's seventeenth-century legal glossary, Trinity College, Dublin MS 1401, *olim* H.5.30

 | DOI:10.1163/9789004755673_002A

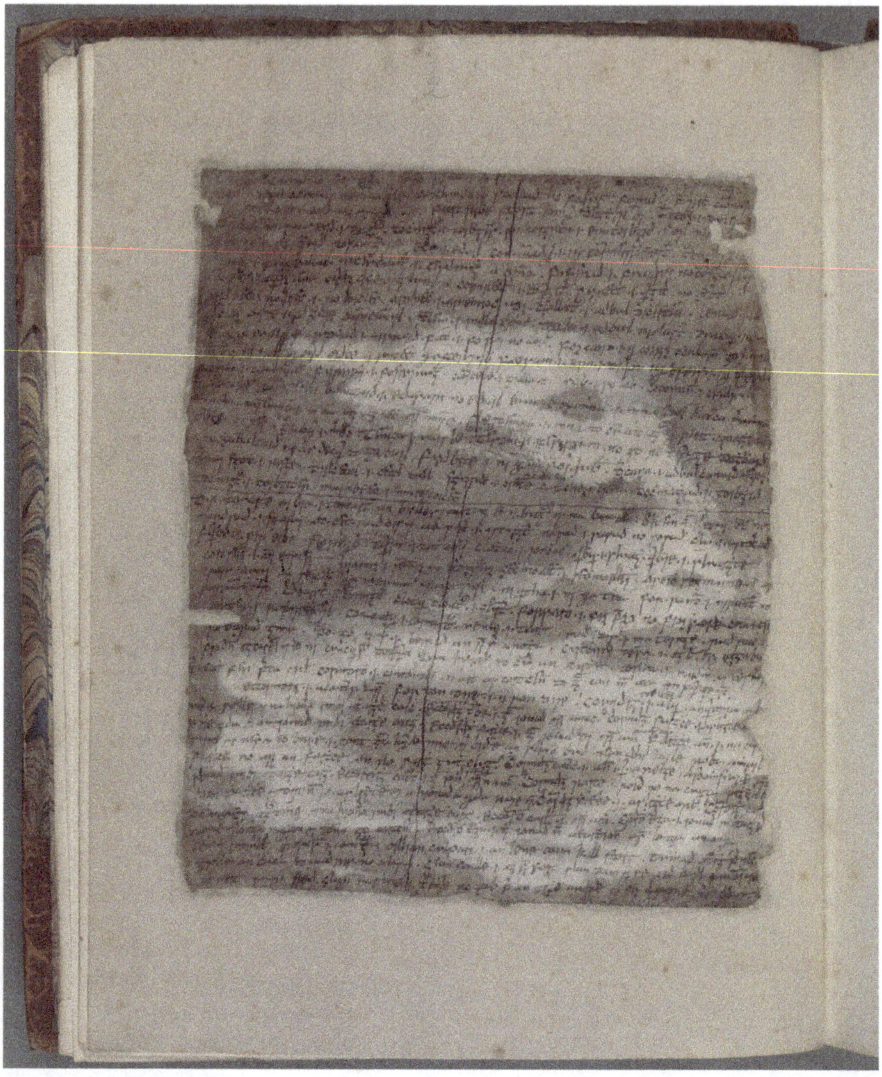

Page 2 of Dubhaltach Mac Fhirbisigh's seventeenth-century legal glossary, Trinity College, Dublin MS 1401, *olim* H.5.30

Page 3 of Dubhaltach Mac Fhirbisigh's seventeenth-century legal glossary, Trinity College, Dublin MS 1401, *olim* H.5.30

Page 4 of Dubhaltach Mac Fhirbisigh's seventeenth-century legal glossary, Trinity College, Dublin MS 1401, *olim* H.5.30

Page 5 of Dubhaltach Mac Fhirbisigh's seventeenth-century legal glossary, Trinity College, Dublin MS 1401, *olim* H.5.30

Page 6 of Dubhaltach Mac Fhirbisigh's seventeenth-century legal glossary, Trinity College, Dublin MS 1401, *olim* H.5.30

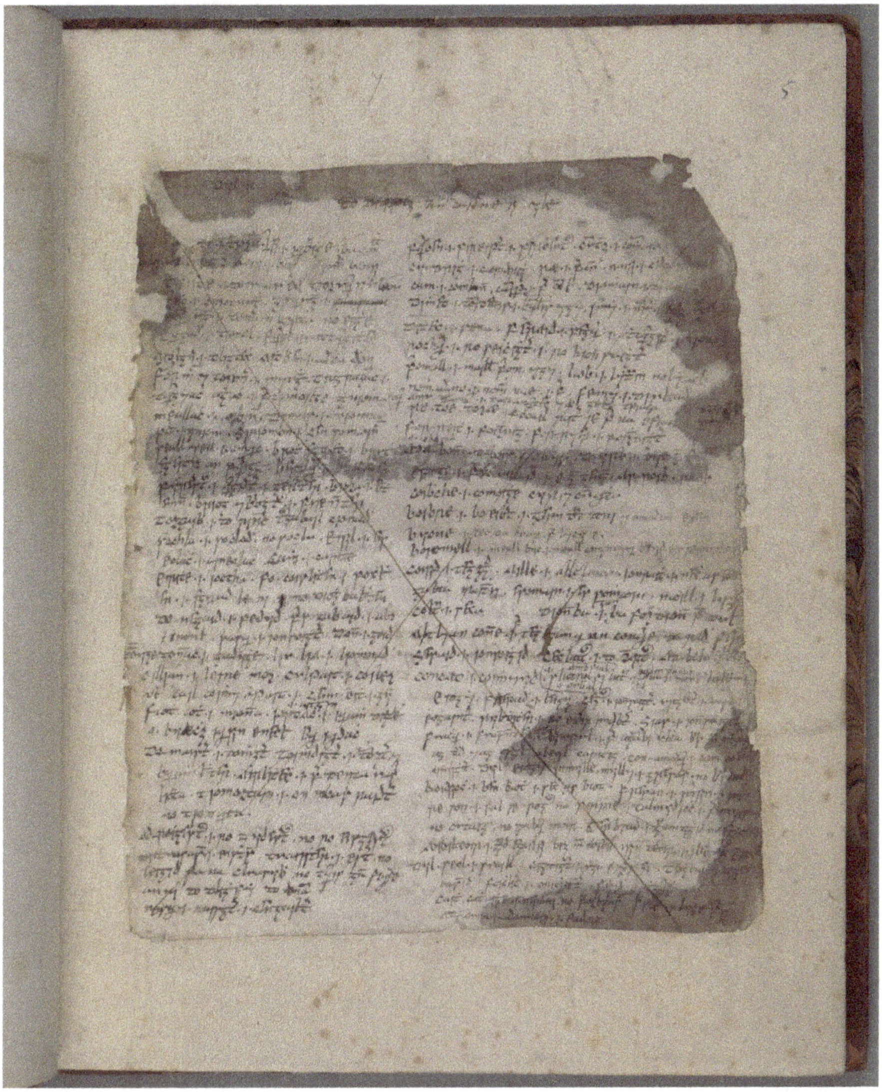

Page 7 of Dubhaltach Mac Fhirbisigh's seventeenth-century legal glossary, Trinity College, Dublin MS 1401, *olim* H.5.30

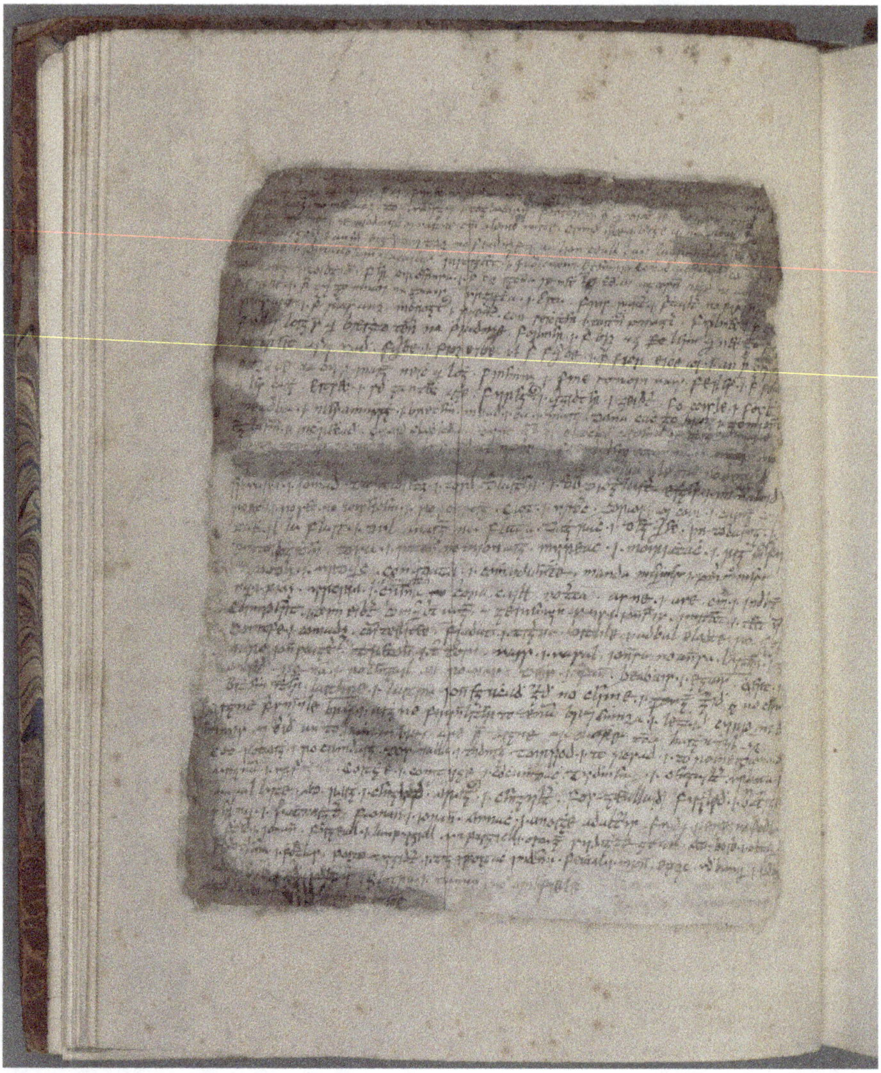

Page 8 of Dubhaltach Mac Fhirbisigh's seventeenth-century legal glossary, Trinity College, Dublin MS 1401, *olim* H.5.30

Page 9 of Dubhaltach Mac Fhirbisigh's seventeenth-century legal glossary, Trinity College, Dublin MS 1401, *olim* H.5.30

Page 10 of Dubhaltach Mac Fhirbisigh's seventeenth-century legal glossary, Trinity College, Dublin MS 1401, *olim* H.5.30

Page 11 of Dubhaltach Mac Fhirbisigh's seventeenth-century legal glossary, Trinity College, Dublin MS 1401, *olim* H.5.30

Page 12 of Dubhaltach Mac Fhirbisigh's seventeenth-century legal glossary, Trinity College, Dublin MS 1401, *olim* H.5.30

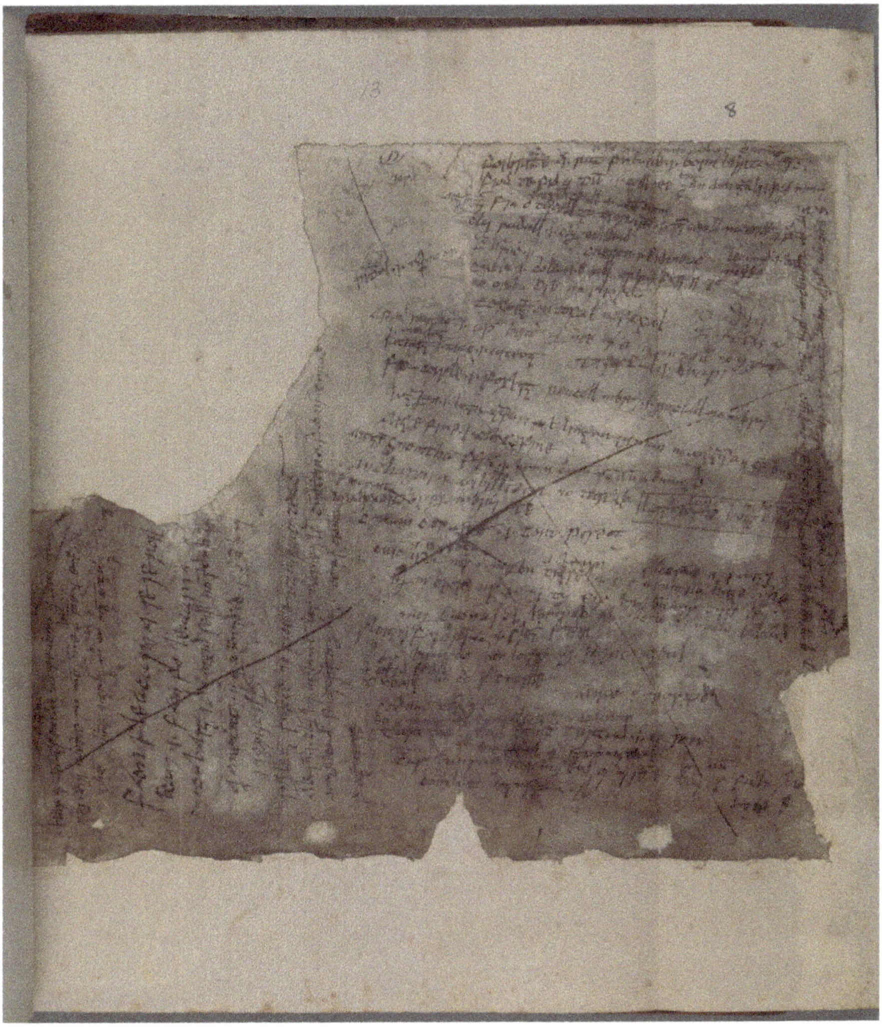

Page 13 of Dubhaltach Mac Fhirbisigh's seventeenth-century legal glossary, Trinity College, Dublin MS 1401, *olim* H.5.30

Page 14 of Dubhaltach Mac Fhirbisigh's seventeenth-century legal glossary, Trinity College, Dublin MS 1401, *olim* H.5.30

Schematics

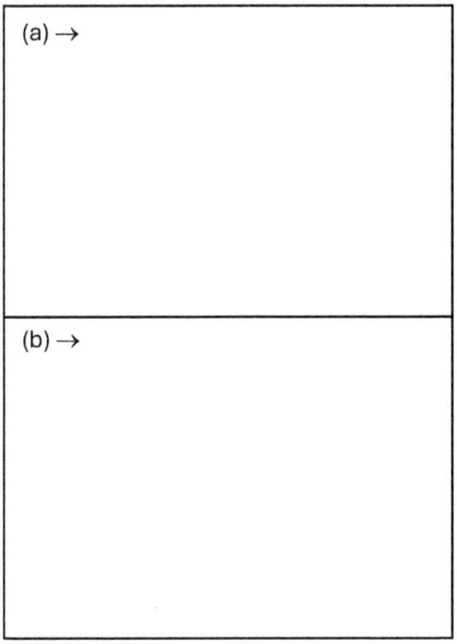

Schematic presentation of page 1

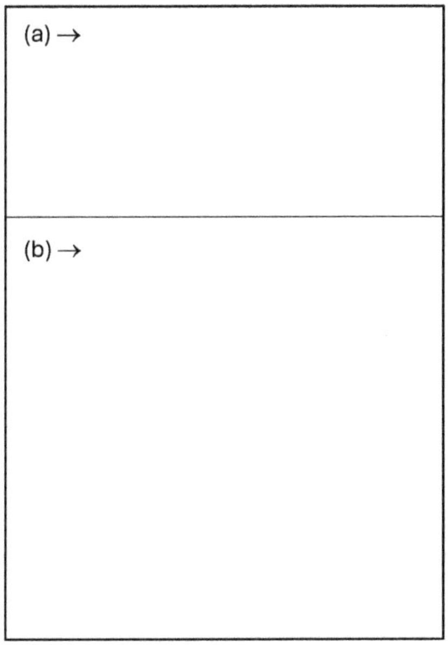

Schematic presentation of page 2

Schematic presentation of page 3

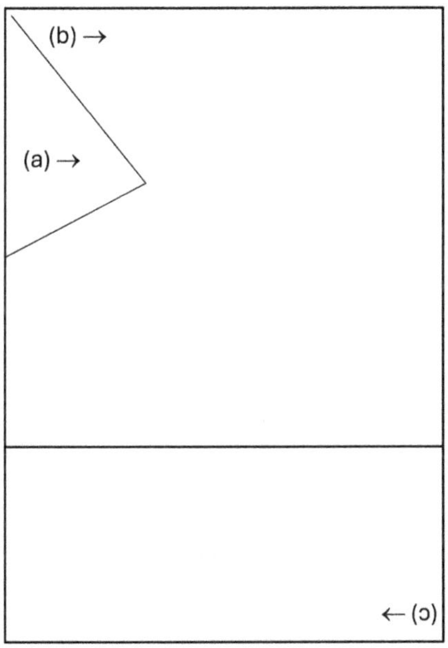

Schematic presentation of page 4

 | DOI:10.1163/9789004755673_002B

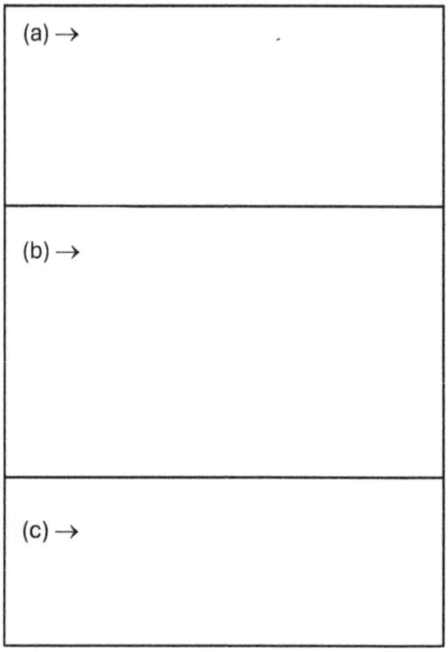

Schematic presentation of page 5

Schematic presentation of page 6

Schematic presentation of page 7

Schematic presentation of page 8

Schematic presentation of page 9

Schematic presentation of page 10

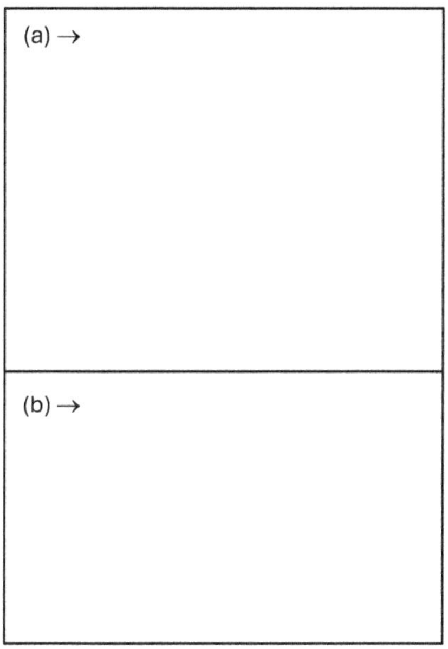

Schematic presentation of page 11

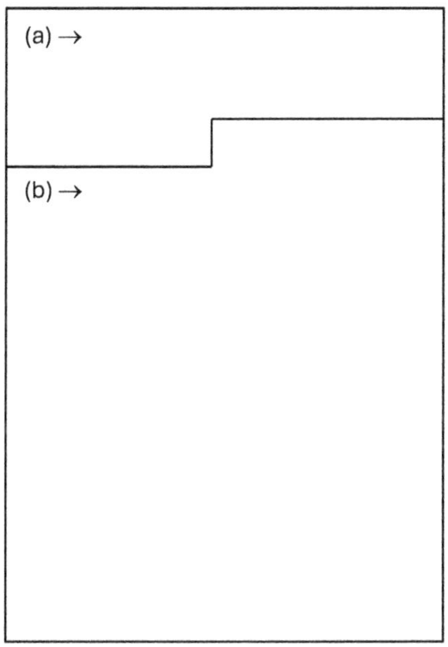

Schematic presentation of page 12

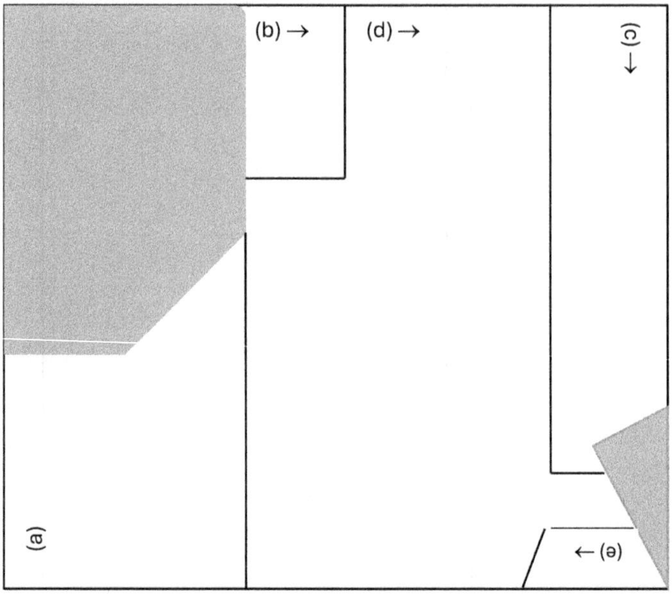

Schematic presentation of page 13

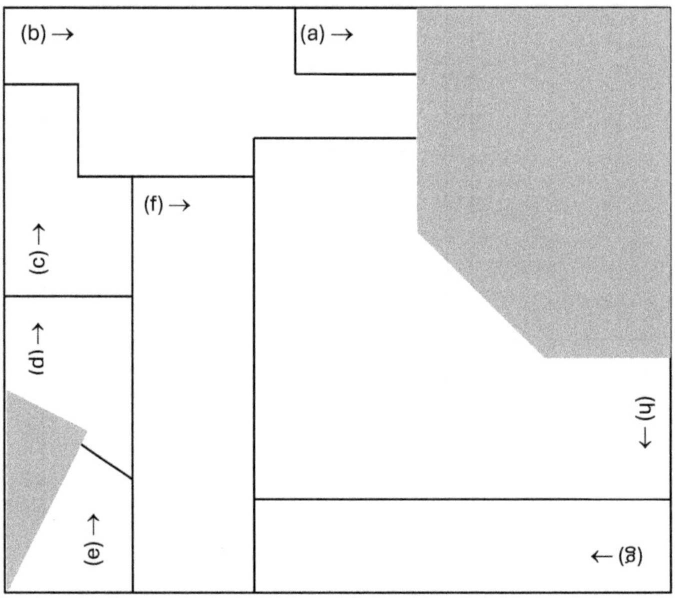

Schematic presentation of page 14

Introduction

1 What Is Dubhaltach's Glossary?

Dubhaltach's Glossary is an Irish legal glossary dating to c. 1643 (Ó Muraíle 1996c: 379) which contains approximately 1,295 entries arranged by textual blocks. The precise number of entries is unknown because the single surviving manuscript witness is badly damaged in several places. Up until now, there has not been a systematic study of the glossary itself or of the manuscript in which it is preserved. The glossary is of the highest importance for a number of reasons. Perhaps the most important reason is that the compiler, Dubhaltach Mac Fhirbhisigh, had access to medieval Irish legal texts which are no longer extant or only survive in fragments. His glossary, thus, provides us with access into a lost world of legal texts and manuscripts. Because of the fact that the glossary was compiled in textual order, it provides us with the opportunity to reconstruct the contents and ordering of some of these lost texts. Many of the headwords in the glossary are not found in modern dictionaries, and many of the glosses contain verbal forms otherwise unattested. The glossary fills in gaps in both our knowledge of early Irish society through the laws, and also our knowledge of the medieval Irish lexicon.

2 Trinity College, Dublin MS 1401 [H.5.30]

The only surviving copy of Dubhaltach's legal glossary is found in TCD MS 1401 (92 ff.). The manuscript catalog description provides the following information: "Duald M 'Firbis's Glossary of the Brehon Laws, 7 ff., with a transcript alphabetically arranged made by Eugene O'Curry in 1840" (Abbott and Gwynn 1921: 265). The manuscript, as it is currently bound, consists of three parts, all of which are paper. The first part consists of one page (f. 1r in the modern MS foliation) which contains two notes. The first note is by Eugene O'Curry, and he gives it first in Irish then (with his orthography and punctuation) in English translation.

> *Ag so inár ndiaiḋ, bloḋ so Ṡánasan Féneaċais an Duḃaltaiġ léiġean̄ta Ṁic Ḟirḃisiġ, ar ṡlioċt a ḋeaġláiṁe féin, ⁊ noċ do ṫionóil ⁊ do sgríḃ se a ttimċeall na bliaḋna dœis an tiġearna, MDCLX. ⁊ anois ar na aiṫsgrioḃaḋ, an ord aibgiṫire, do ċolláiste na tríonóite an áṫ cliaṫ, liomsa Éoġan Ó Cóṁraiḋe. MDCCCXL.*

© KONINKLIJKE BRILL BV, LEIDEN, 2026 | DOI:10.1163/9789004755673_003

> Here follows a fragment of the Brehon law glossary of the learned Duald Mc Firbis, in his own handwriting, and compiled [and written] about the year of our Lord 1660; and now rewritten in alphabetical order for Trinity College Dublin by me, Eugene Curry. AD. 1840.[1]

Immediately after this is the second note:

> [The fragments were found lying between fol. 207 and 208 of H. 2. 15.]

The note is signed by J.H. Todd.[2]

Before turning to the second and third parts of the manuscript, a word should be said about the location where it was found. TCD MS H.2.15, as it was known then, has since been rebound as TCD MS 1316 [H.2.15A] and TCD MS 1317 [H.2.15B]; both of these are composite manuscripts (Abbott and Gwynn 1921: 90–94).[3] Based on the way each of these manuscripts is currently bound and foliated, one can make a very strong case for the legal glossary having been found in what is now TCD MS 1317 [H.2.15B], which contains *inter alia* legal material and other glossaries, in a section owned by Dubhaltach himself (O'Sullivan and O'Sullivan 1962: 64; O'Sullivan 2000: 440 and 446). TCD MS 1317 [H.2.15B] has three different pagination systems in it. Part way through the description, the Trinity College, Dublin manuscript catalog switches between listing the machinated numbers for an item's location within the manuscript (not all of which are on many pages) to listing the penciled numbers (with the occasional typographical error) instead. The catalog description also provides the older ink numbers (written by Edward Lhwyd) in brackets (92–94). Although the Abbott and Gwynn are not using the ink numbers (the third pagination system) in their catalog, that is the system currently used on the Irish Script on Screen website. The ink numbers are referred to by John O'Donovan in his "Supplement to O'Reilly's Irish-English Dictionary" which uses the glossary as one of his sources (*s.v. fresgisin*, "*.i. saoileactain*. Dudley Ferbisse in H.2.15,

1 Immediately above the translation, one line of text has been erased. What can be read through the erasure suggests that it repeats the first line of the translation below it.

2 J.H. Todd was a former librarian at Trinity College, Dublin who worked closely with John O'Donovan and Eugene O'Curry to classify the Irish manuscripts in the library's collection; *Dictionary of Irish Biography*, *s.v.* Todd, James Henthorn https://www.dib.ie/biography/todd-james-henthorn-a8577#:~:text=Todd%2C%20James%20Henthorn%201805%E2%80%93,of%20the%20East%20India%20Company Accessed July 31, 2024.

3 It should be noted that some of the textual and authorial identifications in the catalog are in need of updating, see pp. 3 and 10. Images of both manuscripts are available on the Irish Script on Screen website https://www.isos.dias.ie/. Accessed April 18, 2024.

p. 208, loose sheets."), and also by Petrie (1845: 61, n.f "…a loose sheet of paper in the handwriting of the celebrated Duald Mac Firbis, inserted in a MS. in Trinity College, H. 2. 15. P. 208") (see pp. 62–65). Thus, the glossary would have been found, according to the catalog, in between the end of "an imperfect copy of the *Uraicept*" (Abbott and Gwynn 1921: 93) and the start of a copy of the *Bretha Nemed* (Breatnach 2005: 47). It should be noted that the ink number at the start of this text is 208. The *Bretha Nemed* text was edited by E.J. Gwynn (1942) under the title "An Old-Irish Tract on the Privileges and Responsibilities of Poets;" this text also forms the Appendix to vol. III of D.A. Binchy's *Corpus Iuris Hibernici* (1111–1138), and it is one of the few texts from paper manuscripts he included in the collection. The *Bretha Nemed* text is in Dubhaltach's hand (see the discussion of this text in Ó Muraíle 1996c: 82–86). As noted by Ó Muraíle (1996c: 82), Abbott and Gwynn (1921: 93) omitted to describe the leaf which follows the copy of the *Uraicept* which "appears to be a genealogical poem, while on the verso (p. 158) are various other scribblings by Dubhaltach Óg." This leaf forms the "final folio of the 'old part' of H.2.15B" (Ó Muraíle 1996c: 82). Although Abbott and Gwynn (1921: 93–94) identify the *Bretha Nemed* text as a "fragment of a law glossary" it is not a legal glossary; it is a legal text concerned with poets (amongst other topics); and, while there is a transcript of it by Eugene O'Curry in TCD MS 1338 [H.2.15 no. 3], it is not the same 'glossary' as is found in TCD MS 1401 [H.5.30]. TCD MS 1338 ff. 1–4 is a transcript of *Dúil Laithne* (pp. 116–119 in the current pagination system); ff. 5–26 is a transcript of the *Bretha Nemed* text (p. 208–f. 227^v in the current system; *CIH* 1111.1–1138.37).[4] O'Curry signs his name on the last folio of the transcript (26) and provides the date 1842. The mistake regarding the identification of the legal glossary was corrected in the supplement at the end of Abbott and Gwynn's catalog, where Gwynn states that the glossary in TCD MS 1401 [H.5.30] has nothing to do with the TCD MS 1317 [H.2.15B] text (341–342; and Ó Muraíle 1996c: 82).[5]

The second part of our manuscript consists of the autograph legal glossary itself. The glossary is fourteen pages, the first twelve of which are roughly the same size, i.e. approximately 8″ × 6¼″ (see Plates 1–12). The final two pages are of an irregular shape (see Plates 13–14). All of the pages have areas of writing which are difficult to read, the result of staining, tearing, and possibly the use of a reagent in the nineteenth century (Ó Muraíle 1996c: 87; see the schematics on pp. XXXIII–XXXVI).

4 Both *CIH* and Gwynn use an earlier pagination system which more closely corresponds to what is found in Abbott and Gwynn's catalog.

5 Unfortunately for current scholars, the original catalog error has been uploaded as part of the catalog description on the Irish Script on Screen website.

Based on the style of Dubhaltach's signatures found on page 14 of the manuscript, Ó Muraíle (1996c: 87) has dated the manuscript to "in or around the year 1643" as against O'Curry's date of 1660. Ó Muraíle bases this date by comparison with the style of Dubhaltach's signature in other MSS, for example, the colophon written in TCD MS 1317 at the end of *Dúil Laithne* where Dubhaltach provides the date of May 5, 1643 (Ó Muraíle 1996c: 87 and 372). The evidence provided by Ó Muraíle is compelling, and in what follows this date is accepted.

Dubhaltach writes in a typical seventeenth-century Irish script. Occasionally he switches to roman script when writing words in Latin or English, such as DG 13.d.26.39 *Turtad* and 2.b.7.91 *Venite*, but he does not shift to the Greek alphabet for the one entry which contains a Greek example, i.e. 14.g.1.27 *Ta*[*lent*]*um Lá*[*tene*], *talenton Graeca. Talanntan* [*i*] *nGaoid*[*hilge*].[6] This is not to say that Dubhaltach did not know Greek; there are numerous examples of him making marginal notes in Greek in the version of *Sanas Cormaic* copied by his grandfather in TCD MS 1317 [H.2.15B] (Ó Muraíle 1996c: 81).[7] There are numerous corrections to the manuscript scattered throughout the text, all in Dubhaltach's hand.[8]

The glossary itself comprises pages 1–14 (noted across the top of each mounted page in pencil) (ff. 2r–8v). The pages themselves also have numbering in ink across the top of them. Some of the numbers were written by Dubhaltach, for example, the numeral 4 in the upper right corner of the page once it is turned 180°. On some pages, such as 3, 4, 13, and 14, the entries are written in multiple directions (see pp. XXXIII–XXXVI for the schematic drawings of these pages). The writing is usually in one column, except for page seven which is written in two. Some of the sections have headings which are included in the close transcription of the text. The vertical lines running over the pages of the manuscript give every impression that what we have is a draft of the glossary and that a more polished version existed at one point. In other words, the vertical lines running over the entries suggest that he had crossed out sections of the manuscript after he had copied them to create a clean copy of the glossary. If such a version ever existed, it has not yet been found. Ó Muraíle (1996c: 88) quotes a letter of October 24, 1704 from Ruaidhrí Ó Flaithbheartaigh (Dubhaltach's protégé) to Edward Lhwyd saying that he does not know what became of Dubhaltach's dictionary (Sharpe 2013: 251 (letter 14);[9] see also O'Sullivan 2000:

6 For the system used to number the entries in the glossary, see the Editorial Method.

7 See p. 30–32 for a list of the entries which contain a language other than Irish.

8 For a list of all the marginalia, see Appendix 4 (pp. 447–449).

9 Images of O'Flaherty's letter are available on the Early Modern Letters Online website

439–440 and 444). Edward Lhwyd was a subsequent owner of many of Dubhaltach's manuscripts (Sharpe 2013: 251; O'Sullivan and O'Sullivan 1962; and O'Sullivan 2000: 439).[10] Ó Muraíle (1996c: 87–88) advises caution in assuming that the *Foclóir Féneachais* 'dictionary of jurisprudence' referred to by Dubhaltach in the introduction to his book of genealogies (Ó Muraíle 2003: 1: 168 § 6.5) is the same legal glossary preserved in TCD MS 1401 [H.5.30]. Ó Muraíle (1996c: 87–88 and 95 n. 68) is responding in part to comments by O'Curry in his unpublished manuscript catalogue for the Royal Irish Academy (Ó Muraíle 1996c: 95, n. 68 citing RIA III, facing p. 1081) and (1861: 123) where he states that "… Mac Firbis compiled two others…which unfortunately are now not known to exist: namely, a Glossary of the Ancient Laws of Erinn… Of the former of these, I have had the good fortune to discover a fragment in the library of the Dublin University (class H. 5. 30)." The relevant section of Dubhaltach's introduction to his book of genealogies is worth quoting in full as it is possible that the glossary in TCD MS 1401 [H.5.30] is a draft of his *Foclóir Féneachais* (Ó Muraíle 1996c: 87–88; and 2003: 1: 168 and 169 § 6.5).[11]

> Fiorchoimheud dno adeirim, úair ní headh amháin go rabhsad roilionmar, m*ar* do raidhseam cheana, ag coimeud an cceudna, acht do bhí ord agus dligheadh aca agus orra as nár edir dhóibh (gan dioth adhbhal), bréug na fallás do den*am* ann, m*ar* as lér (i leabhraibh féneachusa na Fódla, agus isna gradaibh fileadh fén) a n-ord agus a ndligheadh, uair ni raibhe laochraidh, na clíar chille na tuaithe in Erinn (gur cumuisgeadh an chrioch) ar nach mbaoí ord airidhe (da ngoirthear gradha .i. cemeanna), agus dligheadh na ngradh sin d'f*h*iachaibh ar gach droing diobh do choimheud fa phén smachta agus a n-onóra do chailleamh (m*ar* do sgríobhsam inar Foclóir Feneachais lab*hr*as go foirleathan orra sin agus ar dligheadh Gaoidhiol i ccoitc*h*inne).
>
> Properly preserved, indeed, I say, for not only were they very numerous, as we have said already, who preserved the same material, but they had and were bound by order and law such that they were unable (without

http://emlo.bodleian.ox.ac.uk/profile/work/8b6d16f0-7c0f-4c29-abee-c4544592c198?sort=date-a&rows=50&dat_sin_year=1704&dat_from_day=24&dat_from_month=10&people=lhwyd&baseurl=/forms/advanced&start=205&type=advanced&numFound=242. Accessed July 31, 2024.

10 Although there is some fluctuation in printed sources regarding the spelling of Edward's surname as Lloyd, Lhuyd, or Lhwyd, the spelling used herein is Lhwyd because it reflects the form of his surname he most often used himself (Roberts 2022: 1–2).

11 The text and translation are both from Ó Muraíle 2003: 1: 168 and 169 § 6.5.

> huge loss) to commit a lie or falsehood in regard to it, as is clear from their order and law (in the law-books of Ireland and in the poetic grades themselves), for there was no band of warriors or learned caste, clerical or lay, in Ireland (until the territory became confused) that had not a certain order (which were called grades, i.e. degrees), and every group of them was obliged to keep the law of those grades under pain of being chastised and losing their honour (as we wrote in our Dictionary of *Féineachas* [= Irish law] which speaks extensively of those matters and of the law of the Gaoidhil in general).

As Ó Muraíle notes:

> This description, with its emphasis on the grades of poets and on the responsibilities of each grade, is reminiscent of nothing so much as the 'tract on the privileges and responsibilities of poets', alias *Breatha Neimheadh Déidheanach*, which, as has been mentioned above, survives only in a transcript by Mac Fhirbhisigh. Whether this is the precise text Dubhaltach had in mind when he refers to his *Foclóir Féneachais*, or another work—perhaps based in considerable measure on that tract—is something which we are no longer in a position to determine. (88)

That being said, the glossary itself has a significant number of entries which derive from *Bretha Nemed Dédenach* (see p. 46) and likely also the no longer extant text(s) *Dúil* and/or *Dúil Roscadach* (these texts were compilations covering a range of topics, including poets and issues of status), and, thus, a much stronger case can now be made that the glossary itself is a draft of the *Foclóir Féneachais*.

The glossary itself seems to have been bound into its current manuscript location after John O'Donovan consulted the glossary for his dictionary materials and after Eugene O'Curry made his alphabetical transcription in 1840. This argument is based on the fact that O'Curry was able to see many of the letters at the extreme edges of the pages which are no longer visible or only partially visible under the current paper frame. Furthermore, most of the material across the top of page 11 currently is obscured under what looks like a semi-transparent white liquid (possibly glue), but the writing was clear to O'Curry at the time of his transcription because he was able to read most of the entries which are now only partially visible.

This brings us to the third part of the manuscript, which is O'Curry's alphabetical transcription. The transcription in O'Curry's handwriting comprises folios 10–92. The writing is normally on the recto of each folio except for the occasional correction on the facing verso. O'Curry includes two notes stating that words in brackets or underlined have been supplied by the context of the entries and that entries which have numbers refer to the old numbers on the manuscript itself. O'Curry's transcription is printed later in this volume.[12] Ó Muraíle (1996c: 87) counts 1,281 separate entries. The count used here is 1,282, which also includes entries which are simply cross-referenced headwords, e.g. 560 *Eccoimdigh. fec coimdidh* and 212 *Breoinde. fec cuig anmanna cat.*[13] If we eliminate those 58 entries which are cross-references, the number of individual glossary entries in O'Curry's transcription is 1,224. It should be noted that O'Curry's transcription includes some cross-references to entries which do not exist in O'Curry's transcription, such as 661 *Findte diblaidhe. fec findte feartsach*. It should also be noted that O'Curry only includes entries when he can read the headword. For example, in entry DG 10.8.12, the headword is illegible, but the gloss itself is clear. It should also be noted that DG 13.d.5.14 *Leamhadh .i. bod mairbhe* was omitted even though it is perfectly legible. One suspects that O'Curry felt that the subject matter (impotence) was not to his liking. In terms of how the arrangement of entries differs from O'Curry's, there are some entries which are listed as two or one entry in O'Curry but combined or separated differently herein; these instances are noted in the close transcription of the glossary. The total number of entries edited herein is 1,295, which also includes entries which are only partially legible. It should also be noted that O'Curry regularly transcribes manuscript long 'e' as ⟨ea⟩, and he regularly adds glide vowels when expanding contracted syllables, such as ⟨aigh⟩ or ⟨uidh⟩. The most important (yet obvious) matter to point out regarding O'Curry's transcription is that it is alphabetical, and, thus, represents a significant rearrangement of the entries as they are found in the manuscript itself. As discussed on page 16, Dubhaltach grouped the entries by text block in the order in which the entries are found in their source texts, similar to what we find in *glossae collectae*. By arranging the entries alphabetically, the textual source blocks are obscured. The above is not meant to be a criticism of O'Curry's transcription; I have relied heavily upon it, especially for entries which have now been obscured by the paper frames.

12 See pp. 367–409.

13 The numbers refer to the entries in O'Curry's transcription.

3 The Ordering of the Manuscript Pages

The order of the pages as currently mounted in the manuscript follows the general order of the material when this can be determined; for example, the material at the bottom of page 11 continues on the top of page 12. What should be borne in mind is that the horizontal lines Dubhaltach draws across some of the pages are significant. They signify that he has changed source texts. For example, the horizontal line across page 2 separates the entries from *Bretha Nemed Dédenach* from the entries which come from a source headed by the abbreviation 'd.r.' (see the discussion on pp. 50–55). Page 4 has been mounted upside down, and once we rotate it 180°, we can see that the entries from *Bretha Nemed Dédenach* are all written in blocks across the tops of pages 2, 4, and 6. The specific textual blocks will be discussed in greater detail in the section on sources (pp. 42–62) and Appendix 2 (pp. 432–435). In some places we can see where Dubhaltach seems to have copied several headwords before adding the glosses, such as DG 7.b.16.76 *Buicne* and DG 7.b.17.77 *Boicmell*.

4 Dubhaltach's Life and Works

In 1671, 'the celebrated antiquary', Dubhaltach Mac Fhirbhisigh, was murdered in a random act of violence by a member of the Crofton family in Co. Sligo (Ó Muraíle 1996c: 287).[14] With his death, Ireland lost a scholar whose tireless efforts to collect the country's historical and legal manuscripts have resulted in the preservation of the majority of the current surviving corpus of early Irish legal texts. Dubhaltach was from a long line of scholars with legal interests (we find his grandfather's name in several early manuscripts), and Dubhaltach himself continued his family's tradition including compiling the legal glossary edited here. Aside from the fact that his glossary has never been edited or translated, Dubhaltach had access to versions of texts which are no longer extant, such as a different version of the *Tract on Marriage and Divorce* to that edited by Kelly (2014), and he had access to at least one legal text of which we have only passing references and occasional quotations (see pp. 50–55). Thus, Dubhaltach provides us with a window onto lost texts, legal terms, and descriptions of some aspects of the functioning of early Irish society not found elsewhere.

14 There are several variants of the spelling of Dubhaltach's name in the primary and secondary sources. Throughout this book, the spelling used by Ó Muraíle 1996c and O'Sullivan 2000 has been adopted; see also Ó Muraíle 1987.

As an avid collector of medieval Irish legal and historical manuscripts, Dubhaltach probably possessed the most thorough understanding of this material of anyone in the seventeenth century.[15] The survival of Ireland's most important legal and historical manuscripts is a result of his efforts as a collector. Dubhaltach's working knowledge of extant manuscripts included familiarity with manuscripts which he himself did not possess. Furthermore, his understanding of the frequently archaic and specialized use of the legal language contained in the oldest layers of the legal texts (dating to c. 650 CE) makes his glossary of particular linguistic significance, especially because the meanings of many of these words are otherwise lost to modern scholarship. The glossary also reveals and clarifies aspects of Irish law which until now have been unknown or poorly understood. Without Dubhaltach's efforts, so much of what we know about early Irish law would not exist. Some of the manuscripts he owned preserve the only complete copies we have of some legal texts, including *Cáin Lánamna* the 'Law of Couples' and *Córus Bésgnai* the 'Arrangement of Discipline'.[16] Thus, his importance to the field as both a compiler and collector cannot be stressed enough. As a result of the relative inaccessibility of both Dubhaltach's Glossary and O'Curry's alphabetic transcription, very little scholarship exists which discusses the glossary at any length; the only significant discussion of the glossary so far is Ó Muraíle (1996c: 87–88).

It is impossible here to provide as comprehensive a study of Dubhaltach's family, education, and professional life as can be found in Nollaig Ó Muraíle's book, *The Celebrated Antiquary Dubhaltach Mac Fhirbhisigh (c. 1600–1671): His lineage, life and learning* (1996c). What follows below relies heavily on this work and others by Ó Muraíle.[17]

Dubhaltach Mac Fhirbhisigh (also known as Dubhaltach Óg to distinguish him from his grandfather, Dubhaltach Mór) was likely born around 1600; the precise year is unknown. He was born in Lacken, Co. Sligo (Ó Muraíle 1996c: 63). Members of his family are mentioned in the annals, particularly in the fourteenth and fifteenth centuries. Notable relatives include: Giolla Íosa Mór,

---

15 This is not to say that he was the only person with such expertise; after all, he likely received part of his education at Baile Mec Aodhagáin at the school run by Flann Mac Aodhagáin (Ó Muraíle 1996c: 78).

16 Both of these texts are found in TCD MS 1316 [H.2.15A], which corresponds to *CIH* 502.7–519.35 and 520.1–536.27, respectively.

17 See Ó Muraíle 1987, 1996a, 1996b, 1997, 2003: 1: 1–9, 2004, and 2012. See also the entry in the Dictionary of Irish Biography https://www.dib.ie/biography/mac-firbhisigh-dubhaltach-og-a5036. Accessed May 16, 2025.

son of Donnchadh, who compiled a now lost collection of annals sometime before 1397, and it is known that he also worked on a compilation of Old and Middle Irish literary texts, which now forms part of the composite manuscript known as the Yellow Book of Lecan (Ó Muraíle 1996c: 6–8); and Dubhaltach's grandfather, Dubhaltach Mór. Like his grandson and several other members of the larger family, Dubhaltach Mór was a scribe and historian. He worked on parts of the sixteenth-century Book of O'Davoren, BL MS Egerton 88, and he also copied the versions of O'Davoren's Glossary and *Sanas Cormaic* 'Cormac's Glossary' found in TCD MS 1317 [H.2.15B] (Ó Muraíle 1996c: 45–48). The fact that Dubhaltach Mór and Dubhaltach Óg share the same name and worked on legal texts and glossaries, some of which are found in the same manuscript, has led to a certain amount of confusion in some earlier works of scholarship. For example, Abbott and Gwynn incorrectly ascribe the TCD 1317 [H.2.15B] versions of O'Davoren's Glossary and *Sanas Cormaic* to Dubhaltach, when they are in fact in his grandfather Dubhaltach Mór's hand (Abbott and Gwynn 1921: 93; and Ó Muraíle 1996c: 371). Dubhaltach's own work then is best viewed as being part of a centuries-old family tradition of scribes, historians, and in Dubhaltach's case, also translator, genealogist, and collector of legal manuscripts, although how many in his collection were already in the family is unknown.

Dubhaltach's earlier life is largely unknown, and virtually nothing is known of him before 1643. In 1643, he was in Ballymacegan, in north Co. Tipperary, in the school run by the Mac Aodhagáin family of lawyers and historians, which included at the time Flann Mac Aodhagáin (Ó Muraíle 1996c: 63) who was acquainted with one of Dubhaltach's later employers, John Lynch, known for his work *Cambrensis Eversus* in which he refutes the many negative claims made by the twelfth-century churchman, Gerald of Wales, against the Irish. *Cambrensis Eversus* famously includes a description by Lynch of the many glossed legal manuscripts he saw which were owned by Dubhaltach (Lynch 1662: 158; translated in Kelly 1850: 2: 374; see pp. 12–13). Virtually nothing is known of Dubhaltach's own personal life, despite how much he tells us about his family otherwise (Ó Muraíle 2003: 9).

The Mac Aodhagáin family acted as lawyers to many of the "ruling families" in "western and central Ireland" (*GEIL* 253) along with copying and glossing many important legal texts. Other post-Norman legal families included the O'Dorans, the O'Davorens, and several others. The composite manuscript TCD MS 1316 [H.2.15A], parts of which were owned by Dubhaltach, contains texts copied by members of this family (O'Sullivan 2000: 440). The point of all of this is to briefly highlight the fact that many of the learned and legal figures at the time were known to each other and spent time in each other's schools and were engaged in copying and compiling some of the same texts. It is not uncommon to find, for example, named scribes involved with copying texts, legal and literary, across multiple manuscripts associated with different learned families (see discussions in O'Sullivan 1999 and 2000).

Returning to Dubhaltach in 1643, it is then that he copied the glossary known as *Dúil Laithne* 'Book of Latin', a copy of which is found in TCD MS 1317 [H.2.15B]. The glossary is made up of material across a wide linguistic range. The legal glossary in TCD MS 1401 [H.5.30] is not related to *Dúil Laithne*, although some Latin does appear in the glossary. During the same year Dubhaltach also copied part of a set of annals which is now known as the Fragmentary Annals of Ireland. 1643 was clearly a busy year for Dubhaltach as he also copied a version of *Bretha Nemed Dédenach* and worked on various other fragments of glossaries, including providing annotations in TCD MS 1317 [H.2.15B] (Ó Muraíle 1996c: 78–96 and 370).

Throughout his career, Dubhaltach was employed by both James Ware and John Lynch mainly to transcribe and translate various historical sources. Dubhaltach transcribed the *Chronicum Scotorum* and produced translations of the Annals of Inisfallen and the Annals of Tigernach (Ó Muraíle 1996c: 227, 247–256, 370–371). It is also important to note that as a result of Dubhaltach's travels throughout Ireland and his associations with other learned legal families and antiquarians, he had access to texts and versions of texts which are no longer extant. He is probably most well-known for his genealogical work, especially *Leabhar na nGenealach* 'Book of Genealogies'. This massive work was completed mostly between 1649 and 1650, but he added material to it over the years (Ó Muraíle 1996c: 166–210).[18]

His life was cut short in January 1671 when he was fatally stabbed at an inn somewhere in or near Doonflin, in west Co. Sligo, by a Thomas Crofton (Ó Muraíle 1996c: 283). While some romantic stories surrounding his death have grown over the years, the exact circumstances which led to the stabbing are unknown, as is the identity of Thomas Crofton. There are multiple potential candidates with this name, but "the precise identity of Thomas Crofton" is unknown (Ó Muraíle 1996c: 287).

18 It is not possible to list every work Dubhaltach compiled, transcribed, or translated here, but there is a comprehensive list in Ó Muraíle (1996c: 370–371 and 381–382).

5 The Structure of the Glossary Entries

Before discussing the structure of the entries in Dubhaltach's legal glossary, a brief overview of some aspects of the early Irish laws and Irish glossaries is necessary so as to put Dubhaltach's Glossary within its larger context.[19]

The earliest extant Irish laws date linguistically to c. 650 CE with the *Senchas Már* 'Great Tradition' being dated most recently to the later years of the seventh century (Breatnach 2011; and Charles-Edwards 2021; Charles-Edwards 2022: 4, n. 7 prefers a date of c. 700 CE), although they are preserved in manuscripts from the twelfth to the seventeenth centuries (*GEIL* 1). The true extent of the early Irish legal corpus is unknown, but the volume of extant legal material far exceeds that which survives of the early English laws. As it is, the semi-diplomatic edition of the medieval Irish laws, the *Corpus Iuris Hibernici*, runs to over 2,300 single-spaced pages (with no translation or supporting annotation). Approximately 800 of those pages consists of texts from manuscripts which "once formed part of the library of Dubhaltach" (Ó Muraíle 1996c: 303; and O'Sullivan and O'Sullivan 1962: 64). The field has largely given primacy to texts found in vellum manuscripts, thus neglecting a large body of previously unedited and unexplored material written on paper because it had been felt that nothing significantly old could be found in paper manuscripts, but it is now known that this is not the case. Binchy's *Corpus Iuris Hibernici*, however, remains the main resource for anyone working with the early Irish laws.[20]

Many of the early legal texts are accompanied by copious interlinear glosses and legal commentary, much like the format found in medieval continental legal manuscripts. The normal pattern of scribal activity in Ireland, however, was to copy the canonical text from manuscript to manuscript with little or no change to the actual text, while copying existing glosses and commentary

19 What follows below relies heavily on the work of Russell 1988b and 1999a, and Taylor-Griffiths 2020. See also Breatnach 1996a.

20 When we talk about law in medieval Ireland, it is easy to forget that the vernacular, secular laws, the so-called Brehon Laws, were not the only legal system operating in the country. Aside from canon law, there were different customs and regulations in the areas with a large Norse presence (Valante 1998). After the Norman Invasion of Ireland in 1169, we see the introduction of English Common Law in the Norman-controlled areas with Gaelic law still in operation outside these areas. In border areas, much like we see in the medieval march in Wales, a mix of the two systems operated. The Gaelic laws eventually got farther and farther pushed to the geographical fringes of the island, and finally under King James I in 1603, the Brehon Laws were deemed to have no authority in Ireland as King James I proclaimed that the Irish people were under the king's protection. Dubhaltach lived right at the turning point of the end of the authority of the native Irish laws (*GEIL* 250–263; Kenny 2007: 9; and Hallinan 2019).

and simultaneously adding more contemporary glosses and commentary to the page. The results are legally and linguistically layered texts such that, in later manuscripts of the seventeenth century, scholars can sometimes find close to 900 years of legal and linguistic change on a single page (*GEIL* 225–231). Glosses and commentary have frequently been ignored or devalued in the field (Binchy 1943: 212), but they offer significant information if one knows how to interpret them. Legal glossaries, of which there are many, have only recently begun to be studied and their significant value to the field recognized (see, for example, Russell 1988b and 1999a; Breatnach 2016; Buckley-Coogan 2019; and Taylor-Griffiths 2020 and 2022).

Glossaries, especially legal glossaries, tend to begin as compilations from glossed texts, but not all types of glossaries are put together the same way. Glossaries tend to begin their life as in-text glosses, in other words, interlinear or marginal glosses found in the manuscripts surrounding the legal texts themselves. Depending on the text, the glosses can be written in multiple hands and over a period of time, or simply copied from one text to a new copy, or a combination of both. Glosses can be lexical or explanatory, etymological or grammatical (Russell 1988b: 16–27; Taylor-Griffiths 2020: 1: 9–7).[21] For example, in an examination of DG 8.8.23 'Urg*artha* .i. crosta. *Airgarthae* 'forbidden', i.e. forbidden', one can see that the lemma is glossed by another word with the same meaning; in other words, the gloss is lexical. The larger context of the source, heptad 49 (*CIH* 45.1–16), is a list of seven people who are not fit to give evidence. The lemma is the participle of *ar-gair* 'forbids'; *eDIL s.v. airgarthae*. Sometimes the semantic connection between the lemma and gloss is less close. For example, DG 4.b.14.22 'Mera*cht* .i. druis. *Meracht* 'excitement', i.e. a hot-blooded person'. If we look at DG 8.12.31 'Finem*hnus* .i. fine iom*h*æin uais. *Finemnus* 'being like a vine', i.e. [< *fine* 'kinsman' + *immáin* 'control' + ⁊ *úais* 'noble'] kinsman of superior control', we find an etymological gloss on the lemma. The meaning of the lemma is uncertain as it is not in *eDIL*, but it seems to be based on *fínemain* 'a vine'; *eDIL s.v. fínemain*. The gloss helps to supply a possible meaning for the lemma as a kinsman who is controlling the legal procedure although not directly involved in it. The image is of the kinsman who has his hands like long tendrils in the legal case, perhaps manipulating those under him. The larger context is a series of citations on people who are not able to give evidence.

21 Although Binchy's disparaging attitude towards etymological glossing is no longer accepted within the field, one would be remiss not to cite his 1943 discussion in "The Linguistic and Historical Value of the Irish Law Tracts" (210–212).

While at first glance etymological glossing in this way may seem cumbersome and unscientific from the modern standpoint of linguistic etymology, etymological glossing played an important role in the medieval scholastic mind-set. In fact, the linguistic relationship between the lemma's meaning and the component parts of the etymological gloss can be quite loose (Russell 2005: 55–60). The model for this type of glossing goes back to Isidore of Seville's *Etymologiae*. We may take as an example the entry on cats (XII.ii.38):

> *Musio appellatus quod muribus infestus sit. Hunc vulgus cattum a captura vocant. Alii dicunt, quod cattat, id est vidat. Nam tanto acute cernit ut fulgore luminis noctis tenebras superet. Vnde a Graeco venit catus, id ed ingeniosus*, apo tou kaiesthai. The mouser (*musio*) is so called because it is troublesome to mice (*mus*). Common people call it the cat (*cattus*) from 'catching' (*captura*). Others say it is so named because *cattat*, that is, 'it sees'—for it can see so keenly (*acute*) that with the gleam of its eyes it overcomes the darkness of night. Hence 'cat' comes from Greek, that is, 'clever' from καίεσθαι ("lit up", i.e. the passive of καίειν "kindle"). (Barney et al.: 2006: 254; for an analysis of the Latin in this entry, see Russell 2008: 26–30; part of the entry is also quoted in OM 211).

In the medieval Irish tradition of etymological glossing in legal texts, there are a handful of words which are regularly used to gloss certain elements in the lemma. Sometimes the etymological gloss is based on meaning, sometimes it is based on sound. The fullest study of these words within the Irish legal glossing tradition can be found in Taylor-Griffiths 2020: 1: 18–144 (see also Binchy 1943: 211–212 [90–91]; Russell 1988b; and Moran 2019: 35–43). Some of the common glossing words used in Dubhaltach's Glossary are presented below (for a fuller account of these and other etymons, see the table in Taylor-Griffiths 2020: 1: 88–90; Table 1 is indebted to that in Taylor-Griffiths 2020 and Moran 2019: 35–43). It should be noted that many of these are restricted to the specific context of Irish legal glossing. It should be noted that we should not understand the etymological aspects of this from modern etymological standards but rather as coming from the Isidorian tradition.

It should also be noted that glosses function within the reference of the meaning and context of the lemma, the glossed word, as it is found in the original base text. Thus, when glosses are pulled out of context, the meanings and explanations can be more challenging to analyse if one does not already know the base text. The first step in the formation of a glossary from a glossed text is the creation of a word-list. Word-lists generally consist of a one-word lemma each followed by a brief explanation. When glosses are pulled from a text and

TABLE 1 Common Glossing Words Used in the Glossary

Etymon	Etymology
ad-	*ada* 'suitable, fitting'
air-/(a)ur-	*úasal* 'noble'
con-	*caín* 'fine, well'
negative prefix *dí-*	*adbal* 'great, mighty, vast'[a]
for-	*fír* 'true'
fris-	*ada* 'suitable'
fris-/frith-	*fír* 'truly'
im-	*éim* 'swift, timely'

a *Adbal* 'great, mighty, vast' is commonly used in the legal texts to form etymological glosses on the negative prefix *dí-*; this likely arose from confusion with the intensifying prefix 2 *dí-*; *eDIL s.v. adbal.*

copied as a list following the order in which the lemmata appear in the base text, an independent text has been created. Such an independent collection of glosses in textual order is also referred to in the literature as *glossae collectae*. This term and 'word-list' refer to the same type of text. In terms of what distinguishes a word-list and a glossary, both are independent, but in glossaries the lemmata have been rearranged in alpha-order. Note that these are in alpha-order and not full alphabetical order. They are principally ordered by first letter only, occasionally also by second letter. Another difference between a word-list and a glossary is that with some of the larger glossaries, such as *Sanas Cormaic* 'Cormac's Glossary' and O'Davoren's Glossary, one can find material from other glossaries added in, so that one ends up with longer glossary entries, entries from multiple sources, and, effectively, other glossaries and/or word-lists being absorbed into these much larger glossaries. In other words, glossaries have the potential to keep growing (Russell 1988b, 1999a: 88–90, and 2023: 192–193; Breatnach 2016; and Taylor-Griffiths 2020: 1: 9–17). One can see this, for example, in the manuscript image of page 81 in the TCD MS 1337 [H.3.18] *Irsan* glossary (edited in Moran 2019: 247–271),[22] where room has been left for more material to be added, and where material has been added by multiples scribes. This glossary illustrates the fact that glossaries are not necessarily the creation of only one person.

22 Images are available on the Irish Script on Screen website. https://www.isos.dias.ie/. Accessed April 24, 2024.

The significance of word-lists and glossaries cannot be overstated. Many of the entries in *eDIL* have the gloss provided in a glossary (not infrequently from O'Davoren's Glossary or *Sanas Cormaic*) as the only source for a word's meaning (see the collection of examples in Arbuthnot 2019). Furthermore, some of these word-lists have been compiled from versions of texts which are no longer extant, thus providing us insight into not only the fact that another version of a text existed, but also some insight into how the text differed from those versions currently extant. For example, Paul Russell, in a recent discussion of his analysis of the glossed extracts from the *Táin* in TCD MS 1337 [H.3.18], pp. 538–539a22, has noted that although it is clear that the glosses come from Recension I, they appear to come from "a text that is not closely related to any of the extant texts" (Russell 2017: 20). Thus, there is much that these word lists and glossaries can tell us, much beyond the meanings or etymologies of words.[23]

In many aspects, Dubhaltach's Glossary is most closely related to O'Davoren's Glossary in that both of them consist of blocks of entries from the same texts. In other words, the entries are grouped by text in the order in which each lemma appears in the source text. Additionally, each of these glossaries list the lemma in the form in which it appears in the source text whereas "other glossaries usually restore a nominative of a noun or a verbal noun in the headword" (Russell 1999a: 88). With O'Davoren's Glossary, the entries have since been arranged in alpha-order, but a glance through the list of sources for O'Davoren's Glossary compiled in *CCIH* (109–156) makes the underlying structure immediate apparent. Not all of the sources for the entries in O'Davoren's Glossary have been identified. Some of which also overlap with entries from Dubhaltach's Glossary (see Appendix 1, pp. 411–431). Clearly both of the glossaries derived entries from several of the same legal texts, although the versions of the texts used by each seem to be different in some cases.

Many of the entries in Dubhaltach's Glossary consist of the following three basic formats. The vast majority of the entries are in Irish with the occasional gloss in English, Latin, and one in Greek although it is not written in the Greek alphabet.[24]

1. The lemma followed by an etymological gloss, which may or may not itself be followed by a non-etymological gloss, such as DG 1.b.10.76: '*Aibhriteodh*

23 These early word-lists are also frequently the forerunners to the modern dictionaries (see the discussion in Griffith et al. 2018: 2–5).

24 Dubhaltach was perfectly capable of writing glosses in Greek as he wrote many glosses in Greek in the margins of the copy of *Sanas Cormaic* copied by his grandfather in TCD MS 1317 [H.2.15B] (Ó Muraíle 1996c: 81). For a list of the entries which contain a language other than Irish, see pp. 30–32

.i. abhratódh no soadh .i. an tan do-fuit a h-abhra dar an súil. Aibritiud 'twinkling of an eye', i.e. [< *1 abra* 'eyelash' + *soud* 'turning'] eyelashes or turning, i.e. when her eyelash falls across the eye'.

2. The lemma followed by a non-etymological gloss, which may be a synonym or a linguistically later form of the lemma, such as DG 1.b.4.55: '*Foichlige .i. fochlaoid .i. tochailt. Foichlide* 'burrowing', i.e. uprooting, i.e. digging up'.
3. Occasionally, we find a descriptive statement followed by a list, such as DG 10.21.54: 5 'An*manna* cat su*nn*... *Cóic anmanna cat sunn* 'Five names of cats here...'.

We find these formats in other types of glossaries as well, especially formats 1 and 2. Textual correspondences with other glossaries are indicated in the edited text and in Appendix 1 (pp. 411–431). There is also the question of how many of the glosses were already found in the material which Dubhaltach compiled from his sources versus how many of the glosses he composed or supplemented himself. This question is not confined to this glossary but is rather a more general question for every glossary. While one could argue that the etymological glosses were found in his source texts as many etymological glosses in legal texts tend to be found in the very earliest linguistic layers (Russell 1988b: 28), there is no way to prove that Dubhaltach himself is not the author of some of these given his extensive knowledge of the legal texts. When the lemma has been glossed with a synonym, it can be harder to determine whether the synonym is found in the source text, was composed by Dubhaltach himself, or carried over from a gloss on another text. Some of the glosses are comparatively later, but a linguistically later form, however, still does not rule out the fact that he could have been using an early text which included a linguistically later layer of glossing. Based on the number of entries in the glossary which are also found wholly or partially in other glossaries and legal texts, on the whole the balance is against Dubhaltach being the author of any but a relatively small number of the glosses. The evidence overwhelmingly suggests he was copying the glosses from his source texts, whether those sources be a glossed version of a text or a collection of glosses already detached from its source text. There is one entry, however, where it is possible that Dubhaltach refers to himself in the first person; it is DG 6.a.12.30 '*Fledh croilighe .*[*i.*] *i gcionn mis, saolim gurob ionann sin cuimniugadh miusa na marbh re h-eglus iocar sin os na marbaibh. Fled crólige* 'funeral feast', i.e. at the end of a month, I suppose that is the same as the [one] month memorial of the dead by the church that is paid for the dead', but that assumes that the gloss in his source was not already written in the first person which could well be the case.

The lemmata normally, in so far as one can tell from the runs of text, follow the order in which they appear in the source text. Dubhaltach compiled the glossary text by text (when this can be determined), thus creating blocks of entries which all come from the same source text. (A discussion of the identified textual blocks is found on pp. 40–61. Sometimes Dubhaltach indicates the source of the blocks of entries, but it should be noted that some of the sources are given as abbreviations, and the expansion of some of them is not certain (a full list of these and other marginalia can be found in Appendix 4, pp. 447–449). For example, the source variously given as 'd.r.', 'Duil .r.', and 'duil' could refer to the texts *Dúil* or *Dúil Roscadach* (*CCIH* 246–253; see the discussion on pp. 50–55). Neither of these texts (it is not entirely clear that *Dúil* and *Dúil Roscadach* refer to different texts) is preserved; there are only scattered references to both of them and the occasional quotation preserved in other texts. As noted in *CCIH* (252), it is quite possible that *Dúil Roscadach* was one of the sources for *Bretha Nemed Toísech*. Of interest regarding the first case study discussed below is that *Dúil Roscadach* is named as a source in one of the glosses in *Bretha for Catślechtaib* (*CIH* 1550.16; Murray 2007: 144). As noted in *CCIH* (249 and 251), not all of these citations are consistent in their referencing. For example, *CCIH* (249) notes that in a similar commentary found in *CIH* 834.17 and 1350.36, the same citation is assigned to *dūil* and *Dūil Roscadha*, respectively. Another example of confusion between the two texts is found in O'Davoren's Glossary, no. 664, where the E version assigns '*.d.*' as the source, and the F version assigns '*dūil .r.*' as the source. In Dubhaltach's mind, it seems likely that *Dúil* and *Dúil Roscadach* represent the same text whether this is true in reality or not.

Despite the issues surrounding the abbreviations 'd.r.', 'Duil .r.', and 'duil', the abbreviation 'b.n.' can be expanded with confidence to *Bretha Nemed* as many of the entries in the textual blocks headed by this abbreviation derive from *Bretha Nemed Dédenach* and follow the same order in which they are found in the surviving text. Dubhaltach does not group all of the entries from a particular source text together. In other words, he does not provide entries only from *Bretha Nemed Dédenach* before moving on to another text. He frequently divides up a page with entries from one source given on the top half and entries from another source given below, frequently divided by a line going across the page.

6 Case Studies

What follows below are three case studies to illustrate how the glossary works and its relationship to other extant legal texts and glossaries. It is hoped that these studies will better orientate the reader to the glossary itself and its relationship to other legal texts and glossaries.

6.1 *Case Study on* DG *4.C.18.95–4.C.19.103 Derived from* Bretha Nemed Dédenach

Bretha Nemed Dédenach is a text which concerns poets and their legal responsibilities and privileges as a result of their elevated social status (Gwynn 1942; *CCIH* 184–188; and *GEIL* 268–269. See p. 46 for further discussion on this text.). DG 4.c.18.95–4.c.19.103 correspond to *CIH* 1118.15–1118.17 (Gwynn 1942: 23.20–22). For convenience, the edited entries are printed below (but without any apparatus).[25]

4.c.18.95 De*ar*cnuid*h* no dercnuid*h* .i. anr*a*d i*ar*sa ní drec*hus* do*n* eal*adh*ain.
Deargnaid nó dergnaid 'undistinguished', i.e. an *ánrad* 'poet of second grade' because he does not face towards poetical skill.

4.c.18.96 Noit*h*gern .i. cli.
Noithgern 'type of poet', i.e. a *clí* 'poet of the third grade'.

4.c.18.97 Olsone, no ollosna .i. can[a].
Olsone, nó ollosna 'type of poet', i.e. *cana* 'poet of the fourth grade'.

4.c.19.98 Saog*h*al .i. dos.
Saegul 'life', i.e. *dos* 'poet of the fifth grade'.

4.c.19.99 Saoircerdne .i. m*a*cfurm*idh*.
Saerceirdne 'free craftsman', i.e. *macfuirmid* 'poet of the sixth grade'.

4.c.19.100 Caoinc*h*erdne .i. foc*h*log.
Caíncheirdne 'good craftsman', i.e. *fochloc* 'a poet of the seventh grade'.

4.c.19.101 Coict*r*iall .i. d*r*isiug.
Cóictríall 'five endeavors', i.e. *drisiuc* 'a poet of the eighth grade'.

4.c.19.102 Taip*h*nem*idh* .i. tam*h*un.
Taipneimed 'sudden noble', i.e. *taman* 'a poet of the ninth grade'.

---

25 For the editorial conventions, see pp. 67–70. A detailed discussion of this group of entries is currently in preparation by the author.

4.c.19.103 Doineim*idh* .i. oblóire.
Doíneimid 'unskilled noble', i.e. *oblaire* 'a poet of the tenth grade'.

A few things are noteworthy about this run of entries. The first is that the lemmata form a list of names for different types of poets which are explained by reference to the more common list of poets found in texts such as *Bretha Nemed Dédenach* (e.g. *CIH* 1124.20–21 and 1125.9–12). The DG entries follow the order in which they appear in *Bretha Nemed Dédenach*. The entries and source text list the poets with the highest level of social status first and proceed in descending order. These words for poets have not been discussed in the secondary literature. Most of them are not in *eDIL*, i.e. *dearcnuidh no dercnuidh*; *noithgern*; *olsone, no ollosna*; *saoircerdne*; *caoincherdne*; *coictriall*; *taiphnemidh*; and *doineimidh* (*saoghal* is in *eDIL*, but it is not defined as a type of poet). Not only are these new words for poets that can be added to *eDIL*, but the entries provide us with definitions of these otherwise obscure words. In this way, Dubhaltach's Glossary expands our knowledge of the medieval Irish lexicon and elucidates an otherwise obscure passage in *Bretha Nemed Dédenach*.

6.2 *Case Study on DG 10.21.54.5 Derived from* Bretha for Catślechtaib

Bretha for Catślechtaib is the twenty-ninth tract within the *Senchas Már* legal compilation (*CCIH* 301). The text is only fragmentarily preserved; the main fragments are printed in *CIH* 1550.15–23 with other extracts and commentary in *CIH* 110.14–21 (see DG 10.21.54 *5 Anmanna cat sunn* for a full list of citations). *CCIH* (301) lists several entries from O'Davoren's Glossary which likely come from the text: 241–241, 421–422, 470(1), 915, 918, 1045, 1109–1110, 1246–1247, 1365, and 1395. The text and all of the other legal references to cats have been edited and translated in Murray 2007 (see also *EIF* 121–124). There is one large entry from Dubhaltach's Glossary concerning cats; it is one of a small number of entries which is presented in list form (see also DG 11.b.2.35–12.a.10.10). It is printed here for convenience in its entirety (for detailed references to other scholarship, the reader is referred to the notes in the edition for this entry).

10.21.54 5 An*manna* cat su*nn* .i. breóinde .i. breo nuall, ⁊ nia t*r*en, no breó án .i. crónan ina in[ne]. ⁊ meoinde .i. mo do-g*h*ni meig*h*il .i. meoain ⟨.i. meig*h*leac*h*⟩ ina in*n*e. Ringcne .i. riac*h*aid nec*h*, ⁊ riac*h*thar é. Cruib*h*ne .i. cruib nia .i. nia tren [a l]*us* a cruibe. *Air*cne .i. a h-*airc* Naoi M*ic* Lai*mh*iac*h*, no a b*air*cne .i. nia t*r*en, tugad*h* a b*air*c Bresail Bric .i. cait b*r*oin*n*geala d*h*uba. Iach .i. fiad*h* c*h*at all*aidh* gabar d*h*' fiad*h* .i. as fiad*h*antas. Folam .i. cat ler mait*h* loim, ⁊ coi*metus* loim go mait*h* ionan*n* e ⁊ an cat cuile a*cht* gur*o*b isi*n* tsenbaile b*hius*, ⁊ folom

> *ar* an mbuaile. Glas-nen*n*ta .i. cat beg b*hius* isi*n* tsenb*h*aile isi*n* nen*n*toig g*h*la[is] ag diotuig*adh* loc*h*ad*h*. Breoin*n*e .i. cat ait*aghius* rig ⁊ tigerna ⁊ *air*c[h]in*n*eac*h*, ⁊ do-ní c*r*onán doib*h*. Meoi*n*de, le meg*h*ile, ⁊ e coim(*h*)*et* i ccuid bid*h* c*r*uib[ne] le coi*met* muilin*n* ⁊ sab*h*aill ⁊ at*ha*. Ringcne le h-*airf*id*edh* clan*n*a na n-*ar*d*air*ec*h*. Da sg*r*iobad*h*, ⁊ iadsan da sg*r*iobad san. B*air*cne .i. cat ban sin.
>
> *Cóic anmanna cat sunn* 'Five names of cats here', i.e. *Breoinne*, i.e. *breó* means 'noise', and *nia* means 'a strong one' [< *breó* 'flame' + *nia* 'warrior'], or wonderful flame [< *breó* 'flame' + *án* 'wonderful'], i.e. purring is its essence. And *meoinne*, i.e. it mews most [< *mó* 'greatest' + *do-gní* 'it does'], i.e. little mew ⟨i.e. mewing⟩ is its essence. *Rincne*, i.e. it torments anyone [< *ríagaid* 'it torments' + *nech* 'anyone'], and it is tormented. *Cruibne*, i.e. [< *crob* 'paw' + *nia* 'warrior'] a strong warrior, i.e. a strong one by virtue of its paw. *Aircne*, i.e. from the ark of Noah Mac Lamíach [< *árc* 'ark' + *Nae* 'Noah'], or from *baircne*, i.e. *nia* 'a strong one' [< *bárc* 'ship' + *nia* 'warrior'], it was brought from the ship of Bresal Brecc, i.e. white-breasted black cats. *Íach*, i.e. an undomesticated wild cat taken from the wild, i.e. from the wilderness. *Folum*, i.e. a diligent good unsheltered cat [< *fó* 'good' + *lomm* 'bare'], and which protects well the unsheltered; it is equivalent to the pantry cat except it is still in the permanent abode, and unsheltered in the cattle-fold. *Glas-nennta* 'nettle-green', i.e. a small cat which is in the permanent abode amongst the green nettles destroying mice. *Breoinne*, i.e. a cat which dwells with king and lord and erenagh, and who purrs for them. *Meoinne*, by mewing, and in its share of food, it is equivalent to a *cruibne* by protecting mill and barn and drying kiln. *Rincne* by entertaining children of the chief nobles. It was written, and they were written there. *Baircne*, i.e. that is a cat for women.[26]

What follows is a comparison, by type of cat, between the information presented in Dubhaltach's Glossary, *Bretha for Catṡlechtaib*, and the relevant entries from O'Davoren's Glossary.

---

26 One should note in passing the argument in *Tromdámh Guaire* (pp. 23–25) between Senchán and Írusán, King of the Cats, where there is some overlap with Dubhaltach's Glossary concerning the names of the cats mentioned in the tale. I should like to thank Anna Chacko for drawing this to my attention.

6.2.1 *Breoinne*
Dubhaltach's Glossary

Bréoinde .i. breo nuall, ⁊ nia tren, no breó án .i. crónan ina in[ne].
Breoinne, i.e. *breó* means 'noise', and *nia* means 'a strong one' [< *breó* 'flame' + *nia* 'warrior'], or wonderful flame [< *breó* 'flame' + *án* 'wonderful'], i.e. purring is its essence.

Breoinne .i. cat aitaghius rig ⁊ tigerna ⁊ airc[h]inneach, ⁊ do-ní cronán doibh.
Breoinne, i.e. a cat which dwells with king and lord and erenagh, and who purrs for them.

Bretha for Catṡlechtaib, CIH 110.14–17; Murray 2007: 146.

BREONE .i. Catt so ⁊ cronan ⁊ comet (no foidh guiteach) aci ⁊ tri bai ind ma tat araen aicci—cronan ⁊ comet. Masa nechtar de is bo ⁊ samaisc no guna beith ni ar c[h]ronan eitir ⁊ is anna ta sein ind in inbaid is mon a sein cometas no is cutruma ris. Masa lughu indas nucu teit dar in ni cometas.
BREONE, i.e. This is a cat and 'she' has purring and protecting (or an inarticulate cry) and three cows are paid for it if it has both, purring and protecting. If it has one of the two, it is a cow and a heifer, or there might not be anything for purring at all and that obtains whenever it is more than or equal to that which it protects. If it is less than this, it does not exceed [in value] the thing which it protects.

O'Dav 241, *CIH* 1475.15–16

Breoinne .i. ainm cait, ut est breoinne .i. cat o andeth esidhe .i. breo an ina inde, cronan ina inde.
Breoinne, i.e. the name of a cat, *ut est* a *breoinne*, i.e. it is a cat from [...], i.e. a wonderful flame in its essence, purring in its essence.

6.2.2 *Meoinne*
Dubhaltach's Glossary

⁊ meoinde .i. mo do-g*h*ni meig*h*il .i. meoain ⟨i. meig*h*leac*h*⟩ ina in*n*e.
And *meoinne*, i.e. it mews most [< *mó* 'greatest' + *do-gní* 'it does'], i.e. little mew ⟨i.e. mewing⟩ is its essence.

Meoi*n*de, le meg*h*ile, ⁊ e coim(*h*)*et* i ccuid bid*h* cruib[ne] le coi*met* muilin*n*, ⁊ sab*h*aill, ⁊ at*ha*.
Meoinne, by mewing, and it is equivalent to a *cruibne* by protecting mill and barn and drying kiln.

Bretha for Catṡlechtaib, *CIH* 1550.15–16; Murray 2007: 145

Meone .i. trenchat do-gni meighligh. Bo cacha rebe .i. di ba ⁊ it inunda ⁊ na .u. *séoit* iar fut fuil i nDuil Roscadhaigh.
A *meone*, i.e. a mighty cat that mews. A cow for each feat, i.e. two cows, and that are equivalent to the five *sets* altogether which are in *Dúil Roscadach*.

CIH 110.18–21; Murray 2007: 146

MEONE .i. Cat cuileadh so ⁊ ma bagabhar tri damha da denumh go riacht a fuidhell imlan daibh, is a denum dun muinntir gu coimhetann o s[h]ein amach, ⁊ da bai ind. Maine faghabar na damha da denum etir no cia bagabar, minip dana risin muinntir a denamh, is bo ind.
MEONE, i.e. This is a pantry cat and if there be found three companies of guests to affirm that their full abundance came to them and its affirmation thenceforth by the household which it protects, and two cows are paid for it. If the companies are not found to confirm it at all or though they be found, if the household does not venture to affirm it, a cow is paid for it.

O'Dav 1246, *CIH* 1516.8

Meoinne .i. ainm cait, *ut est* meoinne is seissidhe cat cuile .i. miu ina inde, no meoan ina inde .i. meghel ine inde.
Meoinne, i.e. the name of a cat, *ut est* a *meoinne*, it is a pantry cat, i.e. a mew in its essence, or a little mew in its essence, i.e. purr in its essence.

6.2.3 *Rincne*
Dubhaltach's Glossary

Ringcne .i. riachaid nech, ⁊ riachthar é.
Rincne, i.e. it torments anyone [< *ríagaid* 'it torments' + *nech* 'anyone'], and it is tormented.

Ringcne le h-airfidedh clanna na n-ardairech.
Rincne by entertaining children of the chief nobles.

O'Dav 1365, CIH 1520.42; Murray 2007: 14

> Rincne .i. cat, ut est rincne is eisside cat mac .i. iarsind-i riachus na macaime becca, no riagait na macaim eissimh.
> *Rincne*, i.e. a cat, *ut est* a *rincne* is a children's cat, i.e. for the reason that it torments the small children, or the children torment it.

6.2.4 *Cruibne*
Dubhaltach's Glossary

> Cruibhne .i. cruib nia .i. nia tren [a l]us a cruibe.
> *Cruibne*, i.e. [< *crob* 'paw' + *nia* 'warrior'] a strong warrior, i.e. a strong one by virtue of its paw.

Bretha for Catṡlechtaib, CIH 1550.17–20; Murray 2007: 145

> Cruipne .i. trenchat a lus a c[h]ruipe—cat sabaill ⁊ muilinn ⁊ atha .i. bis oca n-imc[h]omet a triur. Tuictir co los .i. is amlaidh tuicctir amail bis oc denum eggnama. Di-renur tri sétaib .i. na tri séoit ata ferra bite isin teigh co rosat tri lethuinge.
> *A cruipne*, i.e. a mighty cat [so called] by virtue of its paw. A cat of barn and mill and drying-kiln, i.e. which is guarding all three. Let it be fully understood, i.e. it is thus it is understood in the manner in which it is [while] performing 'feats'. Three *sét*s are paid, i.e. the three *sét*s which are 'best' which are in the bag until they may come to three half-ounces.

O'Dav 422, CIH 1481.21; Murray 2007: 148

> Cruibne .i. ainm cait, ut est cruibne, is eiddide cat sabaill ⁊ muilinn .i. nia [.i.] tren, tren a c[h]ruib e.
> *Crúibne*, i.e. the name of a cat, *ut est* a *crúibne*, it is a cat of barn and mill, i.e. a warrior, i.e. a strong one, strong of paw.

6.2.5 *Aircne* and *Baircne*
Dubhaltach's Glossary[27]

> Aircne .i. a h-airc Nœi Mic Laimhiach, no a bairche .i. nia tren, tugadh a bairc Bresail Bric .i. cait broinngeala dhuba.

27 The entries below understand *baircne* as a variant of *aircne*.

Aircne, i.e. from the ark of Noah Mac Lamíach [< *árc* 'ark' + Nae 'Noah'], or from *baircne*, i.e. *nia* 'a strong one' [< *bárc* 'ship' + nia 'warrior'], it was brought from the ship of Bresal Brecc, i.e. white-breasted black cats.[28]

Baircne .i. cat ban sin.
Baircne, i.e. that is a cat for women.[29]

Cethairṡlicht Athgabálae, CIH 379.11 (cf. *AL* 1: 150.11, 152.32–34); Murray 2007: 147

IM BAIRCNE [.i.] CAT BAN .i. im bairc-nia: nia [.i.] tren, tucad a bairc Bresail Bric i mbit cait bronfinna duba.
CONCERNING A BAIRCNE, i.e. *A CAT FOR WOMEN*, i.e. concerning a ship-warrior: *nia*, i.e. a strong one, it was brought from the ship of Bresal Brecc in which are white-breasted black cats.

O'Dav 242, *CIH* 1475.17–18; Murray 2007: 147

Baircne .i. cat, is eisidhe cat ban .i. baircniadh, a hairc mic Laimiach tuca[d] ar tus, no barcnia [.i.] tren, tucad a bairc Breasail Bric.
Baircne, i.e. a cat, it is a cat for women, i.e. a ship-warrior, from the ark of [Noah] mac Lamíach it was first brought, or a ship-warrior, i.e. a strong one, it was brought from the ship of Bresal Brecc.

6.2.6 *Íach*
Dubhaltach's Glossary

Iach .i. fiadh chat allaidh gabar dh' fiadh .i. as fiadhantas.
Íach, i.e. an undomesticated wild cat taken from the wild, i.e. from the wilderness.

O'Dav 1109, *CIH* 1510.9; Murray 2007: 149

Iach .i. ainm cat, ut est iach do-renar lethdire .i. cat gabur .i. do iatacht.
Íach, i.e. the name of a cat, *ut est* an *íach* which is paid half penalty-fine, i.e. a cat which is brought,[30] i.e. for mousing.

28 This seems to refer to what is commonly called a tuxedo cat.
29 The gloss could also be translated as 'that is a white cat'.
30 The phrase could also be interpreted as 'a cat which is caught'.

6.2.7 *Folum*
Dubhaltach's Glossary

> Folam .i. cat ler mait*h* loim, ⁊ coi*metus* loim go mait*h* ionan*n* e ⁊ an cat cuile a*cht gur*ob isi*n* tsenbaile b*hius*, ⁊ folom *ar* an mbuaile.
> *Folum*, i.e. a diligent good unsheltered cat [< *fó* 'good' + *lomm* 'bare'], and which protects well the unsheltered; it is equivalent to the pantry cat except it is still in the permanent abode, and unsheltered in the cattle-fold.

O'Dav 915, *CIH* 1501.16–17; Murray 2007: 148

> Folumh .i. ainm cait, *ut est* folum, is eisiedi cat buachaillus .i. cometar ccusna buaib isin lis.
> *Folum*, i.e. the name of a cat, *ut est* a *folum*, it is a cat who herds, i.e. who is kept with the cows in the enclosure.

6.2.8 *Glas-nennta*
Dubhaltach's Glossary

> Glas-nen*n*ta .i. cat beg b*hius* isi*n* tsenb*h*aile isi*n* nen*n*toig g*h*la[is] ag diotuig*adh* loc*h*ad*h*.
> *Glas-nennta* 'nettle-green', i.e. a small cat which is in the permanent abode amongst the green nettles destroying mice.

O'Dav 1045, *CIH* 1507.22–23; Murray 2007: 149

> Glas nenta .i. ainm do chat, *ut est* glas nenta do sli sét ina dire; glas nenta .i. bis fon nglasnenaigh, no gabar do nenaigh glais .i. don nenntoig.
> *Glas nenta*, i.e. the name of a cat, *ut est* a *glas nenta* which merits a *sét* for its penalty-fine; *glas nenta*, i.e. which is under the green nettle, or which is brought from a green nettle, i.e. from the nettle.

In the early Irish laws, cats are assigned different values based on their skills, such as mousing; the Welsh laws have similar provisions.[31] There are eight different types of cats listed here (if we collapse *aircne* and *baircne*) despite the

31 Jenkins 1986: 180; *Llyfr Iorwerth* § 131; *Llyfr Blegwryd* 94.8–14; Richards 1954: 92; and Dedio [in preparation].

heading stating that five types of cats are listed. Some of the material overlaps with attested fragments of *Bretha for Catślechtaib* and O'Davoren's Glossary, some of it is not attested anywhere else. *Breoinne* seems to be a ginger cat (based on the etymological gloss) known for its purring (cf. CIH 110.14). It has a value of three cows, but the value is less if it does not have both purring and protecting, i.e. a cow and a heifer, and it could be that the cat has no value if it only purrs. *Meoinne* is described as meowing and protecting the mill, barn, and drying kiln from mice and other pests; the word itself (and likely also *breoinne*) is onomatopoeic. A *cruibne* seems to have a value of three *séts* for guarding barn, mill, drying kiln, and a *meoinne* is worth two cows, one cow for each feat. Dubhaltach seems to equate the *meoinne* with the *cruibne*. A *rincne* is described as a cat for children. This cat might be too young to be a proper mouser. The etymology of the word is uncertain, but it might be related to *rind* 'point, tip' or *rind* 'star' (see Sayers 2015: 6–7 for a full discussion of the possible etymologies). *Aircne* might be a ghost word derived from *bairccne*, a type of cat usually associated with women (see the end of the entry and the discussion in Murray 2007: 147–148). None of the other sources on this type of cat include Noah's name; biblical Noah is referenced here, and Noah's father's name is Lamech (see Murray 2007: 147 for discussion). It is a mystery as to whom Bresal Brecc refers, but the name shows up elsewhere. There are three listed in CGH. One is an "ancestor shared by Laigin and Osraige (118a25–25, p. 19); on p. 101, in the variants from the Book of Leinster and the Book of Lecan, there is an account of his raiding overseas" (Murray 2007: 147). The second is associated with the Dál nAraide, and there might have been a lost tale, *Echtra Bresail*. There is no information on the third one (see O'Dav 242; *Cethairíślicht Athgabálae*, CIH 379.11 and 31–32, 889.23–24, 1903.3; AL 1: 150.11, 152.32–34; SC Y.115, A.6; and Murray 2007: 147–148). *Íach* is an undomesticated wild or forest cat (see O'Dav 1109 and 1395, Murray 2007: 149). The entry in Dubhaltach's Glossary matches nothing else. The word *íach* (an oblique case of *eó*) is also a word for 'salmon'. If there is a connection between the two, it could be to how difficult it is to catch either a salmon or a feral cat with your hands; a wild cat would twist and turn and jump as would a salmon.[32] *Folum* is described as an outdoor cat which is kept outdoors with the cows in an enclosure. Murray (2007: 148) suggests that the name might mean 'bare, unprotected'; cf. *lomm* 'bare, naked, smooth'. Based on the surviving evidence, the *folum* appears to be an outdoor barn cat, thus unsheltered and unprotected (see O'Dav 915 and 1395). Most of the entry does not match anything else. *Glas-nennta* is another outdoor mouser and might refer to a greyish

32 I owe this suggestion to Paul Russell.

striped tabby (see O'Dav 1045; and Murray 2007: 149). There is partial overlap with O'Davoren's Glossary regarding the meaning of the name.

The significance of the above is that the information provided for each type of cat in Dubhaltach's Glossary partially overlaps with information found in other sources, but crucially there is information about each type of cat which is not found elsewhere. This is especially true of the entry on the *íach* as the only solid definition of what type of cat this is; the entry in *eDIL s.v. 2 íach* only defines it as a type of cat without providing any details. With this one entry from Dubhaltach's Glossary, not only can we fill in some gaps in our knowledge of the legal standing of various types of cats, but we also find for the first time a definition of the *íach*.

6.3 *Case Study on* DG *10.13.26–10.21.53 Derived from* **Bretha for Conṡlechtaib**

Immediately preceding the entry on cats, there is also a series of entries concerning different types of dogs. While we are fortunate enough to have Murray's excellent article for the cats, the material on dogs is more difficult to work with as we do not yet have an edited collection of all the material in the laws concerning dogs (see *EIF* 114–121).[33] References to dogs are found scattered throughout *CIH*, but many are found in *Bretha for Conṡlechtaib* (*CIH* 1550.24–1551.12), the thirtieth tract in the *Senchas Már* legal compilation,[34] and O'Davoren's Glossary (*CCIH* 301–302).[35] It should also be noted that the sparsely attested tract *Dúil* (*Roscadach*) also contains information about dangerous dogs (*CCIH* 249; *CIH* 972.30–34). Furthermore, the entries from Dubhaltach's Glossary do not always overlap with the material found in *Bretha for Conṡlechtaib* or other sources concerning dogs.

For convenience, DG 10.16.38–10.17.43 are given below (for detailed discussion on the entries themselves, the reader is referred to the notes in the edition for these entries).

---

33 Some of the types of dogs described in Dubhaltach's Glossary are not discussed in *EIF*.

34 It should be noted that although *Bretha for Conṡlechtaib* follows *Bretha for Catṡlechtaib* within the *Senchas Már*, the entries from *Bretha for Conṡlechtaib* precede the entries from *Bretha for Catṡlechtaib* in Dubhaltach's Glossary.

35 References to dogs are found in *CIH* 1550.24–1551.12, 110.32–113.36, 806.33–807.6, 807.11–16, parts of 1386.4–1396.6, 1268.14–19, 2128.26–33, and there is some overlap with the section on cats and distraint. The following entries in O'Davoren's Glossary (collected in *CCIH* 301) likely come from *Bretha for Conṡlechtaib*: 100, 101, 420, 423, 424, 471, 674, 786–789, 919, 920, 1179, 1248, 1314, 1397, 1472, 1473, and 1598–1600. See also the discussion in Breatnach 1996a: 15–20.

10.16.38 Conair caoimt*achta* .i. conair tiag*ur* isi*n* f[aith]c[h]e.
Conar coimtechta 'accompanying path', i.e. a path by which one goes through the green in front of a residence.

10.17.39 Tacm*h*aisi .i. tacmainge.
Tacmaisi 'of circumference', i.e. of circumference.

10.17.40 Indisi .i. buail*idh* bo.
Indise 'milking enclosure', i.e. enclosure of cows.

10.17.41 M*árus* .i. mo*r* ráid*h*is.
Márus 'he praised', i.e. [< *mór* 'great' + *ráidhis* 'he said'] greatly-he said.

10.17.42 Cana .i. cuilen.
Cana 'whelp', i.e. pup.

10.17.43 Canan*na* .i. cuileoin.
Cananna 'whelps', i.e. whelps.

It is useful to compare DG 10.16.38–10.17.43 against the material in *CIH* 1389.27–38; this is from a commentary on *Bretha for Conślechtaib* concerning offenses by dogs (*EIF* 148; and *CCIH* 63).[36] The material in common with Dubhaltach's Glossary has been underlined.

> *…⁊ ni tacmaing a beol lar tighi co conair cæmtechta, ⁊ cu go trath ⁊ go n-escaire, lan con dligthigh íctar a cin na con-sin.*
>
> *⁊ is iat-so na coin lethdligthigh uili .i. cu go trath gin escaire, ⁊ cu airgter don cuaille crin cuachda, ⁊ cu fænnail, ⁊ cu airgter iter an nómad cleth ⁊ an ursann ⁊ ni cuaille crin cuachda ⁊ tacmaing a beol lar tighi no [conair] cœmtechta.*
>
> *Marus do diandilsi dul fo bi fo cilar crann .i. mor-raiter a dilsi do go luath anti teit fo cli birithi an fordoruis mana raibh crand ina laim .i. espach gin arm ⁊ cu dligthech. Cen eolach reimtuighet aneolach .i. gin eolach do*

36 The passage of commentary is very difficult which is the reason that a translation has not been provided. The point of the example is to show how the entries in the glossary relate to extant legal material.

> *tiacht*[*ain*] *riasna aneolaigh. Athairbe* (?) *lam lonngaille* (?) *.i. da eiber* (?) *go h-ard gona derna gail tre luinne. Gabail itir* (?) *ina comrith canannaib .i. an tan bis a comrith docum a cuilen*…

We can see that material from the first two entries in Dubhaltach's Glossary are found in the commentary in the same order depending on where one thinks the glossing started; the same can be said of the last three (DG 10.17.41–10.17.43) although the grammatical case of the last two differ. The third entry, DG 10.17.40, obviously belongs as part of this sequence of entries, but it is not found in the commentary. It must, however, have belonged with a fuller version of the commentary's source text. Here we can see how Dubhaltach's Glossary helps to fill in textual gaps and increases our knowledge of the original source texts.

The above discussion illustrates both the legal and linguistic importance of Dubhaltach's Glossary and helps to provide the reader with a guide into how the glossary can be used in conjunction with extant sources to fill in the gaps.

7 Entries Which Contain a Language Other Than Irish

While most entries are in Irish, there is a handful of entries in the glossary which have material in other languages: English, Latin, and Greek. Representative entries are listed below. It should also be noted that Dubhaltach shifts to roman script when writing in other languages. Although he knew Greek, he did not employ the alphabet in this glossary. Dubhaltach made numerous annotations in Greek in his grandfather's copy of *Sanas Cormaic*; cf. TCD MS 1317 [H.2.15B], p. 163.

7.1 *English*

13.d.26.39 Turtad .i. eigean ⟨.i. extor[t]ion⟩.
Turtugud 'compulsion', i.e. compulsion, ⟨i.e. *extortion*⟩.

14.f.16.26 Fo-fe, ⁊ fo-fi ⁊ fo-fic*h* .i. fua*cht*naig*adh* .i. ofence.
Fo-fe, ⁊ *fo-fi* ⁊ *fo-fich* 'commits an offence, and commits an offence, and commits an offence', i.e. does injury, i.e. *offence.*

7.2 *Latin*

1.a.10.25 Áindlicet .i. ionglaine no neim*h*cet, licet .i. cetoig[the].
Áindlicet 'not allowed', i.e. uncleanness or not permitted, *licet* 'allowed', i.e. permitted.

1.b.15.91 Góla .i. gorta quasi gula .i. c*r*aos.
Góla 'abyss', i.e. hunger; *quasi* 'as if' *gula* 'opening of the mouth, throat, gluttony', i.e. mouth.

2.b.7.91 Venite .i. tait.
Venite 'come', i.e. come!

4.c.5.46 Forrduain .i. reco*mar*[c] .i. da siolla ⟨on⟩ dunan*n* ut iomco*mar*c flat*h*a feim*h*en, ⁊
casb*air*dne (in) i*ar*co*mar*c .i. t*r*i siolla.
Fordúan 'fordúan', i.e. a meter with a disyllabic ending, i.e. two syllables by which it closes [i.e., a disyllabic ending], *ut* 'like' *iomcomarc flatha feimhen* 'asking a splendid lord', and *casbairdne* of a trisyllabic ending, i.e. three syllables.

4.c.8.57 Miod*h*b*h*a .i. m*e*t*h*on bet*h*a int*e*r bonu*m* et malu*m*.
Midba 'average', i.e. [< *medón* 'middle, center' + *betha* 'life, existence'] a middle life *inter bonum et malum* 'between good and evil'.

5.b.5.37 Deolad*hacht* .i. g*r*asia .i. ní a n-aisgid*h*.
Deolaidecht 'favor', i.e. *gratia* 'favor', i.e. anything being desired.

7.a.21.30 F*r*is-gab*h*aid .i. abstinent.
Fris-gabat 'they restrain', i.e. *abstinent* 'they abstain'.

8.6.17 Iuidig*h*ec*h*t .i. iudiciumm .i. b*r*et*h*em*h*n*us*.
Iúdicecht 'judgement', *iudicium* 'judgement', i.e. judgement.

9.27.87 Coslac*h* .i. luac*h* cúisi .i. luac*h* do b*e*i*r* fe*r* na cuisi do nec*h* oile do cion*n* a cuisi do s*h*esam*h* do, ut d*icitu*r 'sed*h*a gac[h] coslac*h*' .i. an ses*edh* cuid do*n* c*h*úis donti doní *air*ber*t* aonu*air*e i n-*airecht* dá ttig tobac*h*.
Coslach 'payment', i.e. [< *lúach* 'payment' + *cúis* 'matter, case'] payment of a case, i.e. a payment the man of the case gives to someone else on his behalf to defend his case for him, *ut dicitur* 'as it is said' *sedha gach coslach* 'six things for each case', i.e. the sixth share from the case for the one who does the work at once in court when it comes to enforcing.

14.g.1.27 Ta[lent]um Lá[tene], talenton Graeca. Talanntan [i] nGaoid[hilge]. *Talentum Látene* 'talent in Latin', *talenton Graeca* 'talent in Greek'. *Tallann* 'talent' in Irish.

7.3 *Greek*

14.g.1.27 Ta[lent]um Lá[tene], talenton Graeca. Talanntan [i] nGaoid[hilge]. *Talentum Látene* 'talent in Latin', *talenton Graeca* 'talent in Greek'. *Tallann* 'talent' in Irish.

8 Relationship of Dubhaltach's Glossary to Other Irish Glossaries

What follows is a brief synopsis of the other Irish glossaries which have correspondences to the material in Dubhaltach's Glossary.[37] A table showing the correspondences across the glossaries can be found in Appendix 1 (pp. 411–431). There are 20 glossaries with some degree of overlap; sometimes the overlap is exact, sometimes the correspondences are more distant. Aside from Russell 1988b and Mahon 1987, a general overview of some of these glossaries can be found in Arbuthnot, Moran, and Russell 2023. It seems unlikely that Dubhaltach was using any of these glossaries as his immediate sources. Some of the overlap, such as that found with the partial glossary on *Bretha Nemed Dédenach*, eight entries in total, is due to that fact that both of them have the same textual source. In general, this raises questions of how the glossaries, especially the smaller legal *glossae collectae* discussed in Taylor-Griffiths 2020, are related to each other. Appendix 1 (pp. 411–431) shows where runs of entries are found across glossaries, suggesting some degree of interrelatedness amongst them. The greatest degree of overlap, by far, is found with O'Davoren's Glossary and O'Clery's Glossary. The glossary correspondences can broadly be divided into two categories; those with a large and close degree of overlap suggesting one is derived from the other, or that they ultimately go back to the same textual source, and those which only overlap for a few entries, which suggests that although they may share the same ultimate source, they are not very closely related in terms of content. It should be noted that Dubhaltach's Glossary is

37 Within the edited text, there are some entries which have correspondences to more than one version of a glossary entry. For example, DG 1.a.18.42 *Duibell* has correspondences with the D^1 and D^2 versions of *Dúil Dromma Cetta*. Not every example of these types of duplicate correspondences is listed within the edited text. The reader is referred to the Early Irish Glossaries Database to see the full set of these types of duplications. https://www.asnc.cam.ac.uk/irishglossaries/. Accessed July 18, 2024.

contemporary with O'Clery's Glossary, and that O'Davoren's Glossary predates both of these. Dubhaltach's Glossary is not a copy of O'Clery's Glossary, nor is it a copy of O'Davorens' Glossary. Although all three glossaries share lemmata in common, all three of the glossaries are independent compilations. The entries in O'Davoren's Glossary are normally longer than those in O'Clery's Glossary and Dubhaltach's Glossary, and they normally contain textual citations which are largely lacking in both O'Clery's Glossary and Dubhaltach's Glossary. All of the correspondences that I have been able to find are listed in the table in Appendix 1 (pp. 411–431). The glossaries are presented below in decreasing order of correspondences. It should be noted that some of the smaller legal *glossae collectae* are little discussed in the secondary literature.

8.1 *O'Davoren's Glossary*

In terms of overall structure, Dubhaltach's Glossary bears the closest resemblance to O'Davoren's Glossary as both of them are structured in text blocks (see the discussion in *CCIH* 102–105). The textual blocks in O'Davoren's Glossary are harder to see as it has since been arranged in alpha-order, but within each letter-block the textual blocks can be discerned especially in the larger blocks. The text blocks can be seen clearly in the list of sources for the entries in *CCIH* 109–159. It is possible that Dubhaltach may have modeled his glossary on O'Davoren's. As we only have a draft of the glossary, we have no way of knowing whether Dubhaltach eventually arranged the entries in alpha or alphabetical order. O'Davoren's Glossary is extant in two versions which are independent of each other: BL MS Egerton 88, ff. 80ra–93^{rc} (*CIH* 1466.11–1531.24; O'Grady 1926: 108–109; Russell 1988b: 6; Mahon 1987: 51–53, 66–76) (version E) and TCD MS 1317 [H.2.15B], pp. 45–60 (120–135 in the older pagination) (version F).[38] Stokes edited the text twice. He edited the text first in *Three Irish Glossaries*, which does not consider the TCD version (F). The second edition in vol. 2 of *Archiv für celtische Lexicographie* included emended readings from TCD (version F). Version F was copied by Dubhaltach's grandfather, Dubhaltach Mór, who also copied parts of the version in BL MS Egerton 88 c. 1569 (version E) (Ó Muraíle 1996c: 45). Version F lacks the letter *A* and *B*, most of *C*, and the section containing the letters *S*, *T*, and *U* is badly damaged (Abbott and Gwynn 1921: 93; and *CCIH* 100–108). A crucial difference between O'Davoren's Glossary and Dubhaltach's Glossary is that entries in O'Davoren almost always contain a citation from the source text. Some of the entries in Dubhaltach's Glossary might

---

38 Both manuscripts are available on the Irish Script on Screen website http://www.isis.dias.ie. Accessed July 18, 2024.

include a citation from the source text, but whether the citation is from the canonical tract or commentary is not always certain. These entries frequently include an *et cetera* as part of the gloss. There is a total of 276 entries in Dubhaltach's Glossary which have a correspondence, however distant, in O'Davoren's Glossary. Of those 276 entries, 191 have O'Davoren's Glossary as the only other glossary correspondence.

8.2 *O'Clery's Glossary*

O'Clery's Glossary was compiled by Mícheál Ó Cléirigh and published in 1643. As one can see from the date, it is contemporary with Dubhaltach's Glossary. The text has been edited and translated in two parts by Arthur W.K. Miller.[39] The entries are arranged alphabetically. Ó Cléirigh dedicated his glossary to Baothghalach Mac Aodhagáin and mentions several of his sources in his introduction, including *Amhra Choluim Chille*, *Félire Óengusso*, the *Martyrology of Gorman*, and *Foras focal*, and he notes that fact that Seán Ó Maolchonaire and Flann mac Cairbre meic Aodhagáin made glossaries before him. As noted by Knott 1944: 68, the glossary has been "mainly, probably entirely, compiled from older glossaries." On the whole, the language of O'Clery's Glossary is later than what we find in Dubhaltach's Glossary, and it does not contain such the large volume of etymological glosses as we find in both O'Davoren's Glossary and Dubhaltach's Glossary. There are 158 entries in Dubhaltach's Glossary which have a correspondence in O'Clery's. Of those 158 entries, 80 have O'Clery's Glossary as the only glossary correspondence.

8.3 *Sanas Cormaic*

Sanas Cormaic (Cormac's Glossary) exists in seven different manuscript versions, of which only one, H^2 (a fragment), TCD MS 1337 [H.3.18], pp. 76–83 is found in *CIH* (622.13–633.33) (Russell 1988b: 2; Arbuthnot, Moran, and Russell 2023: 366; Mahon 1987: 29–34). All of the versions cited herein are available on the Early Irish Glossaries Database. Whenever an entry from *Sanas Cormaic* has been cited, the text and citation convention found on the database have been followed. Previous editions and translations include those of Stokes, Stokes and O'Donovan, and Meyer. The text exists in both a short and a long version, and it also has shorter and longer versions of some entries.[40] There are 33 entries in *Sanas Cormaic* which have a correspondence in Dubhaltach's Glos-

39 See also Stokes 1900; Gwynn 1907; Gwynn 1909; and Russell 1988: 8–9.

40 There is a large body of secondary literature pertaining to this glossary, not all of which can be referenced here.

sary. Of those 33 entries, all but six also have a correspondence with another Irish glossary. In other words, for only six entries is *Sanas Cormaic* the only other glossary correspondence. Of those remaining 27 entries, only four also have an overlapping correspondence with *Dúil Droma Cetta*. Generally speaking, the entries in *Sanas Cormaic* are longer than the entries in Dubhaltach's Glossary.

8.4 *The Lecan Glossary*

The Lecan Glossary exists in seven manuscript witnesses. Most of the entries consist of single words, and it likely represents "an amalgamation of several short text-glossaries" (Russell 2017: 8–11; Russell 1988b: 7; and Arbuthnot, Moran, and Russell 2023: 370; Mahon 1987: 48–50). Thus, it represents a secondary type of glossary compilation. The text has been edited by Whitley Stokes. There are 17 entries in the version of the Lecan glossary as edited by Stokes which have a correspondence in Dubhaltach's Glossary. Of those 17 entries, for two entries the Lecan glossary is the only other glossary correspondence.

8.5 *Ni Tulach Glossary*

This collection of glossary material is preserved in TCD MS 1337 [H.3.18] (*CIH* 809.3–812.8; Taylor-Griffiths 2020: 1: 164–169). There is a large degree of overlap between this glossary and the *Arra* glossary.[41] There are 17 entries which have correspondences with the *Ni Tulach* glossary. Of those, one entry has the *Ni Tulach* glossary as its only correspondence. It should be noted that of those 17 entries, there is overlap with the *Arra* glossary for 13 of those entries. This glossary lacks an edition and translation.

8.6 *Arra Glossary*

This collection of glossary material is extant in TCD MS 1363 [H.4.22], pp. 60b12–62a (*CIH* 1558.16–1560.27; Taylor-Griffiths 2020: 1: 187–188). As previously noted, there is a large degree of overlap between this glossary and the *Ni Tulach* glossary. There are 13 entries which have correspondences in Dubhaltach's Glossary, all of which also overlap with the *Ni Tulach* glossary. This glossary lacks an edition and translation.

41 See Taylor-Griffiths (2020: 1: 167) for a table which shows the overlapping entries.

8.7 *The Metrical Glossaries*

The Metrical Glossaries "consist of lists of difficult words with very brief, usually non-etymological, explanations set in a metrical form" (Russell 1988b: 8; Mahon 1987: 44–48). The three extant metrical glossaries have been edited by Whitley Stokes in "On the Metrical Glossaries of the Mediaeval Irish." The text is also discussed in Russell 2023. In Dubhaltach's Glossary, there are 12 correspondences with the Metrical Glossaries; of those 12 entries, there are two for which the Metrical Glossaries are the only correspondence.

8.8 *Dúil Droma Cetta*

Dúil Droma Cetta exists in a longer and shorter version, as is the case with *Sanas Cormaic*. There are four MS witnesses found in TCD MS 1337 [H.3.18], pp. 63–75 (*CIH* 604.39–622.12), TCD MS 1337 [H.3.18], pp. 633a–638b (*CIH* 1069.21–1078.14), BL MS Egerton 1782, fol. 15 (incomplete), and TCD MS 1287 [H.1.13], pp. 361–362 (incomplete) (Russell 1988b: 4–5; Russell 1996: 147–149; and Arbuthnot, Moran, and Russell 2023: 358; Mahon 1987: 37–41). The versions of the text cited herein follow what is found on the Early Irish Glossaries Database.[42] The text from TCD MS 1337 [H.3.18], pp. 63–75 has been edited by Whitley Stokes in "Irish Glosses, edited by a member of the Council from a manuscript in the library of Trinity College, Dublin [H. 3. 18, p. 61, col. 1]." There are only ten entries which correspond in any way to entries in Dubhaltach's Glossary. The D[1] version of *Dúil Droma Cetta* seems to be in some ways earlier in date than the longer version of *Sanas Cormaic* and many of the entries are shorter than their *Sanas Cormaic* counterparts, which suggests that *Dúil Droma Cetta* might have been a source for some *Sanas Cormaic* entries (Russell 1996; 159–160; and Arbuthnot, Moran, and Russell 2023: 365).

8.9 *O'Mulconry's Glossary*

This glossary has recently been edited and translated by Pádraic Moran in *De Origine Scoticae Linguae* (*O'Mulconry's Glossary*) (see also Russell 1988b: 5–6; and Arbuthnot, Moran, and Russell 2023: 352–356; Mahon 1987: 34–37). There is a large amount of overlap between the material in O'Mulconry's Glossary and that found in *Dúil Dromma Cetta* and *Sanas Cormaic* (Moran 2019: 53–57; and Arbuthnot, Moran, and Russell 2023: 356). There are eleven correspondences with O'Mulconry's Glossary; for one of these entries, O'Mulconry is the only glossary correspondence.

42 https://www.asnc.cam.ac.uk/irishglossaries/. Accessed July 18, 2024.

8.10 *Bretha Nemed Dédenach Glossary/Aidbriugh Glossary*

The first title is descriptive and given by its first editor, E.J. Gwynn (1942); the second title is derived from the first word in the glossary,[43] which is the convention adopted by Taylor-Griffiths (2020) in her work on these smaller Irish *glossae collectae* and in her edition and translation of the text (2020: 2: 13–39). As the title of the glossary suggests, the glossary's source text is *Bretha Nemed Dédenach*. The glossary is extant in TCD MS 1337 [H.3.18], pp. 61–62 (*CIH* 603.16–604.38; Taylor-Griffiths 2020: 1: 200–227). The entries in the glossary are listed in textual order. The corresponding entries cluster around a group of entries spanning from DG 2.a.1.1 to 2.a.7.25. Eight entries within this range overlap with the *Bretha Nemed Dédenach* glossary. Of those eight, three entries have this glossary as the only correspondence. What is interesting about the *Bretha Nemed Dédenach* glossary is that it has a series of entries at its beginning which do not correspond to any of the extant versions of *Bretha Nemed Dédenach*. The only extant copy of *Bretha Nemed Dédenach* is acephalous (*CCIH* 185), so this glossary appears to be a unique witness to some of the missing material at the beginning of the text (Taylor-Griffiths 2020: 1: 204).

8.11 *Fonnaidh Glossary*

This collection of glossary material is preserved in TCD MS 1337 [H.3.18], pp. 638c–640b (*CIH* 1078.15–1081.36; Taylor-Griffiths 2020: 1: 174–179). There is a large amount of overlap between this glossary and the *Adhart* glossary, which is not discussed in this work (Taylor-Griffiths 2020: 1: 174). There are nine entries with correspondences to the *Fonnaidh* glossary. Six of which do not have any other glossary correspondences. This glossary lacks an edition and translation. It should be noted that in the MS, the note *éitged so sís* is written in *marg. sup.*; note that 5.a.2.12 *Eislis* is found within a block of entries where Dubhaltach has written the word *eidgedh* at the start. As noted in *CCIH* 46, not all of the identifiable citations are from *Bretha Éitged*.

8.12 *Stowe Glossaries*

The Stowe Glossaries edited by Whitley Stokes are a collection of three glossaries found in RIA MS C.i.2 [1234] which may or may not originally belong to the same glossary (Mahon 1987: 50–51). The first is found on ff. 8b–10b and contains entries for the letters A, C, and D. The second glossary is found on f. 29ba. It is entitled *forus focail innso* and contains entries for the letters T and U, but

43 Following Taylor-Griffiths 2020, it might be more appropriate to describe this collection as a *glossae collectae*, a word-list, rather than a glossary.

also some entries beginning with B, C, D, F, L, M, and S. The third glossary in on ff. $30^{a}1$–31^{bs} and contains entries for the letters A, B, C, D, E, F, G, I, and L (Stokes 1907: 268). The glossaries mainly consist of one- or two-word entries. There are five entries for which there is a correspondence with the Stowe Glossaries; for two of those entries, Stowe is the only glossary correspondence.

8.13 *Mat Glossary*

This short collection of glossary material is preserved in TCD MS 1363 [H.4.22], pp. 67a–67b (*CIH* 1565.32–1566.37; Taylor-Griffiths 2020: 1: 188–190). The glossary consists mainly of material from word lists (Taylor-Griffiths 2020: 1: 189). There are four entries with correspondences to this glossary, but note that there are two pairs of entries that are doublets (for doublet entries, see pp. 436–446); the other entry has no other glossary correspondences for any of these entries. The glossary does not yet have an edition or translation.

8.14 *Adhmad Glossary*

This short glossary is preserved in TCD MS 1337 [H.3.18], p. 422 (*CIH* 953.10–954.24; Taylor-Griffiths 2020: 1: 227–251). The "primary base text" for the glossary is *Bretha Nemed Dédenach* (Taylor-Griffiths 2020: 1: 227). All three of the entries for which there are correspondences in Dubhaltach's Glossary (DG 6.b.2.91, 4.c.9.61, and 4.c.10.62) have *Bretha Nemed Dédenach* as their ultimate source. This glossary has been edited and translated by Alice Taylor-Griffiths (2020: 2: 40–64).

8.15 *Breth Glossary*

This collection of glossary material is preserved in TCD MS 1337 [H.3.18], 649b–654b (*CIH* 1092.1–1098.42; Taylor-Griffiths 2020: 1: 179–186). According to Taylor-Griffiths (2020: 1: 179), this glossary itself appears to be a collection of other *glossae collectae* and contains both legal and literary material (2020: 1: 185). In Dubhaltach's Glossary, there are three entries which have correspondences, one of which where the *Breth* glossary is the sole correspondence. It should be noted that for the other two entries, there is overlap with the *Ni Tulach* and *Arra* glossaries in DG 7.b.20.83, and overlap with the *Ni Tulach* glossary in DG 2.b.3.74. This glossary does not yet have an edition or translation.

8.16 *The Glossary in Egerton 158*

BL MS Egerton 158 is a paper manuscript written in Cork by Séamus Ó Broin between 1736 and 1739 (Flower 1926: 221). The text has been edited by Whitley Stokes in "The Glossary in Egerton 158." The alpha-order glossary is on ff. 79^{a}–98^{b}. There are three entries with correspondences to this glossary (DG 6.a.23.42,

7.a.14.21, and 7.a.25.37), but note that two (DG 6.a.23.42 and 7.a.25.37) are doublets (for doublet entries, see Appendix 3, pp. 436–446); the other entry has no other glossary correspondences (DG 7.a.14.21).

8.17 *A Medieval Glossary*

This is the title given by A.I. Pearson in 1942 to the glossary found in TCD MS 1337 [H.3.18], pp. 623–628. It is not found in *CIH* (Russell 1988b: 6–7). According to Russell (1988b: 6–7), some of the entries might derive from *Sanas Cormaic*, but on the whole a range of texts is represented in the entries. There are three entries in Dubhaltach's Glossary which have correspondences with entries in the Medieval Glossary (DG 7.a.2,3, 7.a.7.10, and 9.6.15). There are no entries where the Medieval glossary is the only glossary correspondence.

8.18 *Cotaimside Glossary*

This glossary is preserved in TCD MS 1363 [H.4.22], p. 15 (*CIH* 1540.10–26; Taylor-Griffiths 2020: 1: 186–187). The glossary is quite small, but it does contain material which is not found at the beginning of either the *Ni Tulach* glossary or the *Arra* glossary (Taylor-Griffiths 2020: 1: 186). Dubhaltach's Glossary contains three entries (DG 2.a.5.20, 7.b.27.98, 7.b.33.105) with correspondences in the *Cotaimside* glossary. Of those three entries, two have the *Cotaimside* glossary as its only correspondence. This glossary lacks an edition or translation.

8.19 *Dúil Laithne*

This glossary was copied by Dubhaltach himself in 1643; he tells us this in a colophon on the text (Ó Muraíle 1996c: 372). It is extant in one manuscript, TCD MS 1317 [H.2.15B], pp. 116–117; it is not printed in *CIH*. The text has been edited by Whitely Stokes in *Goidelica: Old and Early-Middle-Irish glosses, prose and verse*. It consists mainly of entries composed of single-word definitions and is not in alphabetical order (Russell 1988b: 7–8). *Dúil Laithne* has 291 entries. There are two correspondences; one of them is the only glossary correspondence for the entry, i.e. DG 13.d.18.29.

8.20 *Irish Glosses*

The title given, by its editor, Whitley Stokes, refers to a collection of Latin declensions accompanied by Irish glosses. Although not a glossary *per se*, it does represent the type of base glossed text from which glosses can be extracted to form *glossae collectae*. The collection is preserved in TCD MS 1315 [H.2.13]. There is one correspondence, DG 1.b.15.91 *Góla*, which contains a Latin word used as an explanation in the gloss.

What becomes apparent in this review of the glossary correspondences between Dubhaltach's Glossary and other medieval Irish legal glossaries, especially when one compares the distribution on the table in Appendix 1 (pp. 411–431), is that there are two main patterns. The first pattern concerns clusters of entries across glossaries which pertain to a specific part of one text. This is what we find with DG 2.a.1, 2.a.3.10, 2.a.4.12–16, 2.a.6.24, and 2.a.7.25, where the entries all have corresponding entries in the *Bretha Nemed Dédenach Glossary/Aidbriugh* glossary. In fact, the only entries from this glossary are found in this cluster. The second pattern is more random, where we find only one or two entry correspondences in another glossary, such as what is found in the *Cotaimside* glossary and *Breth* glossary. O'Davoren's Glossary and O'Clery's Glossary were both compiled from some of the same sources used by Dubhaltach, which explains why there are large number of overlapping entries amongst the three glossaries despite the fact that none of them used another as a source.

9 Analysis of Textual Blocks

Within Dubhaltach's Glossary there are significant continuous text blocks from three major sources, i.e. *Bretha Éitgid*, *Bretha Nemed Dédenach*, and *Dúil* (*Roscadach*).[44] For the most part, Dubhaltach writes an abbreviation for each of these texts at the beginning of the blocks; many of the abbreviations occur at the edges of the manuscript pages, a position which is prone to damage, so it is possible that more abbreviations existed than can be recovered at the present time. While the notation of sources is of enormous importance to the modern scholar, a number of problems still remain in terms of associating DG entries to extant texts. For example, it should be noted that *Bretha Éitgid* is incomplete; despite the fact that copious commentaries associated with the text exist, it is clear that a substantial amount of the original canonical tract does not survive. Although much of the text was edited and translated in *AL* (3: 82–547), the edition is unreliable (*CCIH* 176–182).[45] While *Bretha Nemed Dédenach* has been

44 The following analysis leaves aside the issue of whether *Dúil* and *Dúil Roscadach* are two distinct texts or a short and long version of the same title, similar to the way in which *Bretha Éitgid* is often referred to by *éitgid* within the legal texts themselves. See discussions in *CCIH* 246–253 (where *Dúil* and *Dúil Roscadach* are understood as two distinct texts), and 176–177, respectively, and pp. 50–55.

45 Parts of the text have been edited and translated since; see *CCIH* 180 for a full list of references; McLeod 1996: 281–282, 285–286, and 288–289; McLeod 1999; McLeod 1996c: 346, 347, and 352–353; Binchy 1938: 89–90; *Bretha Déin Chécht* (Binchy 1966a: 1); Simms 1998: 28–29; Scott 1983; Ó Cuív 1975: 10; and Eska 2022: 326–339. See also pp. 43–44.

edited by E.J. Gwynn, the entirety of the text has not been translated (parts of the text have been edited and translated since Gwynn).[46] The most complete copy of the text as preserved in TCD MS 1317 [H.2.15B] is in Dubhaltach's hand. The text is extremely difficult. The lack of a complete modern edition and translation only adds to the difficulty of editing the entries from the text herein (*CCIH* 184–188). Finally, no copy of *Dúil* (*Roscadach*) is known to be extant. There are several references to it within the legal texts, *Sanas Cormaic*, and O'Davoren's Glossary, but nothing beyond passing citations from the text survives. The entries from Dubhaltach's Glossary represent the largest amount of continuous citations from the text, and, thus, is of significant importance as we now have a much better sense of whether the contents of the text do or do not match the contents reported to John Lynch by Dubhaltach himself (see the discussion on pp. 51–52). In fact, Dubhaltach's Glossary helps us to fill in the missing gaps within these and other medieval Irish legal texts.

These three legal texts are not the only texts for which there are significant continuous textual blocks within the glossary, nor are these the only texts for which Dubhaltach has provided the name of his source. Many of the entries in the glossary, however, cannot be traced to a known source. Those entries are listed within the edited text without a putative source, but those blocks which seem to be thematic are discussed below. Many of the entries have linguistic or thematic echoes found in texts spread across the surviving Irish legal corpus, and they are listed in the notes to the edited text even if the entry might not derive from that specific text. What follows is an analysis of those entries for which there is either a significant textual block or a named source within the glossary.[47] The texts below are presented in alphabetical order. See Appendix 2 (pp. 432–435) for a table which sets all of the entry runs against their named source and/or (where possible) their identified source text. Portions of that larger table have been copied within the discussion of each text block below. The following tables collate the manuscript location of the entries, any textual source indicators, entry numbers, and corresponding locations within *CIH*. Further cross-references can be found with the edited entries themselves. If a cell

46 See *CCIH* 185 for a full list of the edited passages as of 2005, which include Breatnach 1981: 58–60; Breatnach 1987: 42–57; Ó Corráin, Breatnach, and Breen 1984: 420–430; "Aithirne's Mother" (Gwynn 1928); Stacey 1994: 40–41; Carey 1990b; Carey 1992: 9–10; Carey 1994: 63–64; Tranter 1997. Since the publication of *CCIH* parts of the text have also been edited and translated in Breatnach 2006; Corthals 2007 [*CIH* 1126.33–1129.32] and 2010 [*CIH* 1129.33–1130.37]; see also the discussion in Corthals 2022.

47 For all of the legal texts discussed below, the reader is referred to the thorough discussions of each text in *GEIL* and *CCIH*.

has been left empty, it indicates that there is not a named source (or abbreviation for that source) associated with a block of entries.

9.1 *Aidbred*

Source named in DG	MS location of named source	Entry run	CIH correspondence
		10.1.1–10.5.4	2168.28, 2169.4–6, 712.13

This fragmentary text is concerned with the recovery of lost and stolen property (Eska 2022: 8–33). At the top of page ten there are a few citations which derive from the commentary to the text. Unfortunately, the top of the page is badly worn and stained, and most of the entries are illegible.

9.2 *Apgitir Chrábaid* 'Alphabet of Piety'

Source named in DG	MS location of named source	Entry run	CIH correspondence
aibgider crab*ad*	8, l. 38	8.38.104	

Apgitir Chrábaid consists of 36 sections and is not an 'alphabet' in the modern sense. Rather, the text is "a short treatise in Old Irish prose concerning the ideal state of Christian conduct and the rewards that ensue therefrom" (Hull 1968: 44). The text is preserved in 18 manuscript witnesses of which only four are complete. As the text is not concerned with legal subject matter, it is not in *CIH*. The one entry which has been identified by Dubhaltach as deriving from the text (§ 10.49) is DG 8.38.104. The larger context of the source passage concerns things which a holy person should avoid, such as being angry, fighting, etc.

9.3 *Bretha Comaithchesa*

Source named in DG	MS location of named source	Entry run	CIH correspondence
		1.a.12.31–1.a.15.36	78.14, 66.37, 75.15, 67.11, 73.36, 579.16, and 198.19
		9.17.53–9.25.76	75.17, 578.1

This text concerns the proper running of a neighborhood and touches upon subjects such as fences, injury to and by livestock, forestry, ploughing, etc. (*AL* 4: 68–159; *GEIL* 273; *CCIH* 292; and complete edition in Charles-Edwards 2022). There is a run of entries on page 9 that comes from *Bretha Comaithchesa* although these are found within a section labeled as coming from *Bretha Éitgid* (see Appendix 2, pp. 432–435). It is possible that there is overlap between the two texts as the entries concern injury. It is also possible that Dubhaltach shifted sources without indicating that he had done so. A run of five entries is found on page 1 of the manuscript, but the source of the larger section within which the entries are found has not been identified. There are also scattered references to the text throughout the glossary.

9.4 *Bretha Éitgid*

Source named in DG	MS location of named source	Entry run	CIH correspondence
e[id]*gedh*	5a, l. 1	5.a.1.1–5.a.6.24	
⟨*edgedh*⟩	5b, l. 2	5.b.1.25–5.b.3.29	265.14 and 267.28
⟨*edgedh*⟩	5b, l. 5	5.b.5.38–5.b.22.46	864.25
edghedh	5c, l. 1	5.c.1.47–5.c.8.61	1175.9, 275.4, 322.34
[*ed*]*gedh*	6a, l. 22	6.a.22.39–6.a.37.84	937.22
édgedh	7b, l. 4	7.b.4.57–7.b.7.61	
édgedh	7b, l. 7[48]		

48 This word seems to bookend the previous block of entries.

(*cont.*)

Source named in DG	MS location of named source	Entry run	CIH correspondence
eidg*edh*	7b, l. 24	7.b.24.91–7.b.26.96	1163.13, 1163.17–19, 325.23 ff., 1212.35 ff., and 2283.1 ff.
eidg*edh*	7b, l. 28	7.b.28.99–7.b.32.104	1177.9, 1180.23
edgaid	9, l. 11	9.12.36–9.47.144	276.3
		10.13.26–10.13.28	312.35–37
*ed*ged	11a, l. 2	11.a.1.2–11.a.28.34	1156. 37, 1399. 17, 1156.39, 1399.22–35, 1157.6, 1399.28, 1157.14–15, 1399.36–37, 1157.15–16, 1399.36–37, 307.12–19, 1629.30–1630.3, 1639.12–23, 1400.21–32, 307.33, 1630.23, 1639.41, 1401.15, 307.35, 1630.25, 1640.1, 1401.18

This text existed in seven different fragmentary versions. Although the text as it survives is not complete, there is a wealth of surviving commentary associated with the textual fragments. It is concerned with injury, whether as a result of negligence or lack of common sense. In many of the examples provided in the text, there is no (or limited) liability attached to the perpetrator (*AL* 3: 82–547; *CCIH* 176–182; *GEIL* 272; McLeod 1999). Many of the entries which are within the blocks labeled *éitgid* do not have a surviving textual source in *CIH*. Thus, Dubhaltach's Glossary helps to fill in some of the gaps in this fragmentary text. It should be noted that Irish legal commentaries are notorious for being borrowed across sources. It is not uncommon to find versions of essentially the same commentary (or quotations from another text) within two or more different texts, especially if the main texts overlap in content. One legal text can also be embedded inside another, such as the version of *Cóic Conara Fugill* embedded inside *Uraicecht Becc* (*CIH* 2257.12–2261.17; *CCIH* 233). As such, it should come as little surprise to find a run of entries (DG 9.17.53–9.25.76) ultimately deriving from *Bretha Comaithchesa* concerning injury done by animals within a textual block which is associated with *Bretha Éitgid*.

9.5 *Bretha for Catślechtaib*

Source listed in DG	MS location of named source	Entry run	CIH correspondence
		10.21.54	See edited text and pp. 50–55

As the title suggests, this text concerns regulations regarding cats (*GEIL* 275; *CCIH* 301; and *EIF* 121–124). All of the legal material related to cats has been edited and translated by Kevin Murray (2007) and the reader is referred to this work for a full list of sources. There is only one entry concerning cats which is found on page 10 (10.21.54); for further discussion, see the case study above on pp. 50–55.

9.6 *Bretha for Conślechtaib*

Source listed in DG	MS location of named source	Entry run	CIH correspondence
		10.13.26–10.21.53	111.22, 1389.27, 1390.25

The text *Bretha for Conślechtaib* is only fragmentarily preserved (*GEIL* 275; *CCIH* 301–302), and, as the title suggests, concerns laws regarding dogs. Many of the types of dogs mentioned in the text are discussed in *EIF* (114–121). The material on dogs is found scattered throughout *CIH*, and there is a section on dogs found within *Bretha Éitgid*. The entries from *Bretha Éitgid* (*CIH* 312.35–37) are found on page 10 within a large section concerning dogs (DG 10.13.26–10.21.53) which seem to derive from various sources although it is possible that many of them derive ultimately from *Bretha for Conślechtaib*. A comprehensive study of this material is lacking, but the material in the glossary entries adds to our understanding of dogs from other legal sources.

9.7 *Bretha Nemed Dédenach*

Source named in DG	MS location of named source	Entry run	CIH correspondence
[b].n.	2a, l. 1	2.a.1.1–2.a.18.66[49]	1111.1–1114.11
b.n.	4c, l. 1	4.c.1.36–4.c.28.136	1114.20–1117.35
			1118.2–1120.11
		6.a.2.4–6.a.4.13	1117.37–1117.42
		7.b.10.65–7.b.18.79	1121.39–1122.16
IS é b.n	9, l. 1	9.1.1–9.1.2	1130.11, 1129.24

This text is the first of a pair of texts, i.e. *Bretha Nemed Dédenach* and *Bretha Nemed Tóisech* (sometimes referred to simply as *Bretha Nemed*). *Bretha Nemed Dédenach* is concerned mainly with poets, their legal responsibilities, and their legal privileges due to their status (Gwynn 1942: 1; *CCIH* 184–188; and *GEIL* 268–269). There is one continuous copy of the text (*CIH* 1111.1–1132.40), which is in Dubhaltach's hand (Ó Muraíle 1996c: 381). Although the text as it survives does contain some glosses, it is clear that Dubhaltach had access to a fuller glossed version of the text, or at least a glossed version of part of the text. The language of the text is very difficult. While Gwynn's edition and textual notes are valuable, he does not translate the text, and the notes are not as full as one would wish for a text of such complexity. Passages from the text have been translated in various secondary sources (see *CCIH* 185 for detailed references and p. 40*n*45). Dubhaltach's Glossary is of immense value in that he provides us with the meanings of many words for which there is no definition provided by *eDIL*. A notable example of this is the list of nine names for types of poets in DG 4.c.18.95–4.c.19.103 (*CIH* 1118.15–1118.17). So far as I am aware, these terms are not discussed in any of the secondary scholarship on poets, and several of the terms are not in *eDIL*. Not only does Dubhaltach provide us with definitions of the terms and their relative order of status to each other, but he also helps solve an otherwise difficult passage in the text, thus aiding future scholars. For further discussion, see the case study on these entries on pp. 19–20.

49 The last two entries in the block do not seem to follow the rest of the sequence although they are related to the text. See the edited text for further details.

9.8 *Bretha Nemed Toísech*

Source named in DG	MS location of named source	Entry run	*CIH* correspondence
		6.a.4.17–6.a.6.24	2213.38–2214.3

This is the first of a pair of texts on poets which comes under the general heading *Bretha Nemed* (*GEIL* 268; and *CCIH* 188–191). There is one continuous copy of the text (*CIH* 2211.1–2232.37), but there is also a glossed copy of part of the text immediately following *Bretha Nemed Dédenach* in TCD MS 1317 [H.2.15B]. It will be recalled that these texts were copied by Dubhaltach himself. This first third of the text has been edited and translated in Breatnach 1989; the version from TCD MS 1317 [H.2.15B] is edited without translation in Gwynn 1942. There is a run of entries from this text on page 6 that comes after a run of entries from *Bretha Nemed Dédenach* (see Appendix 2, pp. 432–435).

9.9 *Cáin Ṡóerraith*

Source named in DG	MS location of named source	Entry run	*CIH* correspondence
		14.h.2.29–14.h.12.35	1772.18–1776.18

This text concerns free clientship (*AL* 2: 194–220; *GEIL* 270; *CCIH* 288–289; Thurneysen 1925a: 238–259). The run of entries on page 14 is not very long (DG 14.h.2.29–14.h.12.35), and the entries cluster around the topic of how to handle the fief of stock if either the client or his lord dies.

9.10 *Cethairšlicht Athgabálae*

Source named in DG	MS location of named source	Entry run	CIH correspondence
Senc*h*as	13e, l. 1	13.d.1.8–13.d.27.40 14.c.4.14–14.d.6.19	370.22–387.5 363.33, 390.20–36

This text concerns distraint, which is the formal legal process of taking someone else's property in order to bring resolution to a legal case (see *GEIL* 177–182). The text exists in two substantial copies although both are missing the ending. The legal text lacks a modern edition and translation (the edition and translation in *AL* 1: 64–305 is unreliable) (*GEIL* 279; and *CCIH* 286–287 for a full list of references).[50] Aside from the runs on pages 13 and 14 of the manuscript, there are numerous references to the text scattered throughout the glossary. Detailed references can be found in the edited text.

9.11 *Cóir Anmann* 'Fitness of Names'

Source named in DG	MS location of named source	Entry run	CIH correspondence
coir an*m*an*n* si*n*	9, l. 4	9.3.10	

This Middle Irish text exists in a long and a short version. It provides explanations of the names of characters who appear in medieval Irish literary and pseudo-historical texts. It should be noted that many of the entries in this collection contain etymological glosses (Arbuthnot 2005: 1). It is not printed in *CIH* because it is not a legal text. The one entry identified by Dubhaltach in the text, entry 9.3.10, is found in section 110 (short version) and 187 (long version). The larger context of the source text concerns Nuadu Fullón who put a spell on a wisp of hair.

50 Parts of the text have been edited in D'Arbois de Jubainville 1895; Thurneysen 1925a: 260–275; Mac Eoin 1981; Binchy 1952: 45–48; and Binchy 1973.

9.12 *Córus Fine*

Source named in DG	MS location of named source	Entry run	CIH correspondence
[c].f.	14h, l. 13	14.h.13.36	744.28–29
c.f.	14h, l. 16	14.h.15.37	161.21–22[51]

This legal text is fragmentary and lacks a modern comprehensive edition and translation, although parts of the text have been edited in passing (see *CCIH* 239 for a full list of references). The text concerns regulations amongst the kindred (*GEIL* 270; and *CCIH* 235–239). It should be noted that the excerpts from the text in TCD MS 1337 [H.3.18], p. 214a (*CIH* 728.17–746.16) begin with the title *Córus Fine* copied by Dubhaltach (O'Sullivan 2000: 442; and *CCIH* 235). There are two entries which have been identified by Dubhaltach as deriving from this text.

9.13 *Di Astud Chor*

Source named in DG	MS location of named source	Entry run	CIH correspondence
		10.31.70–10.48.121	995.15, 1348.24–1357.1, 1196.36–1198.8, 1358.17–38

This text concerns contract law (*GEIL* 277; *CCIH* 244–256; and McLeod 1991). There is a run of entries that comes from *Di Astud Chor* on page 10 (DG 10.31.70–10.48.121). Judging by the way the entries pattern in the glossary (in other words, their attestation pattern within *CIH* is not continuous in places), it appears as if Dubhaltach had access to a more complete version of the text than the parts which survive now. This is especially true of the entries which correspond to later sections of the text. That being said, it has been argued that *Di Astud Chor* itself is a compilation (McLeod 1991: 11; and *CCIH* 245–246), so the entry pat-

51 This passage in *CIH* has not been identified as coming from *Córus Fine*.

tern in Dubhaltach's Glossary might reflect the nature of the text's construction. There are scattered references to the text throughout the glossary and one substantial run of entries on page 10 (DG 10.31.70–10.48.121) which spans almost the entire length of the text.

9.14 *Digest B (56)*

Source named in DG	MS location of named source	Entry run	*CIH* correspondence
		7.b.12.69–7.b.21.85	1381.4–1382.3

For a discussion of the legal digests, see *CCIH* 322–335. There are four digests, A–D, of which A–C are more closely related to each other. Digest B (56) concerns those who can act as a surety. The content overlaps to a certain degree with *Bretha Nemed Dédenach*; the degree of overlap between entries can be seen in Appendix 2 (p. 433). The text in Digest B (56) has been edited and translated by Roland Smith (1932) under the title "The Advice to Doidin" (*CCIH* 62).

9.15 *Dúil (Roscadach)*

Source named in DG	MS location of named source	Entry run	*CIH* correspondence
d.r.	2b, l. 1	2.b.1.67–2.b.23.112	56.30–58.33, 314.21
D.R.	3b, l. 1	3.b.1.23–3.b.39.97	
Duil .r.	5b, l. 4	5.b.4.30–5.b.5.37	
duil .r.	6b, l. 1	6.b.1.87–6.b.3.96	
duil	7b, l. 26	7.b.26.97–7.b.27.98	
duil	7b, l. 28[52]		
duil	7b, *intercol.*, l. 33	7.b.33.105–7.b.36.112[53]	

52 This word seems to bookend the previous block of entries.

53 Due to the placement of the word *dúil*, it is impossible to determine how many of these entries should be associated with that text.

(*cont.*)

Source named in DG	MS location of named source	Entry run	CIH correspondence
d.r.	9, l. 4	9.4.11–9.11.35	
duil .r.	12b, l. 1	12.b.1.11–12.b.30.70	

It should be noted that in almost all of the sections headed by the abbreviations 'd.r.', 'Duil .r.', and 'duil', the text blocks which follow cannot be linked to any of the known extant Irish legal texts, although there are some topical subgroupings which overlap with other texts (see also the brief discussion on p. 41). To add to the potential confusion, it is not entirely clear that *Dúil* and *Dúil Roscadach* refer to different texts. A case for them being two distinct texts was made in *CCIH* (251–252) based on the fact the John Lynch assigns the composition of the final third of *Dúil* to several people, but significantly to Roighni Rosgadach (Lynch 1662: 158; and Kelly 1850: 2: 373), and that a later prologue to *Bretha Éitgid* states that Cenn Fáelad mac Ailello composed a text referred to by the title *Dúil Roscad*. Indeed, the abbreviations Dubhaltach uses, e.gg. 'd.r.', 'Duil .r.', and 'duil', could easily be interpreted as referring to two texts with similar titles. Dubhaltach never expands the abbreviation *.r*. That being said, a case could be made for suggesting that all three abbreviations refer to the same text due to the fact that Roighni Rosgadach's epithet is the same element found in the second half of *Dúil Roscadach*, although linguistically one would expect a different form if it were representing the genitive singular of *Rosgadach*.

At this point, it is worth quoting Lynch's text in full keeping in mind that Dubhaltach was Lynch's source for his list of Irish legal texts (Lynch 1662: 159; trans. Kelly 1850: 2: 375):

> *His subjicimus alium juiris librum* "Dula" *nuncupatum, trībus partibus constantem, quarum prima regi bellum inferri et plures alios injurias per vim fieri vetat. Docet prœterea quœ sint tutelœ ac Asyli jura, qua pœna sint afficiendi qui sanguinem, fuderint ii quibus prœsentibus et annuentibus scelus quodpiam admissum est; quà formâ in scriptum pacta referri debent. In hoc libro conficiendo Cormacus rex supra memoratus et alii elaborarunt.*
>
> *Altera pars, de rebus Ecclesiasticis agit, ac prœsertim de jure sepulturœ, vetatque avitum sepulchrum à quopiam deseri. Deinde prœcipit armenta de satis abigi, et quid de rebus agendum sit, in mari, aut terra fortuitò*

> *repertis tum variæ leges attexuntur. Prior pars Comini Fodui filii Fachnai opus: Posterior Cormaci et Carbrii Hiberniæ regum quorum paulo ante mentionem feci. Ultima pars præscribit honorem qui deferri debeat regi, Episcopo, et literatorum præsidi, ordinique, ac denique diuturno agrorum possessori: rationem etiam indicat qua injuriam cuiquam eorum illatam resarciri oporteat. Hujus operis præter cæteros author est Rognius Rosgadach Uganii regis Hiberniæ filius. Alias etiam res liber ille complectitur.* (Lynch 1662: 158)
>
> 'To these may be added the law treatise called "*Dula*," which consisted of three parts. The first propounds the law against making war on the king, and many other offences committed by force. It also teaches the privileges of sanctuaries and protections, the penalties against those who shed blood, and those who were present at and approved any crime: it prescribed also the legal forms of covenants. King Cormac, with the aid of other scholars, made this compilation.
>
> The second part treats of ecclesiastical matters, especially of the law of sepulture, prohibiting any person from abandoning the burial place of his fathers. It then orders the herds to be kept from the tilled fields, and promulgates various laws on the mode of disposing of things accidentally found on land or sea. Comin Foda, son of Fachtna, was author of the first part: Cormac and Carbry, kings of Ireland, already mentioned, compiled the second. The last division explains the honors due to the king, the bishop, the literary order and their president, and finally to the old landed proprietor: it also prescribes the mode of redress for any injuries that may have been inflicted on them. This work was the compilation of several persons, especially Roighni Rosgadhach, son of Ugoni, king of Ireland. It comprises other subjects besides those I have recorded.' (trans. Kelly 1805: 2: 371 and 373)

Although the text consists of three parts, CCIH (247) has demonstrated that it is not another title for the *Senchas Már*. It should be noted that the second part of *Dúil* as described above is said to have a section on items found on land followed by a section on items found on the sea. DG 2.b.11.99–2.b.20.107 have this same order, where the entries have been assigned to heptad 64 and *Muirbretha*, respectively. It should be noted that these entries are part of a larger text block which Dubhaltach has labeled with the abbreviation on page 2b, line 1, 'd.r.'. Another example of textual ordering is found in DG 2.b.8.95–2.b.18.105 where we have an entry on trapping followed by entries on finding lost items. A passage of commentary in *CIH* 972.30–34 (*CCIH* 249) concerns traps and finds, in the same order; the passage has a marginal note *Dūil sō*. The entries in Dubhaltach's Glossary are from a larger text block headed by the abbreviation 'd.r.' (they are in the same text block as the previous example). It should also be noted that many of the topics found in *Dúil*, as described by Lynch, are also found in Dubhaltach's Glossary. As one can see from the range of sources assigned to many of the entries within the text blocks headed with the abbreviations 'd.r.', 'Duil .r.', and 'duil', there is a significant amount of overlap in the range of subject matter found elsewhere in individual texts printed in *CIH*. Regarding references within individual legal texts to *Dúil* or *Dúil Roscadach*, later glossators and commentators regularly refer to other relevant legal texts by name, and these references are valuable for piecing together the contents of texts which are no longer extant (see *CCIH* 247–253 for a collection of these citations). It is unknown whether Dubhaltach was working with glossed versions of the full texts or a separate glossary derived from the texts. It should be noted that all of the textual citations collected in *CCIH* (251–253) concern topics covered within Lynch's description of the general subjects within the compilation *Dúil*. What should not be overlooked here is the importance of the fact that regardless of whether *Dúil* and *Dúil Roscadach* are actually two texts or one, Dubhaltach's Glossary confirms many of the subject areas covered by the texts as mentioned by Lynch, and this glossary is now the most important source for the structure and contents of the(se) otherwise lost text(s). As one can see from the table above and Appendix 2 (pp. 432–435), a large number of entries in Dubhaltach's Glossary derive from this text.

The first major text block is DG 2.b.1.67–2.b.23.112, within which are subsections which correspond to parts of heptad 64 (DG 2.b.11.99–2.b.18.105) and *Muirbretha/Bretha Éitgid* (DG 2.b.20.106–2.b.20.107) and which follows the order of topics as provided by Lynch for the text *Dúil*. The other entries in this block cover a range of topics including battle, fame, advocates, negligence, and deposit.

The second text block (DG 3.b.1.23–3.b.39.97, 4.b.1.2–4.b.22.35) is arguably the most important within the glossary as it contains legal material relating to women and women's health which is not preserved anywhere else in the extant legal or medical corpus.[54] The section begins with entries concerning fosterage, adultery, a woman's bride-price, forming a marriage contract, reasons for dissolution of a marriage contract, miscarriage, leprosy, and infertility. The entries then move on to the topic of *sleth* 'rape by stealth'. The entries are unusual in

54 Deborah Hayden is currently working on an edition and translation of Irish medical material which will further our understanding of this topic.

their graphic description of the different sexual positions which are covered by the definition of *sleth*; these descriptions are found nowhere else. The section also touches upon the topic of the distance the woman's screams can be heard from the place of assault; it is possible that somewhere here the source text had switched from *sleth* to *forcor* 'rape by violence'. The entries then move to the topic of raising an outcry after the assault and the legal process of prosecuting the assailant. DG 3.b.18.63 and 3.b.18.64 refer to a nun being raped by a monk. The entries continue to discuss the reparation that a king pays to a woman for her rape, then a female attendant, betrothal, loss of virginity, and then two entries on a woman who has sexual assignations in the bushes and a woman who is defined as an itinerant worker and a type of low status concubine. DG 3.b.24.80 has a reference to breastfeeding, a topic which rarely appears in the legal texts.

The next entry (DG 3.b.25.81) is quite lengthy and concerns abortion and contraception; the material covered in this entry appears nowhere else. The material in the entry might derive from Dubhaltach's immediate source, which itself could reflect remedies found in as yet unedited Irish medical manuscripts. The entry begins with a reference to abortion by various means and ends with abstinence. The ancient and medieval medical literature is full of remedies to bring on a late menstrual cycle; it was thought that maintaining a regular cycle was important for having good health and conception, and, thus, the line between bringing on a late menstrual cycle and aborting an early term pregnancy was blurry (Green 2001: 182, n. 144; Green 2005: 54; Riddle 1992: 7–10; Mistry 2015: 18). The entry then goes on to list three remedies for aborting and child or preventing pregnancy: (1) a pottage made of herbs and charms, (2) a thread around the woman's neck, which could refer to a textual amulet, and (3) abstinence. The *Trotula* text (84–86) refers to a womb of a goat, a stone, and the testicles of a male weasel as items which could be worn by the woman who wishes not to conceive (these particular passages are not preserved in the Irish translation of the text: "Handbook of Gynaecology and Midwifery" §17). Abstinence was certainly known as a method of contraception, and sex during menstruation was generally frowned upon (Green 2005: 59; Riddle 1992: 3). It should be noted that the *Tract on Marriage and Divorce* §11 concerns female witnesses being employed to determine whether the wife's statement that she was menstruating was accurate or not. If the husband accused her of lying about this in order to avoid sex (and she was found by the female witnesses to be menstruating), the husband owed his wife the fine of the amount of her bride-price as restitution and the same amount again as a penalty fine and honor-price. If the wife's assertion is proven to be false, she is guilty of sexual avoidance and owes the fine of the amount of her bride-price as a penalty fine and honor-price. What is interesting in the entry is that it refers at the end to her husband paying her the amount of a child's fosterage-fee as a result of preventing conception, which implies that the husband had a role to play in all of this too.

The entries in the text block then discuss miscarriages at varying stages of pregnancy. What should be noted with these is that *eDIL* defines *toglúasacht* as 'abortion' even though it is the verbal noun of *do-gluaisi* 'sets in motion, miscarries'. The entries are ambiguous as to whether they refer to miscarriage (which is not brought deliberately) or abortion (deliberately cased), but *toglúasacht* is translated in the text as 'miscarriage'. The subject of DG 3.b.32.86 is hard to interpret, but it seems to refer to conception and birth. DG 3.b.33.87 concerns childbirth, but the details are not clear. The following two entries concern childbirth and its recovery. The text block then shifts to a love charm, and the woman being instructed in how to bring about harm to her husband or the child in her womb. The final entries concern the household's livestock.

The next large text block comprises DG 5.b.4.30–5.b.5.37. These contain words for a river, a prison, shouting, giving, and hindering.

DG 6.b.1.87–6.b.3.96 refer to topics such as counter-claims, extortion, and guarding.

Two entries, DG 7.b.26.97–7.b.27.98, mention strife and judgement. The other entries on the same manuscript page, DG 7.b.33.105–7.b.36.112, mention topics such as scarcity, death, waste, and a candle-lighter.

DG 9.4.11–9.11.35 cover a range of topics including mire, an assembly of hosts, theft, swearing, marshes, judgement, and driving to and from an assembly.

The final block of entries deriving from this text, DG 12.b.1.11–12.b.30.70, concerns topics which relate to the church such as burial, faith, and an anchorite: also included are references to, amongst other things, a widow, corruption, subjection, residence, expelling, impugning, a pledge, an oath, fines, maintaining a guilty person, harboring a criminal, hereditary serfs, someone outside the kindred, the *aire échta* 'noble of blood vengeance', treaties, tribute, livestock, and compensation.

It is difficult to match entries in Dubhaltach's Glossary to a text which is only preserved in passing references in *CIH*. That being said, other texts do quote *Dúil* (*Roscadach*), and there are textual correspondences (or unknown citations) in other legal texts. The *CIH* references in the table above are thus necessarily sparse. The point of the table is to indicate the large amount of material in the glossary which Dubhaltach indicates comes from *Dúil* (*Roscadach*).

9.16 *Heptad 49*

Source named in DG	MS location of named source	Entry run	CIH correspondence
		8.7.21–8.8.23	45.3–45.4
		8.8.23–8.12.33	1421.18–1422.2

The heptads (*Sechtae*) are a collection of 65 groups of seven items covering a wide range of legal topics (*GEIL* 266; *CCIH* 291–292; and *AL* 5: 118–351). Heptad 49 concerns those who are not considered fit to give evidence. There is a run of entries deriving from heptad 49 on page 8 immediately followed by citations from a larger commentary on people who cannot act as a witness. As noted in *CCIH* (64), these citations surely derive from heptad 49.

9.17 *Heptad 64*

Source named in DG	MS location of named source	Entry run	CIH correspondence
		2.b.11.99–2.b.18.105	56.30–58.33
		9.32.96–9.35.103	55.18, 906.35, 1211.22, and 1853.21–22

Heptad 64 concerns finding lost (or stolen) property. It categorizes finds by their location and sub-divides the locations by 'frequented' or 'unfrequented' places (except for the seventh category which is the sea) (Eska 2022: 33–42). There are two substantial runs of entries from the heptad. The first are on page 2 (DG 2.b.11.99–2.b.18.105) and are found within a larger section identified by Dubhaltach as deriving from *Dúil* (*Roscadach*). We know from John Lynch that there is overlap between the subject matter of this heptad and *Dúil* (*Roscadach*) (see pp. 51–52). This run concerns frequented and unfrequented places. The second run (DG 9.32.96–9.35.103) is found within a larger section identified by Dubhaltach as coming from *Bretha Éitgid*. This run concerns the seven locations of found property, i.e. on a road, in a wood, etc.

9.18 *Liber 2*

Source named in DG	MS location of named source	Entry run	*CIH* correspondence
[li]ber.2.	11a, l. 1		

This rather mysterious notation is found at the top of page 11. It should be noted that Dubhaltach also wrote 'L[iber] 2°' standing for *Liber secundus, Liber alius*, or *Lebor aile* across the top margin of TCD MS 1316 [H.2.15A], p. 43 along with 'Senc[h]*us*'.[55] Dubhaltach owned that section of the manuscript (Ó Muraíle 1996c: 375). The entries which follow this notation in the glossary do not derive from the section of TCD MS 1316 [H.2.15A] which contains a fragment of the heptads.

It is likely a notation for a manuscript source (perhaps indicating a different source) as a section from *Bretha Éitgid* is found at the top of page 11 and the section on categories of women begins at the bottom of the page. In other words, it is not the name of a text.

9.19 *Tract on Marriage and Divorce*

Source named in DG	MS location of source	Entry run	*CIH* correspondence
		4.b.1.2–4.b.22.35	145.33–146.40

The title *Tract on Marriage and Divorce* was given to this fragmentary text on offences committed within marriage by its editor, Fergus Kelly (2014; *CCIH* 306–307). The text covers a range of concerns from betrothal to the proper running of a household. There are scattered references to the text throughout the glossary, but there is one substantial run in the top section of page 4 (DG 4.b.1.2–4.b.22.35). It should be noted that this section of the manuscript is very difficult to read, and many of the entries are illegible. Based on the placement of the run

55 This notation should not be confused with the 'Liber 2°' written by Edward Lhwyd in the upper right corner of TCD MS 1316 [H.2.15A], p. 11.

of entries within the text and CIH (145.33–146.40), the presumption is that the illegible entries at the top of the page derive from the beginning of the text and that the unplaced entries after this also come from the text even though they have not been matched to the printed edition. The subject matter of these later entries is in keeping with that of the text as a whole. The working hypothesis is that Dubhaltach had access to a more complete version of the text with a slightly different glossing tradition (the glosses in the edition do not match up exactly with what is found in the glossary). Furthermore, Dubhaltach's Glossary preserves a better reading of the canonical text in one instance (DG 4.b.10.16).

9.20 *Other Blocks within the Glossary*

9.20.1 Categories of Women

Source named in DG	MS location of named source	Entry run	CIH correspondence
		11.b.2.35–12.a.10.10	

This substantial section of material on pages 11 and 12 (DG 11.b.2.35–12.a.10.10) does not match any other legal material which I have been able to locate. Unlike Dubhaltach's usual method of providing a lemma and gloss, here he gives us a heading followed by a list of entries, which is not unlike the list he provides in the entry on cats (DG 10.21.54).

> [Ad]bar eile d*ar*ob ainm ⁊ ait*h*ne na mbean tet(*h*)a fein *ar* sgat*h* fer; ata d*r*eam diob*h* so, ⁊ ní h-*edh* ata drem oile.

> Other material for which there is the name and characteristic of the women who themselves go under the protection of men; some of these are here, and others are not.[56]

56 Different types of women appear on other pages of the glossary. Some of these types of sexual relationships would have been frowned upon by the church. For different types of women found in the Irish laws, see Power 1936; and Kelly 2009: 68–79 and *passim*. The translation of the entry is difficult to construe as the verb *téit* 'goes' can have sexual undertones as can the phrase *ar scáth* 'in exchange for, under the protection of'. Not all of the women listed here fall into this category. One might be able to translate part of the entry as 'women who themselves have sexual relations under the protection of men'.

This list of types of women is notable for several reasons. The first is that the list focuses on women in the lower levels of society, such as hired workers and vagrants. We also get a glimpse of family life with the entry on the stepmother minding her own children as well of those of her husband. Of note as well is the reference to incest. As remarked by Pamela O'Neill (personal communication, June 2024), we often see the result of incest in the laws, such as the child born of incest being put out to sea, but we do not often hear of incest itself within the laws. There is not a lot of information about these categories of women within the laws. They are all but invisible except in passing references.[57] It should be noted that the top of page 12 is badly worn, and at least five entries are illegible. It is unknown whether Dubhaltach got all of these entries from one source or whether he collected them from a variety of sources. Due to the high number of etymological glosses associated with them, it is likely that he did not compose the entries himself. Almost all of the entries begin with the word *bé*, which is later replaced by *ben*, so the entries do reflect early legal material (on the form *bé*, see Ahlqvist 1980; and Jasanoff 1989). Of the 22 entries which might have originally formed this section of the glossary, 17 are legible. Of those 17 legible entries, 11 appear to be previously unknown legal terms. The entire list of entries is printed below for convenience with the new terms in bold.

- **11.b.2.35** ***Bé foichlide*** 'a hired woman' (but cf. *banamus* 'female hireling')
- **11.b.3.36** ***Bé fothla*** 'a woman of withdrawal' (note that this is not the abducted woman *ben fothlai no forcuir*)
- 11.b.4.37 *Bé foíndel* 'a wandering woman'
- 11.b.5.38 *In carthach* 'the concubine'
- 11.b.5.39 *Bé* [*táide*] 'secret woman'
- **11.b.6.40** ***Bé n-indra*** 'woman of cultivation'/ **11.b.8.41** ***Bé n-indra*** 'woman of cultivation'
- **11.b.9.42** ***Bé n-airnaide*** 'woman of waiting'
- **11.b.10.43** ***Bé fuis i foltaib*** 'a woman of remaining in wealth'
- 11.b.11.44 *Bé carna* 'woman of flesh'
- **11.b.13.45** ***Bé catha*** 'woman of battle'
- DG 11.b.14.46–12.a.2.4 are illegible.
- **12.a.2.5** ***Bé n-indligthech*** 'an unlawful woman'
- **12.a.4.6** ***Bé n-éccomlán*** 'an imperfect woman'
- **12.a.7.8** ***Bé éccendsa*** 'a harsh woman'
- **12.a.9.9** ***Bé da crett*** 'a woman of two shapes'
- **12.a.10.10** ***Bé raiti*** 'a woman of a road'

57 More information on the individual entries can be found within the edited text.

9.20.2 Poem on Epilepsy

Source named in DG	**MS location**	**Entry run**	***CIH* correspondence**
	13.a.1–13.a.3		

Most unusually for a legal glossary, we find a poem and then an entry on epilepsy written at the top of section 13.a; they lack a larger context. The poem consists of four lines. The first and third consist of seven syllables with disyllabic end rhyme; the second has nine syllables (but it is likely that there is elision of two syllables (see Meyer 1909: 11)), the fourth has seven, and both lines have disyllabic end rhyme. The rhyme scheme is thus *abab*. The meter is likely *rannaigecht ḟota recomarcach* ($7^2\ 7^2\ 7^2\ 7^2$) (Murphy 1961: 53). Without a larger context, it appears that the speaker of the poem (Fachtna?), is asking for protection against illness. The entry which follows adds the information that the poem was recited on a day when the author had an attack of epilepsy. As both items form a group and the first is a poem, it was decided not to include the entry as part of the larger glossary.

Ben*nacht ar* an*main* Fa*cht*na/ do*m* sea*ch*na *ar* an ngal*ar* n-egcoir.
A coi*m*de sa, M*ic* Mu[i]*ra*,/ na ⟨leg⟩ inne ar ett*r*eoir.
A blessing on the soul of Fachtna/ to protect me from the unjust illness.
Oh, Lord, Son of Mary,/ do not abandon sense on account of weakness![58]

Glac*ad* talm*haidhacht* .i. gal*ar* mo*r* an la si*n* a*n* gab*us* a*n* rann si*n*.
Glacad talmaidechta 'epilepsy seized', i.e. a great illness on the day in which I recited that poem.[59]

58 The source for the poem is unknown; apparently the poem was recited by someone with epilepsy. It should be noted that Dubhaltach corrected 'featla' to 'fachtna' in the MS.

59 In light of the gloss, the second word of the lemma is likely to be *talmaidecht* 'epilepsy'; *eDIL s.v.* 2 *talmaidecht*. The general sense of the lemma is that despite suffering from an epileptic episode, the composer of the entry was still able to recite the verse written above this in the MS. It is unknown whether Dubhaltach suffered from epilepsy or composed the poem.

9.20.3 Seven Things Which Distance One from Learning

Source named in DG	MS location	Entry run	CIH correspondence
	13.c.1		

This material reads more like a heptad than a glossary entry, and its marginal placement on the page is the reason it was not included as a distinct glossary entry. It lacks a larger context, but it lists nine things (or fewer depending on whether one wishes to group the musical instruments and board games together) which interfere with learning. The items are not surprising as they include music, a faulty pen, board games (*fidchell, búanbach, brandub* are all types of board games), and women.

> Sea*ch*ain se*acht* ngaoi gona an leigin*n* [.i.] ma dail *gur*bad saor, sen, c*r*uit[h] is tiompan, pen*n* c*r*uaid*h* cen*n*dub*h*, fit*h*c[h]ioll, buanf*ach*, brandub[h], b[en].
> *Sechain secht ngae gona in léiginn* 'avoid seven spears which wound learning', i.e. if someone pours [drink] though it may be free, song, harp and timbrel, a black-tipped rough pen, *fidchell, búanbach, brandub*, a woman.[60]

9.20.4 Additional Thematic Clusters

It would be remiss not to say something about the large blocks of entries for which no source is indicated nor can be found, but which on the basis of subject matter seem to form a textual block. Section 1a (DG 1.a.2.4–1.a.16.39) has a cluster of entries concerning harboring an outlaw, the kindred, a physician, the watchman, and livestock. Section 1b has a cluster on offences by and to livestock (DG 1.b.3.51–1.b.10.74). DG 3.a.1.1–3.a.14.22 involve contract law. DG 6.a.7.25–6.a.20.38 concern the church, especially what is owed to it as payment for burial. The entries in DG 7.a.1.1–7.b.4.56 are less easy to categorize, but involve theft, judgement, oaths, sureties, and restitution. The top of page 8, DG 8.1.1–8.7.20, has a section on testimony. DG 8.13.34–8.37.103 cover a wide range of top-

60 O'Curry understands the entire entry as the headword. The translation of the first part of the gloss is tentative; it may refer to drinking.

ics including, oaths, kings, lordship, theft, and judgement. DG 9.1.3–9.3.9 have a section on fosterage fees. The range of topics in DG 10.5.5–10.13.25 includes casting lots, a bed covering, and theft. The range of topics in DG 10.28.55–10.31.69 includes a mouse, wheat, crumbs, a liquid measure, a half-wit, and types of plants. The cluster of DG 13.a.4.1–13.a.12.6 appears to involve providing for someone who is ill. The range of topics in DG 14.b.1.1–14.b.4.10 includes types of dye plants and fosterage. DG 14.c.1.11–14.c.3.13 are also agricultural and include a cloth for a mangy sheep and curds and is similar to the topics we find in DG 14.d.8.20–14.d.10.23. DG 14.f.1.24–14.f.16.26 concern fosterage (clothing and illness). Finally, DG 14.h.17.38–14.h.24.45 have clusters concerning distraint and clientship.

10 The Afterlife of Dubhaltach's Glossary

This section of the Introduction lists, in chronological order as best as can be established, later sources which mention and/or have used Dubhaltach's Glossary.

1. George Petrie (1839). In his address to the Royal Irish Academy, Petrie mentions in passing Dubhaltach's own reference to the glossary and states that, although it had previously been thought to be no longer extant, it might still exist because O'Flanagan had "quoted from it about twenty years since" (13). Ó Muraíle (1996c: 317) suggests that Petrie must be referring to Theophilus O'Flanagan who was working on a "Glossary of the Brehon Laws" around the period 1788–1791, although that work no longer appears to exist.

2. Eugene O'Curry (1840). The first substantive use of the glossary is Eugene O'Curry's alphabetical list of the entries which is currently bound within the same MS as the glossary itself, i.e. TCD MS 1401 [H.5.30]. This list represents a rearrangement of the material as Dubhaltach compiled the glossary in text blocks, not alphabetical order. Whether Dubhaltach himself ever made an alphabetical rearrangement of the material is unknown as no other copies (or versions) of the glossary survive. O'Curry's transcription is not complete. Firstly, he does not include entries when he cannot read the headword, e.g. DG 10.8.12, in which the headword is illegible, but the gloss itself is clear. Secondly, there are some entries which are omitted, e.g. DG 13.d.5.14 *Leamhadh .i. bod mairbhe.* Finally, there are some cross-references in his transcription to entries which are not included in his transcription, e.g. 661 *Findte diblaidhe. fec findte feartsach.*[61] It is likely that O'Curry originally transcribed each entry and then cut the

61 The number refers to the numbered entries of O'Curry's transcription.

entries up into small slips of paper which were then rearranged in alphabetical order before the clean copy of the transcription was made. This is based on the construction of O'Curry's transcription of O'Davoren's Glossary found in Maynooth University, Russell Library MS 79.[62] O'Curry's transcription has subsequently been used by Breatnach (1989) and also in his edition of *Córus Bésgnai*, and by Etchingham (1999) (see below).

3. George Petrie (1845). In his *The Ecclesiastical Architecture of Ireland, Anterior to the Anglo-Norman Invasion*, Petrie translates two of the entries, i.e. DG 13.d.2.9 *Fiodh defidh ar dun* and DG 5.b.22.46 *Minister*. In a note (61, n. f) he mentions that he found the entry:

> … on a loose sheet of paper in the handwriting of the celebrated Duald Mac Firbis, inserted in a MS. in Trinity College, H. 2. 15. p. 208. This leaf is a fragment of Mac Fribis's first draft of his Glossary of the Brehon laws, of which several fragments are to be found scattered among the College MSS.

It is likely that the fragments referred to by Petrie are other glossaries, such as *Dúil Laithne*, rather than fragments of the glossary under discussion. It should be noted that Petrie was a "friend and colleague" of John O'Donovan (Ó Muraíle 1996c: 284).

4. John O'Donovan (?1859×1861). O'Donovan's work with the glossary is best understood as part of the early history of the Royal Irish Academy's *Dictionary of the Irish Language based mainly on Old and Middle Irish*. A dictionary project was first discussed in 1852, and O'Donovan and Eugene O'Curry were approached by the Royal Irish Academy to be the first editors. The start of the work was delayed as both O'Donovan and O'Curry were engaged with the work on the Brehon laws. In 1859 O'Donovan began designing the dictionary, but his work was cut short by his death in 1861 (Griffith et al. 2018: 5). The assumption is that O'Donovan would have known of Dubhaltach's Glossary from either O'Curry or Petrie well before he began using it as a source for his work on the dictionary. O'Donovan's work was later published in 1864 as a Supplement to Edward O'Reilly's *An Irish-English Dictionary* (Griffith et al. 2018: 5).

It is not easy to determine exactly how many entries in the Supplement are directly from Dubhaltach's Glossary. Although O'Donovan provides a list of sources, he is not consistent about how he cites his sources within the entries, some of which refer to Dubhaltach's genealogical work, e.g. *s.v. peillic* 'a bas-

62 I owe this reference to Paul Russell.

ket'.[63] The following is a list of 49 entries from the Supplement which list the glossary as a source.

Sub verba

Adhradh 'adoration'; citation not found, but a cross reference to DG 12.b.23.56 *Aos cairde* is found.

Aghaidh fedil 'a mask'; see DG 13.a.6.2 *Dubhaighid .i. aigid fedil.*

Aibhillteoir 'a pilgrim'; see DG 7.b.32.104 *Aoibhilteoir.*

Aiccither no definition; see DG 10.11.18 *Aiccither .i. uga ésgther.*

Airmitin 'an effort which people make to draw cattle out of a quagmire'; see DG 1.a.12.30 *Airmhidin*

Bósar no definition; lemma not found, but additional citation DG 4.c.8.54 *Adbosaid* found

Bothachus 'cottiership'; lemma not found, but additional citation *bot[h]achus no ar buailid[eacht]* found, but cited as *bothacus on buailideacht* 'during the summer and autumn'. See DG 12.b.21.52 *Bothach.*

Breitheamhnastair 'judicavit'; cites 'Glos Brehon Laws H. 2. 15, p. 208'; this word is not in the Glossary, nor is it in O'Curry's transcription.

Cáirde 'law, right, peace, amity; peace treaty'; cites DG 12.b.23.56 *Aos cairde* entry.

Cliadhra, cliara, cleara, clior, criol 'a bag, wallet'; see DG 9.40.119 *Cliadhra, cléra.*

Coimidecht 'accompanying'; citation not found, but cf. DG 12.b.4.22 *Caoimhthias nó caoimhthes* and DG 5.a.5.20 *Caoimthechtadha.*

Coimpert 'pleading'; citation not found.

Coitsi no definition; but cf. DG 2.b.4.79 *Coitseachtus .i. coimheistachtus.*

Comarlégadh no definition; cites the gloss to DG 12.b.14.46 *Comairlegad .i. an ciontach do legadh fon chaill.*

Comhraite 'design, intentional offence (with malice prepense), actual commission of crime, with malicious intent'; see DG 5.c.4.54 *Comhraite.*

Coslach 'what is paid for defending one's case'; see DG 9.27.87 *Coslach.*

Cubas, brath 'complicity'; see DG 5.c.2.51 *Díchealtach .i. an fer cubus braith .i. an fer bius ag ceilt an uilc.*

Cuimlechtaib 'battles'; cites DG 9.44.137 *Cuimhlechta .i. comsloinnte*, but reads the lemma as *cuimslechta*. O'Curry reads *cuimhleachta.*

Curthóir 'a castigator of children'; cites part of the gloss to DG 13.a.10.5 *Ábhainn.*

Dearlaiter no definition; cites gloss to DG 8.18.45 *Derlaither .i. derb dioghlaither,* which is etymological.

63 It is also possible that some entries were omitted in the compilation of this list; the citations are easy to miss.

Deoraidh 'an exile or stranger within a territory'; cites DG 11.a.22.30 *Deoradh freacair.*
Diongaib gach déigheanach no definition; cites the entire entry for DG 12.b.12.42 *Dionghaibh gach degenach.*
Dithchus no definition; cites gloss to DG 9.3.8 *Diothchus .i. adbar tochus.*
Dithle no definition; cites DG 8.25.67 *Dithle .i. adbhal élaidthe.*
Dubhaighe 'a mask'; cites gloss to DG 13.a.6.2 *Dubhaighid, .i. aigid fedil.*
Eacmaic, ecmaing 'he happened'; cites DG 6.a.30.63 *Do-ecma .i. tegmhus.*
Einech 'the face'; cites *Ar a eineach .i. ar a aighidh* 'Duald Mac Firbis', but this entry is not in the glossary.
Eitsech 'a houseless person'; cites gloss to DG 8.13.33 *Eitsech, .i. duine gan tech.*
Feacht féile 'hospitable entertainment for one night to king, prince, poet, or anyone else'; see DG 11.a.12.17 [*F*]*echt feile.*
Foeighther no definition; not in glossary, but he cites the gloss *.i. fogartar.*
Foilmig, foilngid 'a dog that leaps at one's neck to tear him'; see DG 10.13.26 *Foilngidh.*
Forreith, forreis, foreth 'relieves, is given'; citation not found, but cf. DG 2.a.2.7 *Forrudh.*
Fresgisin no definition; cites the gloss to DG 14.h.4.30 *Fresgisin imscair.* O'Donovan mentions his source as 'Dudley Firbisse in H. 2. 15, p. 208, loose sheets'.
Fuaichne foghla no definition; cites gloss to DG 14.h.19.39 *Fuaichne foghla.*
Fuilleadh 'an addition, augmentation, increase'; citation not found.
Gin tuillmidh, gin tuillmidechta 'consuming mouth, a name for a spendthrift'; see DG 12.b.16.48 *Gintuillmhidecht.*
Gnáithleas 'no definition'; cites the gloss to DG 11.a.12.18 *Gnai*[*th*]*les.*
Iarrath 'the price of fosterage?'; cites the gloss to DG 14.b.4.9 *Iarrath.*
Ionnscuchad graidh 'moving up, to advance'; cites gloss to DG 8.28.77 *Ionnsguchudh gradh no ceíme.*
Nuithear no definition; cites the gloss to DG 1.b.12.83 *Noaighter, núither.*
Seachus no definition; cf. DG 12.b.22.53 *Sechfus.*
Seicill "cu seichill" 'a hound which follows one, but which is not one's own'; see DG 1.a.15.37 *Cu seichill.*
Tairidin 'a mill-race'; see DG 6.a.32.71 *Tairidhin linne muilinn.*
Tairiuc, tairic 'is forthcoming'; cites the gloss to DG 5.c.1.48 *Tairecc.*
Ticsel, tigseal, tixail no definition; cites the gloss to DG 13.d.10.19 *Tigseal.*
Tuidin no definition; cites the gloss to DG 10.6.8 *Tuidhin.*
Turgaire 'inciting, instigating'; cites the gloss to DG 1.b.16.95 *Turgaire.*
Turtgal no definition; cites the gloss to DG 13.d.26.38 *Turtgal.*
Uadhene 'for *fein*'; citation not found.

5. Eugene O'Curry (1861). In his *Lectures on the Manuscript Materials of Ancient Irish History* O'Curry states that he found a copy of Dubhaltach's "Glossary of the Ancient Laws of Erinn" in TCD MS 1401 [H.5.30] (123) (see also pp. 1–2). He provides a revised transcription and translation of DG 5.b.16.43 7 *Caogdac[h]* on pages 494–495 (see also the notes in the close transcription of the glossary p. 331*n*323).

6. Eugene O'Curry (1873). In his *On the Manners and Customs of the Ancient Irish*, O'Curry prints the Irish and translates DG 8.11.30 *Fairbe* (3: 476, n. 500) citing Dubhaltach's Glossary as his source.

7. *eDIL* has three entries which refer to Dubhaltach's Glossary by the old manuscript shelf-mark, H.5.30: *s.vv.* 3 *fochair* 'a branch of poetic science', *foilmer* 'slippery', and *Fúata* 'Ireland'. There are likely more citations in *eDIL* which rely on the definitions provided by Dubhaltach's Glossary, but they are cited under O'Don. Suppl., referring to O'Donovan's Supplement in O'Reilly's dictionary. Dubhaltach is mentioned again *s.v. fethal* 'emblem, halidom, likeness' and *s.v 1 rím* 'counting, number'.

8. Liam Breatnach (1989). In "The First Third of *Bretha Nemed Toísech*" (34, note to §11) Breatnach discusses DG 11.a.6.9 *Eaglus chuir*, DG 11.a.7.10 *Eglus coimdhidin*, and DG 11.a.8.11 *Eaglus con-ranna diobadh. Eglus comhroinnius diobadh an mhanaigh [re] ré trir* and references folios 45–46, which is to O'Curry's transcription of these entries.

9. Colmán Etchingham (1999). In *Church Organisation in Ireland AD 650 to 1000* (167, n. 1), Etchingham mentions that Liam Breatnach drew his attention to the glossary and O'Curry's alphabetical transcription of it. Throughout the book, he has the following references to several of the entries:

(a) p. 167, n. 1, mentions DG 5.b.20.44 *Cathair ataigh*.

(b) p. 282 and n. 1, mention the contents of DG 11.a.7.10 *Eglus coimdhidin*, and DG 11.a.8.11 *Eaglus con-ranna diobadh. Eglus comhroinnius diobadh an mhanaigh [re] ré trir*.

(c) p. 420 mentions DG 11.a.10.15 *Daormhanach*.

(d) p. 430 mentions DG 6.a.7.25 *Manach innerge dethbhire*.

(e) p. 440, n. 2 cites DG 6.a.15.32 *Uinge*… on f. 90, which is from O'Curry's transcription.

(f) p. 441, n. 2 cites and translates DG 6.a.10.28 *Colpa cennaithe*. Etchingham cites f. 31, which is from O'Curry's transcription.

(g) p. 446 refers to DG 11.a.9.14 *Sáormhanac[h]*.

(h) p. 449 discusses and partially translates DG 11.a.6.9 *Eaglus chuir*, DG 11.a.7.10 *Eglus coimdhidin*, and DG 11.a.8.11 *Eaglus con-ranna diobadh. Eglus comhroinnius diobadh an mhanaigh [re] ré trir*.

10. Liam Breatnach's (2017) edition of *Córus Bésgnai* (103) cites and translates the first half of DG 6.a.7.25 *Manach innērge dethbhire*.

11. Charlene M. Eska (2022: 67, n. 58) mentions the entries which originate from heptad 64, e.gg. DG 9.32.96 *Frithe*, DG 9.32.97 *Frithe cat[h]rach*, DG 9.33.98 *Frithe faithe*, DG 9.33.99 *Frithe raite*, DG 9.34.100 *Frithe roeadha no shlebhe*, DG 9.34.101 *Frithe trachta*, and DG 9.35.102 *Frithe fairige*.

12. Alderick Blom (2024: 197) mentions the glossary in passing under the title *Foclóir Féneachais*.

Editorial Method

Each entry has a unique identifying number. The order of the numbering scheme is as follows: page number, section letter, line number of the section, and number of entry for that page. For example, 14.h.2.29 means the entry is found on page 14, section h, line two within that section, and it is the twenty-ninth entry on that page. Entries which O'Curry was able to read but which I have not been able to locate in the manuscript are given the designation OC followed by a numeral. Most pages do not have as many sections as pages 13 and 14. The reader is referred to the section on schematic diagrams (pp. xxxiii–xxxvi) which provides a lettered diagram for each manuscript page, including the direction of writing; some pages have writing going in different directions and occasionally even upside down.

The initial letter of each lemma has been capitalized even when it is not capitalized in the manuscript. Length marks in the manuscript have been retained in the transcription (pp. 310–366) of the text but added or removed in the edited text as appropriate. Word spacing has been normalized in the edited text. Most of the time, Dubhaltach ends each entry with a full stop. The vast majority of the entries are formatted in this way. When an entry ends at the end of a line, whether in a column (as on page 7) or on a page, it is not uncommon for the entry to lack a full stop at its conclusion. The close transcription preserves Dubhaltach's punctuation, but the edited text adds full stops to the end of every entry. Editorial insertions are in [square] brackets, and editorial deletions are in (round) brackets. Dubhaltach himself uses round brackets within his glossary, which have been reproduced in the transcription (where round brackets are otherwise not used) and edited text. While this can be confusing at times, it should be noted that Dubhaltach normally has entire words and phrases in round brackets, but editorial deletions in round brackets tend to be a few letters. Expanded manuscript abbreviations are in *italics* in both the transcription and edited text. The ⟨angled brackets⟩ in the transcription and edited text are used to indicate that the enclosed material has been written above the main line of the text. Otherwise, the angled brackets are used in the standard linguistic convention to refer to a sequence of letters, e.g. ⟨ag⟩, the sequence of letters 'ag'. Where Dubhaltach has underlined a word or phrase in the MS, that has been represented in the transcription but not in the edited text. Manuscript ⟨ꜵ⟩ and ⟨æ⟩ have been transcribed as such, but they have been changed to ⟨ao⟩ and ⟨ae⟩, respectively, in the edited text.

Where letters in the manuscript are not legible, they have been indicated by ellipses within square brackets, e.g. [...]. To the best of my ability, I have

 | DOI:10.1163/9789004755673_004

tried to indicate where there is text, even if it is not legible. There are some entries which O'Curry was able to read which I cannot. Those entries have been included in the transcription and translation as close to their conjectured original position as possible. This has been made possible by the fact that O'Curry includes the manuscript page numbers next to entries which he can only partially read. O'Curry's notes are included with his transcription later in the volume. There are some entries which I have not been able to locate; these are included at the end of the transcription and edition. There are some entries which I have been able to read but were not included in O'Curry's transcription. These entries have been noted in the close transcription of the manuscript and in the notes to the edited text. The notes to the edited text are mainly concerned with the contents of the entry rather than differences between O'Curry's reading of the manuscript and my own. Differences in manuscript readings are confined to the notes in the close transcription so as to keep the notes in the edited text from becoming too unwieldly.

The lemma given in the translation is the corresponding headword in *eDIL*, when possible; frequently the oblique case of a noun as found in the glossary has been kept in the edited text as it provides information about the original source text. No other attempts have been made to normalize the language of the glossary because that would obscure the linguistic diversity within the text.

It should be noted that the orthography of the glossary (when it is not copied exactly from its source) is seventeenth century, as one would expect from a glossary compiled in 1643 or thereabouts. Generally speaking, the same orthographic features of O'Clery's Glossary pertain to Dubhaltach's Glossary as well, e.g. ⟨io⟩ in words such as *grioth* for *grith* and *tionól* for *tinól*, and the use of ⟨sg⟩ for ⟨sc⟩, such as *sgeo* for *sceo* and *sgoth* for *scoth*. Corthals (2010: 64–66) in his edition of the *Áiliu* poems in *Bretha Nemed Dédenach* (CIH 1129.33–1130.37) provides a thorough analysis of the orthographic features of the text, which is relevant to the discussion here as Dubhaltach copied the version of the text preserved in TCD MS 1317. Many of the features that Corthals lists for the *Áiliu* poems in *Bretha Nemed Dédenach* also apply to Dubhaltach's Glossary; for example, ⟨-dh⟩ for ⟨-d⟩ in 1.a.2.4 *anurradh* for OI *anurrad*; ⟨mh⟩ for OI lenited ⟨m⟩ in 1.a.9.22 *coimhchisi* for *comcaisiu*; ⟨m⟩ for OI ⟨mb⟩ in 3.b.20.68 *imert* for *imbert*; ⟨dh⟩ for lenited ⟨g⟩ in 1.a.7.18 *rodhaidhe* for *rodaige*; ⟨gh⟩ for OI lenited ⟨d⟩ in 1.b.8.67 *acluighedh* for *aclaided*; and *air-*, *ar-*, and *aur-* tend to be spelled ⟨ur-⟩ in 3.b.22.73 *urnadma* for *airnadma*, 12.b.1.11 *urnustar* for *arnastar*, 3.b.36.91 *urcuil* for *aurchail*. Also of note is ⟨-id⟩ for OI ⟨-it⟩ in 2.a.10.39 *cuid* for *cuit*.

The component parts of etymological glosses are put within square brackets in the translation following the standard convention for the treatment of etymological glosses (see Moran 2019). All definitions provided in the footnotes are taken from *eDIL* even if *eDIL* is not cited in every instance. When *eDIL* has been cited in the notes, it is because the *eDIL* entry contains additional information relevant to the glossary entry, or it is to disambiguate entries. When a word or entry is too fragmentary to be translated, this has been indicated by ellipses within square brackets, e.g. [...].

Within the notes to the edited text, a distinction is made between 'see' and 'cf.'. When 'see' is used, it indicates that the source which follows it is either the ultimate source for the glossary entry, or that it contains material directly relevant. For example, Dubhaltach copied material neither from O'Davoren's Glossary nor from O'Clery's Glossary, but both glossaries often have identical information as the edited entry. In those instances, 'see' has been used. If a source is preceded by 'cf.', it means that there is a more distant, and less certain, relationship between the edited glossary entry and the indicated source material. All of the textual sources for O'Davoren's Glossary follow what is given in *CCIH* (109–159). Where the source has not been identified, it has been indicated in the notes with 'no id.', short for 'no identification'. As noted above (pp. 32–34) there is frequent overlap amongst some of the entries across Dubhaltach's Glossary, O'Davoren's Glossary, and O'Clery's Glossary. This is likely a result of all three glossaries deriving their entries ultimately from some of the same textual sources. No attempt has been made to retranslate the quoted entries from O'Davoren's Glossary or O'Clery's Glossary. The names of Irish legal texts have been written out in full for clarity and to avoid an excess of abbreviations.

Edited Text and Translation

1.a.1.1 [.]ara .i. [.]sa[.]dibadh.[1]

1.a.1.2 [..]aforfog*h*t as .i. eig*h*em *ar*n[..]p[..] dl[..]oc*ar* as ro [..]ug no [......][2]

1.a.2.3 [...] .i. [..]ur*n*[.] na c*r*ic*h*e sin fes[.][3]

1.a.2.4 Anurr*adh* .i. f*er* [..]t cuigid do eod[.]a[...]a .i. c[.]c [....].
Anurrad 'outlaw', i.e. a man [....][4]

1.a.2.5 Mi[.] .i. a[.]o*us*[..] [..]gigd[.][5]

1.a.3.6 Tuillem*h* an cion*taigh* .i. a cain*achte* ⁊ [.]dib.
Tuillem in cintaigh 'wages of the guilty party', i.e. [.....] and [.][6]

1.a.3.7 Bainleab*aidh* .i. bia*thad* do b*e*i*r* fine di *ar*oile gan oion[.....]s.
Bánlepaid 'white harboring', i.e. refection which a kinsman gives to another without [...].[7]

1.a.4.8 [......] fo luig*h*e cána.
[.....] according to an oath of law.[8]

1 The entry is mostly illegible and is not in O'Curry's transcription.
2 The entry is mostly illegible and is not in O'Curry's transcription.
3 The entry also is mostly illegible and is not in O'Curry's transcription.
4 The remainder of the entry is not legible and might be part of another entry; this entry is not in O'Curry's transcription.
5 The entry is mostly illegible and is not in O'Curry's transcription.
6 The interpretation of the entry is tentative because so much of it is illegible, especially the reading of the gloss. This entry is not in O'Curry's transcription. It is possible that *cainachte* is derived from *cáin* 'fault, blame' and means 'the one who is guilty'; see *Dinneen s.v. cáin.*
7 The interpretation of the lemma is uncertain as it is difficult to determine whether the first element is for 'woman' or 'white'. The context of the entry is unknown, and the entry is not complete because the edge of the MS page is damaged. The reading is uncertain, and the entry is not in O'Curry's transcription. Cf. 12.b.13.43 BANAPAD.
8 The reading is uncertain, and the entry is not in O'Curry's transcription. Cf. 12.b.8.34 LUIGHE CANA.

 | DOI:10.1163/9789004755673_005

1.a.4.9 Bán .i. fíor.
Bán 'pure', i.e. true.[9]

1.a.4.10 Mesio*ch* .i. cui*m*gec[h].
Meisech 'capable', i.e. capable.[10]

1.a.4.11 Adbo .i. toibgel*us*.
Ad-bo 'may proclaim', i.e. ...[11]

1.a.4.12 Aig*he* .i. og*h* ae.
Áige 'head (of the family)', i.e. [< *óg* 'whole, complete, perfect' + *áe* 'of them'] complete one of them.[12]

1.a.4.13 Airecor*us*[..] .i. dui*ne* do[..] [...]c[..]dæirib*h* bia*thus* [..] .i. duine eric anisi da[....]s ce[.]*et*an[.]*rar* cuire cuit*h* [..]l[.][13]

1.a.6.14 [......]ba fialla*ch* go t*r*i nonb*ar*uib*h*, slóg*h* i*ar*mota.
[......] a band of warriors with three times nine men, a host then.[14]

---

9 The reading is uncertain, and the entry is not in O'Curry's transcription. See *Lec. Gl.* 174 *Ban .i. fir.*; O'Cl *Ban .i. fírinne* 'truth'; and *Stowe Gl.* 238 *Ban .i. fir* where the lemma also is explained as 'truth'.

10 The reading is uncertain, and the entry is not in O'Curry's transcription. See O'Dav 1257 (*Cáin Ṡóerraith*; CCIH 145: *Meisi .i. cuimgech, ut est ar ní meisi flaith doniupra feistide .i. uair nocha cuimgech in flaith na tiruairsi de ré ní is gairde na sin: feissti .i. tiruairsi* "Meisi, i.e. competent, ut est 'for the lord is not able to defraud residuaries', i.e. for the lord has no power over the remnant thereof for a time shorter than that; *feissti*, i.e. a remnant."); *Cáin Ṡóerraith* § 6, 248 (CIH 1776.17 and 21, gloss 3; *AL* 2: 212.19 and 24).

11 The reading is uncertain. The entry is not in O'Curry's transcription; the interpretation of the entry is thus tentative as the entry may not be complete. The lemma is interpreted as the 3 sg. pres. subj. of *ad-boind* 'proclaims, gives notice or warning'. The gloss is obscure. It might be derived form of *toibgid*, the later simplex of *do-boing* 'wrests, breaks'; *eDIL s.v. do-boing*. In MI forms of *do-boing* and *ad-boind* are frequently confused; I owe this suggestion to one of the anonymous readers. Cf. 5.a.4.15 AD-BO.

12 The reading is uncertain, and the entry is not in O'Curry's transcription. The gloss is frequently used in legal MSS to gloss the lemma in its meaning *áige fine* 'head of the kindred'; *eDIL s.v. 2 áige*. Cf. 9.31.94 ÁGHA FINE and 13.d.13.23 ÁIGHE FINE.

13 The reading is uncertain because the entry is mostly illegible, and this entry is not in O'Curry's transcription. It is possible that the third letter of the lemma is ⟨n⟩.

14 The beginning of the entry is missing, thus the reading is uncertain; this entry is not in O'Curry's transcription.

1.a.6.15 Corc .i. clan*n* no cinel.
Corc 'family', i.e. family or kindred.[15]

1.a.6.16 o[..]*ar*n [...][16]

1.a.7.17 [.]uid*h* .i. oglu*c*h bi*us* ag dol f*r*ia [..]ll[.]uib.
[...], i.e. a young warrior who is going to his ...[17]

1.a.7.18 Rod*h*aid*he* .i. duine teglom*us* roid*h* .i. cinel d*e*rg.
Rodaige 'a person who gathers madder', i.e. a person who gathers madder, i.e. a kind of red (dye).[18]

1.a.8.19 [T]uid*h*rec[h] ⟨folu⟩ .i. do d*h*era*c*h fola do-[g]ní an liaig*h* ag sgaoil*adh* cuislenn.
Tudrach fola '⟨blood⟩-letting', i.e. to empty blood which the physician does by opening a vein.[19]

---

15 The reading is uncertain, and the entry is not in O'Curry's transcription. See *Metr. Gl.* Supplement *Corc .i. cenel no finda.*; *Lec. Gl.* 358 (M) *Corc .i. ceinel.*; O'Cl *Corc .i. clan* 'children'.

16 The entry is mostly illegible, and the reading is uncertain; this entry is not in O'Curry's transcription.

17 The entry is mostly illegible, and the reading is uncertain; the entry is not in O'Curry's transcription.

18 The reading is uncertain, and the entry is not in O'Curry's transcription; thus the interpretation of this entry is tentative as it may not be complete. The lemma is not in *eDIL* as it stands, but it is interpreted here as 'person who gathers madder' in light of the gloss. There appears to be some confusion between someone who gathers madder used for making red dye, and someone involved with the process of scaling cliffs to harvest produce, such as bird eggs. The second gloss understands *roid* as the word for madder instead of a word for band or rope, hence the gloss *derg* 'red'; it should be noted that the interpretation of *eDIL s.v. ? 1 roid* 'a band or withe (?)' is tentative. Cf. O'Dav 1492 (heptad 54; CCIH 152: *Suainemh .i. tét, ut est cro fir saighes a suainemhnaib .i. in t-allaighe no in roaighe iar teastugud na téti do féin nó da carait* "*Suainem*, a rope, ut est 'the death of a man who advances by ropes', i.e. the cliff-man (?) or the ... after testing the rope by himself or by his friend."); and heptad 54 (CIH 32.1; AL 5: 298.8–300.20; and Eska 2022: 392–393). The interpretation of this entry in O'Dav is also uncertain because of the connection (or not) between *rodaige* and *allaige*. Note, however, that Binchy, CIH 1526, n. i, suggests reading *rodaighe* for *roaighe*. The connection between these two words also is made in commentary to heptad 35: *in rodaide no in t-allaige* 'the builder or the cliff-man (?)' (AL 5: 238.15).

19 The reading is uncertain, and this entry is not in O'Curry's transcription. For the lemma, see *Bretha Éitgid* (CIH 296.30; AL 3: 320.27).

1.a.8.20 Fiac*h* iom*r*aid*h* na gaide .i. a luad ag t*r*iall c[..].
Fíach immráid na gaide 'fine for the intention of theft', i.e. his discussing attempting ….[20]

1.a.9.21 […]inges .i. do cui*mghithiedh* .i. conigsiod.
[…]*inges*, i.e. to be able, i.e. they were able.[21]

1.a.9.22 Coim*hchi*si .i. coi*mh*fec*h*ain.
Comcaisiu 'examining', i.e. jointly-watching.[22]

1.a.9.23 Rergad*air* .i. ro reimn*ighedar*.
Rergadar 'they put', i.e. they arranged.[23]

1.a.9.24 Brot*h* .i. brat*h* do-[g]ni aon*ar*, combrot*h* .i. b*r*at*h* maille re duine eile.
Bruth 'fury', i.e. fury a single person makes, *combruth* 'fury', i.e. fury together with another person.[24]

1.a.10.25 Áindlicet .i. ionglaine no neim*h*cet, licet .i. cetoig[the].
Áindlicet 'not allowed', i.e. uncleanness or not permitted, *licet* 'allowed', i.e. permitted.[25]

---

20 The reading is uncertain because the end of the entry is illegible. For part of the lemma, cf. more distantly *Bretha Éitgid* (CIH 259.25; AL 3: 136.14).

21 The reading is uncertain because the beginning of the entry is illegible; the entry is not in O'Curry's transcription. Both of the glosses look like late forms of *con-icc* 'to be able'; *eDIL s.v. con-icc.*

22 The interpretation of the gloss is tentative. Here it is interpreted as *eDIL s.v. coimḟeithem* 'act of watching', but it is possible that there is also an etymological interpretation of the gloss.

23 The lemma is obscure; see O'Don. Suppl. *s.v. reargadar*, which cross-references *diubracad* and has a quotation from the *Annals of the Four Masters s.a.* 1599 where the verb is interpreted as 'they put or placed'. The interpretation of the lemma here follows that in the *Annals of the Four Masters*. The gloss appears to be a form of *réim(m)nigid* 'advances, arranges'.

24 See *eDIL s.vv. 1 bruth* and *combruth*. Although the entry here does not bear any resemblance to O'Dav 234 (no id.; CCIH 115), both *bruth* and *combruth* appear in that entry as well although the gloss there seems to have misunderstood the lemma.

25 The second half of the entry is not in O'Curry's transcription nor is the headword in *eDIL*. Note that *licet* is Latin (this is based on the fact that it is written in roman script), but cf. *eDIL s.v. licet* 'lawful, allowed, permitted by law' which is derived from Latin *licitum, licet*. Cf. O'Dav 1176 (no id.; CCIH 143: *Licet .i. glanadh no nighi…* "*Licet*, i.e. cleansing or washing…") which echoes the beginning of the entry.

1.a.11.26 [.]sreol[.]c .i. lu*cht* ⟨ł fer⟩ f*aire*.
[.]*sreol*[.]*c*, i.e. a watchman.[26]

1.a.11.27 Ad-c*h*eat*h* .i. ad-c*h*ife*th*.
Ad-cheth 'he could see', i.e. he could see.[27]

1.a.11.28 P*r*oiceptai .i. sermonuig*h*.
Proiceptaid 'preacher', i.e. a preacher.[28]

1.a.11.29 Coim*h*g*h*niom*h* .i. coim*h*g*h*niom*agh*ad*h* cion*adh* ag daran*n* rete fec*ht* ⟨[..]ad[.]⟩.
Comgním 'co-operation', i.e. co-operation in a crime in dividing a thing once ⟨…⟩.[29]

1.a.12.30 *Air*m*h*idin .i. *ar*rac*htus* do-[g]nid daoine ag t*ar*raing b*eth*adh*aigh* as lath*aig*.
Airmidin 'honor', i.e. the strength people make by drawing a living thing from a mire.[30]

1.a.12.31 Fiac*h* duineacait*he* .i. fiac*h* an c*h*ionuid*h* an c*h*a[ith]m*he* do denad*h* duine.
Fíach duinecaithe 'fine of human-trespass', i.e. fine for the crime of trespass which a person did.[31]

---

26 This entry is not in O'Curry's transcription, and the headword is illegible, but *astrolaic* 'astrologer' would fit in the space in the MS.

27 See *eDIL s.v. ad-cí* 'sees'. The headword is the 3 sg. impf. subj; the gloss is a later 3 sg. cond.

28 The gloss is a variant spelling of *sermóntaid*; see *eDIL s.v. sermóntaid, senmóntaid.*

29 The gloss is not included in O'Curry's transcription, and the interpretation of the entry is uncertain. The general sense seems to be acting as an accomplice in a crime. The interpretation of *darann* is conjecture but may refer to the division of stolen goods. It is interpreted as a vn. of **do-ranna* 'divides'; see *eDIL s.v. ar-ranna* 'divides'. I owe this suggestion to Paul Russell.

30 The lemma is an oblique case of *airmitiu* 'honouring, honor'; *eDIL s.v. 1 airmitiu*. The translation of the gloss is tentative. The general sense is that people who have the ability to draw an animal out of a mire are given special status. See O'Don. Suppl. *s.v. airmitin*; and cf. O'Cl *Airmidin .i. onóir* 'honour'.

31 For the lemma, cf. gloss 3, heptad 55 (*CIH* 41.5–6; *AL* 5: 268.24); and *Bretha Comaithchesa* (*CIH* 78.14 and 15, 79.10; *Bretha Comaithcheso* §§ 32, 33, and 38; *AL* 4: 138.23, 146.18, and 152.7). The missing letters are supplied from O'Curry's transcription.

1.a.13.32 *Air*lim .i. leím *air* .i. leim do berid *air*neis *ar* g*h*ort, no *ar* fer, no *ar* clad*h*.
Airlimm 'leaping-trespass', i.e. [< *leímm* 'leaping' + *for* 'on, over'] leaping onto it, i.e. livestock leaps onto a field, or onto grass, or over a ditch.[32]

1.a.13.33 T*air*rsce .i. t*air*iscia .i. ceim[n]iug*adh* do-[g]nid sp*r*e t*ar* fer no gort .⁊c̄.
Tairsce 'crossing-trespass', i.e. crossing-trespass, i.e. stepping which cattle do onto grass or a field, etc.[33]

1.a.14.34 Diog*h*uin feoir eat*ham*(i)ain .i. s*a*rug*adh* fer ferain*n* da ttig somaoin eat*h*a .⁊c̄.
Díguin feóir ethamuin 'trespass of a preserved field of grass', i.e. violation of a grass field from which comes a profit of corn.[34]

1.a.15.35 Brec*h*tán .i. cinel annluin*n*.
Brechtán 'butter', i.e. a type of condiment.[35]

1.a.15.36 Treoir .i. eol*us* no t*r*eóir do-[g]ní nec*h* d'fogl*aigh*ib*h*.
Treóir 'guidance', i.e. knowledge or guidance anyone obtains regarding trespassers.[36]

---

32 The preposition *ar* in the gloss is likely a later usage of *for*, which can mean both 'on' and 'over'; both meanings are used in the gloss; *eDIL s.v. 1 for*. For the lemma, see *Bretha Comaithchesa* (*CIH* 66.37; *Bretha Comaithcheso* § 6; *AL* 4: 78.8). *Airlimm* is a form of cattle-trespass; see *EIF* 137; and cf. 1.a.13.33 TAIRRSCE.

33 The gloss *tairiscia* is obscure; it is possible that it is a later form of the headword or an etymological gloss. For the lemma, see *Bretha Comaithchesa* (*CIH* 75.15; *Bretha Comaithcheso* § 26; *AL* 4: 126.5); and O'Dav 967 (*Bretha Comaithchesa*; *CCIH* 137) where the lemma appears as part of the gloss. *Tairsce* is a less serious variety of grazing-trespass because the livestock do not consume anything; see *EIF* 137; and cf. 1.a.13.32 AIRLIM.

34 For the lemma, see *Bretha Comaithchesa* (*CIH* 67.11; *Bretha Comaithcheso* § 6, gloss j; *AL* 4: 80.7). For the translation 'preserved grass', see the discussion in Charles-Edwards 2022: 14–16. Following Charles-Edwards, it is difficult to determine whether *etha*, the gen. sg. of *ith* 'corn, grain' refers specifically to corn here or more generally to land which has been set aside for a particular use, such as a preserved pasture; *eDIL s.v. ith*. Cf. 4.c.4.40 DIOGHUIN.

35 For the lemma, see *Bretha Comaithchesa* (*CIH* 73.36; *Bretha Comaithcheso* comm. 11 (b)2 (§ 22); *AL* 4: 118.7); and O'Cl *Breachtan .i. cruithneacht, ⁊ fos im úr* 'wheat and also fresh butter'.

36 The translation of the gloss is tentative. The final word, *foglaighibh*, is understand as the dat. pl. of *foglaid* 'one who commits a depredation'; *eDIL s.v. 1 foglaid*. For a possible con-

1.a.15.37 Cu sei*c*hill .i. cú bi*us* ag sei*c*hem ei*c*h o s*h*ealluib*h* o suilib*h* .i. cu do cí duine aga lenm*h*ui*n* ⁊ n*ach* leis fein í.
Cú sechill 'a hound which strays beyond the bounds of its master's territory', i.e. a dog which is following a horse from the glances, from the eyes, i.e. a dog that a person sees following him and it is not his own.[37]

1.a.16.38 Tacomul .i. cengal.
Taccomol 'joining', i.e. binding.[38]

1.a.16.39 Fo*c*huir*adh* [.i.] g*air*m no t*air*ring do-[g]ni ne*c*h *ar* coin.
Fochuiradh 'summoning', i.e. calling or inciting that someone does regarding a dog.[39]

1.a.17.40 Dag do ait .i. an g*r*is gabail.
Daig do áitt 'destructive fire', i.e. the fire of a rafter.[40]

1.a.17.41 Duirb .i. (dae) do*n* robe*t* don orba .i. don ⟨im⟩ feran*n*.
Doirb 'worm', i.e. [< *da n-* 'when' + *ro-bed* 'it is' + *don orba* 'from the land'] when it is from the land, i.e. from ⟨around⟩ the land.[41]

---

text, cf. *Bretha Comaithchesa* (*CIH* 579.16 and 198.19; *Bretha Comaithcheso* XIV/2 (§ 26); *AL* 4: 126.19).

37 See O'Don. Suppl. *s.v. seicill*. The word *seichill* is only found in the phrase *cú sechill*; *eDIL s.v. seichill*. The entry likely originates from *Bretha for Conṡlechtaib*; cf. *CIH* 111.39 and 857.4 (*CCIH* 16). The entry seems to refer to a dog which strays outside of its master's property and follows any person or animal it sees. See O'Don. Suppl. *s.v. seicill*.

38 The lemma is understood as a later m. form of n. *accomol* 'joining, meeting' with the ⟨t⟩ of the m. article *in t-* attached to it as a result of a misreading or misinterpretation of the source text. Cf. 9.6.15 TACOMAL; and *eDIL s.v. taccomol* 'union'. It is also possible that the form arose as a compound of *do* + *accomol*; cf. *comaccomol* 'joining together, uniting, union' < *com* + *accomol*. I owe this suggestion to one of the anonymous readers.

39 The headword is obscure. Based on the gloss, it appears to be a term which refers to someone summing or commanding a dog; see *eDIL s.v. fo-cuir, fo-cuirethar* 'throws, sends, summons'.

40 Regarding the interpretation of the lemma, cf. the similar phrase *teine di āit(t)* discussed in Mac Airt 1956: 263–267; and *eDIL s.v. 1 teine*. The lemma is not listed as one of Mac Airt's examples, which are almost exclusively confined to the annals.

41 The interpretation of the entry is tentative due to the uncertainly of the word *dae*. The headword could be *doirb* 'difficult', or it could be from *dorb* 'small insect or worm'. The latter meaning makes better sense with the gloss. Here and in the following entry in the MS,

1.a.18.42 Duibell .i. [dub] (dae) da n-eibill an teine saig*h*nen.
Duibell 'quick', i.e. [< *dub* 'dark' + *at-bail*(*l*) 'disappears'] darkness when the flash of lightning disappears.[42]

1.a.18.43 Tap .i. obann*n*.
Tap 'sudden', i.e. quick.[43]

1.a.18.44 F*e*r asa he .i. f*e*r ler leis.
Fér asa hé 'grass of his', i.e. he has an abundance of grass.[44]

1.a.18.45 Tad*h*b*h*uis .i. taisbo*n*si.
Tadbáis 'visions', i.e. visions.[45]

1.b.1.46 Fualang .i. teit*h*em*h* no a l*ethét*.
Fúalang 'frenzy', i.e. fleeing or its equivalent.[46]

1.a.18.42 DUIBELL, it looks as if Dubhaltach made a copying error and added *dae* (likely somewhere nearby in his source) to both entries. The interpretation of the gloss *im* is also problematic as it is difficult to determine whether Dubhaltach meant it as a correction to *don*. Both words have been left in the entry due to this uncertainty.

42 See *DDC* D1.262 *Duibell .i. dub dia neipil .i. sáighnén* (*CIH* 613.8 and cf. D2.144, *CIH* 1072.24); I should like to thank Paul Russell for discussion on the interpretation of this entry. The entry in Dubhaltach's Glossary has been emended to match that in *DDC*. As with the discussion of the previous entry, 1.a.17.41 DUIRB on the deletion of *dae*. Cf. O'Cl *Duibeal .i. obann, duibeall .i. udmall no luath* 'sudden, quick or swift'; and O'Dav 595 (*Bretha Nemed Toísech*; *CCIH* 125: *Duibell .i. utmall, ut est duibell lonn lobur* "*Duibell*, i.e. nimble, ut est ..." Stokes does not translate the remainder of the entry.).

43 According to *eDIL s.v. tap*, the headword is only found in glossaries. See *SC* Y.1232 *Tap .i. obann no bidg ut dicitur ni beir tap tigradus is aiti araciallathar tassic an pound.*; *Metr. Gl.* 34 § 23 *'tap' oband*; O'Cl *Tap .i. obann, no bidhg* 'sudden'; and *Bretha Nemed Dédenach* 23.24 (*CIH* 1118.19; *CCIH* 184–188).

44 In the first half of the entry, *he* in interpreted as if it were OI *aí*. The interpretation of this entry is tentative because the context is unknown. The general sense is of owning an abundance of grass.

45 This entry is problematic for a number of reasons. The first is that the case and number of the headword is uncertain; if it is from m. *o*-stem *tadbás* 'vision, image', it could be gen. sg. or nom. pl. The context of the entry is lacking. The gloss appears to be a conflation of *taidbsiu* 'showing, appearance' and a form of *do-aisféna* 'shows, sets forth'. The following sequence of entries in O'Cl should be noted: *Tadhbhad .i. taidhbhsi* 'a vision' and *Tadhbhas .i. taisbénadh* 'to show'. It is possible the Dubhaltach made a copying mistake from his exemplar.

46 For *teithemh*, see *eDIL s.v. teiched, teithed*. For *lethét*, see *eDIL s.v. leithéit*. The entry likely refers to cattle.

1.b.1.47 Ceirt iomain .i. am*h*uil ro imeo*ch*aidis a n-*air*neis fein gan iomain.
Certimmáin 'proper driving', i.e. as they used to round up their own cattle without driving.[47]

1.b.2.48 Iomain ⟨.i. an eall*aigh*⟩ sgor ic an duine .i. na g*h*ort feoir no *ar*b*h*a ⁊ *ar*d ur*char* flesga ⁊ *tr*i desce[im]en*na* o t*h*ire (a) tuai*m* ⟨.i. raoi[..] om[..] *era*d*he* ⁊ [.]acli an l*eth* ber[.] as⟩.
Immáin ⟨.i. ellaig⟩ scor oc in duine 'driving ⟨i.e. of cattle⟩ [into] the person's enclosure', i.e. the field of grass or of corn and a high cast of a rod and three full paces from a mound of the land ⟨i.e. …⟩[48]

1.b.3.49 Sec*htar* cric*h* .i. g*ach* ionad o sin amac*h*.
Sechtar crích 'outside a territory', i.e. every place beyond that.[49]

1.b.3.50 Iomaig*h* .i. iomain .i. tio*m*ain.
Imm-aig 'drives', i.e. driving, i.e. driving.[50]

47 See *Di Choimét Dligthech*, where there is a reference to 'proper driving' (*CIH* 1723.17; *AL* 2: 2.9; *CCIH* 287–288), and also heptad 4 (*CIH* 6.3; *AL* 5: 11). There is a strong likelihood that this entry and the one which follows it in Dubhaltach's Glossary derive from a version of *Bretha Éitged* (*CIH* 1181.28; *CCIH* 176–182). The verb *ro imeochaidis* is the 3 pl. impf. of *imm-tét* 'goes around, encloses, guards'.

48 The entry is difficult to interpret because the interlinear gloss is largely illegible. For the legible part of the gloss, see *Bretha Éitged* (*CIH* 1182.21–22; *CCIH* 176–182). The interpretation of *sgor ic* is uncertain. It is understood here as the vn. of *scuirid* 'unyokes, releases' in its meaning 'enclosure'. The distance of a *deiscéimm* seems to be a full step to one side; *eDIL s.v. deiscéimm*. The interpretation of *túam* is also difficult in that it refers to a 'bend, arch, mound, tomb'; *eDIL s.v. túam*. The larger context of the gloss's source text is to define the term *crích* 'territory, boundary'. The emendation to *o thire tuaim* follows that suggested by Binchy, *CIH* 1182, n. f. The semantic range of *tuaim* encompasses not only 'mound', but also 'grave, tomb, burial mound' which suggests a burial mound is used to mark the boundary of a *crích* 'territory, boundary'. Cf. 1.b.3.50 IOMAIGH.

49 See *Bretha Éitged* (*CIH* 1182.22; *CCIH* 176–182). The entry follows 1.b.2.48 IOMAIN ⟨.I. EALLAIGH⟩ SGORIC AN DUINE in the source text and is understood when taken in conjunction with that entry. The gloss defines the area which is considered beyond the *crích* 'territory, boundary'.

50 Cf. *Bretha Éitged* (*CIH* 1182.23; *CCIH* 176–182) where the lemma is found in a commentary. This entry should be understood within the context of the two previous entries, 1.b.3.49 SECHTAR CRICH and 1.b.2.48 IOMAIN ⟨.I. EALLAIGH⟩ SGORIC AN DUINE. Cf. 6.a.30.65 IOMAIGH.

1.b.3.51 Andom*h*na .i. inde doia*m*h*ne isna cuit*h*ech*a .⁊c̄.
Andomna 'marshes', i.e. [< *ı inne* 'middle, center' + *domne* 'depth, depths'] center of depth in the pits, etc.[51]

1.b.4.52 Iomt*h*ac*h* .i. eimt*h*oinge.
Imthach 'swearing', i.e. [< *éim* 'quickly' + *tongaid* 'swears'] quickly he swears.[52]

1.b.4.53 Follan .i. mait*h* slan.
Follán 'sound', i.e. good, healthy.[53]

1.b.4.54 Cobran*n*a gall .i. coirt*he* bi*us* a c*h*in*n* t*h*ire.
Comranna gall 'divisions by pillar-stones', i.e. a standing stone which is at the end of the land.[54]

1.b.4.55 Foic*h*lige .i. foc*h*laoid .i. toc*h*ailt.
Foichlide 'burrowing', i.e. uprooting, i.e. digging up.[55]

1.b.5.56 Ceat*h*ra .i. caoi doib*h* iot*h*ra.
Cethrae 'cattle', i.e. [< *cáe* 'path, way' + *do* 'to, for, by' + *ithir* 'arable land'] a path by them through arable land.[56]

---

51 The lemma is the nom. pl. of *andomain* 'bog, marshy land'. The interpretation of the gloss is 'land which has depths'. See O'Dav 140 (heptad 37; CCIH 113: *Andomuin .i. ferann ainethaim, ut est andomain tire .i. tír a mbi inne doimne, cuirrig ⁊ seiscenn no moin* "*Andomuin*, i.e. land not arable, ut est *andomain tire* i.e. land in which there is … of depth, marshes and swamp or bog."); heptad 37 (CIH 35.22–23, 36.1, CCIH 113; AL 5: 250.6 and 252.1). For *cuithecha*, see *cuithe* 'pit, trap for animals, well, pool'. Cf. 9.7.19 ANDOMHNA.

52 See *Cáin Ḟuithirbe* (CIH 768.34; CCIH 33). In *Cáin Ḟuithirbe, imthach* is glossed by *imtongat*; here the gloss is etymological; *eDIL s.v. imm-toing* 'swears'. *Imthach* is the vn. of *imm-toing*. For the etymological gloss, see the Introduction, pp. 13–16.

53 The context of the entry is unknown.

54 See the first part of SC Y.683 *Gall i.e. corthe cloiche…*; and O'Cl *Gall .i. coirthe cloiche* 'a pillar stone'. See EIF 409 for a discussion of the types of boundary markers used in early medieval Ireland.

55 For the lemma, see *eDIL s.v. fochlaid* 'borrowing, undermining, uprooting'. See *Cethair-ṡlicht Athgabálae* (CIH 391.9 and gloss 29, 391.15; AL 1: 184.15 and 190.15); and *Bretha Comaithchesa* (CIH 72.2 and gloss 3, 72.5; *Bretha Comaithcheso* §16 and gloss c; AL 4: 96.17 and 98.3) where *fochlaid* is glossed by *tochailt*. Both citations refer to damage done by pigs uprooting or digging into the ground.

56 See heptad 4 (CIH 5.34 and gloss 7, 6.8; AL 5: 136.7 and 16); O'Dav 513 (heptad 4; CCIH 124: *Cethra .i. cae doib ithra, ut est áin cethra as do gort* "*Cethra* 'cattle' i.e. *cae doib ithra*, ut est 'the driving of cattle out of thy cornfield'."). The phrase is not translated by the editors of

1.b.5.57 Lias caor*ac*[h] .i. cr*o* caor*ac*[h].
Lías cáerach 'sheep pen', i.e. sheep fold.[57]

1.b.5.58 Eic*h*las, ⁊ bacg*h*abail .i. ait i mbid eic*h*.
Echlas, ⁊ bacgabail 'stall, and enclosed field', i.e. a place where there are horses.[58]

1.b.6.59 Dic*h*eall diceilt .i. ad*h*bal c*h*eilt.
Díchell dicheilt 'negligence of concealment', i.e. [< *adbal* 'great, vast' + *ceilt* 'concealing'] great concealing.[59]

1.b.6.60 C*ét*ciont*ach* .i. bit*h*ben*ac*[h].
Cétcintach 'first guilty party', i.e. a vicious animal.[60]

1.b.6.61 Direg*ar* .i. dergit*h*er.
Diregar 'is despoiled', i.e. is despoiled.[61]

1.b.6.62 Ruir*mh*id .i. ro *air*m*h*id.
Ruirmid 'he would count', i.e. he would count.[62]

AL or by Stokes, but each suggests that the gloss is etymological. The translation provided here is tentative.

57 Cf. O'Cl *Lias .i. cro bhios ag láoghaibh no ag úanaibh* 'a hut which is for calves or for lambs'; and for similar phrasing cf. heptad 4 (*CIH* 1884.11 and gloss 9, 1884.19; *AL* 5: 136.9 and 23–24).

58 The word *bacghabail* is obscure, but it likely has a similar meaning to *echlas*. Cf. *bacc n-achaid* 'an enclosed field for horses or cattle'; *eDIL s.v. 1 bacc.* It might also refer to an angled bar for holding animals in a field or pen. Cf. heptad 4 (*CIH* 6.1 and gloss 13, 6.12–13, 1884.11 and gloss 10, 19–20; *AL* 5: 136.10 and 24–25) where the lemma is found as part of a gloss; and cf. more distantly O'Dav 1126 (heptad 4; *CCIH* 142: *Inde .i. echlaisc no bac, ut est ain ech fria n-inde* "*Inde*, i.e. halter or staple, ut est 'the driving of horses to their stable'.").

59 A possible source might be heptad 4 (*CIH* 6.2 and gloss 16, 6.13–14, 17, and 1884.12 and gloss 13, 21–22; *AL* 5: 136.10 and 28, and 138.1). *Adbal* 'great, mighty, vast' is commonly used in the legal texts to form etymological glosses on the negative prefix *dí*; this likely arose from confusion with the intensifying prefix *2 dí-*; *eDIL s.v. adbal.*

60 See *Bretha Éitgid* (*CIH* 278.35–36; *AL* 3: 244.6–7) where both the lemma and gloss are found in a commentary concerning pigs.

61 The interpretation of the gloss is tentative. The headword and gloss both appear to be passive forms of *do-rig* 'strips, despoils, exacts payment?'; *eDIL s.v. do-rig.* It is also possible that the verbs are from *dérgaid, dérgid* 'spreads (coverings, a couch), makes a bed'.

62 Both the lemma and gloss are understood as 3 sg. past. subj. forms of *ad-rími* 'counts'; *eDIL s.v. ad-rími.*

1.b.6.63 Toig*h*len[nan] ⟨.i. lendan⟩.
Toglenamon 'clinging to', ⟨i.e. beloved⟩.[63]

1.b.7.64 De sec*h*tmui*ne* .i. se*cht* b*air*gen.
Dé sechtmaine 'on a week-day', i.e. seven loaves.[64]

1.b.7.65 Tuat*h*gabail .i. gabail bi*us ete*r na da t*h*uait*h* amuil ataid h*ua* eric maig*h*e la Mum*h*uin.
Túathgabáil 'territory-seizing?', i.e. [< *túath* 'territory' + *gabál* 'taking, seizing, holding'], a collection which is between the two territories like there are from the compensation of a field by the Munstermen.[65]

1.b.7.66 Aclaig*h*e .i. íoc lóig*h*e.
Acclaide 'rendering liable', i.e. [< *ícc* 'paying' + *lóg* 'fee, wage, payment'] paying a fee.[66]

1.b.8.67 Acluig*h*ed*h* .i. iocuid lóg*h*.
Aclaided 'incurred liability', i.e. [< *íccaid* 'pays' + *lóg* 'fee, wage, payment'] pays a fee.[67]

---

63 The interpretation of the lemma is uncertain, and the missing letters have been supplied from O'Curry's transcription; see *eDIL s.v. toglenamon* 'addition, legal adherence?, possession?'. For the gloss, see *eDIL s.v. lennán.*

64 The lemma is not in O'Curry's transcription. For part of the lemma, cf. *Di Astud Chirt 7 Dligid* (CIH 227.22; AL 5: 438.15; CCIH 293–294).

65 For the lemma and the first half of the gloss, see *Cethairślicht Athgabálae* (CIH 381.25; AL 1: 158.19–20) which is a gloss on the main text. The editors of AL do not translate the lemma, but the immediate context is of three assemblies with the lemma being associated with a food-tribute being collected from a territory. *eDIL s.v. túathgabáil* says the word appears 'in name of a kind of assembly between two 'túath's'. It is also possible that the lemma should be understood as 'territory-distraint' with the food tribute being what is distrained from another territory. The interpretation of the second half of the gloss is obscure, but it might be an example of such a situation in action.

66 For the headword, see *eDIL s.v. acclaid* 'unculpating, rendering liable'; *acclaide* is a variant of *acclaid.* Cf. O'Dav 113 (no id.; CCIH 112: *Aclaid .i. ioc fiach, ut est ar n-aclad im chin a slán .i. arna hiocad eneclann 7 diablad "Aclad,* i.e. paying debts, ut est 'that he should not pay for a crime its *sláns*', i.e. that he should not pay honour-price and double.").

67 The headword is interpreted here as a later 3 sg. pres. impf. of *ad-claid*; *eDIL s.v. ad-claid* 'renders liable'. Cf. O'Dav 113 (no id.; CCIH 112: *Aclaid .i. ioc fiach, ut est ar n-aclad im chin a slán .i. arna hiocad eneclann 7 diablad "Aclad,* i.e. paying debts, ut est 'that he should not pay for a crime its *sláns*', i.e. that he should not pay honour-price and double.").

1.b.8.68 Tallaid .i. tuaslaicid.
Tallaid 'takes away', i.e. dissolves.[68]

1.b.8.69 Gadaig*h* .i. beanuid*h*.
Gataid 'steals', i.e. takes away.[69]

1.b.8.70 Goilid*he* .i. luid*he* ég*he* mar d*e*rt[h]*er* lesi*n* g*r*ein.
Goilide 'eating' (?), i.e. movements of a moon, as it is said, with the sun.[70]

1.b.9.71 Turlais ⟨ɫ tuluid⟩ .i. luaid*h*is.
Tarlais ⟨*nó tuluid*⟩ 'you came ⟨or you came⟩', i.e. you went.[71]

1.b.9.72 Ci*ch*siod .i. ceímn*igh*siod.
Cichsit 'they will go', i.e. they will go.[72]

1.b.9.73 Fesat*ar*, fiasat*ar* .i. fua*cht*naig*te*r.
Fesatar, fiasatar 'they will be injured', i.e. they may be injured.[73]

1.b.10.74 Ciu*chustar* .i. ceimn*ighius*t*ar*.
Cichsiter 'they will be gone', i.e. they will be gone.[74]

---

68 The headword is a later 3 sg. pres. ind. simplex from *do-alla* 'takes away, steals'; *eDIL s.v. 1 do-alla*. The gloss is a later 3 sg. pres. ind. simplex from *do-fúasailci* 'sets free, loosens, dissolves, remits, relaxes'; *eDIL s.v. do-fúasailci*. Cf. O'Cl *Tall .i. goid* 'theft'.

69 The context of the entry is unknown.

70 The interpretation of this entry is tentative. It is possible that the lemma is an astronomical term. The tentative translation is influenced by Mod. Ir. *goileadán* 'persistent, greedy eater'; and Dinneen *s.v. goiledheach* 'one having a good appetite'. Perhaps it refers to the way the moon waxes and wanes, i.e. a quarter moon looks as if someone has taken a bite out of it.

71 As it is difficult to determine whether Dubhaltach meant to correct *turlais* to *tuluid* or simply to list *tuluid* as a variant, I have left both here. The form *turlais* is a 2 sg. pret. of *do-cuirethar* 'puts, sends, comes about'; *eDIL s.v. do-cuirethar*. The form *tuluid* is interpreted as a 2 sg. pret. of *do-tét*; *eDIL s.v. do-tét* 'comes, appears'. The gloss is a 2 sg. pret. of *lúaidid* 'moves, goes'; *eDIL s.v. 1 lúaidid*.

72 The lemma is a 3 pl. fut. of *cingid* 'steps, goes'; *eDIL s.v. 1 cingid*. The gloss is a 3 pl. fut. of *céimnigid* 'steps, goes'. It is common for *céimnigid* to gloss *cingid* in the legal texts; *eDIL s.v. céimnigid*.

73 The interpretation of the entry is tentative. Both of the lemmata appear to be 3 pl. fut. pass. forms of *fichid* 'fights'; *eDIL s.v. 1 fichid*. For the gloss, one would expect a 3 pl. fut. pass. of *fúachtnaigid* 'makes an attack, injures', which is frequently used in the legal texs to gloss *fo-fich* 'attacks, does injury', but the form here could be pres. subj.; *eDIL s.v. fúachtnaigid*.

74 The lemma is understood here as a 3 pl. fut. pass. of *cingid* 'steps, goes'; *eDIL s.v. 1 cingid*.

1.b.10.75 Duinn .i. flaith*e*.
Duinn 'of a ruler', i.e. of a ruler.[75]

1.b.10.76 Aib*h*riteod*h* .i. ab*h*ratód*h* no soad*h* .i. an tan do-fuit a h-ab*hr*a d*ar* an súil.
Aibritiud 'twinkling of an eye', i.e. [< *1 abra* 'eyelid' + *soud* 'turning'] eyelids or turning, i.e. when her eyelid falls across the eye.[76]

1.b.11.77 Seis .i. t*air*is .i. dén co*mnaigh*e.
Seiss 'you should sit', i.e. remain, i.e. do a staying.[77]

1.b.11.78 Seis .i. ionsaigh.
Seis 'you should claim', i.e. claim.[78]

1.b.11.79 T*arrach*taig*h* .i. nec*h* t*arr*aig*h*t*er*.
Tarrachtaig 'kept women', i.e. anyone who is obtained.[79]

The gloss is understood here as a 3 pl. fut. pass. of *céimnigid* 'steps, goes'. It is common for *céimnigid* to gloss *cingid* in the legal texts; *eDIL s.v. céimnigid*.

75 For the lemma, see *eDIL s.v. 2 donn*. For the lemma, cf. *Di Astud Chirt ⁊ Dligid* (CIH 228.14 and comm. 228.24; AL 5: 440.21); and the first part of O'Dav 700 ((2) *Di Astud Chirt ⁊ Dligid*; CCIH 128: *Donn .i. uasal nó brithem nó righ*… "*Donn*, i.e. noble, or a judge, or a king…").

76 The identification of the lemma is uncertain; *eDIL s.v. aibrit(h)iud*. The entry seems to refer to winking. The first gloss appears to be a late plural form of *abra* 'eyelash, eyelid'; *eDIL s.v. 1 abra*. Cf. O'Cl *Abhraid .i. fabhradha* 'eyebrows'.

77 The identification of the lemma is tentative, but it is interpreted here as the 2 sg. pres. juss. subj. of *saidid* 'sits'. The first gloss is a 2 sg. impv. of *do-airissedar* 'stands, remains', and the second gloss consists of the 2 sg. impv. of *do-gní* 'makes, does' and *comnaide* 'remaining, staying'. For the lemma, see *Bretha Nemed Dédenach* (CIH 1126.34) and for the first gloss (CIH 1126.36); see also Corthals 2007: 136, 139, and discussion on 142. I should like to thank one of the anonymous readers for comments on this entry.

78 The interpretation of the lemma is uncertain. It is understood here as a 2 sg. pres. juss. subj. of *saigid* 'seeks, sues, claims' although one would expect a form like *sais*. The verb *ind-saig* 'approaches, advances (a suggestion), seeks, claims' is frequently used to gloss *1 saigid*; *eDIL s.vv. ind-saig ?* and *1 saigid*. It is understood here as a 2 sg. impv.

79 For the lemma, see *eDIL s.v. tarrachtach* 'a kept woman', but that meaning is not secure. In *Cáin Lánamna* it is used to gloss *adaltrach*, so one assumes that the word refers to a secondary wife or concubine. It is difficult here in the glossary to determine whether the lemma is pl. or in an oblique case. For the lemma, see *Cáin Lánamna* § 37, gloss 11 and n. c for further discussion (CIH 519.15; AL 2: 406.8). Thurneysen 1936: 72 suggests that the word should be understood to refer to a woman who is in a sexual relationship where the man visits her. The gloss is more problematic as it is unclear to which verb the gloss belongs. That being said, the meaning suggested by the lemma is 'obtained, seized', *vel sim*, and the gloss might be related to verbs such as *do-roich*; *eDIL s.v. do-roich* 'reaches, gets, acquires'.

1.b.11.80 Dúisi .i. di uaisi .i. mion*na* adbal [ú]aisle.
Dúisi 'treasures', i.e. [< *de* 'of, from' + *úais* 'noble'] from noble things, i.e. venerated objects [< *adbal* 'great, mighty' + *úaisle* 'nobility, dignity'] of great nobility.[80]

1.b.12.81 Ocmoda .i. tad*h*all, adall.
Ocmada 'touchings', i.e. touching, touching.[81]

1.b.12.82 Comaitg*h*es .i. coim*h*d*eacht*.
Comaithches 'neighborhood relationship', i.e. accompanying.[82]

1.b.12.83 Noaig*h*te*r*, núit*h*er .i. ord*er*cuigt*er*.
Nóaighter, núither 'is made known', i.e. is made known.[83]

1.b.12.84 Bad*h*ad*h* .i. ebl*edh*.
Bádud 'extinction', i.e. death.[84]

1.b.13.85 Ad-roille .i. do *air*illn*adh*.
Ad-roilli 'he deserved', i.e. it was deserved.[85]

---

80 The first gloss is etymological on the headword. Although one would normally expect the dat. pl. of *úais* following *di*, cf. O'Dav 750 (*Bretha Nemed Dédenach*; CCIH 130). The second gloss is etymological on the first gloss. For the etymological glosses, see the Introduction, pp. 13–16. Cf. O'Cl *Dúis .i. séd* 'a treasure'; and the beginning of O'Dav 682 (likely from *Muirbretha*; CCIH 128: *Duis .i. uasal*... "*Duis*, i.e. noble…").

81 The form of the lemma appears to be nom. pl., but the original context is unknown. The sense of the headword and both glosses is of touching in a sexual manner. See the beginning of O'Dav 1333 (maybe from *Cáin Ḟuithirbe*; CCIH 147: *Ocmad .i. tadhall*... "*Ocmad*, i.e. visiting…") where Stokes understands *tadall* in its more common meaning of 'visiting'.

82 For the headword and gloss, see *eDIL s.vv. comaithches* and *coimitecht*, respectively.

83 Although the first lemma is not listed in *eDIL s.v. nóïd* 'makes known, spreads fame', it appears to be a variant of the more common sg, pres. pass. represented by *núither*. For the gloss, see *eDIL s.v. airdircigidir* 'celebrates, praises, makes known'. See *Córus Bésgnai* § 28 and gloss 7 (CIH 526.36 and 527.1–3; AL 3: 26.6 and 11). See O'Don. Suppl. *s.v. nuithear*.

84 The lemma is the vn. of *báidid* 'sinks, submerges, wrecks, extinguishes, destroys'; *eDIL s.v. bádud*. The gloss appears to be a vn. of *eplaid*, a later simplex of *ad-bail* 'dies'; *eDIL s.v. atbail(l)*. See *Córus Bésgnai* § 11, gloss 2 (and notes on p. 192) (CIH 522.30–31; AL 3: 12.32); and the second half of O'Dav 136 (*Córus Bésgnai*; CCIH 112: … *.i. urgairit sin cona bi bádh-eibiltin forna dainib* "… i.e. those (payments) forbid a deadly plague to be on human beings.").

85 For the lemma and gloss, see *eDIL s.vv. ad-roilli* and *áiriltnigid*, respectively. The gloss is a late derivative of *ad-roilli*.

1.b.13.86 Dob*hus* .i. droic*h*bes, no deg*h*b*h*és.
Dobus 'evil custom', i.e. a bad custom, or a good custom.[86]

1.b.13.87 Do derlaic .i. do adb*h*al log*h*.
Do derlaic 'he granted', i.e. [< *do* 'to, for' + *adbal* 'great, mighty, vast' + *lóg* 'reward, payment, value, fee'] for a great payment.[87]

1.b.13.88 Anac*ht* .i. aincist*ar*.
Anacht 'he saved', i.e. he saved.[88]

1.b.14.89 Tiomortain .i. cro .i. bas.
Timortain 'death', i.e. death, i.e. death.[89]

1.b.14.90 Dia no dee tré-ág*h* .i. lait*he* na t*t*ri n-ág*h* .i. ag*h ar* ec*h*uib[h], ág*h ar arm*uib*h*, ág*h* for d*h*aoinib*h*.
Día nó dé tré-ág 'day or day of three battles', i.e. the day of the three battles, i.e. a battle of horses, a battle of weapons, a battle of people.[90]

1.b.15.91 Góla .i. gorta quasi gula .i. c*r*aos.
Góla 'abyss', i.e. hunger; *quasi* 'as if' *gula* 'opening of the mouth, throat, gluttony', i.e. mouth.[91]

---

86 For the lemma, see *eDIL s.v. dobés, dobus*. As pointed out by one of the anonymous readers, it is odd that Dubhaltach has *deghbhés* 'good custom' in the gloss and wonders whether Dubhaltach might have mistaken *dobés* for *deghbhés* in his source. It is also possible that *deghbhés* is a misreading of *droghbhés* 'bad custom'.

87 In OI, one would expect the preverb *ro-* instead of *do-*, but *do-* is the regular preverb for the preterite in EMI; McCone 1997: 197; and *eDIL s.v. derlaicid*. *Adbal* 'great, mighty, vast' is commonly used in the legal texts to form etymological glosses on the negative prefix *di*; this likely arose from confusion with the intensifying prefix *2 dí-*; *eDIL s.v. adbal*.

88 The lemma is the 3 sg. pret. of *aingid* 'saves, protects'; *eDIL s.v. aingid*. The gloss appears to be a later form of the verb, likely derived from a later simplex, but the form of the verb is obscure. The interpretation of the gloss is an educated guess based on the lemma.

89 Cf. *Córus Fine* (*CIH* 742.15 and the citations at 684.3–4; *CCIH* 32) where the lemma is found in a commentary. As noted by O'Sullivan 2000: 442 (and *CCIH* 235) Dubhaltach wrote the title of the text in the main MS, TCD MS 1337 [H.3.18].

90 The form of *trí, tré*, in the lemma might be an achaic m. gen. form of the numeral; *eDIL s.v. trí*. The larger context of the entry is unknown.

91 The lemma refers to the open space within a drinking vessel; *eDIL s.v. 2 góla*. The range of meaning for Latin *gula* overlaps with those of *cráes* 'maw, mouth, gluttony'; see *Ir. Gl.* l. 92 *haec gula* 'cráes'. Cf. 5.b.4.32 GÓLA. For the use of *quasi* in etymological glosses, see Russell 2005.

1.b.15.92 Friot*h*g*h*uin .i. gui*n* i n-aig*idh* gona.
Frithguin 'counter-wounding', i.e. a wound in return for a wound.[92]

1.b.15.93 Fosieag*ar* .i. airgit*he*r.
Fo-saigar 'it is attempted', i.e. it is bound.[93]

1.b.16.94 In*n*tec*h* fog*h*lad*h* .i. inte dut*h*uid*h* na ffog*hlaighedh* .i. u*ar*bot*h*a, na coill[id].
Intech foglaig 'scabbard of a plunderer', i.e. [*í* 'that' + *dúthaig* 'belonging to by heredity, natural' + *in* 'the' + *foglaid* 'plunderer'] that inheritance of the plunderer, i.e. dwellings, of the destroyer.[94]

1.b.16.95 Turg*aire* .i. t*air*riach .i. sgr*eth*emla*cht* furailec*ht*tec*h* do b*eth ar* am*a*dan mig*h*niom*h* do de*nam*h.
Turgaire 'inciting', i.e. inciting, i.e. a shouting person who would be commanding a fool to do an evil deed.[95]

1.b.17.96 Fuit*h*b*h*iol .i. fois*h*iob*h*al.
Futhbil 'one who goes to the people with whom there is not a treaty', i.e. going covertly.[96]

92 See *Bretha Cairdi* (CIH 808.29; CCIH 36 and 302).

93 The identification of the headword and its grammatical form are uncertain. It is interpreted here as a 3 sg. pres. pass. of *fo-saig* 'tries, attempts', but cf. *fossaigid(ir)* 'makes stable, establishes, fixes'. The gloss is a 3 sg. pres. pass. of *áirgid*, a later simplex of *ad-rig* 'binds'; *eDIL s.v. ad-rig*.

94 The interpretation of the entry is tentative. It is possible that the gloss is playing with different meanings for 'covering, sheath'. See *eDIL s.vv. dúthaig* and *1 foglaid*.

95 For the gloss *tairriach*, see *eDIL s.v. tairriachad, tairriachtad*. The noun *sgethemlacht* is not listed in *eDIL*, but cf. *scretach* 'crying out, screaming'; the lenition in the glossary seems to be a mistake. Similarly, *furailechtach* is also not in *eDIL*, but cf. the verb *furáilid* 'enjoins, commands' and *furáilem* 'commanding, enjoining'. The entry concerns inciting a fool to commit a crime. The person who does so is legally responsible for any penalties, not the fool; for the law, see *Bretha Éitgid* (CIH 1264.33 and gloss 3, 1264.38–40; AL 3: 156.4 and 11; CCIH 176–182). See O'Don. Suppl. *s.v. turgaire*.

96 The interpretation of the lemma is tentative; *eDIL s.v futhbil* does not provide a meaning. The gloss, however, is provided with the potential meaning 'goes covertly, secret proceeding'; *eDIL s.v. fosiubal*. The lemma and gloss are found in *Bretha Cairdi* (CIH 791.13 and 808.29; CCIH 34 and 36). In both citations from *Bretha Cairdi*, the *fer fuithbil* of the text is described as one who goes to the people with whom there is not a treaty. In other words, this person is a traitor to his own territory.

1.b.17.97 Fuid*h*benn .i. foidub*h*aid.
Fuidben 'deprives', i.e. takes away.[97]

1.b.18.98 Cod*ar*sna .i. co*m*sgaoilt*ach* no co*mthár*sna.
Cotarsnae 'opposite', i.e. scattered or across.[98]

1.b.18.99 Ion*n*lac*h*taid*h* .i. fer d*h*énta ion*n*luig*h*.
Indlachtaid 'attacker', i.e. a man who does attacking.[99]

1.b.18.100 Aorc*h*aid*h* .i. fer dénta coire.
Airchaid 'harmer', i.e. a man who commits an offence.[100]

1.b.19.101 Tél[la]c*h*tac*h* .i. fer do-[g]ní telac*h*.
Tellachtach 'hearthmaker', i.e. a man who makes a hearth.[101]

1.b.19.102 Deocraid*h*tid*h* ⟨.i. sacrilegan⟩ .i. (fer denta toc*r*aíd*h ar* d'Dia) .i. fer do b*hei*r luig*h*e éit*h*ig*h* agan egl*uis*, ⁊ ni tincen*n* [d]lig*hedh*.
Deacraidhtidh 'troublemaker' ⟨i.e. *sacrilegan* 'a wicked person'⟩, i.e. (a man who causes vexation to God), i.e. a man who makes a false oath at the church, and it does not satisfy law.[102]

---

97 The lemma is interpreted as the 3 sg, pres. prototonic ind. of *fo-diben* 'deprives (?)'; *eDIL s.v. fo-diben*. The gloss is interpreted as the 3 sg. pres. ind. of *fodiubaid* 'takes away, diminishes' which is used in legal commentary to gloss *fo-ben*; *eDIL s.v. fodiubaid*. See Digest C (37) (CIH 1940.25; CCIH 77).

98 For the two glosses, see *eDIL s.vv. 1 com-*, *1 scaíltech*, and *comtharsna*, respectively.

99 The interpretation of the lemma is tentative; see *eDIL s.v. indlach*. The literal translation of the gloss is 'man who does attacking'. The form *dénta* is a late sg. rel. form of *do-gní* 'makes, does'; cf. *cirpsire* 'brewer' *.i. fer denta lenna*; see *Lebor Gabhála*, (i) 26.2; and *eDIL s.v. cirpsire*. I should like to thank one of the anonymous readers for this reference.

100 The lemma is interpreted as an agent noun of *airchót* 'harming, injuring'. The word *coire* in the gloss is understood as a form of *caire* 'crime, fault'; see *eDIL s.vv. airchót* and *1 caire*.

101 The lemma is not in *eDIL*, but the form seems to be derived from *eDIL s.v. 1 tellach* 'hearth, fireplace'. I should like to thank one of the anonymous readers for this suggestion.

102 The more modern form is given here as the lemma is not in *eDIL*, which is understood to be derived from *eDIL s.v. deccair*. The interlinear gloss is from Latin *sacriligus* 'one who commits a sacrilege, a profane person'. The sense of the remainder of the gloss is that this is the person who utters a false oath in a church, and either the false oath or the person (the grammar is ambiguous) does not satisfy a legal claim. The form *tincenn* is understood as a MI 3 sg. conjunct form of *tincaid*, a later simplex from *do-incai*; *eDIL s.v. do-incai* 'looks, sees to, satisfies'.

1.b.20.103 Dilsioc*h* .i. duine as diles do gabail no do m*arbadh*, uaide si*n* tig dilsiug*adh* duine indils*igh* cen [c]er[t].
Dílsech 'outlaw', i.e. a person who is without legal protection for seizing or for killing, in respect to those things a proclamation makes an innocent person [someone] without right.[103]

1.b.21.104 Geinite .i. serrac*h* no l*air*.
Geinite 'that which is produced', i.e. a foal or a horse.[104]

1.b.21.105 Áonm*h*ais .i. aonc*h*rut*h*, no aondluim*h*.
Óenmais 'one mass', i.e. one form, or one mass.[105]

1.b.21.106 Táid*hc*hit*h*er .i. teg*ar* no tegt*er*.
Taidchither 'is visited', i.e. someone comes or some people come.[106]

1.b.22.107 Don-rósad .i. do-rónsad.
Don-rósat 'he created', i.e. they made.[107]

2.a.1.1 Br*i*ogac*h* .i. uallac*h*.
Brígach 'powerful', i.e. proud.[108]

103 The sense of the entry is that an outlaw can be seized or killed without the person who does so being legally proclaimed; for the lemma, cf. *Bretha Éitgid* (CIH 1187.20ff.; AL 3: 136.2ff.; CCIH 176–182). The second half of the gloss does not make much sense; it is possible that something has been left out. The missing letters have been supplied from O'Curry's transcription.

104 The identification of the lemma is uncertain; it appears to ultimately be derived from *gainithir* 'is born, is produced'. Cf. *eDIL s.v. ? geiniti* where the citation is from Digest B (43) (CIH 1373.22; CCIH 61). It should be noted, however, that Binchy, CIH 1373, n. i, suggests reading 'ge*n*nti'. Cf. also Dinneen *s.v. geinim* 'I beget, generate'.

105 In MI the usual nom. sg. form of *mass* is *mais*; *eDIL s.v. 1 mass*. Cf. O'Cl *Mais .i. caor* 'a mass'.

106 The lemma is obscure, but it could be a 3 sg. pres. pass. ind. of *do-aithig* 'visits, goes to see'. The two glosses are the sg. and pl. pres. pass. ind., respectively, of *do-icc* 'comes' used impersonally when the agent is indefinite. The plural form is not listed in *eDIL s.v. do-icc*.

107 The lemma is the 3 sg. perf. of *do-fuissim* 'begets, generates' with a nasalizing relative or agreement marker. The gloss is a later 3 pl. perf. of *do-gní* 'makes, does'; for the spelling with *-d*, cf. Keating, *Trí Bior-Ghaoithe an Bháis*, 4686; and see *Aided Con Culainn* 125.3. It is unusual for the number of the lemma and headword not to match, but it is possible that the lemma was mistaken for a 3 sg.; cf. 8.31.81 TÓIRSIOD.

108 See O'Dav 194 (*Bretha Nemed Toísech*; CCIH 114: *Brigach .i. uallach, ut est brigach maith morsésur "Brigach,* i.e. 'proud', ut est 'proud (and) good the heptad'."); and for the lemma, see *Bretha Nemed Toísech* (CIH 2212.30; Breatnach 1989: § 15); and *Bretha Nemed Dédenach* 13.1 (CIH 1111.1; CCIH 184–188). See also the glossary on *Bretha Nemed Dédenach* (CIH 604.21;

2.a.1.2 Fósa[id] [.i.] [..]sinec[109]
Fossaid 'steady', i.e. …

2.a.1.3 I*ar*doc[h] .i. i*ar* digde .i. buidec[h]*us* i*arum*.
Íartach 'restitution', i.e. [< *1 íar* 'after' + *dígde* 'beseeching'] after beseeching, i.e. gratitude afterwards.[110]

2.a.1.4 Ait*h*enaig*h* .i. firenaigid, […]aidig[.].
Aithenaigh 'repays', i.e. makes good, …[111]

2.a.2.5 At*h*m*h*ochta .i. at*h*moaig*h*t*h*e.
Athmochta 'very powerful', i.e. very powerful.[112]

2.a.2.6 Foichmen .i. scoit[h]ad, no fodiub*adh*.
Fochmen 'has attacked', i.e. cutting off, or cutting off.[113]

2.a.2.7 Forrud*h* .i. f*or* rit*h*.
Forrudh 'proceeds', i.e. [< *for* 'on' + *rith* 'running'] on running.[114]

Gwynn 1942: 55, §26; CCIH 28; Taylor-Griffiths 2020: 2: 31 and discussion in 1: 215–216) where the entire entry is found.

109 Too much of the gloss is illegible to make any sense of it. For the lemma, see *Bretha Nemed Dédenach* 13.1 (CIH 1111.1; CCIH 184–188).

110 For the lemma, see *Bretha Nemed Dédenach* 13.2 (CIH 1111.2; CCIH 184–188). See O'Cl *Dighdhe .i. buidheachas* 'gratitude'; and O'Dav 656 (no id.; CCIH 127: *Dighi .i. glanadh, ut est doní molad di dia dighi .i. dia deghnighi, no dia glanadh, no dia buidhechus* "*Dighi*, i.e. cleansing, ut est 'he composes an elegy for her to cleanse her', i.e. to wash her well, or to cleanse her, or to thank her."). Cf. 7.a.26.39 IARDACH.

111 The interpretation of the lemma is uncertain, so I have left the form as it stands in the MS. It is possible that it is a late 3 sg. pres. ind. derived from *ad-fen* 'repays, requites', but there is also the possibility that it is a late 3 sg. pres. ind. of *aithnid* 'recognizes', which comes to replace *ad-gnin*; *eDIL s.vv. 2 aithnid* and *ad-gnin*. The second half of the gloss is illegible. For the lemma, see *Bretha Nemed Dédenach* 13.2 (CIH 1111.2; CCIH 184–188).

112 For the lemma, see *Bretha Nemed Dédenach* 13.3 (CIH 1111.2; CCIH 184–188). The gloss is a later form of the lemma.

113 The lemma is a 3 sg. pres. perf. of *fo-ben* 'attacks, impairs, spoils'; *eDIL s.v. fo-ben*. For the lemma, see *Bretha Nemed Dédenach* 13.4 (CIH 1111.3; CCIH 184–188); and O'Dav 857 (*Bretha Nemed Dédenach*; CCIH 133).

114 The precise identification of the lemma is obscure, so it has been left as it stands in the MS. It is possible that it is a late 3 sg. form of *for-reith* 'runs on, proceeds'. The gloss is etymological, but it could also be the regular 3 sg. pres. form of the verb. There is also a possibility that the lemma is from *fúraid* 'prepares, causes', but this does not sit as well with the etymological gloss. For the lemma, see *Bretha Nemed Dédenach* 13.4 (CIH 1111.3; CCIH 184–188). Cf. O'Don. Suppl. *s.v. forreith, forreis, foreth*.

2.a.2.8 Caom*n*ach*t* [.i.] [....]
Cáemnacht 'fair washing', i.e. ...[115]

2.a.3.9 Sgeo .i. iompoid*h*, no sg*ed*hid*h*.
Sceo 'and', i.e. turning around, or pouring forth.[116]

2.a.3.10 *Secht*[mad] fuit*h*rib*h*e .i. gort, iom*air*[e], d*h*lig*h*t*h*ir b*h*i.
Sechtmad fuithribe 'a seventh of a ridge', i.e. field, ridge, food is owed.[117]

2.a.3.11 Mu*r*t[h]or*adh* .i. duilesg.
Murthorad 'sea-produce', i.e. dulse.[118]

2.a.4.12 [Toisgi]d*h* .i. cait*h*em*h*.
Toiscid 'sustenance', i.e. consuming.[119]

2.a.4.13 Im-desid*h* .i. t*a*rrust*a*r.
Imm-desid 'it was settled', i.e. it settled.[120]

---

115 See *eDIL s.v. ? cáemnacht*. There is no meaning given for this word in *eDIL*; the meaning suggested here is based on that suggested by Stokes in his edition of O'Dav.; the lemma is interpreted as a compound of *cáem* 'fair' and *nacht*, perhaps a vn. of *nigid* 'washes'. The gloss is illegible. For the lemma, see *Bretha Nemed Dédenach* 13.4 (*CIH* 1111.4; *CCIH* 184–188). See also O'Dav 1298 (*Ántéchtae*; *CCIH* 147: *Nocht .i. nighe, ut est saighid De dia caemnocht .i. impo*[*d*] *Dhe dia caomnighi*. "*Nocht*, i.e. a washing, ut est, 'a seeking of God to wash them fairly', i.e. an entreaty of God to wash them well."); *Ántéchtae* (*CIH* 1240.32; *CCIH* 147, n. 188).

116 For the lemma, see *Bretha Nemed Dédenach* 13.4 (*CIH* 1111.4; *CCIH* 184–188). The larger context is the episode where Aithirne praises the river Modarn so that it will return to its normal course.

117 The emendation is based on the reading in the source text; the translation is tentative. For the lemma, see *Bretha Nemed Dédenach* 13.9 (*CIH* 1111.8; *CCIH* 184–188). See also the glossary on *Bretha Nemed Dédenach* (*CIH* 604.23–24; Gwynn 1942: 55, § 28; *CCIH* 28; Taylor-Griffiths 2020: 2: 32 and discussion in 1: 216) which contains part of the entry. See also Mac-Mathuna 1976. The last part of the gloss is obscure, but it could refer to the river Modarn which left food in its wake as it retreated as payment to Aithirne for his praise poem.

118 For the lemma, see *Bretha Nemed Dédenach* 13.11 (*CIH* 1111.9; *CCIH* 184–188). Cf. O'Cl *Murthoradh .i. toradh mara, no muiridhe* 'produce of the sea'.

119 The lemma is not in O'Curry's transcription, but see *Bretha Nemed Dédenach* 13.11 (*CIH* 1111.10; *CCIH* 184–188); see also the glossary on *Bretha Nemed Dédenach* (*CIH* 604.25–26; Gwynn 1942: 55, § 29; *CCIH* 28; Taylor-Griffiths 2020: 2: 32–33 and discussion in 1: 216). The missing letters have been supplied from the source text.

120 The lemma is the 3 sg. perf. of *imm-said* 'surrounds, it was settled, decreed'; the gloss is the 3 sg. pret. of *do-airissedar* 'stands, remains, stops'. For the lemma, see *Bretha Nemed Dédenach* 13.17 (*CIH* 1111.15; *CCIH* 184–188).

2.a.4.14 Toc*h*mus*tar* .i. toib*h*ges.
Tochmastar 'which may be levied', i.e. which he levies.[121]

2.a.4.15 Im-toigren[n] .i. eim*h*t*h*oib*h*gid.
Imm-togrinn 'levies', i.e. [< *éim* 'quickly' + *do-boing* 'levies'] quickly he levies.[122]

2.a.4.16 For-nesa .i. [tin…] tainses.
For-nessa 'spurns', i.e. […] who spurns.[123]

2.a.5.17 R*us* .i. gruaid*h*.
Rus 'face', i.e. cheek.[124]

---

121 Both the lemma and gloss are forms of *do-boing* 'plucks, levies, breaks'; *eDIL s.v. do-boing*. For the lemma, see *Bretha Nemed Dédenach* 13.27 (*CIH* 1111.23; *CCIH* 184–188); the glossary on *Bretha Nemed Dédenach* (*CIH* 604.27; Gwynn 1942: 55, § 30; *CCIH* 28; Taylor-Griffiths 2020: 2: 33 and discussion in 1: 216). Cf. O'Dav 1550 (*Bretha Nemed Dédenach*; *CCIH* 154: *Tochma .i. tobach, ut est acht cidh tochmastar fri ferba filed .i. acht a[n]ní toibges an fili asa briathraibh* "*Tochma*, i.e. a levy, ut est 'except what may be levied from a poet's words', i.e. except that which the poet levies out of his words."); and for the lemma, cf. *Bretha Nemed Toísech* (*CIH* 2227.7–8). Cf. 2.a.18.65 TOCHMUSTAR.

122 For the lemma, see *Bretha Nemed Dédenach* 14.1 (*CIH* 1111.24; *CCIH* 184–188). The lemma (as found here and in the glossary on *Bretha Nemed Dédenach*) provides further confirmation of the missing letters in the source text. The second half of the gloss is a later 3 sg. pres. ind. simplex form of *do-boing*; *eDIL s.v. do-boing*. It is common for the preverb *imm-* to be glossed by *éim* 'swift, timely'; Binchy 1943: 212; and Taylor-Griffiths 2020: 1: 89. See also the glossary on *Bretha Nemed Dédenach* (*CIH* 604.28–29; Gwynn 1942: 55, § 31; *CCIH* 28; Taylor-Griffiths 2020: 2: 34 and discussion in 1: 216); and O'Dav 1551 (*Bretha Nemed Dédenach*; *CCIH* 154: *Togrinn .i. tobach, ut est imtogrinn firenach [fír fili] .i. is em thobgis in firfili in[n]í doberr tarceann a enigh iar fir* "*Togrinn*, i.e. a levy, ut est 'a true poet levies true honour-(price)', i.e. 'tis quickly that the true poet levies what is given for his honour according to truth.").

123 The edges of the pages are worn, and the middle of the entry is illegible. The missing letters have been supplied from O'Curry's transcription. For the lemma, see *Bretha Nemed Dédenach* 14.2 (*CIH* 1111.24; *CCIH* 184–188); the glossary on *Bretha Nemed Dédenach* (*CIH* 604.30; Gwynn 1942: 56, § 32; *CCIH* 28; Taylor-Griffiths 2020: 2: 34–35 and discussion in 1: 216–217); and O'Dav 861 (*Bretha Nemed Dédenach*; *CCIH* 133: *Fornesa .i. tainsem, ut est fornesa cerid n-eicsi .i. dobeir tainsimh for eladhain a n-eces* "*Fornesa*, i.e. censure, ut est 'he contemns the art of poetry', i.e. he puts censure on the science of the poets.").

124 Cf. 2.a.5.18 ROSA which is the next entry in the MS. For the lemma, cf. *Bretha Nemed Dédenach* 14.6; (*CIH* 1111.28; *CCIH* 184–188); and O'Dav 1343 (*Bretha Nemed Dédenach*; *CCIH* 148: *Rús .i. aiged…* "*Rús*, i.e. face…"). See *DDC s.v. rús .i. gruaid…* (*CIH* 619.21); and O'Cl *Russ .i. gruaidh an chinn* 'cheek of the head'.

2.a.5.18 Rosa .i. g*r*uaid*h*e.
Rusa 'faces', i.e. cheeks.[125]

2.a.5.19 Éo .i. édail.
Eó 'salmon', i.e. profit.[126]

2.a.5.20 Con-a*m*ad*hair* .i. ro coi*m*meisio*mnagh*es*thar*.
Con-amadair 'has estimated', i.e. has jointly-estimated.[127]

2.a.5.21 T*ur*baid .i. l*eth*[*s*]g[él].
Turbaid 'exemption', i.e. excuse.[128]

2.a.6.22 [Eallach]ta .i. *ar* na eallac*h*.
Ellachtae 'put together', i.e. for the composition.[129]

2.a.6.23 Incesdnug*adh* .i. cesdnug*adh* a h-in*n*e.
Inchestnugad 'inquiring into', i.e. [< *1 inne* 'nature' + *cestnugud* 'inquiring into, discussing'] discussing its meaning.[130]

2.a.6.24 Fuasnad*h* .i. fuaidr*edh*, no co*m*sgaoil*edh*.
Fúasnad 'impugning', i.e. impugning, or dissolving.[131]

---

125 Cf. 2.a.5.17 RUS. For the lemma, see *Bretha Nemed Dédenach* 14.6 (*CIH* 1111.28; *CCIH* 184–188); and O'Dav 1343 (*Bretha Nemed Dédenach*; *CCIH* 148: *Rús .i. aiged*... "*Rús*, i.e. face...").

126 The identification of the lemma is tentative; there is the possibility that it could be *eó* 'salmon'. See *aoí* in *Bretha Nemed Dédenach* 14.7 (*CIH* 1111.29; *CCIH* 184–188).

127 The lemma is the 3 sg. perf. of *con-midethar* 'estimates, adjudges'; *eDIL s.v. con-midethar*. The gloss might be etymological. For the lemma, see *Bretha Nemed Dédenach* 14.4 (*CIH* 1111.27; *CCIH* 184–188); the *Cotaimside* glossary (*CIH* 1540.10); and Digest D (21) (*CIH* 1982.38; *CCIH* 79). The lemma is also found in the gloss of an entry from the *Ni Tulach* glossary which has been restored by Taylor-Griffiths 2020: 1: 164. Cf. 7.b.27.98 CON-AMADHAIR.

128 The interpretation of the entry is tentative. The missing letters are based on O'Curry's reading of 'lethsg' and the meaning of the lemma. For the lemma, see *Bretha Nemed Dédenach* 14.10 (*CIH* 1112.2; *CCIH* 184–188).

129 The missing letters are supplied from the source text. For the lemma, see *Bretha Nemed Dédenach* 15.3 (*CIH* 1112.27; *CCIH* 184–188); and O'Dav 858 (*Bretha Nemed Dédenach*; *CCIH* 133: *Fuach .i. ran, ut est is í imcomaircir ann, in fuach ellachtda, ar in fers laisin laitneóir is fuach* [*a*] *ainm laisin filid* "*Fuach*, i.e. a stanza, ut est 'this is what is required there, the connected (?) stanza', for the verse with the Latinist is called *fuach* by the (Gaelic) poet.").

130 The interpretation of the lemma is tentative (it is not listed in *eDIL*), but it is based on *cestnugud*, the vn. of *cestnaigid* 'inquires into, discusses'; *eDIL s.v. cestnugud, cesnugud*. The prefix could be *eDIL s.v. 3 in-* 'capable of, fit for, proper for, worthy for'. For the lemma, see *Bretha Nemed Dédenach* 15.4 (*CIH* 1112.28; *CCIH* 184–188).

131 For the lemma, see *Bretha Nemed Dédenach* 15.10 (*CIH* 1112.32; *CCIH* 184–188). See also the

2.a.7.25 An*mchair*des .i. *cair*di*us* an*m*a, *cair*d*us* cic*he*, ⁊ glúine.
Anmchairdes 'spiritual direction', i.e. [< *ainim* 'soul' + *cairdes* 'friendship'] soul friendship, friendship of breast and knee.[132]

2.a.7.26 Coimrec*ht* .i. co*mair*git[h]*er*.
Cumrecht 'was bound', i.e. is bound.[133]

2.a.7.27 Fuirecht .i. *áir*git[h]*er*, no gebt[h]*er*.
Fuirecht 'was bound', i.e. is bound, i.e. will be restrained.[134]

2.a.8.28 Ruid*h*bec*h* .i. ro dib*h*ec*h* .i. ro d*h*oi[c](d)*h*lec*h*.
Ruidbech 'miserly', i.e. [< *2 ro* intensifying prefix + *díbech* 'churlish, grudging, niggardly'] very niggardly, i.e. very niggardly.[135]

2.a.8.29 Ainmec*h* .i. ainém*h*ioc*h*.
Ainmech 'having a blemish', i.e. disfigured.[136]

---

glossary on *Bretha Nemed Dédenach* (CIH 604.32; Gwynn 1942: 56, § 34; CCIH 28; Taylor-Griffiths 2020: 2: 36 and discussion in 1: 217). It should be noted that the glossary on *Bretha Nemed Dédenach* has an entry with the headword, *lai* (CIH 604.31) which corresponds to CIH 1112.32. This lemma occurs in the text in the same line as *fuasnadh*; the headword *lai* is not listed in Dubhaltach's Glossary. For the lemma, and part of the gloss, cf. O'Dav 951 (*Cáin Aicillne*; CCIH 133: *Fuasnad .i. fuaidri nó foeghemh*... "*Fuasnad* ('disturbance'), i.e. opposition or impugning..."); *Cáin Aicillne* § 40 (CIH 492.11).

132 For the lemma, see *Bretha Nemed Dédenach* 15.10 (CIH 1112.33; CCIH 184–188). For the second half of the gloss, see *Bretha Nemed Dédenach* 45.22 (CIH 1133.26). The lemma also is found in a gloss on *fuadnadh* in the glossary on *Bretha Nemed Dédenach* (CIH 604.32; Gwynn 1942: 56 § 34; Taylor-Griffiths 2020: 2: 36).

133 The interpretation of the entry is tentative. The lemma is understood as the 3 sg. pret. pass. of *con-rig* 'binds together, ties'; *eDIL s.v. con-rig*. The gloss is interpreted as a 3 sg. pres. pass. of *comáirgid*, which is often used to gloss forms of *con-rig*; *eDIL s.v. comáirgid*. It is unusual that the tense of the verbs do not match, which is one reason why the interpretation is tentative. It is also possible that the lemma could be *comrecht* 'joint law'; *eDIL s.v. comrecht*. For the lemma, see *Bretha Nemed Dédenach* 15.11 (CIH 1112.34; CCIH 184–188).

134 The lemma is interpreted as the 3 sg. perf. pass. of *fo-rig* 'binds'. *Airgiter* is likely a sg. pres. pass. form of *ad-rig* 'binds' formed from a later simplex, and *gebther* is likely a sg. fut. pass. form of *gaibid*; see *eDIL s.vv. fo-rig, ad-rig*, and *gaibid*. The interpretation of the verbs is tentative. For the lemma, see *Bretha Nemed Dédenach* 15.12 (CIH 1112.35; CCIH 184–188) Cf. 8.13.34 FUIREGAR and 7.a.14.20 FÚIRESTAR.

135 For the lemma, see *Bretha Nemed Dédenach* 15.14 (CIH 1112.36; CCIH 184–188). For the lemma, see the beginning of O'Dav 1346 (*Bretha Nemed Dédenach*; CCIH 148: *Ruidbech .i. meirlech*... "*Ruidbech*, i.e. a robber..."). *eDIL s.v. ruidbech* queries whether the headword should be interpreted as 'very niggardly, miserly' instead of 'robber'. The glosses here suggest the meaning 'very niggardly, miserly'.

136 For the gloss, cf. Mod. Ir. *ainimheach* 'disfigured'. It is possible that the gloss is meant to be

2.a.8.30 Di-ciallat[h]*ar* .i. adbal dic*h*lit*h*er.
Do-cíallathar 'conceals', i.e. [< *adbal* 'great, mighty' + *do-ceil* 'conceals'] greatly it is concealed.[137]

2.a.8.31 Lénaid*h* .i. lio[..].
Lénaid 'impairs', i.e. ...[138]

2.a.9.32 *Ar*dblor caim*he* .i. *ar*dg*h*lor cáintem*h*uil.
Ardblor caime 'high noise of grief', i.e. a high-noise grief-laden.[139]

2.a.9.33 I*n*dlem*h* .i. indile éim*he*.
Intlem 'abundance', i.e. [< *indile* 'property, possessions, cattle' + *éime* 'speed, promptness'] ready cattle.[140]

---

understood etymologically. For the lemma, see *Bretha Nemed Dédenach* 15.15 (CIH 1112.37; CCIH 184–188).

137 The source text reads *do-ciallathar*, and it is possible that the lemma here is a mistake with the incorrect preverb or that Dubhaltach wrote a gloss on *do-cíallathar, diciallathar*, instead of the verb found in the source text. *Adbal* 'great, mighty, vast' is commonly used in the legal texts to form etymological glosses on the negative prefix *dí*; this likely arose from confusion with the intensifying prefix *2 dí-*; *eDIL s.v. adbal.* For the lemma, see *Bretha Nemed Dédenach* 15.16 (CIH 1112.37; CCIH 184–188). Cf. the first part of O'Dav 750 (*Bretha Nemed Dédenach*; CCIH 130: *Dociallathar .i. dichlither, ut est diciallathat airibh airme ochtaib uaisi...* "*Dociallathar*, i.e. is concealed (?), ut est 'numbers (?) are concealed from them by noble eight'..."); and *Bretha Nemed Dédenach* (CIH 1131.33). There is an amount of overlap and possible confusion among the forms of *do-ceil* and *do-cíallathar.*

138 The gloss is likely a synonym for the lemma. In CIH 1112.42 and Gwynn 1942, the missing words in the source text are supplied from O'Dav 1162 (*Bretha Nemed Dédenach*; CCIH 143: *Len .i. bacail, ut est lenaidh logh n-enech .i. bacaid logh n-enech na flatha* "*Len*, i.e. a stopping, ut est 'it hinders (?) honour-price', i.e. it hinders the honour-price of the chief."); the entry in Dubhaltach's Glossary confirms part of that reading. See *Bretha Nemed Dédenach* 15.20 (CIH 1112.42; CCIH 184–188).

139 The second half of the lemma is the gen. sg. of *cuma* 'grief, sorrow'. Although the word is a f. *t*-stem, it does not always show dental inflection; *eDIL s.v. 1 cuma*. The word *caintemhuil* is not in *eDIL*, but it appears to be an adj., 'grief-like', derived from *caíned*, the vn. of *caínid* 'weeping, lamenting' with an adjectival suffix. For the lemma, see *Bretha Nemed Dédenach* 15.20 (CIH 1112.41; CCIH 184–188). Cf. O'Dav 216 ((1) *Bretha Nemed Dédenach*; CCIH 115: *Blor .i. glor, ut est ard blor cumi...* "*Blor*, i.e. noise, ut est 'high the noise of grief'...").

140 For the lemma, see *Bretha Nemed Dédenach* 15.22 (CIH 1113.1; CCIH 184–188). See also O'Cl *Inntliomh .i. ionnmas* 'wealth'; and cf. the first part of O'Dav 1087 (*Bretha Nemed Dédenach*; CCIH 140: *Intlem .i. fagbail no reic no fuillem...* "*Intlem*, i.e. getting, or selling, or interest...").

2.a.9.34 De*ar*la .i. ad*h*bal diolait*he*r.
Derla 'discharged', i.e. [< *adbal* 'great, mighty' + *do-lá* 'puts away, discharges, remits'] greatly it is discharged.[141]

2.a.9.35 Duab*ar* .i. duai[bsech].
Dúabair 'dark', i.e. gloomy.[142]

2.a.10.36 Rélug*adh* .i. foillsiog*adh*.
Rélugad 'manifesting', i.e. manifesting.[143]

2.a.10.37 Ind*edh*ad .i. aisn*edh*id.
Indedhad 'telling', i.e. relating.[144]

2.a.10.38 Fát*h* .i. fo f*hédh* no aoid.
Fáth 'matter', i.e. [< *fo* 'under, according to' + *ed* 'interval, space, time' or + *oíd* 'heed, observation'] for a time or observation.[145]

2.a.10.39 For caoi .i. *ar* coisir o C*h*allain*n* go h-Inid ma*r* b*hius* rí, ⁊ oll*om ar* cuid oidc*he ar* imtec*ht ar* a cceil*ed*uib*h*.
For caí 'on a coshering visit', i.e. for a banquet from New Year's Day to Shrovetide as a king and chief poet go on a circuit of their clients for an evening meal.[146]

---

141 Both verbs in the entry are from *do-lá* 'puts away, discharges, remits'; the lemma appers to be a 3 sg. perf. and the gloss a 3 sg, pres. pass.; *eDIL s.v. do-lá*. For the lemma, see *Bretha Nemed Dédenach* 15.30 (CIH 1113.8; CCIH 184–188); and O'Dav 618 (*Bretha Nemed Dédenach*; CCIH 126: *Derla .i. dilsiugud nó doroilli, ut est nade doenachta derla* "*Derla*, i.e. entitling to or he deserves, ut est …"). For the etymological gloss, see the Introduction, pp. 13–16.

142 The edge of the page is damaged; the missing letters are supplied from the gloss in O'Dav 608 (*Bretha Nemed Dédenach*; CCIH 126: *Duabair .i. duaibsech…* "*Duabair*, i.e. impious…"); see *eDIL s.v. dúabair* 'dark, gloomy, terrible (?)'. For the lemma, see *Bretha Nemed Dédenach* 15.31 (CIH 1113.9; CCIH 184–188).

143 The lemma appears to be a later form of *rélad*, the vn. of *rélaid* 'manifests, reveals'; *eDIL s.v. rélad*. For the lemma, see *Bretha Nemed Dédenach* 16.6 (CIH 1113.15; CCIH 184–188). See also O'Cl *Réuladh .i. foillsiughadh* 'manifestation'.

144 Based on the context of the source text, the lemma appears to be the vn. of *innéidid* 'tells, relates'; see *eDIL s.vv. ind-fét, in-fét* and *innéidid*. For the context, see *Bretha Nemed Dédenach* 16.9 (CIH 1113.18; CCIH 184–188). See also O'Cl *Innéidhim .i. aisnéidhim, no innisism* 'I relate or tell'. For the gloss, one would expect the vn. of *aisnéidid*, a later simplex from *as-indet* 'declares, tells, relates', but the palatal ending here is unexpected for a vn. from *aisnéidid*; see GOI § 723.

145 The word *fédh* is interpreted here as a form of *ed* 'space, interval, time'; *eDIL s.v. 2 ed*. For the lemma, see *Bretha Nemed Dédenach* 16.11 (CIH 1113.19; CCIH 184–188).

146 Although the citation is from *Bretha Nemed Dédenach*, it does not directly follow the pre-

2.a.11.40 Faosam*h* .i. eim*h* .i. didion i*ar* bfeis .i. i*ar* ffesda.
Fáesam 'protection', i.e. [< *2 éim* 'prompt, ready'] prompt, i.e. protection after an evening's entertainment, i.e. after a banquet.[147]

2.a.12.41 Faosam*h* .i. c*ar*adrad*h*.
Fáesam 'protection', i.e. alliance.[148]

2.a.12.42 Fuiri*redh* .i. fosr*ethnugadh*.
Fuirired 'entertainment or refection offered to a lord', i.e. distributing.[149]

2.a.12.43 Caoi*mc*[h]ele .i. giolla t*urusa*.
Cáemchéle 'fair companion', i.e. messenger.[150]

2.a.12.44 Sab .i. so ab.
Sab 'leader', i.e. [< *so* 'good, excellent' + *ap* 'lord'] a good lord.[151]

2.a.12.45 Coccran*n* .i. ciallrun*aigid*.
Cocrann 'casting of lots', i.e. to have a secret purpose.[152]

---

ceding entries in the source text. See *Bretha Nemed Dédenach* 51.7 (CIH 1137.26 and cf. CIH 725.; CCIH 184–188).

147 The lemma refers to the temporary immunity from legal process some have after entertaining someone of high rank; *eDIL s.v. fáes(s)am*. For the lemma, see *Bretha Nemed Dédenach* 16.11 (CIH 1113.19; CCIH 184–188). See also O'Cl *Faosamh .i. comairce* 'protection'; and O'Dav 859 (*Bretha Nemed Dédenach*; CCIH 133: *Faesam .i. foghlaim, ut est co ber breith for fátha faesam* "*Faesam*, i.e. learning, ut est 'how givest thou judgment on a poet's protection'."). Stokes notes that there has been some error because *faesam* means 'protection'. It is possible that the etymological gloss in the entry is not complete.

148 For the lemma, see *Bretha Nemed Dédenach* 16.11 (CIH 1113.19; CCIH 184–188), and see the note on the previous entry.

149 The gloss is the vn. of *fosrethnaigid* 'distributes'; *eDIL s.v. fosrethnaigid*. For the lemma, see *Bretha Nemed Dédenach* 16.11 (CIH 1113.19; CCIH 184–188).

150 For the lemma, see *Bretha Nemed Dédenach* 16.15 (CIH 1113.23; CCIH 184–188). Within the context of the source text, the lemma is found within a list of terms for family relationships, each beginning with *caom-*. The connection between *céile* 'servant, fellow, companion' and the gloss 'messenger' is unclear. The expansion of ⟨.t.⟩ is uncertain, but cf. *cursúr* (for Lat. *cursor*) *.i. gilla turusa* 'messenger' (*The Passions and the Homilies from the Leabhar Breac* 2602; and *Cethairṡlicht Athgabálae*: *do fir taistill .i. in gilla turusa bis for foichill acut* 'thy messenger, i.e. the messenger who thou hast on hire' (AL 1: 160.26–27; CIH 382.18 and 24; CCIH 24)). The examples are taken from *eDIL s.v. turus* 'journey'.

151 For the lemma, see *Bretha Nemed Dédenach* 16.20 (CIH 1113.26; CCIH 184–188).

152 The lemma confirms the reading in CIH 1113.36 and Gwynn 1942: 16.31. The expansion of the gloss is tentative; see *eDIL s.v. cíall*. For the lemma, see *Bretha Nemed Dédenach* 16.31

2.a.13.46 Con-dailid*h* .i. caoinindlig*h*.
Con-dáili 'participates', i.e. [< *caín* 'noble, fair' + *indlid* 'prepares, arranges, arrays'] nobly-prepares.[153]

2.a.13.47 Banataid .i. eda*cht*ain no edáil b*h*an.
Bantáid 'a female thief', i.e. acquiring or profit of women.[154]

2.a.13.48 Bioram*h*na .i. mna bior*ac*[h] b*r*iat[h]*r*ac*h*a.
Biramhná 'sharp-tongued women', i.e. [< *ben* 'woman' + *berach* 'pointed, sharp-tongued'] women of sharp words.[155]

2.a.13.49 Meram*h*ná [.i.] mná mera.
Meramhná 'mad women', i.e. [< *ben* 'woman' + *mer* 'mad, spirited, wild'] mad women.[156]

2.a.14.50 Mu*in*em*h*ná .i. mná b*hius* ag nec*h* isi*n* mui*n*e.
Muinemhná 'thicket women', i.e. women who are with someone in the bracken.[157]

2.a.14.51 Sleit*h*em*h*ná .i. mna do c*hum* a ttiag*ar ar* sleit*h*.
Sleithemhná 'stealth women', i.e. women who have been raped by stealth.[158]

(CIH 1113.36; CCIH 184–188). For the interpretation of the gloss, see *eDIL s.v. rúnugud*; and *Cóic Conara Fugill* 24 § 24.

153 The interpretation of the entry is tentative. For the lemma, see *Bretha Nemed Dédenach* 16.31 (CIH 1113.36; CCIH 184–188).

154 The interpretation of the lemma is conjectural which is why the MS reading has not been emended to reflect the edited text. It is possible that the lemma should be emended to *bangataid* where the form *gataid* is interpreted as an agent noun derived from the vn. of *gataid* 'steals'. For the lemma, see *Bretha Nemed Dédenach* 16.34 (CIH 1113.39; CCIH 184–188). For the glosses, see *eDIL s.v. étachtain, fétachtain* 'acquiring' and *étáil* 'profit, spoils, booty, plunder'.

155 For the lemma, see *Bretha Nemed Dédenach* 16.34 (CIH 1113.39; CCIH 184–188).

156 The adj. *mer* can mean 'mentally deficient, mad, spirited, rash'; *eDIL s.v. mer*. It is difficult to determine which meaning is meant here. For the lemma, see *Bretha Nemed Dédenach* 16.34–35 (CIH 1113.39; CCIH 184–188).

157 The entry refers to women who have sexual assignations behind the bushes; often these women are referred to by the phrase *meirdrech muine* 'bush strumpet'; *eDIL s.v. 1 muine*. For the lemma, see *Bretha Nemed Dédenach* 16.35 (CIH 1113.39; CCIH 184–188).

158 For the lemma, see *Bretha Nemed Dédenach* 16.35 (CIH 1113.40; CCIH 184–188).

2.a.14.52 Codaig*h*e.i. c[oim]t*h*eig*h*e on tes.
Cotaige 'covenant', i.e. coming together from the heat.[159]

2.a.15.53 Giab*air* ł ciabair .i. m*er*d*r*ec*h*.
Gíabur nó cíabar 'harlot', i.e. harlot.[160]

2.a.15.54 Tem*r*ac*h*a .i. uaisle.
Temracha 'high places', i.e. high places.[161]

2.a.15.55 ⟨Condo⟩ tescm*arr* .i. tes*ar*gain, no go ro t*hesa*[i]*r*ge.
⟨Condo⟩ tescomarr 'so that he may rescue them', i.e. rescuing, or that he may rescue.[162]

2.a.15.56 Dog*h*b*h*aid*h* .i. do-g*h*ab*h*áltaid*h* ní as dec*air* do gabail.
Dogbaid 'seizer', i.e. who seizes anything which is difficult to take.[163]

---

159 For the lemma, see *Bretha Nemed Dédenach* 17.2 (CIH 1113.41; CCIH 184–188). Cf. O'Dav 35 (*Bretha Nemed Dédenach*; CCIH 109: *Airginn .i. ben, ut est cenmotha airginn cen ala cnes cotai "Airginn,* i.e. a woman, ut est 'except (or besides) a woman without'…"). Stokes does not translate the last part of the entry. The phrase *cnes cotai* means 'body of covenant'; see *eDIL s.vv. 1 cotach* and *? 1 cotaige*. The interpretation of *coimtheighe*, if the reading is correct, is tentative; it might be a compound of *com-* 'with, together' and a form of *téit* 'going'. I should like to thank one of the anonymous readers for their comments on this entry.

160 For the lemma, see *Bretha Nemed Dédenach* 17.1 (CIH 1113.41; CCIH 184–188). The spelling variation is also found in O'Dav. See also O'Cl *Giabhair .i. meirdreach* 'harlot'; O'Dav 377 (*Bretha Nemed Dédenach* CCIH 119: *Ciabar .i. salach no merdrech, ut est fri coibligi ciabair* "*Ciabar,* i.e. filthy or a harlot, ut est 'with a harlot of copulation' (i.e. a copulating prostitute)."); and SC Y.681 *Giabar .i. merdrech.*

161 It is uncertain whether *temracha* refers to Tara or any high place; *eDIL s.v. temair.* For the lemma, cf. *Bretha Nemed Dédenach* 17.9 *Temrach* (CIH 1114.6; CCIH 184–188) but note *Temracha* (CIH 1113.9); in both instances the word is understood as a placename and capitalized in CIH. As it stands, the lemma is acc. pl. if it is from *temair.* The gloss could also be interpreted as 'nobles'; cf. 6.b.2.91 TEMHAD TEMRACHA. For a summary of the ongoing discussions regarding the interpretation of the word *temair*, see Russell 1988: 15; Mac Giolla Easpaig 2005; Ó Muraíle 2005; Ní Mhaonaigh 2022: 216–218; Theuerkauf 2024a; and cf. Theuerkauf 2024b.

162 For the verbs in this entry, see *eDIL s.v. do-essuirg.* The lemma is a 3 sg. pres. subj.; the source text reads *con do Temhrach tuaithe tescmarr* 'so that he may rescue them, the tribes of Tara'. The sequence *condo* has been displaced from its position in the source text; *condo* is for OI *conda.* The form *tesargain* is the vn.; the final verbal form is from the later MI simplex with stem *te(a)sairg-*. For the lemma, see *Bretha Nemed Dédenach* 17.9 (CIH 1114.6; CCIH 184–188); and O'Dav 1552 (*Bretha Nemed Dédenach*; CCIH 154: *Tescomarr .i. tesarguin, ut est co Temhrach tuaithe tescomarr "Tescomarr,* i.e. rescue, ut est 'so that he may rescue the tribes of Tara'.").

163 The interpretation of the entry is uncertain. The lemma might mean 'humble', but it is also

2.a.16.57 Fuid*h*bit*he* .i. ni *ar* na foidiub*adh*.
Fodbithe 'deprived', i.e. anything regarding deprivation.[164]

2.a.16.58 Der*ch*ana .i. adb*h*al c*h*anaid*h*.
Derchana 'foretells', i.e. [< *adbal* 'great, might' + *canaid* 'sings, chants prophecies'] powerfully he prophecies.[165]

2.a.16.59 Sgor .[i.] c*h*inn*edh*.
Scor 'ceasing', i.e. finishing.[166]

2.a.17.60 Sgot*h* .i. in*n*sge.
Scoth 'word', i.e. statement.[167]

---

possible that it is semantically linked to the gloss, which might give it a meaning of 'one who seizes', i.e. an agent noun, but the interpretation of the gloss is uncertain too; *eDIL s.vv. do-gaib, ? dogbaid*, and *gabáltaid* 'one who holds or seizes'. For the lemma, see *Bretha Nemed Dédenach* 17.10 (*CIH* 1114.7; *CCIH* 184–188).

164 The interpretation of the lemma is uncertain. It might be a past participle of *fo-diben* 'deprives'. The noun *fodiubad* frequently glosses forms of *fo-ben* 'attacks, spoils'; *eDIL s.v. fodiuba, fodiubad* 'cutting off, deprivation'. For the lemma, see *Bretha Nemed Dédenach* 17.11 (*CIH* 1114.8; *CCIH* 184–188).

165 The lemma is likely a 3 sg, pres. form of *do-airchain*; *eDIL s.v. do-airchain* 'foretells, prophesies'. For the lemma, see *Bretha Nemed Dédenach* 17.14 (*CIH* 1114.10; *CCIH* 184–188). For the etymological gloss, see the Introduction, pp. 13–16

166 The lemma has a range of meanings, including 'unyoking, paddock, pasture, camp, band, desisting from, ceasing'. The gloss is interpreted as *cinniud*, the vn. of *cinnid* 'settles, completes, finishes'; *eDIL s.v. cinniud*. For the lemma, see *Bretha Nemed Dédenach* 17.12 (*CIH* 1114.9; *CCIH* 184–188). See also O'Dav 1435 (*Bretha Nemed Dédenach*; *CCIH* 151: *Scor .i. bidh doigh com*[*b*]*a inann ⁊ magh, ut est faenan scor scóthas .i. is cosmail fri mbrechtrad scoth for magh. No is faenan innann lium rocumaidh í ⁊ scoth for scór* "*Scor*, i.e. it is probably the same as field, ut est 'the same as a *scor* that flowers', i.e. it is like the variety of flowers on a field. Or it is, in my opinion, in one and the same way as a flower on a paddock."). Clearly some of the many meanings of *scor* have caused some confusion amongst glossators. Cf. *Lec. Gl.* 21 and M 19; Stokes (93) notes that *scurde* and *scairde* 'definition' are likely misunderstandings of *scor di* 'desisting from' and cites *sgur* (*.i. cindedh*) *in chatha* (TCD MS 1337 [H.3.18], p. 600). 2.a.17.62 SGUIRDE.

167 For the lemma, see *eDIL s.v. 3 scoth*, but note *1 scoth* 'flower, blossom'. For the lemma, cf. *Bretha Nemed Dédenach* 17.12 (*CIH* 1114.8; *CCIH* 184–188). See also O'Cl *Scoth .i. innsce* 'a word'; and cf. O'Dav 1435 (*Bretha Nemed Dédenach*; *CCIH* 151: *Scor .i. bidh doigh com*[*b*]*a inann ⁊ magh, ut est faenan scor scóthas .i. is cosmail fri mbrechtrad scoth for magh. No is faenan innann lium rocumaidh í ⁊ scoth for scór* "*Scor*, i.e. it is probably the same as field, ut est 'the same as a *scor* that flowers', i.e. it is like the variety of flowers on a field. Or it is, in my opinion, in one and the same way as a flower on a paddock.").

2.a.17.61 Tuilc*h*edol .i. cetol toll.
Tulchétal 'forehead-chanting', i.e. [< *toll* 'forehead' + *cétal* 'chanting, reciting'] reciting of foreheads.[168]

2.a.17.62 Sguirde .i. cin*n*te.
Scuirde 'ceased', i.e. finished.[169]

2.a.17.63 Cait*h*che ⟨⁊ caoit*h*em*h*⟩ .i. cion*n*ta.
Caithche ⟨*7 caithem*⟩ 'trespasses and pillaging', i.e. crimes.[170]

2.a.17.64 Toc*h*mag*h*ad .i. toib*h*g*h*id.
Tochmat 'they may levy', i.e. they levy.[171]

2.a.18.65 Toc*h*m*ustar* .i. toib*h*git*h*er.
Tochmastar 'which may be levied', i.e. which is levied.[172]

---

168 The word *tul* covers a range of meanings, including 'protuberance, swelling, forehead, shield'; *eDIL s.v. 1 tul, taul, tel, til*. For the lemma, see *Bretha Nemed Dédenach* 17.13 (*CIH* 1114.9; *CCIH* 184–188).

169 For the lemma, see *Bretha Nemed Dédenach* 17.15 (*CIH* 1114.11; *CCIH* 184–188). See also *Lec. Gl.* 21 *Scurde .i. cindead* and M 19 *Scairde .i. cinnead*; Stokes (93) notes that *scurde* and *scairde* 'definition' are likely misunderstandings of *scor di* 'desisting from' and cites *sgur* (*.i. cindedh*) *in chatha* (TCD MS 1337 [H.3.18], p. 600). Based on the Lecan glosses, we should understand *scuirde* as *scor di* 'desisting from', but cf. *scuirid* 'finishes, desists'. The lemma could be a past part. of *sciurid*, which is how it is understood here. *Cinnte* in interpreted as the past part. of *1 cinnid* 'completes, finishes'. Cf. 2.a.16.59 SGOR.

170 For the first part of the lemma, see *Bretha Nemed Dédenach* 17.15 (*CIH* 1114.11; *CCIH* 184–188).

171 The interpretation of the lemma is based on O'Dav 378 (*Bretha Nemed Dédenach*; *CCIH* 119: *Cona tochmat .i. cona toibgit, ut est cona tochmat a choir cert* "*Cona tochmat*, i.e. so that they may not levy, ut est 'so that they may not levy his right'.") where the entry is headed *cona tochmat*, which *eDIL* lists as a 3 pl. pres. subj. with perfective *com-*. The spelling of the verb in Dubhaltach's Glossary is a later variant. The gloss is the 3 pl. pres. of the later simplex of the lemma *do-boing* 'plucks, breaks, exacts' with orthographic variation of ⟨t⟩ and ⟨d⟩ as one expects the verb to end in ⟨t⟩ = /d/ in the 3 pl.; *eDIL s.v. do-boing*. For the lemma, cf. *Bretha Nemed Dédenach* 17.16 (*CIH* 1114.11; *CCIH* 184–188).

172 Cf. 2.a.4.14 TOCHMUSTAR. The lemma is not in textual order in *Bretha Nemed Dédenach* as would be expected based on the previous entries in Dubhaltach's Glossary (see *CIH* 1111.23). Both the lemma and gloss are forms of *do-boing* 'plucks, levies, breaks'; *eDIL s.v. do-boing*. The lemma is a sg. pass. subj. with perfective *com-*; the gloss is from a later simplex and appears to be sg. pass. pres. subj. Cf. O'Dav 1550 (*Bretha Nemed Dédenach*; *CCIH* 154) where the lemma is found within a gloss.

2.a.18.66 Mainb*th*ec*h* .i. mait*h*t*h*oic[th]ec*h*.
Mainbthech 'wealthy', i.e. good-wealthy.[173]

2.b.1.67 Tomait*h*e ní bia .i. tomait*h* an buille, ⁊ na tug e .i. bag*ar* is na búail.
Tomaithe ní bia 'he may threaten and he may not strike', i.e. threatening the blow, and he did not give it, i.e. threatening and he did not strike.[174]

2.b.1.68 Brait*h*em*h*nac[h] .i. fer do-[g]ní brat*h* nei[ch].
Braithemnach 'betraying', i.e. a person who betrays someone.[175]

2.b.2.69 Mandrad*h* .i. sgaoil*edh*.
Mandrad 'destroying', i.e. destroying.[176]

2.b.2.70 Ad-cet*h* .i. ad-c*h*ífet*h*.
Ad-ceth 'he could see', i.e. he could see.[177]

2.b.2.71 Ad-suit*er* .i. asduig*h*t*er*.
Ad-suiter 'is bound', i.e. is bound.[178]

2.b.2.72 Násad*h* .i. sasad*h*, no sosad*h*.
Násad 'assembly', i.e. satisfaction, or rest.[179]

2.b.2.73 Clú .i. urdc*er*cad*h*.
Clú 'fame', i.e. making known.[180]

---

173 For the lemma, see *Bretha Nemed Dédenach* 39.11 (CIH 1129.12; CCIH 184–188; Corthals 2007: 139 and 141 where the lemma is translated as *reich* 'rich'). Cf. O'Dav 1270 (no id.; CCIH 146) where the lemma is found within a gloss. The gloss here might be etymological.

174 Cf. *Tochmarc Étáine* (524.5) where *tómaithe* is glossed by *bagar*.

175 The lemma is not in *eDIL*. For the lemma, see Digest D (33), CIH 2004.29 and commentary at 1201.7 (on various topics) (CCIH 82 and 50, respectively); and cf. *eDIL s.vv. braithem* and *mraithem* 'betrayer'. The lemma is an adj. here.

176 Cf. O'Cl *Mandradh .i. milleadh* 'destruction'; and the beginning of O'Dav 1255 (no id.; CCIH 145: *Mannar .i. sgailed*… "*Mannar*, i.e. dissolution…").

177 The lemma is the 3 sg. past subj. of *ad-cí* 'sees'; the lemma is a later 3 sg. past subj. of the same verb; *eDIL s.v. ad-cí*.

178 For the lemma and gloss, see *eDIL s.v. ad-suidi* 'stops, hinders, binds, establishes'.

179 *eDIL s.v. 1 násad* notes that the lemma frequently rhymes with *sásad* in poetry. For the lemma, cf. O'Dav 1292 ((2) no id.; CCIH 146: *Nasadh … .i. nó sasadh, ut est sceo nemnasad* "*Nasad*… i.e, or *sasad*, ut est 'and unsatisfying'."); and cf. O'Cl *Nasadh .i. áonach* 'a meeting'.

180 See the first part of O'Dav 466 (*Bretha Nemed Toísech*; CCIH 122: *Clu .i. urdairc*… "*Clú*,

2.b.3.74 F*air*be .i. fír éibe firin*nar*ba.
Fairbe 'a paid advocate', i.e. [< *fír* 'true' + *eipe* 'cutting'] faithful cutting [< *fír* 'true' + *indarba* 'expulsion, banishment, rejection'] of true-expelling.[181]

2.b.3.75 T*air*im .i. tat*h*aoiri*m*.
Tairim 'I blame', i.e. I blame.[182]

2.b.3.76 Clot*h*ac*h* .i. ionc*h*ac*h*.
Clothach 'renowned', i.e reputed.[183]

2.b.3.77 *Ar*b*har* .i. sluag*h*.
Arbar 'army', i.e. host.[184]

2.b.3.78 *Air*b*h*re .i. slúaig*h*te.
Airbre 'armies', i.e. having hosts.[185]

---

i.e. famous…"). The gloss is the vn. of *airdircid* 'extols, magnifies, makes known'; *eDIL s.v. airdircid*. Cf. 9.1.1 CLU.

181 The translation of the entry is tentative. The lemma is cited in *eDIL s.v.* 1 *fairbe ?* from O'Curry 1873: 3: 476, n. 500, which is quoting Dubhaltach's Glossary, 8.11.30 FAIRBE, and cf. *eDIL s.v.* 2 *fairbe* 'cut, strike'. The gloss itself is etymological even though the meaning of *fairbe* is not entirely certain. The sense, based on O'Curry, seems to be that the *fairbe* is someone who is paid to advocate (or draw up?) a case against someone else for a fee. See *CIH* 1421.35 (1417.3–1429.18 is a series of citations on people who are not able to give evidence; *CCIH* 64). Cf. 8.11.30 FAIRBE and 8.14.36 MEADHBHA. There are two similar citations in *Ni Tulach* glossary (*CIH* 811.1–2) and *Breth* glossary (*CIH* 1097.11); *eDIL s.v.* 2 *fairbe*; Taylor-Griffiths 2020: 1: 164–169 and 179–186.

182 See O'Dav 1518 (no id.; *CCIH* 153: *Tairim .i. taithir, ut est ní tairim cluas clothach n-ergna .i. nocha taithirim eistecht na cluaisi cluines in etargna* "*Tairim*, i.e. blame (?), ut est 'I blame (?) not a famous ear of learning', i.e. I do not blame the hearing of the ear that hearkens intellect.").

183 See O'Dav 1518 (no id.; *CCIH* 153: *Tairim .i. taithir, ut est ní tairim cluas clothach n-ergna .i. nocha taithirim eistecht na cluaisi cluines in etargna* "*Tairim*, i.e. blame (?), ut est 'I blame (?) not a famous ear of learning', i.e. I do not blame the hearing of the ear that hearkens intellect.").

184 See O'Dav 88 (*Fél.* Ep. 12; *CCIH* 111: *Arbur .i. slogh, ut est serc ard arbair Isu* "*Arbar*, i.e. a host, ut est 'the lofty love of Jesu's host'."); and cf. *Fél.* Ep. 12. See also *The Poems of Blathmac* where l. 723 has *arbar sluaig* 'the fine host', which, as noted by Carney (1964: 145), literally means 'host of a host'.

185 Cf. O'Cl *Airbhre .i. sluagh* 'army'. For the gloss, see *eDIL s.v. slógdae, slúagdae*.

2.b.4.79 Coitse*achtus* .i. coi*mh*eist*achtus*.
Coitsechtus 'attentiveness', i.e. attentiveness.[186]

2.b.4.80 Sionn*us* .i. [mei]se*mnaghius* no etorgn*ughius*.
Síanus 'meaning', i.e. estimation or interpretation.[187]

2.b.4.81 Sec*h*moall*adh* .i. sec*h*maillig*h*.
Sechmullad 'evading', i.e. evading.[188]

2.b.4.82 Aseic*h* seg*h*maine .i. as sain an ní da seic*h*en*n* an menma ⁊ an tsuil.
Aseich seghmaine '?', i.e. it is distinct that which the mind and the eye follow.[189]

2.b.5.83 Ní *ar*tha .i. ní *ar*atha.
Ní aratha 'anything that surpasses', i.e. that which surpasses.[190]

2.b.5.84 For-randa*r* .i. urran*ntar* no forrua*mnaghth*er.
Fo-rondar 'is reddened', i.e. is reddened or is made red.[191]

2.b.6.85 C*r*edbaig*h*ter .i. c*r*e(m)[in]nig*h*ter.
Credbaigter 'are gnawed', i.e. are gnawed.[192]

---

186 For the lemma, cf. *eDIL s.vv. cotise* and *coitsecht*. For the gloss, cf. *eDIL s.v. coméitsecht*. Cf. O'Don. Suppl. *s.v. coitsi*.

187 The interpretation of the entry is tentative. The first gloss might be a mistake for an abstract noun derived from *meisemnugad* 'judging, appraising'; cf. *meisemnaigid* 'judges, estimates'. For the second gloss, cf. *eDIL s.v. etargnugud* 'interpreting, explaining'.

188 The lemma is a later form of *sechmall* 'evading, neglecting'; *eDIL s.v. sechmall*. The gloss appears to be a variant form of the lemma. For the lemma, see *Di Choimét Dligthech* (*CIH* 1727.5; *AL* 2: 14.10; *CCIH* 287–288).

189 The entry is obscure. It is possible that *aseich* is related to *seic*, giving the sense here of 'that is', or it could stand for *a seich* 'following it', *vel sim*. The form *seghmaine* is thought to contain some form of the root *seich-* 'follow' based on the etymological gloss; *eDIL s.v. seichithir* 'follows, pursues'. The verb *seichenn* is a later conjunct form likely from a simplex verb of *seichithir*, although the *da* in the gloss is unexplained.

190 Both the lemma and gloss are 3 sg. pres. ind. forms of *ar-tá* 'excels, surpasses, remains over' in relative constructions.

191 For the lemma, see *eDIL s.v. fo-roind* 'darkens, stains, reddens'. The first gloss is probably a later form of the lemma. The second gloss is from *forrúamnaigid* 'grows red, makes red'; *eDIL s.v. forrúamnaigid*. Cf. O'Dav 818 (no id.; *CCIH* 132: *Forann .i. foruamna[d], ut est forann slána sella .i. forruamnaighit[h] na suile slana in ferg* "*Forann*, i.e. reddening, ut est 'it darkens sound eyes', i.e. anger reddens sound eyes.").

192 Assuming that a lenition mark has not been omitted, the lemma is a 3 pl. pres. pass. of

2.b.6.86 Cloth*ar* cloat*har* .i. clui*n*ter.
Clothar, *cloathar* 'may hear', i.e. is heard.[193]

2.b.6.87 Forsaid*h* .i. fi*us* f*orusda* no fiors*h*aoid*h*e.
Forsaid 'wise', i.e. knowledge of experience or wisdom.[194]

2.b.6.88 Cota .i. cin*n*[us].
Cóta 'coat', i.e. covering.[195]

2.b.7.89 Rirt*h*er .i. rof*h*iren*naghth*er.
Rirther 'which will be sold', i.e. may be paid.[196]

2.b.7.90 Con-oat*har* .i. coim*étthar*.
Con-othar 'is protected', i.e. is protected.[197]

2.b.7.91 Venite .i. tait.
Venite 'come', i.e. come![198]

---

credba(ig)id 'shrinks, consumes, gnaws'; cf. CIH 1267.5 (from a text on compensation for injuries); CCIH 52; and *eDIL s.v. credba(ig)id.* The gloss is more problematic as it looks as if Dubhaltach misread his source or left out an ⟨i⟩. Although the letters in the MS are clearly ⟨mn⟩ (his ⟨i⟩ normally extends below the base-line), there are enough minims to form ⟨inn⟩; cf. *eDIL s.vv. creinnid* 'gnaws, corrodes, devours' and *creimmid* 'gnaws, bites, corrodes'.

193 Both forms of the headword are 3 sg. pres. subj. of *ro-cluinethar* 'hears'. The gloss is from a later simplex of the same verb; it looks like a 3 sg. pres. pass., although there could be confusion between the subjunctive and later present passive forms; *eDIL s.v. ro-cluinethar*. Cf. O'Cl *Clotha no roclotha .i. do clos no do cualas* 'was heard'.

194 Although both glosses make sense on their own, there is an etymological component to both of them. For the second gloss, see *eDIL s.v. forsaide* 'wisdom, discretion, experience'. Cf. *Bretha Nemed Dédenach* 32.6 (CIH 1124.16; CCIH 184–188) for part of the gloss.

195 The gloss is problematic mainly due to the fact that the edge of the page is damaged. The reading here is taken from O'Curry's transcription. Assuming that the lemma means 'coat, garment', one would expect a gloss with a similar meaning. The form *cinnus* by itself does not make sense here. It is possible that Dubhaltach misread his source, and the gloss should be a form of *cnes* 'skin, surface', perhaps 'covering'; *eDIL s.v. cnes*. The reading as it stands is not secure enough to make a confident emendation.

196 The lemma is a 3 sg. fut. pass. rel. of *renaid* 'sells, barters, exchanges'. The interpretation of the gloss is uncertain. It could be a 3 sg. pres. subj. pass. of *érnigid*; see *eDIL s.vv. érnigid* 'grants, pays' and *as-ren* 'pays away, expends, gives'.

197 The lemma is a 3 sg. pres. pass. of *con-oí* 'protects, preserves, guards'. The verb is later replaced by *coimétaid*; the gloss is a 3 sg. pres. pass. of this later simplex; *eDIL s.v. con-oí.*

198 The lemma is the 2 pl. impv. of Latin *veniō* 'to come'. The gloss is the 2 pl. impv. of *do-tét* 'comes'. This is the only Latin headword in Dubhaltach's Glossary. See also *Auraicept na n-Éces* ll. 140 and 141.

2.b.7.92 Mad*h* t*h*óis .i. ma t*h*oinge.
Madh thóis 'if you may swear', i.e. if you may swear.[199]

2.b.7.93 Rud*h*rac*h* .i. ro-durad*h* gua.
Rudrach 'prolonged', i.e. [< *ro-* intensifying prefix + *dúrad* 'lasting, duration'] great-duration of falsehood.[200]

2.b.8.94 Do-gó sinser .i. beirid an si*n*s*er* a rog*h*a.
Do-goa sinser 'the eldest chooses', i.e. the eldest makes his choice.[201]

2.b.8.95 Cuit*h*c*h*uire te*cht*a .i. ogl*ach* (bi*us* ag gaba[il] fiadh*aigh* i gcuit*ac*[h]) ⁊ do-[g]ní cuac*hairacht* tog*arm*a *ar* an bfiad*h* doc[h]u*m* an cuit*he*.
Cuthchaire téchtae 'lawful trapper', i.e. a vassal (who takes game in a pitfall) and who does pit-hunting by attracting the deer towards the pitfall.[202]

2.b.8.96 Torla .i. naid*h*m, ⁊ desm*erecht air*: cat*h* fer ferta, ⁊ *araile*.
Torla 'bond', i.e. a bond, and an example of it: battle of men of a boundary, etc.[203]

---

199 The lemma and gloss are both 2 sg. pres. subj. forms of *tongaid* 'swears, takes an oath'. The gloss is based on the later simplex, *toingid*; *eDIL s.v. tongaid.*

200 For the lemma, see *eDIL s.v. 1 rudrach.* Cf. O'Cl *Rudhrach .i. fada* 'long'; and see O'Dav 1355 (*Fél.* Prol. 206; CCIH 148: *Rudrad .i. rodura[d] .i. beith co foda for ferann comaidhthech* "*Rudrad,* i.e. great duration, ut est 'to be long on a neighbouring land'."); and SC Y.1089 *Rudrud .i. ro-duradh.*

201 The entry refers to the eldest son choosing his portion of land after the youngest has divided it; GEIL 102. For the lemma, cf. Digest B (1) (CIH 1289.11; CCIH 53; AL 4: 372.15); and for part of the gloss, see *Bretha for Macślechtaib* (CIH 1548.35; CCIH 67).

202 The missing letters have been supplied from O'Curry's transcription. For a discussion of the role of the professional deer-trapper in medieval Ireland, see EIF 279–280. For the lemma, see *Bretha Éitgid* (CIH 322.20 ff., 1158.33; CCIH 178; AL 3: 456.19 ff.); and cf. O'Dav 472 (no id., but there is a possibility that it is from *Osbretha*; CCIH 122, n. 70, 265–266: *Cuithech .i. in fiada .i. clar toll no cep, ut est fer clandas cuithigh i tír a chéili cen athcomarc* "*Cuithech* 'a pitfall', i.e. of the deer, i.e. a holed board or stock, ut est 'a man that digs a pitfall in his tenant's land without asking leave'."). The vn. *togairm* covers a range of meanings including 'calling, provoking, inducing', so it is not necessarily the case that the hunter is 'calling' the deer towards the pit; *eDIL s.v. togairm.*

203 See *Ni Tulach* glossary (CIH 811.15–17); *Arra* glossary (CIH 1559.21–22); and cf. O'Dav 1594 ((2) no id.; CCIH 155: … *Nó torla .i. naidm, ut est ro nenais torla trebar Mac con calma na curadh* "… Or *torla,* i.e. a bond, ut est 'thou shalt bind a bond secure, Mac con the valient of the heroes'."). Based on the entries from the *Ni Tulach* glossary and *Arra* glossary, it is possible that Dubhaltach combined glosses from originally two distinct lemmata. The

2.b.10.97 Coimdid*h* .i. comd*h*úth*ad* .i. áit as coitc*h*en do g*a*c[h] aon ma*r* ata an f*hair*rge, ⁊c̄. Eccoimdig*h* .i. a c*hon*tr*ar*d*ha* si*n*.
Coimtig 'frequented', i.e. belonging equally, i.e. a place which is public for everyone like the ocean is, etc. *Éccoimtig* 'unfrequented', i.e. its opposite.[204]

2.b.11.98 For ton dire .i. *ar* son dire.
For don díre 'in lieu of payment', i.e. instead of payment.[205]

2.b.11.99 1 Coimdig*h* ⟨treib*he*⟩ .i. a l*ár*, a h-*air*m*ed*a, a h-[io]nada soillsi, ⁊ na h-ion*a*da i mbí at*h*aig*h*e c*h*aic*h*. Eccoi*m*dig*h* t*r*ebe .i. g*a*c[h] ionad o si*n* amac[h].
1 Coimtig ⟨treibe⟩ 'frequented place of a dwelling', i.e. its floor, its furniture, its bright places, and the places where everyone frequents. *Éccoimtig treibe* 'unfrequented places of a dwelling', i.e. every place except those.[206]

2.b.12.100 3 Coimdig*h* fait*h*c*h*e .i. a slig*h*t*h*e, a r*ed*he *arda*, ⁊ an t-ionad i mbí at*h*aig*h*e caig*h*. Eccoi*m*dig*h* fait*h*c[h]e .i. g*a*c[h] ionad di osi*n* am*a*c[h]. A*s ed* as fait*h*c*h*e an*n* .i. na c*eth*r[e] guirt as nesa do*n* baile .i. gort g*a*c[h]a h-*air*de ime, ⁊ cid *hé* an sliab*h* bud nesa don baile roba am*h*ail fait*h*c*h*e. No as í an f*h*ait*h*c*h*e: an ro saig*h* guit*h* cluig.
3 Coimtig faithche 'frequented place of a green', i.e. its paths, its high, level places, and the place where everyone frequents. *Éccoimtig faithche* 'unfrequented places of a green', i.e. every place of it except those. This is what is a green then, i.e. the four fields which are closest to the settlement, i.e. a field on each side around it, and though it may be a mountain which is closest to the settlement, it is [con-

---

form *ferta* is the gen. sg. of *fert* 'mound, tumulus, rampart, boundary, grave'; *eDIL s.v. 1 fert.* Cf. 10.10.16 TORLA.

204 Heptad 64 refers to 'frequented' and 'unfrequented' places for finding lost property; *Heptad 64*: 33–42; e.g. 244: 6–7 (*CIH* 56.16; *AL* 5: 320.17–18). For the lemma, cf. O'Dav 581 (no id.; *CCIH* 125).

205 See *eDIL s.v. 1 don*. Cf. O'Cl *Don .i. ar son* 'therefore'.

206 See *Heptad 64*: 33–42, 248.4–7 (*CIH* 56.30–33; *AL* 5: 326.12–15). This and the following several entries are prefaced with roman numerals in the MS. Those numbers have been reproduced here. It should be noted that the order in which they are listed is the order in which they are found in the MS. Some of the missing letters have been supplied from O'Curry's transcription.

sidered] as a green. Or this is what the green is: as far as the voice of a bell reaches.[207]

2.b.15.101 2 Coimdig cat[h]*rach* .i. a h-u*r*l*air*, a relge, a p*r*iom*h*sraide, ⁊ g*a*c[h] ionad*h* i mbí at*h*aig*h*e caig*h*. Eccoi*m*dig*h* cat[h]*rach* .i. g*a*c[h] ion*a*d ⟨in*n*te⟩ osin am*a*c[h].
2 Coimtig cathrach 'frequented place of an enclosure', i.e. its market-place, its churchyard, its main streets, and each place where everyone frequents. *Éccoimtig cathrach* 'unfrequented places of an enclosure', i.e. every place in it except those.[208]

2.b.16.102 4 Coimdig*h* raite .i. (róid no na cu*a*r*t*a ing*h*elta ⟨⁊ g*a*c⟩ idir f*h*ait*h*c*h*e ⁊ dirin*n*) .i. a slig*h*t*h*e, ⁊ a h-ionada *ar*da *r*éd*h*e, ⁊ *araile*.
4 Coimtig raite 'frequented place of rough land', i.e. (road or the circuit of grazing and each [place] between a green and unclaimed land), i.e. its paths, and its high, level places, etc.[209]

2.b.17.103 5 Coi*m*dig*h* s*h*leb*h*e .i. a slig*h*t*h*e, ⁊ *araile*.
5 Coimtig slébe 'frequented place of a mountain', i.e. its paths, etc.[210]

2.b.17.104 6 Coi*m*dig*h* caill[e .i.] a cluaint*h*e, a g*ur*tin*adh*e, ⁊ na h-ion*a*da i mbí at*h*aoig*h*e c*h*aig*h*. Eccoi*m*d*igh* caill*e* .i. o si*n* am*a*c[h].
6 Coimtig caille 'frequented place of a wood', i.e. its glades, its little gardens, and the places where everyone frequents. *Éccoimtig caille* 'unfrequented place of a wood', i.e. except those.[211]

---

207 See *Heptad 64*: 33–42, 250.7–9, 12–13, 15 (*CIH* 57.11–12, 15–18; *AL* 5: 328.3–4, 8–9, 11–12). It should be noted that this entry appears before 2.b.15.101 2COIMDIG CAT[H]RACH in the MS.

208 See *Heptad 64*: 33–42, 248.21, 250.1 (*CIH* 57.4–5; *AL* 5: 326.30–31).

209 See *Heptad 64*: 33–42, 242.1, 252.2 (*CIH* 57.21–22; *AL* 5: 322.10, 328.15–16); and cf. O'Dav 1387 (heptad 64; *CCIH* 149: *Raiti .i. rót, ut est frithe raiti .i. frithe dogabhar ar in rót nó i cuairt ingelta nó itir faithchi ⁊ dirinn. O faithchi imach is ed is raiti ann "Raite,* i.e. a road, ut est 'waif of a *raite*', i.e. a waif that is seized on the road, or in the circuit of grazing, or between a green and a waste (?). From a green out (all but the green?) this is a *raite* there.").

210 This is normally the sixth item in heptad 64 rather than the fifth. See *Heptad 64*: 33–42, 246. (*CIH* 56.9; *AL* 5: 324.16).

211 This location does not normally appear as part of the standard list of seven locations given in heptad 64; one would expect *rofida, vel sim.*, but see *CIH* 56.9 where it is used in commentary. The heptad tends to group the wood and mountain together to count as one of the seven locations; cf. 2.b.17.103 5 COIMDIGH SHLEBHE. For *gurtinadhe*, see *DIL s.v. guirtine* 'a little garden'. See *Heptad 64*: 33–42, 246.1–2 (*CIH* 56.9–10; *AL* 5: 324.17–18).

2.b.18.105 7 Coi*m*d*igh* trag*h*a .i. ionad in at*h*aig*h*id daoine ⁊ longa m*ar*aon, ⁊ ton*n*a go coitcen*n*. Eccoi*m*d*igh* trag*h*a .i. g*a*c[h] ionad n*ach* at*h*aig*h*ion*n* a*cht* longa a n-aon*ar*.
7 Coimtig tráchta 'frequented place of a shore', i.e. a place in which people and boats frequent together, and waves in general. *Éccoimtig trachta* 'unfrequented place of a shore', i.e. each place that but boats alone frequent.[212]

2.b.20.106 Fém*edh* .i. diult*a*d.
Fémed 'refusing', i.e. refusing.[213]

2.b.20.107 *Airíasacht* .i. aont[u]g*hadh*.
Airíasacht 'permission', i.e. consent.[214]

2.b.20.108 Oillian, culpait .i. an léne cona h-all sgóit.
Ollín, culpait 'large linen cloth, hood', i.e. [< *oll* 'great, large' + *lín* 'linen, cloth'] the tunic with its large sheet.[215]

---

212 It should be noted that in this entry, as with the previous entry 2.b.17.104 6 COIMDIGH CAILL[E], Dubhaltach follows the text of the legal commentary (*CIH* 58.30). See *Heptad 64*: 33–42, 246.7–9 (*CIH* 58.30–33; *AL* 5: 324.23–25). It should be noted that Dubhaltach does not include the standard seventh location in the heptad, i.e. the sea, but the sea is not considered to have a 'frequented' or 'unfrequented' place; *Heptad 64*: 262.16 (*CIH* 59.33; *AL* 5: 334: 29).

213 See *Muirbretha/Bretha Éitgid*: 326.5 (*CIH* 314.21; *AL* 3: 422.9). Cf. 7.b.8.64 FÉMEDH.

214 For the gloss, see *eDIL s.v. oentugad* 'conceeding, granting, consenting, agreeing'. See *Muirbretha/Bretha Éitgid*: 326.5, 340.4 (*CIH* 314.21, 959.10; *AL* 3: 422.9); and cf. O'Dav 108 (probably from *Muirbretha*; *CCIH* 111: *Aine .i. aibnes, u test madh airiasacht ar aine oc na bí airiassacht fir cota .i. airechtaighe ar aoibness nó airechtaighe done in fer anfine ar ainechus dó fein im du lar cend na sét cin escail do on fhir bes a aí aei* "Aine (*áine* ?), i.e. delight, ut est 'if there be a consent for pleasure as to which there is no consent of the sharer', i.e. a consent-in-court for pleasure, or a consent-in-court which the non-tribesman gives for his own amusement as to going for the *sét*s without consent of the man whose property they are."); and see also heptad 54 (Eska 2022: 392–393; *CIH* 49.20; *AL* 5: 298.21 ff.).

215 See *Bretha Nemed Toísech* (*CIH* 2218.15); and Digest B (57) (*CIH* 1382.19). Cf. 7.a.24.35 OILLÍAN and 7.a.24.36 CULPAIT. The interpretation of the gloss is uncertain. The general sense is that it is a large tunic made of cloth. For examples of the adj. *oll* 'vast, large' used as a substantive in compounds, see *eDIL s.v. oll*; this assumes MS *all* is a variant of *oll*; *eDIL s.v. 4 all.* The noun *léine* is feminine and has a variant nom. sg. in *léne*; *eDIL s.v. léine*. The noun *scot* 'sheet, sail' is also used in compounds with *lín* 'linen cloth' to refer to a linen cloth or sheet; *eDIL s.v. 2 lín*.

2.b.20.109 Tum*hadh* otraig*h* fri nec*h* [.i.] giolla an c*h*aca do rad ris, no a l*ethét*.
Tummud otraig fri nech 'immersing someone in dung', i.e. 'the boy of dung' he is called, or the like.[216]

2.b.21.110 Slán faille .i. ag si*n* fort slán dam *ar* re cid f*h*aill iom*h*coi*mhét*a do neit im in sréd.
Slán faille 'immunity of negligence', i.e. having that upon you, immunity for me, for a period of time although there is negligence of watching by a champion regarding the troop.[217]

2.b.22.111 Slán n-ait*h*ne .i. treb*air*e ro gaib*h* fer an tig*h*e and-side re fi*us* daingne, no *ar* daingn[e].
Slán n-aithne 'immunity of recognition', i.e. a security which the householder took then to acknowledge a compact, or for a compact.[218]

2.b.23.112 Ea[b]la [....................................][219]

3.a.1.1 [..]b [.]sen[..]e[...]. [..........................][220]

3.a.2.2 [......].i. an cuid a[..]tog*h*a[...]do cia [...] [........]d[...]na gæ[....]s[... ...][221]

3.a.3.3 [Duicheat .i. cuigid [..]]
Dúithche 'of a region' i.e. of a province ...[222]

---

216 The context of the entry is obscure. The general sense of the gloss is to call someone a depreciating epithet associated with excrement. The lemma is understood as *tummud*, the vn. of *tummaid* 'dips, immerses'. For the construction *a lethét*, see *eDIL s.v. leithét*.

217 Parts of the entry are difficult to interpret. It seems to refer to the period of legal immunity although someone has failed in their watch duties. The word *sréd* is problematic. It might be for *spréid* 'cattle, property, stock wealth', in which case the gloss refers to watching property to guard against raiders, and the text would need to be amended to reflect that. It could also be for *sreth* 'strewing, ranks, lines of people, soldiers', in which case the gloss refers simply to watch duties, which is the interpretation adopted here.

218 The translation of the gloss is tentative. It appears to refer to someone who is given immunity in order to seek out a surety who has knowledge of the contract.

219 Both verbs, *aigid* 'drives, impels' and *ailid* 'nourishes, rears, fosters', have future stems in *-ebla*; *eDIL s.vv. aigid* and *1 ailid*. Cf. 9.9.32 EABHLA[...] and 9.11.34 [.]C [..] EABHLA.

220 The entry is mostly illegible and is not in O'Curry's transcription.

221 The entry is mostly illegible and is not in O'Curry's transcription.

222 This entry is in O'Curry's transcription, but I have not been able to find it on the page. The

3.a.3.4 [........................] .⁊. [......................][223]

3.a.4.5 [........].i. cor éisisi .i. eg[.]uisis .i. cor, esi*et*em*h* .i. cor[...], no eccn[e] .i. [.]osnad*h*.[224]

3.a.5.6 [.....] a[..]olanuib, ⁊ [....]anuisge [..][225]

3.a.6.7 [..]ugille *ar* [..]osi dfi*et*b[.][226]

3.a.7.8 [...]fuill*em*a .i. in a[..]gi[.]⁊ urgais, an an*m*aoin, ⁊ an fuillem*h*.
[.....] *fuillema*, i.e. the [...] and exchange of the worthless object, and of the interest.[227]

3.a.7.9 U*r*gais .i. erguid*h*e [ua]is.
Airgais 'exchange of two items of unequal value', i.e. [< *airguide* 'entreating' + *úais* 'noble'] asking a noble.[228]

3.a.8.10 [Urfo]gr*a*ig*h* cuir ⁊ cu*nnar*t[ha] .i. dao[in]e [da nach coir car] cu*n*-*nradha* sin, ma*r* ata m*ai*c, mna, baoit*h* .⁊c̄. [⁊ ni in]an*n* si*n* urfogr*a*ig*h* leabtan*u*sa [.⁊c̄.].
Airḟócraig cuir ⁊ cundartha 'people proclaimed in respect of contract and bargain', i.e. people to whom it is not right to establish that bargain, as are sons, women, fools, etc. and that is not the same as proclaimed people in respect of shelter, etc.[229]

---

interpretation of the lemma is uncertain. It might be a f. gen. sg. substantive of *dúthaig* 'hereditary, native land, district', but the ending is unexplained; *eDIL s.v. dúthaig*.

223 The line is entirely illegible, and nothing in O'Curry's transcription seems to correspond to this location in the MS.

224 This entry is not in O'Curry's transcription. The line is difficult to read, but it concerns contracts; cf. *Di Astud Chor* § 54 (CIH 988.13).

225 The entry is mostly illegible and is not in O'Curry's transcription.

226 The entry is mostly illegible and is not in O'Curry's transcription.

227 This entry is not in O'Curry's transcription. The lemma is missing, the page is damaged, and the context of the entry is unknown.

228 See *Cóic Conara Fugill* § 11 and gloss 10 (CIH 2201.18); for the lemma, see O'Dav 1617 (*Bretha Nemed Toísech*; CCIH 156: *Urgais .i. claochlodh, ut est rath n-aiscid ⁊ urguise nó erguidhi* "*Urgais*, i.e. an exchange, ut est 'stock of gift and entreaty or begging'."); and *Bretha Nemed Toísech* (CIH 2231.33; CCIH 156).

229 The entry is difficult to read due to how badly stained the MS page is. There are three textual sources which are similar to parts, but not all, of the entry. Cf. *Cáin Aicillne* § 38 comm. (CIH 1794.16–29, 2052.38–2053.13; AL 2: 290.1–17); *Di Astud Chor* § 55, comm. (CIH 988.26–37); for part of the gloss, see *Córus Bésgnai* § 9 (CIH 522.1–2). Cf. 3.a.9.11 [URFOGRAIGH

3.a.9.11 [Urfograigh leapandis .i. daoine da nach coir leabaidh do thabhair]t .i. daoine bi*us* i n-ag*adh* dlig*edh*, ⁊ do-[g]ní sin urfog*r*aig*h* cuir ⁊ cun*nartha* diob*h*.
Airḟócraig lepthanais 'people proclaimed in respect of sheltering', i.e. people to whom it is not right to give a bed, i.e. people who are in opposition to law, and that makes them people proclaimed in respect of contract and bargain.[230]

3.a.10.12 [.....]at*ha* no .s. i. diult*adh* no c*r*osad tu*arus*tail do gabail .⁊c̄.
[.....]*atha no .s.*, i.e. refusing or forbidding to take payment, etc.[231]

3.a.10.13 T*áir*cit*her* .i. tat*h*aoir.
Táircither 'is brought about', i.e. is reproached.[232]

3.a.11.14 [...] no fe[...] uenouidir[.] *ar* nec*h* .i. fec[h]em*h*n*us* indlig*h*t*a*c[h].
[...] *no fe*[...] *uenouidir*[.] *ar nech* 'for someone', i.e. illegal indebtedness.[233]

3.a.11.15 As é an roac*h* .i. ge no [in]geall*a* ni a b[riathraib], [nibi] cor i n-eg[mais 'athar].
Is é an roach 'it is he who is the witness to a contract', i.e. though he promises anything by words, it is not a contract in the absence of his father.[234]

LEAPANDIS]. Both entries refer to those with whom it is prohibited to make a lawful contract and those to whom one should not give shelter, respectively. If someone has been proclaimed in respect of shelter, one should not make a contract with that person. It is also possible for someone to be proclaimed in respect of contracts, but not proclaimed in respect of shelter; those people include women and children.

230 The entry is difficult to read due to how badly stained the MS page is. There are two textual sources which are similar to parts, but not all of, the entry. Cf. *Cáin Aicillne* § 38 comm. (*CIH* 1794.16–29, 2052.38–2053.13; *AL* 2: 290.1–17); and *Di Astud Chor* § 55, comm. (*CIH* 988.26–37). See 3.a.8.10 [URFO]GRAIGH CUIR ⁊ CUNNART[HA], the previous entry, for discussion.

231 This entry is not in O'Curry's transcription, and the entry is too fragmentary for the translation to be certain.

232 The lemma is the 3 sg, pres. pass. ind. of *do-áirci* 'brings about, produces, supplies, conducts'; *eDIL s.v. do-áirci*. The gloss might be a 3 sg. pres. pass. ind. of *do-athaíra* 'censures, finds fault with' or a later form of the lemma. Cf. *tathaír* 'blaming, reproaching'. The context of the entry is unknown, and the gloss might make more sense within its larger source context.

233 This entry is not in O'Curry's transcription; the context is unknown, and the reading is not secure.

234 This entry is not in O'Curry's transcription. See *Di Astud Chor* § 57 gloss a (*CIH* 989.7–8, 1195.2–3).

3.a.12.16 [Cia sias] .i. cait i suideab*h*sa.
[*Cía sias*] 'wherever he will claim', i.e. wherever he will claim.[235]

3.a.12.17 Cia lias .i. cait i luideib*h*sa.
Cía lias 'wherever he may leap', i.e. wherever he will leap.[236]

3.a.12.18 Cia er*us* .i. cait i ereoc[hadh].
Cía éras 'wherever he may rise', i.e. wherever he will rise.[237]

3.a.13.19 [...]at[....] bec.[238]

3.a.13.20 Findteferts*a*c[h] .i. ⟨m*a*c⟩ na h-ad*h*altraig*h*e.
Fintiu fertsech 'hereditary land of a spindle', i.e. the son of the *adaltrach*.[239]

3.a.13.21 Findte diabl*ad*h*e* .i. an tseanor*a*c[h].
Fintiu díblide 'hereditary land of a decrepit person', i.e. of the senior.[240]

---

235 The interpretation of the entry is tentative, and the missing letters are supplied from O'Curry's transcription. *Cía* could be interpreted as 'whoever'; *eDIL s.v. 1 cía*. The verb *sias* is interpreted as a sg. fut. rel. of *saigid* 'approaches, claims, reaches, attains'; *eDIL s.v. 1 saigid*. The interpretation of *suideabhsa* is uncertain, however it is likely to be a later future form of *saigid*; McCone 1997: 223–225. Cf. the form *luideibhsa* in 3.a.12.17 CIA LIAS.

236 The interpretation of the entry is tentative. *Cía* could be interpreted as 'whoever'; *eDIL s.v. 1 cía*. The verb *lias* is interpreted as a sg. pres. subj. rel. of *lingid* 'leaps, attacks, rushes'; *eDIL s.v. lingid*. The interpretation of *luideibhsa* is uncertain, however, it is likely a later future form of *lingid*; McCone 1997: 223–225. Cf. the form *suideabhsa* in 3.a.12.16 [CIA SIAS].

237 The interpretation of the entry is tentative, and the missing letters are supplied from O'Curry's transcription. *Cía* could be interpreted as 'whoever'; *eDIL s.v. 1 cía*. The verb *érus* is interpreted as a sg. pres. subj. rel. of *at-reig* 'rises, occurs'; *eDIL s.v. at-reig*. The interpretation of *ereoc[hadh]* is uncertain, however it is likely a later future form of *at-reig*; McCone 1997: 226–227.

238 This entry is not in O'Curry's transcription; most of the entry is illegible.

239 This entry is cross-referenced in O'Curry's transcription but is not included. The interpretation of the entry is uncertain. The context is unknown, but cf. *findtiu dímleithe* in the *Status Tract* (*CIH* 1546.5; *CCIH* 66 and 297–300); the accompanying gloss concerns the kindred's role in the use (or not) of land by an adopted son. The word *fertsach* is interpreted as an adj. derived from *fertas* 'spindle, pole' being used metaphorically of the son of the secondary wife, thus giving a meaning 'heredity land of one like a spindle' although the final syllable is unexpected for a gen. sg. adj. ending in *-ach*; *eDIL s.v. 1 fertas*. It is also possible that the word is from *fersech* 'strong, forcible'.

240 The interpretation of the entry is uncertain. The context is unknown, but cf. *findtiu dímleithe* in the *Status Tract* (*CIH* 1546.5; *CCIH* 66 and 297–300); the accompanying gloss

3.a.14.22 [...][241]

3.b.1.23 .i. M*a*d a [...] do l*eth* ibe ⁊ l*eth*i*a*rr .i. l*eth* biadaid [......]fe[...]l*eth* .i. b[...] afaco .i. mogad*h*[.] do bir*ar ar* an fer d*h*a ndenter.[242]

3.b.2.24 Fuic*h*ec*h*t .i. an gnio*mh* f[erdha] .i. coi*m*ria*ch*tain ⁊c̄.
Fuichecht 'cuckoldry', i.e. the male act, i.e. sexual intercourse, etc.[243]

3.b.2.25 Naid*m* ⁊ urnaidm*h* bi*us* ider fer ⁊ mnaoi .i. naidm*h* .i. coib*h*c*h*e do*n* mnaoi, ⁊ urnaidm*h* ag an f*h*er uirri-si im íoc leis da nden*ad*-si fogail doba n*ar* n[o] olc d*hó*.
Naidm ⁊ airnaidm bís eter fiur ⁊ mnaí 'contract and bond which exists between a husband and a wife', i.e. a contract, i.e. a bride-price for the woman, and a bond that the man has over her regarding payment he has to make if she might cause injury, which is shameful or bad for him.[244]

3.b.3.26 Comt[us .i.] cu*m*aid*h* úais.
Comthus 'partnership', i.e. [< *commaid* 'companionship' + *úais* 'noble'] noble companionship.[245]

3.b.4.27 Do-góad .i. tog*h*aid.
Do-goad 'he might choose', i.e. he chooses.[246]

---

concerns the kindred's role in the use (or not) of land by an adopted son. I should like to thank one of the anonymous readers for this reference.

241 This entry is illegible, and nothing in O'Curry's transcription seems to correspond to this location in the MS.

242 This entry is not in O'Curry's transcription. The reading is not secure enough to attempt a translation of the entry, but the entry concerns being entitled to half maintenance and half fosterage fee.

243 The larger context of the entry is unknown. The missing letters are supplied from O'Curry's transcription.

244 The translation is awkward, but the sense is that the wife has her *coibche* and the husband is responsible for paying compensation for any crime she might commit, and he is also paid compensation for crimes committed against her.

245 See *Coibnes Uisci Thairidne* § 7, gloss 6 (*CIH* 459.25 and 29–30; *AL* 4: 210.4 and 14–15).

246 The lemma is the 3 sg. past. subj. of *do-goa* 'chooses, elects, selects'. The gloss is problematic as a 3 sg. past subj. form is expected. Instead, the gloss appears to be a 3 sg. pres. ind. from the simplex *togaid* (assuming that the form in the MS is not an error); *eDIL s.v. 1 do-goa*.

3.b.4.28 Do-g*h*óidís .i. do t*h*og*h*daois.
Do-gotais 'they might choose', i.e. they might choose.[247]

3.b.4.29 Tuirc*h*reic .i. cid t*h*oir*adh* nes[a] .i. siocla .i. sort ionm*uis* b*erar* do mnaoi i gcoibc*he*.
Turchrecc 'fore-purchase', i.e. thought is be a sooner payment, i.e. *sical*s, i.e. a type of wealth given to a woman in addition to her bride-price.[248]

3.b.5.30 Con-duic*h*et .i. cui*nng*h*id.
Con-daiget 'they ask', i.e. they ask.[249]

3.b.5.31 Aicc .i. íesg.
Aicc 'invoke!', i.e. allow![250]

3.b.5.32 Tec*h*t m*h*uig*he* .i. sealb*h* b*h*eod*h*ile b*hius* *ar* an mag*h*.
Techt maige 'possession of field', i.e. a living possession which is on the field.[251]

3.b.5.33 Tion*n*sgra .i. tionsgedol creice an tsiogail do b*erar* do mnaoi *ar* t*h*oil go n-oige do b*eth* aice.
Tinnscra 'bride-price', i.e. beginning payment of the *sical*s which is given to a woman for the desire for her to be a virgin.[252]

---

247 The lemma and gloss are both 3 pl. past. subj. forms of *do-goa* 'chooses, elects, selects'; *eDIL s.v. 1 do-goa.*

248 The interpretation of the entry is problematic. While the lemma is clear, the first part of the gloss is not; the reading is not secure, and thus, the translation is tentative. The sense of the gloss is of a payment that is made before giving a woman her bride-price. The form *siocla* is interpreted as a late nom. pl. of *sical*, which is frequently used in the plural to refer to the payment made to a woman for her virginity at the time of her betrothal. If she proves not to be a virgin on her wedding night, she has to return the payment; *eDIL s.v. sical.* This payment is made in addition to giving her a bride-price. Cf. 3.b.5.33 TIONNSGRA.

249 Both the lemma and gloss are interpreted as 3 pl. pres. ind. of *con-dïeig* 'asks, seeks, demands' with the gloss being from a later simplex; *eDIL s.v. con-dïeig*.

250 The interpretation of the entry is tentative. The lemma is the 2 sg. impv. of *ad-guid*, which is used for invoking a surety. The gloss is a 2 sg. impv. from either *eiscid* 'allows, concedes' or *eiscid* 'severs', neither of which makes much sense here; *eDIL s.vv. 1* and *2 eiscid.* Cf. 10.11.18 AICCITHER.

251 The entry refers to livestock in the field near a dwelling. For a similar phrase as the lemma, cf. *Cáin Lánamna* § 2, comm. XVII (*CIH* 504.14–15; *AL* 2: 350.14).

252 Cf. 9.43.131 SLABHRA, SLAIBHRE, and 9.43.132 TIONNSGRA. Based on the abbreviation

3.b.6.34 Slab*h*ra tobra .i. sál b*húar* do-b[erar] do mnaoi *ar* coi*met* a genuis di.
Slabrae torbae 'marriage portion of profit', i.e. [< *sál* 'sea' + *búar* 'cattle'] sea of cattle which is given to a woman for preserving her chastity.[253]

3.b.6.35 Taid*h*be .i. taoi eibe *ut* [..].
Taithbe 'dissolution', i.e. [< *tóe* 'silent' + *eipe* 'cutting, incision, selection'] silent cutting *ut* ...[254]

3.b.7.36 M*ar*bt*h*aid*h*be .i. ni ebi*us* a coib*h*ce a ttaoi o m*h*naoi, ⁊ m*ar*b i fen, no a fer, no ce*chtar* doib*h* an*n*.
Marbtaithbe 'dead dissolution', i.e. anything which severs her bride-price in silence from a woman, and she herself is dead, or her husband, or both of them then.[255]

3.b.7.37 Beot*h*aid*h*be .i. ní ebes a c*h*oib*h*ce a ttaoí o mnaoi ⁊ beo i fen sa fer, no as beo ne*chtar* de.

'D.R.' at the beginning of this section of the MS page, the source is likely *Dúil* (*Roscadach*) (*CCIH* 246–253). Cf. O'Cl *Tionnscra .i. coibhche* 'purchase'; and 9.43.133 TIASG. The entry refers to the payment made to a woman for her virginity at the time of her betrothal. If she proves not to be a virgin on her wedding night, she has to return the payment; for the lemma, see *Tract on Marriage and Divorce* § 19 (*CIH* 147.29); *GEIL* 72–73; and *eDIL s.v. sical.* This payment is made in addition to giving her a bride-price.

253 The missing letters are supplied from O'Curry's transcription; there is a dark stain over part of the word. The lemma can refer to both 'stock' and 'marriage portion' which could consist of livestock. The interpretation of MS *tobra* is uncertain. It is understood here as a mistake for *torbae* 'profit, benefit'. The sense of the entry is that this is the payment that she receives for guarding her chastity until (and during) her marriage so that there is no doubt regarding the paternity of any children; cf. *Tract on Marriage and Divorce* § 19 (*CIH* 147.29–36); *GEIL* 72–73; and O'Cl *Slaibhre .i. coibhche* 'dowry, purchase'. Cf. 9.43.131 SLABHRA, SLAIBHRE where the etymological gloss is the same.

254 The interpretation of the entry is tentative. For the use of *tóe* 'silent', *epid* 'cuts', and *eipe* 'cutting, incision' in etymological glosses on *taithbe*, cf. 3.b.7.36 MARBTHAIDHBE and 3.b.7.37 BEOTHAIDHBE. It is possible that we should understand 'silence' here as a metaphor for 'without fuss or contention'.

255 The first half of the gloss is a simplified etymological gloss and hearkens back to the etymological gloss on 3.b.6.35 TAIDHBE. It should be noted that a form of *epid* 'cuts' is also used in an etymological gloss on 3.b.6.35 TAIDHBE and 3.b.7.37 BEOTHAIDHBE. For a similar type of etymological gloss, cf. *Di Astud Chirt 7 Dligid* (*CIH* 239.19; *AL* 5: 474.31). The entry refers to dissolving the marriage contract as a result of the death of one or both parties.

Béotaidbe 'living dissolution', i.e. anything which severs her bride-price in silence from a woman, and she herself and her husband are alive, or either one of them is alive.[256]

3.b.8.38 Cutai*m* .i. co*m*t*h*uiti*m*.
Cutaim 'falling down', i.e. falling down.[257]

3.b.8.39 L*eth*c*h*utaim .i. tuiti*m* .i. coi*m*tuiti*m* do*n* d*a*ra l*eth*.
Lethchutaim 'half falling down', i.e. falling, i.e. falling down by one side.[258]

3.b.8.40 Iomcutai*m* .i. co*m*t*h*uiti*m* doib*h* m*ar* aon .i. don lana*muin*, iolr*adh* na ffoc*ail* si .i. l*et*[h]cutman*n* ⁊ imcut*m*ain*n*.
Immcutaim 'mutually falling down', i.e. falling down by both of them, i.e. for the married couple, it is the sum of the words, i.e. half falling down and mutually falling down.[259]

---

256 The first half of the gloss is a simplified etymological gloss and hearkens back to the etymological gloss on 3.b.6.35 TAIDHBE. It should be noted that a form of *epid* 'cuts' is also used in an etymological gloss on 3.b.6.35 TAIDHBE and 3.b.7.36 MARBTHAID-HBE. For a similar type of etymological gloss, cf. *Di Astud Chirt ⁊ Dligid* (*CIH* 239.19; *AL* 5: 474.31). The entry refers to dissolving the marriage contract while either or both of parties are still alive and linguistically parallels what we find in 3.b.7.36 MARBTHAID-HBE.

257 Both the lemma and gloss are verbal nouns of *con-tuit* 'falls together'; *eDIL s.v. con-tuit*. For the lemma, cf. O'Dav 464 (no id.; *CCIH* 122: *Cutaim .i. tuitim, ut est cid iar coise cuitim fri aliche annscuichthi* "*Cutaim*, i.e. a fall, ut est 'though after a foot's fall it be against immoveable rocks'."); O'Dav 519 (*Bretha Éitgid*; *CCIH* 124: *Cutaim .i. tuitim, ut est bla crann cutaim* "*Cutaim*, i.e. a falling, ut est 'a tree (is) exempt in falling'."); and *Bretha Éitgid* (*CIH* 274.17). It is possible that the sense of the entry is not that of physically falling down (as is the case in the citation from *Bretha Éitgid*), but rather that of something becoming legally forfeit. Cf. 9.25.78 CUTAIM, 3.b.8.39 LETHCHUTAIM, and 3.b.8.40 IOM-CUTAIM.

258 Cf. 3.b.8.38 CUTAIM, 9.25.78 CUTAIM, and 3.b.8.40 IOMCUTAIM. It is possible that the sense of the entry is not that of physically falling down, but rather that of something becoming legally forfeit.

259 The gloss *illrad* is conveying a notion that the lemma, *imcutaim*, includes both of the meanings of *lethcutmann* and *imcutmainn*. The second element of both of those words seems to be derived from *cutaim*. Cf. 3.b.8.39 LETHCHUTAIM and 3.b.8.38 CUTAIM and 9.25.78 CUTAIM. The general sense of the entry is that both members of the married couple are responsible for some aspect of the marriage (or perhaps another type of contract) breaking apart.

3.b.9.41 Domrúid*h* .i. reime deach*aidh* .i. ruid*h* .i. ro faoid.
Domruid 'it has led me', i.e. previously he had led, i.e. he had led, i.e. he had led.[260]

3.b.10.42 Cob*hus* .i. coi*mfh*eis.
Cobás 'increase', i.e. increase.[261]

3.b.10.43 Tog*h*luas*acht* .i. ní do-b*eir ar* mnaoi br*eth* clain*ne* re n-ionb*aidh*.
Toglúasacht 'miscarriage', i.e. something which causes a woman to bear a child before the proper time.[262]

3.b.10.44 Clam*h*doid .i. ben ag mbí lam*h* clam*h*.
Clamdóid 'leprous hand', i.e. a woman who has a leprous hand.[263]

3.b.10.45 Cl*ár* ai*m*rid .i. ben na b*eir* clan*n*.
Clár aimrit 'infertile surface', i.e. a woman who does not bear a child.[264]

---

260 The entry is problematic. The interpretation of the lemma follows that in Carey 1990a: 15, n. 73 (see also McCone 1986b: 8); see *eDIL s.vv. do-fed* 'leads, brings' and *? do-ruid*. For the lemma, see the *Pseudo-Historical Prologue to the* Senchas Már (CIH 341.19; *AL* 1: 12.22; CCIH 286; the lemma is from Dubhthach's judgement which is not included in Carey's edition, but it is translated in Carey 1990a and McCone 1986b). The verb in the first part of the gloss is understood as the 1 sg. perf. of *téit* 'goes'; *eDIL s.v. 1 téit*. The remaining two verbs are interpreted as 3 sg. pret./perf. forms of *do-fed*.

261 It is likely that the lemma and gloss are variant spellings of *cobás* and *comḟás*, both of which mean 'increase'; *eDIL s.vv. cobás* and *comḟás*. It is also possible that the gloss is meant to be interpreted as etymological. The spelling *comfheis* is unexpected; it is possible that the notion of 'increase' was being equated with the notion of spending the night together, < *com-* 'with' + *feiss* 'spending the night'; *eDIL s.v. 2 feis(s), fess*.

262 *eDIL* defines *toglúasacht* as 'abortion'; it is the vn. of *do-gluaisi* 'sets in motion, miscarries'. The sense of *toglúasacht* in this section of the glossary seems to be 'miscarriage' rather than 'abortion'. The line between miscarriage and abortion in the Middle Ages was not always clear. Bodily violence can bring about a miscarriage, but at what point does that shade into abortion or murder of a fetus? Cf. Butler 2015: 193–197 for discussion of the same subject in medieval England. The word *inbaid* refers not only to a proper period of time, but it can also refer to the time of delivery; *eDIL s.v. inbaid*. Cf. 13.d.26.38 TURTGAL.

263 The larger context of the passage is unknown. It should be noted that it is possible that we should not understand *clam* as 'leprous, scurfy', but rather as 'diseased' more generally or 'deformed'. The word *lám* 'hand, arm' is often used to gloss *1 doé* 'arm, hand'; *eDIL s.v. 1 doé* (b).

264 The spelling *aimrit* is a variant of *aimbrit eDIL s.v. aimbrit*. The precise interpretation of *clár* here is uncertain. Perhaps it should be interpreted metaphorically likening the woman to an infertile vessel or barren surface.

3.b.11.46 Din*n*is .i. mion*n*a.
Dindis 'denial by oath', i.e. oaths.[265]

3.b.11.47 Im-rolaid*h* .i. em*h ar* luad*h* fir ag tec*h*t no ag dul doc*hum* a m*h*ná.
Imm-rolaid 'supports', i.e. [< *éim* 'swift, timely' + *ar* 'for' + *lúad* 'moving'] a man who is swift for coming and going to his woman.[266]

3.b.11.48 Dait*h*in .i. ceo, no dait*hin* .i. dat*h* na sine .i. g*r*ian, ⁊ esga.
Daithen 'light', i.e. mist, or light, i.e. the color of the weather, i.e. sun, and moon.[267]

3.b.12.49 Aig*h*néta .i. aig*h*nes no b*r*et[h]em*h*n*us*.
Aigneda 'advocates', i.e. pleading or judgement.[268]

3.b.12.50 Airsinsior .i. firsins*er*.
Arsinser 'ancestor', i.e. [< *fír* 'true' + *senser* 'elder, senior, ancestors'] true ancestor.[269]

3.b.12.51 Sleit*h* .i. coim*h*ria*cht*ain le*n* mnaoi gan fios di.
Sleith 'rape by stealth', i.e. having sexual intercourse with the woman without her knowledge.[270]

---

265 See O'Cl *Dinnis .i luighe, no mionna* 'an oath'; for the lemma, cf. the first part of O'Dav 739 (*Bretha Éitgid*; CCIH 130: *Dinis .i. luigh*… "*Dinnis*. i.e. oath…"), and *Metr. Gl.* 23 § 10 *'Dinnis' ainm do luighe*. Cf. 7.a.10.14 DINNIS.

266 The lemma is interpreted as a 3 sg. pres. ind. from the stem *-la* of *imm-cuirethar* 'carries around, brings, send, supports, endures'; *eDIL s.v. imm-cuirethar*. It is common for the preverb *im(m)-* to be glossed by *éim* 'swift, timely'; Binchy 1943: 212; and Taylor-Griffiths 2020: 1: 89.

267 See O'Dav 692 (likely from *Córus Aithni*; CCIH 128: *Daith*[*en*] *.i. grian ⁊ esca, ut est corus aithne ⁊rl. do tongar dar drucht, dar daithin .i. dar daith sína nó dar dath na sína, dar grein ⁊ dar esca, uair grian ⁊ esca dobeir dath ar na sinaib* "*Daithen*, i.e. sun and moon, ut est 'Regulation of deposits etc. 'one swears by the dew, by the *daithen*'; i.e. by colour (*dath*) of weather (*sín*), or by the colour of the weather, by sun and moon, for sun and moon put colour on the weathers."). The citation in O'Dav lists *Córus Aithni* as a source, but the citation itself does not seem to survive in the fragments from the text printed in *CIH*; CCIH 308. For the lemma, cf. OM 329.

268 For the lemma, see *eDIL s.v. aigne* 'one learned in law; lawyer, advocate, pleader'.

269 It is common for the prefix *ar-* to be etymologized by *fír-* 'true, genuine'; Binchy 1943: 212; and Taylor-Griffiths 2020: 1: 89. The interpretation of the entry is tentative.

270 The context of the passage is unknown. For a discussion of the different types of rape in the early Irish laws, see *GEIL* 134–137; and Oliver 1993.

3.b.13.52 Faoig*he* .i. fóeig*he* ón g*h*láoid.
Fo-égi 'raises an outcry', i.e. raises an outcry by the shouting.[271]

3.b.13.53 Slet*her* .i. teigt*er* doc[h]u*m* mná gan f*hius* di.
Sleither 'people who rape by stealth', i.e. people go to a woman without her knowledge.[272]

3.b.13.54 Sleit*h* t*ar* lónlaingen .i. dul doc[h]u*m* mna gan f*hius* di na deg*h*aid aníar.
Sleith tar lónlaingen 'rape by stealth through a side', i.e. going to a woman without her knowledge from behind.[273]

3.b.14.55 Sl*eth* d*ar* glún .i. idir a d*ha* cois.
Sleith tar glún 'rape by stealth through a knee', i.e. between her two legs.[274]

3.b.14.56 Sl*eth* fo t*h*aob*h* .i. d*ha* cois na mna t*ar* an f*he*r.
Sleith fo thóib 'rape by stealth under a side', i.e. the two legs of the woman across the man.[275]

271 Cf. 3.b.12.51 SLEITH. The entry refers to raising an outcry, presumably once the woman knows that she has been violated.

272 The lemma is not in *eDIL*. The interpretation of the lemma is based on the form of the accompanying gloss. It is possible that the lemma is an impersonal form of a verb derived from *sleith* 'act of raping a sleeping woman', which is the vn. of **selid* 'creeps'; *eDIL s.v. sleith*. This interpretation is only tentative. Cf. 3.b.12.51 SLEITH. The verb *teigter* is interpreted as a later 3 pl. pres. pass. of *téit* 'goes' used impersonally, but the verb has a sexual meaning here. For a discussion of the different types of rape in the early Irish laws, see *GEIL* 134–137; and Oliver 1993.

273 The interpretation of *lónlaigen* is tentative. In O'Dav 1204 (no id.; *CCIH* 144: *Lonlaigen .i. taeb, ut est co fuirim lonlaingen fri lairge luthain .i. a thaeb fri toin na gabla* "Lón-laingen, i.e. a side, ut est 'with a putting of sides to the *luthan* of the thigh', i.e. of his sides to the bottom of the fork."), it is translated as 'side'. The word is a compound of *lón* 'haunch, rump, buttock, hip' and *laingen*, which seems to be derived from *long*; *eDIL s.vv. 1 long* and *2 long*, which is not adequately translated in *eDIL*; cf. O'Cl *Lon loinngen .i.* '[the gullet, O'Conn.]' *.i. sdaidhg bhrághad, dá ngoirthear go coitcheann stéic bhraghad* 'the throat-stalk'. The general sense of the entry is that the woman has been violated from behind. Cf. 3.b.14.55 SLETH DAR GLÚN and 3.b.14.56 SLETH FO THAOBH.

274 Cf. 3.b.13.54 SLEITH TAR LÓNLAINGEN and 3.b.14.56 SLETH FO THAOBH. The lenition of *dha* is unexpected following the 3 sg. f. poss. pron. *a*.

275 Cf. 3.b.13.54 SLEITH TAR LÓNLAINGEN and 3.b.14.55 SLETH DAR GLÚN.

3.b.15.57 C*r*ioc*h* mna fir i n-ai*m*sir a h-égnigt*h*e la fer oile .i. *air*m i gcluint*e*r a h-ég*h*em*h* go a tec*h*.
Crích mná fir i n-aimsir a h-éicnigthe la fer aile 'a married woman's territory at the time of her rape by another man', i.e. a place where her screaming is heard as far as her house.[276]

3.b.15.58 Eatt*air* na mna c*é*t*na* .i. g*a*c[h] ionad o thá si*n* amac*h* genmót*h*a an baile a gclui*n*fid*ha* an ég*h*em*h*.
Edtair na mná cétnae 'the farther distance of the same woman', i.e. each place from there outwards apart from the place where the screaming could be heard.[277]

3.b.16.59 C*r*ioc*h* na contiona .i. i mac*hair*e si*n* ⁊ ionan*n* c*r*ioc[h] riagailt*e*r aca i gcaill.
Crích na continne 'the territory of the contention', i.e. in that cleared field and same territory that is regulated by them in a wood.[278]

3.b.17.60 Fóég*h*em*h* ⟨fogra⟩ tasg adalt*r*aig*h*e, ⁊ t*ur*suig*h*e .i. fog*r*a táisg bi*us* ag an cétmuinti*r* i n-a*m* an egn*igh*th*e*.
Foégem ⟨fogra⟩ tásc adaltraige, ⁊ *toirsige* 'raising an alarm of announcing information of adultery, and of sorrow', i.e. it is for the *cétmuinter* to make an announcement at the time of the rape.[279]

---

276 This entry continues the theme of rape seen in the previous several entries. The sense here seems to be that the woman is violated on her own property and her screams can be heard as far as her house.

277 The interpretation of *eattair* is uncertain. This entry should be understood with 3.b.15.57 CRIOCH MNA FIR I N-AIMSIR A H-ÉGNIGTHE LA FER OILE. It refers to the distance outside of her own property from which her screams can be heard. The lemma is interpreted here as a compound of *ed* 'distance, length' and *tair* 'before, in front, yonder'; *eDIL s.vv. 2 ed* and *1 tair*.

278 The translation of the entry is awkward, but a contrast is being made between a rape which takes place out in the open, such as in a cleared plain, and one which takes place in a concealed area, such as in the woods. The same contrast is found in a commentary concerning the regulation of dogs in *Bretha Éitgid* (*CIH* 312.12–13; *CCIH* 24; I should like to thank one of the anonymous readers for drawing this reference to my attention). The word *contiona* in the MS is interpreted as the gen. sg. of *contan* 'contention, strife', but that interpretation is uncertain; *eDIL s.v. contan*. It is possible that it refers to a rape which is disputed because of its location (cf. the two previous entries), but there is also the possibility that it refers to the location of the rape itself.

279 The interpretation of the entry is tentative in places. The lemma seems to refer to making a legal protest regarding the woman's violation. This assumes that *adaltraighe* is taken as an abstract of *adaltrach* to mean 'adultery' instead of its usual meaning of 'adulterer'

3.b.18.61 Co*mairr* .i. do co*mh*raic.
Comair 'may contend', i.e. for legal confrontation.[280]

3.b.18.62 Tat*h* .i. g*ruth* do ngoirt*er* maot*h*al.
Táth 'cheese', i.e. curds which are called *maethal* 'curds'.[281]

3.b.18.63 Maccaill*ech* .i. caille*ch* dub*h*.
Maccaillech 'young nun', i.e. a black nun.[282]

3.b.18.64 Forcort*har* .i. egn*igh*ter ben .i. do b*r*at[h]*ar* fior-rec*ar* éigne.
For-curthar 'is raped', i.e. a woman is raped, i.e. by a brother rape is [< *fír* 'truly' + *ro-icc* 'reaches, arrives, accomplishes'] truly-accomplished.[283]

3.b.19.65 Ced, no cu⟨ac⟩ad .i. foills*igh*id no in*n*isid.
Ced, nó cu⟨ac⟩ad 'cries or tells', i.e. discloses or tells.[284]

---

or 'secondary wife', but cf. *CIH* 1090.25, which is part of a series of citations on a variety of topics (*CCIH* 46), where it seems to refer to the secondary wife. The form *egnighthe* is interpreted as a participle of *éicnigid* 'compels, violates, rapes'.

280 The lemma is a 3 sg. pres. subj. of *con-ricc* 'meets, encounters, joins', but it can also be used for confronting someone in combat; *eDIL s.v. con-ricc*. Cf. 3.b.16.59 CRIOCH NA CONTIONA and 3.b.17.60 FÓÉGHEMH FOGRA TASG ADALTRAIGHE, ⁊ TURSUIGHE.

281 Cf. 10.41.97 TATH. The lemma refers to a type of cheese made from curds; *eDIL s.v. 1 táth*. The gloss does not seem to fit the context of the surrounding entries in Dubhaltach's Glossary.

282 The context of the entry is unknown, but cf. *Cáin Lánamna* § 37 (*CIH* 519.2) which refers to the rape of nuns; Ní Dhonnchadha 1994–1995: 83. Cf. also O'Dav 415 (*Bretha for Macślechtaib*; *CCIH* 120: *Coipe .i. caille dib* [*ut est*] *mac cope .i. donither re mac caille* "*Coipe*, i.e. a black veil, *mac cope*, i.e. (a son who) is begotten on a *mac caille*.")

283 For the lemma, see *eDIL s.v. for-cuirethar*. The interpretation of the second half of the gloss is tentative mainly due to the uncertainty of *brat*[*h*]*ar*. It could be interpreted here as 'brother', meaning a kinsman (in other words, a case of both rape and incest), or meaning 'friar'. Based on the previous entry, e.g. 3.b.18.63 MACCAILLECH, it is likely that we should understand the word as 'friar'. The gen. sg. of *éicen* 'necessity, compulsion, force, rape', *éigne*, is unexpected, but it could be a later use of the historical gen. sg. For the etymological gloss, see the Introduction, pp. 13–16.

284 The interpretation of the lemma is uncertain. The first part, *ced*, might be related to the verb in the second part, or perhaps to an unattested **con-fét* (I owe this suggestion to one of the readers). The interpretation is uncertain, so no attempt has been made to edit the form. The second part could be a later form derived from a perf. of *ad-fét* 'tells, relates', cf. *ind-fét* 'tells, relates'; *eDIL s.vv. ad-fét, 2 cuad*, and *ind-fét, in-fét*. It is also possible that it is a misreading and should be *2 cuad* 'act of telling, narration'; cf. O'Cl *Cúadh .i. innisin* 'narration'. Cf. 3.b.19.66 AD-CUA.

3.b.19.66 Ad-cua .i. ⟨do⟩ in*n*is.
Ad-cuaid 'told', i.e. told.[285]

3.b.19.67 Ma t*h*ó .i. ma dia ttoinge.
Mathó 'if he swears', i.e. if he swears.[286]

3.b.20.68 Lam*h*c*h*om*air*t .i. com-im*er*t lám*h* .i. basg*hair*e.
Lámchomairt 'clapping hands in lamentation', i.e. [< *com-* 'with, jointly' + *imbert* 'using, employing'] jointly-using of hands, i.e. hand-clapping.[287]

3.b.20.69 Dluethad lam*h* .i. glaca d'iad*h*ad*h* 'ra c*h*ele.
Dlúthad lám 'pressing hands together', i.e. hands clasping each other.[288]

3.b.20.70 Basc .i. baiscm*h*ell*aib* t*r*eas[an] b*r*agad, no usg*ar*.
Basc 'necklace', i.e. necklace with small beads across the neck, or a jewel.[289]

3.b.21.71 Tartad*h* ⟨.i. tortad*h*⟩ rig*h* .i. tornad*h* no glacad*h* do-beir ríg *ar* mnáoi da h-egniugad*h*.
Turtugud ⟨i.e. *tortad*⟩ *ríg* 'protection of a king', i.e. humiliation or seizing which a king pays for a woman being raped.[290]

285 The lemma is interpreted as a later 3 sg. perf. of *ad-fét* 'tells, relates'; *eDIL s.v. ad-fét*. Cf. 3.b.19.65 CED, NO CUACAD.

286 For the verbs, see *eDIL s.v. tongaid* 'swears'; both are 3 sg. The gender of the swearer in the entry is ambiguous. For the tautological formation of *ma* with *día*, see *eDIL s.v. 1 día n-*.

287 See the beginning of O'Dav 1193 (no id.; CCIH 144: *Lamcomairt .i. basgaire… "Lámchomairt,* i.e. handclapping…").

288 Cf. 3.b.20.68 LAMHCHOMAIRT.

289 O'Curry reconstructs the entry as '.i. baiscmhellad[aibh] treas [teas] braghad no asgar [uisgi]'. The interpretation of the entry is uncertain. Here *treas[an]* is interpreted as a late variant of *tre* 'through, across, over' and the def. art.; *eDIL s.v. 1 tre.* Cf. O'Cl *Baiscmhall .i. cruinnmheal* 'an assemblage'.

290 The interpretation of the entry is tentative, and the translation is awkward. The general sense is that the king pays compensation (i.e., what has been seized from a culprit) for the rape of a woman in his territory. Although both lemmata appear to be the 3 sg. impf. subj. of *do-beir* 'gives, brings', in light of OM 866 and O'Dav 1154, both should be understood as forms of *turtugud* 'protection, guarantee of safety'. It should be noted that *eDIL s.v. ? 2 turtugud, turthugud* 'force, violence, compulsion?' cites both the OM and O'Dav entries but suggests that the meaning of the word might be a misinterpretation of *1 turtugud,*

3.b.22.72 Do éc .i. do in*n*is.
Do éc 'told', i.e. told.[291]

3.b.22.73 Ben urnad*ma* .i. adalt*rach* urnad*ma*.
Ben airnadma 'a betrothed woman', i.e. a betrothed *adaltrach*.[292]

3.b.22.74 Cuitil .i. caoi *th*oll .i. for [f]orb*h*as*a*c[h].
Cutal 'empty', i.e. [< *cúa* 'nut' + *toll* 'hollow'] a hollow nut, i.e. of emptiness.[293]

3.b.22.75 Meam*m* .i. pog.
Memm 'a kiss', i.e. a kiss.[294]

3.b.22.76 Ban*ara*d*h* [l]uac*h* .i. ben gab*us* do laim*h* no do-[g]ní ionad mna an tig*h*e.
Banarad lúach 'female attendant of worth', i.e. a woman who undertakes or who takes the place of the woman of the house.[295]

---

turthugud 'protection, guarantee of safety'. Cf. OM 866 *Turtad .i. coimégniugud 'Turtugud* i.e. compulsion'; O'Cl *Tortughadh .i. coimhéigniughadh* 'oppression'; and O'Dav 1154 (*Bretha Nemed Toísech*; CCIH 143: *Leos .i. imdergad no leos .i. bolga ut est asrenar a leos, a tol, a tola, a serbad .i. a ngait a saithiud .i. sermonibus, a turtudh .i. per uim, a togaothad .i. muneribus, a mbrath .i. si quis dicat est* [*s*]*ic* "*Leos*, i.e. shaming. Or *leos*, i.e. bladders, i.e. bags, ut est 'paid for in their shaming, their will, their..., their pilfering (i.e. their theft), their fraud (i.e. *sermonibus*), their compulsion (i.e. *per vim*), their cheating (i.e. *muneribus*), their treachery (i.e. *si quis dicat est sic*)'.") It could be that the lemma should be understood as what the king compels the culprit to pay as compensation along with his general humiliation. The first word of the gloss is uncertain and might be a later form of *tairniud* 'lowering, reducing, humbling', the vn. of *do-airindi*, but it is also possible that the reading is not correct. In the gloss, *ríg*, is understood as a later spelling for OI nom. sg. *rí*.

291 The lemma and gloss are both are interpreted as later 3 sg. pret. forms of *ind-fét* 'tells, relates' and *indisid* 'tells, relates', respectively.

292 Cf. *Cáin Lánamna* § 21 (CIH 512.23 and 512.27–28); and Power 1936: 84–85.

293 See O'Dav 502 (no id.; CCIH 123: *Cutail .i. coach no fas, ut est arna fargaba í cein cutail .i. i cáe tuill no a cae for forbais cutail* (*.i. fas*) *.i. caoch* "*Cutail*, i.e. blind or empty, ut est ..." (the remainder of the entry is not translated by Stokes)); and cf. Eska 2016. The syntax of the gloss suggests we should understand *cúa* as the substantive 'nut' rather than the adj. 'hollow, empty'.

294 See O'Cl *Meam .i. póg* 'a kiss'; the first part of O'Dav 1225 (*Bretha Nemed Toísech*; CCIH 144: *Mem .i. poc*... "*Mem*, i.e. a kiss..."); *Bretha Nemed Toísech* (CIH 2229.15); OM 825 *Memm .i. póg*. *Mem*, i.e. a kiss; and SC YAdd.952 *Mem .i. poc*.

295 The general sense of the entry is that the *banarad* is the female attendant who performs the actions of the woman of the house. The lemma is in an oblique case as *ara* is a dental stem. For the idiom *gaibid do láim*, see *eDIL s.v. lám* IV(d). The inserted ⟨l⟩ is supplied from O'Curry's transcription.

3.b.23.77 Collud*h* n-óig*he* .i. lot óig*he* mna, ⁊ *air* a son si*n* do-ber an fer siocai[l di].
Collud n-óige 'loss of virginity', i.e. loss of a woman's virginity, and it is for that reason that the man gave a *sicail* to her.[296]

3.b.24.78 Be *m*uine .i. ben dan dir b*eth* i mui*ne*.
Bé muine 'bush woman', i.e. a woman for whom it is fit to be in the bushes.[297]

3.b.24.79 Be n-io*m*r*a*ma.i. ben bi*us ar* ionn*r*am*h* o ionad*h* d'ionad.
Bé n-imrama 'wandering woman', i.e. a woman who is serving from place to place.[298]

3.b.24.80 At*h*c[h]or i*ar* bfoltuib*h* .i. at*h*cor do-[g]nid m[*ath*]*air* .i. di (*ar*[...]*ar*-in*n* f*or* an at*air* [...]le[.]) i*ar* san mis c*hi*c*he* .i. i*ar* mb*eth* don cloin*n* re re mís *ar* c*hi*c*h*ib*h* na mna.
Athchor iar foltaib 'restoring according to means', i.e. restoring that the mother does, i.e. from it ([......] to the father [...]) then a month of suckling, i.e. after giving birth to the child for a period of a month on the breasts of the woman.[299]

3.b.25.81 F*r*it*h*bert breit*he* .i. bert f*r*it*h*ir do-[g]ni ben do mill*adh* na clain*ne* bi*us* na broin*n*, ⁊ fos-bert a n-aig*idh* b*r*eit*h*e cl*ainn*e [i]na n-ionb*aidh*, no na ttegmail di *ar* aonc*h*or. At*aid* .3. f*r*it[h]berta b*reith*a an*n* .i. 1 b*r*oc*h*an ⟨.i.⟩ do losuib*h*, ⁊ d'eolosuib*h* do c*ur* a lenib*h* as a*n* mnaoi. 2 snait*he* .i. ima b*r*agaid *con*a teg*h*ma lenaib*h* d*hi*. 3 sog*h*ab*h*ail duile .i. sec*h*na di coim*h*riac*ht*ana i n-ai*m*sir coi*m*perta. An f*r*it[h]b*ert* b*re*-*ithe*. S*éd* erata coi*m*p*er*ta inti .i. sed, da s*éd*, ⁊ t*r*i seoid. m*ar* so: sed do g*r*adib*h* fene, *da séd* do g*radaib* flat*h*a, ⁊ 3 s*éoid* do ri*gaib* c*on*a

296 The missing letters are supplied from O'Curry's transcription. For this payment to a woman to guard her virginity until marriage, see 3.b.5.33 TIONNSGRA.

297 The entry refers to a woman who has sexual assignations in the bushes. In other words, this woman is a type of harlot.

298 This is a type of woman who does itinerant work and is usually considered a class of concubine; *eDIL s.v. 1 bé*. Cf. *Cáin Lánamna* §27 comm. (*CIH* 518.13ff.). Cf. 11.b.2.35 BE FOICHLIGHE.

299 The context of the entry is unknown, and part of it is illegible. Part of the gloss concerns a woman having a period of a month to suckle a child; it is possible that it refers to a wet nurse. Cf. *Ántéchtae* (*CIH* 1240.15) for a similar topic on breastfeeding a child. I should like to thank one of the anonymous readers for comments on this entry.

gcomgradaibh. Seoid sin bentar (don mnáoi) leisin fer ar son firiadhta no toirmesg do chur ar an ccoimpert clainne tegmus etarra.

Frithbert brethe 'obstruction of childbirth', i.e. [< *breth* 'childbirth, bringing forth' + *frither* 'preventative, remedy'] a woman makes a *bertfrithir* 'birth remedy' to harm the child who is in the womb, and she put it inside [her vagina] against delivery of the child at their due time, or not happening to her at all. There are three obstructions of childbirth then, i.e. 1 pottage, i.e. [made] from herbs, and charms to expel her child from the mother. 2 thread, i.e. around her neck so that a child might not happen to her. 3 withholding of desire, i.e. avoidance of sexual intercourse during a time of conception. The obstruction of childbirth. A *sét* of fosterage-fee of conception in respect of it, a *sét*, two *sét*s, and three *sét*s, like this: a *sét* for common grades, two *sét*s for noble grades, and three *sét*s for kings together with the equal ranks. Those *sét*s are given (to the woman) by the man because of barring or preventing the conception of a child which happens between them.[300]

300 See O'Cl *Frithbheart .i. cur an aghaidh* 'opposing'; and for the lemma, cf. O'Dav 1413 (heptad 51; CCIH 150: *Scíath .i. ditin, ut est ata*[*t*] *.uii. frithberta i ndligid ada annsa so aurscíathadh* "*Scíath*, i.e. protection, ut est 'there are seven obstructions in law which are difficult to shield'."); heptad 51 (CIH 46.37; AL 5: 290.17). For discussion of *eolosuibh* 'charms', see Stokes 1903: 45; Plummer 1916: 130; and cf. *Cethairṡlicht Athgabálae* (CIH 421.10; AL 1: 300.15); and heptad 41 (CIH 38.27–28; AL 5: 260.13). The verbal complex *fos-bert* is understood as a 3 sg. pret. of *fo-beir* 'brings under, impairs (?) dips, submerges' with a Class A f. object agreement marker. The form *bert* in the etymological gloss is understand as the vn. *breth*; its unusual form due to its being in an etymological gloss. The entry concerns methods by which a woman can either abort a child or avoid conception all together. The first part refers to the woman inserting something in her vagina as a means of inducing an abortion. For the use of vaginal suppositories (and some other methods, including the use of a charm in conjunction with a potion) as contraception in the middles ages, see Riddle 1992: 93–102; and Arbuthnot 2021. The second part of the entry lists methods of preventing conception, which include taking a potion to induce an abortion (or perhaps bring on a late menstrual cycle), a thread around the woman's neck (perhaps a textual amulet, but see also Riddle 1997: 23 for wearing amulets either to prevent pregnancy or induce an abortion), and avoiding sexual relations entirely or at certain periods of time. The word *sogabail* 'easy holding out' is obscure, but it refers to withholding sexual intercourse, cf. *sogabálta* 'easily handled, managed'; *eDIL s.v. 2 so, su*. It should be noted, however, that during the medieval period it was thought that the time near or immediately after menstruation ended was the 'safe' time to have sexual intercourse if one did not wish to conceive; Riddle 1992: 5, 7. Obviously, advances in medical science have changed this view. It is unclear whether these are measures that the woman takes upon herself, are enforced

3.b.30.82 Co*imp*er*t* fo [co]smaili*us* la*ch*ta .i. dat*h* ban do b*h*eit[h] *ar* ad*h*ba*r* no *ar* g*h*enem*h*ui*n* cl*ainn*e.
Compert fo cosmailius lachta 'semen like milk', i.e. a white color to be there for the makings of or for the conception of a child.[301]

3.b.31.83 Lion*n* tog*h*luas*acht*[a] .i. br*eth* na co*im*perta an tan n*ac*[h] bi a*cht* na lion*n* gan c[or]t*us* geinem*h*na no crot*h*a daon*n*a.
Linn toglúasachta 'fluid of miscarriage', i.e. bringing forth the child when there is nothing except the fluid without proper course of growth or human form.[302]

3.b.31.84 Tog*hluasacht* colla .i. br*eth* leinib*h* m*air*b*h*.
Toglúasacht colla 'miscarriage of a corpse', i.e. bringing forth a dead child.[303]

3.b.32.85 Togl*uasacht* beocu[i]*r*p .i. ambeo re n-ionb*aidh*.
Toglúasacht beocoirp 'miscarriage of a living body', i.e. dead before the proper time.[304]

3.b.32.86 B*r*ioc*h*t fola, fuil foll*us*, ⁊ cu[i]*r*pgne .i. 1 co*imp*er*t* *ete*r b*eth* [i]na fuil ⁊ [i]na lin*n* bain i gcon*n*tab*ar*t *e*t*ur*ra, 2 fuil f*ollus* uirre fen, 3 cuirpg*h*ne .i. gne cuirp daon*na* *air*.
Brecht fola, fuil follus, ⁊ corpgné 'doubt of blood, manifest blood, and physical appearance', i.e. 1 conception being either in its blood or in its white liquid in doubt between them, 2 manifest blood on her her-

upon her by a male partner, or are jointly decided between the couple. For a discussion of contraception and abortion in the medieval world, see Mistry 2015; Riddle 1992 and 1997. I am grateful to Deborah Hayden and one of the anonymous readers for comments on this entry; any errors are my own. For further discussion of this entry, see the Introduction, pp. 54–55

301 The missing letters are supplied from O'Curry's transcription. For the interpretation of *compert* as 'semen', see *eDIL s.v. compert*. The entry refers to the necessity of semen for conceiving a child.

302 The inserted ⟨or⟩ is supplied from O'Curry's transcription. The entry concerns a miscarriage (or abortion) in the early stages of pregnancy. Cf. 3.b.31.84 TOGHLUASACHT COLLA and 3.b.32.85 TOGHLUASACHT BEOCU[I]RP.

303 Cf. 3.b.31.83 LIONN TOGHLUASACHT and 3.b.32.85 TOGHLUASACHT BEOCU[I]RP.

304 It is likely that the entry refers to a miscarriage where the child dies because it was born too early to survive. For *ambeo*, see *eDIL s.v. ambí* where *ambeo* is listed as a reconstructed form although it is found in Dubhaltach's Glossary in the nom. sg. Cf. 3.b.31.84 TOGHLUASACHT COLLA and 3.b.31.83 LIONN TOGHLUASACHT.

self, 3 physical appearance, i.e. it has the appearance of a person's body.[305]

3.b.33.87 Incind*h* co*m*lain*n* gan sgis a*cht* sgeo cneid .i. a*n* lenab*h* i mbi inc*h*in*n* co*mlan*, nac[h] bi sgis aige *ar*na brei*th*, *acht* ag sge*th*, ⁊ ag cned*idh*.
Inchinn comlann cen scís acht scé cneid 'complete brain without distress but it burst a wound', i.e. a child in which there is a complete brain, without having distress after its birth, except vomiting and being wounded.[306]

3.b.34.88 Crucrebaide .i. in geinem*h*ui*n* *ete*r ⟨ł t*ar*es⟩ b*eth* di na fuil follus, ⁊ [i]na dluim cuirpg*h*ne.
Crúcrebaide 'blood of contracting', i.e. the growth [of a fetus] between ⟨or after⟩ being to her [i.e., conception] or manifest blood, and in its mass of physical appearance.[307]

3.b.35.89 Ré f*h*abt*h*a .i. ai*m*sir leig*h*is.
Ré fabtha 'period of illness', i.e. period of healing.[308]

3.b.35.90 Imu*rchur* upt*h*a *ar* d*h*aig*h* ser[ce fir] .i. im[ur]c*hur* piseog.
Immarchor auptha ar dáig serce fir 'carrying a charm for the purpose of [gaining] a man's love', i.e. carrying a charm.[309]

---

305 The interpretation of the entry is uncertain in places, but it refers conception. In the medieval world, there was yet no knowledge of the woman producing eggs, and it was thought that her blood, when mixed with semen, conceived a child over the course of some days. Following the writings of Aristotle, there was thus a period between when a child was conceived and when it became animated; Riddle 1992: 21–22; 1997: 26–31.

306 The interpretation of the entry is uncertain. The general sense is that the child might have a mental disability or has suffered a brain injury. The form *sgeo* is interpreted as a 3 sg. pret. of *sceïd* 'vomits, spews, bursts forth'; *eDIL s.v. sceïd*.

307 The interpretation of the entry is uncertain. The headword is unknown as is the meaning of *cuirpgne*; cf. 3.b.32.86 BRIOCHT FOLA, FUIL FOLLUS, ⁊ CU[I]RPGNE. For the second half of the lemma, cf. *crapad* 'cramping, contracting' although the interpretation here is uncertain. The entry refers to one of the early stages of fetal development. I should like to thank one of the anonymous readers for helpful comments on this entry.

308 Cf. Mod. Ir. *fabht* 'fault, defect, unsoundness'; Dinneen, *s.v. fabht*.

309 The missing letters are supplied from O'Curry's transcription. The entry refers to carrying a love charm; for larger discussion, see Borsje 2010 and 2012. As noted by one of the anonymous readers, it is also possible to interpret *ar dáig serce fir* as 'for the fire of a man's love'.

3.b.36.91 Cosg n-urcuil .i. teg*us*g do-[g]ní ben *ar* anni toir*m*isgt*er* go millen*n* a c[ele no an leanabh bhios na] b*r*oin*n* fen.
Cosc n-aurchail 'instruction of prohibition', i.e. a woman who gives instruction about those things which are forbidden so that she destroys her husband or the child who is in her own womb.[310]

3.b.37.92 Sem*edh* ala b*huar* .i. sem*ed* og f*or* an d*ar*a bu*ar* .i. d*r*oc*h* bla*th* f*or* laoguib*h* an fir [tre connm..].
Séimed ala búar 'calming of the other cattle', i.e. complete calming of the other cattle, i.e. a bad plant afflicting the man's calves by....[311]

3.b.38.93 Creim .i. forbaig*h* .i. ben no crim a ccod*ha* do*na* laoguib .⁊c̄.
Crem 'wild garlic', i.e. of levy, i.e. a woman or wild garlic in a portion [of food] for the calves, etc.[312]

3.b.38.94 Ion*n*ad .i. ni no soc[har tig ..].
Indad 'increase', i.e. anything ...[313]

3.b.39.95 [Eimh ime .i.] fal na timc*h*ell.
Em ime 'protection around it', i.e. the boundary fence.[314]

---

310 The missing words are supplied from O'Curry's transcription. See *Lec. Gl.* 58 *Cusc .i. tecosc.* The entry concerns the woman who provides information about which things would be harmful to a husband or the child in a womb. The verb *millid* has a semantic range including 'ruin, destroy, spoil'. It is not entirely clear whether the subject of *millenn* should be 'it', referring to one of the forbidden items, or 'she' referring to the wife.

311 The interpretation of the entry is tentative, especially as the end of it is illegible. The missing letters are supplied from O'Curry's transcription. The entry concerns calming some of the calves. In the last part of the gloss, it is possible that the calves ate a type of plant which is harmful to them, but this suggestion is tentative; *eDIL s.v. bláth.*

312 The context of the entry is unknown. For the importance of wild garlic in medieval Ireland, see EIF 308–309. See EIF 309 and 320 for discussion of the *crimḟeis* 'garlic feast' which a client is obligated to prepare for his lord before Easter. The word 'ben' might not refer to a woman in this context but rather to a type of edible plant, but I do not have an alternative suggestion. This part of the MS is difficult to read, and it is possible that Dubhaltach made a correction to the text which I cannot see.

313 The context of the entry is unknown. *Indad* can refer to the increase of cattle, young cattle, or any profit generally; *eDIL s.v. indad, indoth.* The majority of the gloss is left untranslated due to uncertainties regarding word boundaries and the amount of the gloss which is missing.

314 For this definition of *eimh*, see O'Reilly, *s.v. eimh.* It is possible that the gloss is etymological but belong to a different lemma.

3.b.39.96 Lias tuig*hith*e .i. c*r*o gam*h*na *ar* na t*h*uig*h*e.
Lías tuigithe 'covered pen', i.e. a calf stall on account of the covering.[315]

3.b.39.97 F[.....]p[....].[316]

4.a.1.1 [.......] g [....]daigin*n* se*r*ce [....]si .i. [.]*éth*uigte se*r*ce.[317]

4.b.1.2 [..........] fa [.........][318]

4.b.1.3 [Meid .i. moid, on[..]]
Méit 'greatness' i.e. desire, ...[319]

4.b.2.4 [....]s[....]g[.......]as [.....][320]

4.b.2.5 [Taoi .i. an...]
Tóe 'silence', i.e. the ...[321]

4.b.3.6 [.....]do [...]a[....]n[....]l[....]be[.....][322]

4.b.3.7 Cli [ceann] .i. ben [nach beir clann tri blia]d[h]na [fuilingidh a fear[....].
Clí cenn 'support of a head', i.e. a woman who does not bear children three years [after] fulfilling her husband...[323]

315 The form *tuighithe* appears to be the past part. of *tuigithir* 'covers'; *eDIL s.v. tuigithir.*

316 The entry is illegible and is not in O'Curry's transcription.

317 This entry is not in O'Curry's transcription. The entry takes up six lines in the upper left corner of page four, and most of it is illegible. For part of the gloss, cf. *Bretha Nemed Toísech* 45.33 (*CIH* 1133.35; *CCIH* 184–188).

318 This entry is not in O'Curry's transcription; the line is illegible.

319 The entry is from O'Curry's transcription, and the translation is uncertain because the reading cannot be verified.

320 This entry is not in O'Curry's transcription; the line is mostly illegible.

321 The entry is from O'Curry's transcription, and the translation is uncertain because the reading cannot be verified. Cf. 4.c.20.109 TAI and 8.18.44 TAOI, TAOIETUS. It is possible that the lemma should be *tai* 'vessel'.

322 This entry is not in O'Curry's transcription; the line is mostly illegible.

323 The interpretation of the entry is tentative because the reading cannot be verified; it is taken from O'Curry's transcription. The entry refers to a woman who has not borne children after three years even though she has fulfilled her marital duties in respect to her husband. The form *fuilingidh* (assuming O'Curry's reading is correct) could be a deriva-

4.b.4.8 E[...] fo[......]e .i. be[....][324]

4.b.5.9 [..............]de[..............]de[.....][325]

4.b.6.10 [...] .i. [.....]tad*h* an og*h* ⁊ [.]a[..]*air*. [..]at[...]aig[...]
[...] i.e. [.....] the virgin and [...][326]

4.b.7.11 [....] .i. ber*thar* fuil misia mna .i. as siad [......]e .i. [....]
[....] i.e. it may be judged [that] a woman is menstruating i.e. ...[327]

4.b.8.12 Mem n-aisi .i. pog da deoin do-geib*h* ben.
Mem n-áise 'a consensual kiss', i.e. a kiss with her consent which a woman gets.[328]

4.b.8.13 Iom*airius* da rud*h*e[d] .i. [....] na [....]t*h*[..].
Amaires da ruided 'suspicion of her shame', i.e. ...[329]

4.b.9.14 Tait*h*m*h*ett .i. iom*r*ad*h* no cui*m*niug*adh*, ⁊ u*r* ait*h*med*h* ma*r* si*n*.
Taithmet 'remembering', i.e. recounting or commemorating, and for commemoration like that.[330]

---

tion of *fuilled* 'filling up, completing', the vn. of *fo-lína* 'fills up, makes up, supplies'; *eDIL s.v. fuilled.*

324 This entry is not in O'Curry's transcription, and the line is mostly illegible.

325 This entry is not in O'Curry's transcription, and the line is mostly illegible.

326 This entry is not in O'Curry's transcription. The entry likely belongs to the *Tract on Marriage and Divorce,* possibly §10 comm. (*CIH* 145.33–34). The passage refers to the man marrying another virgin in the case of a blameless divorce.

327 This entry is not in O'Curry's transcription. Much of the entry is illegible, but it likely belongs to the *Tract on Marriage and Divorce,* possibly §11 comm. (*CIH* 145.38–39). That passage refers to female witnesses testifying whether the wife is menstruating. It is likely that the entry here concerns the same topic. The reading ⟨misia⟩ is uncertain; it is possible that we should read ⟨mista⟩ but it is hard to justify this reading based on the visible letters. It is also possible that the second and third words should be read as one word, possibly for *fíadnaissi* 'witnesses', which would render the translation 'female witnesses are brought'.

328 See O'Cl *Ais .i. deoin* 'wish' and *Meam .i. póg* 'a kiss'; SC YAdd.952 *Mem .i. poc*; OM 825 *Memm .i. póg. Mem,* i.e. a kiss; and *Tract on Marriage and Divorce* §12 (*CIH* 146.5).

329 This entry is not in O'Curry's transcription. I follow the translation in Kelly's edition of the *Tract on Marriage and Divorce* §13 (*CIH* 146.10). It is possible that 4.b.9.14 TAITHMETT belongs with this entry.

330 It is possible that this entry forms part of the previous entry, 4.b.8.13 IOMAIRIUS DA RUDHE[D]. Cf. *Tract on Marriage and Divorce* §13 (*CIH* 146.10).

4.b.9.15 Etla treb*tha* .i. ní goides ben [.......] da fer.
Etla trebtha 'stealing from a household', i.e. anything which a wife steals [.....] from her husband.[331]

4.b.10.16 Saintuillema*r* co clot*h* gan iomc*h*ogu*r* .i. (ioe*ncadh*) [imarcrad] bid*h* do tab*ar*t do mnao[i] [..] goides [..] tuill*adh* clu no cuidec*hus* di o c*ar*aid*h* no o comaigt*ach* sec*h* a fer.
Saintuillemar co cloth cen imchocur 'particularly copious with generosity without consultation', i.e. excess of food which is given by the wife [...] who steals [...] surplus of reputation or company for her from a friend or from a neighbor without the permission of her husband.[332]

4.b.11.17 Neim*h*iomc*h*ogu*r* .i. [iomchogur ⁊c̄. re a] f*er* [fein] [.]o rainig.
Nemimchocur 'non-consultation', i.e. consultation, etc. with her own husband [...] when he came.[333]

4.b.12.18 Diollat lige .i. etac*h* (as fiu l*eth* coib*h*ce a mna) gaibes f*er* i m[naoi] [iar n-ei]rge as [a] [..].
Díllat lige 'bed covering', i.e. covering (which is equivalent to half of his wife's *coibche*) which a man receives from his wife after rising which is ...[334]

4.b.13.19 Rocluic*he* is[in] c*r*i*us* .i. cluit*he* don mnaoi, ⁊ lam fir [i]na c*r*i*us*.
Rocluiche isin cris 'great sport in the girdle', i.e. sport by the wife, and the husband's hand in her girdle.[335]

331 See *Tract on Marriage and Divorce* §14 (*CIH* 146.16).

332 See *Tract on Marriage and Divorce* §15 (*CIH* 146.29). In his edition of the text, Kelly 2014 has a discussion of the corresponding snippet of tract, *no sentulum cloth* (88); the entry in Dubhaltach's Glossary provides a better reading than Oxford, Bodleian Library MS Rawl. B.506. The form *saintuillemar* is interpreted as consisting of *sain* 'different, special', and an adj. formed from *tuillem* 'earning, meriting, deserving', the vn. of *do-slí*; *eDIL s.vv. 1 sain* and *tuillem*. The sense of the entry is that the wife has been overly generous in giving food as hospitality and that she has given an excess without consulting her husband.

333 The missing words are supplied from O'Curry's transcription. Cf. *Tract on Marriage and Divorce* §15 (*CIH* 146.29), and 4.b.10.16 SAINTUILLEMAR CO CLOTH GAN IOMCHOGUR.

334 The missing words are supplied from O'Curry's transcription. See *Tract on Marriage and Divorce* §16 (*CIH* 146.40). The entry refers to the wife needing to supply the covering for the bed as part of her marriage contribution.

335 The entry is obscure, but it has a sexual connotation. The form *is* in the lemma has been emended to *isin*; for other examples of the prep. *i* combined with the dat. sg. article being shortened, see *eDIL s.v. i*. Cf. 4.b.13.20 ROCHLUITHE.

4.b.13.20 Roc*h*luit*he* .i. sp*airn*, ⁊ l[amh fir [i]na crios, nu a fear] [..].
Rochluiche 'great sport', i.e. wrestling, and the husband's hand in her girdle, or her husband...[336]

4.b.14.21 [.. .i. .] friot[h]aig*he* d*r*uis doi[..]n do*n* mnaoi go h-ait diun*air*.
[.. i.e. .] encountering a hot-blooded person [...] by the wife to a very disgraceful place.[337]

4.b.14.22 Mera*cht* .i. d*r*uis.
Meracht 'excitement', i.e. a hot-blooded person.[338]

4.b.14.23 [Golladh fuidhe .i.] faoisid[niughadh ⁊ gollta an ..]ag*h*tig ⟨do⟩-[g]ni an ben t*ar*sna an tig*he* .i. faoisidniug*hadh* di in guilte.
Golad faide 'wailing of a voice', i.e. confessing and weeping of the [...] the wife makes across the house, i.e. confessing by her of the weeping.[339]

4.b.15.24 Fe[abus ruine .i. run] do [denum do mnaoi gan ..] f*e*r an ni b[udh] imd*e*rgad do.
Febas rúine 'excellence of a secret', i.e. a secret which is done by a wife without [...] husband of that which would be a cause of shame for him.[340]

4.b.16.25 Reabac*h* luirge ⟨.i. riabsad*h* an talman do-[g]ni⟩ .i. riabac*h* a talmaide re luirg ben si*n* [bios o] tig do tig*h* [go] [...] [fri a] cele, ⁊ lorg*h* ina laim*h*.
Rébach loirg ⟨.i. ríabsad in talman do-gní⟩ 'tearing of a stick ⟨i.e., striping of the ground that she does⟩', i.e. striped in the ground by

336 The entry is obscure, but it has a sexual connotation. Cf. 4.b.13.19 ROCLUICHE IS CRIUS.

337 This entry is not in O'Curry's transcription, and the context of the entry is obscure. The word *diunair* is interpreted as the intensifying prefix *di-* and *1 nár* 'noble, shameful'.

338 The context of the entry is unknown, but cf. distantly O'Dav 622 (no id.; *CCIH* 126) where Stokes has a different interpretation of the lemma and gloss. This entry might belong with the previous one.

339 The missing words are supplied from O'Curry's transcription. The context of the entry is unknown, and the interpretation is tentative. Perhaps it refers to the wife confessing to an indiscretion. For *faoisidniughadh*, cf. *eDIL s.vv. fo-sisedar* and *faístitiu*.

340 The missing words are supplied from O'Curry's transcription. The entry concerns the wife having a secret (or doing something secretly) which would cause her husband shame if he knew of it. It could also refer to the wife keeping her husband's shameful secret; too much of the entry is missing to be certain.

a woman's stick that is [going] from house to house to [...] to her neighbor, and a stick in her hand.[341]

4.b.17.26 Gu ed ⟨.i. ed brecce⟩ .i. derb*adh* ⟨tre ed brege⟩ sgeoil brege *ar* a fer ga[n adhbar] do-[g]ni ben.
Gáu ét ⟨.i. *ét bréce*⟩ 'false jealousy ⟨i.e. false jealousy⟩', i.e. a wife tests ⟨through false jealousy⟩ a false accusation against her husband without a reason.[342]

4.b.17.27 [Golgaire lenimh .i. bualadh agus comhadh] bid*h* do*n* lesmat[h]*air* on lescl*ainn* go mbid i*n* g*air* guil.
Golgaire lenib 'wailing of a child', i.e. beating and keeping food by the stepmother from the stepchild so that there may be the cry of weeping.[343]

4.b.18.28 Liud*h* sgit*h* .i. ni as sgit*h* le fer do [li]ud f*air* [cen] fer no cen g[..].
Líud scíth 'accusation of refusal', i.e. to accuse the husband of anything which he is unwilling to do without a man or without ....[344]

4.b.19.29 Coib*h*dealac*h* .i. duine ris a mbí coimfial*us*, no coi*m*dealac*hus* gaoil [no caradr]ad [a]g nec[h] [i n]geall fiac*h* .i. ben [bheith]as feic*h* ag h-[é]in*ne* sec*h* a fer.
Coibdelach 'relative', i.e. a person with whom there may be kinship or relationship of kinship or alliance with someone for surety of fines, i.e. a woman is an obligation to anyone apart from her husband.[345]

341 The missing words are supplied from O'Curry's transcription. The identification of *riabsadh* is uncertain; cf. *eDIL s.v. ríabach* 'swarthy, brindled, streaked, striped'. The entry seems to refer to there being stripes in the ground from the woman dragging a stick as she goes from house to house to visit folks. The glossators have understood *rébach* 'that rends or tears, torn, rent' as *ríabach* 'brindled, streaked, striped'. For *talmaide*, see *eDIL s.v. talam* which has a later dental-stem inflection.

342 The missing words are supplied from O'Curry's transcription. The word *derbad* has a range of meanings, including 'proving, proof, testing'; *eDIL s.v. derbad*. The sense of the entry is that the wife brings a false accusation against her husband out of jealousy even though she has no reason to be jealous.

343 The missing words are supplied from O'Curry's transcription. The context of the passage is unknown, but it refers to the stepmother beating and perhaps withholding food from her stepchild. The word *bid* is interpreted as a gen. sg. of *biad* 'food'. I should like to thank one of the anonymous readers for their comments on this entry.

344 The missing words are supplied from O'Curry's transcription. The entry seems to concern accusing the husband of being lazy. The translation is tentative.

345 The missing words are supplied from O'Curry's transcription. The entry refers to the

4.b.20.30 Locc-bergenach .i. loc b*erath*genac*h*, no loc*h*ta sal(a)c*har ar tair*ismec*h* salc*har* go [s]oil[eir] do cac*h* loc suide, luide, tec*h*, ⁊ cuile, ⁊ iad uile, gan sguab*adh* gan glan[adh].
Loc bergenach 'place [?]', i.e. [< *loc* 'place, dwelling' + [?]] place [?], or offence of filth for visibly constant filth for each place of sitting, lying down, house, and pantry, and all of them without sweeping, without cleaning.[346]

4.b.20.31 [Fuarthair … .i. toirmis]g[ios] gniomr*adh* ⁊ lana*mnusa*[dh].
Fúarthair 'is made cold […]', i.e. hindrance for work and sexual relations.[347]

4.b.22.32 Beir geoanach .i. bir briat*h*rac*h* e.
Beir ginach 'a sharp, greedy person', i.e. he is sharp of words.[348]

4.b.22.33 Am*h*nus .i. olc.
Amnas 'cruel', i.e. evil.[349]

4.b.22.34 Io*m*am*h*nus .i. co*m*olc.
Imamnas 'very cruel', i.e. equally bad.[350]

4.b.22.35 Aid*h*c*h*e iodn*aidh*e .i. […][.]aiccib b*hius* ai[.]uir [.]e[.]nenual.
Aidche indaide 'night of expectation', i.e. …[351]

---

financial obligations of the wider kin group regarding unmarried or widowed women. Cf. 6.a.35.81 COIBHDEALAC[H]. The reading [*bheith*]*as* relies on O'Curry's transcription. The ending *-as* may or may no belong with the 3 sg. pres. subj. form of *atta*. If it does, it might be a later analogical rel. ending. The phrase *ag h-*[*é*]*inne* is understood as Mod. Ir. *ag éinne*, which is the equivalent of OI *oc óenduine* 'anyone'. I owe this suggestion to one of the anonymous readers.

346 The missing letters are supplied by O'Curry's transcription. The forms *bergenach* and *berathgenach* are obscure. The entry refers to the wife keeping a filthy house. The MS sequence *salach ar* is likely a mistake for *salchar*; both words have the same general meaning of 'filth'. Cf. 4.b.22.32 BEIR GEONACH.

347 The missing words are supplied from O'Curry's transcription. The entry concerns the house being so cold that it hinders normal activities. For the lemma, see *eDIL s.v.* (*f*)*úaraid* 'becomes cold, makes cold'.

348 The entry is obscure; cf. 4.b.20.30 LOCC-BERGENACH which might be related. Both *beir* and *bir* are understood as forms of *1 bir* 'stake, point, spike'. The word *ginach* means 'greedy, gaping'; *eDIL s.v. ginach.*

349 Cf. O'Cl *Amhnas .i. doilidh, nó amhnáireach* 'shameless'.

350 The context of the entry is unknown.

351 Cf. O'Cl *Iodnaidhe .i. fuireach, no comhnaidhe* 'staying, sojourning'. Too much of the entry is illegible to make sense of it.

4.c.1.36 Fer reime .i. an cainte bi*us* ag ruai*mned* a oile i n-oemas a oile.
Fer réime 'a satirist'(?), i.e. the satirist who causes shame to another on account of the crudity of his satire.[352]

4.c.1.37 F[*er*] raite .i. ap*ad* in raitig[h] dorn na brolla*ch* ó aon lo ama*ch*, no fer *téit* for foriod, ⁊ roba glan fon rod.
Fer raite 'man of a road', i.e. giving notice of the vagrant 'the fist on the breast' from one day onwards, or a man who goes on a mound, and it was clear on the road.[353]

4.c.2.38 Fer fuid*h*re .i. fuid*h*ir crúi elas re dlig*hedh* a fuidre, fuid*h*ir si*n* elós ria na f*h*lait*h* go sedaib*h* a f*h*lat*h*a leis.
Fer fuidre 'tenant at will', i.e. a hereditary *fuidir*-tenant who absconds from the obligation of being a *fuidir*, that *fuidir* who absconds from his lord taking his lord's *sét*s with him.[354]

4.c.3.39 Nos .i. fi*us* nua, no fi*us* naonma[i]*r*, ⁊ nos .i. u*r*d*ar*cug*h*ad*h*.
Nós 'tradition', i.e. [< *fius* 'knowledge' + *núa* 'new, fresh'] new knowledge, or [< *fius* 'knowledge' + *nónbor* 'group of nine people'] knowledge of nine people, and renown, i.e. making known.[355]

---

352 This entry is difficult in a number of different ways, and the interpretation is tentative. The first is the interpretation of gen. sg. *reime*; cf. *eDIL s.vv. 1 réim*(*m*) 'course, way manner', *2 réim*(*m*) 'contortionist, juggler', *3 réim*(*m*) 'shout, cry', and *1 reime* 'thickness, stoutness'. For the lemma, see *Bretha Nemed Dédenach* 17.28 (*CIH* 1114.20; *CCIH* 184–188). Cf. O'Cl *Réim curadh .i. géim curadh. Tug a réim curadh as .i. a gheim curadh, no a ghláodhchuradh* 'hero's shout'. Based on the accompanying gloss, it is possible that the *fer réime* is a satirist *vel sim.* With the gloss, the phrase *a oile* appears twice. The difficulty is whether they mean the same thing each time. The form *oile* could be a later spelling of *1 aile* 'other, second'. It could also be the gen. sg. of *2 ail* 'disgrace, reproach; a type of satire'. The *a* could be a prep. or a poss. pron. There is also the possibility that Dubhaltach made a dittography mistake. The final difficulty is the form *oemas*, the reading of which is not secure due to an ink spot on the MS. It might be a later abstract noun related to the adj. *om* 'raw, rude' and its abstract *oime* 'rawness, crudity'; *GOI* § 261.

353 The entry refers to expelling a vagrant from the community. The phrase *dorn na brollach* refers to expelling an outsider or apprehending a debtor; *eDIL s.v. brollach*; and *Cethairślicht Athgabálae* (*CIH* 369.12; *AL* 1: 128.27; *CCIH* 286–287). For the lemma, see *Bretha Nemed Dédenach* 17.28 (*CIH* 1114.20; *CCIH* 184–188). For the different words for 'road' in medieval Ireland, see Clancy 2007.

354 Cf. O'Cl *Fuidhir .i. fodháor .i. fear tuarastail* 'a hired man'. For a discussion of the *fuidir* tenant, see *GEIL* 33–35, 219. For the lemma, see *Bretha Nemed Dédenach* 17.28 (*CIH* 1114.21; *CCIH* 184–188).

355 The entry contains an amalgamation of two different glossary entries on *nós*, *nós* 'custom

4.c.4.40 Dioghuin .i. sarugadh.
Díguin 'violation of protection', i.e. violation.[356]

4.c.4.41 Tlenamhain cétmuintire neich .i. do ethlodh a chedmuintire and .i. dul go a priomhmhnáoi.
Tlenamain cétmuintire neich 'stealing someone's spouse', i.e. to steal his spouse then, i.e. cohabiting with his spouse.[357]

4.c.4.42 Diamhuin .i. gl[an].
Diamuin 'spotless', i.e. clean.[358]

4.c.5.43 Cuinntestar .i. cuinngither .i. iarrtar.
Cuinntestar 'may be asked', i.e. is asked, i.e. is asked.[359]

4.c.5.44 Toichreachta .i. toichidhe dirge.
Toichrechta 'seeking', i.e. direct seeking.[360]

---

tradition' and *nós* 'fame, renown, reputation'; *eDIL s.vv. 1 nós* and *2 nós*, respectively. For the former, see DDC D1.530 *Nós .i. fis nonbuir .i. tri ríg, tri hespuig, tri filid* (CIH 618.32); O'Cl *Nós .i. naoi fhios .i. fios náonbhair*, etc. '*náoi* (nine) *fios* (knowledge) knowledge of nine persons.'; the beginning of SC Y.970 *Nos .i. nóe-fis .i. fios nonbuir .i. tri righ, tri suid, tri hespuic…*; and *Pseudo-Historical Prologue to the* Senchas Már, § 8 and discussion on p. 26 (CIH 342.17–18; AL 1: 16.25–26; CCIH 286). For the latter, see O'Dav 423 (*Bretha for Conślechtaib*; CCIH 121); where *1 nós* is glossed by *urdarcugud* 'making known', a meaning which matches *2 nós*. For the lemma, see *Bretha Nemed Dédenach* 17.31 (CIH 1114.23; CCIH 184–188). It is possible that *fis nua* in the gloss is a mistake for *nóe fis*.

356 Cf. 1.a.14.34 DIOGHION FEOIR EATHAM(I)AIN. Cf. the beginning of O'Dav 585 (*Bretha Nemed Toísech*; CCIH 125: *Dergoin .i. diguin nó sarugud…* "*Dergoin*, i.e. violation or outraging…"). For the lemma, see *Bretha Nemed Dédenach* 18.5 (CIH 1114.29; CCIH 184–188).

357 See O'Dav 1553 (*Bretha Nemed Dédenach*; CCIH 154: *Tlenamain .i. doetlo, ut est ar tlenamain do cinn a cétmuinntire .i. ar tetlo a cétmuinntire dia cinn .i. dul co cétmuinntir* "*Telnamain*, i.e. he stole, ut est 'for theft as regards his first-wife', i.e. for theft of his first-wife from him, i.e. going in unto a first-wife."). For the lemma, see *Bretha Nemed Dédenach* 18.5 (CIH 1114.30; CCIH 184–188).

358 Cf. 7.b.3.55 DIAMHAIN. See *Lec Gl.* 102 *Di[a]main .i. glan*; cf. O'Cl *Diamhain .i. dí ainimh .i. neamhainmheach* 'without blemish'; and the first part of O'Dav 670 (no id.; CCIH 128: *Diamuin .i. glan…* "*Diamuin*, i.e. pure…"). For the lemma, see *Bretha Nemed Dédenach* 18.10 (CIH 1114.33; CCIH 184–188).

359 For the lemma and first gloss, see *eDIL s.v. con-dïeig* 'asks, seeks, demands'. For the lemma, see *Bretha Nemed Dédenach* 18.11 (CIH 1114.34; CCIH 184–188).

360 The entry is problematic for a number of reasons, and the translation is tentative. The lemma is not in *eDIL*; it is interpreted here as being related to *toichid* 'seeking, suing'; *eDIL s.v. toichid*. For the lemma, see *Bretha Nemed Dédenach* 18.13 (CIH 1114.36; CCIH 184–188) where the larger context concerns poetic knowledge and types of poetic compositions.

4.c.5.45 Duan .i. dúin is indealt .i. aoin siolla.
Dúan 'poem', i.e. a poem which is arranged, i.e. one syllable.[361]

4.c.5.46 Forrduain .i. reco*mar*[c] .i. da siolla ⟨on⟩ dunan*n* ut iomco*mar*c flat*ha* feim*h*en, ⁊ casb*air*dne (in) i*ar*co*mar*c .i. t*r*i siolla.
Fordúan 'fordúan', i.e. a meter with a disyllabic ending, i.e. two syllables by which it closes [i.e., a disyllabic ending], *ut* 'like' *iomcomarc flatha feimhen* 'asking a splendid lord', and *casbairdne* of a trisyllabic ending, i.e. three syllables.[362]

4.c.6.47 L*eth*m*h*io*m*asg .i. droc*h* f*h*ásg isi*n* ran*n* go ruige a leat*h*.
Lethmimasc 'half-*mimasc*', i.e. bad compressing in the stanza as far as its half.[363]

4.c.7.48 Uad*h* .i. egsi.
Úad 'metrical composition', i.e. poetic composition.[364]

4.c.7.49 Aid*h*bsi .i. taisben*adh*.
Aidbse 'chanting', i.e. demonstrating.[365]

---

361 The division of MS *dúinis* is also uncertain; the word *dúinis* is not in *eDIL*; it is possible that *is* is for the copula, and *dúin* is a late form of *dúan* 'song, poem, composition'; *eDIL s.v. dúan*. For the lemma, see *Bretha Nemed Dédenach* 18.14 (*CIH* 1114.37; *CCIH* 184–188).

362 The interpretation of part of the gloss is tentative due to the uncertain reading. The word *feimhen* is understood as a variant of *femenda* 'fine, splendid'; *eDIL s.v. 1 femenda(e)*. The words *fordúan* and *casbairdne* are types of meters; *eDIL s.vv. fordúan* and *1 cas*. For the lemma, see *Bretha Nemed Dédenach* 18.14 (*CIH* 1114.37; *CCIH* 184–188). The ⟨n*n*⟩ might be a mistake; the ⟨in⟩ is likely part of the correction Dubhaltach made to the end of *casbairdne* where he corrected the ending.

363 The word *mimasc* is the name for a type of meter; *eDIL s.v. mimasc*. See O'Dav 1227 (*Bretha Nemed Dédenach*; *CCIH* 145: *Mimasc .i. drochfasc no nath, ut est leth-mimasc ell. Duine .c. c. .i. drochḟasc ann coruicci a leth, ⁊ bidh doigh comad ainm do trost comla é* "Mimasc, i.e. a bad impounding or …, ut est 'a half-*mimasc*…', i.e. a bad impounding there as far as its half, and it seems that it is a name for a doorpost.") where it refers to a type of bolt. There seems to be some confusion between the two meanings of the word across the glossaries. Cf. *eDIL s.v. fáascud* 'pressing, compressing, squeezing'. For the lemma, see *Bretha Nemed Dédenach* 18.16 (*CIH* 1114.38; *CCIH* 184–188).

364 For the lemma, see *eDIL s.v. 2 aí* 'poetic inspiration, learning, metrical composition'; and *Bretha Nemed Dédenach* 18.19 (*CIH* 1114.41; *CCIH* 184–188).

365 For the lemma, see *Bretha Nemed Dédenach* 18.19 (*CIH* 1114.41; *CCIH* 184–188).

4.c.7.50 Gign*igh*t[h]*er* .i. ginf*igh*t[h]*er*.
Gignither 'will come to life', i.e. will come to life.[366]

4.c.7.51 Os .i. og*us*.
Os 'and', i.e. and.[367]

4.c.7.52 *Ar*sit*h*er .i. t*áirr*it*h*er.
Arsither 'would be found', i.e. would be found.[368]

4.c.7.53 Forts*h*esid[h] .i. t*air*isid*h*.
Fortshesidh 'you (pl.) shall sustain', i.e. you (pl.) shall stand.[369]

4.c.8.54 Ad-bosaid .i. obuid.
Ad-bosaid 'you (pl.) shall refuse', i.e. you (pl.) shall refuse.[370]

4.c.8.55 Ad-nesa .i. do-ber táinsíom*h*ad*h*.
Ad-nessa 'reproaches', i.e. he gives a reproach.[371]

---

366 For the lemma and gloss, both 3 sg. fut., see *eDIL s.v. gainithir* 'comes to life, is born'. The gloss is a later form. For the lemma, see *Bretha Nemed Dédenach* 18.26 (CIH 1115.4; CCIH 184–188).

367 For the lemma, see *Bretha Nemed Dédenach* 18.32 (CIH 1115.9; CCIH 184–188).

368 The interpretation of the entry is tentative; it is possible that the entry is corrupt; cf. *airsidhe*, *Bretha Nemed Dédenach* 19.1 (CIH 1115.14; CCIH 184–188). The lemma is interpreted as a sg. past subj. pass. of *ar-icc* 'comes upon, meets, finds'. The gloss is interpreted as a sg. past subj. pass. of *do-airret* 'comes to, finds, gets'; *eDIL s.vv. ar-icc* and *do-airret, do-áirret.*

369 The interpretation of the lemma follows that in Gwynn 1942 (60) where he suggests that the form is the 2 pl. subj. of *for-sech-* 'that you should follow', 'cleave to' (one of the anonymous readers suggests **for-said* 'sustains' as the verb). We should understand the subjunctives here and in the following entry as jussive subjunctives. For the lemma, see *Bretha Nemed Dédenach* 19.4 (CIH 1115.16; CCIH 184–188). The lemma in the edited text has been left as it appears in the MS.

370 The interpretation of the lemma follows that in Gwynn 1942 (60). The lemma is the 2 pl. pres. juss. subj. of *as-boind* 'refuses, rejects'; *eDIL s.v. as-boind*. The gloss is the 2 pl. pres. juss. subj. of *opaid* 'refuses'; *eDIL s.v. opaid, (obbaid)*. For the lemma, see *Bretha Nemed Dédenach* 19.4 (CIH 1115.17; CCIH 184–188). See O'Don. Suppl. *s.v. bósar*. Cf. 4.c.7.53 FORTSHESID[H].

371 Cf. O'Dav 861 (*Bretha Nemed Dédenach*). CCIH 133 identifies the source for the O'Dav citation as CIH 1111.24; *eDIL s.v. for-nessa* notes that the gloss in O'Dav likely belongs with *ad-nessa* rather than *for-nessa* 'tramples, kicks'. For the lemma, see *Bretha Nemed Dédenach* 19.5 (CIH 1115.17; CCIH 184–188).

4.c.8.56 Ad-buib .i. oibéb*h*uid*h*.
Ad-buib 'will refuse', i.e. will refuse.[372]

4.c.8.57 Miod*h*b*h*a .i. m*eth*on bet*h*a int*e*r bonu*m* et malu*m*.
Midba 'average', i.e. [< *medón* 'middle, center' + *betha* 'life, existence'] a middle life *inter bonum et malum* 'between good and evil'.[373]

4.c.9.58 Miod*h*b*h*a .i. toraind.
Midba 'average', i.e. division.[374]

4.c.9.59 Uintsi .i. an*n*so.
Uindsi 'there she is', i.e. here.[375]

4.c.9.60 Cuinni*us* .i. con*nus* .i. con*n*ad*hus* .i. m*ac*, no cui*nnius* on i*arradh*.
Cuindius 'I ask', i.e. reckoning, i.e. wealth, i.e. a son, or I ask from the fosterage-fee.[376]

---

372 The lemma is the 3 sg. fut. of *as-boind* 'refuses'. The gloss is the 3 sg. fut. of *opaid* 'refuses'; *eDIL s.vv. as-boind* and *opaid,* (*obbaid*). For the lemma, see *Bretha Nemed Dédenach* 19.6 (*CIH* 1115.18; *CCIH* 184–188).

373 Cf. *DDC* D1.477 and 478 (*CIH* 617.20–21); OM 822–833; and more O'Dav 1244 (*Status-tract*; *CCIH* 145) where the meaning is 'half'. For the lemma, see *Bretha Nemed Dédenach* 19.15 (*CIH* 1115.26; *CCIH* 184–188). The source of the Latin quotation is unknown. Cf. 4.c.9.58 MIODHBHA.

374 Cf. more distantly *DDC* D1.477 (*CIH* 617.20–21); and OM 822–833; and cf. O'Dav 1244 (*Status-tract*; *CCIH* 145). For the lemma, see *Bretha Nemed Dédenach* 19.15 (*CIH* 1115.26; *CCIH* 184–188). Cf. 4.c.8.57 MIODHBHA.

375 For the lemma, see the discussion in *eDIL s.v. uindim* 'I see, there is, behold'; O'Brien 1932: 162–163; and Russell 1999b. See O'Dav 1618 (*Bretha Nemed Dédenach*; *CCIH* 156: *Uinsi .i. annso, ut est uinsi do dalta* "*Uinsi*, i.e. here, ut est 'here is thy fosterling'."). For the lemma, see *Bretha Nemed Dédenach* 19.21 (*CIH* 1115.29; *CCIH* 184–188).

376 The interpretation of the entry is tentative. For the lemma, which is understood as a 1 sg. pres. ind. of *con-dïeig* 'asks, seeks, demands', see *eDIL s.vv. con-dïeig* and cf. *? cuindius* where no meaning is given. The general sense seems to be of asking for something. For *connus*, see *eDIL s.v. cuntas* 'reckoning, computation', but this is by no means secure. The tentative meaning assigned to *connadhus* is based on O'Reilly, *s.v. conadh* 'rage, fury, firewood, prosperity'. The form *iarradh* could be from *íarraid* 'asks', but is understood here to be a variant spelling of *íarrath* 'fosterage fee' in light of the two following entries (it is possible that the glossator is playing on the similarity of both words); *eDIL s.vv. 1 íarraid* and *íarrath*. See O'Dav 385 (*Bretha Nemed Dédenach*; *CCIH* 119: *Cuindius no cuinnsi .i. cuingim,* [*ut est*] *uindsi cuinnsi nisdring* "*Cuindius* or *cuinnsi*, i.e. I request, ut est …" (Stokes does not translate the remainder of the entry)); and for the lemma, see *Bretha Nemed Dédenach* 19.21 (*CIH* 1115.29; *CCIH* 184–188).

4.c.9.61 Datán [.i.] oide.
Datán 'foster-father', i.e. foster-father.[377]

4.c.10.62 Dat*h*nait .i. mui*m*e.
Datnat 'foster-mother', i.e. foster-mother.[378]

4.c.10.63 Céin .i. fén.
Céin 'himself', i.e. himself.[379]

4.c.10.64 Glenuid*h* .i. lenuid.
Glenaid 'adheres', i.e. adheres.[380]

4.c.10.65 Beit*h*ium .i. bid*h* dam.
Bethum 'I have', i.e. I have.[381]

4.c.10.66 Iorcaid*h* .i. urcoideac*h*, no iut[.] ainf*e*rg*a*c[h].
Airchóid 'let (him) injure', i.e. harmful, or [...] very wrathful.[382]

---

377 See *Metr. Gl.* 28 § 46 *'Datán' ainm gach oide finn*; O'Cl *Daitean .i. oide* 'a guardian, foster-father'; O'Dav 612 (*Bretha Nemed Dédenach*; CCIH 126: *Datan .i. aiti, ut est sóerfad a datan dathnait* "*Datán*, i.e. fosterfather, ut est 'his fosterfather should free the fostermother'."); *Bretha Nemed Dédenach* 19.23 (CIH 1115.32; CCIH 184–188); and *Adhmad* glossary (CIH 954.1–4; Taylor-Griffiths 2020: 2: 51–54 and discussion in 1: 235–239).

378 See *Metr. Gl.* 28 § 46 *'Datán' ainm gach oide finn*; O'Dav 612 (*Bretha Nemed Dédenach*; CCIH 126: *Datan .i. aiti, ut est sóerfad a datan dathnait* "*Datán*, i.e. fosterfather, ut est 'his fosterfather should free the fostermother'."); *Bretha Nemed Dédenach* 19.23–24 (CIH 1115.32; CCIH 184–188); and *Adhmad* glossary (CIH 954.1–4; Taylor-Griffiths 2020: 2: 51–54 and discussion in 1: 235–239). The lemma is also glossed by *muime* in the poem found on pp. 210–213 (212) in TCD MS 1337 [H.3.18]; *eDIL s.v. datnat*; Abbott and Gwynn 1921: 146.

379 For the lemma, see *Bretha Nemed Dédenach* 19.23–29 (CIH 1115.36; CCIH 184–188).

380 For the lemma, see *Bretha Nemed Dédenach* 20.9 (CIH 1116.5; CCIH 184–188).

381 The lemma is understood as the substantive verb with a 1 sg. suffixed agreement marker; *eDIL s.v. atta*. For the lemma, see *Bretha Nemed Dédenach* 20.6 (CIH 1116.2; CCIH 184–188).

382 For the first gloss, see *eDIL s.v. airchóitech*. See O'Dav 1090 (*Bretha Nemed Dédenach*; CCIH 140: *Irchaidh .i. irchoid, ut est irchaid mo menma ma im tir ro .t.t.* "*Irchaid*, i.e. hurt, ut est '... my mind if my land...'."); and for the lemma, see *Bretha Nemed Dédenach* 19.30 (CIH 1115.37; CCIH 184–188). The source text suggests that we understand the lemma as a verb. The interpretation of the verb is tentative. It is understood here as the 3 sg. impv. of *1 airchóitid* 'harms, injures' although one would normally expect to see the verb accompanied by *do* in the source text.

4.c.11.67 Io*rair* .i. *ar*guin *tre* ferg.
Iorair '(he) will be destroyed', i.e. destruction by means of wrath.[383]

4.c.11.68 Ainb .i. aineolac*h*.
Ainb 'ignorant', i.e. ignorant.[384]

4.c.11.69 *Air*b*he* .i. esn*ac*[h].
Airbe 'ribs', i.e. ribs.[385]

4.c.11.70 *Air*bec*h* .i. esn*ac*[h].
Airbech 'ribbed', i.e. ribs.[386]

4.c.11.71 Elge .i. feran*n* no Elg .i. Ére.
Elge 'of Ireland', i.e. land or *Elg*, i.e. *Ére* 'Ireland'.[387]

4.c.11.72 Cond-ag*ar* .i. i*ar*rt*har*.
Con-dagar 'is asked', i.e. is asked.[388]

4.c.12.73 Boimbil, boim .i. aoib*h*in*n*, no sgiat*h*, no boi*m* do b*h*ile sgeit*h*.
Boimbil, boim 'shield-rim, shield', i.e. delightful, or shield, or shield for a rim of a shield.[389]

---

383 The lemma is taken from *rodníorair* in the source text. It is interpreted as a sg. fut. pass. of *oirgid* 'slays'; see GOI §§658 and 665. For the lemma, see *Bretha Nemed Dédenach* 19.29 (*CIH* 1115.37; *CCIH* 184–188).

384 For the lemma, see *Bretha Nemed Dédenach* 20.14 (*CIH* 1116.9; *CCIH* 184–188).

385 The interpretation of the entry is uncertain. The word *airbe* can mean 'fence, pen, ribs' or 'a type of literary composition'; *eDIL s.vv. 1* and *2 airbe*. The gloss is not much help as *esnach* can refer to the ribs or a chorus; *eDIL s.vv. 1, 2,* and *3 esnach*. For the lemma, see *Bretha Nemed Dédenach* 20.19 (*CIH* 1116.13; *CCIH* 184–188).

386 Cf. 4.c.11.69 AIRBHE and discussion for that entry. Cf. *Bretha Nemed Dédenach* 20.19 (*CIH* 1116.13; *CCIH* 184–188).

387 The lemma is gen. sg. in form; *eDIL s.v. Elg*. For the lemma, see *Bretha Nemed Dédenach* 20.19 (*CIH* 1116.13; *CCIH* 184–188). Cf. OC.1 ELG.

388 For the lemma, see *eDIL s.v. con-dïeig* 'asks, seeks, demands'; and cf. See *Bretha Nemed Dédenach* 20.21 (*CIH* 1116.15; *CCIH* 184–188).

389 The interpretation of the entry is tentative. The main issue is how to understand *boim*. The meaning given in *eDIL s.v. boim(m)* 'bit, morsel, fragment' does not fit the glosses; the *eDIL* headword *? boimbil* is not provided with a definition. It could be that the gloss is playing with the range of meanings associated with *boim*. Based on Stokes' translation of O'Dav 221, the meaning 'shield' makes good sense here. The glosses as found here look like an amalgamation of what is found in O'Dav or a similar source. See O'Dav 221 (*Bretha Nemed Dédenach*; *CCIH* 115: *Boim .i. sgiath, ut est boim bil co n-uball airgit .i. sgiath math co*

4.c.12.74 Ro-nétad*h* .i. ro-gonad*h*, no ro-bít*h*.
Ro-nétad 'was injured', i.e. was wounded, or was wounded.[390]

4.c.12.75 Néth .i. dia cat*h*ad.
Néit 'name of a war god', i.e. a god of battle.[391]

4.c.13.76 Do*m*-ig*edh* .i. tig*edh* dam*h*.
Dom-iced 'let it come to me', i.e. let it come to me.[392]

4.c.13.77 Iomorrann .i. im⟨f*h*⟩orran.
Imḟorrán 'great violence', i.e. great violence.[393]

4.c.13.78 Lia .i. comorba.
Lía 'successor', i.e. successor.[394]

4.c.13.79 Lia .i. iomad.
Lía 'flood', i.e. abundance.[395]

---

nae bil fair do airget. Nó .i. aibind, bil aibin mar sin "*Boim*, i.e. a shield, ut est 'a good shield with a boss of silver', i.e. a good shield with a … on it of silver. Or i.e. *aibind* 'delightful': *bil* accordingly (means) 'delightful'."). For the lemma, see *Bretha Nemed Dédenach* 20.25 (CIH 1116.17; CCIH 184–188).

390 The lemma is understood as sg. pret./perf. pass. of *nettid* 'slays, hurts'; *eDIL s.v.* (*?*) *net*(*t*)*id*. The glosses are the sg. pret./pass. pass of *gonaid* 'pierces, wounds, kills', and *benaid* 'strikes, wounds, kills', respectively. For the lemma, see *Bretha Nemed Dédenach* 20.30 (CIH 1116.23; CCIH 184–188).

391 The lemma is the name of a god of war; *eDIL s.v. néit*. Lenited /d/ reduces to /∅/ from MI onwards, which explains the unexpected final ⟨d⟩. See O'Cl *Néid .i. cath* 'a battle'; O'Dav 1289 (*Bretha Nemed Dédenach*; CCIH 146: *Net .i. dia catha, ut est ciaso do ninnaib ro net nar fine .i. ro bith no ro na nairne* "*Nét*, i.e. a god of battle, ut est …." (Stokes does not translate the remainder of the entry.)); SC Y.965 *Neid .i. dia catha la geinti Goideal. Nemon uxor illius .i. a ben sin*. Cf. *Bretha Nemed Dédenach* 20.30 (CIH 1116.23; CCIH 184–188). Cf. 4.c.12.74 RO-NÉTADH.

392 For the lemma and gloss (both 3 sg. impv.), see *eDIL s.v. do-icc* 'comes'. For the lemma, see *Bretha Nemed Dédenach* 21.1 (CIH 1116.24; CCIH 184–188).

393 The lemma and gloss are variant spellings of each other; *eDIL s.v. imḟorrán*. Cf. O'Cl *Iomfhorran .i. cathughadh* 'fighting'; and for the lemma, see *Bretha Nemed Dédenach* 20.31 (CIH 1116.24; CCIH 184–188).

394 Cf. 4.c.13.79 LIA. The glosses for this entry and 4.c.13.79 LIA are differentiating homonyms. For the lemma, see the discussion in *eDIL s.v. 6 lía*. See the beginning of O'Dav 1165 (*Bretha Nemed Dédenach*; CCIH 143: *Lia .i. comarba*… "*Lia*, i.e. successor…"); and for the lemma, see *Bretha Nemed Dédenach* 21.15 (CIH 1116.36; CCIH 184–188).

395 Cf. 4.c.13.78 LIA. The glosses for this entry and 4.c.13.78 LIA are differentiating homonyms. For the lemma, see *eDIL s.vv. 2* and *6 lía*. See part of O'Dav 1166 (*Bretha Nemed Dédenach*;

4.c.13.80 Druis .i. mer*acht*.
Drúis 'of a hot-blooded person', i.e. an emotionally excited person.[396]

4.c.13.81 Guirn .i. suirn, no ait*h*in*n*e .i. gae ornae .i. ga oirgne.
Guirn 'of a firebrand', i.e. of a furnace, or firebrand, i.e. [< *gae* 'spear' + *1 orn* 'slaughter'] spear of slaughter, i.e. spear of destruction.[397]

4.c.14.82 N*ár* .i. naom*h*.
Nár 'honorable', i.e. holy.[398]

4.c.14.83 Derosg .i. derb*h*c*h*in*nedh*.
Derosc 'verdict', i.e. exact determination.[399]

4.c.14.84 Fochrac*h* .i. dui*n*e do-b*er* foic*h*reic celsi*n*e do neoc*h*.
Fochrach 'hireling', i.e. a person who gives a payment of service to someone.[400]

4.c.14.85 Urlata .i. uasal laoite um*h*alóide.
Aurlatu 'obedience', i.e. [< *úasal* 'high, noble, honorable' + *lúaite* 'going'] honorable going of humility.[401]

CCIH 143: *Lia .i. ... No imad uisci...* "*Lia*, i.e. ... Or abundance of water..."); cf. *Bretha Nemed Dédenach* 21.15 (CIH 1116.36; CCIH 184–188).

396 Cf. O'Dav 622 (no id.; CCIH 126) where the lemma is equated with the gloss. For the lemma, see *Bretha Nemed Dédenach* 21.24 (CIH 1117.2; CCIH 184–188). Cf. 4.b.14.22 MERACHT.

397 For the lemma, see *eDIL s.v. gorn* 'firebrand'. See O'Cl *Gorn .i. aithinne teineadh* 'a firebrand'; O'Dav 1036 (*Bretha Nemed Dédenach*; CCIH 139: *Guirn .i. aithinne nó gae oirgne. No gorn .i. [teine] ut est ima ngeiniter guirn* "*Guirn*, i.e. a firebrand, or a spear of destruction. Or *gorn*, i.e. fire, ut est 'round which fires are produced'."); the first part of SC Y.688 *Gorn .i. gai-orn .i. gae orcne .i. aithinde...*; and for the lemma, see *Bretha Nemed Dédenach* 21.26 (CIH 1117.3; CCIH 184–188).

398 Cf. 8.23.58 NÁR. For the use of *nár* as an epithet for heaven, see *eDIL s.v. 1 nár*. Cf. O'Cl *Nar .i. maith* 'good'. For the lemma, see *Bretha Nemed Dédenach* 21.27 (CIH 1117.6; CCIH 184–188).

399 Cf. 9.25.77 DERUSG. See O'Dav 712 (heptad 36; CCIH 129: *Derusc .i. derbchinnedh, ut est la cumail .u. mbo in derusc a dithma* "*Derusc*, i.e. exact determination, ut est 'with a *cumal* of five cows at the end of its delay in pound'."); and heptad 36 (CIH 35.15; AL 5: 240.22). For the lemma, see *Bretha Nemed Dédenach* 22.3 (CIH 1117.13; CCIH 184–188).

400 The *fochrach* is the one who is given a payment for service. The gloss has misunderstood the lemma, but it should be noted that the lemma is not widely attested; *eDIL s.v. fochrach*. Cf. O'Dav 865 (*Bretha Nemed Dédenach*; CCIH 134: *Fochreic .i. fochell, ut est insaig fochrach fochreic .i. in fear foichli a focheall d'fagail* "*Fochreic*, i.e. wages, ut est 'the hireling seeks a wage', i.e. the man who expects to get his hire."); and for the lemma, see *Bretha Nemed Dédenach* 22.16 (CIH 1117.24; CCIH 184–188).

401 Cf. 8.32.86 URLATA. Cf. O'Cl *Urlaitidh .i. umhalóid* 'humility'; O'Dav 1608 (*Bretha Nemed*

4.c.15.86 Dimsi .i. nem*h*maisi.
Dimse 'uncomely', i.e. not beautiful.[402]

4.c.15.87 Ség*h*uin .i. fer gon*us* séig .i. ag*h* all*aidh*, no ség*h*ui*n* .i. *air*e ec*h*ta.
Ségain 'a deer killer', i.e. a man who [< *gonaid* 'peirces, slays' + *ség* 'deer'] slays a deer, i.e. a wild deer, or a champion, i.e. *aire échta* 'lord of blood vengeance'.[403]

4.c.16.88 Buasac*h* .i. bá f*h*esac*h*.
Búasach 'wealthy (in kine)', i.e. [< *bó* 'cow' + *fesach* 'knowing, known'] cow knowing.[404]

4.c.16.89 Airberac*h* .i. nec*h* do-ber oirb*h*ire *ar* nec*h*, ma*r* ata cáinte.
Airbirech 'reproachful', i.e. someone who gives a reproach upon someone, namely a satirist.[405]

4.c.16.90 *Ar*rc*h*ogad*h* .i. seguinid*h*, no cú gon*us* osa.
Arrchogad 'a hound that first finds a deer in hunting', i.e. deer-killer, or a dog which slays deer.[406]

4.c.17.91 *Ar*r .i. fiad*h* no os.
Arr 'stag', i.e. deer or deer.[407]

Toísech; CCIH 156: *[U]rlaiti .i. umhaloid, ut est aes fognama [a]urlaiti* "*Aurlaiti*, i.e. humility, ut est 'obedient servants'."); and *Bretha Nemed Toísech* (CIH 2211.9; Breatnach 1984: 446; Breatnach 1989: § 3). For the lemma, see *Bretha Nemed Dédenach* 22.20 (CIH 1117.27; CCIH 184–188).

402 For the lemma and gloss, see *eDIL s.vv. ? dimse* and *maise*. Cf. SC Y.442 *Dimsi .i. dí-maissi*. For the lemma, see *Bretha Nemed Dédenach* 22.21 (CIH 1117.27; CCIH 184–188).

403 For the meaning of *séghuin*, see O'Reilly, *s.v. seagain* 'deer-killer'. For the lemma, see *Bretha Nemed Dédenach* 22.22 (CIH 1117.28; CCIH 184–188).

404 For the lemma, cf. *eDIL s.vv. ? 1* and *2 búasach*. Cf. O'Dav 225 (*Bretha Nemed Dédenach*; CCIH 115: *Buasach .i. buadach, ut est amail asidhroilli cach buasach biaid* "*Búasach*, i.e. victorious, ut est 'every *buasach* will be as he merits'." Stokes notes that the lemma means 'rich in kine, wealthy'.); and for the lemma, see *Bretha Nemed Dédenach* 22.30 (CIH 1117.35; CCIH 184–188). Cf. Breatnach 1987: 43 where there is a translation of the larger passage from which this entry is found; the last line in which the lemma appears is not translated.

405 For the lemma, see *Bretha Nemed Dédenach* 22.22 (CIH 1117.29; CCIH 184–188).

406 For the meaning of the lemma, see O'Reilly, *s.v. arrchoghaidh* 'the hound that first winds up or comes up with the deer in hunting'. The lemma is not in *eDIL*. Cf. 4.c.17.91 ARR. The gloss *seguinidh* is interpreted here as a derivative of *seagain* 'deer-killer'; cf. 4.c.15.87 SÉGHUIN. For the lemma, see *Bretha Nemed Dédenach* 23.6 (CIH 1118.2; CCIH 184–188).

407 Cf. 4.c.16.90 ARRCHOGADH. The lemma might be extracted from that in 4.c.16.90 ARRCHO-

4.c.17.92 Deog*h*b*aire* .i. sgo*aire*.
Deogbaire 'cupbearer', i.e. brewer.[408]

4.c.17.93 Foircit*h*er .i. fior d*h*é*c*h*ait*h*er.
Foircither 'is surveyed', i.e. [< *fír* 'truly' + *déchaid* 'looks, inspects, examines'] is truly seen.[409]

4.c.17.94 Urano .i. *air*e naoi .i. duine *ar* nec*h* d'fiad*h*nu*is*e *air* no na diaig*h* (c).
Urano 'witness', i.e. [< *aire* 'noble' + *noí* 'nine'] a noble of nine, i.e. a person who acts as a witness for someone or on his behalf.[410]

4.c.18.95 De*ar*cnuid*h* no dercnuid*h* .i. anr*a*d i*ar*sa ní drec*hus* do*n* eal*adh*ain.
Deargnaid nó dergnaid 'undistinguished', i.e. an *ánrad* 'poet of second grade' because he does not face towards poetical skill.[411]

4.c.18.96 Noit*h*gern .i. cli.
Noithgern 'type of poet', i.e. a *clí* 'poet of the third grade'.[412]

4.c.18.97 Olsone, no ollosna .i. can[a].
Olsone, nó ollosna 'type of poet', i.e. *cana* 'poet of the fourth grade'.[413]

GADH. The lemma is not in *eDIL*; see O'Reilly, *s.v. arr* 'a stag, a hind'. Cf. *Bretha Nemed Dédenach* 23.6 (CIH 1118.2; CCIH 184–188).

408 For the lemma, see *Bretha Nemed Dédenach* 23.6 (CIH 1118.3; CCIH 184–188).

409 See the first part of O'Dav 881 (*Bretha Nemed Dédenach*; CCIH 134: *Foircither .i. fírdechar*… "*Foircither*, i.e. let it be truly seen…"); and for the lemma, see *Bretha Nemed Dédenach* 23.8 (CIH 1118.5; CCIH 184–188). For the etymological gloss, see the Introduction, pp. 13–16.

410 The lemma is listed in *eDIL s.v. ? uran* without a definition and citing *Bretha Nemed Dédenach*. Based on the gloss here, it would appear that *urano*, whatever its case may be, means something like 'witness'. The translation of the gloss is tentative. For the lemma, see *Bretha Nemed Dédenach* 23.17 (CIH 1118.13; CCIH 184–188).

411 The lemma appears to be a name for a type of poet. The word *drechus* is obscure; it might be a mistake for *dercais*, the 3 sg. pres. rel. of *1 dercaid* 'looks at, beholds'. It would appear that this part of the gloss is etymologizing the *derc* element of the lemma. For the lemma, see *Bretha Nemed Dédenach* 23.20 (CIH 1118.15; CCIH 184–188). This and the following entries provide alternate names for classes of poets which are not attested elsewhere. The entries in Dubhaltach's Glossary are presented in order of the poets with the highest status first and then listed in descending order as they are given in the source text. See the discussion on pp. 19–20.

412 The lemma is obscure; it is not in *eDIL* nor the other scholarship on poets. For the lemma, see *Bretha Nemed Dédenach* 23.20 (CIH 1118.16; CCIH 184–188). See the discussion on pp. 19–20.

413 The lemma is obscure; it is not in *eDIL* nor the other scholarship on poets. For the lemma, see *Bretha Nemed Dédenach* 23.21 (CIH 1118.16; CCIH 184–188). See the discussion on pp. 19–20.

4.c.19.98 Saog*h*al .i. dos.
Saegul 'life', i.e. *dos* 'poet of the fifth grade'.[414]

4.c.19.99 Saoircerdne .i. macfurm*idh*.
Saerceirdne 'free craftsman', i.e. *macfuirmid* 'poet of the sixth grade'.[415]

4.c.19.100 Caoinc*h*erdne .i. foc*h*log.
Caíncheirdne 'good craftsman', i.e. *fochloc* 'a poet of the seventh grade'.[416]

4.c.19.101 Coictriall .i. drisiug.
Cóictríall 'five endeavors', i.e. *drisiuc* 'a poet of the eighth grade'.[417]

4.c.19.102 Taip*h*nem*idh* .i. tam*h*un.
Taipneimed 'sudden noble', i.e. *taman* 'a poet of the ninth grade'.[418]

4.c.19.103 Doineim*idh* .i. oblóire.
Doíneimid 'unskilled noble', i.e. *oblaire* 'a poet of the tenth grade'.[419]

4.c.20.104 Raed .i. ro éd.
Rét 'a thing', i.e. [< *ro* 'great, complete' + *ed* 'duration'] great duration.[420]

---

414 The lemma is the name for a type of poet. For the lemma, see *Bretha Nemed Dédenach* 23.21 (*CIH* 1118.16; *CCIH* 184–188). See the discussion on pp. 19–20.

415 The lemma is obscure; it is not in *eDIL* nor the other scholarship on poets. For the lemma, cf. *eDIL s.v. ceirdne*; and see *Bretha Nemed Dédenach* 23.21 (*CIH* 1118.16; *CCIH* 184–188). See the discussion on pp. 19–20

416 The lemma is obscure; it is not in *eDIL* nor the other scholarship on poets. For the lemma, cf. *eDIL s.v. ceirdne*; and see *Bretha Nemed Dédenach* 23.21 (*CIH* 1118.17; *CCIH* 184–188). See the discussion on pp. 19–20.

417 The lemma is obscure; it is not in *eDIL* nor the other scholarship on poets. For the lemma, see *Bretha Nemed Dédenach* 23.22 (*CIH* 1118.17; *CCIH* 184–188). See the discussion on pp. 19–20.

418 The lemma is obscure; it is not in *eDIL* nor the other scholarship on poets. For the lemma, see *Bretha Nemed Dédenach* 23.22 (*CIH* 1118.17; *CCIH* 184–188). See the discussion on pp. 19–20.

419 The lemma is obscure; it is not in *eDIL* nor the other scholarship on poets. The translation of the prefix is tentative. For the lemma, see *Bretha Nemed Dédenach* 23.22 (*CIH* 1118.17; *CCIH* 184–188). See the discussion on pp. 19–20.

420 The interpretation of the entry is tentative. For the use of *ro* in etymological glosses, see Taylor-Griffiths 2020: 1: 89. For the lemma, see *Bretha Nemed Dédenach* 23.28 (*CIH* 1118.23; *CCIH* 184–188).

4.c.20.105 Ainb*h*féth .i. ainéol*us*.
Ainféth 'lacking knowledge', i.e. ignorance.[421]

4.c.20.106 Dreteall .i. torc muice.
Drettel 'pet', i.e. male pig.[422]

4.c.20.107 Bainteoluid .i. bang*h*adoig*h*e.
Banteolaid 'female thieves', i.e. female thieves.[423]

4.c.20.108 Fur .i. úir.
Fúr 'earth', i.e. earth.[424]

4.c.20.109 Tai .i. an t⟨an⟩oc loma no cor*ma* .i. tanog, no derbog, no ian cor*ma* no loma.
Tai 'vessel for holding liquid', i.e. the vessel of milk or ale, i.e. vessel, or small pail, or mug of ale or milk.[425]

---

421 For the lemma, see O'Dav 38 (*Bretha Nemed Dédenach*; *CCIH* 110); and *Bretha Nemed Dédenach* 23.30 (*CIH* 1118.24; *CCIH* 184–188).

422 One wonders if the gloss should read *torc peta* 'a pet pig'. See O'Dav 701 ("attributed to *Senchas Már*;" *CCIH* 129: *Drettell .i. peta, amail adeir Senchas [Mór]: na torc arabí treut na dretell .i. in torc peta* "*Drettell*, i.e. a pet, as saith the Senchas Mór: 'neither the boar that is best of the herd, nor the pet', i.e. the pet boar."); and for the lemma, see *Bretha Nemed Dédenach* 23.34 (*CIH* 1118.28; *CCIH* 184–188).

423 Cf. O'Cl *Teol .i. gadaighe* 'thief' *na bainteolaigh .i. na mná do niodh goid, no do niodh gniomha go folaightheach* 'women who steal'; O'Dav 1556 (*Bretha Nemed Dédenach*; *CCIH* 154: *Teol .i. gataide, ut est didis im da banteolaigh Medba .i. im dá baneachlaigh no im da bangataidi nó im da tlenamnaigh do batar ag Meidb, ⁊ ata dethbir 'sa Corus Fine itir thaidhe ⁊ teol* "*Teol*, i.e. a thief, ut est 'thou wilt suppress (?) as to Medb's two she-pilferers', i.e. as to the two she-messengers, or as to the two she-thieves, or as to the two she-robbers whom Medb had. And in the *Corus Fine* ('tribal law'?), there is a difference between *táide* (theft with concealment) and *teol* 'stealing' (without concealment?)"); and for the lemma, see *Bretha Nemed Dédenach* 24.1 (*CIH* 1118.29; *CCIH* 184–188).

424 For the lemma, see the first part of O'Dav 866 (*Bretha Nemed Dédenach*; *CCIH* 134: *Fúr .i. talam*... "*Fúr*, i.e. earth..."); and *Bretha Nemed Dédenach* 24.11 (*CIH* 1118.37; *CCIH* 184–188). See also "Aithirne's Mother" 154; Carey 1994: 63; Gwynn 1928: 155, n. 3, is doubtful of the explanation of the lemma provided in O'Dav.

425 *Tanoc* and *tanog* are variant spellings of the same word, perhaps referring to a small vessel or cup. Cf. *eDIL s.v. taog* which cites O'Dav 1557. It is possible that the forms in Dubhaltach's Glossary are meant to be for *taog*. See O'Dav 1557 (*Bretha Nemed Dédenach*; *CCIH* 154: *Tai .i. derbóg nó taog no ian, ut est f. t. tadbánar toi .i. taisbentar na taoga no na derboga nó in ian loma nó corma* "*Tai*, i.e. a churn or ... or pail, ut est 'f. t. a *toi* is shewn', i.e. the ... or the churns of the pail of milk or ale is displayed."); and for the lemma, see *Bretha Nemed Dédenach* 24.10 (*CIH* 1118.36; *CCIH* 184–188). In "Aithirne's Mother", it is translated as 'milk pail'; see Gwynn 1928: 155, n. 2; and Carey 1994: 63.

4.c.21.110 Fureg .i. fl*edh*.
Fuirec 'preparation', i.e. a feast.[426]

4.c.21.111 Tút*h* .i. balad*h*.
Túth 'smell', i.e. smell.[427]

4.c.22.112 Con-clec*h* .i. do clis.
Con-clich 'jumps', i.e. leaped.[428]

4.c.22.113 Ad-cuitig*h* .i. ro eitig*h*.
At-cuitig 'refused', i.e. refused.[429]

4.c.22.114 Indbertad .i. déna*mh*.
Indbertad 'delivery', i.e. doing.[430]

4.c.22.115 Imdeall .i. b*r*uit*h* (no tab*air*t ne*th*e a h-in*ne* ⟨ł in⟩[h-inne]) fo[r] cludad*h*, clit*h*iug*had*h*, no téig*h*ed*h*, do h-imdilled*h*, ⁊ do h-eim*h*d*h*ailedh (ider coire ⁊ dab*agh*) an coir*m*.
Imdell 'mashing', i.e. brewing (or bringing things properly) under cover, protecting, or warming, for mashing, and for [< *éim* 'timely' + *dáilid* 'portions out, pours out'] a timely pouring out (both cauldron and vat) of the ale.[431]

---

426 Cf. the first part of O'Dav 867 (*Bretha Nemed Dédenach*; CCIH 134: *Fuirec .i. cuirm...* "*Fuirec*, i.e. alefeast..."); and for the lemma, see *Bretha Nemed Dédenach* 24.16 (CIH 1119.1; CCIH 184–188); "Aithirne's Mother" 153; and Carey 1994: 63.

427 For the lemma, see *Bretha Nemed Dédenach* 24.17 (CIH 1119.1; CCIH 184–188); "Aithirne's Mother" 153; and Carey 1994: 63.

428 See O'Dav 398 (*Bretha Nemed Dédenach*; CCIH 120: *Clecht .i. clisiudh* [*ut est*] *conclechtaither é ina brú* "*Clecht*, i.e. playing, ut est 'he leaps in her womb'."); and for the lemma, cf. *Bretha Nemed Dédenach* 24.16 (CIH 1119.1; CCIH 184–188). The interpretation of the gloss is tentative. One could posit an otherwise unattested verb **do-clis* 'leaps', cf. *clisid* 'leaps', or it could be a later pret./perf. form of *clisid*. If it were so, it would be unusual for the tense of the lemma and gloss not to match. See also "Aithirne's Mother" 153; and Carey 1994: 63.

429 Both the lemma and gloss are 3 sg. pret. of *as-toing* 'refuses'; *eDIL s.v. as-toing*. For the lemma, see the first part of O'Dav 39 (*Bretha Nemed Dédenach*; CCIH 110: *Atguitigh .i. era nó etach...* "*Atguitigh*, i.e. denial or refusal..."); *Bretha Nemed Dédenach* 24.19 (CIH 1119.3; CCIH 184–188); "Aithirne's Mother" 153; and Carey 1994: 63.

430 The meaning of the lemma is not entirely secure; *eDIL s.v. indbertad ?*. For the lemma, see *Bretha Nemed Dédenach* 24.21 (CIH 1119.5; CCIH 184–188); "Aithirne's Mother" 153; and Carey 1994: 63.

431 The inserted ⟨r⟩ is supplied from O'Curry's transcription. For brewing in medieval Ireland, see EIF 332–335; and Binchy 1981. The interpretation of *eimhdhailedh* is tentative; it could

4.c.23.116 Lait*h* .i. lion*n*.
Laith 'ale', i.e. ale.[432]

4.c.23.117 Tet*h*raig*h* .i. traig*h*id*h*.
Tethraig 'will have ebbed', i.e. ebbs.[433]

4.c.24.118 Loc[h]*ran*n ⁊ loic*het* .i. an tsoillsi.
Lóchrann ⁊ lóichet 'light and lightning', i.e. the light.[434]

4.c.24.119 Ble[d]*mh*aid*m* .i. glemaidem*h*, no b*ri*s*edh*.
Bláedmaidm 'loud breaking', i.e. manifest breaking, or breaking.[435]

4.c.24.120 Cnom*h*aidm [.i.] b*ri*s*edh* cno.
Cnómaidm 'breaking of a nutshell', i.e. breaking of a nutshell.[436]

4.c.24.121 Tet*h*n[a]t*ar* .i. tait*h*mig*h*id .i. sgaoilid.
Tethnatar 'they will have broken', i.e. releases, i.e. bursts.[437]

---

easily be a variant spelling of *imdilledh*. For the etymological gloss, see the Introduction, pp. 13–16. For the lemma, see *Bretha Nemed Dédenach* 24.22 (CIH 1119.6; CCIH 184–188); "Aithirne's Mother" 153; and Carey 1994: 63.

432 See O'Cl *Laith .i. lionn* 'ale'; and for the lemma, see *Bretha Nemed Dédenach* 24.25 (CIH 1119.8; CCIH 184–188); "Aithirne's Mother" 154; and Carey 1994: 63. The larger passage from which this entry derives is translated and discussed in Breatnach 2005b: 141–142.

433 For the lemma and gloss, see *eDIL s.v. tráigid* 'ebbs, recedes, diminishes'. The larger passage from which this entry derives is translated and discussed in Breatnach 2005b: 141–142 where he suggests that this is an instance where the preterite should be interpreted as a future. Cf. more distantly O'Dav 222 (*Bretha Nemed Dédenach*; CCIH 115); and for the lemma, see *Bretha Nemed Dédenach* 24.25 (CIH 1119.8; CCIH 184–188); "Aithirne's Mother" 154; and Carey 1994: 63.

434 The larger passage from which this entry derives is translated and discussed in Breatnach 2005b: 141–142. Cf. part of the gloss in O'Dav 222 where one of the lemmata appears (*Bretha Nemed Dédenach*; CCIH 115); and for the lemma, see *Bretha Nemed Dédenach* 24.25 and 26 (CIH 1119.8 and 9; CCIH 184–188); "Aithirne's Mother" 154; and Carey 1994: 63.

435 For the lemma, see *eDIL s.vv. bláed* 'shout, cry' and *bledmaidm*. It should be noted that ⟨dh⟩ has been expunged after ⟨ble⟩ in TCD MS 1317 [H.2.15B]; Gwynn 1942: 24, n. 4. The larger passage from which this entry derives is translated and discussed in Breatnach 2005b: 141–142. For the lemma, see *Bretha Nemed Dédenach* 24.26 (CIH 1119.9; CCIH 184–188); "Aithirne's Mother" 154; and Carey 1994: 64.

436 The lemma is not listed in *eDIL*. The larger passage from which this entry derives is translated and discussed in Breatnach 2005b: 141–142; I follow Breatnach's translation of the lemma. For the lemma, see *Bretha Nemed Dédenach* 24.27 (CIH 1119.10; CCIH 184–188); "Aithirne's Mother" 154; and Carey 1994: 64.

437 For the lemma, see *eDIL s.v. 1 teinnid, tennaid* 'cuts, cracks, breaks'. The larger passage from

4.c.25.122 Tud*hc*h*a*id*h* .i. dodeac*h*uid.
Tudchaid 'he came', i.e. he came.[438]

4.c.25.123 Át*h* téc*ht*a .i. inad dlig*hthach* no ait no baile.
Áth téchtae 'a suitable ford', i.e. a lawful place or position or settlement.[439]

4.c.25.124 Frecm*airc* .i. fior f*h*iafraige.
Frecmarc 'inquiring', i.e. [< *fír* 'true' + *fiafruige* 'inquiring'] true inquiring.[440]

4.c.25.125 Miodc*h*ui*ne* .i. ag leaguib*h*.
Midchuine 'medical treatment', i.e. by physicians.[441]

4.c.26.126 Coiglig*he* .i. caoi acla[ighe] .i. caoi loca loig*he*.
Coicclige '?', i.e. [< *cáe* 'path' + *aclaide* 'gentle'] gentle path, i.e. [< *cáe* 'path' + *loca* 'lock of hair' + *lige* 'lying down, sleeping, resting'] path of hair of resting.[442]

4.c.26.127 Mi*us*cait*h* .i. malla*cht*.
Miscad 'curse', i.e. curse.[443]

---

which this entry derives is translated and discussed in Breatnach 2005b: 141–142 where he suggests that this is an instance where the preterite should be interpreted as a future. For the lemma, see *Bretha Nemed Dédenach* 24.27 (*CIH* 1119.9; *CCIH* 184–188); "Aithirne's Mother" 154; and Carey 1994: 64. Cf. 6.a.22.40 TETHNATTAR.

438 The lemma and gloss are both 3 sg. perf. forms of *do-tét* 'comes'. For the lemma, see O'Cl *Tudhchaidh .i. tainicc* 'he came'; *Bretha Nemed Dédenach* 24.29 (*CIH* 1119.12; *CCIH* 184–188); "Aithirne's Mother" 154; and Carey 1994: 64.

439 For the lemma, see *Bretha Nemed Dédenach* 25.1 (*CIH* 1119.14; *CCIH* 184–188); "Aithirne's Mother" 154; Carey 1994: 64; Gwynn 1928: 156, n. 18, suggests emending *áth* 'ford, open space between two objects' to *fáth* 'cause, reason, subject matter, affair' and translates *áth téchta* as 'fitting occasion'.

440 For the etymological gloss, see Dinneen *s.v. fiafruighe* 'inquiring, inquiry'. For the lemma, see *Bretha Nemed Dédenach* 25.8 (*CIH* 1119.19; *CCIH* 184–188).

441 For the lemma, see *Bretha Nemed Dédenach* 25.7 (*CIH* 1119.19; *CCIH* 184–188).

442 The missing letters are supplied from O'Curry's transcription. Cf. *eDIL s.v. coicclige* where no definition is provided, but there is a cross-reference to *cocluiche* 'playing a game?'. The two etymological glosses are difficult to interpret in light of the fact that there are multiple meanings associated with each of the component words. Thus, the interpretation of the entry is tentative at best. Hopefully in the future a scholar will produce an edition of the source text which will resolve this problem. For the lemma, see *Bretha Nemed Dédenach* 25.12 (*CIH* 1119.24; *CCIH* 184–188).

443 Cf. the beginning of *SC* Y.859 *Miscath .i. mí-innsci....* See *Lec. Gl.* 310 *Misca[i]th .i. mallacht*;

4.c.26.128 Biolf*hot*h*ach* .i. gan fot*hach*.
Bilfotach 'free from glanders', i.e. free from glanders.[444]

4.c.26.129 Gre*ch* .i. cnu.
Grech 'nut', i.e. nut.[445]

4.c.26.130 Baidsid*he* .i. fer do-[g]ni baisd*he*d, ma*r* ata oll*amh* baisdi*us* grada *ar* na fil*edh*ib*h*.
Baítside 'baptizer', i.e. a man who makes a baptism, namely an *ollam* 'chief poet' who baptizes ranks on the poets.[446]

4.c.27.131 Foirb*h*led .i. f*or* f*h*ill*edh* na fil*idacht*a .i. duan, ⁊ f*or*duan .⁊c̄.
Forbled 'undergrowth (?)', i.e. [< *for* 'on' + *filliud* 'bending, folding, turning'] for folding the practice of poetry, i.e. *dúan* 'poem', and *fordúan* 'a type of stanza', etc.[447]

O'Cl *Mioscaith .i. mallachd* 'a curse'; O'Dav 1211 (no id.; *CCIH* 144: *Miscaid .i. mallacht, ut est miscaid fri ceird cainti* "*Miscaid*, i.e. a curse, ut est 'a curse against the satirist's art'."); and for the lemma, see *Bretha Nemed Dédenach* 25.15 (*CIH* 1119.26; *CCIH* 184–188).

444 See O'Dav 206 ((2) *Bretha Nemed Dédenach*; *CCIH* 114: *Nó bil .i. slán, ut est each, dá boin bil-fotach .i. slán cen ḟothach* "Or *bil*, i.e. sound, ut est 'a horse, two cows, free from glanders', i.e. sound without glanders."); and for the lemma, see *Bretha Nemed Dédenach* 25.21 (*CIH* 1119.31; *CCIH* 184–188). Glanders is an infectious disease primarily affecting horses: UC Davis Veterinary Medicine Center for Equine Health https://ceh.vetmed.ucdavis.edu/health-topics/glanders. Accessed July 4, 2024.

445 See *SC* YAdd.727 *Grech .i. cnú*; and for the lemma, see *Bretha Nemed Dédenach* 25.26 (*CIH* 1119.35; *CCIH* 184–188). The larger passage from which the entry derives is translated in *Uraicecht na Ríar* 44–45.

446 For the lemma, see *eDIL s.v. ? baitsid(e), ? baitse.* The interpretation of the lemma is based on the gloss. For the lemma, see *Bretha Nemed Dédenach* 25.27 (*CIH* 1119.37; *CCIH* 184–188). The larger passage from which the entry derives is translated in *Uraicecht na Ríar* 44–45 except for this word.

447 For the lemma, see *Bretha Nemed Dédenach* 25.31 (*CIH* 1119.39; *CCIH* 184–188). The larger passage from which the entry derives is translated in *Uraicecht na Ríar* 44–45 where the lemma is understood as a dat. pl. of *forbul* 'undergrowth'. The first part of the gloss is etymological. The second half of the gloss quotes *Bretha Nemed Dédenach* 18.14 (*CIH* 1114.37); cf. 4.c.5.45 DUAN and 4.c.5.46 FORRDUAIN. The first gloss raises questions about the reading of the lemma. If we follow the reading in *Bretha Nemed Dédenach*, the first etymological gloss does not make linguistic sense as it depends on the lemma ending in [d]. If we retain the reading in Dubhaltach's Glossary, we end up with a word which is not found in *eDIL*. There is likely some confusion in the transmission of the glosses to the text.

4.c.27.132 Tora*ch*ta .i. do-ro*ach*t, no do-ria*cht*.
Torachta 'reached', i.e. reached, or reached.[448]

4.c.28.133 Uid*h*bre*th* .i. guib*h*re*th*.
Úidbreth 'false judgement', i.e. false judgement.[449]

4.c.28.134 Oimb*h*re*th* .i. guibre*th* om*h*.
Ombreth 'raw judgement', i.e. a raw false judgement.[450]

4.c.28.135 [In]oimblig*h* .i. blig*h*id*h* a h-in*n*e.
In-omblig 'levies', i.e. levies properly.[451]

4.c.28.136 F*air*ben .i. firin*n*[e] *ar* b*é*in no firen.
For-ben 'strikes', i.e. [< *fírinne* 'justice' + *ar* 'for' + *béin* 'striking'] justice for striking or just.[452]

5.a.1.1 Deoltaoide .i. gaid.
Deóltaide 'sucking theft?', i.e. theft.[453]

5.a.1.2 Tiomg*aire* .i. i*ar*raid*h*.
Timgaire 'asking', i.e. asking.[454]

---

448 The lemma is the part. of *do-roich* 'reaches, attains, acquires'. The glosses are earlier and later 3 sg. pret. forms, respectively; *eDIL s.v. do-roich* and cf. *torachta* 'cyclic, circular, complete'. For the lemma, see *Bretha Nemed Dédenach* 26.5 (*CIH* 1120.5; *CCIH* 184–188).

449 The interpretation of the lemma is based on the gloss as no definition is given in *eDIL s.v. úidbreth ?*. For the lemma, see *Bretha Nemed Dédenach* 26.10 (*CIH* 1120.10; *CCIH* 184–188).

450 The lemma is understood as a compound of *om* 'raw, crude, immature, rude, unrefined' and *breth* 'judgement'; *eDIL s.v. om*. The sense is of a judgement given in haste without proper reflection which proves to be false. For the lemma, see *Bretha Nemed Dédenach* 26.11 (*CIH* 1120.10; *CCIH* 184–188).

451 See *eDIL s.v. in-omblig* 'milks, exacts, levies' and the discussion in Gwynn 1942: 222. See the first part of O'Dav 1119 (*Di Brethaib Gaire*; *CCIH* 141: *Inombligh .i. bluighid no toibgid*… "*Inomblig*, i.e. mulcts or levies…"). For the lemma, see *Bretha Nemed Dédenach* 26.11 (*CIH* 1120.10; *CCIH* 184–188).

452 Cf. 7.b.1.48 FAIRBEN. The text has the prototonic form of the verb. For the lemma, see *Bretha Nemed Dédenach* 26.11 (*CIH* 1120.11; *CCIH* 184–188).

453 The interpretation of the lemma is tentative because the reading of the first part of the word is uncertain. Perhaps the first element is *deól* 'sucking', but how this makes sense within a wider context is obscure although it could refer to stealing milk from cows in a field.

454 See *Metr. Gl.* 24, § 19 '*Tiomghoire*' *iarruidh*.

5.a.1.3 Aig*he* .i. aimsir.
Áige 'time', i.e. point of time.[455]

5.a.1.4 M*airn* .i. brat*h*.
Mairn 'betraying', i.e. betraying.[456]

5.a.1.5 Midis .i. [measaid.]
Midfess 'who will judge', i.e. would judge.[457]

5.a.2.6 [Dear] .i. esgit*he*r.
Doír 'unfree', i.e. is allowed.[458]

5.a.2.7 Seoid gabla .i. seoid gab*hlaigh*ter isi*n* eric .i. d*airt* .i. *ceithri* sgreab*ail* a luac*h*.
Séoit gabla 'forked *séts*', i.e. *séts* which are divided for the *éric* 'fine', i.e. a yearling heifer, i.e. four scruples its worth.[459]

5.a.2.8 D*ar*taid [.i. ...].
Dartaid 'yearling bullock', i.e. ...[460]

5.a.3.9 [Col]p[thach] .i. *sé* sg*r*iab*ail*.
Colpthach 'two-year-old heifer', i.e. six scruples.[461]

455 The context of the entry is unknown; *eDIL s.v. 3 áige*.

456 See O'Cl *Mairn .i. brath* 'betrayal'.

457 The missing word is supplied from O'Curry's transcription. The parse of the lemma and gloss is tentative, but both are interpreted as 3 sg. forms of *midithir* 'judges'; *eDIL s.v. midithir*. Normally one would expect the lemma to reflect an older form of the verb, but in this entry the lemma is the MI 3 sg. fut. rel. One would expect to see the *f*-future in the gloss if the lemma is MI, but instead the form appears to be the OI 3 sg. cond.

458 The interpretation of the entry is tentative because the reading of the lemma is not certain. The lemma is supplied from O'Curry's transcription. The lemma could also be for *dér* 'tear, weeping'; the context of the entry is unknown. The gloss is understood as the 3 sg. pres. pass. of *eiscid* 'allows, concedes'; *eDIL s.v. 1 eiscid*.

459 See *GEIL* 115 for a discussion of the lemma and *EIF* 61 for the value of a *dairt*. The entry refers to the honor-price of the *fochloc*, who ranked seventh of the seven poetic grades. See *Uraicecht Becc* (*CIH* 2320.6; (also in *Uraicecht na Ríar*, 155); *AL* 5: 58.18); *Díre*-text 6 § 6 (*CIH* 922.20–21; *CCIH* 41).

460 If this entry follows the pattern of the surrounding entries, the gloss should state that the *dartaid* has a value of anything from two to four scruples; its value varied depending on the time of year; *EIF* 60–61.

461 For the value of the *colpthach*, see *EIF* 62.

5.a.2.10 Sam*usg* [.i.] da sg*r*eb*al* dég.
Samaisc 'three-year-old dry heifer', i.e. twelve scruples.[462]

5.a.2.11 Lulg*ach* .i. *ceithri* sg*r*eab*ail fichet*.
Lulgach 'milch cow', i.e. 24 scruples.[463]

5.a.2.12 Eislis .i. ailsiod*h* lesa.
Éislis 'neglect', i.e. [< *áilsed* 'neglect, negligence' + *1 les* 'relief, redress, matter, case, hospitality, care'] neglect of redress.[464]

5.a.2.13 Combac*h* .i. coi*m*b[riseadh].
Combach 'breaking', i.e. breaking.[465]

5.a.3.14 Ca .i. cin*us*.
Cáe 'house', i.e. covering (?).[466]

5.a.4.15 Ad-bo .i. urfog*r*aid*h*.
Ad-bo 'may proclaim', i.e. proclaims.[467]

5.a.4.16 Im*h*de .i. eim*h*d*h*idnig*h*.
Imm-dích 'protects', i.e. [< *éim* 'timely, prompt' + *dítnid* 'protects'] quickly-protects.[468]

---

462 For the value of the *samaisc*, see EIF 63–64.

463 For the value of the *lulgach*, see EIF 64–65.

464 See the *Fonnaidh* glossary (CIH 1079.27–28; CCIH 46; and Taylor-Griffiths 2020: 1: 174–179); and cf. *Cáin Aicillne* § 26 (CIH 487.19 and 32; AL 2: 268.24). It is possible that the gloss is not etymological (or later was not understood to be etymological) as there are a handful of examples from the legal texts where *áilsed* and *les* are found in the same clause; *eDIL s.vv. áilsed* and *1 les*.

465 The missing letters are supplied from O'Curry's transcription. See O'Cl *Combach .i. coimh-briseadh* 'breaking'.

466 The form *cinus* by itself does not make sense here. It is possible that Dubhaltach misread his source, and the gloss should be a form of *cnes* 'skin, surface', perhaps 'covering'; *eDIL s.v. cnes*. Cf. 2.b.6.88 COTA and 5.b.2.27 IORCHA, IAR CHA.

467 The lemma is the 3 sg. pres. subj. of *ad-boind* 'proclaims, gives notice'; *eDIL s.v. ad-boind*. Cf. O'Dav 89 (no id.; CCIH 111: *Adbo* (*.i. urfocraim*) *.i. obaim nó atboinn nó atbois, ut est atbois a réir britheman* "*Adbo* (i.e. I proclaim), i.e. I refuse, or he proclaims it, or thou shouldst proclaim it, ut est 'thou shouldst proclaim it in obedience to the judge'."). Cf. 1.a.4.11 ADBO.

468 For the gloss, see *Bechbretha* § 54, gloss f (CIH 457.2; AL 4: 202.9). It is common for the preverb *im*(*m*)- to be glossed by *éim* 'swift, timely'; Binchy 1943: 212; and Taylor-Griffiths 2020: 1: 89.

5.a.4.17 Manchuine .i. lu*cht* coi*m*id*heachta*, ⁊ coi*m*[eadtha].
Manchaine 'service due from a tenant', i.e. attendant and custodian.[469]

5.a.5.18 [R]o-fesad .i. fu*achtnaigh*id.
Ro-fessad 'might injure', i.e. injures.[470]

5.a.5.19 For-uast*ar* .i. fua*chtnaigh*[th]er.
For-uastar 'may be injured', i.e. is injured.[471]

5.a.5.20 Caoi*mthe*cht*a*d*h*a .i. coi*m*ide*acht*ad*h*a .i. lu*cht* coi*m*id*acht ar* son bi*us* d'aontoisg.
Coímthechtaide 'attendants', i.e. attendants, i.e. an attendant whose purpose is for that.[472]

5.a.6.21 Dérac*h* .i. lomr*adh*.
Dérach 'stripping', i.e. stripping.[473]

5.a.6.22 Glin*ne* .i. daingen.
Glinne 'security', i.e. security.[474]

5.a.6.23 Treab*air*e d'fir ub*h*an .i. fulang.
Trebaire d'fiur amáin 'surety for only one man', i.e. supporting.[475]

5.a.6.24 Ciol*ar*[n] .i. c[orn].
Cilorn 'vessel', i.e. goblet.[476]

469 The entry refers to the tenant's obligation to serve as an attendant or guard for his lord.

470 The lemma appears to be the 3 sg. past. subj. of *fo-fich* 'trespasses, does injury' which is frequently glossed by *fúachtnaigid* 'is aggressive, does injury'; *eDIL s.v. fo-fich.*

471 The lemma is understood as the 3 sg, pres. subj. pass. of *fo-fich* 'trespasses, does injury' which is frequently glossed by *fúachtnaigid* 'is aggressive, does injury'; *eDIL s.v. fo-fich.*

472 The context of the entry is unknown. See O'Don. Suppl. *s.v. coimidecht.*

473 See the *Ni Tulach* glossary (*CIH* 810.14; *CCIH* 149; and Taylor-Griffiths 2020: 1: 164–169) and the *Arra* glossary (*CIH* 1560.16; *CCIH* 68; Taylor-Griffiths 2020: 1: 187–188).

474 See the *Fonnaidh* glossary (*CIH* 1079.27 and 28; *CCIH* 46; and Taylor-Griffiths 2020: 1: 174–179).

475 The interpretation of the entry is tentative because the reading of some of the words is uncertain. The division of the lemma is tentative and understands *ubhan* to be a form of *amáin* 'only' which has a form *amhán*; *eDIL s.v. amáin.*

476 The missing letters are supplied from O'Curry's transcription. Assuming that O'Curry's

5.b.1.25 [Fer medh]ongoide l*eth*e .i. f*er* aga mbí ⟨fios⟩ an gadaige.
Fer medongaite leithe 'a half [unlawful] receiver of stolen goods', i.e. a man who has knowledge of the thief.[477]

5.b.1.26 Fer m*edh*ongoide láin .i. f*er* [a]ga mbi fios an gad[aige] ⁊ [na] goide mále [*read* meirle].
Fer medongaite lain 'a fully [unlawful] receiver of stolen goods', i.e. a man who has knowledge of the thief and of the stolen goods.[478]

5.b.2.27 Iorcha, i*ar* ch*a* .i. landaoir, ca .i. tec*h* .⁊c̄.
Airchae, íar chae 'out-office, back house', i.e. storeroom, house, i.e. house, etc.[479]

5.b.2.28 Mís eim*h*glethe .i. mí a ndentaoi eim*h*gle .i. suid*h*iug*adh* cána no ca*ir*de no dlig*edh* .⁊c̄.
Mís éimgléthe 'a month of prompt deciding', i.e. a month in which a prompt decision is made, i.e. establishing law or treaty or tribute, etc.[480]

5.b.3.29 Sgenman*n*a .i. n*eth*e sgin*nius* do*n* in*n*eoin on ord gaba*n*.
Scenmanna 'slippings off', i.e. things which slip off from the anvil by the work of a smith.[481]

---

reading of *corn* is correct, the lemma *cilar* 'error?' does not make sense, but emending to *cilarn* brings the lemma into semantic alignment with the gloss; *eDIL s.v. ? cilar.*

477 See *Aidbred* § 4, comm. 148.8 (CIH 2169.38).

478 The missing letters are supplied from O'Curry's transcription. See *Aidbred* § 4, comm. 150.1–2 (CIH 2170.6–7). The form *mále* in the MS does not make sense here, so it has been emended to *meirle* 'stealing, robbing, robbery'; *eDIL s.v. meirle.*

479 Cf. O'Dav 1107a (no id.; CCIH 141: *Ircha .i. cuiltech no aircecal no tech in bídh* "*Ircha*, i.e. a kitchen, or room, or pantry (lit. 'the house of the food')."). See DDC D2.64 *Cae .i. tech. ut dicitur ceardcae .i. tech cearda* (CIH 1071.14); O'Cl *Cai no ca .i. teach* 'a house'; and SC YAdd.365 *Cai .i. tech, unde dicitur cerdcha .i. tech cerda.* For the meaning of 'house' for *cáe* in glossaries, see *eDIL s.v. cáe.*

480 The interpretation of *eimglethe* and *eimgle* is tentative. Both appear to consist of *éim* 'prompt, ready, timely' and a form of *gléid* 'makes clear, clears up, decides, concludes'; *eDIL s.vv. gléid* and *gléthe.* The sense of the entry is that there is a month where legal matters are decided quickly, perhaps at an assembly. The lemma looks as if it itself is an etymological gloss, perhaps on *imgléod* 'act of deciding, ratifying'; see the Introduction, pp. 13–16. *Bretha Éitgid* (CIH 258.32; AL 3: 132.14) which refers to ten days for proclaiming a treaty and a month for ratifying it.

481 For the lemma, see *eDIL s.v. sceinm* 'springing, flying off'. For things slipping off an anvil, see *Bretha Éitgid* (CIH 265.14 and 267.28; AL 3: 176.16 ff. and 188.21).

5.b.4.30 Tret*h*nac*h* .i. trenton*nac*[h].
Trethnach 'stormy', i.e. powerful-billowy.[482]

5.b.4.31 Ub*ha*, ab*ha* .i. ab*h*an*n*.
Uba, aba 'river', i.e. river.[483]

5.b.4.32 Góla .i. gúala.
Góla 'prison', i.e. prison.[484]

5.b.4.33 Blaoid*h*is .i. béicis.
Bladis 'shouted', i.e. shouted.[485]

5.b.4.34 Ruib*h*en .i. tuillid.
Ruiben 'remains', i.e. increases.[486]

5.b.5.35 Iodnac*har*, iod*h*nag*ar* .i. tiodnaict[h]*er*.
Indnachar, indnagar 'is given', i.e. is given.[487]

5.b.5.36 Derbana*r* .i. diuba*rtar*.
Derbanar 'is hindered', i.e. is deprived.[488]

---

482 See *Breth* glossary (*CIH* 1098.1–2; *CCIH* 46; and Taylor-Griffiths 2020: 1: 179–186). The larger passage from *Breth* glossary which contains both the lemma and gloss is translated in O'Curry 1861: 617.33.

483 The entry contains three later variant nom. sg. forms of *ab* 'river'; *eDIL s.v. 1 ab*.

484 Cf. 1.b.15.91 GÓLA. The gloss is a later spelling of the lemma; *eDIL s.v. 2 góla* 'pit, prison, drinking vessel'.

485 The interpretation of the entry is tentative. The lemma appears to be a 3 sg. pret. of a verb related to *bladaigid* 'praises' and *1 blá* 'shout, cry, report, fame'; see Dinneen *s.v. blaodgaim* 'I shout, I boast'. The gloss is the 3 sg. pret. of *béiccid* 'cries, roars, bellows'; *eDIL s.v. béiccid*.

486 The interpretation of *ruiben* is problematic. According to *eDIL s.v. ruiben*, the meaning is 'stays, abides, remains', but here it is glossed by *tuilled* 'increasing', which matches the gloss in O'Dav 1368 (no id.; *CCIH* 149: *Ruib .i. tuilled, ut est ní torc ruchtach ruiben i cru isil uirc .i. nocha tuillem in torc roechtach nó romór i cru in uirisil* "*Ruib*, i.e. addition, ut est 'no strong boar grows in a low pig's stye', i.e. the very daring (?) or very large boar does not increase in the stye of the very low one.") where Stokes translates *ruiben* 'as grows'. For the lemma, cf. *Ni Tulach* glossary (*CIH* 809.6–9; *CCIH* 149; and Taylor-Griffiths 2020: 1: 164–169).

487 Both lemmata appear to be sg. pres. pass. forms of *do-indnaig* 'gives, bestows, grants'; *eDIL s.v. do-indnaig*. I am hesitant to restore the preverb in the case because the lemmata may reflect a later formation without the preverb.

488 The lemma is understood as a 3 sg. pres. pass. of *do-rorban* 'hinders, obstructs, prevents'; *eDIL s.v. 2 do-rorban*. The gloss is understood as a 3 sg. pres. pass. of *do-opir* 'takes away, deprives, defrauds', *eDIL s.v. do-opir*.

5.b.5.37 Deolad*hacht* .i. g*r*asia .i. ní a n-aisgid*h*.
Deolaidecht 'favor', i.e. *gratia* 'favor', i.e. anything being desired.[489]

5.b.5.38 Deoin .i. corr *u*[i]sge.
Deóin 'well', i.e. well of water.[490]

5.b.6.39 Coic, coc*aire*, fert*h*ig*h*is .i. fer do-b*er* tene ⁊ *us*ge do*na* h-aoideiduib*h*, ⁊ isi*n* ⟨*nó* agan⟩ egl*us* bios.
Coic, cocaire, ferthigis 'cook, cook, steward', i.e. a man who carries fire and water to the guests, and at the church also.[491]

5.b.6.40 Lánc*h*at*h*aig*h* .i. lánad*h*oin.
Lánchathaig 'fully warlike', i.e. fully ...[492]

5.b.13.41 T*r*i ioma*r*e, no díre bios ag fulang na h-eaguilsi .i. cé*t*ran*n*, cuingeall, ⁊ ud*h*b*air*t: cé*t*ran*n* .i. flesg lai*m*e ⁊ orba laime na man*ac*[h] fein do benatt*ar* as coill *ar* na t*h*iod*h*nacal da n-erlam*h* ó t*h*osac*h*; cuingell .i. ni geallt*ar* do*n* egl*us* isi*n* cionuid do-[g]nit[h]*er* ria; udb*air*t .i. feran*n* iodbai*r*t na h-uasuil na mb*eth*aid*h* *iar* t[r]osg*adh* do D*h*ia ⁊ dona naom*h*uib*h*.
Trí immaire, nó díre bís oc fulang na h-ecailse 'three divisions or payment which support the church', i.e. *cétrann* 'first share', *coingell* 'stipulation', and *udbairt* 'offering': *cétrann* 'first share', i.e. the monks' own land and patrimony which they took from a wood in respect to the bestowal from their possession from the beginning; *coingell* 'stipulation', i.e. that which is pledged to the church for the crime which is committed against it; *udbairt* 'offering', i.e. donated land of the noble during his lifetime after fasting to God and to the saints.[493]

---

489 Note that Dubhaltach uses Latin *gratia* in the gloss to explain the lemma.

490 For the lemma, see *Bretha Éitgid* (CIH 864.25; CCIH 39). For the lemma and part of the gloss, cf. O'Dav 669 (*Bretha Nemed Dédenach*; CCIH 127: *Deoin .i. fuaran nó corr nó tibrait, u test ailiu uisci ⁊rl.* "*Deoin*, i.e. a well, or pool, or spring, ut est 'I beg for water &c.'."); and for the lemma, see *Bretha Nemed Dédenach* 41.19 (CIH 1130.36; CCIH 184–188; Corthals 2010: 78 and 80 where it is translated as 'well (??)'; see the note on 89).

491 See O'Cl *Coca .i. cócaire* 'cook'. The word *aoideiduibh* is understood at the dat. pl. of *oígi* 'stranger, guest'; *eDIL s.v. oígi.*

492 The entry is obscure. Both the lemma and gloss appear to be gen. sg. compounds where the first element is *lán* 'full, whole'. The second element of the lemma might be from *cathach* 'bellicose, vehement'; *eDIL s.v. 1 cathach.* The second element of the compound is obscure.

493 For similar content, cf. distantly *Ni Tulach* glossary (CIH 809.13–14; CCIH 149; and Taylor-

5.b.10.42 Ceng*ar* .i. ceimn*igh*t[h]*er*.
Cengar 'is stepped', i.e. is stepped.[494]

5.b.16.43 7 Caogdac[h] .i. ain*m* g*r*aid t*r*e ma*r* c*h*an*us* na t*r*i *cóic*a salm: fog*h*laint*idh*, deisgibal, st*aru*ide, foirc*etlaigh*, sáoi canoine, d*r*uimcli. Ag si*n* na sec*h*t ng*r*aid egna. 6 Fog⟨laintig*h*⟩ .i. f*er* ag a mbi eol*us* i ndeic*h* leabr*aibh* d'foc*h*oir aige, ui*m*e si*n* goirt*er* de f*er* tiachtana foc*h*oireac*h*. 5 Desgib*al* .i. f*er* ag a *m*bi eol*us* foc*h*oire uile .i. *da* leab*har déc* na foc*h*oirec*h*. 4 St*ar*uide .i. f*er* ag a *m*bi *trícha* d'aice*acht*uib*h* nao*m*ta ina f*h*ogloim. 3 F*or*c*et*l*aid* .i. f*er* ag a *m*bi g*r*amadac*h*, crosan ⁊ siollaob*ha*, ⁊ rim*he*, ⁊ ret*ha* na bl*iad*na, ⁊ ret*ha* g*r*ene, ⁊ esga. 2 Saoi canoine .i. f*er* ag a mbi eol*us* canoine, ⁊ can*us* sgela Iosa .i. b*r*eit[h]*er* nDe (isi*n* inad glan i mbi) .i. ecna cadluic canoine. 1 D*r*uimcli .i. f*er* ag a mbí eol*us* iomlan na h-egna on leab*ar* as mó da ngoirt*er* Cuilmen, g*us* [in] leab*har* as lug*h*a da ngoirt*er* deic*h* b*r*et*h*ir, ina ndeac*h*raigt*er* .i. i ndeg*hchoir*igh*th*er an tiomna mait*h* do-rin*n*e Día do Maoisi.
7 *Cóictach* 'cleric of a certain grade', i.e. a name of a grade because he chants the three times fifty psalms: *foglainntid*, *deiscipul*, *staraige*, *forcetlaid*, *suí canóine*, *druimchlí*. These are the seven grades of wisdom. 6 *Foglainntid* 'a student', i.e. a man who has knowledge of the ten books of science, because of that he is called a man who is learning science. 5 *Deiscipul* 'disciple', i.e. a man who has knowledge of the whole of science, i.e. the 12 books of science. 4 *Staraige* 'historian', i.e. a man who has 30 holy lessons in his learning. 3 *Forcetlaid* 'teacher', i.e. a man who has [knowledge of] grammar, composition, and meters, and arithmetic, and the courses of the years, and the courses of the sun and of the moon. 2 *Suí canóine* 'expert of canons', i.e. a man who has knowledge of canons, and who tells the Gospel story of Jesus, i.e. the word of God (in the pure place in which he is), i.e. wisdom of catholic canon. 1 *Druimchlí* 'man of learning', i.e. a man who has complete knowledge of the wisdom from the greatest book which is called *Cuilmen*, to the smallest book which is called

Griffiths 2020: 1: 164–169). The entry concerns three different ways in which the church receives income. The first is from the land which the monks own themselves as part of their own property or inheritance. The second type of income is that of fines for any crime committed against the church. The third is land which a noble person donates to the church during their lifetime.

494 The verb *céimnigid* 'steps, goes, proceeds' frequently glosses *cingid* 'steps, goes, proceeds'; *eDIL s.v. céimnigid.*

Deich Bríathar 'Ten Words' in which are arranged, i.e. in which [< *deg* 'good' + *córaigid* 'arranges'] is well-arranged the good Testament which God made for Moses.[495]

5.b.20.44 Cat*hair* ataig*h* .i. cat*hair* i n-aitcen*n* cac*h* a s*hochar*, ⁊ a d*hochar*: cat*hair* ataig*h* t*h*all i gcion*n* cille: cat*hair* ataig*h* an *airch*in*nigh*: cat*hair* ataig*h* .i. cat*h*aoir eps*coip*.

Cathair ataig 'city of refuge', i.e. [< *cathair* 'city' + *ad-teich* 'flees to, resorts to'] a city into which each flees his advantage and his disadvantage: city of refuge yonder at the end of the churchyard: city of refuge of the monastic superior: city of refuge, i.e. episcopal see.[496]

5.b.22.45 Fet*h*aol .i. mion*n*, ma*r* ata, clog, c*r*os, bacc*h*all, ministe*r* no soisgel .⁊c̄.

Fethal 'halidom', i.e. venerated object, namely bell, cross, crozier, service-set, or gospel, etc.[497]

---

495 See *Uraicecht Becc* (CIH 2332.2–6; AL 5: 102.19); a status tract related to *Uraicecht Becc* (CIH 687.3–6; CCIH 30); a glossed paragraph "on the seven grades of ecclesiastical scholars" (CIH 2101.1–9; CCIH 84); cf. distantly O'Dav 639 ("a citation from a passage on ecclesiastical scholars"; CCIH 127); cf. distantly O'Dav 1302 ("a citation from a passage on ecclesiastical scholars"; CCIH 147); and see O'Curry 1861: 494–495 where this entry is edited and translated. The translation here follows O'Curry. *Cuilmen* is the name given to the *Origines* or *Etymologiae* of Isidore of Seville; *eDIL s.v. cuilmen*. *eDIL s.v. 1 rím* cites Dubhaltach's Glossary for the meaning 'number'. For the meaning assigned to *crosan*, see *eDIL s.v. crosánacht* 'composition of *crosán*' (composition consisting of verse and alliterative prose). The end of the entry refers to the ten commandments.

496 For the phrase meaning 'city of refuge', see *eDIL s.v. attach* 'refuge, praying, request'. The translation of the entry is not smooth, and it is possible that we should understand the phrase *cathair ataig* as 'sanctuary'. If we do, then the second part of the gloss refers to the physical limit of sanctuary provided by the church. The use of *sochar* and *dochor* here is unusual as both normally refer to advantageous and disadvantageous contracts, respectively. Perhaps we should understand them as referring to 'good' and 'bad' people and circumstances more generally or situations which might not be to the church's advantage or disadvantage. The verb *aitcenn* is understood as a later 3 sg. pres. from of a simplex derived from *ad-teich* 'flees to, resorts to, prays to'; its vn. is *attach*, thus the first gloss is at least partly etymological. That being said, one would not expect such a late verbal form in an etymological gloss. For a discussion of the *cathair ataig*, see Etchingham 1999: 167 and n. 1 which mentions this entry in passing as part of a larger discussion of the *cathair ataig*, which seems to refer to "a church settlement of particular eminence, since it has *seniors* 'seniors' who have a judicial function."

497 Cf. 8.36.100 FEATHAL. For the lemma, cf. O'Dav 899 ((2) no id.; CCIH 134); the *Ni Tulach* glossary (CIH 810.13–14); and the *Arra* glossary (CIH 1560.15–16); Taylor-Griffiths 2020: 1: 164–169 and 187–188, respectively. The word *minster* can refer to the case used to carry

5.b.22.46 Minist*er* .i. mion*na* aisdir bi*us ar* aisd*er* isi*n* túait*h* le tab*air*t mion*n* *ar* c*h*ach. ⁊c̄.
Meinstir 'reliquary', i.e. [< *mind* 'relic' + *astar* 'journeying, travel'] traveling relics which are for traveling in the community for bringing venerated objects for everyone, etc.[498]

5.c.1.47 Díre*ch*, ⁊ dera*ch* .i. lomr*adh*.
Dírech, ⁊ *derach* 'stripping', i.e. stripping.[499]

5.c.1.48 Tairecc .i. torra*cht*ain.
Tairecc 'coming', i.e. coming up to.[500]

5.c.1.49 Súilte*ch* .i. fer sellce*acht*a .i. seallac[h].
Súiltech 'looking on', i.e. onlooker, i.e. onlooker.[501]

5.c.1.50 Erent*ac*[h] .i. f*er* f*or*a n-ern*aigh*t[h]*er* fia*ch*.
Erentach 'paid', i.e. a man for whom a fine is paid.[502]

---

vessels and other items for the Divine Service, but also to any case used for carrying the Host, relics, or any venerated item; *eDIL s.v. meinistir*. Cf. 5.b.22.46 MINISTIR. See Wycherley 2015: 172 and 209.

498 Cf. 8.36.100 FEATHAL and 5.b.22.45 FETHAOL. The entry refers to a case used for carrying relics or other venerated objects around the community. The entry is translated in Petrie (1845: 341) as "*Ministear*, i.e. traveling relics which are carried about in a district to administer oaths to all."

499 See the *Ni Tulach* glossary (CIH 810.14–15); and the *Arra* glossary (CIH 1560.16–17); Taylor-Griffiths 2020: 1: 164–169 and 187–188, respectively. For the lemma, cf. O'Dav 591 (*Bretha Nemed Toísech*; CCIH 125); and *Bretha Nemed Toísech* (CIH 2219.24). It is possible that we should understand the lemma with the meaning of 'uncovering' or 'disclosing'. Cf. 5.a.6.21 DÉRACH.

500 For the lemma and gloss, see *eDIL s.vv. tairecc* and *toracht, torachtu, torachtain*. Cf. O'Don. Suppl. *s.v. tairiuc, tairic*.

501 The interpretation of the lemma is tentative; see *eDIL s.vv. sellc(h)echt, seilligecht* and *? suiltech*. For a discussion of the culpable onlooker, see GEIL 154–157. For this and the following lemma, see CIH 858.8 and 2123.5; both citations are part of collections of citations and commentary from various texts (CCIH 39 and 86–87, respectively). Note that *eDIL s.v. ? suiltech* cites both of the passages from CIH 858.8 and 2123.5.

502 The interpretation of the lemma is tentative, but it likely concerns the paying of fines on behalf of someone else. For this and the previous lemma, see CIH 858.8 and 2123.5; both citations are part of collections of citations and commentary from various texts (CCIH 39 and 86–87, respectively). Note that *? suiltech* cites both of the passages from CIH 858.8 and 2123.5.

5.c.2.51 Díc*h*ealtac*h* .i. an fer cub*us* brait*h* .i. an fer bi*us* ag ceilt an uilc.
Dícheltach 'hidden', i.e. the man [who is] complicit of a treachery, i.e. the man who is concealing the wrongdoing.[503]

5.c.3.52 Tuid*h*in aosa escána .i. t*ár*gad*h* an lo*cht*a ná bí isi*n* riagail.
Tuidin áesa escána 'leading people who are outside of canon law', i.e. bringing the people who are not within the rule.[504]

5.c.3.53 Ealgn*us* .i. eolgnais.
Elgnas 'malicious injury', i.e. malicious injury.[505]

5.c.4.54 Com*h*raite .i. an t*urchar* do-b*he*r duine t*re* ferg, ⁊ g*ur*ob ail leis a guin.
Comraite 'intention', i.e. the death a person causes through anger, and it is his desire to injure him.[506]

5.c.4.55 Duinet*h*aid*h*e .i. táites d'i*m*irt *ar* an dui*ne* *ar* na marb*adh* .i. a f*h*olac*h* an cuirp m*air*b d'eis a m*ar*bt*h*a.
Duinetáide 'murder with concealment of the body', i.e. theft of moving by the person after the killing, i.e. his hiding the dead body after killing him.[507]

5.c.6.56 Fog*h*ail t*r*ebdire .i. fogail do dena*m* isna t*r*ebaib*h* i n-*air*illn*aigh*ter dire.
Fodail trebdíre 'distribution of compensation for stealing from a house', i.e. to make a distribution amongst the households when compensation is deserved.[508]

503 For the first part of the gloss, see *Bretha Éitgid* (*CIH* 1175.9; *CCIH* 50); and O'Don. Suppl. *s.v. cubas, brath* 'complicity'. This person is guilty of complicity through prior knowledge; *eDIL s.v. 1 cubus*.

504 The interpretation of *escána* is difficult, and I owe the following suggestion to one of the anonymous readers. The reader suggests that the word could be based on the negative prefix *ess-* and *cáin* 'law, rule', creating an *i*-stem adj. *escáin* 'outside of canon laws'. Considering that *ríagal* in the gloss often refers to monastic rules and frequently glosses *cáin*, this lends further support to the proposed interpretation of *escána*.

505 For the lemma, see *Bretha Éitgid* (*CIH* 275.4; *AL* 3: 226.23); O'Dav 767 (*Bretha Nemed Dédenach*; *CCIH* 130); and *Bretha Nemed Dédenach* 33.22 (*CIH* 1125.18; *CCIH* 184–188).

506 For this meaning of *turchar*, see Dinneen *s.v. torcher* 'fall, departure, death' and *eDIL s.v. 1 do-tuit* 'falls, perishes'. The sense is that the offender set out to kill the other person. See O'Don. Suppl. *s.v. comhraite*.

507 The entry refers to hiding the dead body after killing someone. For the first gloss, see *Ántéchtae* (*CIH* 1244.15; *CCIH* 51); and for the lemma, cf. heptad 55 (*CIH* 50.1; *AL* 5: 300.23).

508 Cf. distantly *Bretha Éitgid* (*CIH* 322.34; *AL* 3: 458.12).

5.c.6.57 Roch bi .i. ro b*hi*.
Roch bí 'and is wont to be', i.e. is wont to be.[509]

5.c.7.58 Pliun .i. t*air*isiom*h*.
Pliún 'inert' (?), i.e. continuing.[510]

5.c.7.59 Toit*h*fliun .i. t*air*risiom*h*, no fuillid*he*, cos*m*ail ⁊ pliun.
Tophliún 'inertia', i.e. continuing, or increasing, similar to *pliun* 'inert'.[511]

5.c.7.60 Egl*us* l*eth*dire .i. egl*us* n*ac*[c] bí [i]na dlig*hedh* t*r*e ttesdan*n*, l*eth*dire uait*he*.
Eclas lethdíre 'church of half-compensation', i.e. a church which is not in its law in respect of testimony, half-compensation from it.[512]

5.c.8.61 Eagl*us* na foltmaisi .i. egl*us* i mbi óglaoc*h* l[..] na cen*n* uirre leis *ar* maisioc*h* folt *air*.
Eclas na foltmaisi 'the church of the untonsured', i.e. a church in which there is a young man [...] the head on him he has for beauty of hair on him.[513]

6.a.1.1 [Forbuain] indlig[htheach], no forrge, no forr*ac*[h] indlig[htheach] .i. ni do b[h]uain da ceilib[h] do[n] r[h]ig t*ar* an ni d[ligeas].

---

509 For the archaic connective -*ch*-, see Binchy 1960: 77–94. The example from Dubhaltach's Glossary is not included in Binchy's inventory of examples (a search of *CIH* does not find the textual source).

510 The lemma is difficult; cf. *eDIL s.vv. do-pliúna* 'is torpid' and *tophliú(i)n* 'sluggishness, inertia'; and Stüber 2010: 129, n. 6. Although otherwise unattested, the lemma is likely related to one of these words, i.e. 'sluggish, inert', especially considering the meaning of the gloss. Cf. 5.c.7.59 TOITHFLIUN.

511 Cf. 5.c.7.58 PLIUN. For the lemma, see the section on prescriptive rights in *CIH* 751.11 (*CCIH* 32).

512 The interpretation of this entry is tentative for a few reasons. The first is the interpretation of *na* which seems out of place, hence the emendation. The second is the interpretation of *tesdann*; the meaning 'testimony' is by no means certain; *eDIL s.v. ? testan*. It is unclear whether the entry refers to a church which does not carry out the rites fully or properly.

513 In *eDIL s.v. fotlmaise*, the entry discusses whether the word means 'tonsure, state of being tonsured' or 'untonsured'. Even though the entry here is incomplete, the gloss suggests the meaning 'untonsured'. The interpretation of the gloss is tentative due to the missing word.

Forbuain indligthech, nó forrge, nó forrach indligthech 'unlawful exaction, or overbearing, or unlawful oppressing', i.e. to obtain anything from his clients by the king beyond that to which he is entitled.[514]

6.a.2.2 R[uice,] ruca .i. ruaid*h* cec*h* imdergt*h*a.
Ruice, ruccae 'shame', i.e. blush of each reproach.[515]

6.a.2.3 Bos .i. bá fi*us* .i. fi*us* mait*h*.
Bas 'palm of the hand', i.e. [< *báe* 'profit' + *fis* 'knowledge'] profit knowledge, i.e. profitable knowledge.[516]

6.a.2.4 Eallac*h* .i. suidiug*adh*, no or[dúghadh].
Ellach 'joining', i.e. placing, or arranging.[517]

6.a.3.5 [Cicht] .i. [rinnai]g*h*e.
Cicht 'engraver', i.e. engraver.[518]

6.a.3.6 Sg*r*ipt .i. sg*r*ibnid*h*.
Script 'writing', i.e. scribe.[519]

---

514 The missing words are supplied from O'Curry's transcription. The word *forbuain* seems to be a variant of *forbach*; *eDIL s.v. forbach* 'an extraordinary levy, exaction, extortion'. The sense refers to anything which a lord or king exacts from his clients beyond that which he is lawfully due. For part of the lemma and gloss, cf. *Cáin Ḟuithirbe* (CIH 761.35–38; CCIH 33); the gloss is not translated in the edition of the text. Cf. 6.b.2.93 FORBHACH.

515 The missing letters are supplied from O'Curry's transcription. Cf. the last part of O'Dav 64 (no id.; CCIH 110: *Ail… .i. ma dia tucthar ruice ruadh-imdergtha fair* "*Ail…* i.e. if the red blush of reproach is inflected upon him."); and SC YAdd.1110 *Rucce* (*.i. nairi*) *.i. ruadcheo, ł quasi ru-tige*; and see *Lec. Gl.* 256 *Ruice .i. imdergad.*

516 The word *bas* can also refer to measures of quantity or distance; *eDIL s.v. 1 bas*. Cf. O'Cl *Ba .i. maith* 'good'.

517 For the lemma, see *Bretha Nemed Dédenach* 22.32 (CIH 1117.37; CCIH 184–188); and O'Cl *Eallach .i. suidhiughadh* 'sitting'.

518 The missing test is supplied from O'Curry's transcription. See *Ántéchtae* (CIH 2181.17; CCIH 88); O'Dav 367 (*Bretha Nemed Dédenach*; CCIH 119: *Cicht .i. geibiach .i. rindaighe,* [*ut est*] *cicht scriptor* "*Cicht*, i.e. an embroiderer, i.e. an engraver…"); DDC D1.157 *Cicht .i. geibire .i. rindaire*; SC M.246 *Cicht .i. gebiach .i. rinnaire*; and for the lemma, see *Bretha Nemed Dédenach* 22.35 (CIH 1117.40).

519 See *Ántéchtae* (CIH 2181.17; CCIH 88); O'Dav 1434 (*Bretha Nemed Dédenach*; CCIH 151: *Script .i. scribnide, ut est ócht scrip.* Stokes does not translate the entry.); and for the lemma, see *Bretha Nemed Dédenach* 23.1 (CIH 1117.40).

6.a.3.7 Culma[i]*re* .i. c*air*pteoir.
Culmaire 'chariot-maker', i.e. chariot-maker.[520]

6.a.3.8 C*r*uitig*h* .i. c*r*uit*e*re.
Cruittig 'of a harper', i.e. harper.[521]

6.a.3.9 Cuislen*n*aig*h* .i. f*e*t*h*ánac*h*.
Cuislennaig 'of a piper', i.e. piper.[522]

6.a.3.10 Gnae .i. oib[inn].
Gnóe 'beautiful', i.e. delightful.[523]

6.a.4.11 [...]er[.....]nt*e*r.[524]

6.a.4.12 B*r*on*nus* .i. sof*hius* b*r*on*n*.
Bronnas 'who bestows', i.e. [< *so* 'good, excellent' + *fius* 'knowledge' + *bronn* 'gift'] good knowledge of gifts.[525]

6.a.4.13 Bert .i. b*reith*em*h*nus.
Bert 'judgement', i.e. judgement.[526]

---

520 For the lemma, see *Bretha Nemed Dédenach* 23.1 (CIH 1117.41; CCIH 184–188); *Lec. Gl.* 512 *Culmairi .i. cairptheoir*; *Metr. Gl.* 32, § 9 *is 'culmaire' guch cairbtheóir*; O'Cl *Culmhaire .i. sáor dhéunmha carabid, no cairptheoir* 'a man who makes chariots'; SC Y.320 *Culmaire .i. cairptheoir*; and *Stowe Gl.* 292 *culmaire .i. cairpteor.*

521 The form of the lemma is uncertain; it might be a gen. sg. or nom. pl. of *cruitach* 'hunch-backed', perhaps another word for a harper; see *eDIL s.v. 1 cruitt* 'harper'; and Dinneen *s.v. cruitheach.* For the lemma, cf. *Bretha Nemed Dédenach* 23.2 (CIH 1117.41; CCIH 184–188).

522 The lemma appears to be the gen. sg. of *cuislennach* 'piper. For the lemma and gloss, see *eDIL s.vv. cuislennach* and *fetánach.* For the lemma, see *Bretha Nemed Dédenach* 23.2 (CIH 1117.41; CCIH 184–188).

523 See O'Cl *Gnaoi .i. aoibhinn* 'delightful''; the first half of O'Dav 1023 (*Bretha Nemed Dédenach*; CCIH 138: *[G]no[e] .i. airdirc nó aibind, ut est gnoe imbuil cerdach*... "*Gnoe*, i.e. conspicuous or delightful, ut est '*gnoe imbuil cerdach*'..."); and for the lemma, see *Bretha Nemed Dédenach* 23.2 (CIH 1117.42; CCIH 184–188). See also *eDIL s.v. oíbind* 'pleasant, delightful'. One would expect the gloss to be similar to that found in O'Cl and O'Dav.

524 The entry is not in O'Curry's transcription. Much of the entry is illegible, but it is likely one of the words at CIH 1117.42 based on the entries before and after it in Dubhaltach's Glossary; cf. 6.a.3.10 GNAE and 6.a.4.12 BRONNUS. Cf. *Bretha Nemed Dédenach* 23.2–3 (CIH 1117.42; CCIH 184–188).

525 The lemma appears to be the 3 sg. pres. ind. rel. of *2 bronnaid*; and cf. *eDIL s.v. 2 bronnad.* For the gloss, see O'Reilly *s.v. bronn* 'gift'. For the lemma, see *Bretha Nemed Dédenach* 23.3 (CIH 1117.42; CCIH 184–188).

526 Cf. 8.27.75 BERT. Cf. the beginning of O'Dav 280 (no id.; CCIH 117: *Bert .i. breth*... "*Bert*, i.e.

6.a.4.14 *Air*illn*edh* .i. dlig*edh*.
Airillned 'deserving', i.e. deserving.[527]

6.a.4.15 Ad-ren .i. iocaid*h*.
Ad-ren 'pays', i.e. pays.[528]

6.a.4.16 Ad-ealla .i. aid*h*[l]id.
Ad-ella 'visits', i.e. visits.[529]

6.a.4.17 Breas .i. *ar*dfoll*us*.
Bres 'blow', i.e. highly manifest.[530]

6.a.5.18 Sruit*h* .i. uasal.
Sruith 'venerable', i.e. noble.[531]

6.a.5.19 I*ar*ngl*us* .i. i*ar* ngleo f*h*esa.
Íarnglus 'after-glow', i.e. [< *íar* 'after' + *glé* 'brightness' + *fis* 'knowledge'] after brightness of knowledge.[532]

6.a.5.20 I*ar*soillsi gl*us* .i. soillsi i*ar*ngl*us*a [....]ll[.] soillsi.
Íarsoillsi glus 'glow of after-light', i.e. light of after-glow [...] light.[533]

6.a.6.21 Clio*th*c*h*a, clucha .i. clut*h*ma[i]*r*e .i. tet[h]a.
Clithcu, cluchu 'more sheltering', i.e. more sheltered, i.e. warmer.[534]

---

a judgment...") where *bert* is treated as a noun meaning *breth* 'judgment'. For the lemma, see *Bretha Nemed Dédenach* 23.3 (*CIH* 1117.42; *CCIH* 184–188).

527 The lemma is a later derivative of *áirillnigid* 'merits, deserves'; *eDIL s.v. áiriltnigid.*

528 For the lemma, cf. *Cáin Ḟuithirbe* (*CIH* 773.25).

529 The gloss is the later simplex of the lemma; *eDIL s.v. ad-ella* 'visits, approaches'.

530 For the gloss, which is normally used for *airdslechta* 'a form of assault' and *ardracht*; see *eDIL s.vv. airdslechta* and *? ardracht*; and cf. the first part of O'Dav 115 (*Di Brethaib Gaire*; *CCIH* 112, 307–308: *Ardslechta .i. ardfollus*... "*Ardslechta*, i.e. highly manifest..."); and for the gloss, see *Bretha Nemed Toísech* (*CIH* 2213.40).

531 For the lemma, see *Bretha Nemed Toísech* (*CIH* 2213.38 and 2214.2).

532 For the lemma, see *Bretha Nemed Toísech* (*CIH* 2214.2); more distantly, cf. *SC* Y.689; O'Dav 1024 (*Bretha Nemed Toísech*; *CCIH* 138); and Digest B (1) (*CIH* 1291.17; *CCIH* 53; and *AL* 4: 376.22). The entry refers to old age. Cf. 6.a.5.20 IARSOILLSI GLUS. The lemma is translated as 'dotage of old age' in *Uraicecht na Ríar*, 23 (21.23); the larger source passage is edited and translated in *Uraicecht na Ríar*, 20–28.

533 Cf. distantly Digest B (1) (*CIH* 1291.18; *CCIH* 53; *AL* 4: 376.22). The entry refers to old age. Cf. 6.a.5.19 IARNGLUS.

534 The interpretation of *clucha* as a variant of *clithcu*, the comp. of *clithach*, is tentative. The

6.a.6.22 Ainfig*h* .i. gan fig*he*.
Anfud 'tempest', i.e. without stillness.[535]

6.a.6.23 Sging .i. iomd*ad*h.
Sceng 'bed', i.e. of a bed.[536]

6.a.6.24 Imsging .i. [...] iom[.]d[.].
Imscing 'apartment', i.e. ...[537]

6.a.7.25 Mana*ch* innerge det*h*b*h*ire .i. man*ach* img*h*es ona eagl*us* dut*hchus* doc[h]u*m* egluisi oile da adnacal inte, no d'i*arraidh* coth*aighthe* tre ria*chtan*u*s* .i. di-ait[h]b*erair* eirge aisde a h-in*n*e, ma*r* si*n* in*n*erge cattuctatad*h* ma det*h*bir no in*n*det[h]bir.
Manach indéirge dethbire 'monastic tenant of justifiable desertion', i.e. a monastic tenant who leaves from his native church to another church for his burial there, or to seek sustenance out of necessity, i.e. [< *dí-* neg. pefix + 2 *aithbiraid* 'reproaches, blames'] he is without being reproached departing from it for a reason, namely desertion of a [?] whether justifiable or not justifiable.[538]

---

word *cluthmaire* is a Mod. Ir. comp. form of the adj. *cluthmar*, a late form of *cluthar*. The word *tet[h]a* is interpreted as the EMI comp. *tethu*, equivalent to Mod. Ir. *teo* 'warmer'. I owe this suggestion to one of the anonymous readers. For the lemma, see *Bretha Nemed Toísech* (CIH 2214.2). The larger source passage is edited and translated in *Uraicecht na Ríar* 20–28; the lemma as at 21.24.

535 For a discussion of the form of the lemma (dat. sg. of *anfud*), see *Uraicecht na Ríar*, 26, note to line 24. For the lemma, see *Bretha Nemed Toísech* (CIH 2214.3). The larger source passage is edited and translated in *Uraicecht na Ríar* 20–28; the lemma as at 21.24. The word *fighe* is understood as a form of *féth* 'calmness, stillness'; *eDIL s.v. 3 féth*.

536 See *Dúil Laithne* 196 *Sceng .i. iomda* 'torus'; *Lec. Gl.* 488 *Sgeng .i. lebaid*; O'Cl *Sceng .i. leaba, no both bheag ina mbí leaba* 'a bed, or small booth in which is a bed'; SC Y.1151 *Sceng .i. imdæ, unde dicitur imsceng .i. both bec imma timchellæ imdæ. inde dicitur ferr imsoing adbar il.* For the lemma, cf. *Bretha Nemed Toísech* (CIH 2214.3). The larger source passage is edited and translated in *Uraicecht na Ríar* 20–28. Cf. 6.a.6.24 IMSGING from which the lemma here is derived. The gen. sg. form of the gloss is unusual; *eDIL s.v. 2 imdae*.

537 See SC YAdd.790 *Imscing .i. tech tech becc a talla imdæ* and Y.1151 *Sceng .i. imdæ, unde dicitur imsceng .i. both bec imma timchellæ imdæ. inde dicitur ferr imsoing adbar il*; and for the lemma, see *Bretha Nemed Toísech* (CIH 2214.3). The larger source passage is edited and translated in *Uraicecht na Ríar* 20–28; the lemma is at 22.25. The gloss is illegible, but one would expect something similar to what is found in SC; cf. *2 imdae* 'apartment'. Cf. 6.a.6.23 SGING.

538 The interpretation of *cattuctatadh* is obscure. The second half of the gloss might refer to a young monastic pupil being taken back regardless of the reason for desertion. The first

6.a.9.26 At[h]*air* an*n*oide .i. at[h]*air* egl*us*e dut[h]c*hus* do nec*h*.
Athair andóite 'father of a mother-church', i.e. father of a church which is native to someone.[539]

6.a.10.27 Cro rig*h*, ⁊ senaid*h* .i. c*r*uin*n*iog*adh*, no dail an rig*h* no an tsenuid*h*.
Cró ríg ⁊ senaid 'enclosure of a king and of a synod', i.e. assembling, or meeting of the king or of the synod.[540]

6.a.10.28 ⟨Colpa⟩ cennait*h*e .i. cen*n* snait*h*e saog*h*ail no cen*n* aig*h*e .i. aimsire .i. ai*m*sir, is an*n* ioc*us* an colpa cen*n*ait*h*e da ngoirt*e*r colpa cen*n*ad*air*te.
Colpthach cennaithe 'two-year-old heifer of last payment', i.e. end of the thread of life or the end of time, i.e. of time, i.e. time, it is then that he pays the two-year-old heifer of last payment which is called the two-year-old heifer of the final pillow.[541]

6.a.12.29 Se*acht*b*air*gen .i. b*air*gen ioc*us* an m*ar*b*h* i gcion*n* se*acht*m*ui*n*e deis a b[h]ais.
Sechtbairgen 'seven loaves', i.e. bread which the deceased pays for at the end of a week after his death.[542]

6.a.12.30 Fl*edh* croil*ig*h*e .[i.] i gcion*n* mis, saolim g*ur*ob ionan*n* si*n* cui*m*niug*adh* mi*us*a na m*ar*b*h* re h-egl*us* ioc*ar* si*n* os na m*ar*b*aibh*.

---

part of the entry is edited and translated in *Córus Bésgnai*, 103. For the larger context, see *Córus Bésgnai*, 292 (CIH 91.24; CCIH 14). On monks abandoning their church, see the discussion in Etchingham 1999: 429–430 (which mentions this entry).

539 Taking *athair* 'father' as 'founder' would make better sense here, although the word might refer to a monastic title; *eDIL s.v. 1 athair*. Cf. O'Cl *Annóid .i. eaglas* 'church'; and *Córus Bésgnai*, § 75, 238.12 (CIH 1818.26).

540 The context of the entry is unknown.

541 The entry is edited and translated in Etchingham 1999: 441, n. 2 (I follow his translation); and see 440–444 for discussion of what is due to the church as payment for burial. The amount varied depending on the wealth of the deceased; the minimum was the clothing worn by the deceased. Cf. *Anfuigell* § 54 comm. (CIH 2162.38) for similar material.

542 For the lemma, see *Anfuigell* § 54 comm. (CIH 2162.39). CIH 2162.38–39 is translated and discussed in the *Tract on Marriage and Divorce*, 118–121; see also § 35 (CIH 149.31–36) for a similar passage. Cf. *Di Astud Chirt ⁊ Dligid* (CIH 133.5–9). Etchingham 1999: 441 edits and translates the version of the passage from *Anfuigell* (CIH 984.27); see 440–444 for discussion of what is due to the church as payment for burial.

Fled crólige 'funeral feast', i.e. at the end of a month, I suppose that is the same as the [one] month memorial of the dead by the church that is paid for the dead.[543]

6.a.14.31 Re com*h*loig*h*t*h*e .i. ai*m*sir ⟨no⟩ *cair*de fa fiacaib*h* co*m*log*uis* an feicem*h* donti *ar* a mbí fiac*h* aige.
Ré comloigthe 'period of mutual concession', i.e. time or respite concerning fines of mutual adjustment of the debtor by the one to whom he owes a fine.[544]

6.a.15.32 Uinge diubaid*h* n-uire ⟨don eglus teide⟩ .i. *air*ged uam*h*a no leabt*h*a .i. diub*h*aid .i. adbal eibe na h-uire .i. i mbúain no i ndena*m* na h-uaig*h*e do*n*a daoinib*h*-si, deor*aidh*, mur*c*u[i]*r*t*h*e, faoi*n*dl*edh*aig*h*, fu*r*fog*r*aig, ⁊ taisdeall*aigh*, si*n* uat*h*a maille se*acht*b*air*gin. Lainbiath*adh* g*ach* graid*h* a fl*edh* croil*ige*, no *sechtmad* log*h* e[nech]. Se*acht*m*adh* loig*h*e enec*h* g*ach* g*r*aid a se*acht*b*air*gen no a se*acht*m*adh* lainbiath*adh*.
Uinge díupaid n-úire 'an ounce for digging a grave ⟨for the church to which he goes⟩', i.e. the value of a grave or of a resting place, i.e. digging, i.e. [< *adbal* 'great, vast' + *eipe* 'cutting'] great cutting of the grave, i.e. for cutting or for making the grave for these people: [for the] exile, castaway, vagrant, proclaimed person, and traveler, [the fee for cutting the grave is due] from them along with the seven loaves. Full refection of each grade for his funeral feast, or a seventh of his honor-price. A seventh of the honor-price of each grade is [equivalent to] seven loaves or is [equivalent to] a seventh of full refection.[545]

---

543 For the lemma, see *Anfuigell* § 54 comm. (CIH 2162.39). CIH 2162.38–39 is translated and discussed in the *Tract on Marriage and Divorce* (Kelly 2014: 118–121); see also § 35 (CIH 149.31–36) for a similar passage. Cf. *Di Astud Chirt ⁊ Dligid* (CIH 133.5–9). Etchingham 1999: 441 edits and translates the version of the passage from *Anfuigell* (CIH 984.27); see 440–444 for discussion of what is due to the church for burial. The amount varied depending on the wealth of the deceased. Unusually in this entry, Dubhaltach uses the first person in the explanation, assuming that the gloss in his source was not written in the first person.

544 See *Bretha Nemed Dédenach* 33.18 (CIH 1125.23; CCIH 184–188). For *comloguis*, which is interpreted as a gen. sg. of an abstract noun, cf. *eDIL s.vv. comlóg* and *comlogad*.

545 See the *Tract on Marriage and Divorce* § 35 (CIH 149.31–36) and discussion at 118–121; and for similar material cf. *Di Astud Chirt ⁊ Dligid* (CIH 133.7). See Etchingham 1999: 440–444 for a discussion of some of these passages and of what is due to the church for burial; this entry is mentioned in passing on 440, n. 2. The amount varied depending on the wealth of the deceased; the minimum was the clothing worn by the deceased.

6.a.18.33 Rúsg nd*air*ti .i. *ru*sg diosg no *etram*.
Rúsc dairte 'covering of a yearling heifer', i.e. shelter or light covering.[546]

6.a.19.34 Fertag*ar* .i. adnaicter.
Fertagar 'is buried', i.e. is buried.[547]

6.a.19.35 Ion*n*ota*cht* .i. tosac*h* .i. tec*h*t in*n*.
Inotacht 'beginning', i.e. beginning, i.e. [< *techt* 'going' + *i n*- 'in, into'] going in.[548]

6.a.19.36 Ionforb*air*t .i. fas, no bisioc*h*.
Inḟorbairt 'increase', i.e. growing, or increase.[549]

6.a.20.37 Anailge .i. sam*h*laig*h*t*h*e.
Anailge 'analogy', i.e. compared.[550]

6.a.20.38 Éit*h*em*h*lac*hus* .i. cosmúil*acht*, no (no) t*ar*raing [cosmailecht] (colm*hacht*) b*hius* eidir n*et*hib*h*, ⁊ go h-*air*ide *ede*r danaib*h*, no cerduib*h* .⁊c̄.
Fethemlachas 'expert skill', i.e. similarity, or drawing similarity between things and that is particular between poets, or artisans, etc.[551]

6.a.22.39 Coinsi .i. caoin-gn*ús* dia soad*h* g*a*c[h] nda[t]h.
Cuinsiu 'face', i.e. [< *caín* 'fine, good, fair' + *gnúis* 'face'] fair-face towards which each person would turn.[552]

---

546 See the *Tract on Marriage and Divorce* § 34 (CIH 149.27). As discussed in Kelly 2014: 117, the phrase *rusc dairtei* 'receptacle (?) of a yearling heifer' is difficult to interpret. The gloss suggests *rúsc* should be interpreted as 'covering', and perhaps this refers to a shroud or other covering for the dead body; *eDIL s.v. rúsc*.

547 The lemma appears to be a sg. pres. pass. of *fertaid*, although the form suggests a verb similar in shape to *fertaigid*; *eDIL s.v. fertaid* 'makes a burial mound, buries'. Considering the previous entries in the glossary, e.g. 6.a.18.33 RÚSG, it is possible that this entry comes from the *Tract on Marriage and Divorce*.

548 The context of the entry is unknown.

549 For the second gloss, see *eDIL s.v. bisech* 'increase, addition, improvement'.

550 The lemma is understood as a form of *analach*; *eDIL s.v. analach, analag* 'analogy'.

551 For the lemma, see *Uraicecht Becc* (CIH 2277.20; CCIH 315–318). It is possible that *colmacht* is a mistake for *cosmailecht* which makes better sense within the context of the gloss. I owe this suggestion to one of the anonymous readers.

552 The ⟨t⟩ is supplied from O'Curry's transcription. The interpretation of the second part of the gloss is tentative; *eDIL s.v. 1 dath*. For the lemma, see *Bretha Nemed Toísech* (CIH

6.a.22.40 Tet*h*natt*ar* .i. roten*n*sat*ar*, no rot*h*esgsat.
Tethnatar 'they have cut', i.e. they broke, or they destroyed.[553]

6.a.22.41 Foid*h*erc .i. foirreil.
Fodirc 'visible', i.e. clearly visible.[554]

6.a.23.42 Bit*h* .i. guin.
Bíth 'wound', i.e. wound.[555]

6.a.23.43 Cota-imtiagad .i. comaitg*h*eth*ad*(*h*).
Cota-imtiagat 'they accompany them', i.e. they accompany.[556]

6.a.23.44 Taith .i. an gru*th* tait*h*.
Táth 'a kind of cheese', i.e. the pressed curds.[557]

6.a.23.45 Faigneoir .i. cerd cait*h*es an sdan rena f*h*aingnib*h*.
Faigneoir 'scabbard-maker', i.e. an artisan who applies the tin to the scabbards.[558]

2218.10); and see the *Fonnaidh* glossary (CIH 1079.29–31; CCIH 46; and Taylor-Griffiths 2020: 1: 174–179). The entry in Dubhaltach's Glossary closely follows the text in the *Fonnaidh* glossary. It should be noted that Dubhaltach wrote his source as [*ed*]*gedh* immediately preceeding the lemma. It should also be noted that the *Fonnaidh* glossary has the heading *éitged so sis* on TCD MS 1337 [H.3.18], p. 638, *marg. sup.*; Taylor-Griffiths 2020: 1: 174. Cf. O'Cl *Cainse no caoinse .i. ághaidh* 'face'.

553 For the lemma, see *Bretha Nemed Toísech* (CIH 2218.11); and see the *Fonnaidh* glossary (CIH 1079.33; CCIH 46; and Taylor-Griffiths 2020: 1: 174–179). The larger passage from *Bretha Nemed Toísech* (CIH 2218.11) is edited and translated in *Cáin Ónae*, 42. The entry in Dubhaltach's Glossary closely follows the text in the *Fonnaidh* glossary. It should be noted that Dubhaltach wrote his source as [*ed*]*gedh* immediately preceeding the start of this section of the page. It should also be noted that the *Fonnaidh* glossary has the heading *éitged so sis* on TCD MS 1337 [H.3.18], p. 638, *marg. sup.*; Taylor-Griffiths 2020: 1: 174. Cf. 4.c.24.121 TETHN[A]TAR.

554 For the lemma, see *Bretha Nemed Toísech* (CIH 2218.11).

555 See O'Cl *Bíth .i. guin* 'a wound'; *Lec. Gl.* 53: *Bith .i. guin*; "The Glossary in Egerton 158" 708 *bith .i. guin*; and cf. Digest B (57) (CIH 1382.21–22; CCIH 62). The lemma is the vn. of *benaid.* Cf. 7.a.25.37 BÍTH.

556 The lemma is understood as the 3 pl. pres. of *con-imthet* with a Class B 3 pl. object agreement marker; *eDIL s.v. con-imthet* 'accompanies'. The gloss is less straightforward and is understood as a later 3 pl. pres. of *con-éitet* 'goes with, accompanies'; *eDIL s.v. con-éitet.*

557 Cf. 3.b.18.62 TATH.

558 The lemma is not in *eDIL*. It is understood as an agent noun derived from *faigen* 'a sheath, scabbard', thus 'one who makes sheaths, scabbards'; *eDIL s.v. faigen*. For the lemma, cf. distantly *Cáin Íarraith* (CIH 1759.18; AL 2: 146.18; CCIH 288).

6.a.24.46 Ceobat*h* .i. an muir nem*hair*gsion*adh* b*hius* fá c*h*éo.
Ceóbath 'mist-sea', i.e. the sea which is under mist is not easily seen.[559]

6.a.24.47 Do-roac*h*t .i. do-roait*h*ed*h*.
Do-roacht 'came', i.e. went to see.[560]

6.a.24.48 Do-roilg*edh* .i. doro-log[adh].
Do-rolged 'had been forgiven', i.e. had been forgiven.[561]

6.a.25.49 Ad ro-g*r*eim .i. ro ing*r*eim.
Ad ro-grainn 'persecuted', i.e. persecuted.[562]

6.a.25.50 Ad-glenad .i. ad*h*a glanuid*h*, no glenoid, no t*h*eglomuid.
Ad-glennat 'they examine', i.e. [< *ada* 'suitable' + *glanaid* 'cleanses'] suitable he cleanses, or adheres, or brings together.[563]

6.a.25.51 Eigceall .i. d*r*oic*h*iall.
Éccíall 'lack of sense', i.e. lack of sense.[564]

---

559 For the lemma, cf. *Bretha Nemed Toísech* (CIH 2226.1); O'Dav 358 (*Bretha Nemed Toísech*; CCIH 119: *Ceobath .i. muir [beg .i.] inber mbeg .i. muir n-Erenn 7 Alban, [ut est] ar is lethe ler ceobath corbaid* (?) "*Ceobath*, i.e. a small sea, i.e. a little estuary, i.e. the sea of Ireland and Scotland, ut est 'for a mainsea is wider than a *ceobath*…(?)'.") and the second half of 1151 (*Bretha Nemed Toísech*; CCIH 142) which repeats O'Dav 358. Although the entries in O'Dav suggest that the lemma means 'small sea', the gloss provided here states it is a sea covered by mist. The form *nemhairgsionadh* is problematic. It is interpreted as a negative prefix combined with a form of *aircsiu* 'looking on', perhaps an abstract noun; the expansion of the final syllable is uncertain.

560 The lemma is the 3 sg. pret. of *do-roich* 'reaches, comes to, arrives'. The interpretation of the gloss is tentative. It is understood as a 3 sg. pret. of *do-aithig* 'visits, goes to see, frequents'. See *eDIL s.vv. do-roich* and *do-aithig*, respectively. It could also be the case that the gloss is a later variant of the lemma.

561 The missing letters are supplied from O'Curry's transcription. The lemma is understood as a 3 sg. perf. pass. of *do-luigi* 'forgives, remits'. The gloss is understood as a variant of the lemma; *eDIL s.v. do-luigi*.

562 The interpretation of the lemma and gloss is tentative. They are both understood to be 3 sg. pret. forms of *in-greinn* 'persecutes, pursues with hostile intent', cf. vn. *ingreimm*; *eDIL s.v. in-greinn*.

563 The interpretation of the entry is tentative mainly due to the uncertainty of the meaning of the lemma; cf. *eDIL s.v. as-gleinn* 'investigates, examines'. For the etymological gloss, see the Introduction, pp. 13–16.

564 The context of the entry is unknown.

6.a.25.52 G*a*c[h] ae .i. g*a*c*h* og*h*ae dib*h*.
Cech áe 'each of them', i.e. [< *cach* 'each' + *óg*(*a*)*e* 'completeness, wholeness'] each complete person of them.[565]

6.a.26.53 An*m*chaide .i. cait*h*ium*h* an*m*a go h-áit*h* no go h-ad*h*a.
Anmcaide 'life-holiness', i.e. [< *caithem* 'spending, enjoying, consuming' + *ainim* 'life' + *1 áith* 'sharp, keen' + *ada* 'suitable'] spending of life keenly or suitably.[566]

6.a.26.54 Fubtad*h* .i. fodiub*adh* b*e*t*h*a.
Fubthad 'threatening', i.e. deprivation of life.[567]

6.a.26.55 Fuadac*h* do t*a*rr .i. ben torr*a*c[h] fuaid*igius* fer leis.
Fúatach do tharr 'abducting of a belly', i.e. a pregnant woman whom a man carries away with him.[568]

6.a.27.56 Guat*h*asg .i. tasg gúa a len*n*ain, no neic*h* as ionmui*n* le do tab*air*t doc[h]u*m* na mna.
Gáutháse 'false announcement', i.e. giving the woman a false announcement of her spouse, or of anyone who is a beloved person by her.[569]

---

565 The context of the entry is unknown. It is difficult to determine whether to read *oghae* or *ogh ae* in the gloss (or perhaps even *ogae* for *2 áige* 'head (of a family)'). If we read *ogh ae*, it leaves *dibh* stranded as *ae* would have the same meaning in this clause.

566 The interpretation of the lemma is uncertain; cf. O'Dav 470 ((2) no id.; CCIH 122); and *eDIL s.v. anmchairde* 'confessor' where it is queried whether *anmcaide* in O'Dav is for *anmchairde*. It is entirely possible that the lemma here should be corrected to *anmchairde* as well. The phrase *sreath anmchaide* in O'Dav (untranslated by Stokes) is also found in a series of glosses from *Uraicecht Cóel* (CIH 786.14; CCIH 33). I should like to thank one of the anonymous readers for this reference. The gloss, which is etymological, suggests *anm-* should be interpreted as deriving from *eDIL s.v. ainim*(*m*) 'soul, life'. For the etymological gloss, see the Introduction, pp. 13–16. The identification of *áith* as *1 áith* is tentative. *eDIL s.v. ? aith* notes that this word is frequently used in etymological glosses, but no translation is provided; it is unclear whether this should be an entry distinct from *1 áith*. Within the entry here, however, *áith*, like *ada*, is glossing *-id-* within the lemma.

567 Cf. the first part of O'Dav 930 (no id.; CCIH 136: *Fuba .i. fubthad nó fobiubadh* "*Fuba*, i.e. terrifying or undermining."); and O'Cl *Fubtadh .i. bagar* 'a threat'.

568 The entry refers to the abduction of a pregnant woman.

569 The entry refers to a woman who is given false information about her husband or other loved one.

6.a.28.57 Ua*th*b*h*as .i. dub*h*aig*h*ed*h*, no an luc*h* etorra, ⁊ a léne, no an erc luacra do*n*a mnaib ben*us* si*n*.
Úathbás 'terror', i.e. growing dark, or the mouse between her [body] and her tunic, or the lizard for the women who strike that.[570]

6.a.29.58 Mir méne .i. g*r*[*e*]im*h* as mian leis an mnaoi t*h*orr*aigh*.
Mír méine 'a desired morsel', i.e. a morsel which is desired by the pregnant woman.[571]

6.a.29.59 D*r*ut*h*lac*h* .i. laoc*h*d*r*ut[h]a .i. fer l*eth*c*h*ui*nn*.
Drúthlach 'a foolish man', i.e. [< *láech* 'layman' + *2 drúth* 'imbecile'] a male imbecile, i.e. a man of half-sense.[572]

6.a.29.60 Naoi .i. et*har*.
Noe 'boat', i.e. a boat.[573]

6.a.29.61 Fo-glen .i. deg*h*len.
Fo-glen 'adheres', i.e. adheres.[574]

6.a.30.62 Do-*air*r .i. t*arraigh*t[h]er.
Do-airr 'may get', i.e. is seized.[575]

6.a.30.63 Do-ecma .i. tegm*hus*.
Do-ecma 'may happen', i.e. may happen.[576]

---

570 The entry refers to things which induce terror in women, including a dark night, a mouse in the house, and a reptile. The use of 3 pl. *etorra* for expected 3 sg. *etir* is unusual, but it is not uncommon for the plural form to be used in anticipation of the second object when it coordinates with the first; see *eDIL s.v. eter, etir* I (a). The final phrase of the gloss is awkward in that it is difficult to determine whether we should envision women struck by terror or women who are trying to hit the mouse or lizard, although the active verb suggests the latter.

571 The lemma has the later f. gen. sg. of *mían* 'desire, object of desire'. The form of *la* here, i.e. *leis*, in the type of construction found in the gloss is late MI or EMI; *eDIL s.v. la*. The entry refers to a pregnant woman's craving for a particular type of food. For the lemma, see *Cethairślicht Athgabálae* (*CIH* 387.30; *AL* 1: 174.z and 176.1). For pica in medieval Ireland, see *GEIL* 154; and the text on pica translated in Ó Corráin 2002: 33–34 (from *Bretha Éitgid*, *CIH* 940.11–941.24, and 1256.2–1257.37).

572 For the lemma, see *Bretha Nemed Toísech* (*CIH* 2230.4).

573 The context of the entry is unknown.

574 For the lemma, see *eDIL s.v. do-glen* 'clings, cleaves, adheres to'.

575 The lemma is the 3 sg. pres. subj. of *do-airicc* 'comes, finds, gets'; *eDIL s.v. do-airicc*.

576 The lemma is a 3 sg. pres. subj. of *do-ecmaing* 'hits, happens'; the gloss is understood as a

6.a.30.64 S*édr*a*c*[h] .i. t*r*en, nertma*r*.
Sedrach 'vigorous', i.e. strong, vigorous.[577]

6.a.30.65 Iomaig*h* .i. iomain.
Imm-aig 'drives', i.e. driving.[578]

6.a.30.66 Ad-rire .i. iocaid*h*.
As-riri 'may pay', i.e. pays.[579]

6.a.30.67 Urnasg .i. ua[sal]-fonasg.
Airnasc 'bond', i.e. [< *úasal* 'high, noble' + *fonasc* 'tie, bond'] noble-bond.[580]

6.a.31.68 Taisealb*adh* .i. taisben*adh*.
Taiselbad 'showing', i.e. showing.[581]

6.a.31.69 U*r*co*n*n .i. uas*a*l-c*h*odn*a*c[h].
Airchonn 'person of rank', i.e. [< *úasal* 'high, noble' + *codnach* 'adult, lord'] noble-lord.[582]

6.a.31.70 Ni h-ois .i. na faom*h*, ni h-og*har* .[i.] ní faomt*har*.
Ní h-ais 'you may not lend', i.e. do not accept, is not lent, i.e. is not accepted.[583]

---

later 3 sg. pres. subj. form of the same verb. See O'Don. Suppl. *s.v. eacmaic, ecmaing* where the gloss is translated as 'that happens'.

577 The lemma is not in *eDIL*, but cf. *s.v. 2 sedlach* 'vigorous (?)'.

578 Cf. 1.b.3.50 IOMAIGH. The gloss is the vn. of the lemma.

579 The lemma as it stands in the MS is the 2 sg. fut. of *as-ren* 'pays', however the gloss is the 3 sg. pres. ind. of *íccaid* 'pays'. The lemma has been edited to the 3 sg. fut. to match the gloss; it is not uncommon for ⟨e⟩ and ⟨i⟩ to be used interchangeably in later orthography. See *eDIL s.vv. as-ren* and *1 íccaid*. Cf. 6.a.4.15 AD-REN.

580 The missing letters are supplied from O'Curry's transcription. Although the primary meaning of *airnasc* is 'ring, collar', it likely means 'bond' here; *eDIL s.v. airnasc*. For the lemma, see *Cáin Ḟuithirbe* (*CIH* 772.12; *CCIH* 212–218); this extract is not included in the edited portions of the text. For the etymological gloss, see the Introduction, pp. 13–16.

581 See O'Cl *Taisealbadh .i. taisbhénadh* 'showing'.

582 For the etymological gloss, see the Introduction, pp. 13–16. See *Cethairṡlicht Athgabálae* (*CIH* 410.29 and 32; *AL* 1: 258.26 and 272.27).

583 The lemma is understood as a 2 sg. pres. subj. of *oidid* 'lends, offers'.

6.a.32.71 T*airi*d*h*in lin*n*e muilin*n* .i. clad*h* con*n*m*hus* an t-*us*ge leisi*n* muilean[n].
Tairiden linne muilinn 'watercourse of a mill pond', i.e. a ditch which contains the water for the mill.[584]

6.a.32.72 Clad*h* fot*h*[*b*]aid*h* mona .i. gáin*n*ir mona.
Clad fótbaig móna 'ditch of a turf-bog', i.e. [?] of peat.[585]

6.a.33.73 Ap[th]ain .i. ebiltin.
Apthain 'death', i.e. death.[586]

6.a.33.74 *Árchú* lom*h*na .i. cu *ar*a mbi lomán da cengal.
Árchú lomna 'leashed slaughter-hound (guard dog)', i.e. a dog on whom there is a leash for binding it.[587]

6.a.33.75 Ruib do-meal*ar* .i. ba, ⁊ caoir[e].
Rop do-melar 'an animal which is eaten', i.e. cows and sheep.[588]

6.a.34.76 Ruib na doi*m*eal*ar* .i. capuill, ⁊ muca.
Rop ná tomelar 'an animal which is not eaten', i.e. horses and pigs.[589]

---

584 Cf. *Coibnes Uisci Thairidne*, p. 76 (*CIH* 458.36; *AL* 4: 218.29; *CCIH* 296). The verb *connmhus* is understood as the 3 sg. pres. rel. of *coinnmid*, a later simplex of *con-gaib* 'contains, maintains, supports, keeps'; *eDIL s.v. con-gaib*. See O'Don. Suppl. *s.v. tairidin*.

585 For the lemma, see *Coibnes Uisci Thairidne*, §13 (*CIH* 461.29–30; *AL* 4: 220.10; *CCIH* 296). For a discussion of turf-cutting in medieval Ireland, see *EIF* 396–397. The interpretation of *gáinnir* is obscure.

586 Cf. 10.15.33 APTHA. The lemma is the gen. sg. of the vn. of *ad-bath* (see *at-bail(l)*); *DIL s.v. apthu*. The gloss appears to be the dat. sg. of *epeltu*, the vn. of *at-bail(l)*. For the gloss, cf. *CIH* 700.13 (a text on wounding) which Breatnach 2005a: 30 characterizes as "late" (*CCIH* 30).

587 Cf. 10.19.48 ÁRCHU. See *Cethairślicht Athgabálae* (*CIH* 402.8 and 18–19; *AL* 1: 232.4 and 234.25–27); and *EIF* 114–117. See O'Cl *Archu .i. cú bhios ceangailti* 'a dog that is chained'.

588 Cf. 9.13.37 RUIB DO-MEALAR and 9.13.38 RUIB NÁ TO-MEALAR. See the *Mat* glossary (*CIH* 1566.1–2; *CCIH* 69; and Taylor-Griffiths 2020: 1: 188–190).

589 Cf. 9.13.37 RUIB DO-MEALAR and 9.13.38 RUIB NÁ TO-MEALAR. See the *Mat* glossary (*CIH* 1566.2–3; *CCIH* 69; and Taylor-Griffiths 2020: 1: 188–190). This entry and the preceding one should be understood within the context of prohibited and non-prohibited goods in the Bible; see Deuteronomy 14: 4–6 and Leviticus 11: 3. The rule is that animals with cloven hooves which chew their cud are permitted to be eaten, others are not. Pigs were an important part of the medieval Irish economy and were regularly eaten; see *EIF* 79–88.

6.a.34.77 Féisi .i. muc.
Feisi 'sows', i.e. a pig.[590]

6.a.34.78 Citriug, ⁊ treteall .i. an*m*an*n*a do caoir*ibh*.
Citriog, ⁊ tretall '*citriog* and *tretall*', i.e. names for sheep.[591]

6.a.35.79 Tasc*ar*t*h*a .i. an cait*h*cliat*h*.
Tascartha 'things cast up', i.e. bulwark.[592]

6.a.35.80 Forcraid*h*, aigbele, ⁊ *ét*toll*us* .i. lo*ch*t*a* na ndénta n*a*c[h] dioráit*h*.
Forcraid, aicbéile, ⁊ etallas 'excess, danger, and defect', i.e. the occupants of the buildings which are not lawfully constructed.[593]

6.a.35.81 Coib*h*dealac[h] [.i.] duine aga *m*bí coi*m*d*h*eala, no gaol re nec*h*.
Coibdelach 'relative', i.e. a person with whom there may be kinship, or a relationship with someone.[594]

6.a.36.82 Am*h*uis rúin, ⁊ raid*h*, ⁊ iomagall[ma] .i. am*h*uis ⟨bid⟩ ma*r* si*n* ag tigerna.
Amuis ruin, ⁊ raid, ⁊ imacallma 'confidential, and conversational, and council attendants', i.e. attendants like that whom a lord has.[595]

6.a.37.83 Ro-rir .i. do-rorec.
Ro-rir 'sold', i.e. sold.[596]

---

590 For the lemma, see *Cethairšlicht Athgabálae* (CIH 375.12; AL 1: 140.37); and cf. O'Dav 1026 ((2) no id.; CCIH 138). See *eDIL s.v. 1 feis* 'sow'.

591 Cf. 9.26.80 CITRIOGHA. On the importance of sheep in medieval Ireland, see EIF 67–77. It is possible that *treteall* is for *treitell* 'pet, favorite'; *eDIL s.v. treitell*; and EIF 125.

592 The lemma is understood as the nom. pl. of *tascar* 'stuff cast up by the sea, gear, belongings'; *eDIL s.v. turscur, tascar*. The entry is difficult to interpret, but the general sense provided by the gloss is of a defensive mound of belongings or things cast up by the sea. For the lemma, cf. CIH 864.25 which is from a collection of citations and glosses from various sources (CCIH 39).

593 See *Bretha Éitgid* (CIH 931.28–29; AL 3: 166.19–20).

594 Cf. 4.b.19.29 COIBHDEALACH.

595 For the lemma, see *Uraicecht Becc* (CIH 1607.22; AL 5: 72.24; CCIH 70). The form *amhuis* could be gen. sg. or nom. pl.; *eDIL s.v. amus* 'hireling, attendant, mercenary'. The translation of the lemma is tentative. Cf. 9.41.123 AMHUS ALA TUAITHE.

596 The lemma is the 3 sg. pret. of *renaid* 'sells, barters, exchanges'. The gloss is understood as a later 3 sg. pret. of *reccaid* 'sells, barters, exchanges'; see *eDIL s.vv. renaid* and *1 rec(c)aid*, respectively.

6.a.37.84 Ni ria .i. na rec.
Ní ria 'you may not sell', i.e. do not sell.[597]

6.a.37.85 Ar-aid*he* .i. *ar* son.
Ar-aide 'because of', i.e. because of.[598]

6.a.37.86 Dénm*hech* .i. dis*h*om*h*aoinec*h*.
Dénmech 'unprofitable', i.e. [< *dí-* negative prefix + *somaínech* 'profitable, precious, valuable'] unprofitable.[599]

6.b.1.87 *Air*benat*har* .i. ion*nar*bt[h]*ar*.
Airbenathar 'is expelled', i.e. is expelled.[600]

6.b.1.88 Frio*th*aige .i. fior-ion*n*saig*h*id*h*.
Frithaigid 'counter-claim', i.e. [< *fír* 'truly' + *indsaigid* 'approaching, seeking, claiming'] truly-claiming.[601]

6.b.1.89 Sich .i. ionsaig*h*id*h*.
Sich 'declared', i.e. claiming.[602]

6.b.1.90 Aill .i. uasal.
All 'cliff', i.e. high.[603]

---

597 The lemma is understood as the 2 sg. pres. subj. of *renaid* 'sells, barters, exchanges' used with jussive meaning. The gloss is understood as a 2 sg. impv. of *reccaid* 'sells, barters, exchanges'; see *eDIL s.vv. renaid* and *1 rec(c)aid*, respectively.

598 For the lemma, see *eDIL s.v. 3 aí.*

599 The interpretation of the lemma is tentative. It appears to be the antonym of *2 soinmech* 'prosperity'. For the lemma, see *Bretha Éitgid* (CIH 937.22; CCIH 41).

600 The interpretation of the entry is tentative. The lemma appears to be a 3 sg. pres. pass. of *ind-árban* 'drives out, expels, rejects' without the preverb. The gloss is a 3 sg. pres. pass. of *indarbaid*, a later simplex of *ind-árban*; *eDIL s.v. ind-árban.*

601 See the section on counter-claims at CIH 1199.31 and 36 (CCIH 50); *eDIL s.v. frithaigid* 'encountering, disallowal, counterplea'. For the etymological gloss, see the Introduction, pp. 13–16.

602 The lemma is the 3 sg. pret. of *seichid* 'assets, declares'. Cf. 6.b.1.88 FRIOTHAIGE which also has the same gloss. I should like to thank one of the anonymous readers for comments on this entry.

603 See *Lec. Gl.* 35 *Aill .i. uasal* and 202 *Aill .i. uasal*; O'Dav 65 (no id.; CCIH 110: *Aill .i. uassal, ut est aill for breth, breth for enech .i. is uasal in brethemnus brethemhnus forsna eneclannuibh* "*Aill*, i.e. noble, ut est 'a noble decree is a judgment of honour', i.e. noble is the decree, a decree on the honour-price."); and *eDIL s.v. 1 all* 'cliff, foundation, basis'. It is possible that the meaning of *all* has broadened to include anything high, lofty, and, thus, noble.

6.b.2.91 Tem*h*ad tem*r*ac*h*a .i. eblid na h-uaisle.
Temad temracha 'death of a noble person', i.e. death of the noble.[604]

6.b.2.92 Fu[i]reg*ar* .i. *air*git[h]*er*.
Fuiregar 'is bound', i.e. is bound.[605]

6.b.2.93 Forb*h*ac*h* .i. forb*h*uain .i. ní ben*us* ri t*ar* dlig*h*[edh] ⟨da che[le]⟩.
Forbach 'extortion', i.e. exaction, i.e. anything a king takes away beyond that which he is entitled from his client.[606]

6.b.3.94 Conai*meacht* .i. do caoin ai*m*sig*edh*.
Conaimeacht 'with hostility', i.e. for [< *caín* 'fine, well' + *aimsiged* 'striking, pleading'] fine-striking.[607]

6.b.3.95 Com*h*ad*h* .i. coi*m*[eada]d*h*.
Comad 'guarding', i.e. guarding.[608]

---

604 The interpretation of the entry is tentative. The form *temhad* is understood as the vn. of *temaid* 'dies' followed by the gen. sg. of *temrach*, an adj. derived from *temair* 'high place, eminence' used substantively, thus, 'a preeminent person'; *eDIL s.vv. ? temaid* and *temair*. See the discussion on *rotemadh* in Talyor-Griffiths 2020: 1: 242. The word *eblid* is understood as a vn. of *eplaid* 'dies', a later simplex of *at-bail*; *eDIL s.v. at-bail(l)*. For the first part of the lemma, cf. distantly O'Dav 1554 (*Bretha Nemed Dédenach*; CCIH 154); *Bretha Nemed Dédenach* 19.30 (CIH 1115.38; CCIH 184–188); and the *Adhmad* glossary (CIH 954.9; Taylor-Griffiths 2020: 2: 57 and see discussion in 1: 227–251). Cf. 2.a.15.54 TEMRACHA. For a summary of the ongoing discussions regarding the interpretation of *temair*, see Russell 1988: 15; Mac Giolla Easpaig 2005; Ó Muraíle 2005; Ní Mhaonaigh 2022: 216–218; and Theuerkauf 2024a; and cf. Theuerkauf 2024b.

605 The missing letter is supplied from O'Curry's transcription. The lemma is understood as the 3 sg. pres. pass. of *fo-rig* 'detains, keeps, binds'. The gloss is understood as the 3 sg. pres. pass. of *ad-rig* 'binds'; *eDIL s.vv. fo-rig* and *ad-rig*, respectively. See *Bretha Comaithchesa* (CIH 76.31 and 36; *Bretha Comaithcheso* §18, gloss e; AL 4: 128.13 and 130.8).

606 The missing letters are supplied from O'Curry's transcription. Cf. 6.a.1.1 [FORBUAIN] INDLIG[GTHEACH], NO FORRGE, NO FORRACH INDLIG[HTHEACH].

607 The lemma might be corrupt which is why it is left as it reads in the MS. It might be a compound of *co-* 'with' and *námadach* 'hostile, inimical'; *eDIL s.v. námadach*. For the etymological gloss, see the Introduction, pp. 13–16.

608 The missing letters are supplied from O'Curry's transcription. The vn. *comad* has a range of meanings including 'keeping, guarding, preserving'; *eDIL s.vv. 1 comad* and *con-oí*. The MS form *coimheadadh* is interpreted as a vn. of *coimétaid* 'keeps, guards'; *eDIL s.v. 1 coimétaid*. Cf. 8.6.18 COMHAD. Cf. *Cethairṡlicht Athgabálae* (CIH 415.18 and gloss 8, 415.29–31, AL 1: 284.40).

6.b.3.96 Forcmad*h* .i. fiorcoim*h*[eadadh].
Forcmad 'keeping', i.e. [< *fír* 'truly' + *coimétad* 'keeping'] truly-keeping.[609]

7.a.1.1 Feiste .i. tioru*air*si .i. i*ar*draig*he*.
Feistid 'heir', i.e. remainder, i.e. children.[610]

7.a.1.2 Bá .i. m*aith*.
Bá 'benefit', i.e. good.[611]

7.a.2.3 I*m*bed .i. [is] e briug*hus* baoisi .i. bág*h* [no] iom*a*d baoisi.
Imbed 'abundance', i.e. it is an abundance of folly, i.e. boast or excess of folly.[612]

---

609 The missing letters are supplied from O'Curry's transcription. The lemma is interpreted as a vn. of *forcmaid*, a later simplex of *for-comai* 'keeps, preserves'; *eDIL s.v. for-comai.* The MS form *coimheadadh* is interpreted as a vn. of *coimétaid* 'keeps, guards'; *eDIL s.v. 1 coimétaid.*

610 See the last part of O'Dav 1257 (*Cáin Ṡóerraith*; CCIH 145: *Meisi…feissti .i. tiruairsi.* "*Meisi…feissti*, i.e. a remnant.") and the first part of 896 (*Bretha Nemed Toísech*; CCIH 134: *Feistidh no deisti .i. tiruairsi… Fesitid* or *deisti*, i.e. remainder…) where *feistid* 'a residuary legatee, heir' and *deisti* 'remnant', are given as variants of the same lemma; cf. 8.27.73 DÉIS, 7.a.3.4 DÉISTE, and 14.h.12.35 DÉISDE, FESDHIDE, NO ESDIDE. The F version of O'Dav states that *Dúil Roscadach* is the source for the remainder of the gloss (CCIH 251). Stokes 1904: 347, suggests that *festid* means "1. What English lawyers call a personal representative, and 2. The debts due to the deceased." O'Rahilly 1913: 285–286 suggests that *feiste* (which might not be the actual lemma here) is from ME *feste* 'firm, fixed, secure'; see also *eDIL s.vv. feiste* and *festid.* The glosses suggest the lemma is not the ME loanword *feiste*. *Tioruairsi* refers to anyone or anything which remains, whether it be physical remains, such as relics, or a person who remains after the death of a family member or lord. *Iardraighe* refers to any 'issue, offspring' or those who remain to inherit; *eDIL s.v. íartaige, íardaige, íardraige, íardraoi.* A possible source for the entry is CIH 1461.14–23, which is part of a selection of citations and commentary from *Di Choimét Dligthech.* Although *feiste* does not appear in either the quoted tract or commentary, *deiste* and *tiruairsi* do (CCIH 65 and 287–288).

611 The last word of the entry is *maith*, but O'Curry misses the head word in the *marg. sin.* at the start of the line below, thus combining this entry with that of 7.a.2.3 IMBED. See O'Cl *Ba .i. maith* 'good'; and for the lemma cf. O'Dav 279 (*Tract on Marriage and Divorce* and *Cáin Íarraith*; CCIH 116–117). Miller 1879–1880: 369 lists *Fél.* Nov. 13 as a reference for the entry in O'Cl, but there is nothing relevant in *Fél.* under that date. It could be that the editor was linking the O'Cl lemma to the variant *ba* of *ma* in the *Leabhar Breac* version of that text.

612 The word *no* is supplied from O'Curry's transcription. For the first part of the gloss, see O'Dav 266 (no id., but also in *MG* §272; CCIH 116: *Briughus .i. umat, ut est ar is é briughus baisi i[n]sin na tét i mba* "*Briugus*, i.e. abundance, ut est 'for that is an abundance of folly that goes not into…'"); and *MG* §272; and for the gloss also cf. O'Dav 196 (*Bretha Nemed*

7.a.3.4 Déiste .i. déis as ed tioru*air*sin béos.
Deistiu 'remnant', i.e. a tenant who is still a remainder.[613]

7.a.4.5 Grio*th* .i. crio*th*nug*hadh*.
Grith 'shaking', i.e. shaking.[614]

7.a.4.6 Gu*air*iug*hadh* .i. g*air*iug*adh* .i. denam g*arrth*a no éigh[m]e.
Gúairiugud 'false imprisonment', i.e. shouting, i.e. shouting or screaming.[615]

7.a.6.7 T*ar*gad .i. tionol.
Tárcud 'collecting', i.e. gathering.[616]

7.a.6.8 F*air*ge .i. at*h*t*air*git*h*er.
Fairge 'is offered', i.e. is paid.[617]

Toísech). This entry is difficult for a number of paleographical reasons. The first is that the reading of the lemma is not secure. The second is that it is difficult to determine whether the ⟨e⟩ at the start of the entry is meant to be a 3 sg. m. indep. pron., or whether it is meant to be a negative prefix. It is likely that it is meant to be interpreted as a pronoun due to the fact that a similar entry in O'Dav 266 has *ut est ar is é briughus baisi*; see also *MG* § 272. It is also possible that the ⟨e⟩ was meant to be crossed out as there is a lot of extra ink around the letter; it could be that the ⟨e⟩ was written over another letter.

613 For the lemma, see the first part of O'Dav 896 (*Bretha Nemed Toísech*; CCIH 134: *Feistidh no deisti .i. tiruairsi*… "*Fesitid* or *deisti*, i.e. remainder…"). The F version of O'Dav 896 states that *Dúil Roscadach* is the source for the remainder of the gloss (CCIH 251). It is also possible to translate the entry as 'land which is still a remainder'. The length mark in the lemma is likely based on analogy with *déis* 'tenant, land' which follows it. *Tioruairsin* refers to anyone or anything which remains, whether it be physical remains, such as relics, or a person who remains after the death of a family member or lord. The *n*-stem ending is unexpected, but it is possible that there has been confusion between *tiruairse* and original *n*-stem *túairse* as both words have overlapping meaning. A possible source for the entry is CIH 1461.14–23, which is part of a selection of citations and commentary from *Di Choimét Dligthech*, although it should be noted that the entry itself is not an exact match for either the quoted tract or commentary. This entry concerns inheritance. Cf. 8.27.73 DÉIS, 7.a.1.1 FEISTE, and 14.h.12.35 DÉISDE, FESDHIDE, NO ESDIDE.

614 See *eDIL s.vv. 1 grith* and *crithnugud, crithugud*. *Grith* is often confused for *crith* 'trembling'.

615 See *eDIL s.v. gúairiugud*. *eDIL* proposes an etymology of the lemma as consisting of *gú* 'false' + *airíadad* 'excluding, barring'. The lemma also is found in the *Ni Tulach* glossary (CIH 811.30), the *Arra* glossary (CIH 1559.33), at CIH 2080.41 (citations on assault; CCIH 83), and in *Bretha Nemed Toísech* (CIH 2218.38). None of these citations preserve the entry as it is found here. The entry seems to be making an etymological link between the elements *gúair-* and *gáir-* 'cry', i.e. the cries of grief that a falsely imprisoned person makes.

616 See O'Cl *Targadh .i. tionól, no cruinniughadh* 'a congregation or gathering'.

617 The lemma is problematic. It appears to be derived from a simplex of the verb *do-fairget*

7.a.7.9 Aid*h*ilgn*ech* .i. dlig*h*t*h*e*ch*.
Aidilccnech 'needy', i.e. lawful.[618]

7.a.7.10 Aid*h*b*h*en .i. ad*h*b*ha* d*h*íona.
Aidbden 'representative', i.e. [< *adba* 'abode' + *dín* 'protection'] abode of protection.[619]

7.a.8.11 Fórm*ac*[h] ⁊ tórm*ac*[h] .i. m*é*tug*hadh*.
Fórmach ⁊ *tórmach* 'increase and increment', i.e. increasing.[620]

7.a.8.12 Tiug*h*ragac*h* .i. t*air*ged*h*ac*h* ag*h*ac*h* .i. fer t*h*ionoilte g*h*niom*ha* t*air*.
Tiugradach 'causing damage', i.e. [< *táircedach* 'causing' + *ágach* 'warlike, given to fighting'] causing fighting, i.e. a man mustered for causing insult.[621]

7.a.10.13 Meallac*h* .i. aoibin*n*.
Mellach 'pleasant', i.e. delightful.[622]

'offers', but the regular simplex of this verb is *taircid*; cf. *feraid* 'grants, supplies'. The translation of the lemma is based on the meaning of the gloss. *Attairgid* 'pays, repays, renders; assembles' is itself formed from *ath* and *tairgid*, according to *eDIL s.v. attairgid*. It should also be noted that some forms of the vb. *do-fairget* appear as *targad* which is the lemma immediately before this entry in the manuscript; cf. 7.a.6.7 TARGAD. See O'Dav 887 (3) (*Bretha Éitgid*; CCIH 134: *Feraid…ferga .i. atairgither*. "*Feraid*…[…], i.e. is paid back.")

618 The lemma also is found in the *Ni Tulach* glossary (CIH 811.30) and the *Arra* glossary (CIH 1559.33). It is possible that the gloss is meant to be etymological, but it is not obvious.

619 See O'Cl *Aidhbhean .i.adhbha dhíona, no teughdhais dhíona* 'abode'; and for the lemma cf. O'Dav 185 (no id.; CCIH 114); and MG § 244. The *aidbden* was a noble whose duty it was to act as an intermediary between his lord and a lord of higher status; Thurneysen 1928: 23 and 62; and cf. *Críth Gablach* l. 412.

620 See the first half of O'Cl *Fórmach .i. tórmach .i. médughadh* 'increase'. *eDIL s.v. formach* suggests that the lemma in O'Cl is derived from the verb *do-formaig* whose regular vn. is *tormach*. The source of the text accompanying the entry in O'Cl has not been identified.

621 *Tiugradach* appears to be derived from *tiugrad*, which is defined by *eDIL* as 'last person responsible (?); person who causes damage through negligence or who does not interfere to avert it'. The meaning here is rather more abstract and hinges on the sense of causing damage while not actually doing the injury itself. The phrase *tairgedhach aghach* etymologizes ⟨-agach⟩ in *tiughragach* as 'warlike, given to war', and the entry uses the circumstance of assembling men for fighting as an example of the lemma's meaning; see Dinneen, *s.v. -tairgeadhach*. One would expect the gen. sg. of *ágach* rather than the nom., but it is also possible that the form is gen. pl. *tionoilte* is the part. of *do-inóla* 'gathers, musters, assembles'.

622 See O'Cl *Meallach .i. aoibhinn* 'delightful'. The lemma also is found in the *Ni Tulach* glossary (CIH 811.32) and the *Arra* glossary (CIH 1559.35).

7.a.10.14 Dinnis .i. mionna.
Dindis 'denial by oath', i.e. oaths.[623]

7.a.11.15 Io*ch*t .i. gniom*h*.
Icht 'deed', i.e. act.[624]

7.a.11.16 Siniomon .i. sen som*h*aoin*e*c[h].
Siniomon 'cinnamon', i.e. [< *sen* 'old' + *somaínech* 'profitable, valuable'] an old valuable item.[625]

7.a.12.17 S*h*eall ⁊ sell .i. am*har*c.
Seall 'glance' and *sell* 'glance', i.e. looking.[626]

7.a.12.18 Brot*h*sguad*h* .i. brut*h* sgeit*hius* an f*hair*rge.
Brodscuad 'rubbish', i.e. [< 1 *bruth* 'heat, mass, fury, boiling' or *1 brod* 'bit of straw', + *sceïd* 'vomits, spews'] bits of rubbish which the sea spews up.[627]

7.a.13.19 Bérd*air* .i. b*reith*emn*agt*er.
Bertair 'are judged', i.e. are judged.[628]

---

623 See O'Cl *Dinnis .i. luighe, no mionna* 'an oath'; for the lemma, cf. the first part of O'Dav 739 (*Bretha Éitgid*; CCIH 130: *Dinnis .i. luighe…* "*Dinnis*, i.e. oath…"); and *Metr. Gl.* 23 § 10 *'Duine' ainm do luighe lán*. For discussion of denial by oath, see *GEIL* 200–201. Cf. 3.b.11.46 DINNIS.

624 For the equation of *icht* and *gním*, see *SC* Y.891; and cf. *Cóic Conara Fugill* H § 14.

625 The word *siniomon* is either a loan from English 'cinnamon' or Latin 'cinnamomum'; see *eDIL s.vv. cinamon* and *sinomum*, respectively. The gloss is etymologizing the element *sin* of the lemma as OI *sen* 'old'.

626 The two lemmata are variant spellings of each other. The lenition of the first lemma in the entry is unexpected, but it should be borne in mind that the entry was extracted from a lenited context in its source text.

627 Cf. *sceith*, which is used specifically of that which the sea casts forth. The entry refers to items of refuse, such as foam, vegetation, or rubbish, which the sea has cast ashore. For the lemma and a similar explanation of the lemma, cf. O'Dav 270 (no id.; *CCIH* 116: *Brotscuad .i. spreigal, ut est brotscuadh la feirge feidm .i. amail spreigal na fairrgi is amlaid ata in atber sim in tan bis go feirg* "*Brodscuad*, i.e. rubbish, ut est 'rubbish produced by the working of anger (but perhaps read *fairrge* 'sea')', i.e. what he says when he is angry is thus, like the rubbish of the sea." where the 'he' may refer to a *dóerbard*; see *Bretha Nemed Dédenach; CIH* 1132.30 where the lemma is used disparagingly of the compositions of the *dóerbard*, a type of law-status poet). I owe the identification of the O'Dav entry to Paul Russell. Cf. OM 765: *Is brod scuad .i. is brodsce úan*. 'It is *brod scuad* 'rubbish?', i.e. the foam is … (?)'.

628 The length mark in the MS could be a suspension mark. For *breithemnagter*, see *eDIL s.v. brithemnaigid*.

7.a.14.20 Fúirest*ar* .i. *air*gid*h*ter .i. geib*h*ter.
Fuirestar 'is bound', i.e. is bound, i.e. is restrained.[629]

7.a.14.21 Biora .i. b*reith*em*h*n*aidh*.
Bera 'judge', i.e. judge.[630]

7.a.15.22 Briog*h* ⁊ briog*h*t[h]*ar* .i. fírén*aigh*t*h*er.
Bríg 'authority' and *brigthar* 'is judged', i.e. is justified.[631]

7.a.16.23 Torgaib*h* .i. do rin*ne* t*or*gabail cionad*h*.
Torgaib [*do-rogaib*] 'he commits a crime', i.e. he committed a crime.[632]

7.a.17.24 Sochla .i. soc*h*lad*h*, no soc*h*lú.
Sochla 'renowned', i.e. renowned, or renown.[633]

7.a.17.25 Eisil .i. eiséolac*h* .i. ainéolac*h*.
Essel 'ignorant', i.e. without knowledge, i.e. ignorant.[634]

7.a.18.26 Cám*h* .i. cáinte.
Cám, i.e. satirist.[635]

---

629 The lemma is a sg. pres. pass. subj. form of *fo-rig* 'detains, prolongs, binds'. *Airgidhter* is likely a sg. pres. pass. subj. form of *ad-rig* 'binds', and *geibhter* is likely a sg. pres. pass. subj. form of *gaibid*; see *eDIL s.vv. fo-rig, ad-rig,* and *gaibid.* For the lemma, cf. the gloss in O'Dav 826 ((1) *Di Astud Chirt 7 Dligid*). Cf. 8.13.34 FUIREGAR and 2.a.7.27 FUIRECHT.

630 See *eDIL s.v. ? bera;* and "The Glossary in Egerton 158" 750 *Beara*, 'a judge'. The gloss is understood as possibly an agent noun of *breth* or one of its derivatives, thus 'one who judges'.

631 The first lemma also is found in the *Ni Tulach* glossary (CIH 811.31) and the *Arra* glossary (CIH 1559.34). For the first lemma, cf O'Dav 297 (no id.) where it has a different meaning. For the second lemma, see 268 (no id.: *Brighther .i. raiter no brithemnaigther, ut est crolí bais brighther do cach iarna miadh "Brighter*, i.e. is said or is judged, ut est '(a fine for) death-maim is adjudged to every one according to his dignity'."). For the second lemma, see also *Bretha Nemed Dédenach* 41.7 (CIH 1130.25; CCIH 184–188; Corthals 2010: 77 and 80 where it is translated as 'be asserted'; see the note on 87).

632 For the lemma, see *eDIL s.v. do-rogaib.*

633 The form *sochlú* reflects the etymology of *sochla* as *so* 'good' and *clú* 'reputation'; *eDIL s.v.* 1 *sochla.* See O'Cl *Sochla .i. sochéillidh, no sochlú-ach* 'sensible, or renowned'; and for the lemma, cf. O'Dav 1422 (*Bretha Nemed Toísech*; CCIH 150). The form *sochladh* is unexplained. It is possible that Dubhaltach misread his source text (or that the source text already contained the mistake); the intended form might *sochlach* 'famous, renowned'.

634 See O'Cl *Eisil .i. eiséolach, no nemheolach* 'ignorant'.

635 See DDC *Cámh .i. cainte.* For satire in medieval Ireland, see McLaughlin 2008.

7.a.19.27 Éiri*the* .i. ioctha.
Éirithe 'paid', i.e. paid.[636]

7.a.19.28 Fo-coisli*the*r .i. foxl*aigh*t*er* .i. sg*ar*ad*h* le ní, no diog*h*bal*aigh*ter.
Fo-coislither 'is carried off', i.e. is taken away, i.e. parting with anything, or is taken away.[637]

7.a.21.29 Do-n-egaid .i. feduid.
Do-n-egat 'that they lead off', i.e. they lead.[638]

7.a.21.30 Fris-gab*h*aid .i. abstinent.
Fris-gabat 'they resist', i.e. *abstinent* 'they abstain'.[639]

7.a.22.31 Sas*ar* .i. ionsoig*h*t[h[*er*.
Sasar 'may be claimed', i.e. may be claimed.[640]

7.a.22.32 Don*n* .i. goid.
Donn 'theft', i.e. theft.[641]

---

636 The form *éirithe* is the past part. of *as-ren* 'pays'. It should be noted that the lemma preserves the older participle stem without the nasal; *eDIL s.vv. as-ren* and *érnid*. The form *ioctha* is the past part. of *íccaid* 'pays'.

637 The form *diogbalaighter* is likely a pres. pass. sg. of verb **dígbálaigid*, derived from *dígbál*, the vn. of *do-gaib* 'takes away, removes, lessens, diminishes'.

638 The lemma is likely a 3 pl. pres. act. ind. of *do-aig* 'drives off, drives away'. The nasalization could arise from an infixed pron. or from the lemma being extracted from a nasalizing context, such as a nasalizing relative clause. The ending *-id* for OI *-at*, but cf. 7.a.21.30 FRIS-GABHAID where the gloss suggests that the verb should be 3 pl. On the use of *-d* for *-t* see *goid* for *gait*, 7.a.22.32 DONN. The form *feduid* is interpreted as the 3 pl. pres. act. ind. of *feidid* with 3 pl. *-id* for *-at*.

639 The ending of the lemma is interpreted as 3 pl. pres. act. ind. for OI *-at*. The form could also be 2 pl., but that interpretation is not supported by the gloss. On the use of *-d* for *-t* see also *goid* for *gait*, 7.a.22.32 DONN. It should be noted that the meaning of the lemma is provided by Latin *abstinent*, a 3 pl. pres. act. ind. of *abstinēre*. Cf. 7.a.21.29 DO-N-EGAID.

640 The lemma and definition are from *saigid* and *ind-saig*, respectively; *eDIL s.vv.* 1 *saigid* and *ind-saig ?*. For the gloss, cf. O'Dav 1469 (*Di Astud Chirt 7 Dligid*; CCIH 151).

641 See O'Dav 704 (*Cáin Aicillne*; CCIH 129: *Donn .i. flaithemnus no gait, ut est ar trian a duinn 7 a mesci .i. trian in neich tuilles a dond a flaithemnas do, nó trian na herca atá a ngait a seoit* "*Donn*, i.e. chiefship or theft, ut est 'for the third of his *donn* and his drunkenness', i.e. the third of what his *donn*, his chiefship, entitles him to: of the third of the eric which is due for stealing his treasure (at a banquet, when he is intoxicated).") and the gloss in 1587 (no id.; CCIH 155: *Torcla .i. cluinsin, ut est do neoch forsa torclaither donn nó taidhe riamh 7rl. .i. forsa cluinter gait* "*Torchla*, i.e. a hearing, ut est 'to anyone of whom pilfering or theft may have been heard previously' etc., i.e. of whom stealing is heard."). *Goid* is for OI *gait*.

7.a.23.33 Do*nn*uig*h*e, do*nn*ac*h* .i. gaduig*h*e.
Donnaige 'thievishness', *donnach* 'thief', i.e. thief.[642]

7.a.23.34 Líu, lia .i. liom*h*nad*h*.
Líu, lía 'I accuse', i.e. accusing.[643]

7.a.24.35 Oillían .i. léine m*h*ór.
Ollín 'item of clothing', i.e. large linen cloth.[644]

7.a.24.36 Culpait .i. coiler ut [est] cail coim*hét*, ⁊ pait .i. cenn.
Culpait 'hood', i.e. *coilér* 'collar' *ut est cail* means 'protection', and *pait* 'pate', i.e. head.[645]

7.a.25.37 Bít*h* .i. gui*n*.
Bíth 'wound', i.e. wound.[646]

7.a.26.38 Faot*h*, aot*h* .i. mion*na*.
Fáeth 'oath', *óeth* 'oath', i.e. oaths.[647]

---

642 For the first lemma and more distantly the gloss, cf. O'Dav 1588 ((1) no id.; CCIH 155).

643 Both of the lemmata are variant spellings of the 1 sg. pres. act. ind. absolute of *líid* 'charges, accuses'; *eDIL s.v. líid*. The form *liomnadh* is likely a vn. derived from *líamnaid*. Cf. Digest B (57) (CIH 1382.12 ff., especially 1382.15–16).

644 The lemma is not in *eDIL*. The lemma is etymologized as consisting of *oll* 'great, large' and *lín* 'linen, cloth'. Cf. *Bretha Nemed Toísech*, CIH 2218.15 and Digest B (57) (CIH 1382.19). This entry and the next (*culpait*) occur twice in CIH in two versions of the same passage, 1382.19 (Digest B (57)) and 2218.15 (*Bretha Nemed Toísech*); in the latter the order is as here, but in the former the order is reversed. One reason, apart from the gloss, for thinking that *oillián* is an item of clothing is its link with *culpait* 'hood, cowl'. Cf. 2.b.20.108 OILLIAN, CULPAIT.

645 Irish *culpait* is from Latin *culcita*; *eDIL s.v. culpait*. See DDC *s.v. culpait* and SC Y.249. Cf. *Bretha Nemed Toísech* (CIH 2218.15) and Digest B (57) (CIH 1382.19). This entry and the previous (*oillían*) occur twice in CIH in two versions of the same passage, 1382.19 (Digest B (57)) and 2218.15 (*Bretha Nemed Toísech*); in the former the order is as here, but in the latter the order is reversed. The word *cail* is regularly glossed by *coimét* 'protection'; *eDIL s.v. 1 cail*. The second element is *pait(t)*; its primary sense is 'container for liquid' but such terms are frequently used colloquially for 'head' (cf. French *tête* < Latin *testa* 'pot'). Cf. 7.a.24.35 OILLÍAN and 2.b.20.108 OILLIAN, CULPAIT.

646 See O'Cl *Bíth .i. guin* 'a wound'; *Lec. Gl.* 53: *Bith .i. guin*; "The Glossary in Egerton 158" 708 *bith .i. guin*; and cf. Digest B (57) (CIH 1382.21–22; CCIH 62). The lemma is the vn. of *benaid*. Cf. 6.a.23.42 BITH.

647 The lemma *fáeth* is a compound of *fo* and *oeth*; *eDIL s.v.* 1 *fáeth* ?; and Breatnach 1990a: 11, n. 43. See O'Cl *Aoth .i. mionn* 'oath'; *Metr. Gl.* 9 § 4 *'Áoth' minn*; and Digest B (57) (CIH 1382.25–26). Cf. 9.8.23 FAOTH.

7.a.26.39 Iardac*h* ⟨.i. ait*h*gin⟩ .i. i*a*ram*h* dig*h*de .i. buidec*hus* i*ar*sin enecl*ann* ber*ar* i*ar*dac*h*.
Íartach 'restitution', ⟨i.e. restitution⟩, i.e. [< *íaram* 'afterwards' + *dígde* 'asking pardon'] afterwards pardon, i.e. good-will after the honor-price which is taken as restitution.[648]

7.a.28.40 Do-maist*er* .i. tom*hais*t*er*.
Do-maister 'is devised', i.e. is estimated.[649]

7.a.28.41 Toimdig*h*t*er* .i. to*mhais*t*er*, ⁊ b*a*ram*hlaigh*t*er*.
Toimtigter 'is deemed', i.e. is estimated, and is opined.[650]

7.a.29.42 Airlít*h*ec*h* .i. f*er* denta uas*a*l liot*h*a.
Airlithech 'obedient person', i.e. a person who follows a noble.[651]

7.a.30.43 Tiomortain .i. on mbas raidt*er* no tiom*ar*ta.
Timortain 'death', i.e. from the [word] *bás* 'death' it is said or shortened.[652]

7.a.32.44 Ad-roig*h*est*ar* .i. ro guidest*ar*, no ro eisgest*ar*.
Ad-rogestar 'sureties are invoked', i.e. he asked, or he asked.[653]

7.a.33.45 Urt*h*uasa*cht* .i. eist*echt*.
Airthúasacht 'keeping silent', i.e. listening.[654]

7.a.33.46 Tuaisit*h*er .i. est*er*, no leigid*h* fa na cluasuib*h*, no t*air*is ga*n* fiarf*ho*-*ghidh* an ni do dlig*hfedh* do d*e*na*m*.

648 For the lemma, cf. *CIH* 1384.9 and 19 (citations with commentary "on accusing a person of wrongdoing"; CCIH 63). Cf. 2.a.1.3 IARDOC[H].

649 See *eDIL s.vv. do-maisi* and 1 *toimsid, toimsigid*. Cf. Digest B (57) (*CIH* 1383.7–8).

650 See *eDIL s.vv. toimtnigid*, 1 *toimsid, toimsigid*, and *baramlaid*, respectively. Cf. *CIH* 1384.19 (citations with commentary "on accusing a person of wrongdoing;" CCIH 63).

651 See *eDIL s.v. airlithe*. For *liotha* cf. *eDIL s.vv. lenaid* and *líth*. Cf. *CIH* 1384.40 (citations with commentary "on accusing a person of wrongdoing;" CCIH 63).

652 The first part of the gloss should be understood as etymologizing ⟨mort⟩ in the lemma as Latin *mort* 'death'. The context of the entry is unknown, but cf. Digest B (56) (*CIH* 1381.17).

653 See *eDIL s.vv. ad-guid, guided*, and 1 *eiscid*, respectively.

654 See *CIH* 949.32; the entry forms part of a glossary fragment from the *Lecan Glossary* (CCIH 41; Russell 1988: 7).

Túaisither 'silence is kept', i.e. is heard, or allows according to the ears, or in addition without asking about what he should do.[655]

7.a.36.47 Nas*ar* .i. naisgt*er* .i. cengailt*er*.
Nasar 'may be bound', i.e. is bound, i.e. is bound.[656]

7.b.1.48 F*air*ben .i. fíreipt*her* .i. fírbent*ar*.
For-ben 'strikes', i.e [< *fír* 'truly' + *as-ben* 'smites'] is truly-smote, i.e. [*fír* 'truly' + *benaid* 'strikes'] are truly-struck.[657]

7.b.1.49 Cu*m*t*hus* .i. com*hm*ait*hius*.
Comthus 'partnership', i.e. equal excellence.[658]

7.b.2.50 Cuindrig*h* .i. caoindrig*h*.
Cuindrig 'controls', i.e. [< *caín* 'finely' + *dírgid* 'directs, guides'] finely controls.[659]

7.b.2.51 Rae .i. feran*n*.
Róe 'level ground', i.e. land.[660]

7.b.2.52 Naisi .i. cenguilsi.
Naisi 'bond', i.e. bond.[661]

7.b.3.53 Cam .i. comlan*n*.
Cám 'battle', i.e. battle.[662]

---

655 The translation of the entry is tentative.

656 The lemma appears to be a sg. pres. pass. subj. of *naiscid* 'binds'; *eDIL s.v. naiscid.*

657 Both of the glosses etymologize the element of the preverb *for-* (*fair-* as it is given in the MS) as *fír-* 'true, genuine', and thus create new pass. verb forms built from the conjunct form of *as-ben* (or from *eipid*, the later simplex of *as-ben*) and *benaid*, respectively; *eDIL s.vv. as-ben* and *benaid*; Binchy 1943: 212; and Taylor-Griffiths 2020: 1: 88, 93, 99, 102, 107, and 133–136. Cf. 4.c.28.136 FAIRBEN.

658 Cf. O'Don. Suppl. *s.v. cumthus*. Cf. Digest B (39) (*CIH* 1371.15).

659 The lemma appears to be the 3 sg. pres. prototonic form of *con-dírig* 'checks, controls, adjusts'; *eDIL s.v. con-dírig*. The definition provides a variant spelling of the lemma, but it also etymologizes the deuterotonic form of the lemma. Cf. Digest B (39) (*CIH* 1371.15).

660 This entry does not appear in O'Curry's transcript. See *Cethairślicht Athgabálae*, *CIH* 356.8 and 34; and O'Cl *Rae .i. fearann* 'a field'.

661 The lemma appears to be deverbative from *naiscid* 'binds'. While *cengul* 'bond' is well attested, the ending *-si*, which matches the end of *naisi*, is unexplained. Cf. O'Cl *Nas .i. ceangal* 'a bond'.

662 See *SC* YAdd.375: *Cam .i. comlnad*; and O'Cl *Cam .i. comhlann* 'battle'.

7.b.3.54 Cai*mper* .i. fer co*mlainn*.
Caimper 'champion', i.e. man of battle.[663]

7.b.3.55 Diam*h*ain .i. diainim.
Diamuin 'unblemished', i.e. [< *dí-* negative prefix + *ainim* 'blemish, defect'] unblemished.[664]

7.b.4.56 Dim*h*ed*h* .i. toi*mh*den*n*is .i. b*aramluigh*is.
Díbaid 'having no male issue', i.e. he supposed, i.e. he conjectured.[665]

7.b.4.57 Im*edh* .i. ni*medh* .i. egl*us*.
Imbed 'abundance', i.e sanctuary, i.e. church.[666]

7.b.4.58 Tregan, dit*h*ec*h* .i. séna.
Trécun 'foresaking', *díthech* 'oath of denial', i.e. denying.[667]

7.b.5.59 Feraid .i. feg*air* .i. at*htairg*id*h* .i. tionol.
Feraid 'supplies', i.e. is brought, i.e. pays, i.e. collecting.[668]

7.b.6.60 Roch*air* .i. ro seic*h*ig*h*ter .i. ro h-ion*n*saig*h*ter.
Rochar 'be declared', i.e. is asked, i.e. is claimed.[669]

663 It is possible that the gloss is partially etymologizing the lemma as *cám* 'battle' and *fer* 'man'; cf. 7.b.3.53 CAM. See *Bretha Nemed Dédenach* 14.22 (*CIH* 1112.14; *CCIH* 184–188); O'Cl *Caimper .i. fear morchomhlainn* 'a champion'; for the lemma, cf. O'Dav 376 (*Bretha Nemed Dédenach*; *CCIH* 119); and *SC* YAdd.376 *Caimpar .i. comlainntec.*

664 See O'Cl *Diamhuin .i. dí ainimh .i. neamhainmheach* 'without blemish', and *SC* YAdd.498 *Diamain .i. di-anim*; and for the lemma, cf. O'Dav 670 (no id.; *CCIH* 127). Cf. 7.b.3.55 DIAMHUIN.

665 The entry might concern inheritance. The meaning of the lemma is uncertain as it has a range of meanings including 'destruction, death, and inheritance'. Both of the verbal forms appear to be 3 sg. preterites. See *eDIL s.vv.* 1 *díbad*, *toimtnigid*, and *baramlugad*, respectively. Cf. *CIH* 857.22–26 and Digest C (14) (*CIH* 1925.28).

666 The interpretation of the lemma is uncertain. The association between the lemma and the first gloss might result from confusion between *nemed* and the form of the lemma after the article as it was originally a n. noun. For the first gloss, cf. *SC* Y.962; and OM 830.

667 See O'Cl *Ditheach .i. séna* 'poor'. See discussion in *GEIL* 200–201.

668 The form *fegair* is interpreted as a 3 sg. pres. pass. of *feidid*; *eDIL s.v. feidid*. The lemma is found in the same quotation as the following item in the MS, 7.b.6.60 ROCHAIR in O'Dav. 887 (discussed by Binchy 1966b: 230). For the lemma, cf. O'Dav 887 ((1) no id.; *CCIH* 134) and 1112 (no id.; *CCIH* 141).

669 The verbal form *ro seichighter* is uncertain. It is likely that it is a sg. pass. of *saigid*, *ro-saig*, or *seichid*. Forms of *ind-saig*, later *innsaigid*, frequently gloss *saigid* in the legal texts; *eDIL*

7.b.7.61 Fr*i*omall .i. maill*id* fr*i*om.
Frimall 'incites', i.e. incites against me.[670]

7.b.7.62 Laob*h* .i. l*eth*tr*o*m, no l*eth*taob*h*.
Láeb 'bias', i.e. biased, or biased.[671]

7.b.8.63 No*m*ad*h* nó .i. nom*adh* nae .i. fer.
Nómad nó 'ninth descendant', i.e. ninth person, i.e. a person.[672]

7.b.8.64 Fém*edh* .i. diultad*h* aniu t*ar* am*arac* .i. tar a n-*air*tec*h* ⁊ do geb*air* tfiac*h*a.
Fémed 'refusing', i.e. refusing today for tomorrow, i.e. for restoring them and your fines will be paid.[673]

7.b.10.65 Re toe torae .i. focail raiter re fer na bfiac*h*.
Ré tóe torae 'a period of silence which may come', i.e. words which are said to the debtor.[674]

---

s.v. ind-saig ?. The lemma is found in the same quotation as the previous item in the MS, 7.b.5.59 FERAID in O'Dav 887. See O'Dav 887 ((1) no id.; *CCIH* 134: *Feraid .i. atairgid, ut est feraid insci di na rochar arra* "*Feraid*, i.e. returns, ut est 'he gives her an oath that the thing due is not attained'.") and 1112 (no id.; *CCIH* 141: *Insci .i. luighe, ut est feraidh insci di na rochar arru*... "*Insci*, i.e. oath, ut est 'he gives her an oath that the thing due is not obtained...'."). Binchy (1966: 230) understands the *rochar* in O'Dav 887 as a perfective pres. subj. pass. of *seichid* 'says', although he states that a form of *saigid* would make better sense. Binchy translates the first part of the gloss as 'he makes a statement if the consideration cannot be declared (?)'. It is unlikely that the lemma here is the same as the *rochair* found in the *Gormac* glossary § 20 (*CIH* 1568.26) which is a later 3 sg. pret. of *do-tuit* 'falls'.

670 The lemma is not in *eDIL*. Based on the meaning provided and of the existence of verbs such as *muillid, fomuillid*, and *1 inmuillid*, all of which mean 'incites', it is possible that *friomall* is a verbal form derived from **frimuillid*; *eDIL s.vv. muilid, fomuillid*, and 1 *inmuillid*.

671 See *eDIL s.vv.* 4 *láeb, lettrom*, and *lettáeb*, respectively. For the lemma, see O'Cl *Laobh .i. claon* 'oblique' *laoibhrí .i. rí claon* 'an unjust king'; and cf. O'Dav 1174 (no id.; *CCIH* 143: *Laebh .i. lenad*... "*Laebh*, i.e. following...").

672 Normally a *fuidir* can leave his lord, but if the status of *fuidir* has been inherited beyond four generations and nine men, the *fuidir* can no longer leave his lord; *Críth Gablach*, ll. 326–327; Binchy 1984; *GEIL* 33–35; and Charles-Edwards 1993: 406. Cf. O'Cl *Nae .i. duine* 'a man'.

673 The question is whether the lemma represents *fémed*, the vn. of *fo-émid*, or *féimded*, the vn. of *éimdid*; both words mean 'refusing'; *eDIL s.vv. fém(m)ed* and *féimded*. For the gloss *airtech*, see *eDIL s.v. airtach*. See O'Cl *Feimdheadh .i. diultadh* 'refusal'. Cf. 2.b.20.106 FÉMEDH.

674 See *Bretha Nemed Dédenach* 29.28 (*CIH* 1122.32; *CCIH* 184–188); and O'Cl *Ré, no ad ré .i. do éirigh* 'he arose'.

7.b.10.66 Du*ar* .i. dui*ne*.
Dúar 'a type of poet', i.e. a person.[675]

7.b.11.67 For-reit*h* .i. foir*igh*nig*h*.
Fo-reith 'he helps', i.e. he helps.[676]

7.b.11.68 For-r*eith*er .i. foir*igh*nig*h*ter.
Fo-reither 'he is helped', i.e. he is helped.[677]

7.b.12.69 Ada-bonn ⟨.i. obaim⟩.
Ada-boind 'he refuses', ⟨i.e. I refuse⟩.[678]

7.b.12.70 Ad-bois .i. obais.
At-bois 'you may refuse it', i.e. you may refuse.[679]

---

675 The meaning of the lemma in this entry is dependent on the meaning of the definition. The usual meaning of *dúar* is 'word, stanza', but it is also used in the compound *dúarfine* to refer to a poet; *eDIL s.v. dúar*. Cf. *Bretha Nemed Dédenach* 16.27–28 (*CIH* 1113.33; *CCIH* 184–188); and for the lemma, cf. O'Cl *Dúar .i. ran no focal. Duairfhine .i. fileadha dobhrígh gurab fine focal iad, oir as ionann dúar 7 focal* 'a stanza or word. *Duairfhine*, poets; because they are the tribe (*fiñe*) of words (*focal*), for *dúar* and *focal* (word) are the same'; O'Dav 582 (*Bretha Nemed Dédenach*; *CCIH* 125) and 583 (*Bretha Nemed Dédenach*; *CCIH* 125); and more distantly *SC* B.304. The *SC* entry cites *Bretha Nemed* as its source.

676 Although there are headwords in *eDIL* for both *fo-reith* 'helps' and *for-reith* 'proceeds', *fóirithnigid* 'helps' is regularly used to gloss *fo-reith* in legal commentary; *eDIL s.v. fóirithnigid*. It is not uncommon for *fo-reith* and *for-reith* to be confused; *eDIL s.vv. for-reith* and *for-reith*. See *Bretha Nemed Dédenach* 29.29 (*CIH* 1122.33; *CCIH* 184–188).

677 These are the 3 sg. pass. forms of the verbs given in 7.b.11.67 FOR-REITH. *Fóirithnigid* 'helps' is regularly used to gloss *fo-reith* in legal commentary; *eDIL s.v. fóirithnigid*. See *Bretha Nemed Dédenach* 29.29 (*CIH* 1122.33; *CCIH* 184–188).

678 The verbs *ad-boind* and *as-boind* are frequently confused, especially as the outcome of the pre-tonic syllable with a 3 sg. infixed pronoun would be the same for each verb, but the definition provided by *opaid* 'refuses' resolves the any ambiguity in determining the lemma; *eDIL s.vv. ad-boind, as-boind*, and *opaid*; *GOI* § 834.b; Plummer 1926–1928: 127–128; Smith 1932: 79, n. 3; *Bretha Crólige* § 18; and Russell 1988a: 101. See *Bretha Nemed Dédenach* 28.26 (*CIH* 1121.39; *CCIH* 184–188); Digest B (56) (*CIH* 1381.4); and O'Dav 89 (no id.; *CCIH* 111: *Ad-bo* (*.i. urfocraim*) *.i. obaim nó atboinn nó atbois, ut est atbois a réir britheman* "*Adbo* (i.e. I proclaim), i.e. I refuse, or he proclaims it, or thou shouldest proclaim it, ut est 'thou shouldest proclaim it in obedience to the judge'."). It is unusual for the gloss not to match the lemma in person and number, but it should be noted that both Digest B (56) and O'Dav 89 have the 3 sg. pres. form alongside a 1 sg. pres. form.

679 For the verbal forms in this entry, see the discussion on 7.b.12.69 ADA-BONN. These verbal forms are not found in the same section of text as 7.b.12.69 ADA-BONN. See O'Dav 89 (no id.; *CCIH* 111: *Ad-bo* (*.i. urfocraim*) *.i. obaim nó atboinn nó atbois, ut est atbois a réir brithe-*

7.b.12.71 Díuirb .i. du*in*e g*an* fera*nn*.
Díoirb 'a person without inheritance', i.e. a person without land.[680]

7.b.13.72 Eítnge .i. fer d*roch* urlap*ra* .i. e g*an* teng*aid*.
Etnge 'unfit to plead', i.e. a man bad at pleading, i.e. [é 'he' + *cen* 'without' + *tengae* 'tongue'] one who is without a tongue.[681]

7.b.13.73 As-roib .[i.] ro ob.
As-roib 'he may refuse', i.e. he refused.[682]

7.b.14.74 Coib*h*che .i. com*h*oig*h*e cuir ⁊ cu*nnarth*a.
Coibche 'contract', i.e. [< *com-* 'joint' + *óge* 'wholeness, completeness' + *cor* 'contract'] joint-completion of a contract and bargain.[683]

7.b.15.75 Boibre .i. bo eib*er*t .i. geim d*r*ut[h] do-[g]ni, ⁊ amadan eisein.
Boibre 'a kind of fool', i.e. [< *bó* 'cow' + *epert* 'speaking'] cow speaking, i.e. he makes a wanton lowing [sound], and he is a simpleton.[684]

---

man "*Adbo* (i.e. I proclaim), i.e. I refuse, or he proclaims it, or thou shouldest proclaim it, ut est 'thou shouldest proclaim it in obedience to the judge'.")

680 The meaning of the lemma is taken from its etymology, i.e. *dí-* (negative prefix) and *orba* 'patrimony, heritage (of land), real estate'; *eDIL s.v. orb(b)a*. See *Bretha Nemed Dédenach* 28.29 (CIH 1122.1; CCIH 184–188); Digest B (56), CIH 1381.3. For the lemma, cf. O'Dav 1317 (no id.; CCIH 147).

681 For the etymological gloss, cf. *eDIL s.v. étenga* 'dumb, unfit to plead'. See *Bretha Nemed Dédenach* 28.29 (CIH 1122.1; CCIH 184–188); Digest B (56) (CIH 1381.4); and cf. O'Cl *Etnge .i. edteangtha .i. duine balbh* 'i.e. *edteangtha* (tongueless) a dumb man'; and OM 473: *Etngad .i. cen t[h]engad. 'Etngad* 'tongueless', i.e. without tongue'.

682 The lemma appears to be a 3 sg. pres. subj. of *as-boind* 'refuses' with *ro-* expressing possibility; *eDIL s.v. as-boind*; and GOI § 531. See *Bretha Nemed Dédenach* 29.2 (CIH 1122.8; CCIH 184–188); Digest B (56) (CIH 1381.8; "The Advice to Doidin": 73); and cf. O'Dav 89 (no id.; CCIH 111). Cf. 7.b.12.69 ADA-BONN and 7.b.12.70 AD-BOIS.

683 The entry is a common gloss on *coibche*; cf. *Di Astud Chor* § 15, gloss a; and cf. CIH 990.25, 1195.19–20, 1353.6, 2047.2. Cf. *Bretha Nemed Dédenach* 29.4 (CIH 1122.10); and Digest B (56) (CIH 1381.11; "The Advice to Doidin": 73).

684 This is one of a group of entries in the glossary which concern those of unsound mind. Within the context of *Bretha Nemed Dédenach*, those of diminished mental capacity are placed within the category of those who should not act as a surety to a contract. See *Bretha Nemed Dédenach* 29.10 (CIH 1122.15; CCIH 184–188); Digest B (56) (CIH 1381. 18 and 21; "The Advice to Doidin" 73; and Smith 1932: 80); and cf. O'Dav 316 (*Bretha Nemed Dédenach*; CCIH 117: *Boibre .i. bo-abartach, abairt amail in mboin* "*Boibre*, i.e. cow-behavior, behaving like the cow."). It should be noted that the material from Digest B (56) here and for the following two entries in the MS is a close match to the text as it appears in both Dubhaltach's Glossary and O'Dav. Both the entry here and O'Dav 316 etymologize *boibre* as containing

7.b.16.76 Buicne .i. ceo da b*h*uaic. Fer le*th*cui*nn* e.
Buicne 'halfwit', i.e. [< *búaic* 'top, head' + *ceó* 'mist'] a mist from his head. He is a half-witted man.[685]

7.b.17.77 Boicmell .i. meall buic .i. meall congnai ima b*r*ag*h*uid .i. in reindinic.
Boicmell 'a kind of fool', i.e. [< *boc* 'soft' + *mell* 'swelling'] soft swellings, i.e. a swelling of horn around his throat, i.e. the buffoon.[686]

7.b.18.78 Coisid .i. teg*us*g*a*d.
Coisid 'they control', i.e. they instruct.[687]

7.b.18.79 Aille .i. alleluia.
Aille 'hymn of praise', i.e. alleluia.[688]

7.b.18.80 Ionráit*h* .i. nec*h* as io*n*gab*th*a i rait*high*i*us*.
Inráith 'capable of acting as a surety', i.e. anyone who is to be taken as a surety.[689]

---

bó 'cow' as the first element in the lemma. It should also be noted that this entry and the next two in the MS, i.e. 7.b.16.76 BUICNE and 7.b.17.77 BOICMELL, are found consecutively in O'Dav and numbers 316, 317 (*Bretha Nemed Dédenach*; CCIH 117), and 318 (*Bretha Nemed Dédenach*; CCIH 117). Most of the definitions of these lemmata have an etymological element and should be understood thusly and not literally.

685 See the discussion on 7.b.15.75 BOIBRE and 7.b.17.77 BOICMELL. See *Bretha Nemed Dédenach* 29.10 (*CIH* 1122.15; CCIH 184–188); Digest B (56) (*CIH* 1381.18–19, 21; "The Advice to Doidin" 73; and Smith 1932: 80); and cf. O'Dav 317 (*Bretha Nemed Dédenach*; CCIH 117: *Buiceall .i. bis 7 ceo da bhuaic, in cainti no in fer lethchuinn* "*Buiceall*, i.e. one who is with a fog from his cap, the satirist, or the half-witted man.").

686 See the discussion on 7.b.15.75 BOIBRE and 7.b.16.76 BUICNE. See *Bretha Nemed Dédenach* 29.10 (*CIH* 1122.15; CCIH 184–188); Digest B (56) (*CIH* 1381.19–20 and 21; "The Advice to Doidin" 73; and Smith 1932: 80–82); and cf. O'Dav 318 (*Bretha Nemed Dédenach*; CCIH 117: *Bocmeall .i. fo mbit na mill buic bragha. No is boc ar merdacht mella congna* "*Bocmell*, i.e. (one) under whom are the soft lumps of the neck. Or he is a he-goat for madness (who has) lumps of horn.").

687 If we assume that the lemma is in some way connected to the text of the previous several entries as they appear in the MS, e.g. 7.b.15.75 BOIBRE, 7.b.16.76 BUICNE, then the matching text in *Bretha Nemed Dédenach* 29.11 (*CIH* 1122.15) is *ionchoisiod* and in Digest B (56) (*CIH* 1381.20; "The Advice to Doidin" 73) is *incoiset*. The larger textual context involves people who should not act as sureties because their memory is not reliable.

688 See *Bretha Nemed Dédenach* 29.12 (*CIH* 1122.17; CCIH 184–188); Digest B (56) (*CIH* 1381.26; "The Advice to Doidin" 74); and cf. O'Cl *Aille .i. moladh* 'praise'. The larger textual context of the entry is that clerics should not act as sureties *uair uatuaslaici int ailleluighi uil*[*e*] *aca-san* 'for the hymn of praise dissolves the oath by them'; *CIH* 1381.26; "The Advice to Doidin" 74 and 77.

689 The lemma does not have a headword in *eDIL*, but see *Críth Gablach*, l. 130. It is derived

7.b.19.81 Esomain .i. es som*h*aoin.
Esamain 'fearless', i.e. [< *es-* (neg. prefix) + *somaín* 'benefit, profit'] profitless.[690]

7.b.19.82 Naoill .i. luig*h*e.
Noíll 'oath', i.e. oath.[691]

7.b.20.83 Col*tr*a .i. sec[d]a.
Coltra 'firm', i.e. stiff.[692]

7.b.20.84 Dion*n*ba .i. ⟨gan⟩ ba for dion*n*, f*or* d[t]ul*ach*.
Dindba 'poor', i.e. ⟨without⟩ [< *dind* 'height' + *bó* 'cow'] cows on a height, on a hill.[693]

---

from *in-* 'capable of' and *ráith* 'surety'; *eDIL s.vv.* 3 *in-* and 1 *ráth*. The verbal form *iongabtha* is the verbal of necessity of *in-gaib*; *eDIL s.v. in-gaib*. It is possible that the second half of the gloss etymologizes the lemma. The lemma does not appear in the source text, i.e. *Bretha Nemed Dédenach*, where the surrounding lemmata in the glossary are found, but it makes sense within the larger textual context.

690 The lemma and the following glossary entry in the MS, 7.b.19.82 NAOILL, form a phrase in Digest B (56) (*CIH* 1381.37; "The Advice to Doidin" 74, 78; and Smith 1932: 84), *is essomain noillach*. See also O'Dav 772 (probably from *Bretha Nemed Dédenach*), 781 (1) (no id.), and 799 ((1) no id. (2) probably *Bretha Nemed Dédenach*; *CCIH* 130 and 131) where the lemma is equated with *lasamain* 'flaming'; the entries in O'Dav emphasize the suddenness with which a man takes an oath, as if he were on fire. O'Dav 781 (1) quotes the text in Digest B (56): *Esomain .i. obann no lasamain, ut est is esomain maillech .i. lasamain fri tabairt luighi* "*Esomain*, i.e. sudden or flaming, ut est 'he is a sudden swearer', i.e. he is on fire ot take an oath." The sense is that this person takes an oath too quickly. The lemma is likely derived from *es-* (neg. prefix) and *omun* 'fear'. Cf. 7.b.19.82 NAOILL.

691 See the discussion on 7.b.19.81 ESOMAIN. The lemma and the previous glossary entry in the MS, 7.b.19.81 ESOMAIN, form a phrase in Digest B (56) (*CIH* 1381.37; "The Advice to Doidin" 74, 78; and Smith 1932: 84). *Noíllach* in the source text is the gen. sg. of *noíll*. Cf. O'Dav 781 (1) (no id.; *CCIH* 131).

692 See Digest B (56) (*CIH* 1381.39; "The Advice to Doidin" 75, 78; and Smith 1932: 84); *Ni Tulach* glossary (*CIH* 811.36); *Breth* glossary (*CIH* 1097.19); *Arra* glossary (*CIH* 1559.39); and O'Dav 460 (no id.; *CCIH* 122: *Coltra .i. secda nó slatrata, ut est is coltra fri imrisin .i. is secda no is slatrata ac ime fri son na firinne* "*Coltra*, i.e. stiff or bold, ut est 'he is *coltra* for contention', i.e. he is stiff or bold at a fence against the truth."). The form *secda* is from *sectha*, the part. of *seccaid*; *eDIL s.v. sectha*. Smith 1932: 78 translates the text in BL MS Egerton 88: *is coltra fri himrisan .i. is secdha é imrisan na firinne* 'he is stubborn in contention, i.e. he is bold at quarrelling with the truth'.

693 See Digest B (56) (*CIH* 1381.34–35 and 1382.1; "The Advice to Doidin": 74, 75, 77, 78; and Smith 1932: 84); and for the lemma cf. O'Dav 672 (no id.; *CCIH* 128). The lemma is found in two places within Digest B (56). Both times the lemma is defined in the text as someone who is too poor to act as a surety. In relation to the order in the glossary in which the lemmata

7.b.21.85 Ailtl*eth*an con*are* .i. fer teg*hleth*an *ar* an con*air* e da rad*h* fri(e)r.
Altlethan conaire 'broad-housed of a path [of legal procedure]', i.e. this man is to be called a man of broad-house on the path [of legal procedure].[694]

7.b.22.86 Sesaid .i. ionsoig*h*id.
Sesaid 'you (pl.) should claim', i.e. claim.[695]

---

are found relative to their source textual order, one would want to match the entry in the glossary to the citation in CIH 1382.1, however, the meaning provided in CIH 1381.34–35, *ag na bi ba ar thulchaib* 'who has no cows on hills' (Smith 1932: 77) is a better match for the meaning provided in Dubhaltach's Glossary although it looks like it might be originally an etymological gloss. It is possible that *for dionn* 'on a height' was originally a gloss on *for tulach* 'on a hill'. The ⟨d⟩ in *dulach* is unexpected and might be a mistake for ⟨t⟩. Although Digest B (56) (CIH 1382.1) and O'Dav 672 largely agree textually, neither of them preserves the entry as it is found here.

694 See Digest B (56) (CIH 1382.2–3; "The Advice to Doidin" 75, 78; and Smith 1932: 84); *Ni Tulach* glossary (CIH 811.37); and *Arra* glossary (CIH 1559.39–40). Cf. O'Cl *Ailt .i. teagh* 'house'. There are a number of issues with the interpretation of this entry. The lemma could be a compound of *alt* 'joint, shape, manner' or *alt* (*ailt*) 'house' and *lethan* 'broad, wide'; *eDIL s.vv.* 1 *alt*, 3 *alt*, and *lethan*, respectively. Smith 1932: 78 translates the text in BL MS Egerton 88 *is alt lethan conaire i.e. is lethan a tegh arin conaire* 'he is broad-jointed (?) in (legal) procedure, i.e. his house is broad on the road'; he notes (84) that O'Donovan (Brehon Law Transcripts) translated the text as 'who is broad-housed on the road', which follows the glossator's interpretation of the phrase. One of the issues with interpreting *fer teghlethan* as 'man who is broad as a house' is that one would expect *tige* instead of *tegh-*; interpreting *tegh-* as a form of *tiug* 'thick', i.e. 'a man which is thick and broad', would still result in an interpretation where someone is creating an obstruction. That all of the sources agree on interpreting *ailt* as 'house' suggests we should follow the same here, although it should be noted that one of the characteristics of Irish glossing is that sometimes multiple meanings are being interpreted simultaneously by the glossators. Regardless of how one translates the lemma, the sense is that this person is one who obstructs legal procedure. In other words, he metaphorically sets up an obstruction on the path of legal procedure. This entry is contextually within a larger group of people in the source text who are described as being unsuitable to act as a surety. It should be noted that *do +a+ rádh* is an EMI form of *ráidid* 'speaks, says'; *eDIL s.v. ráidid*; and Gwynn and Lloyd 1904: 16.9.

695 The interpretation of the lemma is tentative. It is understood as a 2 pl. juss. subj. of *saigid* 'approaches, sues, claims'; cf. O'Dav 1469 (*Di Astud Chirt 7 Dligid*; CCIH 151: *Sas .i. innsaighid, ut est dia sasar fir slan brethe senchaidhe .i. madia n-innsaighther doreir firinne na senchaide* "*Sas*, i.e. if truth of a sound judgment of historians be sought, ut est 'if it be searched according to the truth of the historians'."). The verb *ind-saig* 'approaches, seeks, claims, sues' frequently glosses *saigid* in legal texts and has a later simplex *indsaigid*; it is understood here as a 2 pl. impv.; *eDIL s.v. ind-saig ?*. Cf. 7.b.24.92 SEGAR, 1.b.11.78 SEIS, and 7.b.25.95 SIAS.

7.b.22.87 Cec*h*latt*ar* .i. do *conn*c*at*t*ar*.
Cechlatar 'they will hear', i.e. they saw.[696]

7.b.22.88 Ad-bela .i. ebi .i. ba[s].
Ad-béla 'he will die', i.e. cutting (?), i.e. death.[697]

7.b.23.89 Conóad .i. coim*hét*uid.
Conóat 'they guard', i.e. they guard.[698]

7.b.23.90 Slatra ⁊ lat*ra* ⟨.i. ambfial⟩ ⟨.i. anb*h*al⟩ .i. ⟨láidir, dana⟩ *quasi more latrom*.
Slatra 'strong' and *latra* 'mighty', ⟨i.e. shameless⟩, ⟨i.e. shameless⟩, i.e. ⟨strong, bold⟩ *as if more latronum* 'in the manner of thieves'.[699]

7.b.24.91 Frepad*h* .i. leig*hius*.
Frepad 'cure', i.e. cure.[700]

7.b.24.92 Seg*ar* .i. ion*n*saigt*er*.
Segar 'let it be investigated', i.e. is sought.[701]

---

696 The lemma is problematic. The gloss provides the meaning 'they saw', but the lemma itself looks like it was derived from a future form of *ro-cluinethar* 'hears' but without the preverb; for the first part of the lemma, cf. O'Dav 380 (no id.; *CCIH* 119).

697 For the lemma, cf. Digest B (52) (*CIH* 1378.31). The first gloss is problematic due to the uncertainty of the reading. It is found on the damaged left side of the MS page, and it is difficult to determine what, if anything has been lost. It is also uncertain whether the final letter is actually ⟨i⟩. It is possible that the word should not be interpreted as *eipe* 'cutting', but rather as a sg. fut. form of *at-bail*, such as *-epéla*. I should like to thank one of the anonymous readers for comments on this entry.

698 The verb *coimétaid* 'keeps, guards, watches' replaces *con-oí*; *eDIL s.vv. con-oí* and 1 *coimétaid*. Cf. O'Cl *Connaoi .i. coimhédaidh no cumhdaighidh* 'keeping or protecting'; and for the lemma, cf. *Di Astud Chor* (*CIH* 1356.15).

699 See the glossary of words mainly from *Tecosca Cormaic* at TCD MS 1337 [H.3.18], p. 539b7 where *anbial* is glossed by *anfial*, which is found in *TC* § 13.19; and O'Cl *Slait ⁊ latra .i. laidir* 'strong'. The last part of the entry etymologizes *latra*, cf. *latrann* 'thief', from Latin *lātro* 'thief'. The gen. pl. of *lātro* should be *latronum*, but it looks as if a suspension mark has been left out. Cf. 8.37.103 SLATRA.

700 See O'Cl *Freapadh .i. leigheas* 'cure'; the first part of O'Dav 1001 (no id.; *CCIH* 138: *Freptha .i. leghas*… "*Freptha*, i.e. healing…"); *Fonnaidh* glossary (*CIH* 1079.17); and *CCIH* 46. It should be noted that Dubhaltach wrote his source as *eidgedh* immediately preceeding the lemma. It should also be noted that the *Fonnaidh* glossary has the heading *éitged so sis* on TCD MS 1337 [H.3.18], p. 638 in *marg. sup.*; Taylor-Griffiths 2020: 1: 174.

701 Cf. 7.b.24.93 URGNAIGHTER, 7.b.25.94 RUIBHDHITHER, 7.b.22.86 SESAID, 1.b.11.78 SEIS,

7.b.24.93 Urgn*aigh*ter .i. uasal f*h*og*h*ainter.
Urgnaiter 'let attendance be given', i.e. [< *úasal* 'lofty, noble' + *ar-fogni* 'serves, prepares'] nobly let it be served.[702]

7.b.25.94 Ruib*h*d*h*it*h*er .i. ro eidis imdib*h*ter.
Ruibdither 'he may have been pierced', i.e. [< *ad-cota* 'accepts, agrees' + *imm-díben* 'excises, circumcises'] that he agreed that he has been cut.[703]

7.b.25.95 Sias .i. ion*n*saigter.
Sias 'who will claim', i.e. is claimed.[704]

---

and 7.b.25.95 SIAS. The verb *ind-saig* 'approaches, seeks, claims, sues' frequently glosses *saigid* in legal texts and has a later simplex *indsaigid*, which is found in the entry here; *eDIL s.v. ind-saig ?.* See *Bretha Éitgid* (*CIH* 1163.13 and gloss 1, 1163.17–19, 325.23, 1212.35, and 2283.1 and 5; *CCIH* 176–182); *Fonnaidh* glossary (*CIH* 1079.18–19); *CCIH* 46; and O'Dav 1487 (*Din Techtugud*; *CCIH* 152: *Segar .i. indsaighter, ut est ata teora haimsera in segar étechta* "*Segar*, i.e. there are three times in which unright is reached."). It should be noted that the next four entries in Dubhaltach's Glossary follow the same textual order in which they are found in *Bretha Éitgid* (*CIH* 1163.13–14). A version of the source text from NLI MS G 11 (*CIH* 2283.1 ff.) is edited and translated in Binchy 1938: 80–81; I follow Binchy's translations here.

702 See 7.b.24.92 SEGAR. Following Binchy 1938: 81, the lemma is interpreted as the sg. pass. impv. of *ar-fogni* 'serves, prepares'. The verbal form *foghainter* is interpreted as the sg. pass. impv. of *fo-gní* 'serves, renders service'. See *Bretha Éitgid* (*CIH* 1163.13 and gloss 1, 1163.17–19, 325.23, 1212.35, and 2283.1 and 5; *CCIH* 176–182). It should be noted that the previous and following entries in Dubhaltach's Glossary follow the same textual order in which they are found in *Bretha Éitgid* (*CIH* 1163.13–14). A version of the source text from NLI MS G 11 (*CIH* 2283.1 ff.) is edited and translated in Binchy 1938: 80–81; I follow Binchy's translations here.

703 The lemma appears to be a sg. pres. pass. subj. of *benaid* 'strikes, wounds'; Binchy, 1938: 81, n. a. The translation of the remainder of the entry is tentative as it does not appear in the source text, however, it seems to be etymologizing the lemma; *eDIL s.vv. ad-cota* and *imm-díben*. It should be noted that forms of *imm-díben*, such as the sg. pret. pass, *immeruidbed*, echo the structure of the lemma. See 7.b.24.92 SEGAR and 7.b.24.93 URGNAIGHTER. See *Bretha Éitgid* (*CIH* 1163.14 and gloss 1, 1163.17–19, 325.23, 1212.35, and 2283.2 and 7; *CCIH* 176–182). It should be noted that the previous two entries in Dubhaltach's Glossary follow the same textual order in which they are found in *Bretha Éitgid* (*CIH* 1163.13–14). A version of the source text from NLI MS G 11 (*CIH* 2283.1 ff.) is edited and translated in Binchy 1938: 80–81; I follow Binchy's translations here.

704 Cf. 7.b.24.93 URGNAIGHTER, 7.b.25.94 RUIBHDHITHER, 7.b.22.86 SESAID, 1.b.11.78 SEIS, and 7.b.24.92 SEGAR. The lemma is interpreted as the sg. fut. rel. of *saigid* 'approaches, seeks, claims, sues'. The verb *ind-saig* 'approaches, seeks, claims, sues' frequently glosses *saigid* in legal texts and has a later simplex *indsaigid*, which is found in the entry here;

7.b.26.96 Fúa*char* .i. fúa*cht*n*aig*ter.
Fúachar 'is inflicted', i.e. is inflicted.[705]

7.b.26.97 Brasul .i. fer aga *m*bí ulc*h*a bras m*ar* ulgar ag d*r*ud ⁊ ag osg*hladh* a beoil c*h*aintig*h*.
Bresal 'strife', i.e. a man who has a large [< *ulcha* 'beard' + *bras* 'boastful, forceful'] boastful beard like one who talks closing and opening his satirical mouth.[706]

7.b.27.98 Con-amad*hair* .i. caoín no co*m*aimsig*h*ter.
Con-amadair 'had judged', i.e. [< *caín* 'well'] well or it is obtained.[707]

7.b.28.99 Inm*h*uille, muill*edh* .i. gresa*cht*, no b*r*usdad.
Inmuille 'inciting', *muillid* 'inciting', i.e. inciting, or urging.[708]

---

eDIL s.v. ind-saig ?. See *Bretha Éitgid* (CIH 1163.13 and gloss 1, 1163.17–19, 325.23, 1212.35, and 2283.1–4; CCIH 176–182); and *Fonnaidh* glossary (CIH 1079.20; and CCIH 46). It should be noted that the previous three entries in Dubhaltach's Glossary follow the same textual order in which they are found in *Bretha Éitgid* (CIH 1163.13–14). A version of the source text from NLI MS G 11 (CIH 2283.1 ff.) is edited and translated in Binchy 1938: 80–81. It should be noted that the entry from the *Fonnaidh* glossary and Dubhaltach's Glossary quote a word from the main text of *Bretha Éitgid*, *sias* (the lemma here), which is not found in the extant versions of the text. Cf. 8.24.63 SAIS.

705 Cf. 7.b.25.95 SIAS, 7.b.24.93 URGNAIGHTER, 7.b.25.94 RUIBHDHITHER, and 7.b.24.92 SEGAR. See *Bretha Éitgid* (CIH 1163.14; 325.23, 1212.35, and 2283.2; CCIH 176–182); cf. *Fonnaidh* glossary (CIH 1079.39–42; and CCIH 46). It should be noted that the previous four entries in Dubhaltach's Glossary follow the same textual order in which they are found in *Bretha Éitgid* (CIH 1163.13–14). A version of the source text from NLI MS G 11 (CIH 2283.1 ff.) is edited and translated in Binchy 1938: 80–81; I follow Binchy's translation.

706 The translation of the entry is tentative. Cf. Digest B (56) (CIH 1381.35; "The Advice to Doidin" 74, 77; and Smith 1932: 84). MS *brasul* has been interpreted as *bresul* in light of the material in Digest B (56): *bes combrasul .i. as bras oc sithladh urlabra triana ulcha* 'who is over-loquacious, i.e. he who is skilled in straining eloquence through his whiskers' (Smith 1932: 77). The general sense is that this person should not act as a surety due to the untrustworthiness of what they say, i.e. straining their speech through their beard, or because they create strife by their words. The interpretation of MS *ulgar* is based on Mod. Ir. *allagar* 'talk, shout'; *Foclóir Gaeilge-Béarla s.v. allagair.*

707 For the lemma, cf. *Bretha Nemed Dédenach* 14.4 (CIH 1111.27; CCIH 184–188); the *Cotaimside* glossary (CIH 1540.10); and Digest D (21) (CIH 1982.38; CCIH 79). It is common for the preverb *con-* to be glossed by *caín* 'good, well, fine'; Binchy 1943: 212; and Taylor-Griffiths 2020: 1: 88. Cf. 2.a.5.20 CON-AMADHAIR.

708 For the lemmata, cf. *Bretha Éitgid* (CIH 334.25, 1177.9; CCIH 50); CIH 1391.1 ff. (CCIH 63); and O'Cl *Muilleadh .i. greasachd* 'exhorting'. For the form *brusdad*, see *eDIL s.v. brostad.*

7.b.29.100 Báoidsioc*h* .i. ben b*h*aot*h* .i. sec*h* as baot[h].
Baítsech 'harlot', i.e. a wanton woman, i.e. [< *sech* 'that is to say' + *báeth* 'foolish'] that is to say *báeth* 'foolish'.[709]

7.b.29.101 Fresán .i. imr*i*sin .i. ime re son .i. fál re fog*ur* na firinn*e*.
Fresán 'strife', i.e. strife, i.e. [< *imm* 'around, concerning' + *ré* 'time' + *són*, an anaphoric pronoun] around that time, i.e. a fence against the sound of the truth.[710]

7.b.30.102 Talmuidioc*h* .i. fer mire no cut*h*aig*h*, no gal*air* m*h*oir.
Talmaidech 'an epileptic person', i.e. a man of madness or of fury, or of great illness.[711]

7.b.31.103 Terbsad .i. greamuig*h*id no sgaoilid.
Terbsat 'they separated', i.e. they seize or they divide.[712]

7.b.32.104 Aoib*h*ilteoir .i. grad*h* egailsi bi*us* m*ar* aoibil isin teoir .i. i leigen*n* crab*aidh*.
Oíbelteóir 'recluse', i.e. a religious grade who is like a flame in the contemplative life, i.e. in studying piety.[713]

---

709 The term *báeth* is used for anyone who is considered not legally incompetent. This category of people includes women, children, sons of living fathers, those of unsound mind, unransomed captives, and slaves; GEIL 68. For the lemma, cf. O'Dav 306 (*Di Astud Chirt ⁊ Dligid; CCIH* 117).

710 The lemma is not in *eDIL*. The lemma is falsely segmented from *imresan* 'strife, feud, contention' (sometimes also attested as *imbressan*), the vn. of *imm-fresna* 'contends, disputes'; *eDIL s.v. imresan*. In the legal texts the word *fresan* is frequently found in the phrase *im fresan fiadnaise* 'conflict of evidence' (which could be an etymological gloss on *imresan*); AL 6 *s.v. fresan*; e.g. CIH 357.29, 1249.7 and 1668.10. It is, however, found by itself in CIH 1570.38. The second part of the definition etymologizes *imresan* as consisting of *imm* 'about, concerning', *⁊ ré* 'time', and *són*, an anaphoric pronoun. It is possible that we should understand *son* as *són* 'sound', but that would leave the *re* unaccounted for.

711 For the lemma, see *Bretha Éitgid* (CIH 1180.23, CCIH 50); and O'Dav 1508 ((2) *Bretha Éitgid*; CCIH 153).

712 The lemma might be a 3 pl. pret. from *terbaid* 'separates', which is a later simplex from *do-eipen* 'excise, forfeits'; *eDIL s.vv. terbaid* and *do-eipen*. For a form of the lemma, cf. O'Dav 1517 (no id.; CCIH 153).

713 The first part of the definition provides the etymology of *oíbelteóir*, which was originally two distinct words, *oíbell* 'flame' and *teóir* 'contemplative life'; *eDIL s.v. oíbelteóir*. For the lemma, cf. CIH 1570.26 (a section concerning testimony; CCIH 69); Digest D (21) (CIH 1984.8); and O'Dav 86 (no id.; CCIH 111). See O'Don. Suppl. *s.v. aibhillteoir*.

7.b.33.105 Seol .i. suaill.
Séol 'scarcity', i.e. little.[714]

7.b.33.106 Aigdig*ht*[h]*er* .i. uga eisgit*h*er.
Aicdigther 'is invoked', i.e. [< *óg* 'whole, complete' + *eiscid* 'allows, concedes'] completely it is allowed.[715]

7.b.33.107 Tiog*h*baid*h* .i. deige[nach] bas*aig*id*h*.
Tiugbad 'death', i.e. [< *déidenach* 'last' + *básaigid* 'puts to death, kills'] last he puts to death.[716]

7.b.34.108 Foic*h*liter .i. oirc*h*illa*igh*ter.
Foichliter 'they are prepared', i.e. they are prepared.[717]

7.b.34.109 F*ed*hid*h* .i. at*h*t*airgidh*.
Feidid 'he brings', i.e. he pays.[718]

7.b.35.110 Cáit*h*, cáthaigh[th]e .i. nem*h*ni, no f*or* orb f*h*ás*a*c[h].
Cáith 'waste', *caithaigthe* 'wasted', i.e. nothing, or on waste land.[719]

7.b.35.111 F*r*esl*uig*e .i. luig*h*e f*r*is.
Freslige 'lying beside', i.e. lying next to him.[720]

---

714 For the lemma, cf. *Ni Tulach* glossary (CIH 809.5–6); the *Cotaimside* glossary (CIH 1540.12); and O'Cl *Suaill .i. beag* 'small'.

715 See heptad 58 (AL 5: 308.24, CIH 52.7 and gloss 5, 52.11–14) where the lemma is glossed by *ugu-eisced*. The interpretation of the entry, especially the lemma, is uncertain. The lemma might be a 3 sg. pres. pass. ind. form of a verb derived from *aicde*, the vn. of *ad-guid* 'invokes a surety'. It is common for the preverb *aig-* to be glossed by *óg* 'whole, complete'; Taylor-Griffiths 2020: 1: 88.

716 The translation of the translation of the definition is tentative as the excerpt is out of context.

717 The verb *ar-foichlea* 'gets ready, prepares' has a later simplex, *oirchilligid*, which is found here; *eDIL s.v. ar-foichlea*.

718 In legal commentary *attairgid* 'pays, repays, renders' is frequently used to gloss *feidid* 'brings, leads, applies'; *eDIL s.v. attairgid*. The general semantics is that one brings a payment. For the lemma, cf. *Bretha Nemed Dédenach* 29.19 (CIH 1122.24; CCIH 184–188); *Ni Tulach* glossary (CIH 810.26); and *Arra* glossary (CIH 1558.27).

719 The first lemma is straightforward; the second lemma has been emended as a participle of *caithid* 'spends, consumes', but it is also possible that the lemma is derived from a secondary verb derived from *cáith*. The form *fororbfhásach* is problematic. The expansion of the suspension mark of the first ⟨f⟩ is uncertain, as is the division of the word into one, two, or three words. Thus, the translation is tentative.

720 The gloss provides an etymology of *freslige*, i.e. lying against. For the lemma, cf. O'Dav

7.b.36.112 Ad-anna .i. adannaig*h* .i. fadoig.
Ad-annai 'he lights', i.e. candle-lighter, i.e. lighting.[721]

8.1.1 [...].i.[.]aingen.[722]

8.1.2 Cis .i. cia, no caidiad.
Cis 'which', i.e. what, or what are?[723]

8.1.3 Coinin l*eth* .i. caoin[....].
Coinín leth 'rabbit half', i.e. [< *caín* 'fair, well'] fair ...[724]

8.1.4 Ceallad .i. [t]emceall*ad*, no teglom*ad*.
Ceallad 'surrounding', i.e. surrounding, or gathering.[725]

8.1.5 *Conotar* .i. coi*m*[h]e[d].
Conoatar 'they are guarded', i.e. guarding.[726]

8.2.6 [D]roc*h* .i. dorc*h*a, no nem*h*sol*us*.
Droch 'bad', i.e. obscure, or unclear.[727]

8.2.7 Faor .i. fuirec*h*, no foir*idh*in.
Fáer 'delay', i.e. delaying, or helping.[728]

1005 (no id.; CCIH 138) and 1011 (no id.; CCIH 138); and *Críth Gablach* l. 234 (CIH 564.33).

721 Cf. *Críth Gablach* l. 524 (CIH 569.17). The second gloss is a form of *atúd*, the vn. of *ad-daí* 'kindling, lighting'. It is also possible that the gloss is a MI form of *ad-daí*.

722 This entry is not in O'Curry's transcription. The upper corner of the page is torn and worn, and the lemma is illegible, but the gloss might be *caingen* 'suit, claim'.

723 See *eDIL s.v.* 1 *cía*.

724 Both the transcription and translation of this entry are tentative due to the fact that the MS is badly worn across the top of the page and the text is illegible in places. This entry is not in O'Curry's transcription, and it is possible that this entry belongs with the preceding one.

725 This entry is not in O'Curry's transcription, and the lemma is not in *eDIL*. The lemma appears to be a vn. from a verb **cellaid* 'surrounds', derived from the same route found in *do-immchella* 'goes around, surrounds' < **to-imb-cell-*; *eDIL s.v. do-imchella*. For the second gloss, see *teclamad* 'collecting, assembling' The reading of the entry is tentative as parts of it are illegible.

726 The lemma is the 3 pl. pres. pass. ind. of *con-oí* 'protects, guards', and *coimét* is it's vn.; *eDIL s.v. con-oí*. See "A Poem on the Airgialla" §10. Cf. 7.b.23.89 CONÓAD.

727 The reading of the lemma is uncertain as parts of it are illegible; I follow O'Curry's reading. See O'Cl *Droch*.

728 See O'Dav 903 (no id.; CCIH 135: *Faer .i. fuirech .i. fiadnaise cen fae .i. cen fuirech or cin*

8.2.8 Dí*thech*, coindircle .i. c*air*deml*acht*.
Díthech 'oath of denial', *condircle* 'partiality', i.e. friendliness.[729]

8.3.9 Laobad*h* .i. saob*h*ad*h*.
Láebad 'perverting', i.e. deceiving.[730]

8.3.10 Miod*h*[lach .i.] m*ed*hon laoc*hus*, no met*h*lac*hus*.
Midlach 'one incapable of bearing arms', i.e. [< *medón* 'middle' + *láechas* 'valor'] middle valor, or [< *meth* 'feeble, failure, wasting' + *láechas* 'valor'] feeble valor.[731]

8.3.11 Do-luaisg*et* .i. tog*h*luais*et*.
Do-luaisget 'they remove', i.e. they move.[732]

8.3.12 Fer dit*h*re .i. fer *ar* doit*h* re, no *ar* dóit*h* tíre.
Fer díthre 'a landless man', i.e. [< *Fer* 'man' + *ar* 'for' + *díth* 'loss, lack' + *ré* 'time'] a man for lack time, or [< *ar* 'for' + *díth* 'loss, lack' + *tír* 'land]' for lack of land.[733]

---

fhoirithin n-uirre o neoch "*Faer*, i.e. act of delaying, staying, ut est 'witness without delay', i.e. without delaying or without support to it from anyone.").

729 The link between the first lemma and the remainder of the entry is unclear. It is possible that the gloss to *díthech* was skipped when Dubhaltach was compiling the glossary. Cf. 7.b.4.58 TREGAN, DITHECH and 8.3.9 LAOBADH which follows this entry in the MS, all of which concern evidence. See discussion in *GEIL* 200–201.

730 Cf. the previous entry in the MS, 8.2.8 DÍTHECH, COINDIRCLE. Both of these entries concern giving false testimony out of partiality towards someone involved in a legal case. For the lemma, cf. *Cethairślicht Athgabálae* (*CIH* 385.17 and gloss 32, 385.29–30, *AL* 1: 166.29–30).

731 I follow O'Curry's reading of the lemma; the MS is worn and part of the lemma is illegible.

732 The translation of the lemma is tentative. For the lemma, see Digest A (16) (*CIH* 1150.35, *CCIH* 49); Digest D (21) (*CIH* 1984.7, *CCIH* 79–80); and *CIH* 1570.1 (a section concerning testimony; *CCIH* 69) where *doluaiscet* is glossed by *togluaiscet*; *eDIL s.vv.* ? *doluaiscet* and *do-gluaisi*, respectively. The larger passage in the source text concerns categories of people whose sole testimony without other witnesses is sufficient; normally the evidence of a single person would not be considered valid; *GEIL* 203.

733 See Digest A (16) (*CIH* 1150.37); and *CIH* 1570.5 (a section concerning testimony; *CCIH* 69). The larger passage in the source text concerns categories of people whose sole testimony without other witnesses is sufficient; normally the evidence of a single person would not be considered valid; *GEIL* 203. The sense here is that the landless man has nothing to gain by providing false testimony.

8.4.13 Ben f*r*ia h-uait*h*ne .i. re n-iod*h*nuib*h*, ⁊ uait*h*ne cin*n* a lenib*h* uait*he*.
Ben fria h-úaithne 'a woman in labor', i.e. at the time of birth, and delivery of the child's head from her.[734]

8.4.14 Cimidi*h* i rae .i. b*r*aig*he ar* na gabail i rae ca[tha].
Cimmid i rói 'captive in battle', i.e. a prisoner after being captured on a battlefield.[735]

8.5.15 T*r*i b*r*iat*r*a (an egcui*nn*) .i. an mic big do-[g]ni t*estus* no fiad*hnuse* .i. an lion ceall, an la sun*nr*adac*h*.
Trí bríathra (an éccoind) .i. an maic big do-gní testas nó fíadnaise 'three testimonies (of the minor), i.e. of the young child who gives testimony or evidence', i.e. the number of the churches, the specific day.[736]

8.5.16 Easp*uc etir* a p[ars] ⁊ a cailioc*h* .i. idir a ablai*n* ⁊ a cailis.
Espoc etir a phars ⁊ a chailech 'a bishop between his Host and is chalice', i.e. between his consecrated wafer and his chalice.[737]

---

734 See *Aidbred* §1, comm. (*CIH* 2164.2) (Dubhaltach owned the main MS for this text, TCD MS 1387 [H.5.15]; O'Sullivan 1999: 277; and O'Sullivan 200: 439) and *CIH* 1269.32–33; Digest D (21) (*CIH* 1984.10 and 1986.26ff., *CCIH* 79–80); and *CIH* 1570.6 (a section concerning testimony; *CCIH* 69). The larger passage in the source text concerns categories of people whose sole testimony without other witnesses is sufficient; normally the evidence of a single person would not be considered valid; *GEIL* 203; and Eska 2022: 12.

735 The missing letters are supplied from O'Curry's transcription. For the interpretation of the entry, see *eDIL s.v.* 1 *brága*. See Digest D (21) (*CIH* 1984.11 and 1986.21ff., *CCIH* 79–80); and *CIH* 1570.5 (a section concerning testimony; *CCIH* 69). The larger passage in the source text concerns categories of people whose sole testimony without other witnesses is sufficient; normally the evidence of a single person would not be considered valid; *GEIL* 203.

736 See *CIH* 1363.32–33 (a section on evidence, *CCIH* 60); *CIH* 1570.7–8 and gloss 14, 1570.24–25 (a section concerning testimony; *CCIH* 69); and *Cáin Domnaig* ll. 46–47. For discussion on evidence provided by children, see *GEIL* 205; and Kelly 2020: 147. One of the few situations where evidence by children is considered valid is regarding the breaking of Sunday laws. The text at *CIH* 1363.32–33 lists the three testimonies (only two are given in Dubhaltach's Glossary); the testimony not listed here is *in lín fer* 'the number of men'. In the MS, the closing parenthesis is after *big*.

737 See Digest A (16) (*CIH* 1150.35–36); *CIH* 1570.2 (a section concerning testimony; *CCIH* 69); Digest D (21) (*CIH* 1984.14, *CCIH* 79–80); *Aidbred* §1, comm. *CIH* 2164.2–3, and *CIH* 1269.34–35. The larger passage in the source text concerns categories of people whose sole testimony without other witnesses is sufficient; normally the evidence of a single person would not be considered valid; *GEIL* 203; and Eska 2022: 12.

8.6.17 Iuidig*hecht* .i. iudiciumm .i. b*re*t*h*em*h*n*us*.
Iúdicecht 'judgement', *iudicium* 'judgement', i.e. judgement.[738]

8.6.18 Com*h*ad .i. coi*mé*t*u*id*h*.
Comad 'guarding', i.e. guarding.[739]

8.6.19 Co-nae .i. c[o]*m* [...].
Con-oí 'he protects', i.e. ...[740]

8.7.20 Do-boing .i. toibg*h*id*h*.
Do-boing 'he exacts', i.e. he exacts.[741]

8.7.21 Fer cuitc*h*ernsa .i. fer bi*us* i gcu*m*a re nec*h* h-i*mon* do*m*an [.i.] ag cosn*am* rig*h*e no abdaine.
Fer cuitchernsa 'man of equal rank', i.e. a man who is a rival against someone contending for power, i.e. contending for kingship or abbotship.[742]

8.8.22 Fer fuiche .i. fer *tét* go mnaoi na gnais.
Fer fuiche 'cuckold', i.e. a man who goes to the wife for sexual intercourse.[743]

8.8.23 Urg*ar*t*h*a .i. c*r*osta.
Airgarthae 'forbidden', i.e. forbidden.[744]

---

738 This entry might not belong to the same source text as the previous entries in the MS, but cf. the Latin citation on judgement in Digest A (16) (*CIH* 1150.38–39).

739 See *Cethairślicht Athgabálae* (*CIH* 415.18 and gloss 8, 415.29–31, *AL* 1: 284.40). Cf. 6.b.3.95 COMHADH.

740 The transcription and translation of the definition are tentative as the end of the page is badly worn and part of the word is illegible. The missing letter is supplied from O'Curry's transcription.

741 The definition is the 3 sg. pres. of the later simplex of the lemma *do-boing* 'plucks, breaks, exacts'; *eDIL s.v. do-boing*.

742 See heptad 49 (*CIH* 45.3 and gloss 8, 45.12–13, *AL* 5: 284.19). The sense of the entry is that the *fer cuitchernsa* is someone who is a rival for a position of power. The larger context of the source, heptad 49, is a list of seven people who are not fit to give evidence. This entry is part of a larger group of entries concerning evidence.

743 See heptad 49 (*CIH* 45.3, *AL* 5: 284.16). The sense of the entry is that another man is having sexual relations with his wife. The larger context of the source, heptad 49, is a list of seven people who are not fit to give evidence.

744 See heptad 49 (*CIH* 45.4, *AL* 5: 284.7); and cf. *CIH* 1421.18–21, which is part of a series of cita-

8.8.24 Fris-ráilter .i. frit*h*áilter, no fír-in*n*lit[er].
Fris-ráilter 'they are provided for', i.e. they are provided for, or [< *fír* 'truly' + *indlid* 'prepares, arranges'] truly-they are provided for.[745]

8.9.25 Riach*t*aig*he* .i. fer riach*t*an*us*.
Ríachtaige 'need', i.e. man of need.[746]

8.9.26 Mb*h*rog*hthar* .i. firen*igh*ter.
Brogthar 'is proved', i.e. is justified.[747]

8.9.27 Con-seic*h*it*h*er .i. tait*hnemhach* ionsaigter.
Con-sechither 'is corrected', i.e. pleasantly it is sought.[748]

---

tions on people who cannot act as witnesses (CCIH 64). The larger context of the source, heptad 49, is a list of seven people who are not fit to give evidence. The lemma is the participle of *ar-gair* 'forbids'; *eDIL s.v. airgarthae.*

745 I follow O'Curry's reading of the final word; the MS is worn and part of the writing is illegible and possibly lost. See *Corus Fine* (CIH 729.30; and cf. CIH 2206.31). Dubhaltach has written the heading 'Cor*us* Fine' in *marg. sup.* of TCD MS 1337 [H.3.18], p. 214, which is the start of the set of excerpts from the text; CCIH 235; and O'Sullivan 2000: 442. The extract which corresponds to the entry in Dubhaltach's Glossary is found on p. 215a, CIH 729.30–32. It should be noted that 'frisrailt*er*', which glosses MS 'frisrailidar', is not in Dubhaltach's hand. The context of the citation in CIH 2206.31–32 suggests that the topic continues that of the previous glossary entries, i.e. those who are not fit to act as witnesses. Out of context, it is difficult to determine the exact sense of the lemma and entry more generally. It could be that we are meant to understand it in terms of a list, i.e. the names of those people who cannot act as a witness are provided. Such a list is found at CIH 1421.22 ff. (1417.3–1429.18 is a series of citations on people who are not able to give evidence; CCIH 64), and it is likely that this and the previous entry and several which follow it in Dubhaltach's Glossary come from this part of BL MS Egerton 88, or a MS which has a similar group of citations; the lemmata in Dubhaltach's Glossary are not an exact match for what is found in BL MS Egerton 88.

746 The lemma is not in *eDIL*. The meaning provided here is based on the meaning of *ríachtanus* 'need, necessity'; *eDIL s.v. ríachtanus*. See CIH 1421.24 (1417.3–1429.18 is a series of citations on people who are not able to give evidence; CCIH 64), and it is likely that this and the surrounding entries in Dubhaltach's Glossary come from this part of BL MS Egerton 88, or a MS which has a similar group of citations; the lemmata in Dubhaltach's Glossary are not an exact match for what is found in BL MS Egerton 88.

747 The lemma is from *brogaid* 'establishes, proves, justifies', a MI form of *mrogaid* 'advances, extaneds'; *eDIL s.vv. brogaid* and *mrogaid*. For the lemma, cf. *Bretha Nemed Dédenach* 27.23 (CIH 1121.9); and CIH 1089.14 (CCIH 46). See CIH 1421.26 (1417.3–1429.18 is a series of citations on people who are not able to give evidence; CCIH 64), and it is likely that this and the surrounding entries in Dubhaltach's Glossary come from this part of BL MS Egerton 88, or a MS which has a similar group of citations; the lemmata in Dubhaltach's Glossary are not an exact match for what is found in BL MS Egerton 88.

748 The lemma appears to be a 3 sg. pres. pass. of *con-secha* 'corrects, restrains', but the palatal-

8.9.28 Fuillmec*h* .i. fer ga[ch] fuill*edh* loig*hacht ar* breig do den*am* na f*h*iadn*ui*se.
Fuillmech 'profiteer', i.e. person [who receives] every additional payment for lying about the evidence.[749]

8.10.29 Foilmer .i. fer b*hius* ag leim *ar* nec*h* go foi[l] ag breit*h* a s*et* uad*h*.
Foilmer 'slippery', i.e. a person who is attacking someone cunningly to take his property from him.[750]

8.11.30 F*air*be .i. fior eibe ut [est] fer f*air*be .i. fer fior eibe aoi .i. an fer bi*us* ag fior-ebe na cuisi i n-aig*idh* neic*h ar* log*h*.
Fairbe 'a paid advocate', i.e. [< *fír* 'true' + *eipe* 'selecting, cutting'] faithful cutting, *ut est* a person who advocates, i.e. a person who faithfully advocates a lawsuit, i.e. the person who faithfully advocates the case against someone for a fee.[751]

---

ization is unexpected if the form were OI; *eDIL s.v. con-secha*. The meaning provided is difficult to reconcile with the gloss, but the general sense seems to be that a mutually agreeable solution is being sought by legal remedy involving correct procedure. It is possible that the gloss is etymological in some way. See *CIH* 1421.29 (1417.3–1429.18 is a series of citations on people who are not able to give evidence; *CCIH* 64), and it is likely that this and the surrounding entries in Dubhaltach's Glossary come from this part of BL MS Egerton 88, or a MS which has a similar group of citations; the lemmata in Dubhaltach's Glossary are not an exact match for what is found in BL MS Egerton 88.

749 See *CIH* 1421.32 (1417.3–1429.18 is a series of citations on people who are not able to give evidence; *CCIH* 64), and it is likely that this and the surrounding entries in Dubhaltach's Glossary come from this part of BL MS Egerton 88, or a MS which has a similar group of citations; the lemmata in Dubhaltach's Glossary are not an exact match for what is found in BL MS Egerton 88.

750 The lemma is one of three citations from Dubhaltach's Glossary in *eDIL s.v. foilmer*. The first half of the entry is also found in BL MS Egerton 88 (*CIH* 1421.32–33), and it is an etymology of the lemma, which has a range of meanings including 'unreliable, flighty'. *CIH* 1417.3–1429.18 is a series of citations on people who are not able to give evidence (*CCIH* 64), and it is likely that this and the surrounding entries in Dubhaltach's Glossary come from this part of BL MS Egerton 88, or a MS which has a similar group of citations; the lemmata in Dubhaltach's Glossary are not an exact match for what is found in BL MS Egerton 88.

751 The lemma is cited in *eDIL s.v.* 1 *fairbe ?* from O'Curry 1873: 3: 476, n. 500, which is quoting Dubhaltach's Glossary; cf. *eDIL s.v.* 2 *fairbe* 'cut, strike?'. The entry itself is etymological even though the meaning of *fairbe* is not entirely certain. The sense, based on O'Curry, seems to be that the *fairbe* is someone who is paid to advocate (or draw up?) a case against someone else for a fee. See *CIH* 1421.35 (1417.3–1429.18 is a series of citations on people who are not able to give evidence; *CCIH* 64), and it is likely that this and the surrounding entries in Dubhaltach's Glossary come from this part of BL MS Egerton 88, or a MS which has a sim-

8.12.31 Finem*h*nus .i. fine iom*h*aoin uais.
Finemnus 'being like a vine', i.e. [< *fine* 'kinsman' + *immáin* 'control' + ⁊ *úais* 'noble'] kinsman of superior control.[752]

8.12.32 Feiles*ac*[h] .i. f*er* fea[llas] *ar* les c*h*aig*h*.
Felesach 'frivolous', i.e. a person who betrays everyone for profit.[753]

8.13.33 Eitsec*h* .i. ré gan tec*h* aige.
Eistech 'houseless', i.e. anyone who does not have a house.[754]

8.13.34 Fuireg*ar* .i. *air*gid*h*t[h]er .i. geibt[h]*er*.
Fuiregar 'is bound', i.e. is bound, i.e. is restrained.[755]

---

ilar group of citations; the lemmata in Dubhaltach's Glossary are not an exact match for what is found in BL MS Egerton 88. Cf. 2.b.3.74 FAIRBE and 8.14.36 MEADHBHA.

752 The meaning of the lemma is uncertain as it is not in *eDIL*, but it seems to be based on *fínemain* 'a vine'; *eDIL s.v. fínemain*. The entry is etymological and helps to supply a possible meaning for the lemma as a kinsman who is controlling the legal procedure although not directly involved in it. The image is of the kinsman who has his hands like long tendrils in the legal case, perhaps manipulating those under him. See *CIH* 1421.35 (1417.3–1429.18 is a series of citations on people who are not able to give evidence; *CCIH* 64), and it is likely that this and the surrounding entries in Dubhaltach's Glossary come from this part of BL MS Egerton 88, or a MS which has a similar group of citations; the lemmata in Dubhaltach's Glossary are not an exact match for what is found in BL MS Egerton 88.

753 Cf. *eDIL s.v.* 2 *felesach*. See the first half of O'Dav 897 (no id.; *CCIH* 134: *Feles .i. fellas for les... "Feles* 'vanity', i.e. what betrays advantage..."); and *CIH* 1422.1 (1417.3–1429.18 is a series of citations on people who are not able to give evidence; *CCIH* 64), and it is likely that this and the surrounding entries in Dubhaltach's Glossary come from this part of BL MS Egerton 88, or a MS which has a similar group of citations; the lemmata in Dubhaltach's Glossary are not an exact match for what is found in BL MS Egerton 88.

754 The lemma is not in *eDIL*, but cf. *s.v. etsad, estad, autsad, itsad*. The meaning of the lemma is taken from the explanation provided. The meaning of *ré* is tentative as it could refer to a space of time as well as an indefinite number of people; *eDIL s.vv.* 1, 2, and 3 *ré*. The lemma is also listed in O'Don. Suppl. *s.v. eitsech*. See *CIH* 1422.2 (1417.3–1429.18 is a series of citations on people who are not able to give evidence; *CCIH* 64), and it is likely that this and the surrounding entries in Dubhaltach's Glossary come from this part of BL MS Egerton 88, or a MS which has a similar group of citations; the lemmata in Dubhaltach's Glossary are not an exact match for what is found in BL MS Egerton 88. Cf. 12.b.7.32 EITSECH.

755 The lemma is the 3 sg. pres. pass ind. of *fo-rig* 'detains, binds'. *Airgidhther* is likely a sg. pres. pass. subj. form of *ad-rig* 'binds', and *geibhther* is likely a sg. pres. pass. subj. form of *gaibid*; see *eDIL s.vv. fo-rig, ad-rig*, and *gaibid*. Cf. 7.a.14.20 FÚIRESTAR and 2.a.7.27 FUIRECHT.

8.13.35 Fo-coisle .i. fox*ladh*.
Fo-coisle 'takes away', i.e. taking away.[756]

8.14.36 Meadb*ha* .i. mesamnuig*h* .i. bret*h*em*h*.
Midba 'judge', i.e. judge, i.e. judge.[757]

8.14.37 Mead*h* .i. bá .i. mait*h*.
Med 'measure', i.e. good, i.e. good.[758]

8.14.38 Dána các*h* go h-iat*h* .i. go mion*na*.
Dánae cách co h-íath 'everyone is bold until an insignia', i.e. until emblems of rank.[759]

8.15.39 Églaim*m* .i. inc*h*rec*h*ad*h*.
Eclaimm 'examination', i.e. finding fault.[760]

---

756 For the lemma, see *Cethairṡlicht Athgabálae* (*CIH* 379.11; *AL* 1: 150.11); for a distant comparison with the lemma, cf. O'Dav 829 (*Bretha Nemed Toísech*; *CCIH* 132); and *Bretha Nemed Toísech* (*CIH* 2212.2; Breatnach 1989: § 7; *CCIH* 132). Cf. 13.d.11.20 FO-COISLE.

757 The lemma is not given the meaning 'judge' in *eDIL s.v. midba*(*e*); it is given the meaning 'middle cut, average'; the word is historically a compound of 3 *mid* and the vn. of *ben-* 'cuts, strikes'. In the entry on *fairbe*, there is a similar etymology involving cutting which develops into a word for advocate; *fairbe* is historically a compound containing the vn. of *ben-* 'strikes, cuts'; *eDIL s.v.* 2 *fairbe*. Based on the evidence from *fairbe* and the meanings provided in the entry, *meadhbha* is given the meaning 'judge' here. It should also be noted that the word appears in the title of a legal text *Midba Breth* in the pseudo-historical prologue to the *SM*. The text itself does not survive (*CIH* 1655.25; *CCIH* 71 and 265; and *AG* 36.3). For the lemma, cf. O'Dav 1213 (*Bretha Déin Chécht*; *CCIH* 144) and 1244 (*Status-tract*; *CCIH* 145); 1244 is the more relevant of the two as the *midbae* is said to be the one who measures every estimation. The word *mesamnuigh* is not listed in *eDIL*, but cf. *eDIL s.vv. meisem, mesam* 'an estimate, judgement' and *meisemnaigid* 'judges'. Cf. 2.b.3.74 FAIRBE and 8.11.30 FAIRBE.

758 The connection between the lemma and the glosses is not entirely clear, but it looks as if the entry is in origin an etymological gloss on the previous entry 8.14.36 MEADHBHA. Alternatively, the lemma belongs with the previous entry and there has been a copying mistake. Here *bá* is interpreted as a variant of *fó*, which is frequently glossed by *maith*; *eDIL s.v.* 1 *fó*. Cf. O'Cl *Ba.i. maith* 'good' and *Fó .i. maith*; and *Metr. Gl.* 9 § 4 *'Fó' ainm do mhaith is do mhíadh*.

759 The context of this entry is unknown, and the interpretation is tentative. For the first part of the lemma, cf. *TC* § 31.19; and cf. *Metr. Gl.* 9 § 4 *'Áoth' minn, ocus 'íath' ferann*. Cf. 3.b.11.46 DINNIS, 7.a.10.14 DINNIS, and 7.b.23.90 SLATRA ⁊ LATRA.

760 The interpretation of the lemma is uncertain. It could be for *eclaimm* 'investigation, examination'; *eDIL s.v. eclaimm*.

8.15.40 C*ar*aid claoc*h*lod*h*a .i. duine aga *m*bí claoc*h*lod*h* *cair*desa re a *th*igerna maille (in) [fri] tab*artus* do tab*air*t do*n* tigerna .⁊c.
Caraid claechlóda 'mutual friends', i.e. a person who has a mutual friendship with his lord together with giving a gift to the lord, etc.[761]

8.16.41 Lu*cht* codaig*h* naoim*h* no firen .i. len*us* daon naom am*h*áin, no lu*acht* aon patruin.
Lucht cotaigh naoimh nó fírén 'people of holy or righteous covenant', i.e. who only follow one holy person, or a people of one patron.[762]

8.17.42 Feall *ar* c*h*olb*h*a .i. faell *ar* anti bi*us* *ar* colb*h*a a lebt*h*a no ang*ar* do.
Fell ar colba 'deceit by a support', i.e. deceit by the one who is a support of his bed or undutiful to him.[763]

8.18.43 Sruaim .i. iomud.
Srúaim 'large quantity', i.e. large quantity.[764]

8.18.44 Taoi, taoiet*us* .i. tosd.
Tóe 'silence', *taitius* 'stealth', i.e. silence.[765]

8.18.45 Derlait*h*er .i. derb diog*h*lait*h*er.
Derlaither 'it is put away', i.e. [< *1 derb* 'truly' + *dedlain* 'severs, separates'] truly it is separated.[766]

---

761 The translation of the entry is tentative. The general sense of the lemma is of a mutual friend, which the entry explains as someone who has a mutual friendship with a lord involving them both giving gifts to each other. *Caraid* is a later nom. sg. of *cara* 'friend'; *eDIL s.v.* 1 *cara*. For *clœchlod*, see *eDIL s.v. coímchloud*. The emendation of *in* to *fri* is based on the common prepositional phrases formed with *immallé*, i.e. 'together with, jointly'.

762 The context of the entry is unknown.

763 The translation of the entry is tentative. The entry is about betrayal of someone who is a member of one's household or otherwise in a position of trust. The interpretation is complicated by the range of meanings for both *colba* 'part of a house, support, outer edge of a bed' and *lepaid* 'harborage, house-room, bed', thus the betrayal could be more specifically adultery; *eDIL s.vv. colba* and *lepaid*. The word *angar* is understood to be for 2 *ingor* 'undutiful'. For the gloss, cf. *Gúbretha Caratniad* § 33, gloss 2 (CIH 2197.1).

764 In glossaries *srúaim* 'stream' takes on the meaning 'large quantity' and is frequently glossed by *imbad*; *eDIL s.vv. srúaim* and *imbed, imbad*. See the first part of O'Dav 1464 ((1) no id.; CCIH 151: *Sruaim .i. imat*… "*Sruaim*, i.e. abundance…"); and *Lec. Gl.* 126 *Srua*[*i*]*m .i. imad*.

765 See O'Cl *Tai, no taoi .i. tosdach* 'silent'. Cf. 4.b.2.5 [TAOI].

766 See *eDIL s.vv.* 1 *do-lá* and *dedlaid*. For the lemma, cf. O'Dav 676 (probably from *Bretha Cairdi*; CCIH 128). See O'Don. Suppl. *s.v. dearlaiter*.

8.18.46 Esges .i. im u*m*aloid.
Éscus 'promptness', i.e. regarding humility.[767]

8.19.47 Roeach .i. ro sec*h*, no roiseic*h*em .i. ro ionsaig*adh*.
Roäch 'witness to a contract', i.e. he declared, or I declared, i.e. he advanced.[768]

8.19.48 Clot*h* .i. uirderc.
Cloth 'famous', i.e. famous.[769]

8.19.49 Córáoi .i. áoi cóir .i. caing*an* cóir.
Córae 'lawsuit', i.e. [< *2 áe* 'law-suit' + *cóir* 'proper, correct'] a just lawsuit, i.e. a just lawsuit.[770]

8.20.50 Gab*h*ail la flait*h* .i. dul a n-aig*id* na flat*h*a.
Gabál la flaith 'seizing by a lord', i.e. going against the lord.[771]

8.20.51 Dag*h*rac*h* .i. deg*hair*ec*h*.
Dagrach 'good chief', i.e. [< *dag* 'good' + *1 airech* 'chief, leader, noble'] good chief.[772]

8.20.52 Im-tobaing .i. éim*h*toibg*h*it*h*er.
Im-toboing 'he mutually exacts', i.e. [< *2 éim* 'prompt, ready' + *toibgid* 'exacts'] swiftly it is exacted.[773]

---

767 Cf. O'Cl *Umhalóid .i. umlachd* 'humility'.

768 See O'Dav 1338 (*Bretha Nemed Toísech*; CCIH 148: *Roach .i. ro sechad fiadan nó rosechad briathar, ut est for mac ⁊ rath ⁊ roach* "*Roach*, i.e. utter futility of a witness or utter futility of words, ut est 'on a son and a surety and a *roach*'."); and *Di Astud Chor* § 57 (CIH 989.5, 1194.32); and *Bretha Nemed Toísech* (CIH 2230.11; CCIH 89). The *roach* is an inferior/invalid witness to a contract. What is unclear in all of this is whether an earlier glossator misunderstood the meaning of *roäch*; in other words, perhaps the verbs should be closer to what we find in O'Dav 1338 rather than a variation on the standard glossing of *saigid* by *seichim no indsaigim*; *eDIL s.v. ind-saig* ?.

769 For the form *uirderc*, see *eDIL s.v. airdirc*. See *Stowe Gl.* 260 *Cloth .i. oirrdric*; and cf. O'Cl *Cloth .i. clu* 'fame'. Cf. 8.22.55 NODH.

770 The context is unknown.

771 The context of this entry is unknown.

772 Neither the lemma nor the gloss is in *eDIL*. The interpretation of the lemma is based on the gloss.

773 The lemma is not in *eDIL*, but it is a compound verb formed of the prefix *imm-* 'around,

8.21.53 Tósa .i. imden*adh*, no mion*n*aig*ad*.
Tosa 'he may swear', i.e. proving, or swearing.[774]

8.21.54 Muire[dh]ac*h* .i. moiriat*h*ac*h* .i. rig*h* moi*r* ferui[nn].
Muiredach 'lord', i.e. lord, i.e. [< *mór* 'great, large' + *rí* 'king'] great king of a territory.[775]

8.22.55 Nodh .i. urd*air*c.
Nóad 'making known', i.e. well-known.[776]

8.22.56 Con*árd*h*ata .i. com*h*aididn*igh*th*e*.
Conardata 'equally-acknowledged', i.e. equally-acknowledged.[777]

8.22.57 Manda m*air*m*h*esa .i. iom*ad* moi*r* mesa.
Manna moirmesa 'of an abundance of large mast', i.e. a large quantity of mast.[778]

---

about mutually' and *do-boing* 'wrests, levies, recovers, exacts'; *eDIL s.vv.* 3 *imm-*, *im-* and *do-boing*. It is common for the preverb *im-* to be glossed by *éim* 'swift, timely'; Binchy 1943: 212; and Taylor-Griffiths 2020: 1: 89. The form *toibghither* is a 3 sg. pres. pass. ind. from *toibgid*, a later simplex of *do-boing*.

774 The general meaning of the lemma is clear from the glosses provided, but its precise parse is less certain. It appears to be a 3 sg, pres. subj. of *tongaid* 'swears'; for the lemma, cf. *Bretha Nemed Dédenach* 23.12 (CIH 1118.8; CCIH 184–188). The word *imdénad* is a later form of *imdénam*, and *minnaigad* is a later denominative from 1 *minn*; cf. *eDIL s.vv. imdénam*i and *minnaigid*. The final syllable of *minnaigad* has been expanded as *-ad* to create a vn. to match the vn. *imdénad*, but the palatal ⟨g⟩ would suggest that the final syllable could be expanded as *-id*, forming a 3 sg, pres. ind., 'he swears'.

775 The word *moiriathach* is interpreted as a form of *muiredach*. The translation of the second half of the entry is tentative as it is out of context. The missing letters in the gloss are supplied from O'Curry's transcription. See the first part of O'Dav 1273 (no id.; CCIH 146: *Muiredach .i. righ*... "*Muiredach*, i.e. king...").

776 The interpretation of the lemma is based on O'Cl *Nódh .i. oirdheirc* 'famous'; and O'Dav 1287 (heptad 33; CIH 30.8; CCIH 146: *Noudh .i. athnugud no urdarcugud*... "*Noudh*, i.e. renewing or making conspicuous..."). Cf. 8.19.48 CLOTH.

777 The lemma appears to be a compound of *con-* and *ardata* 'acknowledged'; *eDIL s.v.* ? *ardata*; and cf. more distantly O'Dav 1301 (no id., perhaps a pleading; CCIH 147: *Nardata .i. aitin*... "*Nardata*, i.e. recognition..."). The gloss is similarly a compound of *com-* and the past. part. of *aititnigid* 'acknowledges'; *eDIL s.v. aititnigid*.

778 For the lemma, see *eDIL s.v.* 2 *mann*. See the first part of O'Dav 1233 (no id.; CCIH 145: *Mann .i. imat*... "*Mann*, i.e. abundance...") and 1234 ((3) no id.; CCIH 145: *Mann*...*Nó mann .i. imad, ut est uasal aradren mann marmesa .i. imad mesa co mór* "*Mann*... Or *mann*, i.e. abundance,

8.23.58 N*ár* .i. fíor.
Nár 'honorable', i.e. true.[779]

8.23.59 Uircria .i. crena ⟨.i. cennach⟩, c*r*iona, caill*ech*, no t*er*ca.
Archria 'you wither', i.e. you buy ⟨i.e. buying⟩, you wither, elderly woman, or scarcity.[780]

8.23.60 Asné .i. asé.
Asné 'which is he', i.e. it is he.[781]

8.23.61 Om*h* .i. indlig*thech*.
Om 'raw', i.e. unlawful.[782]

8.24.62 Coimpert .i. coim*h* eibt*er*, coim*air*b*er*tnug*adh*, ⁊ gei*n*nem*h*iun*n*.
Compert 'conception', i.e. [< *cáem* 'well, suitable' + *ibid* 'drinks, suckles'] well they may be suckled, being born, and birth.[783]

8.24.63 Sais .i. ion*nsaigh*is.
Sáis 'he may claim', i.e. that he claims.[784]

---

ut est 'a noble who buys up plenty of great mast', i.e. abundance of mast greatly."); and cf. O'Cl *Mann .i. biad* 'food'.

779 Cf. O'Cl. *Nar .i. maith* 'good'; and for the lemma, cf. O'Dav 1283 (*Bretha Nemed Toísech*; CCIH 146) and 1290 (*Bretha Nemed Dédenach*; CCIH 146). Cf. 4.c.14.82 NÁR.

780 The entry is difficult for a number of reasons. The lemma itself could be a 2 sg. pres. ind. from *airchraid*, a later form of *ara-chrin* 'decays, withers'; *eDIL s.v. ara-chrin*. The first gloss, *crena*, looks like the 2 sg. pres. ind. of *crenaid* 'buys' (and it is glossed as such here and in O'Cl), but it could also be from the verb *crainnid* 'gnaws, corrodes, devours', which makes sense considering the remainder of the glosses in the entry; *eDIL s.vv. crenaid* and *creinnid*. Cf. O'Cl *Crean .i. ceannach* 'purchase'.

781 See *eDIL s.v.* 1 *é, hé*. The lemma is understood as containing a nasalizing rel. clause with the copula.

782 See *Di Astud Chirt ⁊ Dligid* (CIH 225.18–19, 35, CCIH 293–294; AL 5: 432.2 and 434.6) which refers to the three raw unlawful morsels.

783 It is common for the prefix *com-* to be glossed by *cáem*; see Taylor-Griffiths 2020: 1: 88; and *eDIL s.v.* 1 *cáem*. Although neither the verb *comairbertnaigther* nor its vn. *comairbertnugud* is defined in *eDIL*, the sense seems to be 'brings forth, gives birth'; it is also found in heptad 47 (CIH 43.16; AL 5: 276.24).

784 The verb *ind-saig* 'approaches, seeks, claims, sues' frequently glosses *saigid* in legal texts and has a later simplex *indsaigid*, which is found in the entry here; *eDIL s.v. ind-saig* ?. The entry is out of context, thus, there is the possibility that the lemma could be a conjunct 2 sg., pres. subj. form, but for the gloss to be 2 sg., it would have to be preterite, which is less likely in this case. Cf. 7.b.25.95 SIAS.

8.24.64 Imitec[h]t .i. tec[h]t ui*m*[e].
Immitecht 'wandering', i.e. [< *imm* 'around, about' + *techt* 'going'] going about.[785]

8.25.65 Coindfe .i. comad*hus*, coi*m*d*h*eilit*h*ec*h*.
Coindfe 'proper', i.e. proper, sharing with.[786]

8.25.66 Fiad*h*at .i. tigerna.
Fíadat 'of a lord', i.e. of a lord.[787]

8.25.67 Dit*h*le .i. adb*h*al élaidt*h*e.
Díthle 'theft', i.e. great absconding.[788]

8.25.68 Ro-sgot[h] .i. ro ion*n*saig*h*ter.
Ro-scoth 'he said', i.e. it was claimed.[789]

8.26.69 Tret*h*on*n* .i. t*r*i t*r*eoín.
Trethan 'fury', i.e. [< *trí* 'three' + *trén* 'strong man'] three strong-men.[790]

---

785 *Uime* is a later form of *imm* 'around, about'; *eDIL s.v.* 1 *imm, imb*. For the lemma more distantly, cf. O'Dav 1002 (no id.; CCIH 138).

786 The final word in the entry is not in *eDIL*, and the meaning is uncertain. Although one would expect a meaning along the lines of 'fitting, suitable, proper', it appears to be related to *con-dáili* 'shares'. It is also possible that it is a mistake for *comdligthech* 'equally legitimate'. Cf. DDC *Cuindisem .i. coindfe arisma .i. dun co trebaib*; O'Cl *Comhdhas .i. comhadhas or coimdhlightheach*… 'suitable or lawful…'; for the lemma, cf. O'Dav 473 (likely from *Bretha Cairdi*; CCIH 122); and *Fonnaidh* glossary (CIH 1079.3); and cf. CIH 1980.28 (CCIH 46).

787 There is no context for the lemma or gloss, but both appear to be in the gen. sg. See O'Cl *Fiadh .i. tighearna* 'lord'.

788 The gloss provided is common for the lemma, and the general sense is stealing something of value. See *Di Astud Chirt 7 Dligid* (CIH 228.14 and 18, 231.15 and 19, 958.16, 1869.32; CCIH 24 and 42; AL 5: 440.21 and 26). Cf. O'Don. Suppl. *s.v. dithle*.

789 The lemma appears to be the 3 sg. pret. of the verb **scothaid* 'says' based on *scoth* 'word, saying, speech'; *eDIL s.vv.* 3 *scoth* and cf. *miscad* 'curse, malediction' and *roscad* 'legal maxim or aphorism'. The verb *ind-saig* 'approaches, seeks, claims, sues' frequently glosses *saigid* in legal texts and has a later simplex *indsaigid*, which is found in the entry here; *eDIL s.v. ind-saig* ?. The meaning in this entry refers to advancing a suggestion, thus, saying something. Cf. *Lec. Gl.* 272 *Scoth .i. indsce*; O'Cl *Scoth .i. innsce* 'word'; SC Y.859 *Miscath .i. mí-innsci. Scath .i. innsei, amail atá Duil Roscadach*; and for the lemma, cf. *Bretha Nemed Dédenach* 17.12 (CIH 1114.8; CCIH 184–188).

790 Although *trethan* usually means 'sea, storm', it also has metaphorical meanings such as 'uproar, fury, thundering', which seems to be the sense here. For the lemma, cf. O'Cl *Treathan .i. ton* 'wave'; O'Dav 1576 (*Fél.* June 3; CCIH 155); and heptad 54 (CIH 49.10; AL 5: 298.8–300.20; and Eska 2022: 392–393).

8.26.70 Uais .i. uasal, ion*n*sa, no an*n*sa.
Úais 'noble', i.e. noble, hard, or difficult.[791]

8.26.71 Lúiter.i. tionoilt*er*.
Luiter 'is moved', i.e. is gathered.[792]

8.27.72 Ro-ná .i. ro cengail, ut [est] ro-nas.
Ro-na 'he may bind', i.e. he bound, *ut est* it was bound.[793]

8.27.73 Déis .i. feran*n*.
Déis 'land', i.e. land.[794]

8.27.74 Beab*h*ais .i. ég*h*ais.
Bebais 'he died', i.e. he died.[795]

8.27.75 Bert .i. b*r*it*h*em*h*n*agh*t*h*is.
Bert 'he judged', i.e. he judged.[796]

8.28.76 Laithne .i. Laitin.
Laithne 'of Latin', i.e. Latin.[797]

8.28.77 Ion*n*sguc*h*ud*h* g*r*ad*h* no ceíme .i. árdug*adh* g*r*aid*h* .⁊c[.] no ceim[e].
Indscuchud grad nó ceime 'changing ranks or degree', i.e. raising rank, etc. or degree.[798]

---

791 The lemma and the last two glosses are found in their unidentified source text; see CIH 1578.24 (CCIH 69); cf. O'Cl *Uais .i. uasal*... 'noble....'

792 The lemma is from *luïd* 'moves' which was early replaced by 1 *lúaidid*; *eDIL s.v. luïd*. The form *tionoilter* is from *tinóilid*, a later simplex of *do-inóla* 'gathers, musters, collect'; *eDIL s.v. do-inóla*. For the lemma, cf. heptad 24 (CIH 24.6; AL 5: 210.25).

793 See *eDIL s.v. naiscid* 'binds, secures'. In the gloss, we see the use of *ro-* to form preterites whereas it is used for the subjunctive in the lemma. For the lemma, cf. O'Dav 1378 (no id.; CCIH 149).

794 Cf. 14.h.12.35 DÉISDE, FESDHIDE, NO ESDIDE and 7.a.3.4 DÉISTE. Cf. O'Cl *Dés .i. fearann* 'land'.

795 Cf. O'Cl *Beabhais no adbath .i. fuair bás* 'he died'.

796 For the lemma, cf. O'Dav 280 (no id.; CCIH 117) although there *bert* is a noun. The gloss is tentatively understood as the 3 sg. pret. of *brithemnaigid* 'adjudges'. Cf. 6.a.4.13 BERT.

797 See *eDIL s.v. Laiten*.

798 See. O'Don. Suppl. *s.v. ionnscuchad graidh*. The general sense of the entry is to move upwards in social status. The form *gradh* might be a mistake for the gen. sg. *graidh*, and *ceíme* appears to be a later gen. sg. of *céim* 'step, rank, degree'. The first part of the entry is found also in *Uraicecht Becc* (CIH 1595.18; AL 5: 22.28).

8.29.78 Aig*h*ne fris-n-in*n*le br*eth* .i. aig*n*ne fir-in*n*lit*h*er do dena*m* br*eth*em*h*-n*us*a .i. legaid*h* cuirp an br*e*[ith]em*h*nuis, ⁊ berid*h* an t-ollam*h*an br*eth*, ase si*n* aigne as onor*agh*e do*n*a h-aig*h*ne*d*aib*h* .⁊c.
Aigne fris-n-indlea breth 'an advocate whom judgement encounters', i.e. an advocate who [< *fír* 'truly' + *indlid* 'prepares'] truly-prepares to make a judgement, i.e. he reads the body of the law, and the *ollam* gives judgement, it is he who is an *aigne* who is an honorer of the advocates, etc.[799]

8.31.79 Cod-ródaig*h* .i. ro c*h*um*h*daig*h*.
Cot-rodaig 'he preserved it', i.e. he preserved it.[800]

8.31.80 Dos-n-alla .i. didnig*h*.
Dos-n-alla 'he takes them away', i.e. he protects.[801]

8.31.81 Tóirsiod .i. do rósad .i. do roin*n*e.
Toirsed 'he would attain', i.e. he had created, i.e. he had made.[802]

8.31.82 Daon .i. duin[e].
Doén 'person', i.e. person.[803]

8.32.83 Urgna*m* .i. urf*h*og*h*na*m*h.
Aurgnam 'preparing', i.e. extra service.[804]

8.32.84 Coitg*h*e .i. comtuige .i. co*m*c*h*um*h*dac*h*.
Cotga 'covering', i.e. covering, i.e. mutually-covering.[805]

---

799 See *Cethairṡlicht Athgabálae* (CIH 896.19 and 33; CCIH 40; and Breatnach 1990a: 11–12); and *Uraicecht Becc* (CIH 1614.35–37; AL 5: 100.22–24). The interpretation of the entry is tentative; see the discussion in Breatnach 1990a.

800 The lemma is a 3 sg. pret. of *con-utainc* with a Class B 3 sg. object agreement marker. The form *ro chumhdaigh* is a 3 sg. pret. of *cumtaigid*, a later simplex of *con-utainc* 'builds, preserves, protects'; *eDIL s.v. con-utainc, con-utaing*.

801 See *eDIL s.vv. do-alla* and 2 *dítnid*.

802 See *eDIL s.vv. do-roich, do-fuissim*, and *do-gní*.

803 The missing letter is supplied from O'Curry's transcription. For the lemma, cf. O'Dav 342 (*Bretha Nemed Toísech*; CCIH 118).

804 Both the lemma and gloss refer to the work involved with providing service, usually in preparing food and drink; *eDIL s.vv. aurgnam* and *airḟognam*; cf. *Cáin Lánamna* § 11 and gloss 1 (CIH 507.29); and O'Cl *Urgnamh .i. fleadh* 'feast'.

805 The lemma is an early form of *comthuige*, which glosses it here; *eDIL s.v. comthuige*. For the first gloss, see *Cáin Ḟuithirbe* (CIH 771.38–39; CCIH 214).

8.32.85 Túid*h*men*ar* .i. cengailt[h]er.
Tuidmenar 'is bound', i.e. is bound.[806]

8.32.86 Urlata .i. uasal lúite.
Aurlatu 'obedience', i.e. [< *úasal* 'high, noble, honorable' + *lúaite* 'going'] honorable going.[807]

8.33.87 Ad-raig*h* .i. cenglaid*h*.
Ad-rig 'he binds', i.e. he binds.[808]

8.33.88 Árag*ar* .i. cenguilt[h]*er*.
Áragar 'is bound', i.e. is bound.[809]

8.33.89 Fos-geallaid*h* .i. fuig*h*lid*h* .i. b*r*iat*r*aigig.
Fos-gellaid 'he pronounces a verdict on it', i.e. he pronounces a verdict, i.e. he judges.[810]

8.34.90 Sern*ar* .i. s*r*eat*h*naig*h*t[h]*er*.
Sernar 'is arranged', i.e. is arranged.[811]

8.34.91 Fáonán .i. ionan*n*.
Fáenan 'the same', i.e. the same.[812]

---

806 The lemma is a 3 sg. pres. pass. of *do-dímen* 'binds, makes fast'; *eDIL s.v. do-dímen*. For the lemma, see Digest B (1) (*CIH* 1289.38; *CCIH* 53; *AL* 4: 374.28).

807 The definition is an etymological gloss on the lemma; *eDIL s.v. lúaite*. Cf. O'Cl *Urlaithe .i. ésgaidh* 'quick' and *Urlaitidh .i. umhalóid* 'humility'; and O'Dav 1608 (*Bretha Nemed Toísech*; *CCIH* 156: *[U]rlaiti .i. umhaloid, ut est aes fognama "Aurlaiti,* i.e. humility, ut est 'obedient servants'."). Cf. 4.c.14.85 URLATA.

808 For the lemma, see *Bretha Nemed Toísech* (*CIH* 2226.22; *CCIH* 89). The gloss confirms that the lemma is not a form of *at-reig* 'rises'. Cf. 8.33.88 ÁRAGAR.

809 For the lemma, see *Bretha Nemed Toísech* (*CIH* 2226.22; *CCIH* 89). Cf. *Bretha Nemed Dédenach* 13.23 (*CIH* 1111.19; *CCIH* 184–188). Cf. 8.33.87 AD-RAIGH.

810 The lemma and both glosses carry the same semantic range of pronouncing a judgement, judging, and speaking; *eDIL s.vv. fo-gella, 2 fuiglid*, and *bríathraigid*. For the lemma, see *Bretha Nemed Toísech* (*CIH* 2226.22; *CCIH* 89).

811 For the gloss, cf. Digest B (11) (*CIH* 1303.15–16; *CCIH* 55). For the lemma, see *Bretha Nemed Dédenach* 40.4 (*CIH* 1129.34; *CCIH* 184–188; Corthals 2010: 75 and 78 where the lemma is translated as 'is displayed'); and see O'Dav 1444 (*Bretha Nemed Dédenach*; *CCIH* 151: *Sernar .i. gabtair… .i. srethnaighther… "Sernair,* i.e. is recited… i.e., let it be distributed…") where both the lemma and gloss are found as part of a larger entry. The verb *sreth(n)aigid* frequently glosses *sernaid*; *eDIL s.v. sreth(n)aigid*. Cf. 10.45.116 SERNAR.

812 See O'Cl *Faon .i. faonann .i. ionann* 'the same'; and for the lemma, cf. O'Dav 159 (no id.; *CCIH* 113). Cf. 8.35.94 FRITHID.

8.34.92 Annac*h* .i. ánoig*h*e adalt*r*ais.
Andach 'badness', i.e. of incomplete fornication.[813]

8.34.93 Fuada .i. eire, no fodla.
Fúata 'Ireland', i.e. *Ériu* or *Fódla*.[814]

8.35.94 F*r*it*h*id .i. ionan*n*.
Frithid 'the same', i.e. the same.[815]

8.35.95 Fuigeall .i. lanfuigioll.
Fuigell 'judgement', i.e. final decision.[816]

8.35.96 Urfuigioll .i. ordug*adh* suidig*h*te geall.
Airḟuigell 'preliminary decision', i.e. established order of pledges.[817]

8.35.97 Ad-boib .i. obt*har*.
Ad-boib 'he will refuse', i.e. is refused.[818]

---

813 Cf. *Fél.* February 16; O'Cl *Andach .i. olc* 'evil' and *Andagh .i. old no peacadh* 'evil or sin'; and O'Dav 71 (*Fél.* Prol. 237 and *Fél.* Feb. 16; *CCIH* 110). The entry is best understood in the citation from *Fél.* February 16 where the fornication with the Devil is not completed.

814 This is one of three entries in *eDIL* which cites TCD 1401 by the shelf mark H.5.30; the dictionary is actually citing O'Curry's transcription and not the MS itself. Both of the glosses are also words for 'Ireland'. For the lemma, see *Cáin Fhuithirbe* (49; *CIH* 776. 40); and for the lemma and first gloss, see O'Dav 902 (*Cáin Ḟuithirbe*; *CCIH* 138; *Fuata .i. ere*… '*Fuata*, i.e. a burden…').

815 Cf. 8.34.91 FÁONÁN. *eDIL s.v. 2 frithid* cites Peter O'Connell's Irish-English dictionary as the source for this citation. O'Connell himself simply notes his source as an 'Old Glossary' without further details; see BL MS Egerton 83, p. 389. The entry in O'Connell is one of the later additions that has been squeezed in between other lines; it is written in smaller letters and in a lighter shade of ink. See https://www.dib.ie/biography/oconnell-peter-o-conaill-peadar-a6577 accessed February 2, 2023. Most of O'Connell's dictionary was absorbed into O'Reilly's dictionary where the lemma is also found. The relationship between O'Connell's dictionary and Dubhaltach's Glossary is a subject which will be taken up in the future by the author.

816 Cf. O'Cl *Fuigheall no fughall .i. breitheamhnas* 'judgment'.

817 For the gloss, see *Urchuillti Bretheman* § 5 (Thurneysen 1930: 362–364; Thurneysen 1933: 129; Smith 1934: 25; *CIH* 2103.2; *CCIH* 85 and 280). The gloss is from a list of things forbidden to judges. See also *GEIL* 268.

818 For the lemma, see *eDIL s.v. as-boind*; and *Bretha Nemed Dédenach* 19.6 and 28.25–26 (*CIH* 1115. 18 and 1121.38–39; *CCIH* 184–188).

8.36.98 Fodo[-]tlena .i. ḟoet*h*lás.
Fodo-tlena 'who may steal it', i.e. who steals.[819]

8.36.99 Forto-tuigidt*her* .i. tig i ffortac*h* imden*m*a.
Fordo-tuigidther 'who covers it', i.e. [< *do-icc* 'comes' + *i* 'in, for' + *fortach* 'over-swearing'] he who comes in order to provide overriding testimony.[820]

8.36.100 Feat*h*al .i. mion*n*, egc*us*c.
Fethal 'appearance', i.e. distinguishing characteristic, appearance.[821]

8.36.101 Ud*h*ban*ar* .i. iod*h*b*ar*[tar].
Adbonar 'notice is given', i.e. is offered.[822]

8.37.102 Ad-uid*h*bre .i. ad*h*a iod*h*b*h*ras.
A*d-id*[*-i*]*bre* 'who may offer it', i.e. [< *ada* 'suitable, fitting' + *idbraid* 'offers'] fitting that he offered.[823]

8.37.103 Slatra .i. dánáu, no ainbḟiele.
Slatra 'stronger', i.e. bolder, or more shameless.[824]

---

819 See *Di Astud Chirt 7 Dligid* (CIH 235.2 and 10–11; CCIH 293–294; AL 5: 462.3 and 14). The verb *fo-etlan* frequently glosses *fo-tlen*. The form here is a 3 sg. rel. from a later simplex; *eDIL s.vv. fo-tlen* and *fo-etlan*.

820 See *Di Astud Chirt 7 Dligid* (CIH 235.3; CCIH 293–294; AL 5: 462.3). The sense of the gloss is that someone has made an oath which overrides that of others; the translation of the gloss is tentative; *eDIL s.v. for-tuigethar*.

821 See O'Dav 899 (no id.; CCIH 134: *Fethal .i. cumdach comartha nó minn, ut est imdénat som la fethla, ocus cach lasa mbiat fethla .i. ecusc no comartha* "*Fethal*, i.e. a shrine, or mark, or relic, ut est 'they prove with relics', and 'every one who has insignia', i.e. appearance or mark."); the *Ni Tulach* glossary (CIH 810.13–14); and cf. the *Arra* glossary (CIH 1560.15–16). For the second gloss, see SC Y.669 *Feuthal .i. eugasg*; and O'Cl *Feathal .i. éccosc, nó Cuma* 'face or form'. While *fethal* and *mind* can also refer to a halidom, the inclusion of *éccosc* suggests that the meaning here is 'distinguishing characteristic or appearance'; *eDIL s.vv. fethal, mind,* and *éccosc*, respectively. Cf. 5.b.22.45 FETHAOL.

822 For the lemma, cf. *Bretha Nemed Toísech* (CIH 2221.37; CCIH 89); *eDIL s.vv. ad-boind* and *ad-opair*. The translation of the entry is tentative as the reading of the gloss is not secure. The missing letters are supplied from O'Curry's transcription.

823 The lemma is particularly problematic. It appears to be the 3 sg. pres. subj. of *ad-opair* 'offers up, sacrifices, grants' with a Class C n. object agreement marker; cf. the form in "An Irish Penitential" 154 § 4, *madidipre* 'if he offers it'. For the etymological gloss, see the Introduction, pp. 13–16. The second half of the gloss is a 3 sg. pret. *idbraid*, a later simplex of *ad-opair*; *eDIL s.v. ad-opair*.

824 See *Lec. Gl.* 141 *Slatra .i. dana*; and Meyer 1910: 311 § 12. The lemma and glosses are all com-

8.38.104 Daifenn .i. fu*ar*uige, no su*ára*g*h*e.
Daithfenn 'rejection', i.e. coldness, or meanness.[825]

9.1.1 Clu .i. u*r*dercad*h*.
Clú 'fame', i.e. making known.[826]

9.1.2 Clo, cluas*ach* .i. [....]ge
Clú 'fame', *clúasach* 'pleasing to hear', i.e. ...[827]

9.1.3 *Ar* a l*eth* iarait*h* .i. fi[...]*us* si du[...........]
Ar a leth íarraith 'for half fosterage of him', i.e. ...[828]

9.1.4 [.....] .i. s*et*ran [..].[829]

9.2.5 Siride .i. siort*h*oir bi*us* ag sired*h* aide no aite.
Sirite 'those who wander', i.e. a wanderer who is [< *siriud* 'wandering' + *áitt* 'place, abode' + *nó* 'or' + 2 *aite* 'abode, dwelling'] wandering a place or abode.[830]

---

paratives; see *eDIL s.vv. 3 slat, slait, 1 dánae*, and *ainfíal*, respectively. Cf. 7.b.23.90 SLATRA ⁊ LATRA. I should like to thank one of the anonymous readers for comments on this entry.

825 The meaning of the lemma is uncertain; *eDIL s.v. ? daithfenn*. See *Apgitir Chrábaid* 'Alphabet of Piety' §10.49. The variant spelling *daifenn* is also found in the version edited in Meyer 1901: 450.3. The interpretation of the first gloss is tentative; it is interpreted as an abstract noun based on *1 úarach* 'cold, chilly'. Dubhaltach writes 'aibgider crabad' before the entry.

826 See O'Dav 466 (*Bretha Nemed Toísech*; CCIH 122: *Clú .i. urdairc, ut est clu conmider ar(?) a cil* "*Clú*, i.e. famous, ut est 'fame is judged...'"); and *Bretha Nemed Dédenach* 40.20 (CIH 1130.11; Corthals 2010: 77 and 79 where it is translated as 'reputation'). For the second half of the O'Dav entry, cf. *Bretha Nemed Toísech* (CIH 2228.30; CCIH 89 and 122). The gloss is the vn. of *airdircid*. Cf. 2.b.2.73 CLÚ.

827 The entry is not in O'Curry's transcription. This entry is difficult as the gloss is illegible. The first lemma is interpreted as a variant spelling of *clú* 'fame'; cf. 9.1.1 CLU and 2.b.2.73 CLÚ. For the second lemma, see *Bretha Nemed Dédenach* 39.25 (CIH 1129.24; Corthals 2007: 139 and 142 where it is translated as *anzuhören* 'to listen').

828 The entry is not in O'Curry's transcription. The interpretation of this entry is tentative because so much of the line is illegible.

829 The entry is not in O'Curry's transcription. The reading is very tentative.

830 The entry refers to wandering cattle. For the lemma, cf. the phrase *sechem sirite* 'following those who wander'; *eDIL s.v. sechem. Sirite* is the 3 pl. pres. rel. of *sirid* 'wanders'; for *siorthoir*, interpreted here as 'wanderer', cf. Mod. Ir. *sirtheoir* 'seeker, petitioner, beggar'. See O'Dav 1407 (no id.; CCIH 150: *Seichme siriti .i. in tellach*[read *in t-ellach*] *lenas duine cen chet do, ut est* [*annsom tighradus ⁊rl.*] *sechme siriti ala crich .i. na sirthoraigh bid ag siredh aiti no aide* [*leg aige?*] *tar in crich no as in crich* "*Sechem siriti*, i.e. the [cattle] (family) that follows

9.2.6 Forraid*h* .i. foirid*h*.
Foraid 'he helped', i.e. he helps.[831]

9.2.7 Cuirioc*h* [.]occe .i. [t]on*n* c*r*iot*h*aig no [loitbert]a[i]g*h*.
Cuirrech 'marsh' [.....] .i. quaking or harmful bog.[832]

9.3.8 Dio*thchus* .i. adb*ar* to*chus*.
Díthchus 'possessions', i.e. the makings of property.[833]

9.3.9 Dringes .i. d*r*emnis.
Dringes 'who climbs', i.e. who climbs.[834]

9.3.10 Dlaoi fulla .i. an draoi Fullan .i. an cuid dola b*r*io*cht* for dlaoi do cur duin*e ar* [.......] [l]a si*n* d*r*aoi si*n* do h-oil*edh* Nuad*h*a Fullon, ⁊ uaide ain*mnigh*ter dlaoi fulla. Coir An*mann* si*n*.
Dlaí fulla 'hair of vagrancy', i.e. [< *druí* 'druid' + *fullón* 'handsome'] the druid Fullón, i.e. the one who put a spell on a wisp [of hair] to set

a man without his leave, ut est 'a most difficult *tigradus* etc.'." Stokes does not translate the reminder of the entry.); CIH 1326.36 (CCIH 150); and *Di Choimét Dligthech* (CIH 1743.16–17; CCIH 287–288; and AL 2: 72.29). I should like to thank one of the anonymous readers for suggestions and comments on this entry.

831 The lemma is interpreted as a 3 sg. pret. of *fo-reith* 'helps'; the gloss is the 3 sg. pres. of *foirid* 'helps, remedies'.

832 Most of this entry is illegible. O'Curry reads the first word as 'luirioch'. It is possible that the first word should be *cuirrech* 'marsh, fen' (in the MS, it looks like a ⟨c⟩ was made over a ⟨b⟩), and the final word of the gloss might be the gen. sg. of *lottbertach* 'harmful, destructive'; see *eDIL s.v. lott* 'ruin, injury, damage'; EIF 182 and 395–396; and cf. *Findśruth Fíthail* (CIH 166.38 and 2139.18; CCIH 20 and 88). The passage of commentary mentions 'quaking bogs' as an accidental cause of death to livestock. Cf. O'Dav 514 (heptad 5; CCIH 124; CIH 6.24; AL 5: 138.12: *Cechair .i. cec[h]air a huachtar ⁊ uisce a hichtar ⁊ lathach .i. lathach a hichtar ⁊ uisce a huachtar, is i a ndeithber. Nó cechair .i. tonda crithir ⁊ sruth for a huachtar ⁊ uisce ⁊rl. for a hichtar, ⁊ laith .i. feith ⁊ uisce for a huachtar* "*Cechair*, i.e. marsh (is) its upper part and water its lower part, but *lathach*, i.e. slough its lower part and water its upper part. Or *cechair*, i.e. a quagmire (?), and a stream on it surface and water etc. on its bottom, and *laith*, i.e. a bogstream and water on its surface."). Although the phrase *tonn crithech* means 'bog', the gloss suggests that we understand both adjectives as describing *tonn*. It is unclear whether *tonn* still retains its common meaning of 'wave' here, or whether we are to understand the gloss as providing either two terms different types of bogs or two terms for 'bog'.

833 For the meaning of the lemma, see the bibliography in *eDIL s.v. díthchus*. For the lemma, see *Di Ḟodlaib Cenéoil Túaithe* (CIH 432.17; CCIH 25). See O'Don. Suppl. *s.v. dithchus*.

834 For the lemma, see *eDIL s.v. dringid* 'climbs', the vn. of which is *dréim*. The verb *dréimnigid*, based on the vn. *dréim*, frequently glosses *dringid* in the legal texts; *eDIL s.v. dréimnigid*.

a person […] that druid who fostered Nuada Fullón, and from which it is called *dlaí fulla* 'hair of vagrancy'. That is from *Cóir Anmann*.[835]

9.4.11 Lai*th*, lat*hach* .i. sraid*h* .i. uisge [ina] h-u*achtar* ⁊ cec*hair* [i]na h-io*chtar*.
Laith 'puddle', *lathach* 'mire', i.e. way, i.e. water in the upper part and quagmire in the lower part.[836]

9.5.12 Cec*hair* .i. cec*hair* [i]na h-u*achtar* ⁊ *us*ge [i]na h-io*chtar* .i. dubt*h*on-n*a*c.
Cechar 'quagmire', i.e. quagmire in the upper part and water in the lower part, i.e. dark brown.[837]

9.5.13 Com*m*or cuan .i. ionad ina com*m*[ar]….
Commar cúan 'assembly of hosts', i.e. the place in which [there is] an assembly …[838]

---

835 Parts of the entry are illegible. The missing letter is supplied from O'Curry's transcription. See *Cóir Anmann* 'Fitness of Names' 110 (short version) and 187 (long version). The entry in the glossary is very similar to that of the source text, but not identical. For the lemma, cf. *Córus Bésgnai* § 9, gloss 12; and McCone 1986a: 16. The noun *cuit* 'share, portion' is interpreted here in its pronominal use; *eDIL s.v. cuit* (7). The form *dola* is interpreted as the 3 sg. pret. of *fo-ceird, ro-lá*; for *do h-oiledh* see *eDIL s.v.* 1 *ailid*. For the MI interchange of the preverbs *do-*, *ro-*, and *no-*, see McCone 1997: 197.

836 The meaning of the first lemma is taken from the second lemma. See O'Dav 514 (heptad 5; *CCIH* 124: *Cechair .i. cec[h]air a huachtar ⁊ uisce a hichtar ⁊ lathach .i. lathach a hictar ⁊ uisce a huachtar, is í a ndeithber. Nó cechair .i. tonda crithir ⁊ sruth for a huachtar ⁊ uisce ⁊rl. for a hichtar, ⁊ laith .i. faith ⁊ uisce for a huachtar* "*Cechair*, i.e. a marsh (is) its upper part and water its lower part, but *lathach*, i.e. slough its lower part and water its upper part. This is the difference. Or *cechair*, i.e. a quagmire (?), and a stream on its surface and water etc. on its bottom, and *laith*, i.e. a bogstream and water on its surface."); and heptad 5 (*CIH* 6.24, 1884.30 and 34–35; and *AL* 5: 138.11). Cf. O'Cl *Ceachair .i. lathach* 'dirty'. Cf. 9.5.12 CECHAIR.

837 See O'Dav 514 (heptad 5; *CCIH* 124: *Cechair .i. cec[h]air a huachtar ⁊ uisce a hichtar ⁊ lathach .i. lathach a hictar ⁊ uisce a huachtar, is í a ndeithber. Nó cechair .i. tonda crithir ⁊ sruth for a huachtar ⁊ uisce ⁊rl. for a hichtar, ⁊ laith .i. faith ⁊ uisce for a huachtar* "*Cechair*, i.e. a marsh (is) its upper part and water its lower part, but *lathach*, i.e. slough its lower part and water its upper part. This is the difference. Or *cechair*, i.e. a quagmire (?), and a stream on its surface and water etc. on its bottom, and *laith*, i.e. a bogstream and water on its surface."); and heptad 5 (*CIH* 6.24, 1884.30 and 34–35; and *AL* 5: 138.12). Cf. O'Cl *Ceachair .i. lathach* 'dirty'. Cf. 9.4.11 LAITH, LATHACH.

838 The interpretation of the phrase is uncertain as *cúan* could be the gen. pl. of *cúan* 'river, waters' or the gen. pl. of the m. *o*-stem inflection of *cú* in its meaning 'band, troop'; *eDIL s.vv.* 2 *cúan* and *cú*, respectively. Thus, the gloss could be interpreted as a meeting place of

9.5.14 A[..] .i. gaduig*hedh*.
[....], i.e. thieving.[839]

9.6.15 Tacomal .i. acomal .i. cengal.
Taccomol 'joining', i.e. joining, i.e. binding.[840]

9.6.16 Do[ṡ]ec*h*ma .i. doiṡec*h*anta.
Doṡechma 'unavoidable', i.e. unavoidable.[841]

9.6.17 In*n*tec*h*, ⁊ buaile gal*air* .i. ait imbi gal[ar].
Inntech 'compound for sick animals', and *búaile galair* 'cow-pen of disease', i.e. place where there is disease.[842]

9.7.18 [Im]toi*n*git .i. em*h*-*th*oinge[t].
Imtoingit, 'they swear' i.e. [< *éim* 'swift, timely' + *tongaid* 'swears'] promptly they swear.[843]

9.7.19 Andom*h*na .i. inde doi*m*ne.
Andomna 'marshes', i.e. [< *inne* 'center' + *domain* 'deep, depths'] middle of depth.[844]

---

rivers or a place where hosts assemble. The entry in interpreted in light of heptad 5 (CIH 6.24, 1884.30 and 36, 1885.1; and AL 5: 138.12 and 19) where the editors of AL understand the phrase as referring to companies.

839 The entry is not in O'Curry's transcription, and the lemma is illegible. The gloss concerns theft.

840 The form and meaning of the lemma are uncertain, but it could be a later m. form of n. *accomol* 'joining, meting' with the ⟨t⟩ of the m. article *in t-* attached to it as a result of a misreading or misinterpretation of the source text. For the second gloss, cf. the first part of O'Dav 577 (*Met. Dind.* 1: 28.2; CCIH 125: *comol .i. cengal*... "*Comol*, i.e. tying..."); O'Cl *Comhal gle .i. coimhcheangal a ngléo* 'joining in battle'; MG § 259 *Comol .i. ceangal*...; and *Met. Dind.* 1: 28.2 Cf. 1.a.16.38 TACOMUL.

841 See Borsje and Kelly 2003: 37 for a discussion of the range of attested forms of the lemma. For the gloss, cf. Mod. Ir. *dosheachanta* 'unavoidable'. I should like to thank one of the anonymous readers for the Mod. Ir. comparandum.

842 The missing letters are supplied from O'Curry's transcription. The context of the entry is unknown. The interpretation of the lemma is based on the gloss. It might be related to *intech* 'sheath; used of the wattling round stakes in a fence'; *eDIL s.v. 1 intech*.

843 The entry is not in O'Curry's transcription, and the lemma is illegible. See O'Dav 1512 (*Di Astud Chirt ⁊ Dligid*; CCIH 153) where *eim toingit* is an etymological gloss on *imtongat*; and *Di Astud Chirt ⁊ Dligid* (CIH 228.15 and 36; CCIH 153; AL 5: 440.22 and 442.7); *eDIL s.v. imm-toing*. One would expect the lemma to be a form of *imm-toing*. For the etymological gloss, see the Introduction, pp. 13–16.

844 The lemma is the nom. pl. of *andomain* 'bog, marshy land'. See O'Dav 140 (heptad 37; CCIH

9.7.20 Crioc*h* g*an* dicelt .i. g*an* falac*h*.
Crích cen díchelt 'land without hidden spaces', i.e. without hiding.[845]

9.7.21 For-tuig*h*iter .i. fíor-t*h*uig*h*iter .i. fir-*m*io[nnaightear].
For-tuigiter 'are covered', i.e. [< *fír* 'true, truly' + *tuigithir* 'covers'] truly they are covered, i.e. truly they are sworn.[846]

9.8.22 [..ig]igis .i. ina*edh*ris.[847]

9.8.23 Faot*h* .i. luig*h*e .i. min*n*a.
Fáeth 'oath', i.e. oath, i.e. oaths.[848]

9.8.24 Áin .i. iomaig*h* .i. iomain.
Áin 'driving', i.e. drives, i.e. driving.[849]

9.8.25 Ruig*hledh* .i. ro fuig*hledh*.
Ruigled 'a judgement was given', i.e. a judgement was given.[850]

9.8.26 F*r*iosg*art* .i. f*r*eg*r*ais.
Fris-gart 'he answered', i.e. he answered.[851]

113: *Andomuin .i. ferann ainethaim, ut est andomain tire .i. tír a mbi inne doimne, cuirrig 7 seiscenn no moin* "*Andomuin*, i.e. land not arable, ut est *andomain tire* i.e. land in which there is…of depth, marshes and swamp and bog."); heptad 37 (*CIH* 35.22–23, 36.1; *CCIH* 113; *AL* 5: 250.6 and 252.1). Cf. 1.b.3.51 ANDOMHNA.

845 The context of the entry is unknown.

846 The missing letters are supplied from O'Curry's transcription. The glosses on the lemma both etymologize the element of the preverb *for-* as *fír-* 'true, genuine', and thus create new pass. verb forms; *eDIL s.v. for-tuigethar*; and Taylor-Griffiths 2020: 1: 89. The reading of the last gloss relies on O'Curry's transcription. The sense of 'cover' here is to protect or take an oath for; See *Di Astud Chirt 7 Dligid* (*CIH* 235.3 and 11–12; *CCIH*24; *AL* 5: 462.3 and 14–16).

847 The reading is very uncertain, and this entry is not in O'Curry's transcription.

848 Cf. 7.a.26.38 FAOTH, AOTH. The lemma *fáeth* is a compound of *fo* and *oeth*; *eDIL s.v.* 1 *fáeth* ?. See the discussion in Breatnach 1990a: 11, n. 43.

849 See *Bretha Comaithchesa* (*CIH* 205.15 and 17; *Bretha Comaithcheso* § 42; *AL* 4: 156.20 and 158.7); cf. O'Cl *Ain .i. táin* 'plunder'; and for the second gloss, cf. O'Dav 66 (no id.; *CCIH* 110).

850 Both the lemma and the gloss are understood as 3 sg. perf. pass. forms of *fo-gella*, but the lemma appears to be the prototonic form.

851 The gloss is from a later simplex of the lemma *fris-gair*; *eDIL s.v. fris-gair, -frecair*. See O'Cl *Friscart .i. freagrais* 'he answered'.

9.8.27 Foruail [....]
Foróil 'abundance' ...[852]

9.9.28 [..]ob*h*liugs[.][853]

9.9.29 *Air*be .i. fal.
Airbe 'fence', i.e. fence.[854]

9.9.30 Filc ⟨.i. maith⟩ .i. foill secd*ha* .i. in cuaille.
Felc 'brittle', ⟨i.e. good⟩, i.e. frail brittle, i.e. the stake.[855]

9.9.31 Ága ⟨ł ionag*ha*⟩ .i. iomáin amac*h*, o tág*ha* .i. iomáin amuic*h*.
Aige ⟨*nó ionagha*⟩ 'driving ⟨or driving to⟩', i.e. driving out, from [the word] *taga* 'he should drive back', i.e. driving in.[856]

9.9.32 Eab*h*la[...]
Ebla 'will drive' ...[857]

9.10.33 [..]ac[..]e .i. iono*cht*. a[...] adeir, ⁊ an m[.] as uga do-g[n]e lona menmu ac denam.
[.......], i.e. leaving, i.e. [...] it says, and the [...] which is a choice he may make ...[858]

---

852 The reading of the lemma is tentative, and the remainder of the line is illegible. The lemma is interpreted as a form of *eDIL s.v. foróil, furóil, fuláir* 'abundance, excess'.

853 It is uncertain if this word belongs with the previous entry; most of it is illegible, and it is not in O'Curry's transcription.

854 The context of the entry is unknown.

855 See O'Dav 819 (no id.; CCIH 132: *For*[*r*]*ualatar .i. ro lingestar, ut est for*[*r*]*ualatar findairbi filc fill .i. ro comlingestar no ro lebhlingssetar na heich ar in finnairbi ⁊ sí seacda. Filc seacda da réir sin* "*Forrualatar*, i.e. have jumped, ut est 'horses have jumped a brittle white paling', i.e. the horses have leaped or have jumped the white paling, and it brittle. According to that *filc* means 'brittle'.").

856 The entry might be corrupt; *eDIL s.v. do-aig*. The gloss on the lemma has not been edited. It is possible that it is a mistake for *imaga*, the 2 sg. pres. subj. of *imm-aig* 'drives'. See O'Dav 66 (no id.; CCIH 110: *Agh .i. imain amach, ut est ma imaga taga .i. imain amuigh* "*Aga*, i.e. drive (cattle) out, ut est 'if *imm-aga* 'thou drive out', *taga* 'drive in'."). There is no context for the entry, but it seems to involve driving cattle to and fro.

857 The entry is not in O'Curry's transcription. The remainder of the line is illegible. Both of the verbs *aigid* 'drives, impels' and *ailid* 'nourishes, rears, fosters' have future stems in *-ebla*; *eDIL s.vv. aigid* and *1 ailid*. Considering the subject matter of the surrounding entries, 'will drive' is likely the meaning here. Cf. 2.b.23.112 EA[B]LA and 9.11.34 [.]C [..] EABHLA.

858 The reading of this entry is too tentative to attempt a translation, and it is not in O'Curry's

9.11.34 [.]c [..] eab*h*la .i. taebuail anuig.[859]

9.11.35 Aig, taig .i. im na h-ec*h*uib*h*, ⁊ im na caoirib*h*, m*ar* si*n* g*ath* uaitugud.
Aig, taig 'go, come', i.e. regarding the horses, and regarding the sheep, like a stream taking [something] away.[860]

9.12.36 Timine .i. sadail nec*h* as time da fine.
Timíne 'weakling', i.e. anyone who is afraid of his kindred is indolent.[861]

9.13.37 Ruib do-meal*ar* .i. ainm*nighthe* at*h*cogn*us* a ccuid m*ar* taid ba, caoir[e], ⁊ gob*air* ⁊c̄.
Ruip do-melar 'animals which are eaten', i.e. so named for chewing their share again such as cows, sheep, and goats, etc.[862]

9.13.38 Ruib ná to-meal*ar* .i. ain*mnighthe* [...]
Ruip ná to-melar 'animals which are not eaten', i.e. so named ...[863]

9.14.39 Et*h*or .i. fer do-[g]ni t*r*i an f*h*ail.
Ethar (?), i.e. a man who makes a third of an enclosure.[864]

---

transcription. It is possible that this entry is a continuation of the one from the previous line.

859 The reading of this entry is too tentative to attempt a translation, and it is not in O'Curry's transcription. Both of the verbs *aigid* 'drives, impels' and *ailid* 'norishes, rears, fosters' have future stems in *-ebla*; *eDIL s.vv. aigid* and *1 ailid*. It is possible that the last word is from *aingid* 'saves, protects, serves'. Cf. 2.b.23.112 EA[B]LA and 9.9.32 EABHLA[....].

860 See O'Dav 67 (no id.; *CCIH* 110: *Aigh .i. eirigh, ut est aigh taigh .i. tair doridhis .i. eirigh go Cormac ⁊ tair doridhisi uadh* "*Aig*, i.e. go, ut est 'go, come', i.e. come again, i.e. go to Cormac and come again from him."). The second part of entry is not in O'Curry's transcription. The sense of the second part of the gloss is that the coming and going of the animals is like a stream ebbing and flowing or taking and depositing items from its bank.

861 The translation of the gloss is tentative.

862 See the *Mat* glossary (*CIH* 1566.1–2; *CCIH* 69). It should be noted that the lemma is singular in the *Mat* glossary. See *eDIL s.v. athchocnaid*. Cf. 6.a.33.75 RUIB DO-MEALAR and 9.13.38 RUIB NÁ TO-MEALAR.

863 See the *Mat* glossary (*CIH* 1566.1–3; *CCIH* 69). It is possible that the illegible text on the remainder of the line followed the same pattern as 9.13.37 RUIB DO-MEALAR and provided the names of specific animals which do not chew their cud. Cf. 6.a.34.76 RUIB NA DOIMEALAR.

864 The entry is out of context and, thus, the gloss seems to bear little relation to the meaning 'boat' of the lemma as it stands. It is possible that the beginning of the lemma is missing because the side of the page is damaged, cf. *clethra, clethra* 'shelter, protection'.

9.14.40 Íre .i. ferann.
Íriu 'land', i.e. land.[865]

9.14.41 Mét na n-ireann .i. na b*h*ferann.
Mét na n-írenn 'the size of the lands', i.e. of the lands.[866]

9.14.42 Buirisg .i. bior asa eisg .i. poll b*eth* na l*ar*.
Buiresc 'end', i.e. [< *bir* 'stream' + *esc* 'water'] stream from its water, i.e. a hole that may be in the ground.[867]

9.14.43 Cenn ⁊ costac*air* .i. [..]*ar*[....]ca .i. a c*h*en*n* de fen.
Cenn 'head' and *costagair* 'is established', i.e. [.......] i.e. his head from himself.[868]

9.15.44 Maol macha .i. cuaille maol am*h*uil mac*h*ad*h*.
Mael macha 'bare milking enclosure', i.e. a post bare as a milking enclosure.[869]

9.15.45 Cátaid*h* .i. úaislétaid*h*.
Cátaid 'dignity', i.e. dignity.[870]

---

865 See the first part of O'Dav 1079 (no id.; CCIH 140: *Iriu .i. ferann...* "*Íriu*, i.e. land..."); and Digest A (4) (CIH 1141.15; CCIH 48). Cf. O'Dav 1080 (no id.; CCIH 140: *Irraind .i. ferann...* "*Írind*, i.e. land..."); and O'Cl *Irionn .i. fearann* 'land'.

866 See the first part of O'Dav 1080 (no id.; CCIH 140: *Irraind .i. ferann...* "*Írind*, i.e. land..."); and O'Cl *Irionn .i. fearann* 'land'. Cf. O'Dav 1079 (no id.: CCIH 140: *Iriu .i. ferann...* "*Íriu*, i.e. land..."); and Digest A (4) (CIH 1141.15, CCIH 48).

867 Both explanations of the lemma refer to a well or spring, i.e. the source of the water, a hole in the ground. See *Di Astud Chirt ⁊ Dligid* (CIH 231.10 and 13–14); and O'Dav 308 (*Di Astud Chirt ⁊ Dligid*; CCIH 117: *Buiresc .i. forcenn,* [*ut est*] *siniu sencuimne co buiresc in betha .i. brissiud betha. No co buireisc .i. eisc uisque, go tiachtain uisque taran mbith. Nó buiresc .i. anma co forcend* "*Buiresc*, i.e. an end, ut est 'older than the memory of the old to the end of the world', i.e. the destruction of the world. Or to *barr-eisc*, that is top of *esc* 'water', till the coming of water over the world. Or *buiresc*, i.e. of a soul to the end.").

868 Both the reading and the translation are tentative due to how much of the manuscript is damaged. It could be that this is really two entries. It is possible that the lemmata and gloss should be interpreted as referring to the head of a kindred or the end of a matter.

869 The context of the entry is unknown, and the interpretation is tentative. The gloss might be partially etymological.

870 See O'Cl *Cataidh .i. eneaclann no uaisle* 'honour, or nobility'. The lemma might be a later dental nom. sg. or it could be in an oblique case; the same applies to the gloss; *eDIL s.v. cáttu* and *úaislidetu*, respectively.

9.15.46 Odh*ar* .i. oin*edh* no oint[h]*er* .i. tugt[h]*ar* [í]asa*cht*.
Odar 'let it be loaned', i.e. let him loan or let it be loaned, i.e. let a loan be given.[871]

9.16.47 Bradaid*h* .i. foxl*aidh*.
Brataid 'carries off', i.e. carries off.[872]

9.16.48 Lios .i. ima mbí an clad*h*.
Les 'courtyard', i.e. around which there is the rampart.[873]

9.16.49 Airlisi .i. ima mbí an taile an fál.
Airlise 'area outside a domestic enclosure', i.e. around which there is the battlement of the fences.[874]

9.16.50 Sui, saoi .i. on tsoad*h* .i. iompod*h*.
Suí, saoi 'turn', i.e. from the [word] *soud* 'turning', i.e. turning.[875]

9.17.51 Indorsa .i. in*n*osa no an u*air*-si.
Indorsa 'now', i.e. now or now.[876]

9.17.52 Medla, máda, ra*cht*, sas, féis, ⁊ tuir*edh* .i. an*m*an*n*a do m*h*uic.
Medla, máta, rucht, sas, feis, and *tuired*, i.e. names for a pig.[877]

---

871 The lemma is the 3 sg. pres. subj. pass. of *oidid* 'grants, lends'; *eDIL s.v. oidid*. The glosses *oinedh* and *oint[h]er* are interpreted as 3 sg. impv. and pass. impv. of the same verb as the lemma. For the lemma, see O'Dav 1303 (no id.; CCIH 147); and *Bretha Éitgid* (CIH 1190.37; CCIH 50). I should like to thank one of the anonymous readers for comments on this entry.

872 The second gloss appears to be a simplex derived from *fo-coisle(a)* 'takes away, carries off'. See the first part of O'Dav 276 (no id.; CCIH 116: *Brataidh .i. foxlaidh no beridh… "Brataid,* i.e. abducts or takes…").

873 Cf. O'Cl *Lios .i. teagh, no baile* 'a house or town'.

874 The context of the entry is unknown, and the interpretation of the gloss is tentative. It seems to suggest that there are fences surrounding the *airlise*; EIF 368–369.

875 The lemmata are understood as variant spellings of the 2 sg. impv. of *soïd* 'turns'. For this use of the n. sg. art. in the gloss, see Beatnach 1990b. The context of the entry is unknown.

876 See O'Dav 1117 (probably from the *Tract on Marriage and Divorce*; CCIH 141: *Indorsa .i. in uair so, ut est is trian i trian frithgnama do mnai indorso "Indorsa,* i.e. at this hour, ut est ''tis a third of attendance by the woman now'.").

877 Cf. O'Dav 360 (*Bretha Nemed Toísech*; CCIH 119: *Comhlachtaidh ainm do orc muice .i. leana[id] dia lacht .i. dia mathair .i. cumain lais a lacht. Comlachtaid cimcidh .i. antan cinges. Ar is ocht n-anmanna in[n]a muc, comlachtaid, scuithid, foir, cro, cuin[d]eol, lupait ceis, deil "Cumlachtaid,* i.e. a name for a sow's pigling, i.e. it follows its milk (*lacht*), i.e. its mother, i.e. it remembers her milk. *Comlachtaid cimcid* (is its name) when it goes (to the

9.17.53 Metoll.i. fogail do-[g]ni an m*h*uc mor da ngoirt*er* medla.
Métal 'belly', i.e. trespass which the large sow does if pigs are called.[878]

9.18.54 Ruired .i. ro feraid.
Ruired 'was inflicted', i.e. was inflicted.[879]

9.18.55 Cec*h*laid, clasaid .i. toc*h*luid.
Cechlaid 'it dug', *clasaid* 'it digs', i.e. it uproots.[880]

9.18.56 Ingelt .i. gle*th* a h-in*ne*.
Ingelt 'grazing', i.e. [< *gleth* 'grazing' + ⁊ *inne* 'properly, naturally'] grazing properly.[881]

---

teat). For there are eight names of swine, *comlachtaid, scuithid, foir, cro, cuindeol, lupait, céis, deil*.") for a list of eight pigs, none of which overlap with the ones listed here; *Bretha Nemed Toísech* (CIH 2227.39). Only the *máta* is discussed in the section on pigs in *EIF* 79–88. See O'Cl *Rucht .i. muc* 'a pig'; and cf. O'Dav 1241 (no id.; CCIH 145: *Main .i. lesugud, ut est cuich in mait ro mainighis .i. cuich in muc ro leasaighis* "*Main*, i.e. benefiting, ut est 'whose is the pig which thou hast supported?', i.e. whose is the pig which thou hast benefited?"). The words *sas* and *tuiredh* are not listed in *eDIL* as names for pigs. *Medla* 'paunch, belly' is used of the belly of animals that are eaten; *eDIL s.v. metal*. *Máta* is an archaic and poetic word for a pig; *eDIL s.v. 2 mát, máta*. *Rucht*'s meaning comes from the entry in O'Clery; *eDIL s.v. ? 3 rucht*. *Sas* might be related to *sásad* 'satisfying, food'. *Feis* is also an archaic and poetic word for a sow; *eDIL s.v. 1 feis*. *Tuired* is problematic because the word as it stands is the name for an ailment associated with the forelegs of horses.

878 For damage caused by pigs trespassing on someone's land; cf. *Bretha Comaithchesa* (CIH 72.1–35; *Bretha Comaithcheso* §§16–18); and *EIF* 142–143. The translation of the second half of the explanation is tentative as *medla* can refer to the pigs themselves or their belly; *eDIL s.v. métal*. Cf. DG 9.17.52 MEDLA, MÁDA, RACHT, SAS, FÉIS, ⁊ TUIREDH. The verb *goirter* is understood as the 3 pl. pres. subj. pass. of *gairid* 'calls, summons'. It could be that the entry refers to damage which the sow does when someone imitates the sound of her piglets squealing; see the discussion in *EIF* 81 and n. 107; *Bretha Éitgid* (CIH 943.36–37; CCIH 41; this passage is not translated in *AL*).

879 The lemma and gloss are both sg. perf. pass. forms of *feraid* 'supplies, performs'. It is also possible that the lemma is *ruiriud* 'cattle-trespass, stampede' and that the glossator misunderstood the lemma. Cf. *Bretha Comaithchesa* (CIH 77.38, 78.7, and 579.34; and *Bretha Comaithcheso* §§29–30).

880 This entry seems to follow on from the previous few in the manuscript which all concern pigs and the damage that they cause; cf. 9.17.53 METOLL. Cf. *Bretha Comaithchesa* (CIH 72.1–9 and 576.16ff.; *Bretha Comaithcheso* §§16, and Satellite v).

881 See O'Cl *Gleith .i. caitheamh, no ingeilt*… 'feeding or grazing…'.

9.18.57 Fer iondraic [...][.i.][..]dic*h*e.
Fer indraic 'trustworthy person', i.e. ...[882]

9.19.58 Cl*eth*e lui ⟨.i. na ngrad Fene⟩ .i. se*cht* ccin*n* gan cois, no aon gas *con*a cian*n*.
Cléithe luí 'a large branch', ⟨i.e. of the *Féni* grades⟩, i.e. seven heads without a trunk, or one sprig with its head.[883]

9.19.59 M*edh*ontaid*he* lui .i. se*cht* gais gan a ccen*n*a.
Medóndae luí 'moderate branch', i.e. seven sprigs without their heads.[884]

882 On the trustworthy witness, see *GEIL* 56, 202–203. Cf. *Bretha Comaithchesa* (*CIH* 580.19; *Bretha Comaithcheso*, Satellite XVII.11).

883 This and the following three entries refer to categories of degrees of damage associated with cutting trees and edible plants. The gloss refers to non-noble plants; the value of various plants and trees are separated in categories of 'noble' and 'common'; Kelly 1976; and 1999. This material is not found in *Bretha Comaithchesa* or the fragments of text and commentary associated with *Fidbretha*. That being said, the lemma is also found in glosses associated with *Bretha Comaithchesa* where they are concerned with fines for damage to fence posts. The lemma is translated as 'serious minor matter' in *Bretha Comaithcheso* (*CIH* 204.1–5 and 1858.3–8, commentary 21; and Charles-Edwards 2022: 416). The order of offences as found in Dubhaltach's Glossary is in the reverse order than those found in *Bretha Comaithchesa*. It should be noted, however, that the *Fidbretha* commentary presents a system of equating one large tree to a number of smaller ones as a means of assessing fines for damage, which is similar to what we find here where one whole sprig with its top is equated to the tops of seven without their trunks. See the discussion in Eska 2025. It is possible that these four entries come from a version of *Bretha Comaithchesa* or *Fidbretha* which is no longer extant. Cf. 9.19.59 MEDHONTAIDHE LUI, 9.20.60 LÚ LUI, and 9.20.61 FUIRIREDH LUI. Cf. O'Cl *Lui .i. geg* 'branch'; and O'Dav 1159 (no id.; *CCIH* 143: *Lui .i. gega no gesca, ut est fuil for a lui lam fuire .f.* "*Lui*, i.e. branches or boughs, ut est 'there is on his branch a hand...'.").

884 One would expect the form *medóndae* instead of *medhontaidhe*, but the lenited /d/ has been reduced to ⟨∅⟩ in this position. This and the previous and following two entries refer to categories of degrees of damage associated with cutting trees and edible plants. This material is not found in *Bretha Comaithchesa* or the fragments of text and commentary associated with *Fidbretha*. That being said, the lemma is also found in glosses associated with *Bretha Comaithchesa* where they are concerned with fines for damage to fence posts. The lemma is translated as 'moderately minor matter' in *Bretha Comaithcheso* (*CIH* 204.1–5 and 1858.3–8, commentary 21; and Charles-Edwards 2022: 416). Cf. the discussion on 9.19.58 CLEITHE LUI, 9.20.60 LÚ LUI, and 9.20.61 FUIRIREDH LUI. Cf. O'Cl *Lui .i. geg* 'branch'; and O'Dav 1159 (no id.; *CCIH* 143: *Lui .i. gega no gesca, ut est fuil for a lui lam fuire .f.* "*Lui*, i.e. branches or boughs, ut est 'there is on his branch a hand...'.").

9.20.60 Lú lui .i. se*cht* nda[...]e no se*cht* slap*air*, ni riagailt*er* lu lui na m*ed*-*h*ontaid*h* lui, *acht* do l*us*, do *gair*leoig, ⁊ do praisig*h*.
Lú luí 'a small branch', i.e. seven [..] or seven bandages, a minor matter nor a moderately minor matter are regulated, but by herb, by garlic, and by cabbage.[885]

9.20.61 Fuirir*edh* lui .i. bui*nn*e go ccen*n* no se*cht* ccin*n* gan buinne.
Fuirired luí 'refection branch', i.e. a stalk with a head or seven heads without a stalk.[886]

9.21.62 Ag*h* .i. bo.
Ag 'bovine', i.e. cow.[887]

9.21.63 *Et*, ed .i. ailbin bo.
Éit, *éd*, 'a herd of cattle', i.e. a small herd of cows.[888]

9.21.64 Ima-dic*h*et .i. em*h*-d*h*idnid.
Ima-dichet 'which they ward off', i.e. [< *éim* 'quickly' + *didnid* 'they protect'] they quickly-protect.[889]

---

885 This and the previous two and following entries refer to categories of degrees of damage associated with cutting trees and edible plants. The meaning of the first part of the gloss is unclear. This material is not found in *Bretha Comaithchesa* or the fragments of text and commentary associated with *Fidbretha*. That being said, the lemma is also found in glosses associated with *Bretha Comaithchesa* where they are concerned with fines for damage to fence posts. The lemma is translated as 'minor matter' in *Bretha Comaithcheso* (*CIH* 204.1–5 and 1858.3–8, commentary 21; and Charles-Edwards 2022: 416). Cf. the discussion on 9.19.58 CLETHE LUI, 9.19.59 MEDHONTAIDHE LUI, and 9.20.61 FUIRIREDH LUI. Cf. O'Cl *Lui .i. geg* 'branch'; and O'Dav 1159 (no id.; *CCIH* 143: *Lui .i. gega no gesca, ut est fuil for a lui lam fuire .f.* "*Lui*, i.e. branches or boughs, ut est 'there is on his branch a hand…'.").

886 This and the previous three entries refer to categories of degrees of damage associated with cutting trees and edible plants. This material is not found in *Bretha Comaithchesa* or the fragments of text and commentary associated with *Fidbretha*. Cf. the discussion on 9.19.58 CLETHE LUI, 9.19.59 MEDHONTAIDHE LUI, and 9.20.60 LÚ LUI. Cf. O'Cl *Lui .i. geg* 'branch'; and O'Dav 1159 (no id.; *CCIH* 143: *Lui .i. gega no gesca, ut est fuil for a lui lam fuire .f.* "*Lui*, i.e. branches or boughs, ut est 'there is on his branch a hand…'.").

887 See *Bretha Comaithchesa* (*CIH* 194.17; *Bretha Comaithcheso* § 18, gloss b, source B; *AL* 4: 108.13); and O'Cl *Agh .i. bó* 'cow'.

888 See *Bretha Comaithchesa* (*CIH* 194.18; *Bretha Comaithcheso* § 18, gloss b, source B; *AL* 4: 108.13); and O'Cl *Éd no éid .i. áirnéis, no spréidh* 'cattle'.

889 See *Bretha Comaithchesa* (*CIH* 71.1 and 3; *Bretha Comaithcheso* § 12, gloss a, source A; *AL* 4: 92.25 and 94.2); and cf. the first part of O'Dav 714 (*Bretha Comaithchesa*; *CCIH* 129: *Dichet .i. ditin…* "*Dichet*, i.e. protection…"). For the lemma, see *eDIL s.v. imm-dích*. It is common for

9.21.65 Sec*hnus* n-*air*gsin .i. do c*h*i an dui*n*e a spred*h* ar foguil ⁊ sec*hnnaidh* iad sa n-oidc*he*, ⁊ ní f*h*idir gu áit i rabatt*ar*.
Sechnais n-airgsin 'he avoided looking on', i.e. the person sees his cattle being plundered, and he yields them in the night, and he does not know where they were.[890]

9.22.66 Faill n-aididin .[i.] faill do [den]a*m* u*m*pa i*ar* n-aididniug*adh*.
Faill n-aititin 'neglect of acknowledgement', i.e. neglecting to do something about it after acknowledging.[891]

9.22.67 Legad do luide .i. leigen do*n* sp*r*ed*h* luid*h*e san fer.
Legad do luige 'allowing to lie down', i.e. allowing the cattle to lie down in the grass.[892]

9.23.68 Feis ⟨i bfeis⟩ .i. i mbuail*idh* no i n-at*h*lompu*r*e coitcin*n*.
Feis i bfeis 'spending the night ⟨in accommodation⟩', i.e. in a cowshed or in a common bare pasture.[893]

9.23.69 Feis i bfual .i. i n-at*h*buail*idh* s*h*alaig.
Feis i bfúal 'spending the night in urine', i.e. in a dirty disused milking-stead.[894]

9.24.70 Feis i n-andom*h*ain .i. bid i lenmui*n* isi*n* tsesgin*n*, no isi*n* derg moin, no isi*n* luit*h*, ⁊ et*h*aid an fer ime.

---

the preverb *imm-* to be glossed by *éim* 'swift, timely'; Binchy 1943: 212; and Taylor-Griffiths 2020: 1: 89.

890 For *sellach*, the crime of looking on, see *GEIL* 154–157. *Do-chí* is a later 3 sg. pres. of *ad-cí* 'sees'; *eDIL s.v. ad-cí*. I should like to thank one of the anonymous readers for comments on this entry.

891 The ⟨den⟩ are supplied from O'Curry's transcription. It could be that a word or two has been left out of the explanation of the lemma as the translation does not make much sense as it stands. The general sense is that one has acknowledged something, such as witnessing a crime, but then done nothing about it. For the lemma, cf. *Bretha Nemed Toísech* (*CIH* 963.28; *CCIH* 42).

892 On lying-down trespass, cf. *Bretha Comaithchesa* (*CIH* 66.37, 576.4, and 677.36; *Bretha Comaithcheso* § 6 and Satellites II and III); and *EIF* 136.

893 For the lemmata, see *CIH* 983.38 (citations from a range of texts; *CCIH* 43); *Di Astud Chirt ⁊ Dligid* (*CIH* 236.17–19; *AL* 5: 468.9–10); and for part of the gloss, cf. O'Dav 964 (*Bretha Comaithchesa*; *CCIH* 137). The general sense is that the animal spends the night in a clean cowshed or bare-pasture.

894 See *CIH* 983.39 (citations from a range of texts, *CCIH* 43); *Di Astud Chirt ⁊ Dligid* (*CIH* 236.17–19; *AL* 5: 468.9–10). The general sense is that the animal spends the night in a dirty cow-shed.

Feis i n-andomain 'spending the night in a bog', i.e. being stuck in the marsh, or in the red bog, or in the mire, and it [the animal] eats the grass around it.[895]

9.24.71 Coib*h*nit*h*er .i. cui*m*r*igh*t[h]*er*.
Coimnither 'is impounded', i.e. which is bound.[896]

9.25.72 Gealtat*har* .i. ing*h*ilt[h]*er*.
Geltathar 'is grazed', i.e. is pastured.[897]

9.25.73 Ime .i. fal.
Imbe 'fence', i.e. fence.[898]

9.25.74 Ed*á*rb*h*a .i. ba bí*us* etorra .i. *air*b*h*e no fál.
Etarbae 'fence', i.e. [< *ba* 'fence' + *eter* 'between'] a fence which is between them, i.e. hedge or fence.[899]

9.25.76 Fagh .i. sliab*h*.
Fag 'land', i.e. a mountain.[900]

9.25.77 Der*usg* .i. cin*nedh* d*h*ireac*h*.
Derosc 'verdict', i.e. just penalty.[901]

---

895 See CIH 983.40 (citations from a range of texts, CCIH 43). It is possible that *derg* could be from *derc* 'berry' and that the cow might have wandered into the bog to eat bilberries, etc.; *eDIL s.v.* 3 *derc*. It is also possible that *derg* is being used as an intensifier. The general sense is that the animal spent the night stuck outdoors. Cf. 9.23.69 FEIS I BFUAL and 9.23.68 FEIS I BFEIS.

896 For the lemma and gloss separately, cf. *Bretha Comaithchesa* (CIH 578.1; *Bretha Comaithcheso*, Satellite VIII); and *Di Astud Chor* § 36 (CIH 1357.6; CCIH 60). For the verbs, see *eDIL s.v.* 2 *cuimnigid(ir)* and *con-rig*, respectively.

897 See *eDIL s.v. gelid* and *ingeltid*, respectively. Dubhaltach indicates lenition sporadically, so it is difficult to determine whether each verb should be sg. pass. or pl. pass.

898 See *Bretha Comaithchesa* (CIH 65.12 and 15; *Bretha Comaithcheso* § 5 and gloss c).

899 See the second half of O'Dav 281 (no id.; CCIH 117: *Boing… .i. cia coimmbrister in ba bis etarru .i. ailedha ⁊ airbedha "Boing…* i.e. though the *ba* (fence?) that is between them is broken, i.e. stakes and railings.") and 327 (no id.; CCIH 118: *Ba .i. fal, etarba damscuithe "Ba*, i.e. a hedge, a fence of oxen (and) small animals."). Cf. *Bretha Comaithchesa* (CIH 579.28; *Bretha Comaithcheso*, Satellite XV).

900 For the lemma, cf. the first part of O'Dav 967 (*Bretha Comaithchesa*; CCIH 137; *Fagh .i. ferann… "Fag*, i.e. land…") and *Bretha Comaithchesa* (CIH 75.17; *Bretha Comaithcheso* § 26; and discussion in Charles-Edwards 2022: 224–225). It is uncertain what type of land *fag* describes, but the sense seems to be generally uncultivated or poor high land.

901 For the lemma, cf. O'Dav 697 (*Bretha Comaithchesa*; CCIH 128); and *Bretha Comaithchesa*

9.25.78 Cutai*m* .i. tuiti*m*.
Cutaim 'falling down', i.e. falling.[902]

9.26.79 Cit .i. cáora.
Cit 'sheep', i.e. sheep.[903]

9.26.80 Cit*r*iog*h*a .i. uán .i. troig*h* .i. clan*n* cite.
Citriga 'lamb', i.e. a lamb, i.e. offspring, i.e. offspring of a sheep.[904]

9.26.81 Cetem*h*uin .i. caora som*h*aoin.
Cétamain 'May', i.e. sheep of profit.[905]

9.26.82 Uainc*h*en*n* .i. fuan b*hius* mu*n* ccen*n* .i. srián.
Úanchend 'lamb-head', i.e. a covering that is around the head, i.e. a bridle.[906]

9.27.83 Adbalud .i. eblid .i. bás*aigh*id.
At-balad 'it would die', i.e. it would die, i.e. he would slay.[907]

(CIH 72.4 and 7; *Bretha Comaithcheso* §16 and gloss e). Cf. O'Dav 712 (heptad 36; CCIH 129: *Derusc .i. derbchinnedh, ut est la cumail .u. mbo in derusc a dithma* "*Derusc*, i.e. exact determination, ut est 'with a *cumal* of five cows at the end of its delay in pound'."); and heptad 36 (CIH 35.16; AL 5: 240.22). Cf. 4.c.14.83 DEROSG.

902 See O'Dav 464 (no id.; CCIH 122: *Cutaim .i. tuitim, ut est cid iar coise cuitim fri ailche annscuichthi* "*Cutaim*, i.e. a fall, ut est 'though after a foot's fall it be against immovable rocks'.") and 519 (*Bretha Éitgid*; CCIH 124: *Cutaim .i. tuitim, ut est bla crann cutaim* "*Cutaim*, i.e. falling, ut est 'a tree (is) exempt in falling'."); and, cf. *Bretha Eitgid* (CIH 274.17). Cf. 3.b.8.38 CUTAIM.

903 See "Amergin Glungeal's Mystical Poem" in TCD MS 1337 [H.3.18], p. 50; Abbott and Gwynn 1921: 144. Cf. OM 220 *Cit .i. ouis, unde citén dicitur .i. agnus* "*Cit*, i.e. sheep, from which is said *citén*, i.e. lamb."; and similarly *Irsan* 70. Cf. EIF 68.

904 The lemma is not in *eDIL*. It seems to be a formation of *cit* 'sheep' and 3 *traige* 'offspring, descendants'; cf. O'Cl *Trogh .i. clan* 'children'. The last part of the gloss is partially etymological. Cf. 6.a.34.78 CITRIUG, ⁊ TRETEALL. See the discussion on sheep in EIF 67–77.

905 The explanation of the lemma is a partial etymology of the lemma where *cit* 'sheep' is understood as standing for the first element *cet-* and *somaín* 'profit, benefit' is understood as the second element *-mhuin*.

906 The interpretation of this entry is uncertain. Perhaps the lemma is a name for a type of bridle.

907 The lemma and first gloss are deuterotonic and prototonic forms of the 3 sg. impf. subj. of *at-bail(l)* 'dies'; *eDIL s.v. at-bail(l)*.

9.27.84 Derc n-át*h*a .i. toll *cair*iol*ach* át*h*a.
Derc n-átha 'hole of a drying-kiln', i.e. flame-knowledgeable hole of a drying kiln.[908]

9.27.85 Teingléir .i. tengaid*h* léir.
Teingléir 'abundant fire', i.e. [< *tengaid* 'tongues' + *léir* 'assiduous, earnest'] earnest tongues.[909]

9.27.86 Lua*mh*n*acht* .i. lua*mairacht*.
Lúamnacht 'pilotage', i.e. piloting.[910]

9.27.87 Coslac*h* .i. luac*h* cúisi .i. luac*h* do b*ei*r f*e*r na cuisi do nec*h* oile do cion*n* a cuisi do s*h*esam*h* do, ut d*icitu*r 'sed*h*a g*a*c[h] coslac*h*' .i. an ses*edh* cuid do*n* *ch*úis donti doní *air*ber*t* aonu*air*e i n-*air*e*cht* dá ttig tobac*h*.
Coslach 'payment', i.e. [< *lúach* 'payment' + *cúis* 'matter, case'] payment of a case, i.e. a payment the man of the case gives to someone else on his behalf to defend his case for him, *ut dicitur* 'as it is said' *sedha gach coslach* 'six things for each case', i.e. the sixth share from the case for the one who does the work at once in court when it comes to enforcing.[911]

---

908 This entry is obscure; it is possible that the gloss is meant to be etymological. For drying kilns, see the discussion in *EIF* 241–242.

909 The lemma is obscure, but *tengleir* is found in Meyer 1907: 3: 294 § 6 (ACL).

910 The lemma is not widely attested. The context of the entry is unknown.

911 The lemma is difficult as it is open to more than one interpretation; *eDIL s.v. coslach* does not provide a definition of the word in English, but it refers to Thurneysen 1925b: 341. The form *coslag* appears in *Gúbretha Caratniad* § 31 where Thurneysen translates it as *Besorgungs-Lohn*. In his discussion of the form (1925b: 341), he proposes an etymology of the word as *cos* 'foot' + *lóg* 'price, amount' giving the literal meaning of *coslach* as *Fuss-Lohn* 'foot-wage', and suggests that the term is the payment for work which requires one to be on one's feet, in contrast to *lámtorad* 'handiwork' which is work that one did while sitting; see also *LEIA s.v. coslach*. The form *coslaige* is found in *Bretha Comaithcheso*, Satellite VI where it is translated as 'herders' (see also the note in Charles-Edwards 2022: 311); perhaps here we can see a semantic broadening of the term from the wage someone is paid to the term used for those, such as herders, who would have been paid a *coslach*. Thurneysen 1925b: 341, n. 1 notes that a different definition (which he disagrees with) appears in O'Don. Suppl. *s.v. coslach* where the definition is given as 'what is paid for defending one's cause' (the meaning of 'cause' in the definition is equivalent to 'case' now); the source O'Donovan cites for this definition is Dubhaltach's Glossary. Part of the confusion lies in the fact that the gen. sg. of *cos* 'foot' can appear as *coisi*, and the gen. sg. of *1 cúis* 'matter, case' can appear as *cúisi*. It should be noted that Dubhaltach's use of length marks

9.29.88 Cad*h*na .i. caingne.
Cadna 'of a case', i.e. of a case.[912]

9.29.89 Tl*us* .i. tuill*edh* uais do b*erar* risi*n* ní bi*us* esbad*hach*.
Tlus 'property', i.e. [< *tuilled* 'addition, increase' + *úas* 'higher, surpassing, noble'] noble addition which is given for anything which is lacking.[913]

9.30.90 Com*hair*sior .i. at*hchomhair*ct[h]*er*.
Comairsar 'is inquired', i.e. is asked.[914]

9.30.91 Dime, ⁊ diomt*ha* .i. on didion.
Dime 'may cover', and *dimtha* 'could be covered', i.e. by the covering.[915]

9.30.92 Solam*h* .i. luat*h*.
Solam 'quick', i.e. quick.[916]

9.30.93 Uball fab*h*aill (i).i. uball bi*us ar* fos*h*iub*h*al for anuall f*or* an tuin*n* .i. uball tui*nn*e.

does not always conform to modern usage, but he does write length marks for some of the forms in this entry. Although the term *coslach* is interpreted here as the payment made for someone who argues a case on behalf of someone else (with there being further semantic broadening of the term *coslach* to also include not only herders and the like, but also those who stand on their feet to argue a case in court; both herders and advocates act to defend one's property and interests), it could also be interpreted as 'herder'. If one were to interpret *coslach* as 'herder', the first part of the gloss would be translated as the etymological gloss 'payment of a foot' (which could well be the standard etymological gloss on the lemma), but the remainder of the entry is difficult to interpret from an agricultural-labor perspective. Whatever *coslach* may actually mean, it is interpreted as a wage paid to an advocate by Dubhaltach.

912 The meaning of the lemma is obscure; the interpretation given here is based on the meaning of the gloss; *eDIL s.v. caingen*.

913 See O'Dav 1595 (no id.; CCIH 155: *Tlus .i. tuilled uais* "*Tlus*, i.e. a noble addition."); and for the lemma, cf. O'Dav 1530 (*Bretha Nemed Toísech*; CCIH 153).

914 The lemma might be a form of the sg. pres. pass. subj. of **com-arc-*, for which see *eDIL s.v. comairser*. The gloss is from *athchomarcaid*, a later simplex of *ad-comairc* 'asks'; *eDIL s.v. ad-comairc*.

915 For the lemmata, see *eDIL s.v. 1 do-eim* 'covers, shelter, protects'. The gloss could also be interpreted as 'from the [word] *dítiu* "covering"'. I should like to thank one of the anonymous readers for comments on this entry.

916 Cf. O'Cl *Solamh .i. ésgaidh* 'quick'.

Uball fabaill 'moving object', i.e. a round object that is [< *fosiubal* 'going covertly'] going excessively proudly on the sea, i.e. 'a sea apple'.[917]

9.31.94 Ág*h*a fine .i. óg*h* ae b*híus ar* an ffine. Flait*h* gelf*h*ine sin.
Ágae fine 'head of a kindred', i.e. [< *óg* 'whole, complete, perfect' + *áe* 'of them'] complete one of them who is before the kindred. That is chief of the *gelfine* 'kindred'.[918]

9.31.95 Fo-c*h*erd, fo-c*h*eird .i. do c*h*uir.
Fo-cerd, fo-ceird 'puts', i.e. puts.[919]

9.32.96 Frit*h*e .i. ní do amuig*h* ag dol i mug*h*a, ut [est] 'frit*h*e treb*h*e' .i. ní dogab*ar* isi*n* treb*h* t*h*all.
Frithe 'a found item', i.e. anything from outside going astray, as *frithe trebhe* 'something found in a house', i.e. anything which is found inside the house.[920]

9.32.97 Frit*he* cat[h]*rach* .i. i l*ar* an cille no an duine.
Frithe cathrach 'something found in an enclosure', i.e. in the middle of the church or the fort.[921]

9.33.98 Frit*he* fait*he* .i. *ar* an f*h*ait*h*c*h*e i gcu*airt* ingelta.
Frithe faithche 'something found on a green', i.e. on the green in a grazing district.[922]

---

917 The lemma could be a proverbial saying, but the context here is unclear; *eDIL s.v. uball, ubull*. Although the primary meaning of *uball* is 'apple, fruit', here it is being used of any round object in general. The entry seems to refer to an object being carried along by the sea. Part of the gloss is obscure and might be etymological.

918 For the role of this figure see Charles-Edwards 1993: 39, 82, 95, 426–427, and 476. Cf. 13.d.13.23 ÁIGHE FINE.

919 The context of this entry is unknown. The lemmata are variant forms of the 3 sg. pres. ind. of *fo-ceird*; the gloss is a later formation from the same verb.

920 The ultimate source of the entry is heptad 64 (*AL* 5: 320–341; Eska 2022: 33–42 and 238–269; *CIH* 55.18–61.7 (especially 55.18 and 21–22); *CCIH* 291–292). The material in Dubhaltach's Glossary is not an exact match to the material from any of the other extant versions of the heptad. The verb *dogabar* is the sg. pres. pass of *fo-gaib* 'finds, discovers, obtains'. The preverb *fo-* is frequently replaced by *do-* after the OI period; *eDIL s.v. fo-gaib*.

921 The ultimate source of the entry is heptad 64 (*AL* 5: 320–341; Eska 2022: 33–42 and 238–269; *CIH* 55.18–61.7 (especially 55.18 and 22); and *CCIH* 291–292). The material in Dubhaltach's Glossary is not an exact match to the material from any of the other extant versions of the heptad.

922 The ultimate source of the entry is heptad 64 (*AL* 5: 320–341; Eska 2022: 33–42 and 238–269;

9.33.99 F*rithe* raite .i. dogab*ar* *ar* an rod i gcu*air*t ingelta idir fait*h*ce ⁊ dirin*n*.

Frithe raite 'something found on rough land', i.e. it is found on the road in a grazing district between a green and unclaimed land.[923]

9.34.100 Fri*th*e roead*h*a no s*h*leb*he* .i. ní dogab*ar* isi*n* roif*h*iod*h* no isi*n* sliab i gcu*air*t ingelta.

Frithe roeda nó shlebe 'something found in a wood or on a mountain', i.e. something found in the wood or on the mountain in a grazing district.[924]

9.34.101 F*rithe* trach*ta* .i. isi*n* tráig*h* gab*ar*.

Frithe trachta 'something found on the shore', i.e. it is found on the shore.[925]

CIH 55.18–61.7 (especially 55.18 and 22–23); and CCIH 291–292). The material in Dubhaltach's Glossary is not an exact match to the material from any of the other extant versions of the heptad. The form *faithe* is a variant gen. sg. of *faithche*; *eDIL s.v. faithche, faidche.*

923 The ultimate source of the entry is heptad 64 (*AL* 5: 320–341; Eska 2022: 33–42 and 238–269; CIH 55.18–61.7 (especially 55.19 and 23); and CCIH 291–292). The material in Dubhaltach's Glossary is not an exact match to the material from any of the other extant versions of the heptad. The verb *dogabar* is the sg. pres. pass of *fo-gaib* 'finds, discovers, obtains'. The preverb *fo-* is frequently replaced by *do-* after the OI period; *eDIL s.v. fo-gaib*. Although the word *raite* is frequently translated as 'road', it can also refer to uncultivated land. The meaning 'rough land' in this context is taken from *EIF* 540; see additional discussion in Eska 2020: 241, n. 10. For the different types of roads, see *Róda, cis lir-side?*; and Clancy 2007. See also O'Dav 1387 (heptad 64; CCIH 149: *Raiti .i. rót, ut est frithe raiti .i. frithe dogabhar ar in rót nó i cuairt ingelta nó itir faithchi ⁊ dirinn. O faithchi imach is ed is raiti ann* "*Raite*, i.e. a road, ut est 'waif of a *raite*', i.e. a waif that is seized on the road, or in the circuit of grazing, or between a green and a waste (?). From a green out (all but the green?) that is a *raite* there.")

924 The ultimate source of the entry is heptad 64 (*AL* 5: 320–341; Eska 2022: 33–42 and 238–269; CIH 55.18–61.7 (especially 55.19 and 23–24); CCIH 291–292); and see O'Dav 1388 (heptad 64; CCIH 149: *Roed .i. rofidh na caille, ut est frithe roedha nó sleibe* "*Roed*, i.e. the great wood of the forest, ut est 'a waif of a great wood or of a mountain'."). The material in Dubhaltach's Glossary is not an exact match to the material from any of the other extant versions of the heptad. For discussion on the range of variant forms of *ruud, rúd*, see Thurneysen 1923: 5; and *eDIL s.v. ruud, rúd*. The verb *dogabar* is the sg. pres. pass of *fo-gaib* 'finds, discovers, obtains'. The preverb *fo-* is frequently replaced by *do-* after the OI period; *eDIL s.v. fo-gaib*.

925 The ultimate source of the entry is heptad 64 (*AL* 5: 320–341; Eska 2022: 33–42 and 238–269; CIH 55.18–61.7 (especially 55.19 and 24); and CCIH 291–292). The material in Dubhaltach's Glossary is not an exact match to the material from any of the other extant versions of the heptad.

9.35.102 F*rithe* fa*ir*ige .i. isi*n* f*hair*ige imuig*h* geibt*h*er.
Frithe fairge 'something found in the sea', i.e. it will be found out on the sea.[926]

9.35.103 Ollob*hair* aigsi*n* .i. folab*air*t do-[g]ní nec*h* ag faigsi*n* n*eth*e, ⁊c̄.
Allabair aicsin 'reporting seeing', i.e. someone reports seeing something, etc.[927]

9.36.104 Ocht*rach* .i. ot*rach*.
Ochtrach 'dung', i.e. dung.[928]

9.36.105 Oil .i. aoil no pluic.
Óil 'cheek', i.e. cheek or cheek.[929]

9.36.106 Ruid*hedh* .i. imde*arga*d*h*.
Ruided 'blushing', i.e. blushing.[930]

9.36.107 Miod*h*bac*h* .i. fer miod*h*b*adh*.
Midbad 'middle-huts', i.e. *fer midboth* 'man of middle-huts'.[931]

---

926 The ultimate source of the entry is heptad 64 (*AL* 5: 320–341; Eska 2022: 33–42 and 238–269; *CIH* 55.18–61.7 (especially 55.19–20 and 24–25); and *CCIH* 291–292). The material in Dubhaltach's Glossary is not an exact match to the material from any of the other extant versions of the heptad.

927 The ultimate source of the entry is heptad 64 (*AL* 5: 320–341; Eska 2022: 33–42, 278, and 288; *CIH* 906.35, 1211.22, and 1853.21–22; *CCIH* 291–292); and O'Dav 144 (heptad 64; *CCIH* 113: *Allobhair .i. folabra, ut est ar allobair n-aidsina*. Stokes does not provide a translation of the entry.). The material in Dubhaltach's Glossary is not an exact match to the material from any of the other extant versions of the heptad. The entry concerns making a report that a lost item had been seen floating on the water. The form *folabairt*, if it is not a mistake for *folabrad*, appears to be a vn. formed by combing elements of *labairt* 'speaking' (a late vn. of *labraithir*) and *fo-labrathar* 'speaks in an undertone'; *eDIL s.v. fo-labrathar* and *labairt*.

928 The gloss is a later form of the lemma; *eDIL s.v.* 1 *ochtrach*.

929 The first gloss is a later form of the lemma; *eDIL s.v. óil*, (*oíl*). *Pluic* is the f. of *pluc*; *eDIL s.v.* 2 *pluc*.

930 Although the context of the entry is not known (cf. the previous entry in the MS, 9.36.105 OIL), blushing is normally associated with shame or disgrace, usually the result of satire.

931 The lemma is understood a mistake for a form of *midboth* 'middle-huts' (of which *midbad* is also a variant); *eDIL s.v. midbad*. The *fer midboth* had limited legal capabilities due to the fact that his father was still alive; *GEIL* 82–83. Cf. O'Dav 1213 (*Bretha Déin Chécht*; *CCIH* 144: *Midbach .i. eorna na n-en ebar deogh dia sugh. Nó maetheorna na n-innsi, ut est grainne midbaigh do aire are nó idhbaich* "*Midbach*, i.e. the barley of the birds, a drink is drunk from sucking it. Or the soft barley of the islands, ut est 'a grain of *midboth* to an *aire*-

9.36.108 *Sára* saml*adh* .i. saml(*adh*)ad*h* as *sár* .i. dui*ne* do sam*h*lug*adh* fri ní as mesa inas e fein .i. re coin no re cec*hair*.
Sára samladh 'insults of comparisons', i.e. comparing which is an insult, i.e. comparing a person with anything which is worse than himself, i.e. like a dog or a quagmire.[932]

9.37.109 Deorad*hus* .i. diorat*hus* .i. nem*h*cin*t*ad*h*.
Deoradas 'state of being an outsider', i.e. an outsider, i.e. without crimes.[933]

9.38.110 D*arm*na .i. *dáir* maoine do-[g]nid t*airbh*.
Darmna 'heat', i.e. [< *dáir* 'bulling' + *main* 'livestock'] bulling of livestock which bulls do.[934]

9.38.111 *Air*m i ttot*h* .i. inad i tt*airing*.
Airm i toth 'place where it may fall', i.e. place where it draws.[935]

9.38.112 Mad ois .i. da n-éisgísi.
Mad ois 'if you lend', i.e. if you allow.[936]

---

ard-chieftain....'") and CIH 2305.9 and 27–28, but that interpretation of the lemma does not make sense here in light of the explanation given in the gloss.

932 The context of the entry is unclear. The general sense refers to comparing someone to something unpleasant as a means of insulting them.

933 The word *deorad* can mean 'exile, outsider, outlaw, wanderer, pilgrim', i.e. anyone not local to a specific area. As such, they have limited legal capabilities and need someone else to act on their behalf. The first gloss is a variant spelling of the lemma, and the second gloss suggests that we understand the lemma in its meaning of 'pilgrim, keeper or relics'; *eDIL s.v. deorad*; *GEIL* 5, 160, 170, and 223; and Kelly 2011: 167–169.

934 The lemma is not well attested. *EIF* 151, n. 109, notes that the only attestation of the word is found in *Bretha Éitgid* (*CIH* 276.3; *AL* 3: 230.25); and O'Dav 741 (*Bretha Éitgid*; *CCIH* 130: *Darmna .i. dair na maine no na cethra* "*Darmna*, i.e. the bulling of the property or the cattle.").

935 The translation of the verb in the gloss is tentative. It is understood here as the 3 sg, pres. ind. of *tairrngid*, a later simplex of *do-srenga* 'draws, drags, pulls', but the semantic connection with the lemma is unclear. It is also possible that the suspension mark in the MS should be over the ⟨g⟩ rather than the ⟨i⟩ (it is ambiguous in the MS). For the lemma, cf. O'Dav 158 (maybe from *Córus Íubaile*; *CCIH* 113).

936 See the citation from a text on animal offenses at *CIH* 1578.33 (*CCIH* 68); and cf. O'Dav 1310 (no id.; *CCIH* 147: *Ois .i. eisci no aonto, ut est mad ois do tharb do oen na comaighthech* "*Ois*, i.e. a grant or agreement, ut est 'if thou lendest thy bull to one of the neighbours'."). The verb *eiscid* 'allows, concedes' is frequently used to gloss *oidid* 'lends, grants, offers' in legal texts; *eDIL s.v. eiscid* and *oidid*. Both the lemma and gloss are 2 sg. pres. subj. of their respective verbs. Cf. 9.38.113 OIDHTHE.

9.38.113 Oid*h*the .i. éisgid*h*si.
Oidthe 'you (pl.) lend', i.e. you (pl.) allow.[937]

9.39.114 Dít*h* .i. dit*h*im .i. díot*h*.
Díth 'end of a grace period', i.e. delay in pound, i.e. end of a grace period.[938]

9.39.115 Siasra .i. reimn*igh*th*e* no ⟨ion⟩saig*h*th*e*.
Siasra 'will enforce', i.e. was regulated or was enforced.[939]

9.39.116 Coiccenuid .i. rún no coccub*us* u*m* cionuid*h*.
Coiccinaid 'co-crime', i.e. [sharing] secret or shared-knowledge about a crime.[940]

9.39.117 At*h*rola .i. la asa h-ait*h*le .i. ní do t*h*iom*ar*gui *ar* nec*h*.
Athrola 'he entrusted', i.e. in his custody afterwards, i.e. anything enforced on someone.[941]

---

937 The interpretation of the lemma and gloss are tentative; here they are both taken to be the 2 pl. pres. ind. of *oidid* 'lends, grants, offers' and *eiscid* 'allows, concedes', respectively; *eDIL s.v. oidid* and *eiscid*. Cf. 9.38.112 MAD OIS which immediately precedes this entry in the MS.

938 The lemma is equated with *díthim*, a legal term used for the period of time when the distrained property is in the pound and has not yet become of the process of gradually becoming the property of the plaintiff; *GEIL* 177–182. The second gloss is a later spelling of the lemma.

939 The interpretation of the lemma is uncertain and may be a mistake for a passive form of the 3 sg. fut. of *saigid* 'attains, claims, enforces' although one would expect *siasar*; *eDIL s.v.* 1 *saigid*. It is possible that Dubhaltach made a copying mistake.

940 The lemma is not in *eDIL*. The context of the lemma is unknown, but it refers to secret crimes or knowledge of a secret crime. The second half of the gloss might by etymological. Cf. *Bretha Nemed Dédenach*, 54 §10 (*CIH* 603.31); O'Dav 390 (*Bretha Nemed Dédenach*; *CCIH* 119: *Coic .i. rún nó comairle* [*ut est*] *ni cuala coic nuin* "*Coic*, i.e a secret or counsel, ut est 'thou heardest no evil secret'."); *SC* B.225; and O'Cl *Coic .i. rún* 'secret'. Although the word *coic* is explained in glossaries as 'secret', it might be better to understand the lemma as **com-* + *cinaid* 'co-crime' rather than 'secret-crime'; *eDIL s.v.* 2 *coic*. This interpretation has also influenced the understanding of *coccubus* as consisting of **com-* + *cubus*. For the phonology of *com-* in composition, see *GOI* §330. I should like to thank one of the anonymous readers for suggestions regarding the interpretation of this entry.

941 The interpretation of the entry is tentative. The lemma is the 3 sg. perf. of *ad-cuirethar* 'restores, entrusts'; and for the lemma, cf. O'Dav 104 (no id.; *CCIH* 111); *eDIL s.v. ad-cuirethar*. For the second gloss, see *eDIL s.v. do-immoirg*, but the verbal form is unexplained.

9.40.118 *Air*ite .i. gab*h*áil.
Airite 'received', i.e. receiving.[942]

9.40.119 Cliad*h*ra, cléra .i. bolg no c*r*ió l, no tíag*h*.
Cliadra, cléra 'bag', i.e. satchel or bag, or wallet.[943]

9.41.120 Lob*har* .i. dui*n*e t*r*og*h*.
Lobur 'weak', i.e. a weak person.[944]

9.41.121 Laoch .i. an t-*air*e ec*ht*a.
Láech 'warrior', i.e. the lord of slaughter.[945]

9.41.122 Fuag*ar*t[h]aid*h* .i. an fu*r*fogra*idh*.
Fúacarthaid 'herald', i.e. the one who proclaims.[946]

9.41.123 Am*hus* ala tuait*he* .i. deor*aidh*.
Amus ala túaithe 'hireling of another territory', i.e. an outsider.[947]

9.41.124 Direc[h]t(*h*)aid .i. iond*r*aig*aidh*.
Direchtaid 'despoiler', i.e. plunderer.[948]

---

942 The lemma is the part. of *ar-eim* 'accepts, receives'; *eDIL s.v. airite*.

943 The lemmata both appear to be forms of *criöl* 'bag, receptacle, casket', but it is unclear whether they are nom. sg. or in an oblique case. Here they are being interpreted as variant nom. sg. forms; *eDIL s.v. criöl* and *cliadra, cléra*. It is possible that the ⟨d⟩ in some forms arose as a hiatus filler and that ⟨cl⟩ in some forms arose from distant metathesis. All three of the glosses are more or less synonymous. See O'Don. Suppl. *s.v. cliadhra*.

944 The lemma covers a range of meanings, 'weak, infirm, sick, afflicted', but it is not being used here to refer to someone not capable of legal action; *eDIL s.v. lobur, lobor*.

945 For the role of the *aire échta* in society, see *GEIL* 127; Binchy 1941 (1970 reprint with addenda) in *Críth Gablach*, pp. 70–72; McLeod 1987: 46–50; 2004: 114–133; and 2013: 101–114.

946 Both the lemma and gloss are agent nouns. The second gloss is understood as an agent noun from *furfócra* 'notice, proclaiming'.

947 The lemma makes a distinction between someone hired from outside the territory versus one hired locally. Cf. 6.a.36.82 AMHUIS RÚIN, ⁊ RAIDH, ⁊ IOMAGALL[MA].

948 The lemma looks like an agent noun derived from *do-rig* 'strips bare, despoils, exacts payment?'; *eDIL s.v. do-rig*. The final meaning, confined to the legal texts, is listed as uncertain in *eDIL*. The gloss is likely an agent noun derived from *ind-reith* 'invades, lays waste, plunders'; cf. *indred*, its vn. It is also possible that the gloss should be read as *indredach* 'given to invading or plundering'; the edge of the MS is damaged.

9.42.125 Dru*th* .i. go rat*h*.
Drúth 'a fool', i.e. with grace.[949]

9.42.126 Díoc*hus*g .i. a[i]nm*he*r gan rat*h*.
Díchosc 'a person without legal remedy', i.e., a very fierce person without grace.[950]

9.42.127 Ad*h*ma .i. aid*h*me .i. cul*adh* no glés.
Adma 'skillful', i.e. skilled, i.e. equipment or apparatus.[951]

9.42.128 Ang*ar* .i. iongor.
Angar 'undutiful', i.e. undutiful.[952]

9.42.129 Dimeltaid .i. f*e*r adbal-cait*h*m*h*ec*h*.
Dímeltaid 'a used-up person', i.e. a much-consuming person.[953]

9.43.130 Faol*us* .i. fuilngnis.
Fulus 'young animals', i.e. supporter.[954]

---

949 For the interpretation of the gloss, see *Córus Bésgna* §9, gloss 10, and the note on p. 190 (*CIH* 522.2 and 9; *AL* 3: 12.1); and cf. *Bretha Crólige* §12, gloss 10, and the note on p. 59 (*CIH* 2289.10 and 23). For those of unsound mind, see *GEIL* 91–94. Cf. 9.42.126 DÍOCHUSG.

950 The lemma is not in *eDIL*. It appears to be formed by the negative prefix *dí-* and *cosc* 'reproving, correction, punishment, preventing, remedy, legal remedy'; *eDIL s.v. cosc*. When taken in conjunction with 9.42.125 DRUTH, the sense of the lemma is that of someone of unsound mind who is very wild and unpredictable in their actions. For the gloss, cf. *Bretha Crólige* §12, gloss 9, and the note on p. 59 (*CIH* 2289.10 and 23); see also *Córus Bésgna*, p. 190. For those of unsound mind, see *GEIL* 91–94.

951 Cf. O'Cl *Adhma .i. eolach* 'wise' and *Aidhme .i. uradh trealamh, uirnis no culaidh* 'dress'.

952 The lemma is a variant of 2 *ingor* 'undutiful, impious'; *eDIL*. For another example of the interchange between *angar* and *ingor*, cf. 8.17.42 FEALL AS CHOLBHA.

953 The general sense of the entry is that someone has been overly lavish and generous to the point of having used up or given away all their resources. The lemma is not in *eDIL*; cf. *eDIL s.v. dímelte* 'used up, consumed, worn out, decrepit'.

954 The lemma seems to be from *fulus* 'young of animals, produce, offspring'. The gloss is not in *eDIL*, but it seems to be either for *fuilngech* 'supporter' or related to *fuilngid* 'one who supports, a champion'; *eDIL s.vv. fuilngech* and 1 *fuilngid*. The general sense of the entry is that which can be used as a means of economic and/or household support. In the MS, Dubhaltach inserted the ⟨n⟩ of the gloss later with a reference mark. It is possible that he meant to cross out the ⟨g⟩ following the ⟨g⟩ but neglected to do so. It is also possible that as part of this correction process he forgot the write the suspension mark over the ⟨s⟩.

9.43.131 Slab*h*ra, slaib*h*re .i. sal b*huar* .i. bu*ar* tig t*ar* sal.
Slabrae, slaibre 'livestock', i.e. [< *sál* 'the sea' + 1 *búar* 'cows, cattle'] a sea of cows, i.e. cows which come across the sea.[955]

9.43.132 Tion*n*sg*r*a .i. tin*n*sget*a*l.
Tinnscra 'bride-price', i.e. beginning.[956]

9.43.133 Tiasg .i. tin*n*sg*n*a.
Tíasc 'beginning', i.e. beginning.[957]

9.44.134 Com*h*lun*n* .i. coi*m*líon.
Comlann 'equal number', i.e. equal number.[958]

9.44.135 Fuilac*h* .i. fulang.
Fulach 'supporting', i.e. supporting.[959]

9.44.136 Dam*h*rad*h* .i. b*eth ar* dáim*h*.
Dámrad 'retinue', i.e. to be in a retinue.[960]

---

955 The lemmata are variant spellings of each other. The second gloss explains the etymological gloss on the lemmata. The headword can also mean 'marriage portion, dowry', and it could be that the entry refers to a marriage portion which consists of foreign livestock; *eDIL s.v. slabrae, slaibre*. Cf. 3.b.5.33 TIONNSGRA and 3.b.6.34 SLABRA TOBRA where the etymological gloss is the same.

956 Cf. 9.43.131 SLABHRA, SLAIBHRE. The gloss is understood in the entry as being etymologically related to the lemma, although the interpretation is less clear. It is possible that the lemma should be for *tinnscna* 'beginning', which is a variant of *tinnscetal*, the vn. of *do-inscanna* 'begins'; *eDIL s.v. do-inscanna*. It is easy to confuse the forms of ⟨r⟩ and ⟨n⟩ in Irish MSS. If we do not emend the lemma, the entry refers to the payment made to a woman for her virginity at the time of her betrothal. If she proves not to be a virgin on her wedding night, she has to return the payment; *Tract on Marriage and Divorce* §19; GEIL 72–73; and *eDIL s.v. sical*. This payment is made in addition to giving her a bride-price. Cf. O'Cl *Tionnscra .i. coibche* 'purchase', 9.43.133 TIASG, and 3.b.5.33 TIONNSGRA.

957 Cf. 9.43.132 TIONNSGRA. The reading of the gloss is uncertain. *Tinnscna* 'beginning' is a variant of *tinnscetal*, the vn. of *do-inscanna* 'begins'; *eDIL s.v. do-inscanna*. Cf. O'Dav 1564 (*Bretha Nemed Dédenach*; CCIH 154: *Tiasc .i. tinnscna, ut est tiascai i n-anmain Dé* "*Tiasc*, i.e. begin, ut est 'commence it (?) in God's name'."); *Bretha Nemed Dédenach* 38.1 (CIH 1128.15; Corthals 2007: 138), but it is uncertain whether the citation from Dubhaltach's Glossary is taken from this text.

958 See O'Dav 561 (no id.; CCIH 125: *Comlunn .i. comlín, ut est fo comlunn gena* "*Comlunn*, i.e. equal number, ut est ...").

959 The gloss, *fulang*, later came to replace *fulach*; *eDIL s.v. fulach*.

960 See *eDIL s.vv. dámrad* and *dám*.

9.44.137 Cuim*h*lec*h*ta .i. comsloin*n*te.
Comṡlechta 'of common lineage', i.e. of common stock.[961]

9.44.138 Osuic .i. uga .i. tog*h*a le h-os .i. re bel .i. biad*h*.
Osaic 'hospitality', i.e. [< *uccu* 'wish, desire'] wish, i.e. [< *toga* 'desire' + *ós* 'mouth'] desire by a mouth, i.e. by mouth, i.e. food.[962]

9.45.139 Cotuig*h*e tionc*h*uir [.i]. ní do cur fon tion .i. fon taob*h* da coim*h*teg*h*ad*h*.
Cotuige tinchoir 'a bed covering', i.e. anything to put under the soft part of the body, i.e. under the side for their mutual warming.[963]

9.45.140 Cum*al* sec*h*tm*adh* m*ar*b*h*t*h*a .i. an sectm*adh* cuid do*n* coirpdire [.i]. oir sec*h*t coirpdire g*ach* urr*adh* i gcoitcin*ne* *ar* na m*ar*b*adh*.
Cumal sechtmad marbtha 'a seventh *cumal* for killing', i.e. the seventh part of the body-fine, i.e. because the body-fine of each freeman in general is seven [*cumal*s] after their being killed.[964]

9.46.141 Biad*h*m*h*oc*h* .i. biad*h* go moc*h*.
Biadmhoch 'early food', i.e. food early.[965]

---

961 The entry refers to kinsfolk who share common ancestry. According to the note for O'Dav 528 (*Di Astud Chirt 7 Dligid*; CCIH 124: *Comlechta .i. comluigi nó comliudh… "Comlechta*, i.e. copulation or accusation…"), the form *cuimlechta* could be the gen. sg. of **com-lecht* 'co-bed'. This interpretation of the lemma does not make sense here with the meaning provided by the gloss in Dubhaltach's Glossary. See also *Di Astud Chirt 7 Dligid* (CIH 230.24; *AL* 5: 448.1 and 3). It should be noted that O'Don. Suppl. *s.v. cuimlechtaib* provides the definition 'battles' and cites 'H 2 15, p. 36, col. b'; he lists the lemma for Dubhaltach's Glossary as *cuimslechta*.

962 Although *osaic* refers to the religious act of washing the feet of others, it also has the more general meaning of providing attendance, i.e. hospitality, for guests; *eDIL s.v. osaic*.

963 The entry refers to some form of warm bed covering. Although *tinchor* more commonly refers to a marriage contribution, it can also refer to household goods and equipment more generally and also to a bed. In this entry, it is possible that the bed covering was contributed as part of the goods necessary to set up the household.

964 The term *corpdíre* 'body-fine' is normally used to refer to the fine for causing bodily harm, and *éraic* 'body-fine, fixed penalty for homicide' is used as the term for the fine of seven *cumal*s, which along with the victim's honor-price, are paid to the victim's kindred; *GEIL* 126 and 131–133. The legal texts are not always consistent in their usage of these terms and both can refer to fines associated with injury or death.

965 The lemma is not in *eDIL*, but the sense is that of eating a meal early or perhaps food or a food render which is ready early. It is possible that the gloss is etymological as one would expect an adverb to modify a verb. The interpretation of the entry is tentative.

9.47.142 To .i. an tab*air*t.
Tó 'he may swear', i.e. the payment.[966]

9.47.143 As-do .i. b*ei*reid*h* oca.
As-do 'he may refuse', i.e. he may delier the wish.[967]

9.47.144 Suier[...] [.i.] an ta[..][968]

10.1.1 [...]e[.......]rite[.......]c[....]fot[h] n-ionais .i. [...] [.........]ecium[.]ta mil[.]s[..] indile[.] ti[..]t*er*[.]ag [.]ec*h*[.]nos .i. fot*h* n-io[nais] .i. ai[d]brait*er* ag nec*h* *iar* no[..][...]reimdilsi .i. ani ⟨...⟩ fot*h*uig*h*ter ⟨aidbraid⟩ do dilsiug*ad* roi*mh*e ria*m* ag nec*h* [.]en*e*tt[.]uaid, no roi*mhe* e fein da roim*he*.
[...] claim of growth, i.e. [..............], i.e. claim of growth, i.e. it is claimed by one according to [...] prior right, i.e. that which ⟨...⟩ is established ⟨claiming⟩ to surrender before that previously by someone [...], or before that he himself for it previously.[969]

10.4.2 F[o]t*h*[a] c[o]m[*h*]*ar*da .i. fot*h* creca go reimdilsi, no fot*h* n-ionais aca m*ar*aon.
Fotha comarda 'equal claims', i.e. a claim of purchase with prior right, or they both have a claim of growth.[970]

---

966 The context of the entry is unknown. The lemma is the 3 sg. pres. subj. of *tongaid* 'swears'; cf. O'Dav 1588(1) (no id.; *CCIH* 155).

967 The entry is not in O'Curry's transcription, and the interpretation of the entry is tentative because the reading of the gloss is uncertain. The lemma is the 3 sg. pres. subj. of *as-toing* 'refuses'. The word *beireidh* is interpreted as a 3 sg. pres. subj. of *beirid* 'carries, brings', and *oca* is understood as *uccu* 'wish, desire, choice'. I should like to thank one of the anonymous readers for comments on this entry.

968 This entry is not in O'Curry's transcription. The bottom of the page is worn and damaged.

969 The entry is not in O'Curry's transcription, and it is uncertain how many entries are on the first three lines of the page because it is so badly worn. It is clear, however, that the entry (or entries) concern(s) establishing right to a disputed possession, particularly livestock. The two broad types of claims include a claim of purchase and a claim of growth; the second refers to the livestock being born while in one's possession. The material likely comes from the commentary associated with *Aidbred* § 3, from sources A and F (*CIH* 2168.28–2169.6 and 1271.25–33, respectively). Dubhaltach owned TCD MS 1387 [H.5.15], which contains the main MS source for *Aidbred*. Cf. *CIH* 727.31–32 for similar content.

970 The missing letters are supplied from O'Curry's transcription. See *Aidbred* § 3, commentary from sources A and F (*CIH* 2169.4–6 and 1271.25–33, respectively). Dubhaltach owned

10.4.3 Fot*h*a l*ethar*da .i. fot*h* creca go rei*m*[dilsi, no foth] n-ionais ag an d*ar*a de, no fot*h* creca nama ga aroile.
Fotha letharda 'unequal claims', i.e. a claim of purchase with prior right, or one of them has a claim of growth, or the other one only has a claim of purchase.[971]

10.5.4 Tad*h*at .i. gaduig*h*e.
Tadat 'thieves', i.e. thieves.[972]

10.5.5 F*or*ngaire .i. f*or*[con]g*ra* [... ⁊c an] ceimn*ugh*ad*h*.
Forngaire 'command', i.e. command [...] etc., the stepping.[973]

10.6.6 C*ran*nuigid*h* .i. cuirid c*ran*n*ch*or.
Crannaigid 'he casts lots', i.e. he casts lots.[974]

10.6.7 Tat*h*ad .i. ata liom.
Tathat '[I] accord you', i.e. I have.[975]

10.6.8 Tuid*h*in .i. c*ruin*n*iug*ad*h* no tuinid*h* .i. orlaim*h* no se[..]
Tuidin 'proof', i.e. gathering or ownership, i.e. ready or ...[976]

TCD MS 1387 [H.5.15], which contains the main MS source for *Aidbred*. Cf. CIH 727.31–32 (citations from a variety of texts; CCIH 32).

971 See *Aidbred* § 3, commentary from sources A and F (CIH 2169.4–6 and 1271.25–33, respectively). Dubhaltach owned TCD MS 1387 [H.5.15], which contains the main MS source for *Aidbred*. Cf. CIH 727.31–32 (citations from a variety of texts; CCIH 32).

972 See *Aidbred* § 3, tract from source P (CIH 712.13), where the lemma has the same gloss as found in Dubhaltach's Glossary.

973 Both the lemma and the first gloss are used as the vn. of *for-congair*; *forcongra* is used in MI and later; *eDIL s.vv. forngaire, forgaire* and *forcongra*, respectively. Cf. 10.45.118 FORNGAIRE. See O'Cl *Forngaire .i. furáileamh* 'a command'. It is possible that the second gloss belongs with another entry as it is difficult to reconcile its meaning with the rest of the entry. The writing on the left side of the MS page is very faint. O'Curry also was uncertain whether the gloss belonged with *forngaire*.

974 For the legal process of casting lots, see GEIL 208–209. The verb *cuirid* 'causes, has done' replaces earlier *fo-ceird*; *eDIL s.v. cuirid*.

975 Cf. the *Fonnaidh* glossary (CIH 1081.7 and 8; CIH 46; and Taylor-Griffiths 2020: 1: 174–179) 'Tathat .i. ata agat. Tathu*m* .i. ata agam.'; and the dialogue between Fachtnae and Sogan (CIH 590.34; CCIH 27; and Meyer 1918: 365.13). The form *tathat* has a 2 sg. suffixed pron.; *eDIL s.v. attá* 'is'. I should like to thank one of the anonymous readers for comments on this entry.

976 The remainder of the entry is lost due to damage at the edge of the page. See O'Don. Suppl. *s.v. tuidin*.

10.7.9 [....]a*nith* .i. is daoisaoct ase as .*cét*.giallna.[977]

10.7.10 Saoit*he* .i. ni as saot*h* le nec*h* m*a*r ata diub*air*t.
Saithe 'distress', i.e. anything which is a hardship for someone as if it is a loss.[978]

10.7.11 Cui*nn*dfec[h] .i. c[..] .i. cuidb*h*ide no [...]
Cuindbech 'empty', i.e. [...], i.e. ridiculous or ...[979]

10.8.12 [...] .i. sasal ions*h*i*n*d.
[...], i.e. that is...[980]

10.9.13 [Caitheamh] tola mna .i. fer d'faoid*h*ec*h*tain le .i. do dul cuigt*he*, ma do foad*h*, ma do faoid*eth*, muna ffoa, muna f*h*o, muna ffoa[dh]: ⟨sin uile o d*h*ul cuigt*he*⟩.
Caithem tola mná 'enjoying sexual intercourse with a woman', i.e. a man spending the night with her, i.e. to go to her, if he spends the night, if he spends the night, if he does not spend the night, if he does not spend the night: ⟨all of that from [the phrase] *dul cuicce* 'going to her'⟩.[981]

10.10.14 Culla*th* [a]ge .i. edac*h* leab*th*a do ber ben d*h*ocu*m* fir ant*an* naisgt*e*r iad ma-le.

---

977 This entry is not in O'Curry's transcription. The reading is very uncertain, thus, no translation is attempted.

978 The context of the entry is uncertain, but it might belong with previous entries which come from *Aidbred*, which concerns lost and stolen property and how to get said property back into one's own possession.

979 Although the entry is incomplete, it might refer to contracts which are considered null and void. For the lemma, cf. *Ántéchtae* (CIH 1249.9 and 19; CCIH 51); and cf. CIH 727.30 (citations from a variety of texts; CCIH 32); *Bretha Nemed Toísech* (CIH 2220.27); SC Y.387: *Cuindfiuch .i. fas .i. cuinnfiuch ni co cetchura*; and O'Dav 349 (*Bretha Nemed Toísech*; CCIH 118: *Cuinnbech, .i. fas, ut est cuinnbech ní co cét-churu...* "*Cuinnbech*, i.e. void, ut est 'void is anything up to the first contracts'...").

980 The lemma is illegible, and the reading of the gloss is uncertain. The entry is not in O'Curry's transcription.

981 The first word and missing letters are supplied from O'Curry's transcription. The context of the entry is unknown. The general sense is of spending the night with a woman enjoying sexual relations. The form *faoidhechtain* is the vn. of *foaid* 'spends the night'. The verbs in the gloss are all forms of *foaid*; *eDIL s.v. foaid*. The string of verbs in the gloss is unusual as they are all from the same verb. Perhaps Dubhaltach is presenting us with a range of variant spellings. The form *cuigthe* is understood as *1 co* 'to' with a 3 sg. f. suffixed. pron.

Culaith occai 'furnishings she has', i.e. a bed covering that a woman gives to a man when they are betrothed together.[982]

10.10.15 Toit*h*len .i. do étlod.
Toithlen 'stealing', i.e. to steal.[983]

10.10.16 Torla .i. naidm.
Torla 'bond', i.e. a bond.[984]

10.11.17 [...]d[..] c[.]ac*h* .i. ait*h*ec*h* .i. deglaoc*h*.
[.......], i.e. commoner, i.e. good-layman.[985]

10.11.18 Aiccit*h*er .i. uga ésgt[h]*e*r.
Aiccither 'you may see', i.e. [< *uccu* 'wish, selection, choice' + *eiscid* 'allows, concedes'] a wish may be granted.[986]

10.11.19 Do-r*ar*aic .i. ro t*air*gist*er*.
Do-ráraic 'he brought', i.e. he brought.[987]

10.11.20 Doit*h*c*h*en .i. dáit*h* .i. luait*h*cíonad.
Daithchin 'swift-crime', i.e. swift, i.e. swift-crime.[988]

10.12.21 [....]*ed* .i. au*m*egaig*hed*.[989]

---

982 The interpretation of the lemma is based on Dinneen, *s.v. culaith* 'clothes, apparel, attire, furniture'. The reading of the lemma is tentative because edge of the page is very worn.

983 The lemma appears to be a form of *tothla* 'stealing, illegal sexual intercourse', the vn. of **to-tlen-*; *eDIL s.v. tothla*.

984 See O'Dav 1594 ((2) no id.; *CCIH* 155: *Nó torla .i. naidm*... "Or *torla*, i.e. a bond..."); the *Ni Tulach* glossary (*CIH* 811.15); the *Arra* glossary (*CIH* 1559.21). Cf. 2.b.8.96 TORLA.

985 The entry is not in O'Curry's transcription. The edge of the MS is damaged, and the lemma is illegible.

986 Cf. 3.b.5.31 AICC. See O'Don. Suppl. *s.v. aiccither .i. uga eiscther*. It is possible that *ésgt[h]er* is from *2 eiscid* 'cuts off, severs', but this interpretation is harder to reconcile with the lemma.

987 For the lemma and gloss, see *eDIL s.v. do-áirci* 'causes, brings about'; both forms are 3 sg. perf. ind. In legal contexts, the verb can also mean 'conducts, brings, leads'. For the lemma, see *Fél.* Aug. 1.

988 The lemma appears to be a compound of *daith* 'swift, ready, prompt' and *cin* 'guilt, crime, levy'.

989 The reading is tentative, and the entry is not in O'Curry's transcription.

10.12.22 Laith*rech* laig*h*en .i. lat*hair* in ro h-eillg*edh* e.
Láthrach láigen 'place of spears', i.e. a place where it has been claimed.[990]

10.12.23 Im-id-rub*air*t .i. do-rinne imb*e*rt.
Imid-rubairt 'he had placed it', i.e. he had placed.[991]

10.12.24 Dioc*h*unduil .i. coi*m*tec*htus* .i. [....] .i. mugugad*h*.
Dichundail 'inconstant', i.e. accompaniment, i.e. [....] i.e. destroying.[992]

10.13.25 Roc*h*ma .i. ro at*h*cuma.
Rochma 'he wounded', i.e. he wounded.[993]

10.13.26 Foilngid*h* .i. cu do ni foileim *ar* nec*h*.
Foilngid 'a springer', i.e. a dog which makes a leap on someone.[994]

---

990 The entry seems to refer to setting a spear in the location where one is making a claim, assuming that the interpretation of *laighen* should be understood here as 'spears'. Cf. O'Dav 1130 (*Din Techtugud*; CCIH 142: *Inlolaigh .i. ro heillged...* "*Inolaig*, i.e. has been claimed..."); *Din Techtugud* (CIH 209. 29 and 33). Based on *inlolaigh* in O'Dav and *inlolaid* in *Din Techtugud*, it could be that the second half of the lemma here is a misreading for a form of *in-loing* 'puts in a claim'; *eDIL s.v. in-loing.*

991 This entry is problematic for a number of reasons. The lemma is a 3 sg. perf. of *immbeir* 'places, uses' with a Class C n. object agreement marker. The context of the entry is unknown. The second word in the gloss might be read as 'riune', but that form is not an Irish word. The MS reading 'miebter' has been emended to 'imbert' in order to make sense of the word; the reading of this word is not secure.

992 The interpretation of the entry is tentative, especially as the lemma is not in *eDIL* and the second gloss is illegible.

993 The interpretation of the lemma is uncertain. It is possible that it is a variant form of the 3 sg. pret./perf. of *ad-cuimben* 'strikes, wounds' without the preverb. The gloss is also a 3 sg. pret./perf. form of *ad-cuimben*; *eDIL s.v. ad-cuimben.*

994 See *Bretha for Conślechtaib* (CIH 111.22). The larger context within *Bretha Éitgid* (CIH 312.35–37) is the three dogs checked in trespass. This entry and the following two are found there; 10.13.27 CU CON and 10.13.28 CU L[OIRGE]. See also *AL* 3: 414.25; O'Dav 471 (*Bretha for Conślechtaib*; CCIH 122: *Clothra .i. ní cluinter ac a crothad amail atá ma[d] cú foilm[n]ech bid urfogra cluic nó clothra fo a bragait .i. cluigin im a bragait nó ní aile atcluinfither ac a crotha[d] intan ticfa do dénam fogla* "*Clothra*, i.e. something that is heard when shaken, ut est 'if a springing dog, let there be the notice of a bell or of a rattle under his neck', i.e. a little bell round his neck or something else which, when he shall come to commit trespass, will be heard a-shaking."); *Bretha Nemed Toísech* (CIH 2228.18–20); and Breatnach 1996a: 17. The lemma is an epithet for a dangerous dog; *EIF* 148. See O'Don. Suppl. *s.v. foilmig, foilngid.*

10.13.27 Cu *con* .i. cu na ccuilen.
Cú con 'a dog of dogs', i.e. a dog with pups.[995]

10.13.28 Cu l[oirge] .i. cu ris na gabann g*r*eim lorg.
Cú loirge 'a sleuth-hound', i.e. a dog against which a track does not prevail.[996]

10.14.29 Cu ot*r*aig*h* .i. (madr*ad* gerr) as i-side an cu f*r*isa ngaib*h* maoit*hfh*lesg.
Cú otraig 'a yard dog [lit. dunghill dog]', i.e. (a terrier) that is the dog over which a soft rod prevails.[997]

10.14.30 Cot-ris*edh* .i. do [...] no do cengolad*h*.
Cot-rised 'he should have bound it', i.e. to [...] or he should bind.[998]

10.15.31 Fes*edh* .i. fua*cht*na*igh*f*edh*.
Fesed 'it would fight', i.e. it would attack.[999]

---

995 See *Bretha Éitgid* (*CIH* 312.35–37) for the three dogs checked in trespass. This entry and the previous and following one are found there; 10.13.26 FOILNGIDH and 10.13.28 CU L[OIRGE]. See also *AL* 3: 414.25; *Bretha Nemed Toísech* (*CIH* 2228.18–20); and Breatnach 1996a: 17. This material originally comes from the fragmentary text *Bretha for Conślechtaib*.

996 The sense is that the dog will trace anything without losing the track. See *Bretha Éitgid* (*CIH* 312.35–37) for the three dogs checked in trespass. This entry and the previous and following one are found there; 10.13.26 FOILNGIDH and 10.13.27 CU CON. See also *AL* 3: 414.25; *Bretha Nemed Toísech* (*CIH* 2228.18–20); and Breatnach 1996a: 17. This material originally comes from the fragmentary text *Bretha for Conślechtaib*.

997 The literal meaning of the lemma is 'dunghill dog', but it should be understood as the 'yard dog'; *EIF* 116; Binchy 1973: 78 § 4; and Murray 2007: 151. The sense is that the dog is not very fierce. See *CIH* 1390.7, which is part of a collection of citations from various texts, one of which is *Bretha for Conślechtaib* (*CCIH* 63). I should like to thank one of the anonymous readers for comments on *madrad gerr*; cf. Mod. Ir. *madra gearr* 'terrier'.

998 The lemma is a 3 sg. past subj. of *con-rig* 'binds' with a Class B n. object agreement marker; cf. O'Dav 489 (no id.; *CCIH* 123: *Cotreisin .i. cuimrech, ut est madh cen conn cotat comnart cotreisi[n] .i. ma[d] cin codhnach calma aca cuibrech co secda. Ocus atá sa corp cétna: con-res do cuimne .i. do coin is cuimnech um indliged do denum* "*Cot-reisin*, i.e. a fetter, ut est 'if I should fetter him without a hard, strong adult', i.e. if without a brave person *sui iuris* (I should be) tying him tightly. And in the same text is: 'thou shouldst tie up thy *cuimne*, i.e. thy hound that is mindful (*cuimnech*) to commit illegality'."). O'Dav 489 is not listed in *CCIH* with a source; it is likely we can add *Bretha for Conślechtaib* to that list. See 10.15.32 CON-REIS below which is the second half of the entry in O'Dav. The middle of the gloss is illegible, but it is possible that it originally contained another word meaning 'bind'.

999 The lemma is a 3 sg. past subj. of *fichid* 'fights'. Cf. *Bretha for Conślechtaib* (*CIH* 1550.33; *CCIH* 67).

10.15.32 Con-reis .i. cui*m*rig*h*si no cuib*r*ig*h*.
Con-reis 'you should bind', i.e. bind or bind.[1000]

10.15.33 Apt*h*a .i. ebiltin.
Apthu 'death', i.e. death.[1001]

10.15.34 *Air*bir .i. t*air*b*h*ir.
Airbir 'plead', i.e. surrender.[1002]

10.15.35 Fec*h*ad .i. fec*h*aid.
Fechad 'they fight', i.e. they fight.[1003]

10.16.36 Fresluide .i. p*r*eapuide.
Freslaide 'a hostile one', i.e. a springer.[1004]

10.16.37 Cu lomna .i. cu danad *árach*, lom*h*an ima gob.
Cú lomna 'a dog on a leash', i.e. a dog for whom there is a binding, a leash around its muzzle.[1005]

1000 The words in the entry are all forms of *con-rig* 'binds, ties'; the lemma is the 2 sg. pres. juss. subj., and the glosses are from later simplex forms of the verb and are 2 sg. impv. Cf. O'Dav 489 (no id.; *CCIH* 123: *Cotreisin .i. cuimrech, ut est madh cen conn cotat comnart cotreisi*[*n*] *.i. ma*[*d*] *cin codhnach calma aca cuibrech co secda. Ocus atá sa corp cétna: conres do cuimne .i. do coin is cuimnech um indliged do denum* "*Cot-reisin*, i.e. a fetter, ut est 'if I should fetter him without a hard, strong adult', i.e. if without a brave person *sui iuris* (I should be) tying him tightly. And in the same text is: 'thou shouldst tie up thy *cuimne*, i.e. thy hound that is mindful (*cuimnech*) to commit illegality'."), which concerns tying up a dog if it is prone to commit an illegality. For the first half of the entry in O'Dav, see 10.14.30 COT-RISEDH. O'Dav 489 is listed in *CCIH* without a source; it is likely we can add *Bretha for Conślechtaib* to that list.

1001 The lemma is the vn. of *ad-bath* (see *at-bail*(*l*)); *DIL s.v. apthu*. The gloss appears to be the dat. sg. of *epeltu*, the vn. of *at-bail*(*l*). For the gloss, cf. *CIH* 700.13 (a text on wounding) which Breatnach 2005a: 30 characterizes as "late"; *CCIH* 30. It is unusual for the lemma and gloss to be in different cases, unless the dat. sg. of *epeltu* has been reinterpreted as the nom. sg. It is also possible that the final letter in the MS should be read as ⟨u⟩. Cf. 6.a.33.73 AP[TH]AIN.

1002 The lemma is the 2 sg. impv. of *ar-beir* 'lives, eats, uses, pleads'. The gloss is the 2 sg. impv. of *do-airbir* 'bends, lowers, yields, surrenders'.

1003 O'Curry does not print the gloss; the reading is tentative. Both verbs appear to be 3 pl. pres. ind. of *fichid* 'fights', conjunct and absolute, respectively.

1004 The translation is tentative. The lemma might be the agent noun in *-aige* derived from the adj. *freslach* 'contending, hostile', which itself is derived from *frestlaid* 'attends on, receiving or encountering an attack'. The gloss might be similarly formed, i.e. an agent noun derived from **prepach*, itself derived from *prepaid* 'starts, bounces'. See *eDIL s.vv. frestlaid* and *prepaid*, respectively.

1005 See *CIH* 312.14 and 1389.26, both of which refer to a dog tied to a stake some distance

10.16.38 Conair caoimt*acht*a .i. conair tiag*ur* isi*n* f[aith]c[h]e.
Conar coimtechta 'accompanying path', i.e. a path by which one goes through the green in front of a residence.[1006]

10.17.39 Tacm*h*aisi .i. tacmainge.
Tacmaisi 'of circumference', i.e. of circumference.[1007]

10.17.40 Indisi .i. buail*idh* bo.
Indise 'milking enclosure', i.e. enclosure of cows.[1008]

10.17.41 M*á*r*us* .i. mo*r* ráid*h*is.
Márus 'he praised', i.e. [< *mór* 'great' + *ráidhis* 'he said'] greatly-he said.[1009]

10.17.42 Cana .i. cuilen.
Cana 'whelp', i.e. pup.[1010]

---

from the doorway and pathway so that it cannot bite anyone; *EIF* 148. Cf. *CIH* 572.26, a fragment on wandering animals, which refers to a dog without a leash (*CCIH* 26). Cf. 10.16.38 CONAR CAOIMTECHTA and 10.17.39 TACMHAISI.

1006 See *CIH* 1389.28; *EIF* 148; and cf. 10.16.37 CU LOMNA and 10.17.39 TACMHAISI. The lemma refers to the pathway in front of a residence.

1007 The gloss has the gen. sg. of *tacmang* in its meaning 'circumference'. See *CIH* 1389.32 where the nom. sg. is found. This and the previous two entries, 10.16.37 CU LOMNA and 10.16.38 CONAR CAOIMTECHTA, refer to a dog being leashed away from the house and pathway. According to *EIF* 148, the glossator envisions a circular house with "wattling woven around vertical stakes."

1008 Both the lemma and gloss appear to be in the dat. sg. Cf. *Stowe Gl.* 439 *Inis .i. buaile.*

1009 See *CIH* 1389.33 (citations on offences by animals; *CCIH* 63) where the lemma is glossed with *mor-raiter* as it is here. The lemma is interpreted as a 3 sg. pret. from *móraid* 'makes great, exalts, magnifies, increases', based on the etymological gloss, but that interpretation is tentative, especially as it does not fit well within its larger source context.

1010 See *CIH* 1389.37–38 (citations on offences by animals; *CCIH* 63); *Di Astud Chirt 7 Dligid* (*CIH* 238.26 and 30); Murray 2007: 150; and cf. O'Dav 529 (*Di Astud Chirt 7 Dligid*; *CCIH* 124: *Cano .i. cuilen mic tire, ut est cis lir dia ro suided comdire? Gédh, corr* [*caitin, cailech*], *cano* "*Cano*, i.e. a wolf's cub, ut est 'what is the number (of animals) for which equal fine has been settled? A goose, a heron, a kitten, a cock, a wolf's cub.'"). In *Di Astud Chirt 7 Dligid* the lemma is glossed as *cuilen cen gnim* 'a pup without activity'; cf. the material on cats below. In the F version, TCD MS 1317 [H.2.15B], of O'Davoren's Glossary there is added: *.i. cuilen mic tire is uada ata fotha canainde*. The source *Fotha Canainde* has yet to be identified; it is not in *CCIH*. It might be possible that this is the title of a tract on canines or wolves which is no longer extant. Dubhaltach's grandfather copied this version of O'Davoren's Glossary, and Dubhaltach himself made notes in the margins. The inflection of *cana* varies. See also O'Cl *Cana .i. cuilén* 'a little dog'.

10.17.43 Canan*na* .i. cuileoin.
Cananna 'whelps', i.e. whelps.[1011]

10.17.44 Cirde .i. [ai]d no tesguid.
Cirrthe 'mangled', i.e. observation or he cuts.[1012]

10.18.45 Cuimnett*ar* .i. do coim*m*ion*naghedar* .i. do at*h*cu*m*at*ar*.
Cuimnettar 'they are cut', i.e. they are cut, i.e. they are cut.[1013]

10.18.46 Puibl[a]i[d] .i. tesgad*h*.
Puiblaid (?), i.e. cutting.[1014]

10.18.47 Cu na tt*r*i ngnio*m* .i. lorg*airacht* goide, gabalt[aige] [....] legt*er*, ⁊ diongbail fir fo*r*rain ide*r* da f*h*iall*ach* .i. da *cet*[h]*er*n.
Cú na trí gním 'dog of the three tasks', i.e. tracking theft, seizing [...] they are destroyed, and protecting a man under attack by two warrior bands, i.e. two fighting men.[1015]

10.19.48 *Á*r*ch*u .i. cu bi*us* f*or* *ar*a*ch* .i. cengal.
Árchú 'slaughter-hound (guard dog)', i.e. a dog which is on a leash, i.e. binding.[1016]

1011 Cf. *CIH* 1389.37–38 (citations on offences by animals; *CCIH* 63).

1012 The missing letters are supplied from O'Curry's transcription. Cf. O'Dav 787 (likely from *Bretha for Conṡlechtaib*; *CCIH* 131: *Eses .i. tescad, ut est diles don coin tria fraigidh nó for dorus acht ni doesister .i. acht na ro tescait ní* "*Eses*, i.e. cutting, ut est '(it is) lawful for the hound (to go) through the wall or by the door, provided it be not severed', i.e. provided nothing has been cut."); the entry states that it is lawful for the dog to go through the wall or door provided it (the leash?) is not severed. The entry in Dubhaltach's Glossary might not be complete. The interpretation of the lemma and first gloss are tentative. The lemma is interpreted as the past part. of *cirrid* 'mangles, maims'.

1013 The entry is problematic for a number of reasons. The lemma might be from *cummaid* 'wounds, shapes, devises'; cf. *con-ben* 'smites, cuts off, hacks'. The first gloss might be a later deponent from *con-ben*. The second gloss appears to be from *ad-cuimben* 'strikes, cuts, wounds'.

1014 The missing letters are supplied from O'Curry's transcription. The lemma is obscure, but one assumes that its meaning must be similar to that of its gloss, which is a variant spelling of *tescad* 'cutting, smiting', the vn. of *do-esc* 'cuts, severs, destroys'; *eDIL s.v. tescad*.

1015 See *CIH* 186.37 (concerning compensation for injury to or by dogs; *CCIH* 23), 1390.25, 30, 34–35 (citations on offences by animals; *CCIH* 63); *EIF* 116; and *CCIH* 23 where it is suggested that it is possible that this citation may be from *Bretha for Conṡlechtaib*.

1016 See heptad 37, concerning difficult pledges, (*CIH* 35.21 and 30–31; *AL* 5: 250.4); *EIF*

10.19.49 Aba*ch* .i. cnu*mhus* .i. feis a[.....]all*aid* ia*r*ra ní s*h*eduig*h*es t*ar* na locaib*h*.
Apach 'entrails', i.e. which it gnaws, i.e. trespass [...] a wild animal seeking something which wanders across the localities.[1017]

10.20.50 Do*chtair* .i. coisgter .i. múi*nter*.
Dochtair 'is restrained', i.e. is restrained, i.e. is taught.[1018]

10.20.51 Collúd*h* .i. collód*h* .i. soad*h* do *ch*olla.
Collud 'destruction', i.e. destruction, i.e. [< *coll* 'destruction' + *soud* 'turning'] turning to destroy.[1019]

10.20.52 Muiltt*er* .i. leit[h]ir, no f*r*islaig*h*ter.
Muillter 'is incited', i.e. is known, or is arranged.[1020]

10.21.53 Tóirb*h*enad .i. [to]ir*ith*ni[ge]d.
Toirbenad 'he used to help', i.e. he used to help.[1021]

114–117; and *Cethairślicht Athgabálae* (CIH 402.8 and 18–19; AL 1: 232.4 and 234.25–27). Cf. 6.a.33.74 ÁRCHÚ LOMHNA.

1017 For the lemma, cf. CIH 1395.35 (citations on offences by animals; CCIH 63); and EIF 178. Perhaps this is in reference to wild dogs or wolves roaming the countryside. It is also uncertain whether this is one entry or two due to the fact that the end of one line and the beginning of the next is illegible. O'Curry does not print the majority of the gloss. The first gloss is interpreted as a 3 sg. pres. ind. rel. of a later simplex related to *cnaïd* 'gnaws, consumes' and its vn. *cnám*; cf. Mod. Ir. *creim* 'gnaw'.

1018 For the lemma, cf. O'Dav 674 (likely from *Bretha for Conślechtaib*; CCIH 128: *Docht .i. tost .i. ní fócair nech a*[*l*]*la dochtair, alla brostair* "*Docht*, i.e. silence [rectius 'silent'], ut est 'no one proclaims the day he is restrained, the day he is egged on'."); and *Bretha for Conślechtaib* (CIH 1390.25, citations on offences by animals; CCIH 63). The verb *múinter* is glossing *coisgter* (from *con-secha* 'corrects, reproves, restrains') with its meaning 'corrects' rather than on the lemma. *Coisgter* itself, with the meaning 'restrains', is glossing the lemma.

1019 See CIH 1390.26 (citations on offences by animals; CCIH 63). The context is the destruction of a track.

1020 For the second gloss, cf. O'Dav 1005 (no id.; CCIH 138: *Freisligh .i. firindeall…* "*Fresligi*, i.e. true arrangement…"); cf. *Bretha Éitgid* (CIH 268.12 ff.; CCIH 24; AL 3: 192.9); and EIF 178. The first gloss might be a 3 sg. pres. pass. of *lethaid* 'spreads out', but it can be used figuratively of things known; *eDIL s.v. lethaid.* The entry might be a reference to a dog fight.

1021 The missing letters are supplied from O'Curry's transcription. The gloss is obscure, but it might be from *tóirithnigid* 'helps, relieves', which is used in legal texts to gloss *do-rorban* 'happens, arrives, profits, helps'; the word has been edited to reflect this interpretation. O'Curry reads 'toirighnid', but it is difficult to make sense of word. Both forms are understood as the 3 sg. impf. ind.; *eDIL s.vv.* 1 *do-rorban* and *tóirithnigid.*

10.21.54 5 An*manna* cat su*nn* .i. breóinde .i. breo nuall, ⁊ nia t*r*en, no breó án .i. c*r*óna*n* ina in[ne]. ⁊ meoinde .i. mo do-g*h*ni meig*h*il .i. meoain ⟨.i. meig*h*leac*h*⟩ ina in*ne*. Ringcne .i. riac*h*aid nec*h*, ⁊ riac*hthar* é. Cruib*h*ne .i. cruib nia .i. nia tren [a l]*us* a cruibe. *Air*cne .i. a h-*airc* Naoi M*ic* Lai*mh*iac*h*, no a b*air*cne .i. nia t*r*en, tugad*h* a b*air*c Bresail B*r*ic .i. cait b*r*oin*n*geala d*h*uba. Iach .i. fiad*h* c*h*at all*aidh* gaba*r* d*h*' fiad*h* .i. as fiad*h*ant*a*s. Folam .i. cat ler mait*h* loim, ⁊ coi*metus* loim go mait*h* ionan*n* e ⁊ an cat cuile a*cht* gu*r*ob isi*n* tsenbaile b*hius*, ⁊ folom *ar* an mbuaile. Glas-nen*n*ta .i. cat beg b*hius* isi*n* tsenb*h*aile isi*n* nen*n*toig g*h*la[is] ag diotuig*adh* loc*h*ad*h*. Breoin*n*e .i. cat ait*aghius* rig ⁊ tigerna ⁊ *air*c[h]in*n*eac*h*, ⁊ do-ní c*r*onán doib*h*. Meoi*n*de, le meg*h*ile, ⁊ e coim(*h*)*et* i ccuid bid*h* c*r*uib[ne] le coi*met* muilin*n* ⁊ sab*h*aill ⁊ at*h*a. Ringcne le h-*air*fid*edh* clan*n*a na n-*ar*d*air*ec*h*. Da sg*r*iobad*h*, ⁊ iadsan da sg*r*iobad san. B*air*cne .i. cat ban sin.

Cóic anmanna cat sunn 'Five names of cats here', i.e. *Breoinne*, i.e. *breó* means 'noise', and *nia* means 'a strong one' [< *breó* 'flame' + *nia* 'warrior'], or wonderful flame [< *breó* 'flame' + *án* 'wonderful'], i.e. purring is its essence. And *meoinne*, i.e. it mews most [< *mó* 'greatest' + *do-gní* 'it does'], i.e. little mew ⟨i.e. mewing⟩ is its essence. *Rincne*, i.e. it torments anyone [< *ríagaid* 'it torments' + *nech* 'anyone'], and it is tormented. *Cruibne*, i.e. [< *crob* 'paw' + *nia* 'warrior'] a strong warrior, i.e. a strong one by virtue of its paw. *Aircne*, i.e. from the ark of Noah Mac Lamíach [< *árc* 'ark' + *Nae* 'Noah'], or from *baircne*, i.e. *nia* 'a strong one' [< *bárc* 'ship' + *nia* 'warrior'], it was brought from the ship of Bresal Brecc, i.e. white-breasted black cats. *Íach*, i.e. an undomesticated wild cat taken from the wild, i.e. from the wilderness. *Folum*, i.e. a diligent good unsheltered cat [< *fó* 'good' + *lomm* 'bare'], and which protects well the unsheltered; it is equivalent to the pantry cat except it is still in the permanent abode, and unsheltered in the cattle-fold. *Glas-nennta* 'nettle-green', i.e. a small cat which is in the permanent abode amongst the green nettles destroying mice. *Breoinne*, i.e. a cat which dwells with king and lord and erenagh, and who purrs for them. *Meoinne*, by mewing, and in its share of food, it is equivalent to a *cruibne* by protecting mill and barn and drying kiln. *Rincne* by entertaining children of the chief nobles. It was written, and they were written there. *Baircne*, i.e. that is a cat for women.[1022]

1022 Some of the missing letters are supplied from O'Curry's transcription. This is one of

10.28.55 Luc*h*l[a]m*h*a .i. lam*h*aid*h* luc*h*.
Luchláma 'mouse-paws', i.e. he catches a mouse.[1023]

10.28.56 Rórdam*us* .i. ro im*r*aidm*h*is.
Rórdamas 'we should incur', i.e. we should consider.[1024]

Dubhaltach's longer entries; see the discussion on pp. 50–55. Most of the material in this entry is from the fragmentary text *Bretha for Catšlechtaib*. Material on cats can be found in CIH 1550.15–23, 110.14–21, 379.11, 889.23–24, 1903.3, 238.26–30, 1837.15, 23–24, 709.37–39, 897.37–39, 789.18–24, 1628.26–28, 1208.41–1209.2, 113.33–36, 1901.25, 290.32–36, SC Y.115, SC B.95, and O'Dav 241, 242, 421, 422, 470 (1), 915, 918, 1045, 1109, 1110, 1246, 1247, 1365, 1395 (*Bretha for Catšlechtaib*). The discussion on pp. 50–55 lists the citations from O'Davoren's Glossary relevant to this entry. The *bairche* is the subject of SC Y.115: *Barcne .i. cat ban, fobith is a mbairc dusfucad 'Bairche*, i.e. a cat for women, because it is from a ship it was brought' (translation from Murray 2007: 148) and SC B.95: *Bairche .i. catt boineand ar (fobíth) is ambairc dosfucad 'Bairche*, i.e. a female cat, because it is from a ship it was brought' (translation from Murray 2007: 148). The word *rincne* is also the subject of SC Y.1084: *Rincne quasi quinqui. Unde dicitur Ferchess mac Mosecis dixit intan boi Find ua Baiscui oc airim cach coicir ar n-uair do sluag Luigdech maic Macniadh do chuinchidh ind fennedo .i. Ferchis. Adacht Ferchess tren foa chnamæ sech Find ⁊ dollieicci in slig for Lugaid conidromarb ⁊ asbert occa rincne quasi carincue rus rig .i. ar ba heth atbeired Find beus o'trimed cach coicer a uair. Rincni quasi quinque 'Rincne* as if *quinque* 'five'. Thus is said: Ferchess son of Moshéices (?) said [it] when Finn úa Baíscne was counting every five people in turn of the host of Lugaid mac Macniad, seeking the warrior, Ferchess. Ferchess went as fast as he could past Finn and he casts the spear at Lugaid so that he killed [him] and he said on that occasion: '*rincne quasi carincne, riis rig*', for that is what Finn used to say also when he counted every five people in turn. *Rincne* as if *quinque*' (translation from Arbuthnot 2012: 78). In her discussion of the SC entry, Arbuthnot suggests that the lemma originally referred to a type of "aggressive cat" with five sharp claws which would explain the Latin word glossing it. From there, the entry referring to a type of cat "is conflated with an account of the killing of Mac Con," in which account *rincne* refers to a spear (2012: 79 (for quotatioons) and 70). For the early Irish laws related to cats, see Murray 2007; and EIF 121–124. In the early Irish laws, cats are assigned different values based on their skills, such as mousing. There are more than five different types of cats listed here. Some of the material overlaps with attested fragments of *Bretha for Catšlechtaib* and O'Dav, while some of it is not attested anywhere else. For the verb form *da sgriobadh*, see *SnaG* 408; pret. pass. sg. and pl. forms look the same in EMI.

1023 The entry concerns catching a mouse. The lemma, *luchlámha* 'mouse-paws' might refer to a type of cat. For the gloss, see *eDIL s.vv. lamaid* 'dares, ventures' and *1 lámaid* a variant of *lámaigid* 'touches, handles'. Note that the previous entry in the glossary concerns cats: 10.21.54 5 ANMANNA CAT SUNN. I should like to thank one of the anonymous readers for comments on this entry.

1024 The expansion of the final syllable of the lemma is tentative. The verb is a 1 pl. past subj. of *reithid* 'runs, becomes due'; *eDIL s.v. reithid*. The gloss is the 1 pl. past subj. of *imm-rádi* 'considers, mentions'; *eDIL s.v. imm-rádi*.

10.28.57 Taosnam*hadh* .i. tumad*h*, n[o] fliuch*adh ar*áin.
Taosnamad 'pouring', i.e. dipping, or wetting of bread.[1025]

10.29.58 T*uir*enn .i. *c*ruit*h*ne*acht*.
Tuirenn 'wheat', i.e. wheat.[1026]

10.29.59 Cic*h*sime .i. ceimn*igh*imne.
Cichsimme 'that we shall proceed', i.e. we shall proceed.[1027]

10.29.60 Con-et*ha* .i. coim*eta*.
Con-etha 'that he may obtain', i.e. that he may obtain.[1028]

10.29.61 ⟨Buicne .i. ceo d*ha* buaic .i. cáinte.⟩
⟨*Buicne* 'halfwit', i.e. [< *búaic* 'top, head' + *ceó* 'mist'] a mist in his head, i.e. satirist.[1029]⟩

10.29.62 Ol .i. oll .i. mo*r*.
Ól 'liquid measure', i.e. great, i.e. big.[1030]

10.29.63 Lat .i. slat.
Lat 'robbery', i.e. robbery.[1031]

1025 The missing letter is supplied from O'Curry's transcription. The interpretation of the lemma is uncertain. It might be derived from *taescaid* 'pours out, bales' and related to *taesc* 'spurt, flow'; see *eDIL s.vv. taescaid* and *taesc*; and cf. Mod. Ir. *taosc* 'bail, pump, drain'. The glosses suggest a meaning related to dipping or wetting a piece of bread.

1026 See Meyer 1905: 488 § 8, the poem is found in TCD MS 1337 [H.3.18], but it is not in *CIH*; and O'Cl *Tuireann .i. cruithneachd* 'wheat'.

1027 The lemma is the 1 pl. fut. rel. of *cingid* 'steps, proceeds, goes'; *eDIL s.v.* 1 *cingid*. The gloss appears to be the 1 pl. fut. rel. of *céimnigid* 'steps, proceeds, goes' although one would expect the ending to be *-imme*; *eDIL s.v. céimnigid*.

1028 The interpretation of both the gloss and lemma are uncertain. Both look as if they might be 3 sg. pres. subj. forms of *ad-cota*. Cf. 2.b.7.90 CON-OATHAR.

1029 Cf. 7.b.16.76 BUICNE. See the discussion on 7.b.15.75 BOIBRE and 7.b.17.77 BOICMELL. See *Bretha Nemed Dédenach* 29.10 (*CIH* 1122.15; *CCIH* 184–188); Digest B (56) (*CIH* 1381.18–19, 21; "The Advice to Doidin" 73; and Smith 1932: 80); and cf. O'Dav 317 (*Bretha Nemed Dédenach*; *CCIH* 117: *Buiceall .i. bis 7 ceo da buaic, in cainti no in fer lethchuinn* "*Buiceall*, i.e. one who is with a fog from his cap, the satirist, or the half-witted man.").

1030 For the *ól* as a measure of liquid capacity, see *EIF* 578–579.

1031 The interpretation of the lemma is tentative. On the basis of the variation between *latra* and *slatra* 'strong', the lemma is interpreted here as a variant of *slat* 'robbery'; cf. *latra* 'robber, thief'; *eDIL s.v. latrann*. Cf. 8.37.103 SLATRA.

10.29.64 Du*mh*a .i. io[nad].
Duma 'mound', i.e. place.[1032]

10.30.65 Bru*ar* .i. spuillec*h ar*áin.
Bruar 'crumbs', i.e. cuttings of bread.[1033]

10.30.66 B*ruar* sraife .i. iomad sraib*h*.
Bruar straife 'bits of sloe', i.e. an abundance of sloes.[1034]

10.30.67 *Air*gedluib .i. luib *air*gid.
Airgetluib 'silver-plant', i.e. silver plant.[1035]

10.30.68 Fot*h*b*h*la .i. fod*h*eid*h*b*h*le .i. diailbe .i. deroile.
Fothla 'deducting', i.e. deducts, i.e. kindliness, i.e. smallness.[1036]

10.31.69 Fíí, ⁊ híí .i. d*r*ung no d*r*eam, no gibe ní *ar* chena, na mbi iolr-*adh*.

1032 The missing letters are supplied from O'Curry's transcription. The lemma refers to a burial mound. For the lemma, cf. O'Dav 751 (no id.; CCIH 130: *Dumha .i. imat*... "*Duma*, i.e. much..."). In the entry from O'Davoren's Glossary, the lemma is interpreted as a large pile or heap; *eDIL s.v.* 1 *duma* and *imbed, imbad.*

1033 The gloss refers to small fragments of bread, i.e. crumbs. The interpretation of *spuilleach* is tentative. It seems to be derived from a verb similar to Mod. Ir. *spól* 'joint (a piece of meat), cut into pieces'. Cf. 10.30.66 BRUAR SRAIFE.

1034 Cf. 10.30.65 BRUAR. The interpretation of *sraife* and *sraibh* is tentative. It is possible that both are gen. sg. variants of *straif* 'sloe', but how to construe the meaning with *bruar* 'crumbs, bits' is difficult; *eDIL s.vv. straif* and *bruar*. Cf. *Bretha Déin Chécht* § 9 (CIH 2307.21–23); and EIF 258. As discussed by Kelly in EIF 258 and McManus 1988: 159–160, *sraif* means 'sulfur' and should be interpreted not as one of the three foreign herbs as they are given in *Bretha Déin Chécht*, but rather as the passage is interpreted in *Uraicecht Becc* (CIH 1610.9–10, AL 5: 84.9–10), as three foreign herbs and sulfur, orpiment, etc. Cf. 10.30.67 AIRGEDLUIB.

1035 The identification of this plant is unknown. It is possible that the lemma is a misinterpretation of *airgetlam* 'orpiment'; cf. *Bretha Déin Chécht* § 9 (CIH 2307.21–23); and EIF 258. As discussed by Kelly in EIF 258 and McManus 1988: 159–160, it has been suggested that the list of three foreign herbs given in *Bretha Déin Chécht* should be understood as it is given in *Uraicecht Becc* (CIH 1610.9–10, AL 5: 84.9–10), as three foreign herbs and sulfur, orpiment, etc. Cf. 10.30.66 BRUAR SRAIFE.

1036 The lemma is a variant of *fothla* 'withdrawing, deducting', the vn. of *fo-tlen*; *eDIL s.v. fothla*(*e*). The first gloss is a variant of *fo-dedla* 'subdivides, separates, deducts'; *eDIL s.v. fo-dedla.* The interpretation of *diailbe* is uncertain because the reading of the word itself is uncertain. The interpretation of it as a form of *dailbe* 'kindliness' is difficult to reconcile with the rest of the entry; *eDIL s.v. dailbe.*

Fíí ⁊ *h-íí* 'other and another', i.e. crowd or indefinite number of people, or whatever thing in addition, that which is not an abundance.[1037]

10.31.70 Cele saorf*h*lat*h*a .i. saoirc*h*ele.
Céile saorfhlatha 'client of a free lord', i.e. a free client.[1038]

10.31.71 Ma[nac*h*] riagla .i. saorman*ac*.
Manach ríagla 'a monastic client bound by rule', i.e. a free monastic client.[1039]

10.32.72 Desid*h* .i. t*a*rr*ustar*.
Desid 'it has come into effect', i.e. it has been established.[1040]

10.32.73 Fris-com*hair* .i. fior-coi*medhtur*.
Fris-comair 'it is guarded against', i.e. [*fír* 'truly' + *coimétaid* 'keeps, guards'] it is truly-guarded.[1041]

10.32.74 Ad-suit*er* .i. astuig*h*t*er*.
Ad-suiter 'it is established', i.e. it is established.[1042]

1037 Both lemmata are variants of each other, but the headword itself is uncertain. It might be an abbreviation for *aile* 'other, second'. The words *drong* and *drem(m)* refer to an indefinite number of people, but *drong* refers to a more definite number than *drem(m)*; *eDIL s.v. drong*.

1038 See *Di Astud Chor* §1 (CIH 995.15, 1348.24; AL 5: 356.6–7; and CCIH 60). As noted in CCIH 249, a passage containing the lemma is ascribed to the text *Dúil* in a commentary on the Introduction to the *Senchas Már* (CIH 1660.25). CCIH 246 and 249 suggests that *Di Astud Chor* §1 derives from *Dúil*.

1039 See *Di Astud Chor* §1 (CIH 1348.27; AL 5: 356.12–13; and CCIH 60). CCIH 246 and 249 suggests that *Di Astud Chor* §1 derives from *Dúil*.

1040 The lemma is a 3 sg. perf. of *saidid* 'sits, settles down, remains, adopts'. The gloss is a 3 sg. perf. of *do-airissedar* 'remains, endures'; *eDIL s.vv. do-airissedar* and *saidid*. See *Di Astud Chor* §1 (CIH 1348.32; AL 5: 356.21; and CCIH 60). CCIH 246 and 249 suggests that *Di Astud Chor* §1 derives from *Dúil*.

1041 See *Di Astud Chor* §1 (CIH 1348.35–36; AL 5: 356.25; and CCIH 60). The form of the lemma is rarely attested; in his edition of *Di Astud Chor*, McLeod emends MS *friscomair* to *fris-congair* 'overrules' (as two other MS witnesses have that form). The lemma is interpreted here as a sg. pres. pass. ind. of *fris-comai* 'governs, guards against, keeps'. The verb *coimedhtur* is the sg. pres. pass. ind. of *coimétaid*, a later simplex of *con-oí* 'protects, guards, keeps'. The gloss here is similar to gloss l in McLeod's edition, i.e. *fircoimetaid* 'truly-guards'. CCIH 246 and 249 suggest that *Di Astud Chor* §1 derives from *Dúil*. For the etymological gloss, see the Introduction, pp. 13–16.

1042 The gloss is a later 3 sg. pres. pass. form of *ad-suidi*; *eDIL s.v. ad-suidi*. See *Di Astud Chor* §2 (CIH 1349.1; and CCIH 60).

10.32.75 Fégad*h* .i. fec*h*ain súl.
Fégad 'looking at', i.e. inspecting by eyes.[1043]

10.32.76 Im[chisin] .i. eim*hdh*ec*h*sain *ar*a m*h*enmuin.
Imcisin 'examining', i.e. [*éim* 'timely, swift' + *déchsain* 'viewing, examining'] timely-examining by his mind.[1044]

10.33.77 Secfaid*h* .i. sec*h*mallaid*h*.
Secfaid 'he will enforce', i.e. he neglects.[1045]

10.33.78 Cor go ffi*us*, go ttreb*aire* .i. cun*nradh* go ffi*us* diub*ar*ta ag nec*h*, ⁊ treb*aire* (.i. urr*adh* aniu) re co*m*all an cun*n*at*h*a.
Cor co fis, co trebaire 'a contract with knowledge, with suretyship', i.e. a bargain with knowledge of overpayment by someone, and suretyship (i.e. a surety present) for fulfillment of the bargain.[1046]

10.34.79 Cuidig fesa ⁊ treab*aire* .i. an c*h*uid do*n* cun*nradh* in*ar* fe[as] diub*ar*t do b*eth*, ⁊ ⟨cuid⟩ treba[i]*re* .i. an cuid le ffuil an urr*adh* i n-urr*adhus* a coi*m*líon*n*ta. Gan f*hius*, gan treb*air*e a c*h*ontr*a*rda si*n*.
Cuitig fesa ⁊ trebaire 'share of knowledge and of suretyship', i.e. the share of the bargain in respect to there being overpayment, and a ⟨share⟩ of suretyship, i.e. and share the surety has for [acting as a] surety for its completion. Without knowledge, without suretyship is its opposite.[1047]

10.36.80 Nec*h* dia*m*ba cu*m*a a ebirt, ⁊ a aigde .i. duine ag*ar*ob ionan*n* an ní adeir se, ⁊ an ní b*híus* na inntin, g*ur*ob m*ar* adeir se b*hius* an ní rec*us*, no nac*h* ccelion*n* mait*h* na olc da mbi isin sed rec*us* .⁊c̄.

1043 See *Di Astud Chor* § 2 (*CIH* 1349.4; and *CCIH* 60).

1044 The missing letters are supplied from O'Curry's transcription. See *Di Astud Chor* § 2 (*CIH* 1349.4; and *CCIH* 60). The etymological gloss is not found in other extant versions of *Di Astud Chor*. For the form of the etymological gloss, see the Introduction, pp. 13–16.

1045 The relationship between the lemma and gloss is obscure. See *eDIL s.vv. 1 saigid* and *sechmi-ella, sechmo-ella*; the gloss might be a 3 sg. pres. ind. of a later simplex form of *sechmi-ella*. The lemma is not found in *Di Astud Chor* like the surrounding entries.

1046 See *Di Astud Chor* § 2 commentary [a] (*CIH* 1349.10; and *CCIH* 60). The gloss here does not repeat what is found in the commentary.

1047 The ⟨as⟩ are supplied from O'Curry's transcription. See *Di Astud Chor* § 2 commentary [h] (*CIH* 1349.25; and *CCIH* 60). The gloss here does not repeat what is found in the commentary.

Nech díamba cummae a epirt, ⁊ a aicde 'Anyone whose word will be as good as his bond', i.e. a person for whom that which he says is as good as that which is the intention, so that just as he says that the thing will be that he sells, he does not conceal [whatever] good or bad which may be in the valuable that he sells, etc.[1048]

10.37.81 Cria .i. cenn*n*.
Cria 'you may buy', i.e. buy.[1049]

10.38.82 Ria .i. rec.
Ria 'you may sell', i.e. sell.[1050]

10.38.83 Taid*h*cria .i. tait*h*cen*n*ac*h* ł aith[cennach].
Taithchria 'he may buy back', i.e. recall a purchase or redemption.[1051]

10.38.84 Iom*ar*r .i. tio*mar*gui*n*.
Immar 'he may coerce', i.e. compelling.[1052]

1048 See *Córus Bésgnai* § 3, gloss 4 (*CIH* 520.25; *AL* 3: 4.15; and *CCIH* 290). The sense of the entry is that the person is trustworthy, and the item they are selling is exactly as good or as bad as they say it is. Based on the surrounding entries, one would expect this entry to derive from *Di Astud Chor*.

1049 The lemma might be the conjunct form of the 2 sg. pres. subj. of *crenaid* 'buys, purchases'. The gloss appears to be the 2 sg. impv. of *cennaigid* 'buys, purchases'. Cf. 10.38.83 TAIDHCRIA; and *Di Astud Chor* § 8 and gloss a (*CIH* 1351.39–1352.1; and *CCIH* 60); and Digest D (15) (*CIH* 1963.33; *CCIH* 79).

1050 The lemma might be the conjunct form of the 2 sg. pres. subj. of *renaid* 'sells, barters'. The gloss appears to be the 2 sg. impv. of *recaid* 'sells, barters'. Cf. 10.38.83 TAIDHCRIA; and *Di Astud Chor* § 8 and gloss a (*CIH* 1351.39–1352.1; and *CCIH* 60); and Digest D (15) (*CIH* 1963.33; *CCIH* 79).

1051 The lemma is the 3 sg. pres. subj. prototonic form of *do-aithchren* 'buys back, redeems'. It is difficult to tell whether the correction of *taithcennach* to *aithcennach* is an actual correction or a second gloss. See O'Dav 1520 (no id.; *CCIH* 153, n. 217: *Tathcria .i. in cunnrad doberar tarais, ut est [ni tagra F] ní tathcria ma ro ria .i. ni tuca amuich é ma ro recais amach* "*Tathcria*, i.e. the bargain which is given beyond it, ut est 'thou shouldest not sue, though shouldest not buy back (?) if thou sell', i.e. do not bring it in if thou has sold it out."), it is quite likely that at least part of the entry is from *Di Astud Chor*; and *Di Astud Chor* § 8 and gloss a (*CIH* 1351.39–1352.1; and *CCIH* 60).

1052 The lemma appears to be the 3 sg. pres. subj. prototonic form of *imm-oirg* 'constrains, coerces'; *eDIL s.v. 2 imm-oirg*. The gloss is the vn. of *do-immoirg* 'compels'; *eDIL s.v. tomorcon*. For the gloss, cf. the first part of O'Dav 1591 (no id.; *CCIH* 155: *Toirec .i. timarguin*... Stokes does not provide a translation); and *Di Astud Chor* § 9 and gloss b (*CIH* 1352.4–5; and *CCIH* 60).

10.38.85 Acht .i. cu*nn*taba*r*t.
Acht 'exception', i.e. doubt.[1053]

10.38.86 Cías*ar* .i. céimn*igh*ter.
Cíasair 'it may be proceeded with', i.e. it is proceeded with.[1054]

10.38.87 Tat*h*luig*h*ter .i tait*h*mig*h*ter.
Tathluither 'is released', i.e. is dissolved.[1055]

10.39.88 Ad-road .i. do-roc*hair*.
Ad-roth 'has fallen', i.e. has fallen.[1056]

10.39.89 Cu*m*sgug*udh* .i. co*m*sgaoil*edh*.
Cumscugud 'changing', i.e. dissolving.[1057]

10.39.90 Fom*hus* .i. foi*m*esum*h*nu*gh*ad*h*.
Fomus 'estimating', i.e. estimating.[1058]

10.39.91 Tuid*h*mid*h*e .i. astuig*h*t*h*e.
Tuidmide 'should be bound', i.e. should be bound.[1059]

1053 See O'Dav 166 (no id.; CCIH 113: *Acht .i. conntabairt, ut est is teol, is taighe cin acht* "Acht, i.e. doubt, ut est 'it is purloining, it is theft without doubt'."); and for the gloss, cf. *Di Astud Chor* § 9 and gloss b (CIH 1352.5; and CCIH 60). Cf. 14.b.2.2 ACHT.

1054 For the gloss, cf. the first part of O'Dav 392 (*Bretha Nemed Dédenach*; CCIH 119: *Ceird .i. ceimniugud no cing...* "*Ceird*, i.e. a stepping or walking..."). The verb *céimnigid* 'steps, proceeds, goes' is a frequent gloss on *cingid* 'steps, goes, proceeds'; *eDIL s.v. céimnigid*. See *Di Astud Chor* § 12 and gloss b (CIH 1352.21–22; and CCIH 60).

1055 For the lemma and gloss, see *eDIL s.vv. tathluither* and *taithmigid*, respectively. See *Di Astud Chor* § 13 and gloss a (CIH 1352.26–27; and CCIH 60).

1056 The interpretation of the lemma here follows that in *Di Astud Chor* § 15, e.g. a 3 sg. perf. subj. of *ad-tuit* 'falls'; see McLeod's discussion of the form (209). The gloss is a 3 sg. perf. of *do-tuit* 'falls'. See *Di Astud Chor* § 15 and gloss b (CIH 1353.7; and CCIH 60).

1057 See *Di Astud Chor* § 18 and gloss a (CIH 1353.21–23; and CCIH 60).

1058 The gloss might be a late vn. derived from *fo-midethar* 'judges, makes an estimate'. The usual vn. of *fo-midethar* is *fomus*; *eDIL s.v. fo-midethar*. See *Di Astud Chor* § 18 cf. gloss e (CIH 1353.35; and CCIH 60).

1059 The lemma is interpreted here as the verbal of necessity of *do-dímen* 'binds, makes fast, fixes'. The gloss is the verbal of necessity of *fastaigid*; *eDIL s.v. astaigthi*. See *Di Astud Chor* § 20 and gloss c (CIH 1354.7 and 991.27; and CCIH 60) where the syntax of the larger textual contexts suggest that both forms are verbals of necessity rather than past participles. See O'Dav 1522 (*Di Astud Chor*; CCIH 153: *Tuidmithe .i. fastaighthi, ut est*

10.39.92 Ion*n*longad .i. io*m*fuilng[et].
In-longad 'they impose', i.e. they sustain.[1060]

10.40.93 Tiondain, no tiodain .i. tiod*h*naic.
Tindin, nó tidin 'he may bestow, or he may bestow', i.e. he bestows.[1061]

10.40.94 Ni *air*b*h*e .i. ni raib*h*e.
Ní aurba 'is not an exception', i.e. there was not.[1062]

10.40.95 Ad-roir .i. ad*h*a ro oirg.
Ad-roir 'he may attack', i.e. [< *ada* 'suitable, fitting' + *oirgid* 'kills, punishes'] suitable that he attacked.[1063]

10.40.96 Meisi .[i.] cui*m*geach.
Meisi 'competent', i.e. capable.[1064]

10.41.97 Tat*h* .i. tait*h*mech.
Táth 'joining', i.e. dissolving.[1065]

---

tuidhmithe cach cor doninnlaic bel 7 lam 7 tenge "*Tuidmithe*, i.e. fastened, ut est 'binding is every contract to which mouth and hand [and tongue] contribute'.").

1060 Although the verb *in-loing* 'joins, unites, imposes' is well-attested, it is possible that the lemma is a misreading of *ní dlongat* 'they do not tear apart'. See *Di Astud Chor* § 23 and gloss d (*CIH* 1354.31–32; and *CCIH* 60).

1061 The lemmata are understood as 3 sg. prototonic pres. subj. forms of *do-indnaig* 'gives, bestows, grants'; *eDIL s.v. do-indnaig*. See *Di Astud Chor* § 24 and gloss c (*CIH* 1355.5; and *CCIH* 60). The gloss is the 3 sg. pres. ind. of *tidnaicid* a later simplex from *do-indnaig*. I should like to thank one of the anonymous readers for comments on this entry.

1062 See *Di Astud Chor* § 27 and gloss f (*CIH* 1356.4; and *CCIH* 60).

1063 The lemma is the 3 sg. pres. subj. of *ad-reith* 'attains, attacks, arrests'; *eDIL s.v. ad-reith*. That being said, it is quite possible that the lemma is a mis-segmentation of a MS *arnachat roir*; see *Di Astud Chor* § 28 (*CIH* 1356.7; and *CCIH* 60). The form *roir* would be for *-roírea*, the 3 sg. pres. subj. of *feraid* 'suffices, laments', which is how the form is interpreted by McLeod; see *eDIL s.v. feraid*. For the etymological gloss, see the Introduction, pp. 13–16.

1064 The word *cuimgech* 'able, capable' is a common gloss on *meisi* 'competent, legally qualified'; *eDIL s.v. meise, meisi*. See SC Y.951 *Meisi .i. cuimgech*; and the first part of O'Dav 1257 (*Cáin Ṡóerraith*; *CCIH* 145: *Meisi .i. cuimgech*… "*Meisi*, i.e. competent…"); cf. *Cáin Ṡóerraith* (*CIH* 1776.17 and 21; *CCIH* 145). It is possible that *meisi* is a misinterpretation of a MS *tatmeisi*; cf. *eDIL s.v. do-aithbig* 'dissolves, annuls'; and see *Di Astud Chor* § 28 and gloss d (*CIH* 1356.9–10; *CCIH* 60).

1065 See *Di Astud Chor* § 28 and gloss d (*CIH* 1356.9–10; *CCIH* 60). Cf. 3.b.18.62 TATH. The entry makes sense when understood within the context of the source text (reproduced from McLeod's edition). Tract: *Ní taithbis-siu táth condartho íar ngréne góligiu* 'You

10.41.98 *Ar-gair* .i. urg*air*id*h* .i. cros*adh*.
Ar-gair 'hinders', i.e. hinders, i.e. forbidding.[1066]

10.41.99 Bailiud*h* .i. élód*h* a ba, as mait*h*.
Bailiud 'derangement', i.e. escape of its profit, from its good.[1067]

10.41.100 Ad-dai*mh*ed .i. aididn*igh*id.
Ad-daimet 'they acknowledge', i.e. acknowledges.[1068]

10.41.101 Bret*h* .i. b*h*ret*h*ema[n].
Breth 'judgement', i.e. of a judge.[1069]

10.42.102 Com*ha* .i. na b*h*féc*h*em*h*an.
Comad 'preserving', i.e. of the claimants.[1070]

10.42.103 Coiccert .i. na h-*air*ech*t*a.
Coicert 'decision', i.e. of the court.[1071]

10.42.104 Blaid*h*re .i. bal re ré.
Blaidre 'unintentionally defrauding', i.e. prospering before time.[1072]

---

should not dissolve the joining of a bargain after sunset'; gloss d: *.i. nocha cuimgeach é taithmech un cunnartha iar luighe gúa don grein* 'i.e. he is not capable of the dissolution of the bargain after the false reclining of the sun'. In Dubhaltach's Glossary, the gloss should be glossing the verb *tiathbis*, *vel sim.*, rather than *táth*.

1066 The first gloss is a later simplex of the lemma; *eDIL s.v. ar-gair*. See *Di Astud Chor* § 34 and gloss d (*CIH* 1356.37–38; *CCIH* 60).

1067 See *Di Astud Chor* § 34 and gloss d (*CIH* 351.22–23 and 1356.38; *CCIH* 60).

1068 It is unusual that the verbal numbers in the entry do not match. See *Di Astud Chor* § 35 (*CIH* 1357.1; *CCIH* 60).

1069 The missing letter is supplied from O'Curry's transcription. See *Di Astud Chor* §§ 43 and 44, and 44 gloss b (*CIH* 786.25 and 1196.36; *CCIH* 50). The lenition of the gloss is unusual. The gloss could be either gen. sg. or gen. pl.; both forms are identical.

1070 See *Di Astud Chor* § 43 (*CIH* 1196.37; *CCIH* 50). The gloss is not found in other versions of the text.

1071 See *Di Astud Chor* § 43 (*CIH* 1196.37; *CCIH* 50). The gloss is not found in other versions of the text.

1072 See O'Dav 299 (no id.; *CCIH* 117: *Blaidhre .i. in diubairt anfesa, ut est dofuaslaici cach mblaidhre .i. uatuaslaici gach ní na bi bal ri re do gallraib buna no in diubairt anfesa* "*Blaidre*, i.e. the fraud of ignorance, ut est 'every *blaidre* dissolves', i.e. every thing releases, which is not *bal* (?) for a time (*ré*) from radical diseases: or the fraud of ignorance."), although it is possible that the entry might derive from a version of *Di Astud*

10.42.105 Neg*har* .i. nig*h*ter.
Negar 'is absolved', i.e. is absolved.[1073]

10.42.106 Suiter, no soat*har* .i. iompóit*her*.
Soiter, nó saothar 'is overthrown, or is overthrown', i.e. is revoked.[1074]

10.42.107 Imced[adh .i.] ém*h*d*h*é*ch*ad*h*.
Imcedad 'examining', i.e. [< *éim* 'timely, swift' + *do-éccai* 'looks at, sees'] timely-he looks.[1075]

10.43.108 Saoit*he* .i. b*r*eg*airacht* (as saot*h* le nec*h*) nó diub*airth*.
Suíthe 'knowledge', i.e. deceit (out of his wealth by someone) or defrauding.[1076]

10.43.109 Con-derb*har*a .i. coi*m*d*h*iub*r*a.
Con derbara 'that he may defraud', i.e. [< *cáem* 'prompt, ready' + *do-opir* 'deprives, defrauds'] promptly he may defraud.[1077]

10.43.110 Amne .i. am*h*l*adh* so.
Amne 'thus', i.e. thus.[1078]

Chor; and cf. *Di Astud Chor* § 43 (CIH 1197.3; CCIH 50). It is possible that the gloss is meant to be etymological.

1073 The gloss appears to be derived from a later form of *nigid* 'washes, absolves'.

1074 Both of the lemmata are interpreted a 3 sg. pres. pass. forms of *soïd* 'turns around, changes, overthrows'; *eDIL s.v. soïd.* The gloss is a 3 sg. pres. pass. of *impóid*, a later simplex of *imm-sói* 'turns around, changes, revokes, annuls'; *eDIL s.v. imm-sói.* Based on the surrounding entries, one would expect this entry to derive from *Di Astud Chor.*

1075 The missing letters are supplied from O'Curry's transcription. This entry is difficult for a number of reasons, not least of which is the uncertain reading of the lemma. The lemma might be for *imchachad* 'looking' or a form of *imm-acci* 'inspects, looks at'. The second half of the gloss appears to be the 3 sg. pres. ind. prototonic form of *do-éccai.* It could be that the lemma is similarly formed. It is common for the preverb *im*(*m*)- to be glossed by *éim* 'swift, timely'; Binchy 1943: 212; and Taylor-Griffiths 2020: 1: 89. Cf. *Di Astud Chor* § 49 and Digest D (15) (CIH 1963.35; and CCIH 79).

1076 The sense of the entry is that someone has knowledge of the deceitful nature of the contract. Based on the surrounding entries, one would expect this entry to derive from *Di Astud Chor.*

1077 The entry is difficult because the interpretation of the lemma and gloss is unclear. It looks as if Dubhaltach took the entry from *Di Astud Chor* § 45 (CIH 1197.10), *arnacon derbara.* The gloss might have an incorrect suspension mark; cf. *Di Astud Chor* § 45, gloss j (CIH 1197.11), *coindiubra* 'houndishly-deprived'.

1078 See *eDIL s.v. amein*; and *Di Astud Chor* § 50 (CIH 755.32).

10.44.111 Sen*arus*g .i. sein*chin*n*edh* óg*h*.
Senárusc 'old stipulation', i.e. a full old offence.[1079]

10.44.112 Fo-suid*h* .i. astaid*h* go t*re* f*hius* mait*h*.
Fo-said 'he decides', i.e. he binds by means of good knowledge.[1080]

10.44.113 Do-rait*hm*a*cht* .i. ro s*re*t*h*n*ig*h*edh*, no ro tait*hm*i*g*h*edh* .i. ro sgaoi[le-dh].
Do-raithbecht 'it has been released', i.e. it has been dispersed, or it has been released, i.e. it has been released.[1081]

10.45.114 Roc*h*ad .i. ro ionsaig*h*id*h*.
Rochad 'they attain', i.e. they reached.[1082]

10.45.115 Inc*h*ren*ar* .i. c*re*ac*ar* a h-in*n*e.
Increnar 'is bought', i.e. its real value is bought.[1083]

10.45.116 Sern*ar* .i. s*re*t*h*n*agh*t*ar*.
Sernar 'is arranged', i.e. is arranged.[1084]

1079 The noun *senárosc* can also mean 'proverb'; cf, O'Cl *Seanarasg .i. seanfhocal* 'a proverb'; and *eDIL s.v. senárosc*. Based on the surrounding entries, one would expect this entry to derive from *Di Astud Chor*.

1080 The interpretation of the lemma is tentative. It might be the 3 sg. pres. ind. of *saidid* 'sits, settles, decides' with prosthetic ⟨f⟩. The context of the entry is unknown, so it is possible that ⟨fo⟩ should be interpreted in a relative context. The overall sense is binding a contract to the extent that one has reliable knowledge of the terms and conditions. Based on the surrounding entries, one would expect this entry to derive from *Di Astud Chor*.

1081 The missing letters are supplied from O'Curry's transcription. The lemma is the sg. pret./perf. pass. of *do-aithbig* 'dissolves, opens, loosens'. The glosses are also sg. pret./perf. passives; see *eDIL s.vv. sreth(n)aigid*, *taithmigid*, and *scaíled*, respectively. All of the verbs have a similar range of meanings including a notion of dissolving, dispersing, and/or releasing. See *Di Astud Chor* § 50 (CIH 987.22 and 1197.29; CCIH 43 and 50). The glosses are not found in other versions of the text.

1082 The lemma might be a 3 pl. pres. ind. of *ro-saig* 'reaches, attains'; *eDIL s.v. ro-saig*. See *Di Astud Chor* § 52 and gloss n (and discussion on p. 240) (CIH 1198.11; and CCIH 50).

1083 See *Di Astud Chor* § 52 and gloss j (CIH 1198.7–8; and CCIH 50).

1084 See Digest B (11) (CIH 1303.15–16; CCIH 55); cf. *Bretha Nemed Dédenach* 40.4 (CIH 1129.34; CCIH 184–188; Corthals 2010: 75); and see part of O'Dav 1444 (*Bretha Nemed Dédenach*; CCIH 151: *Sernair .i. … .i. srethnaighther…* "*Sernair*, i.e. is recited…, i.e. let it be distributed…"). The verb *sreth(n)aigid* frequently glosses *sernaid*; *eDIL s.v. sreth(n)aigid*. Cf. 8.34.90 SERNAR. Considering the surrounding entries, one would expect to find the lemma in a version of *Di Astud Chor*, but cf. *Di Astud Chor* § 52, gloss o (CIH 1198.13).

10.45.117 M*a*c beoat[h]*ar* .i. m*a*c i ttesg*air*[e].
Mac béoathar 'son of a living father', i.e. a son under proclamation.[1085]

10.45.118 Forng*aire* .i. f*orcon*gra.
Forngaire 'direction', i.e. command.[1086]

10.45.119 Dlig*hedh* aond*acht*[a, no] ioldac*h*ta .i. bi*us ete*r cen*n* is mem*r*u, do b*righ* g*ur*ob aon an cen*n* i l*eth* ris na mem*r*uib*h*, ⁊ g*ur*ob iol[ardha an] mem*air* i l*eth* ris [an cceann].
Dliged oendachta, nó ildachta 'entitlement of unity or plurality', i.e. which is between a head and [the] members, because the head was singular in regard to the members, and the members were multiple in regard to the head.[1087]

10.47.120 [Na .iiii. mna] dligt*hac*[h]a .i. c*é*tm*uin*ter go m*a*ca ⁊ c*é*tm*uin*ter gao*n* m*a*ca, [⁊] adaltr*ach* go m*a*ca, ⁊ be cuitgernsa [⁊ in mac gor].
Na ceithri mná dligthacha 'the four lawful women', i.e. a spouse with sons, and a spouse without sons, and a concubine with sons, and a woman of condominium with the dutiful son.[1088]

10.48.121 [...].i. [.]saidcer cra[...][1089]

11.a.1.1 Fren .i. frem*h*.
Fren 'root', i.e. root.[1090]

1085 Most contracts made with the son whose father is still alive are not considered valid; *GEIL* 80–81. See *Di Astud Chor* § 54 and gloss n (*CIH* 1198.19; and *CCIH* 50).

1086 See *Di Astud Chor* § 54, gloss o (*CIH* 988.24; and *CCIH* 43); and O'Cl *Forngaire .i. furáileamh* 'a command'. Cf. 10.5.5 FORNGAIRE.

1087 The missing letters are supplied from O'Curry's transcription. See *Di Astud Chor* § 1, commentary n (*CIH* 1358.32–33; and *CCIH* 60); and *Findśruth Fíthail*, (*CIH* 2131.24–25; and *CCIH* 88). I should like to thank one of the anonymous readers for detailed comments on this entry.

1088 O'Curry does not print the gloss. The reading is tentative. See *Di Astud Chor* § 1, commentary k (*CIH* 1358.17–38; and *CCIH* 60); and see the discussion in Power 1936: 84–86. It should be noted that *mac* can refer to a son or to any child regardless of gender. The ⁊ 'and' in the final clause is interpreted as 'with' because it makes better sense with the preceding conditions. Fo this use of *ocus*, see *eDIL s.v. ocus* d (2).

1089 O'Curry does not print the gloss, and the reading is tentative. The reading of the last line is uncertain because the bottom of the page is missing.

1090 The lemma and gloss are variants of each other.

11.a.1.2 [Deoraidh aigenta .i. an deoraigh…]
Deoraid aicenta 'natural pilgrim' i.e. the pilgrim….[1091]

11.a.2.3 [Mainch… .i. ma … don] [t]aob*h* am*ac*[h] [do ni neach].
Mainch…. i.e. …. from outside which someone does.[1092]

11.a.3.4 Annoit [.i. eagluis duthchuis….. .i. eagluis an pharráisde i gcomhuigh-eann neach, no as neasa do neach ar fineachas .r.]
Andóit 'mother-church', i.e. hereditary church […]i.e. the parish church in […] someone, or which is closest to someone's hereditary land …[1093]

11.a.4.5 [Eachtrannus .i. neach téid amach inn ionad eachtrann.]
Echtrannus 'foreigner', i.e. anyone who goes out in a foreign place.[1094]

11.a.5.6 Escom*h*an, iongglan .i. excomunicatus.
Escoman, inglan 'polluted, impure', i.e. *excommunicatus* 'excommunicate'.[1095]

11.a.5.7 Ara-c*h*eala .i. *air*c[heallus no … eas no goidea]s.
Ara-chela 'who may steal', i.e. who steals or […] or who takes away.[1096]

11.a.6.8 Taoidid*h* .i. taoit*h*nig*h*id*h*.
Táidid 'steals', i.e. steals.[1097]

1091 The entry is supplied from O'Curry's transcription. The entry has the later m. nom. sg. form of *deorad* 'outsider, exile, stranger, pilgrim'; *eDIL s.v. deorad.* The interpretation of the entry is tentative.

1092 The entry is supplied from O'Curry's transcription. The interpretation of the entry is tentative. Based on the surrounding entries, it is likely that the lemma is a form of *mainche* 'monastic family or community; service rendered to a monastic community or its head'.

1093 The entry is supplied from O'Curry's transcription. The interpretation of the entry is tentative; I do not know how to expand the final letter of the gloss. See O'Cl *Annóid .i. eaglas* 'church'.

1094 The entry is supplied from O'Curry's transcription. The lemma is not in *eDIL*.

1095 See O'Dav 769 (*Bretha Nemed Dédenach*; CCIH 130: *Escoman .i. inglan, ut est imachomracht co mbiadh n-escomna* "*Escoman*, i.e. impure, ut est 'he asked (?) that there should be impurity'."); and cf. *Bretha Nemed Dédenach* (CIH 1112.34; and CCIH 130).

1096 The missing letters are supplied from O'Curry's transcription. The context of the entry is unknown.

1097 The gloss appears to be a later verb derived from the lemma.

11.a.6.9 Eagl*us* c*h*uir .i. at*hair* .i. egl*us* cuires cuir *ar tus ar* an man*ac*[h] andoi[d] [um leit*h*]t*r*iun an c*het*m*h*anaig*h*.
Eclas chuir 'a church of contract', i.e. a father, i.e. a church which places the initial contract on the monastic tenant regarding the 1/6 of the first monastic tenant.[1098]

11.a.7.10 Egl*us* coi*m*d*h*idin .i. egl*us* ga mbiter na comaididin re ré desi an t-[ath]*air* [⁊ an mac] l*eth*t*r*i[a]n ma man*ac* m*ac* manaig*h*.
Eclas comdidan 'church of acknowledgment', i.e. a church which has the acknowledgment for the lifetime of two people, the father and the son 1/6 if the monastic tenant is the son of a monastic tenant.[1099]

11.a.8.11 Eagl*us* con-ran*na* diobad*h*. Egl*us* com*h*roin*nius* diob*adh* an m*h*anaig*h* [re] ré t*r*ir .i. at*air*, m*ac* ⁊ ua.
Eclas con-ranna díbad 'a church which shares an inheritance'. *Eclas comroinnas díbad an mhanaig re ré trír* 'a church which shares the monastic tenant's inheritance for the lifetime of three people', i.e. a father, son, and grandson.[1100]

11.a.9.12 Ro-negam .i. riocfam.
Ro-n-ecam 'to which we reach', i.e. we shall reach.[1101]

1098 The missing letters are supplied from O'Curry's transcription. See the discussion of this entry in Etchingham 1999: 449. Cf. 11.a.7.10 EGLUS COIMDHIDIN and 11.a.8.11 EAGLUS CON-RANNA DIOBADH. EGLUS COMHROINNIUS DIOBADH AN MHANAIGH RE RÉ TRIR. The interpretation of *andoid* is tentative; see *eDIL s.v. 1 andóit*. The entry concerns the church's share in the inheritance of its dependents. See *Bretha Nemed Toísech* (*CIH* 2212.16–17; Breatnach 1989: § 11 and note on p. 34).

1099 The missing letters are supplied from O'Curry's transcription. According to Etchingham 1999: 282 and 449 (which reference this entry), this entry, 11.a.6.9 EAGLUS CHUIR, and 11.a.8.11 EAGLUS CON-RANNA DIOBADH. EGLUS COMHROINNIUS DIOBADH AN MHANAIGH RE RÉ TRIR, refer to the church's share in the inheritance of its dependents. See *Bretha Nemed Toísech* (*CIH* 2212.16–17; Breatnach 1989: § 11 and note on p. 34).

1100 According to Etchingham 1999: 282 and 449 (which reference this entry; it is translated on 449), this entry, 11.a.6.9 EAGLUS CHUIR, and 11.a.7.10 EGLUS COIMDHIDIN, refer to the church's share in the inheritance of its dependents. See *Bretha Nemed Toísech* (*CIH* 2212.16–17; Breatnach 1989: § 11 and note on p. 34).

1101 See O'Dav 1394 (no id.; *CCIH* 149: *Ronecam .i. gusa roichem, ut est comsoer cach recht roneccam .i. is comsoer o gach richt duine gusa ricfam siosana* "*Ro-n-ecam*, i.e. to which we reach, ut est 'equally noble is every kind of person whom we reach', i.e. it is equally noble of every kind of person to whom we shall come down here.").

11.a.9.13 Dlom*h*aim .i. raid*h*im.
Dlomaim 'I declare', i.e. I say.[1102]

11.a.9.14 Sáorm*h*anac[h] .i. an dec*h*mad*h* [m]ac, no an *cétnae* tuiste.
Sáermanach 'free monastic client', i.e. the tenth son, or the first offspring.[1103]

11.a.10.15 Daorm*h*ana*ch* .i. man*ach* crui, gola ⟨.i. prisun⟩, gob*h*la ⟨.i. na croiche⟩, gill do bas, ⁊ manac*h* nuna.
Dáermanach 'base monastic client', i.e. a monastic client [saved from] slaying, and a pit ⟨i.e. prison⟩, and a gibbet ⟨i.e. of the gallows⟩, saved from death, and a monastic client [saved from] famine.[1104]

11.a.11.16 [A]*n*ma*n*na breit*he* .[i.] bret*h*, ri*ar*, coigert, *et*ercert, ⁊ comha *ut dicitur* tre chom*ha* .i. t*r*esi*n* mbreit*h* d*ar*ab ain*m* comha.
Anmanna breithe 'names of judgements', i.e. *breth, ríar, coicert, etercert,* and *coma ut dicitur* 'as it is said' by judgement, i.e. by the judgement which is called *coma.*[1105]

11.a.12.17 [F]echt feile .i. ced oid*h*che aoid*h*ig*h*echt duine (go tig*h* duine oile) ma ri, oll*am*, fl*aith*, no gibe cinel duine e.
Fecht féile 'visit of hospitality', i.e. a person's one night's hospitality (to the house of another person) if the person is a king, chief poet, lord, or whatever type of person.[1106]

1102 The context of the entry is unknown.

1103 For a discussion of free monastic tenants, see *GEIL* 33 and 39. This entry is mentioned in Etchingham 1999: 446. See *Córus Fine* (*CIH* 746.15).

1104 See *Córus Bésgnai* §9 and gloss 3 (*CIH* 522.1 and 6–7; *AL* 3: 10.24); *Córus Fine* (*CIH* 746.15–16); cf. *Fuidir-tract* §7 and gloss 6 (*CIH* 428.10–11 and 19; *AL* 5: 360.15); O'Dav 1052 (*Fuidir-tract*; CCIH 139: *Gola .i. cuithe, ut est fuidir crui ⁊ gola .i. o cuithi donesairg, ⁊ dom doigh is e sin in prison* "*Gola*, i.e. a pit, ut est 'a tenant of enclosure and gaol', i.e. from a pit he rescues him, and it seems to me it is the prison."). See the discussion in Etchingham 1999: 420 (which mentions this entry).

1105 The missing ⟨a⟩ is supplied from O'Curry's transcription. The entry lists five words which mean 'judgement'.

1106 The missing letter is supplied from O'Curry's transcription. O'Don. Suppl. *s.v. feacht féile* cites Dubhaltach's Glossary and TCD MS 1336 [H.3.17] col. 127, *Di Choimét Dligthech* (*CIH* 1730.37–1731.20), as his sources. Cf. 11.a.12.18 GNAI[TH]LES and 11.a.13.19 FOLACH N-OTHRASA.

11.a.12.18 Gnai[th]les .i. gac*h* aoidig*h*ec*h*t on c*het*-adaig*h* amac*h*.
Gnáthles 'customary need', i.e. each evening's hospitality from the first night onwards.[1107]

11.a.13.19 Folac*h* n-ot*hr*asa .i. iomf*h*ulaing no frit[h]eol*adh* duine b*hius* i n-ot*h*ras.
Folach n-othrusa 'sick-maintenance', i.e. supporting or serving a person who is on sick-maintenance.[1108]

11.a.14.20 [Fer] máma mog*h* .i. an fer gab*us* do laim*h* ma*m* ⁊ gnio*m* an d*h*uine bi*us* loite do dena*m ar* a s*h*on fe*dh* a luide ot*hrus*.
Fer máma mod 'a substitute', i.e. the man who sets about the service and work of the person who is injured to do on his behalf during the time that the injured person is on sick-maintenance.[1109]

11.a.15.21 [Fer o]guib*h* toguib*h* .i. fer a t*h*ogbala na s*h*uide ⁊ na leab*adh*, ⁊ in a gluas*acht ar* cena f*hedh* a ot*hrus*a.
Fer ócaib tócaib 'a nurse-tender', i.e. a person lifting him into a seat and into a bed, and moving him on his behalf during the time [the injured person is] on sick-maintenance.[1110]

1107 The missing letters are supplied from O'Curry's transcription. This is one of the few entries where *eDIL s.v. gnáth* cites O'Donovan's Supplement as its source; O'Don. Suppl. *s.v. gnáithleas* cites Dubhaltach's Glossary as his source. Cf. 11.a.12.17 [F]ECHT FEILE and 11.a.13.19 FOLACH N-OTHRASA

1108 Cf. 11.a.12.18 GNAI[TH]LES and 11.a.12.17 [F]ECHT FEILE.

1109 The missing word is supplied from O'Curry's transcription. See the commentary on *Slicht Othrusa* (*CIH* 1213.17 and 1214.23; *AL* 3: 472.6 and 474.17; *CCIH* 51, 180–182, and 303). Some of the same material is also found in commentaries on *Bretha Éitgid* (*CIH* 1634.36 and 1635.34; *CCIH* 71) and *Cethairšlicht Athgabálae* (*CIH* 369.17; *AL* 1: 130.6; *CCIH* 287). The entry describes the substitute who is found to perform the regular work of the injured man during his period of recovery. For the elements of the lemma, see *eDIL s.vv. 1 mám* 'obligation, service, duty, function' and *mod* 'manner, function, work, service'. Binchy 1938: 115, n. 4, suggests that both words are gen. pl., giving a literal meaning of "man of duties of (= and) works" (see also the general discussion of this person's role on 115–117).

1110 The missing letters are supplied from O'Curry's transcription. See the commentary on *Slicht Othrusa* (*CIH* 1214.23, 27, and 1213.18; *AL* 3: 472.7, 474.18 and 24; *CCIH* 51, 180–182, and 303). Some of the same material is also found in commentaries on *Bretha Éitgid* (*CIH* 1634.37 and 1635.34; *CCIH* 71) and *Cethairšlicht Athgabálae* (*CIH* 369.17; *AL* 1: 130.7; *CCIH* 287). The entry concerns providing the injured person with someone to help them sit up, lay down, and generally assist them moving around. The phrase *fer ócaib tócaib* is composed of **ocaib* and *do-fócaib*, each meaning generally 'raises, lifts up'

11.a.16.22 [Sl]iocht a roisg .i. eol*us* bra*th* b*hius* ag suil an f*hagh*l*aidh*e *ar* ní *air*ide do lot no do goid.
Slicht a ruisc 'mark of his eye', i.e. knowledge that a thief is reconnoitering something to damage or to steal.[1111]

11.a.16.23 Dergabad .i. urfog*r*a de[th]nes*a*c[h] gan maill, ⁊ banabad*h*, ní ass maille inás.
Dergapaid 'harboring a person after they have committed a crime, lit. 'red harboring'', i.e. proclaiming hastily without delay, and *bánapaid* 'harboring a person before they have committed a crime, lit. 'white harboring'', it is not as urgent.[1112]

11.a.17.24 Lán n-aoinf*h*ir .i. láinf*h*iac*h* b*hí*us *ar* aon duin*e* am*h*ai*n*.
Lán n-óenḟir 'full [fine] of one man', i.e. a full fine will be [levied] on one person alone.[1113]

11.a.18.25 Rio*th* go moirseisior, no go cuig*er* .⁊c. .i. iomlaine na ffiac*h*, no d*h*i-oluid*hacht* an milltenuis do-[g]ni an cuidea*cht*[a] do buain (do buain) do g*a*c aon dib*h* go moirses*e*r, go cuig*e*r, no gibe nuim*e*r adeir dlig*edh* .⁊c.

(*tócaib* is interpreted as the deuterotonic 3 sg. pres. ind. of *do-fócaib*). The phrase is used in the legal texts to 'refer to the man employed to lift the patient and lay him down'; *eDIL s.v. ocaib, (? ócaib)*; and *AL* 3: 472, n. 1. Binchy 1938: 119, n. 2 (general discussion on 119–120 and 126) suggests that the phrase possibly has the literal meaning "a man who moves [the patient] hither and thither," comparing it to the phrase *áin, táin* 'drive in, drive out' (also *aig, taig*) used generally of moving something hither and thither. Both interpretations cover the semantic range of **ocaib* and *do-fócaib* and encompass the activities of a nurse assisting a patient in daily activities.

1111 The missing letters are supplied from O'Curry's transcription. The passage refers to a thief scoping out property to damage or steal it. The sense of the phrase 'at the eye of the thief' is that the thief is looking at something, in this case with dishonorable intent. For the lemma and part of the gloss, see *CIH* 1397.41 (citations concerning guilt by association and liability for the crimes of others; *CCIH* 63) where the liability in that passage is on the part of the person who is aware that the thief is looking for something to damage or steal. I should like to thank one of the anonymous readers and Paul Russell for comments on this entry.

1112 The missing letters are supplied from O'Curry's transcription. See *CIH* 1398.21 and 1406.12–13 (citations concerning guilt by association and liability for the crimes of others; *CCIH* 63–64). The entry refers to harboring criminals after or before they have committed a crime. Cf. *Córus Bésgnai* §66 (*CIH* 1817.3). Cf. 12.b.13.43 BANAPAD and 12.b.13.44 DERGAPAD.

1113 See *Bretha Éitgid* (*CIH* 1156. 37, 1399. 17 and 20; *AL* 3: 408.20; and *CCIH* 50).

Rith co mórṡeiser, nó co cóicer .⁊c. 'liabilities of fines up to seven people, or up to five people, etc.', i.e. the totality of the penalties, or payment of the damage which the company does for injury for each one of them up to seven people, up to five people, or whatever may be the number of people the law says, etc.[1114]

11.a.20.26 Lán an c*h*iontaig*h* .i. lainf*h*iac*h* dleg*ar* don ciont*a*c[h].
Lán in chintaig 'the guilty person's full [fine]', i.e. the full fine is owed by the guilty person.[1115]

11.a.20.27 Faoindleg*hach* .i. fer n*a*c ttig fa dlig*edh* cor*us*a fine.
Foíndledach 'vagrant', i.e. a person who does not observe the law of the ordering of the kindred.[1116]

11.a.21.28 Urfog*rach* .i. fer b*hius* re dena*m* uilc go ffog*rann* an t-inbleog*h*an as neasa uaid e .i. an lu*cht* gaoil as goire d*hó*.
Urfocrach 'proclaimed person', i.e. a person who previously did an evil deed so that the kinsman who is closest to him proclaims him, i.e. the kinsman who is most loyal to him.[1117]

11.a.22.29 Fuinm*h*aell, no fuinb*h*eall .i. foinbleogn*as*, teglom*as*, no tionoiles.
Fuinmbell, nó fuinbell 'who humored', i.e. who coaxes, who collects, or who gathers.[1118]

11.a.22.30 Deor*adh* f*r*eacair .i. deor[ad] do-[g]nit*er* do urr*adh* ma*r* so .i. fer si*n* d*ho*-[g]ní minicniug*ad* cionta ⁊ ní f*het*uid a f*h*ine a cionta d'ioc do

1114 The missing ⟨a⟩ is supplied from O'Curry's transcription. See *eDIL s.v. mórfeiser*. The phrase *do buain* has been repeated twice; this is likely a mistake. See *Bretha Éitgid* (*CIH* 1156.39, 1399.22–35; *AL* 3: 408.28; and *CCIH* 50). The larger context of the entry concerns the liability due from each member of a group of people for harboring a criminal.

1115 See *Bretha Éitgid* (*CIH* 1157.6, 1399.28; *AL* 3: 410.7; and *CCIH* 50).

1116 See *Bretha Éitgid* (*CIH* 1157.14–15, 1399.36–37; *AL* 3: 410.19–21; and *CCIH* 50).

1117 See *Bretha Éitgid* (*CIH* 1157.15–16, 1399.36–37; *AL* 3: 410.22; and *CCIH* 50). For *gaoil*, see *eDIL s.v. 1 gáel* 'kinship, relationship'.

1118 The interpretation of the lemma is uncertain; cf. *eDIL s.v. fo-inmlig* 'humors', although the meaning is not entirely secure. Perhaps, in light of the glosses, we should understand it as 'coaxing'; cf. *foínblegon* 'humoring (?), mildness, coaxing', the vn. of *fo-inmlig*. For the lemma (as *dofuinmell*) and the second gloss, see *CIH* 1397.26 (citations concerning guilt by association and liability for the crimes of others; *CCIH* 63).

gnait*h*, ⁊ as aml[aid c]uirid a cion dib*h*, ⁊ do-[g]níd deor*adh* freac*air* de .i. do-b*er* a f*h*ine .uii. ccu*m*ala do f*h*lait*h*, sec[h]t mbl*iad*na féne do egluis [⁊] da c*h*umail c*hair*de do gac[h] l*eth* do na c*eithr*e l*eth*ib*h* .i. risi*n* a ffuil comcu*air*d c*air*de do*n* ciont*a*c, ⁊ saor iad ma*r* si*n* *air*a [c]iont*a*b*h*, ⁊ na diaig*h* si*n* da ttug*adh* nec*h* dia f*h*ine bos g*r*ain, no urg*h*a sgrie, no ingelt da ecuib*h* na fera*n*n *ar* c*air*d[e, f]uill*adh* a cion orra aris.

Deorad frecair 'outlawed stranger', i.e. a native freeman is made into an outlaw like this, i.e. that person who frequently commits crimes and his kindred is not usually able to pay for his crimes, and thus his head [of kindred] casts [him] off from them, and he makes an outlawed stranger of him, i.e. his kindred gives seven *cumal*s to a lord, [seven *cumal*s for] seven years of penance [are paid] to the church, and two *cumal*s for peaceful relations [are paid] to each side of the four sides [i.e. each of the four neighbors], i.e. with which there is a mutual peaceful relationship for the crime, and they are free like that from his crimes, and after that if one of the kindred should give [him] a measure of grain, or the use of a knife, or grazing for his horses on the land [which is also used by those neighbors with whom there are] peaceful relations, his head [of kindred] should pay for them [i.e. pay the amount the kindred paid to exonerate themselves for his crimes] again.[1119]

11.a.27.31 Faic*h*ill .i. tu*ar*u*s*tal.
Foichill 'wage', i.e. wage.[1120]

The first gloss is understood as a 3 sg. pres. ind. rel. perhaps derived from a later simplex of *fo-inmlig* or its verbal noun.

1119 Some of the missing letters are supplied from O'Curry's transcription. See *Bretha Éitgid* (CIH 307.12–19, 1629.30–1630.3, 1639.12–23, 1400.21–32; AL 3: 380.27–382.10; CCIH 176–182). For the lemma, cf. O'Dav 996 (*Cáin Ḟuithirbe*; CIH 138). The translation of the lemma follows that given in AL 3: 380.27. The section of tract with which the entry is paired reads *Cid dogni deorad do urrad?* 'What makes an outlaw of a native freeman?' The entry details the amounts the local lord, church, and neighbors are to be paid in advance for any crimes the outlawed kinsperson might commit after he has been proclaimed an outlaw by the kindred. These advance payments exonerate the kindred from any future liability. If a kinsman gives the outlaw grain, a knife to use, or lets him graze his horses on land owned by a kinsman, the payments need to be made again. See O'Don. Suppl. *s.v. deoraidh.*

1120 The lemma is both a dat. sg. form and also a MI nom. sg. form of *fochell*; *eDIL s.v.* 2 *fochell.* See O'Cl *Faichill .i. tuarastal* 'wages'; *Bretha Éitgid* (CIH 307.33, 1630.23, 1639.41, 1401.15; AL 3: 384.17; CCIH 176–182).

11.a.27.32 Faill tiom*airg*th*e* ag rig*h* .i. gan an ciont*ach* do t*h*iom*ar*gad*h* ré *etghedh* duine *air*ith*e*.
Faill timaircthi ag ríg 'neglect of restraining by a king', i.e. he did not restrain the guilty party against negligence to a particular person.[1121]

11.a.28.33 Dlig*edh* cenn*d*ac*ht*a .i. dlig*hedh* uac*htar*(*us*)ánac*ht*a, no tigerna*m*-l*acht*[a].
Dliged cennachta 'rule of headship', i.e. rule of authority, or lordship.[1122]

11.a.28.34 Ead*ar*f*h*lait*h* .i. foit*h*tigerna .⁊c̄
Etarflaith 'intermediate chief', i.e. sub-lord.[1123]

11.b.2.35 Be foichlide ⟨.i. ben foiclig*h*t*e*r a tig*h* a tech⟩ .i. ben bi*us* fochol-caoi .i. for claon con*air*, *air*m i bfaoi aidc*h*e, ní f*h*aoi *ar*oile an be n-iomra*m*a.
Bé foichlide 'a hired woman', ⟨i.e. a woman who is hired from house to house⟩, i.e. [< *ben* 'woman' + *fochell* 'wage' + *cáe* 'way, path'] a woman who is [on the] wage-road, i.e. on the wrong road, where she spends the night, on the other hand, the *bé n-imrama* does not spend the night.[1124]

11.b.3.36 Be fot*h*la ⟨i. dia bfoetlonn ni da s*edh*uib*h* sec*h* an p*r*iom mnaoi .i. a m*et* an airech⟩ .i. ben dia bfot[l]enan*n* a cele a t*r*eabad sech an ben n-*ar*uis .i. an airec*h*.

1121 See *Bretha Éitgid* (CIH 307.35, 1630.25, 1640.1, 1401.18; *AL* 3: 384.19–20; CCIH 176–182).

1122 The headword *tigernamlacht* is not in *eDIL*. For the lemma, see *Cáin Lánamna* § 2, comm. XVIII, MS A (*CIH* 504.17; *AL* 2: 350.16).

1123 For the lemma, cf. *CIH* 1200.1 (citations from various texts; CCIH 50).

1124 For a similar lemma and gloss regarding a man, cf. *Di Astud Chirt ⁊ Dligid* (*CIH* 237.35 and 238.1, 1420.26; *AL* 5: 468.1 and 470.26–27). This type of woman is not discussed in Power 1936, but cf. *banamus* (Power: 1936: 105). This entry seems to refer to an itinerant woman who hires herself out for wages. It could also refer to an itinerant prostitute. The similar text in *Di Astud Chirt ⁊ Dligid* is equally as opaque. For female itinerant workers more broadly, cf. Karras 2012: 82–83. A *bé n-imrama* 'wandering woman' is classed as a type of concubine. This entry is preceded by the following heading in the MS: [Ad]bar eile d*ar*ob ainm ⁊ ait*h*ne na mbean tet(*h*)a fein *ar* sgat*h* fer; ata d*r*eam diob*h* so, ⁊ ní h-*edh* ata drem oile. 'Other material for which there is the name and characteristic of the women who themselves go under the protection of men; some of these are here, and others are not'. See the discussion in the Introduction on pp. 58–59.

Bé fothla 'a woman of withdrawal', ⟨i.e. when he takes away anything from her valuables without the consent of the female head of the household, i.e. for the concubine's amount⟩, i.e. a woman from whom her husband takes away from her household without the consent of the woman of the house, i.e. the concubine.[1125]

11.b.4.37 Be faoindil .i. ben fon indile i tt*h*ig urd[al]ta.
Bé foíndel 'a wandering woman', i.e. [*fo* 'under, less than, little' with acc. sg. art. + *indile* 'property, possessions'] a woman of little property in an appointed house.[1126]

11.b.5.38 In c*ar*t*h*ac*h* .i. dormuine.
In carthach 'the concubine', i.e. concubine.[1127]

11.b.5.39 Be [táide] .i. ben teid[e] ⟨*ar* faoindel asa tig*h*⟩ i ccom*m*d*h*ail fir ele [t]*ar* cen*n* a f(*h*)ir fein .i. in c*ar*t*a*c[h] .i. dor*m*uine.
Bé [táide] 'secret woman', i.e. [< *ben* 'woman' + *téit* 'goes'] a woman who goes ⟨wandering from her house⟩ to meet another man in spite of her own husband, i.e. the *carthach* 'concubine', i.e. a concubine.[1128]

11.b.6.40 Be n-ion*n*ra .i. ben bi*us* i rin*n* na rae e, an ban *air*gec*h* .i. ben [b]i*us* for *air*ge ion*n*ra i gcom*us* *air*ge, ⁊ ag dena*m* trebt*h*a fo ion*n*amail mog*h*a daoíre.

1125 The missing letter is supplied from O'Curry's transcription. The sense of the entry is that the husband is stealing from his wife's property to support his *airech* 'concubine'. See Power 1936: 95. Cf. *Críth Gablach* ll. 18 and 48 (*AL* 4: 298.18 and 314.24). The *airech* receives *séts* at the inducement of the man and is considered to be in a legal union with him.

1126 The missing letters are supplied from O'Curry's transcription. This type of woman has no fixed abode and likely refers to an outlaw or vagrant. It is also possible that she is an itinerant worker.

1127 See Power 1936: 94–99. The *carthach* receives no property from the man, and her status is lower than the *airech*'s. The *dormuine* is often equated with the *carthach*, but her status is lower; she is, however, of higher status than the *bé n-imrama* and *bé n-indlis*. Cf. *Bretha Crólige* § 56 and gloss 3 (*CIH* 2301.23 and 25).

1128 It is quite likely that the second element of the lemma is missing as *bé* by itself refers to a woman generally rather than specifically to a married woman in an illicit relationship with another man. It is possible that the word *táide* 'of a secret' was omitted; see Power 1936: 99–100; and *Cáin Lánamna* § 36 and gloss 2 (*CIH* 518.22 and 28–29).

Bé n-indra 'woman of cultivation', i.e. [< *ben* 'woman' + *i* 'in, on, at' + *rind* 'end' + *róe* 'level piece of ground'] a woman who is at the end of the cultivated ground, the dairymaid, i.e. a woman who is at the cultivated summer milking place controlling the summer milking place, and cultivating after the manner of an unfree male servant.[1129]

11.b.8.41 [B]e n-an*n*ra .i. ben bi*us* an*n* isi*n* re .i. mat[h]*air* na ndilec[h]tad, bi*us* go macuib*h* ⁊ go lescl*ainn* iomd*h*a leis a cele deg[aid] ⁊ a meic aige i n-iona[d] a fir.

Bé n-indra 'woman of cultivation', i.e. [< *ben* 'woman' + *ann* 'there, then' + *i* 'in, on, at' + *róe* 'level piece of ground'] a woman who is there on the cultivated ground, i.e. the mother of the orphans who is with many children and stepchildren with her later spouse and he has begotten her children instead of her husband.[1130]

11.b.9.42 [Be] n-urnuide .i. ben aontum*na* b*hius* ag urnuide a cele go h-ai*m*sir n-*airch*enn .i. urnaid*m* n-iodnuide, no urnaid*hm* ad*h*all .i. f*r*i re ima tab*air*t.

Bé n-airnaide 'woman of waiting', i.e. an unmarried woman who is waiting for her husband until a fixed time, i.e. a waiting betrothal, or a visiting betrothal, i.e. [waiting] for the time for her to be given.[1131]

11.b.10.43 Be f(*h*)uis i ffoltaib*h* .i. ben bios i bfoisdine (go bfol*adh* toc*hus*a aice) *ar* cion*n* [cai]c*h* do coim*het* a h-enig .i. an p*r*im-ben.

Bé fuis i foltaib 'a woman of remaining in wealth', i.e. a woman who is in a dwelling (with wealth of property in her possession) ready for each [eventuality] for preserving her honor-price, i.e. the head-woman.[1132]

1129 Cf. *CIH* 955.22 (citations from various texts; *CCIH* 42). The general sense of the entry is that this woman is at the summer milking place and in charge of milking and caring for the cattle; *EIF* 44, n. 126. Cf. 11.b.8.41 [B]E N-ANNRA.

1130 The lemma here is a variant of the previous one; see 11.b.6.40 BE N-IONNRA. The sense here is that this woman has children of her own and stepchildren all living with her current husband. I should like to thank one of the anonymous readers for comments on this entry.

1131 This woman has been betrothed, but the marriage process has not been finalized. For this type of betrothal, see *Tract on Marriage and Divorce* § 2 and pp. 55–56.

1132 This woman has enough of her own property to maintain her own honor-price. The

11.b.11.44 Be c(*h*)*ar*na .[i.] ben b*hius* im baoisi cuigir, no nonb*air* [ar]a cc*ar*nuid fir iom*dha*, t*riar* i n-aonlo no i n-aon oidc*he* os *air*d, no cuig*er* fo c*hleth*, no nonb*air ar* [f]ud a bet*ha* d'feraib*h* taid*he*.

Bé carna 'woman of flesh', i.e. a woman who is in the wantonness of five people, or nine people concerning her carnal knowledge of many men, three men in one day or in one night openly, or five men secretly, or nine men throughout her life regarding men in secret.[1133]

11.b.13.45 Be cat*ha* .i. ben t*r*esa ccuirt*er* cat*h* teng*ann*, *ar* olc*us* a teng*ann*, no do-[g]ni [cath a t]eng*ann* go ccuirt*er* cat*h* ui*m*pe, no ben do b*eredh* cat*h* am*h*[ail] do b[er]*edh* [Meadhbh Cruachan].

Bé catha 'woman of battle', i.e. a woman through whom a battle of a tongue is waged, on account of the wickedness of her tongue, or a battle which her tongue makes so that a battle is waged because of her, or a woman who could give battle such as Medb of Cruachan would give.[1134]

11.b.14.46 [..................][1135]

12.a.1.1 [....]aor [..]b[.].[1136]

---

lenition of *fhuis* is unusual, but sometimes a *punctum* can be used to indicate nasalization.

1133 The missing letters are supplied from O'Curry's transcription. The lemma is a phrase for a harlot. The general sense of the entry is that the woman has the wantonness of five or nine normal women. For the lemma and similar gloss, see *Di Astud Chirt 7 Dligid* (*CIH* 230.14, 16–18; *CCIH* 24); and Digest B (15) (*CIH* 1306.4; *CCIH* 55). For the form *carnuid*, see *eDIL s.v. carna(ig)id*. It is possible that there is a preposition missing before the last two words of the gloss. See Power 1936: 108. The lenition of *charna* is unusual, but cf. the first half of O'Dav 213 (*Bretha Nemed Dédenach*; *CCIH* 114: *Bé charna .i. merdrech, ar dia ndech in ben co cuicir is bé charna* "*Bé carna*, i.e. a harlot, for if the woman go with five men she is a *bé carna*."); and *Bretha Nemed Dédenach* (*CIH* 603.25) where the lenition is not present. For the use of a sg. with *imdae* 'many, numerous, abundant', see *eDIL s.v. 1 imdae*. I should like to thank one of the anonymous readers for comments on this entry.

1134 The entry contains two definitions of the lemma. The first is that this is the woman who stirs up trouble due to her wicked tongue. The second is that of a woman who starts a physical battle, such as Medb of Cruachan.

1135 The line is illegible, and it is possible that this material belongs with the end of the previous entry. This line is not included in O'Curry's transcription.

1136 Too much of the entry is illegible to make any sense of it; it is not included in O'Curry's transcription.

12.a.1.2 Be [.....] [.]c bri[.] atac*h*.
Bé [.....][1137]

12.a.1.3 Be [.]n[..][.....]olc ɫ n[...]ac.
Bé ...[1138]

12.a.2.4 [....]*ar* [.]t[.] [..]bc c[..] ag [....][1139]

12.a.2.5 Be n-ind[lightheach] .i. ben as indlig*htac*[h] do ne[ch] [do beith aige ara] fial*us*ag risi*n* fer .i. an ben coibdealac[h] .i. ben oile f*r*is a coibdeal*aigh* no in dlig*ed* lan[amnusa].
Bé n-indligthech 'an unlawful woman', i.e. a woman who is unlawful for someone to be with her on account of her kinship to the man, i.e. the female kinswoman, i.e. another woman [should be] with him outside of kinship [to him] or in accordance with the rule of marriage.[1140]

12.a.4.6 Be n-eccomlan .i. ben nac*h* comlan do nec*h* (do nec*h*) aige im guin, im goid, no im gal*ar* coisi no [laime .i. bean ni(m)] slan lam *ar* gaid .i. ben gat*hach* no baclam[a]c[h], no as eccomlan d'f*e*r aga *m*bi [no as.......]
Bé n-éccomlán 'an imperfect woman', i.e. a woman who is not complete for someone to be with her because of being wounded, because of loss, or because of illness of foot or hand, i.e. a woman whose hand is not complete because of loss, i.e. a deprived woman or maimed in a hand, or who is imperfect for a man who is with her or who is ...[1141]

1137 Too much of the entry is illegible to make any sense of it, and it is not included in O'Curry's transcription.

1138 Too much of the entry is illegible to make any sense of it, and it is not included in O'Curry's transcription.

1139 Too much of the entry is illegible to make any sense of it, and it is not included in O'Curry's transcription. It might belong with the previous entry.

1140 The missing letters are supplied from O'Curry's transcription. The translation of the final gloss is tentative. The general sense of the entry is that this woman is too closely related to the man to be in a lawful relationship.

1141 The sense of the entry is that the woman is maimed and cannot carry out household duties. For similar content, cf. *Cethairṡlicht Athgabálae* (CIH 375.9; CCIH 24); GEIL 85.

12.a.6.7 [Bé tog]a .i. ben comar*b*a fo-sisith*ar* a h-at[h]*ar* indrota[..] faoisidaid an[.]a[.]es*are*[........]
Bé toga 'woman of choice', i.e. a female heiress whom her father acknowledges [....] acknowledgement the ...[1142]

12.a.7.8 [Be ei]g*h*ensa .i. ben bi*us* i bfirgen*us* uais amuil bi*us* ban *air*cinn*a*c[h] p*r*imc[haithr]e m[ar] cen*n*[....]
Bé éccendsa 'a harsh woman', i.e. a woman who is in a state of hard wrath like one who is a female head of a nunnery ...[1143]

12.a.9.9 Be da cret .i. an ben as uaisle dib*h* aga *m*bí da c*r*eit da[.........] [no] ria fior ⁊ c*ar*pa[t] ep*acht* no ruadi do m*a*c *cair*de.
Bé da crett 'a woman of two shapes', i.e. the woman most noble of them who has two shapes for her [...] or for her husband and chariot of a [...] or redness for a treaty child.[1144]

12.a.10.10 Be rait[i] .i. an ben as apad do [.........] ceilib*h* ann ⁊ do b*eredh* Me*dh*b*h* C*r*uac[h]an, ⁊ [.........] mac a bra*thar* ma beg ⁊c̄.
Bé raiti 'a woman of a road', i.e. the woman who is proclaimed for [...] spouses there and Medb Cruachan would give, and [...] child of her brothers if young, etc.[1145]

12.b.1.11 Urn*us*t*ar* .i. baoi ag urn*aid*e.
Arnastar 'may be bound', i.e. who was waiting.[1146]

12.b.1.12 Aois toga .i. aois to [...]
Áes toga 'age of choice', i.e. age of ...[1147]

1142 The interpretation of the entry is tentative because so much of the line is illegible, and it is not included in O'Curry's transcription. Cf. *Díre-tract*, §9 (CIH 922.24–26; CCIH 295); Power 1936: 104, 107–108; *GEIL* 76, 104–105.

1143 Both the transcription and translation are tentative as the entry is difficult to read and the end is missing. Some of the missing letters are supplied from O'Curry's transcription. The general sense is that a severe and difficult woman is likened to the head of a monastic house.

1144 Both the reading and the translation of this entry are tentative. One possible interpretation is that this is the noble woman who brokers peace between two families and, as such, has two roles. This is based on the meaning of *crett* 'frame, body, trunk'.

1145 Too much of the reading is tentative to supply a secure translation. It is possible that the entry refers to a female outlaw or vagrant.

1146 The specific context of the entry is unknown.

1147 The entry refers to the age at which a girl is able to consent to marriage. The gloss presumably repeats the meaning of the lemma.

12.b.2.13 *Airc*[h]ennc[h]a .i. fir*chinn*te.
Airchendcha 'fixed', i.e. [< *fír* 'truly' + *cinnte* 'definite, fixed, appointed'] truly-settled.[1148]

12.b.2.14 Toraid .i. ⟨on⟩ torra*cht*ain .i. tainig.
Toraid 'results', i.e. from *torachtain* 'arriving at', i.e. it arrived.[1149]

12.b.2.15 Fert*ar* .i. fertaig*h*ter .i. adnaicter.
Fertar 'they are buried', i.e. they are buried, i.e. they are buried.[1150]

12.b.2.16 Creadal ⟨.i. cr*edmus*⟩ .i. credm*he*.
Credal 'devout', ⟨i.e. belief⟩, i.e. of faith.[1151]

12.b.3.17 Anch*ara* de .i. ain*m* do*n* aoibilteior.
Ancharae Dé 'anchorite of God', i.e. a name for a recluse.[1152]

12.b.3.18 Feadb*h* .i. baint*r*eabt[h]*ach*.
Fedb 'widow', i.e. widow.[1153]

12.b.3.19 Fec*h*aid .i. fua*cht*naig*h*id.
Fechait 'they fight', i.e. attacks.[1154]

1148 See *eDIL s.vv. airchendach* and *airchendchaide*; and cf. O'Cl *Ercheannchaidhe .i. fírchinnte* 'fixed, settled'.

1149 The case of the lemma is difficult to determine; it could be a gen. sg. or acc. pl. of *torad*; *eDIL s.v. torad*. For this use of the n. sg. art. in the gloss, see Beatnach 1990b.

1150 The first gloss might be a later verb derived from *fertaid* 'makes a burial mound for, buries', rather than being from *fertaigid* 'endows with miraculaous power (?)'; *eDIL s.v. fertaid* and *fertaigid*. The second gloss is a later simplex derived from *ad-anaig* 'buries, entombs'; *eDIL s.v. ad-anaig*. Cf. the first part of O'Dav 961 (heptad 57; *CCIH* 137: *Fert .i. ulad cumdachta*... "*Fert*, i.e. a covered tomb...").

1151 Cf. O'Cl *Creadhal .i. cráibhdheach* 'pious'; O'Dav 446 (*Fél.* Feb. 4; *CCIH* 121: *Credal.i. creidmech no braibjthech .i. o ní is credulus* "*Credal*, i.e. believing or devout, from *credulus*."); *Fél.* Feb. 4; and *Stowe Gl.* 35 *Creadail .i. creidmech*.

1152 For the gloss, see *eDIL s.v oíbelteóracht*. Cf. 13.d.15.25 ANCHARAI. Cf. O'Don. Suppl. *s.v. aibillteoir*.

1153 The context of the entry is unknown.

1154 For the lemma, see *eDIL s.v.* 1 *fichid* 'fights'. The verb *fúachtnaigid* 'is aggressive, injures, makes an attacks' is frequently used to gloss *fo-fich* 'does injury, attacks'; *eDIL s.v. fo-fich*, which notes that O'Cl *Feachaid .i. dochuireadar* 'they put' seems to be missing its object, i.e. put to fight. It is possible that the gloss should be for *fúachtnaigit* 'they attack'.

12.b.3.20 Ailed*h* .i. ellned*h*.
Éiled 'corruption', i.e. corruption.[1155]

12.b.4.21 Fionn .i. cionad*h*.
Finn 'just', i.e. liabilities.[1156]

12.b.4.22 Caoim*hth*ias *nó* caoim*hth*es .i. caoi*m*te*chtacht*aig*h* .i. do-[g]ni coi*m*-id*acht*.
Coímthas nó coímthes 'who accompanies', i.e. attendant, i.e. he accompanies.[1157]

12.b.4.23 Coi*m*riad .i. coi*m*imt*acht*, no comic[h]e*m*níug*h*[adh].
Comríad 'subjection', i.e. accompanying, or progressing together.[1158]

12.b.5.24 Fon*n* fri fon*n* .i. bon*n* fri bon*n*.
Fonn fri fonn 'sole against sole', i.e. sole against sole.[1159]

12.b.5.25 Utsad*ha* .i. iostad*ha* .i. aite soid*h* no ionad*h* co*mnaigh*e.
Autsad 'residence', i.e. dwelling-place, i.e. [< *2 aite* 'abode, dwelling' + *soud* 'turning, returning'] place of returning or place of remaining.[1160]

1155 The identification of the lemma is uncertain. It could be a variant spelling of *eDIL s.v. éilned, éil*(*l*)*ed* 'pollution, corruption, defilement', or it could be a mistake for *trúailned* 'corruption, pollution, defilement', the vn. of *trúailnid* 'corrupts, pollutes, defiles'; *eDIL s.v. trúailned.* Cf. O'Cl *Eillneadh .i. truailleadh* 'pollution'.

1156 The context of the entry is unknown, but the lemma likely should be taken in the sense of something which is morally just, true, or fair; *eDIL s.v.* 1 *finn*. Cf. O'Cl *Fionn .i. firinne* 'truth'.

1157 The lemmata are variants of the same verb, but the headword is uncertain. It is possible that the lemmata are a reanalysis of the second element of *do-coímthet* 'accompanies' as a weak simplex verb. Cf. O'Cl *Caoimtheacht .i. coimhidheacht* 'protection'. See O'Don. Suppl. *s.v. coimidecht*.

1158 The missing ⟨adh⟩ are supplied from O'Curry's transcription. Cf. *CIH* 1269.20 (a passage on a judge's retinue and entitlements; *CCIH* 52). The glosses seem to understand the lemma as consisting of *com-* 'with' and *1 ríad* 'riding'. For the first gloss, see *eDIL s.v. coimitecht*; for the second, see *eDIL s.v. comchéimniugad*. Cf. See O'Don. Suppl. *s.v. coimidecht*.

1159 See O'Dav 816 (no id.; *CCIH* 132: [*F*]*onn .i. druim no bonn, ut est sal fri sal, fonn fri fonn .i. do bonn i n-inadh buinn ind fir it dhegaid, no druim cechtar dhé fri araile* "*Fonn*, i.e. back or sole, ut est 'heel against heel, sole against sole', i.e. thy sole in the place of the sole of the man after thee. Or back of each of the two against the other."); and *CIH* 1396.23 (citations concerning guilt by association and liability for the crimes of others; *CCIH* 63–64). The lemma is a later variant of *eDIL s.v.* 1 *bonn*.

1160 The context of the entry is unknown.

12.b.5.26 Sgiolla .i. daosg*air*, oba*nn*.
Scillu 'suddenly', i.e. bold, sudden.[1161]

12.b.6.27 I*arrair* .i. i*arradh*.
Íarair 'seeking', i.e. seeking.[1162]

12.b.6.28 T*air*fent*ar* .i. tairpent*ar*.
Tairfentar 'may be shown', i.e. may be shown.[1163]

12.b.6.29 Terbad*h* .i. ion*nar*ba no delug*adh*.
Terbad 'separating', i.e. expelling or separating.[1164]

12.b.6.30 Frecur .i. fiorat*h*c*h*ur.
Frecor 'impugning', i.e. [< *fír* 'true' + *athchor* 'renouncing, handing back'] true-renouncing.[1165]

12.b.7.31 Dodan-iongaib .i. diongb*hus*, no do-[g]ni a d*h*iongbail.
Dodan-ingaib 'that he removes it', i.e. who removes, or who removes it.[1166]

12.b.7.32 Eitsec*h* .i. duine gan tec*h*.
Eistech 'houseless', i.e. a person without a house.[1167]

1161 A See *Lec. Gl.* 200 *Scill .i. obann*; *Metr. Gl.* 27 § 38 *'Sgill' obann…*; O'Cl *Sgill .i. obann* 'sudden'; O'Dav 1408 (*Ántéchtae*; CCIH 150: *Scille .i. obann, ut est cia conscara scille .i. cia scara rit é co hobann* "*Scille*, i.e. sudden, ut est 'though he separates suddenly', i.e. though he severs him from thee suddenly."); *Ántéchtae* (CIH 1245.27 and 1245.37–1256.1; and CCIH 150).

1162 The likely sense of the lemma and gloss is pursuing a legal claim.

1163 Both the lemma and gloss are prototonic 3 sg. pres. pass. subj. forms of *do-aisféna* 'shows, exhibits'; *eDIL s.v. do-aisféna*.

1164 See O'Cl *Tearbadh .i. dealughadh* 'to separate'; and the first part of O'Dav 1517 (no id.; CCIH 153: *Terbadh .i. indarba no deluged…* "*Terbud*, i.e. banishing or separating…").

1165 See the first part of O'Dav 998 (no id.; CCIH 138: *Frecur .i. firathchur… "Frecur*, i.e. true-putting-back…"). It is common for the pre-verb *fris-* to be glossed by *fír-* 'true, genuine'; Taylor-Griffiths 2020: 1: 89. The lemma *frecor* is the vn. of *fris-cuirethar*; *eDIL s.v. frecor*.

1166 The lemma is interpreted as the 3 sg. pres. ind. of *do-ingaib* 'wards off, takes away' with a m. Class C object agreement marker. Based on the glosses, it is likely the lemma was taken from a nasalizing relative clause in the base text. The first word in the gloss is a later simplex of the lemma; *eDIL s.v. do-ingaib*. The second half of the gloss contains its vn. used with *do-gní*.

1167 For the lemma, read *eistech* 'houseless, a houseless person'. Cf. 8.13.33 EITSECH. See CIH

12.b.7.33 Cuidig*h* geill .i. luac*h* tob*h*aig*h*.
Cuitig geill 'share of a pledge', i.e. fee of enforcing.[1168]

12.b.8.34 Luig*he* cana .i. mion*na* do tab*air*ter b*eth* umal do*n* riag*h*ail.
Luige cána 'oath of law', i.e. oaths which are given by the one who is obedient to the law.[1169]

12.b.8.35 Ba na forb*h*aig*he* .i. ba an luac*h* tobaig.
Bó na forbaige 'the cow of the additional levy', i.e. a cow [is] the fee of enforcing.[1170]

12.b.9.36 Com*h*logad ruis .i. laig si*n* e, no com*mait*h*em*h* ber*ar* do*n* dui*ne* *ar* a mbi fiach.
Comlogad ruis 'mutual concession of shame', i.e. those are payments, or equal remission is given to the person who owes a fine.[1171]

12.b.10.37 Fiac*h* lesaig*hthe* .i. fiac[h] biata[d] ⁊ lesaig*hth*e na ccion*tach*.
Fíach lesaighthe 'liability of maintaining', i.e. liability of feeding and maintaining the guilty person.[1172]

12.b.10.38 Fer didin .i. fer bi*us* ag didin an c*h*in*taigh*.
Fer dídin 'man of protection', i.e. a man who is protecting the guilty person.[1173]

1422.2 (citations concerning people who cannot give evidence; CCIH 64); and O'Don. Suppl. *s.v. eitsech*.

1168 The entry concerns contracts. The lemma could be in an oblique case with later velar inflection, but it could also be a nom. sg.; *eDIL s.v. cuit*. Cf. heptad 66 (CIH 62.37; AL 346.20).

1169 Cf. O'Cl *Luighe .i. mionna* 'oaths'.

1170 The entry refers to an additional fine levied by a leader; *eDIL s.v. forbach*.

1171 The interpretation of this entry is tentative. The difficulties are with *ruis*: it could be from *rus* 'shame', *rús* 'knowledge', or *ros* 'knowledge'. The division of MS *laigsine* is also uncertain.

1172 For the lemma, see *Ántéchtae* (CIH 1247.5, 2180.8); *Cethairṡlicht Athgabálae* (CIH 1455.9, 1720.13); and CCIH 51, 65, 71, and 88, respectively. The citation from CIH 2180 is found in TCD MS 1387 [H.5.15] which Dubhaltach owned. The sense of the entry seems to be that as a result of feeding and providing protection to the guilty party, the protector owes the claimant fines for doing so. I should like to that one of the anonymous readers for comments on this entry.

1173 The context of the entry is unknown. For the lemma, cf. *Cethairṡlicht Athgabálae* (CIH 1455.8, 1720.11; CCIH 65 and 71).

12.b.11.39 Toc*h*uir*edh* ⟨.i. ciond⟩ .i. an cuir*edh* ⟨.i. ciond⟩ cugad.
Tochuiriud 'invitation' ⟨.i. ciunn 'from a head (of family or leader)'⟩, i.e. the invitation ⟨i.e. from a head⟩ to you.[1174]

12.b.11.40 Tom*us* .i. tuair*im*.
Tomus 'considering', i.e. likelihood.[1175]

12.b.11.41 A ccuib*h*di*us* .i. i n-u*m*l*acht*, i n-aontu*g*a[d] do dlig*hedh*. Egcuibdi*us* a c*h*ontr*ardha* si*n*.
I cuibdius 'in agreement', i.e. in submission, in agreement [in regard] to law. *Éccuibdes* 'not in agreement' is its opposite.[1176]

12.b.12.42 Diong*h*aib*h* g*ach* degen*ach* .i. gibe nec*h* aga ruib*h*e an cion*tach* ⟨da biath*ad* no da cuim*h*dac*h*⟩ fa deir*adh*, diol*adh ar*a son.
Dingaib cach déidenach 'every last person who wards off', i.e. whichever person by whom the criminal ⟨was being fed or being protected⟩ last, compensation on account of that.[1177]

12.b.13.43 Banapad .i. biath*adh* an cion*taigh* re nden*am* cion*adh*.
Bánapaid 'white harboring', i.e. feeding the guilty party before committing a crime.[1178]

12.b.13.44 Dergap*ad* .i. an biath*adh* i*ar* nden*am* cion*adh* do*n* ciontac[h].
Dergapaid 'red harboring', i.e. the feeding after a crime has been committed by the guilty party.[1179]

1174 The context of the entry is unknown. Perhaps the entry concerns the head of the family inviting the guilty party to come under his protection. Cf. 12.b.10.38 FER DIDIN.

1175 The context of the entry is unknown. In Mod. Ir. *tuairim* means 'opinion' which is likely how the gloss should be understood. I should like to thank one of the anonymous readers for pointing this out.

1176 The semantic range of the lemma also includes paying for something jointly and/or equally; cf. heptad 1 (which has a monastic context; *CIH* 1882.1–2; and *AL* 5: 122.24). I should like to that one of the anonymous readers for comments on this entry.

1177 The context of the entry is unknown. The sense of it concerns the person who was last feeding and supporting the guilty party. See O'Don. Suppl. *s.v. diongaib gach déigeanach*.

1178 Cf. 11.a.16.23 DERGABAD and 12.b.13.44 DERGAPAD. See *CIH* 721.16–17, 803.4–5, 1398.21 and 1406.12–13 (all of which are collections of citations covering topics such as guilt by association and harboring a criminal; *CCIH* 31, 35, and 63). Cf. *Córus Bésgnai* § 66 (*CIH* 1817.3). The entry refers to the less serious offence of unwittingly harboring a criminal before they committed a crime.

1179 Cf. 12.b.13.43 BANAPAD and 11.a.16.23 DERGABAD. See *CIH* 721.17–18, 803.5–6, 1398.21,

12.b.14.45 Dergs*aru*g*adh* .i. dorn do buai*n* as b*r*ollac*h* a*n* cion*taigh*, cid*h* re nde*nam*, cid i*ar* nden*am*, cion*adh*.
Dergsárugud 'red violating', i.e. striking a fist against the breast of the guilty party, whether before the crime or after the crime.[1180]

12.b.14.46 Com*air*legad .i. an cion*tach* do legad*h* fon c*h*aill.
Comairléciud 'allowing', i.e. allowing the guilty party to be at large.[1181]

12.b.15.47 Coim*h*ríom*h* in*n*sge f*air* .i. co*mh*aig*h*nes a n-ag*aidh* an biod*h*b*hadh* no an coint*aig*.
Comrím insce fair 'synchronizing a statement about it', i.e. a common argument against the culprit or the guilty party.[1182]

12.b.16.48 Gintuillm*h*id*echt* .i. gin toi*mh*lide*cht* .i. gin toi*m*li*us* .i. it*h*es a ferann, no i bes no c*h*ait[h]es re a bele [é].
Gintuillmidecht 'extravagance', i.e. [< *gin* 'mouth' + *toimlidecht* 'consumption'] mouth consumption, i.e. [< *gin* 'mouth' + *toimlid* 'consumes'] a mouth which consumes, i.e. who devours his land, or in which he is or who consumes before his lips.[1183]

---

and 1406.12–13 (all of which are collections of citations covering topics such as guilt by association and harboring a criminal; CCIH 31, 35, and 63). Cf. *Córus Bésgnai* § 66 (CIH 1817.3). The entry refers to the more serious offence of harboring a criminal after they have committed a crime.

1180 The entry refers to the process of apprehending a criminal or expelling an outsider; *eDIL s.v. brollach*. See CIH 721.18–19, 803.7–8, and 1406.14–15 (all of which are collections of citations covering topics such as guilt by association and harboring a criminal; CCIH 31, 35, and 63). Cf. *Cethairślicht Athgabálae* (CIH 1747.35–37; AL 2: 88.19–20). The interpretation of the gloss is tentative. Usually, the phrase *dorn i mbrollach* refers to the apprehending a criminal or outsider. It is possible that the gloss either has a different idiom for the same action or refers to performing an act of violence upon the offender.

1181 The entry refers to allowing the guilty party to escape. See CIH 721.19 and 1406.15 (both of which are collections of citations covering topics such as guilt by association and harboring a criminal; CCIH 31 and 63). See O'Don. Suppl. *s.v. comarlégadh*.

1182 The context of the entry is unknown, but it likely continues the topic of harboring a criminal seen in the previous entries. The interpretation of this entry is tentative. It is possible that the entry refers to having a legal statement from the various witnesses which contains no contradictions and which can be used against the criminal.

1183 The final word is supplied from O'Curry's transcription. The interpretation of the entry is uncertain. It seems to concern the spendthrift whose extravagance uses up his ancestral land; *eDIL s.v. gintuillmidecht*. It is also possible that the lemma should be read as *gin tuillmhidecht* 'without merit'; *eDIL s.v. tuillmidecht*; and AL 6: *s.v. gin-tuillim*. For the lemma, cf. *Uraicecht Becc* (CIH 1594.17; AL 5: 20.4–5). See O'Don. Suppl. *s.v. gin tuillmidh, gin tuillmidechta*.

12.b.17.49 Senc*h*let*he* .i. luc*ht* lanamna b*hius* ag lenmui*n* do t*r*i g*h*lunuib a ndiaig*h* a c*h*eile, ⁊ o b*eth* ⟨ma*r* si*n*⟩ agan at[h]*air* ⁊ agan m*a*c ⁊ agan ua. As *eter* le slio*cht* an t*r*ir si*n* gan iadsan na a sli*cht* do leigen do gnat*h*, ⁊ [s]eincl*eth*e na da[oin]e sin.

Senchléithe 'hereditary serf', i.e. a follower who adheres to three generations consecutively, and the father and the son and the grandfather are all ⟨like that⟩. It is likely that those three people are within that class without them ever leaving their class, and those people are hereditary serfs.[1184]

12.b.19.50 Ioc cana ⟨*nó* congbail, no gabail⟩ re h-ainffine .i. ma*r* do rach*adh* duine ona fine fa riagail cana ⁊ fine oile ⟨.i. dlig*edh* cor*us*a fine tugt*e*r isi*n* cain sin⟩.

Ícc cána ⟨nó congbáil, nó gabáil⟩ fri h-ainfine 'compensation as a legal requirement ⟨or sustaining, or maintaining⟩ in respect of someone outside the kindred', i.e. as a person from the kindred would submit to the rule of law and of another kindred ⟨i.e. law of the arrangement of the kindred which is given in that law⟩.[1185]

12.b.20.51 Gníad*h* .i. focal cuirt*er* *ar* son an *air*ec[h] e*cht*a .i. an f*e*r risa ndent*ur* com*air*le an gnio*mh*a no an e*cht*a do dena*m* ⁊ do be*ir* com*air*le do cac*h* cu*m* an gnio*mh*a.

Gníad 'a doer', i.e. a word used for the *aire échta* 'noble of blood vengeance', i.e. the man with whom counsel of the action or committing of the slaughter is done, and he gives counsel to each one with a view to the deed.[1186]

1184 The missing ⟨oin⟩ are supplied from O'Curry's transcription. The *senchléithe* becomes such when his immediate ancestors have occupied the same land for three generations. They are not slaves but are bound to the lord and the land; GEIL 35–36. I should like to thank one of the anonymous readers for comments on this entry.

1185 It is difficult to determine whether the reference to *corusa fine* is to the legal text *Córus Fine* or is a general reference to the arrangement of the local kindred.

1186 The interpretation of the lemma is tentative. It could be interpreted as the 3 sg. impf. ind. of *gníid* 'acts, does, makes', or it could be an oblique case of *gnía* 'worker'; *eDIL s.v. gníid* and 3 *gnía*, respectively. In either case, the lemma refers to someone who gets things done. See O'Cl *Gníadh .i. foghantaidh, no fear dhénta foghainte* 'a man who does service'. For discussion of the *aire échta* and theories on his role in early Irish society, see the legal glossary in *Críth Gablach, s.v. aire échta*; GEIL 127; McLeod 2004 amd 2013. Here, the *aire échta* is interpreted as someone who advises the people under his protection who are to carry out the action of vengeance.

12.b.21.52 Bot*hach* .i. daor fuidir .i. daor bot*hach* bi*us* *ar* bot[h]*achus* no *ar* buailid[eacht] *ar* fe*dh* sam*h*ruid*h*, no fog*h*m*air*.
Bothach 'crofter', i.e. *doír fuidir* 'base tenant', i.e. a base crofter who is in a state of being a *bothach* 'crofter' or in a state of having a *buaile* 'byre' throughout summer or autumn.[1187]

12.b.22.53 Sec*h*f*us* .i. ion*n*saig*h*fes.
Sechfas 'who will declare', i.e. who will claim.[1188]

12.b.22.54 Baile ata tall .i. Senc[h]*us* Mo*r*.
Baile at-tá tall 'where that is', i.e. *Senchas Már*.[1189]

12.b.23.55 Caom*h*sad .i. d'fasad.
Comḟosad 'rest', i.e. to halt.[1190]

12.b.23.56 Aos c*air*de .i. an drong bi*us* fon statuid sio*th*cana dá ngoirt*er* c*air*de. Sio*th* no riagail ordoig*h*id lu*cht* crice no d*ha* ⟨⁊c.⟩ *etar*ra fein, ⁊ bí cáin fo Eirin*n* uile ⟨⁊ cac*h*⟩ ag adrad di.
Áes cairde 'people governed by a treaty', i.e. those who are under the statute of a compact of peace which is called a *cairde* 'treaty'. Peace or rule that people of the territory or two ordain, ⟨etc.⟩ between themselves, and it is a treaty throughout all of Ireland ⟨and everyone⟩ observing it.[1191]

12.b.25.57 G*r*in, g*r*iun .i. fera*nn*.
Grin, *griun* 'of land, [on] land', i.e. land.[1192]

1187 The word *fogmar* is a later form of *fogamar* 'autumn'; *eDIL s.v. fogamar*. For the *bothach*, see GEIL 35. As noted in GEIL 35, *Críth Gablach* l. 580 (CIH 570.15), equates someone who is a *dóerbothas* with *dóerḟuidrius*. See O'Don. Suppl. *s.v. bothachus*.

1188 The lemma is the 3 sg. fut. rel. of *seichid* 'asserts, declares'. Cf. O'Don. Suppl. *s.v. seachus*.

1189 The entry possibly cites the *Senchas Már* as the source of some of the surrounding glossary material, perhaps that which follows although the entries have not been sourced to a specific text.

1190 The lemma is interpreted as a form of *comḟosad* 'rest, truce'; *eDIL s.vv. comḟosad* and *comsad*. For the gloss, see *eDIL s.v. fossad* 'stationary, halting, staying, abiding'.

1191 This entry is cited in its entirety in *eDIL s.v. cairde*, which cites O'Don. Suppl., which in turn cites this glossary, as its source. The entry appears to refer to a compact of peace or some form of governance which has authority throughout all of Ireland. See O'Don. Suppl. *s.vv. adhradh, cáirde*.

1192 Both lemmata are from *grian* 'earth, land'; they are the gen. sg. and dat. sg., respectively. See O'Cl *Grían .i. fearann* 'land'.

12.b.25.58 Im-ruim*ethar* .i. ro reimnig*hethar* in iomar*bus*.
Imm-ruimdethar 'transgresses', i.e. the transgression was proceeded.[1193]

12.b.25.59 Urrad*us* ⟨.i. cionta⟩ .i. *air* arát*hus* .i. a c*h*ionta.
Aurradus 'native law', ⟨i.e. crimes⟩, i.e. [< *ar* 'for, because' + *ar-reith* 'capture, overtake'] because it may overtake, i.e. his crimes.[1194]

12.b.26.60 Iomglan mis ⟨ano a cont*r*ar*dha*⟩ .i. neimhg*h*laine bi*us ar* nec*h ar* fe*dh* mis t*r*e bia*thad* ciont*aigh* f*r*i re deachm*aigh*e .i. cion an ciont*aigh* go cen*n* mi*us*a .i. do b*eth* ar tí biat*hus* e *ar* fe*dh* deic*h* la.
Inglan mís 'unclean months' ⟨*ano* 'year' is its opposite⟩, i.e. impurity which is for someone for the duration of a month for feeding a criminal for a space of ten days, i.e. the criminal's crime until the end of a month, i.e. for the one who feeds him for the duration of ten days.[1195]

12.b.27.61 Tu*cht* .i. gne.
Tucht 'manner', i.e. manner.[1196]

12.b.27.62 Rag*h*b*ha* .i. ro gab*ha*.
Rogba 'he may take', i.e. he may take.[1197]

1193 For the gloss, see *eDIL s.v. réim(m)nigid*. *Iomarbus* is the vn. *imm-ruimdethar*; it is possible that part of the gloss is an etymological gloss on the lemma; *eDIL s.v. immarmus, immormus, immorbus*. For the first part of the gloss, cf. *Cethairślicht Athgabálae* (CIH 413.22 and 25–26; *AL* 1: 282.16); and O'Dav 944 (probably from *Di Choimét Dligthech*; CCIH 136).

1194 The lemma is straightforward, but the first gloss is not. It is likely that it contains an etymological gloss on *aurradus* 'native law, surety, guarantee', which might be composed of *air* 'for' + a form of *ar-reith* 'captures, overtakes', but the second element is not satisfactorily explained in the verb's paradigm; *eDIL s.v. ar-reith*. Cf. *Cethairślicht Athgabálae* (CIH 412.10; *AL* 1: 274.29).

1195 The lemma is almost certainly a mistake for *inglan* 'impure, unclean'; to understand the lemma as *immglan* 'very pure' does not make sense in light of the gloss; *eDIL s.vv.* 1 *inglaine* and 1 *inglan*. See O'Cl *Ingglaine .i. neamhghloine* 'impurity' and *Ingglan .i. neamhghlan* 'impure'.

1196 See *Metr. Gl.* 19 § 59 *'Tucht' gach gné....*

1197 The lemma and gloss are both 3 sg. pres. subj. forms of *gaibid* 'takes'.

12.b.28.63 Cob*hach* .i. coib*h*fiac*hach*.
Cobach 'tribute', i.e. [< *com-* 'equally' + *fíachach* 'liable to penalty or fine'] equally liable.[1198]

12.b.28.64 Matbosaide .i. mad iangabasid*he*.
Mad-bo-saide 'well he may exact', i.e. well he may reprove.[1199]

12.b.28.65 Lias .i. do laog*h*aib*h* ⁊ caoirib*h*.
Lías 'pen', i.e. for calves and sheep.[1200]

12.b.28.66 Mac*h*ad*h* .i. do indilib*h*, ⁊ d'eac*h*aib*h*.
Machad 'milking enclosure', i.e. for cattle, and for horses.[1201]

12.b.29.67 Tos*ach* cána .i. i*ar* n-esc*air*e .i. ffogu*r* cana.
Tosach cána 'beginning of a law', i.e. after public notice, i.e. promulgation of law.[1202]

12.b.29.68 A ndegh*adh* cána .i. i ffoirc*h*enn sec*h*t mbliadan i tt*us* a h-at*h*núidig*h*t*h*e.
A ndegad cána 'after a law', i.e. at the end of seven years from the beginning of its renewal.[1203]

1198 For the gloss, see *eDIL s.v. comḟiachach* and cf. *comḟiach* 'equal debt, liability', which is the ultimate etymology of the lemma; Thurneysen 1928: 13; and *eDIL s.v.* 1 *cobach.*

1199 See *eDIL s.vv. boingid* and *in-gaib*. The lemma is interpreted as the prefix *mad-* 'well, good', the 3 sg. pres. subj. of *boingid* 'breaks, strikes, cuts, exacts' followed by an anaphoric pron. The gloss similarly consists of *mad-*, the 3 sg. pres. subj. of *in-gaib* 'reproaches, censures, reproves, receives, constructs' followed by an anaphoric pron. I should like to thank one of the anonymous readers for comments on this entry.

1200 Cf. O'Cl *Lias .i. cro bhios ag láoghaibh no ag úanaibh* 'a hut which is for calves or for lambs'.

1201 The *machad* is normally used for milking cows, so horses are not expected as part of the gloss; *eDIL s.v.* 1 *macha, machad.*

1202 The entry refers to the proclamation of a promulgated law. In the second gloss, *fogur* is used in its wider semantic sense of sounds generally and 'report, rumor'; in other words, anything which can be heard; *eDIL s.v. fogur*. Cf. 12.b.29.68 ANDEGHADH CÁNA.

1203 Cf. 12.b.29.67 TOSACH CÁNA. The form *deghadh* is MI; *eDIL s.v. dead.* The sense seems to be that the promulgated law will expire at the end of seven years unless it is renewed. For discussion of the potential seven-year limit on *cánai*, see Charles-Edwards 2000: 563.

12.b.30.69 Éric .i. fíriac.
Éric 'compensation', i.e. [< *fír* 'true' + *ícc* 'paying'] true-paying.[1204]

12.b.30.70 Céin m*hair*da .i. an ccéin m*hair*id.
Céin mhairte 'as long as they live', i.e. the period of time that they live.[1205]

13.a.4.1 Faon fleacain .i. re re roilecan .i. faon fo leacain.
Fáen fleacain 'weak of *fleacain*', i.e. before time of *roilecan*, i.e. [< *fáen* 'weak' + *fo* 'under' + *lecca* 'cheek, jaw'] weak under jaw.[1206]

13.a.6.2 Dub*h*aig*h*id .i. aigid fedil no s*echtea*rdub*h*áin.
Dubaigid 'darkens', i.e. mask or outer darkness.[1207]

13.a.7.3 *Ar*a n-et*h*at .i. *ar*a n-u*r*nuid*h*id .i. *ar*a *m*b*eth* in oiricill.
Ara n-ethat 'in order that they eat', i.e. in order that he sustains, i.e. in order that there may be provision.[1208]

13.a.9.4 Inbleog*an* saic*h*t*h*e no sáoit*h*e .i. gallraig*h*teac*h*.
Inbleogan saethe nó saithe 'kinsman-surety of illness or of sickness', i.e. ailing.[1209]

13.a.10.5 Áb*h*ain*n* .i. cl*ár* b*hius* (ag bual*adh* bas dáoine) le cúrt*h*oir .i. fer do-[g]ní cúrad .i. gredad*h* sm*acht*aig*h*te *ar* m*a*caib do-[g]ní cion*n*ta.

1204 The context of the entry is unknown.

1205 The lack of context makes the entry difficult to interpret. The general sense is of persisting/living for a long period of time. The adj. *cían* 'long, enduring, a long time', acc. *céin*, can be used as a preverb to *maraid* 'lasts, persists, survives', but this is distinct from the adverbial phrase *céin máir* 'a long time'; GOI § 892; *eDIL s.vv. cían* and *maraid*.

1206 The interpretation of this entry is tentative. The entry is preceded by a poem and entry on epilepsy. See the discussion in the Introduction on p. 60.

1207 The first half of the gloss is interpreted as 'mask'; *eDIL s.v. fethal* 'emblem, halidom, appearance'. The final word of the gloss is interpreted here as a compound of *sechtar* 'outside' and *dubán* 'darkness', thus referring to something that changes the face on the outside, such as a mask; O'Reilly, *s.v. dubán*. On the use of masks to frighten horses, see *Cethairślicht Athgabálae* (CIH 383.15; AL 1: 164.15). See O'Don. Suppl. *s.vv. aghaidh fedil* and *dubhaighe*. *eDIL s.v. fethal* refers to Dubhaltach as a source.

1208 The context of the passage is unknown. The verb in the lemma is interpreted as the 3 pl. pres. ind. of *ithid* 'eats'.

1209 The second word in the lemma is interpreted as a gen. sg. form of *saeth* 'distress, hardship, disease, illness'; *eDIL s.v. saeth*.

Abann 'scourge', i.e. a wooden board (for beating a person's palm) which a chastiser has, i.e. a person who does the chastising, i.e. a punishment beating for boys who commit crimes.[1210]

13.a.12.6 Fog*h*nisse [...]
Fognisse 'is subject to' ...[1211]

13.b.2.7 Indul .i. u*air*, no óir.
Indall 'in the future', i.e. when, or when.[1212]

13.d.1.8 Foib*h*rit*h*e .i. rat*h* fubaid*h*e ⟨.i. fo ba .i. fo mait*h* an n*eth*e do roi(m)[n]*n*e⟩ .i. boim berrta .⁊c̄.
Fobrithe 'payment', i.e. wage of shaving ⟨i.e. [< *fó* 'good' + *bá* 'profit, benefit, good'] good profit, i.e. [*fó* 'good' + *maith* 'prosperity, good, prosperity'] good profit of the matter regarding hair⟩, i.e. shaving morsel, etc.[1213]

13.d.2.9 Fiod*h* defid*h* *ar* du*n* .i. coill dee *ar* ⟨ł ag⟩ an dún ga *m*bi .i. fid*h* nim*edh*.
Fid de-ḟid ar dún 'sacred wood at a fort', i.e. a sacred wood which is on ⟨or at⟩ a fort, i.e. a sacred tree.[1214]

13.d.3.10 Ait*h*gin g*ach* fed*h*a o t*air*c*h*ell ⟨.i. timceall⟩ go diorain*n* ⟨.i. adb*al* rinn⟩ .i. ti*m*ceall na coill*idh* *ar* fad.

1210 There is the possibility that *ábhainn* could be the headword. *eDIL s.v. cúrthóir* cites O'Don. Suppl. as its source, which in turn cites this glossary; O'Don. Suppl. *s.v. curthóir*. The participle *smachtaighte* 'punished, corrected' is difficult to construe. For the first part of the gloss, cf. *Cáin Íarraith* (*CIH* 1768.20; *AL* 2: 186.7).

1211 The interpretation of the lemma is uncertain. It could be derived from *fo-gní* 'serves, is subject to, avails'; *eDIL s.v. fo-gní*. It is also possible that the lemma should be divided as *fo-ghni sse*. The remainder of the line in the MS is empty; it is possible that Dubhaltach started this entry and did not finish it.

1212 The interpretation of the lemma is uncertain. It might be a form of *indal*, which itself is given the uncertain meaning 'in the future' in *eDIL s.v. indal*; cf. O'Dav 817 for the lemma (no id.; *CCIH* 132). The tentative dictionary definition matches the explanation provided by the gloss; *eDIL s.v.* 2 *úar, úair* (III).

1213 The last gloss refers to the wages paid for shaving. For the lemma and part of the gloss, see *Cethairṡlicht Athgabálae* (*CIH* 370.22–23; *AL* 1: 132.19–20).

1214 See *Cethairṡlicht Athgabálae* (*CIH* 371.23–24; *AL* 1: 134.21) where the lemma is part of a gloss on the main text. The entry is translated in Petrie 1845: 61 n. f as: "*Fiodh defid* on the Dun, i.e. the sacred *wood* on or at the *dun*, i.e. a *Fidh nimheadh*."

Aithgein cach feda ó thairchell ⟨.i. timchell⟩ co *ndírainn ⟨.i. adbal rind⟩* 'restitution of each wood from the border ⟨i.e. boundary⟩ to the mountain ⟨i.e. vast point⟩', i.e. as far as the boundary of the wood.[1215]

13.d.4.11 Cl*ár* sadall .i. cl*ar* diallaid.
Clár sadall 'saddle trees', i.e. saddle tree.[1216]

13.d.5.12 Fer lesac*h* .i.
Fer lesach 'legal representative', i.e.[1217]

13.d.5.13 Cresion .i. *cr*eidmeac*h*.
Crésen 'pious', i.e. faithful.[1218]

13.d.5.14 Leam*h*ad*h* .i. bod m*air*b*he*.
Lemad 'rendering impotent', i.e. a lifeless penis.[1219]

13.d.6.15 Crela .i. *cr*íola .i. *cr*o iall orba fertsi si*n* ⁊c̄., no orba *cr*uib*h* no sliosda.

1215 See *Cethairślicht Athgabálae* (CIH 371.26; AL 1: 134.23–24) where the lemma is part of a commentary on the main text.

1216 The legal passage refers to making saddle trees and other household equipment from whale bones. For the second word in the gloss, see *eDIL s.v. díallait* 'saddle'. See *Cethairślicht Athgabálae* (CIH 371.31; AL 1: 134.30) where the lemma is part of a gloss on the main text.

1217 Dubhaltach did not finish the entry. The entry refers to a woman's legal guardian. See *Cethairślicht Athgabálae* (CIH 374.12; AL 1: 140.7–8) where the lemma is part of a gloss on the main text. The phrase is found frequently in the legal texts.

1218 See *Cethairślicht Athgabálae* (CIH 377.12; AL 1: 144.27) where the lemma is part of a gloss on the main text. For the gloss and lemma, respectively, cf. O'Dav 446 (*Fél.* Feb. 4; CCIH 121) and 447 (*Fél.* Feb. 4; CCIH 121); *Fél.* February 4.

1219 This entry is not included in O'Curry's transcription. The entry refers to rendering a husband impotent as a result of spells being cast against him. See *Cethairślicht Athgabálae* (CIH 388.11; AL 1: 180.26) where the lemma is part of a gloss on the main text; and for the lemma; cf. O'Dav 930 (probably from the *Tract on Marriage and Divorce*; CCIH 136). On the use of charms to render a male partner impotent, see the discussions in Borsje 2010 (the lemma is translated on 183); see also Borsje 2021: 12–16; and Mistry 2015: 138–139. The larger context of the entry concerns a series of ways in which a woman can use magical means to render a partner impotent or induce an abortion. It should be noted that impotence was grounds for divorce; GEIL 74.

Crela 'receptacles', i.e. receptacles, i.e. [< *1 cró* 'inheritance' + *1 íall* 'thong, strop, leash, shoe-string'] inheritance of strings that is property of a spindle, etc., or property of hand or thigh.[1220]

13.d.8.16 Toxaig*ad* [.i.] on toxal no foxal.
Toxaigad 'seizing', i.e. from [the word] *toxal* 'carrying off' or *foxal* 'taking away'.[1221]

13.d.9.17 Apad raitig*h* .i. ap*adh* bert*er ar* nec[h] ⁊ e *ar* an rod no *ar* slig*h*e.
Apad raitig 'a vagrant's notice', i.e. a notice is given on someone, and he is on the road or on a path.[1222]

13.d.10.18 Iatiaig*h* ⟨.i. mealog⟩ .i. tiac*h* .i. aiteog.
Íadaig 'a bag', ⟨i.e. a bag⟩, i.e. wallet, i.e. bag.[1223]

13.d.10.19 Tigseal .i. buain.
Tíscál 'taking', i.e. depriving.[1224]

1220 The entry refers to property, be it household items or land, which a daughter owns outright either as a result of her own efforts, or as part of her marriage gift or inheritance. See *Cethairślicht Athgabálae* (CIH 378.21–22; AL 1: 148.4–5) where the lemma and part of the gloss are found within a gloss on the main text. The last part of the gloss refers to land acquired by one's "own exertions and which may be given to a son or daughter" (EIF 416–417); see the larger discussion on female inheritance in EIF 415–417.

1221 The lemma appears to be a vn. derived from *do-fochsla* 'seizes, caries off'; *eDIL s.v. do-fochsla*. Considering the surrounding entries, one would expect the entry to derive from a version of *Cethairślicht Athgabálae*.

1222 The entry refers to giving to someone who does not have a residence. See *Cethairślicht Athgabálae* (AL 1: 284.33) where the lemma is part of a gloss on the main text; (cf. CIH 415.22–24; I cannot find all of the material from the AL citation in CIH); and see *Di Choimét Dligthech* (CIH 1748.9; AL 2: 90.9; CCIH 287–288) for the lemma as part of a commentary.

1223 The lemma could be acc. or dat. sg; *eDIL s.v. íadach*. The meaning of *mealog* is uncertain; *eDIL s.v.* ? *melog*; as is *aiteog*; AL 6, *s.v. aiteog* suggests 'string' which is used to tie a bag, but *aiteog* glosses *iadag* in BL MS Harley 432. For the lemma and the last gloss, see *Cethairślicht Athgabálae* (CIH 379.9 and 25–26; AL 1: 152.24–25). For the lemma, cf. O'Dav 1110 (probably from *Bretha for Catślechtaib*; CCIH 141).

1224 Considering the surrounding entries, one would expect this entry to derive from *Cethairślicht Athgabálae*. For the lemma, cf. O'Dav 1515 (*Di Astud Chirt ⁊ Dligid*; CCIH 153); *Di Astud Chirt ⁊ Dligid* (CIH 243.33; AL 5: 490.8; CCIH 153). Cf. 13.d.18.30 TIGSEL. See O'Don. Suppl. *s.v. ticsel, tigseal, tixail.*

13.d.11.20 Fo-coisle .i. foxluig*h*.
Fo-coisle 'takes away', i.e. takes away.[1225]

13.d.11.21 Reac*h*oll mBr*eth* .i. roic*h*iall na mbr*eth*.
Recholl Breth 'shroud of judgements', i.e. [< *ro-* emphasizing part. + *cíall* 'wisdom, good sense, intelligence'] great-wisdom of the judgements.[1226]

13.d.12.22 Lug*arm*an .i. luga g*arm*an *nó* lingua g*ar*man no an g*arm*an ce*n* b[i]u(i)r.
Lúgarman 'spool-stick', i.e. [< *luga* 'smaller' (see *bec*, comp. corresponding to *lú*) + *garman* 'weaver's beam, club'] a smaller stick or [< *lingua* 'tongue' + *garman* 'weaver's beam, club'] *lingua* 'tongue' stick or the stick without a point.[1227]

13.d.13.23 Áig*h*e fine .i. cen*n*e fine.
Áige fine 'head of a kindred', i.e. heads of the kindred.[1228]

13.d.14.24 Ait[h]gi*n* snomtha f*edh*a .i. buain c*r*oin*n* d[e]na c*r*annuib.
Aithgein snomtha feda 'restitution for stripping the bark off a tree', i.e. removing the wood from the trees.[1229]

13.d.15.25 Ancharai .i. aoib*h*illt*h*eoir no deor*adh* De.
Ancharae 'anchorite', i.e. recluse or pilgrim of God.[1230]

1225 Cf. 8.13.35 FO-COISLE. For the lemma, see *Cethairślicht Athgabálae* (CIH 379.11; AL 1: 150.11); for a distant comparison with the lemma, cf. O'Dav 829 (*Bretha Nemed Toísech*; CCIH 132); and *Bretha Nemed Toísech* (CIH 2212.2; Breatnach 1989: §7; CCIH 132).

1226 For the lemma, see *Cethairślicht Athgabálae* (CIH 380.5; AL 1: 154.11); O'Dav 1389 (*Tosach Bésgnai*); *Tosach Bésgnai* (CIH 215.3; CCIH 149 and 293); and discussion of the title in Eska 2016.

1227 The interpretation of the entry is reliant on AL 1: 152.16–17. The lemma and gloss are found in *Cethairślicht Athgabálae* (CIH 379.7 and 21, and see note i).

1228 For the lemma, see *Cethairślicht Athgabálae* (CIH 380.6; AL 1: 154.12). The gloss appears to be plural, unless we should read it as *cenn na fine* 'head of the *fine*'; the grammatical context of the lemma is unambiguously singular. Cf. 9.31.94 ÁGHA FINE.

1229 For part of the lemma, cf. *Cethairślicht Athgabálae* (CIH 383.8; AL 1: 164.2) where it is part of a gloss on the main text. For damage to trees, see EIF 385–387.

1230 Cf. 12.b.3.17 ANCHARA DE. Considering the surrounding entries, one would expect the

13.d.15.26 Laoig*h*tec[h] no laoig*h* a lias ⟨.i. laoig*h* i tec[h] no cro⟩.
Lóegtech nó lóeg i lías 'calf-house or calf in a pen' ⟨i.e. calf in a house or enclosure⟩.[1231]

13.d.16.27 I*ar*masait .i. i*ar* mbr*eth* cl*ainn*e.
Iarmasait 'valuables', i.e. after judgement of kindred.[1232]

13.d.17.28 Cneam*h* cosaite .i. sort piseog.
Cnám cosaíte 'a bone of strife', i.e. a type of spell.[1233]

13.d.18.29 Cuic*h* apa nos m*ar*ba ⟨.i. piseoga⟩.
Coich apa nos-marba 'a bone that kills them', ⟨i.e. spells⟩.[1234]

13.d.18.30 Tigsel ⟨.i. buain⟩ .i. i*n* guimin ⟨.i. croce*nn*⟩ ro h-oige[d] ⟨.i. fuaig*edh*⟩ ui*m*pe.
Tíscál 'taking', ⟨i.e. depriving⟩, i.e. the hide ⟨i.e. hide⟩ that was sewn ⟨i.e. was sewn⟩ around her.[1235]

---

entry to derive from *Cethairṡlicht Athgabálae*. For the gloss, cf. *Bretha im Ḟuillemu Gell* (CIH 472.13; AL 5: 408.14) where it is a gloss on the main text.

1231 In view of the surrounding entries, one would expect the entry to derive from *Cethairṡlicht Athgabálae*.

1232 The interpretation of the entry is uncertain, especially as Dubhaltach corrected the original lemma. The lemma might be a plural form of *íarmaisi* 'valuables', or it could be from *íarbháis* 'posthumous'. Without a clear understanding of the lemma, it is difficult to arrive at the correct interpretation of the gloss, thus the translation is tentative. In view of the surrounding entries, one would expect the entry to derive from *Cethairṡlicht Athgabálae*.

1233 See *Cethairṡlicht Athgabálae* (CIH 388.9–10; AL 1: 180.24) where the entry is part of a gloss on the main text. The entry refers to a type of charm put in the marriage bed to make a husband impotent. For discussion of this entry and its larger context, see Borsje 2010: 180–182; Borsje 2021: 12–16; and Mistry 2015: 138–139. Cf. 13.d.18.29 CUICH APA NOS MARBA.

1234 For the interpretation of *coich* as 'bone' see *Dúil Laithne* § 23. Cf. 13.d.17.28 CNEAMH COSAITE. It is possible that the entry refers to giving a dog an enchanted morsel to test the efficacy of the spell; cf. *Cethairṡlicht Athgabálae* (CIH 388.15; AL 1: 180.31); and see Borsje 2010: 186.

1235 Cf. 13.d.10.19 TIGSEAL and 13.d.20.32 MARB-CNAI. For the lemma and most of the gloss, see *Cethairṡlicht Athgabálae* (CIH 890.32–33; CCIH 40); and cf. *Cethairṡlicht Athgabálae* (CIH 386.20; AL 1: 174.28). The larger context concerns stripping the dead, and here might refer specifically to stripping the shroud off the corpse as, for example, *colainn* 'corpse' is a fem. *i*-stem.

13.d.19.31 I*ar*mbre*th*[emn]us .i. ní t*ar* éis bre*th*em*h*nuis tuill*adh* leis.
Íarmbrethemnas 'final judgement', i.e. something after a judgement in addition to it.[1236]

13.d.20.32 M*ar*b-cnai .i. lomrad olla .i. ciro cnu olla .i. lomrad.
Marbcnaí 'covering of the dead', i.e. stripping of wool, i.e. a sheep fleece of wool, i.e. stripping.[1237]

13.d.21.33 Sloig*hedh* fuidre*ch*ta .i. slog*h* fuidir.
Slógad fuirdrechta 'a hosting of *fuidir*-tenants', i.e. a company of semi-freemen.[1238]

13.d.22.34 T*r*eas bunsac[h] [.i.] bon[n] loisg *ar* sgiat[h] ngeal.
Tress bunsach 'a battle of sticks', i.e. [< *1 bonn* 'sole of the foot, foot' + *losc* 'lame, crippled'] a lame foot in front of a bright shield.[1239]

13.d.23.35 Dubaig*idh* no cert f*or* cuaille ⟨.i. oig*h*id fedil⟩.
Dubaige nó ceirt for cúaille 'a mask or rag on a pole', ⟨i.e. a mask⟩.[1240]

13.d.24.36 Aire .i. trosgad*h*.
Aire 'against it', i.e. fasting.[1241]

1236 For the lemma, see *Cethairšlicht Athgabálae* (CIH 386.35; *AL* 1: 176.18) which is part of a gloss on the main text.

1237 The interpretation of *ciro* is uncertain because the reading is uncertain; cf. O'Reilly *s.v. círe* 'sheep'. For the lemma, see *Cethairšlicht Athgabálae* (CIH 386.22 and cf. 36; *AL* 1: 174.30 and 176.20). The entry refers to stripping the woolen shroud off of a corpse. Cf. 13.d.18.30 TIGSEL.

1238 On the obligations of the *fuidir* to his lord, see *GEIL* 33–35. The entry refers to the military service a *fuidir* owes his lord. For the lemma, see *Cethairšlicht Athgabálae* (CIH 386.39; *AL* 1: 176.24) which is part of a gloss on the main text.

1239 The entry refers to scaring the timid. Cf. 13.d.27.40 TREAS BUNSACH ⟨BONN AR SGIATH NGEAL⟩ .⁊C. and 13.d.23.35 DUBAIGIDH NO CERT FOR CUAILLE. For the lemma, see *Cethairšlicht Athgabálae* (CIH 387.5; *AL* 1: 178.1) where it is part of a gloss on the main text.

1240 Cf. 13.d.22.34 TREAS BUNSAC[H], 13.d.27.40 TREAS BUNSACH ⟨BONN AR SGIATH NGEAL⟩ .⁊C., and 13.a.6.2 DUBHAIGHID. For the lemma, see *Cethairšlicht Athgabálae* (CIH 387.6; *AL* 1: 178.1–2) where it is part of a gloss on the main text.

1241 The interpretation of the lemma is tentative, but it is based on the larger context of *Cethairšlicht Athgabálae* (CIH 366.17 (and gloss 2) and 367.7 (and gloss 4); *AL* 1: 116.15 and 118.7) where the tract refers to someone being fasted against. In these sections of the main text, *aire* must be understood as the preposition *ar* with a 3 sg. m. and n. suffixed pronoun. Both of the associated glosses contain *troscad* 'fasting'.

13.d.25.37 Codnac*h* t*airg*t*he*
Codnach táircthe 'a legally competent adult brought it about'[1242]

13.d.26.38 Turtgal .i. gail egent*ach* ⟨bi*us ar* m*h*naoi re br*eth* cloin*ne*⟩.
Turtgal 'violence', i.e. a violent injury ⟨that is done to a woman to [bring about] the birth of a child⟩.[1243]

13.d.26.39 Turtad .i. eigean ⟨.i. extor[t]ion⟩.
Turtugud 'compulsion', i.e. compulsion, ⟨i.e. *extortion*⟩.[1244]

13.d.27.40 T*r*eas bunsac*h* ⟨bon*n ar* sgiat*h* ngeal⟩ .⁊c., .i. m*ar* bud*h* as ⁊ en*n* b*eth* treas an*n acht* fallas com*h*lut*h* ngusgan*n*ail.
Tress bunsach, ⟨*bonn ar scíath ngel*⟩ .⁊c. 'a battle of sticks, ⟨a foot before a bright shield⟩, etc.', i.e. just as shoe and track there would be a battle there except for deceit circulating false reports.[1245]

14.b.1.1 Liasrad*h* .i. dénam lias no cro do laoguib et ceteri.
Líasrad 'tending of folds or pens', i.e. making a pen or fold for calves, etc.[1246]

1242 The interpretation of the entry is tentative as it is incomplete, unless it belongs with the following entry in the MS. The lemma refers to a legally competent adult who causes something to happen. The phrase also can be used of an inciter; *eDIL s.v. tárcud, táirciud.* Cf. *Cethairślicht Athgabálae* (*CIH* 366.17 (and gloss 2) and 367.7 (and gloss 4); *AL* 1: 116.15 and 118.7) where it might be possible for the entry here to refer to the legally competent adult who instigated the fasting referred to in this part of the potential source text. More distantly, cf. *Cethairślicht Athgabálae* (*CIH* 387.15; *AL* 1: 178.14) which refers to a legally competent adult instigating an action.

1243 The entry refers to inflicting an injury on a pregnant woman such that it brings about premature labor. For the lemma, see *Cethairślicht Athgabálae* (*CIH* 387.37; *AL* 1: 180.9) where it is part of a gloss on the main text. See O'Don. Suppl *s.v. turtgal.* Cf. Butler 2015: 193–197 for discussion of the same subject in medieval England. Cf. 3.b.10.43 TOGLUASACHT.

1244 See *eDIL s.v. ? 2 turtugud, turthugud.* Cf. OM 866 *Turtad .i. coimégniugud.* '*Turtugud*, i.e. compulsion'.; and for the lemma, cf. part of O'Dav 1154 (*Bretha Nemed Toísech*; *CCIH* 143). I am reluctant to emend the lemma as both OM and O'Dav have *turtad vel sim.* This is one of the few instances where Dubhaltach uses an English gloss. In view of the source of the surrounding entries, one would expect the entry to derive from *Cethairślicht Athgabálae.*

1245 The interpretation of the entry is tentative as the reading of the gloss is uncertain in places. The general sense seems to concern circulating rumors or a false fight. Cf. 13.d.22.34 TREAS BUNSAC[H] and 13.d.23.35 DUBAIGIDH NO CERT FOR CUAILLE. For the lemma, see *Cethairślicht Athgabálae* (*CIH* 387.5; *AL* 1: 178.1) where it is part of a gloss on the main text. For *enn*, see *eDIL s.v. 1 eng* 'track, trace'.

1246 For the lemma, cf. *Cáin Lánamna* § 11 gloss 3 (*CIH* 508.11; *AL* 2: 364.18).

14.b.2.2 Acht .i. [a]chtug*adh* dlig*ed*.
Acht 'stipulation', i.e. a stipulation of law.[1247]

14.b.2.3 *Air*esg, ⁊ *arus*g .i. cin*n*iod*h* dligt[h]*ech*.
Áiresc, ⁊ *árosc* 'condition', i.e. lawful agreement.[1248]

14.b.3.4 Faor .i. foirit*h*in no cob*air* g*h*eill.
Fáer 'delay', i.e. helping or assistance of a surety.[1249]

14.b.3.5 Urcorat*har* .i. at*h*cuirit[h]er .i. faidig*h*t[h]er.
Urcorathar 'is extended', i.e. is restored, i.e. is prolonged.[1250]

14.b.4.6 Coic[h] .i. de*ar*g.
Coich 'red', i.e. red.[1251]

14.b.4.7 Dunn .i. róid*h*.
Donn 'brown', i.e. brown-red.[1252]

14.b.4.8 Líog*h* .i. dat*h*.
Líg 'beautiful', i.e. color.[1253]

1247 For the lemma, cf. *Cáin Lánamna* §1 gloss 10 (*CIH* 502.23; *AL* 2: 342.22). Cf. 10.38.85 ACHT.

1248 For the lemma, cf. *Cáin Lánamna* §1 gloss 10 (*CIH* 502.23; *AL* 2: 342.22).

1249 See *Di Choimét Dligthech* (*CIH* 1751.16; *CCIH* 71); and Digest D (6) (*CIH* 1953.37–38; *CCIH* 78); *AL* 2: 100.18 and 102.4.

1250 See *eDIL s.vv. ar-cuirethar* and *fotaigid*, *fataigid*. See Digest D (6) (*CIH* 1953.36; *CCIH* 78). The entry might derive from material associated with *Di Choimét Dligthech* (*CIH* 1751.16; *CCIH* 71). Cf. 14.b.3.4 FAOR.

1251 See O'Dav 533 (no id.; *CCIH* 124: *Coic .i. der, ut est doformaig donn roidh cethraime, doformaig coic trian* [*.i. derg og roid*, F] "*Coic*, i.e. red, ut est 'dun *roid* increases (the value of cloth) a fourth, red increases it a third'."). Cf. 14.b.4.7 DUNN. This and the following entry concern dyes. For the historical development of Irish color terms, see Ó Fionnáin 2023: especially 19–31 for Old Irish color terms.

1252 See O'Dav 533 (no id.; *CCIH* 124: *Coic .i. der, ut est doformaig donn roidh cethraime, doformaig coic trian* [*.i. derg og roid*, F] "*Coic*, i.e. red, ut est 'dun *roid* increases (the value of cloth) a fourth, red increases it a third'."). *Donnroid* is a reddish-brown dye; *EIF* 268. Cf. 14.b.4.6 COIC[H]. This and the previous entry concern dyes. For the historical development of Irish color terms, see Ó Fionnáin 2023: especially 19–31 for Old Irish color terms.

1253 See *eDIL s.v. 1 lí* for the use of *líg* as the nom. sg. in glossaries. See O'Dav 1197 ((1) no id.; *CCIH* 144: *Lig .i. dath, ut est meser liga asa sóiri ⁊ asa suthain .i. mesemnacht in datha ar a mét is sóer do nech a beith ⁊ ar a marthanaigi* "*Líg*, i.e. colour, ut est 'thou shouldst

14.b.4.9 I*arr*at*h* .i. luac*h* oilemna.
Íarrath 'fosterage-fee', i.e. payment of fosterage.[1254]

14.b.4.10 Cumd[ach] meic g*ac* graid .7c .i. cen*nach* ber*ar* do nec*h* do c[h]ion*n* an m*ai*c do coim*hét* i n-ai*m*sir aonaig*h*, no re a at*hcar* for a at*hair* i*ar* ndiailtre, no luac[h] a(c) coim*et*ec*h*ta do b*h*erid do macaib*h* na (na) ngrad*h* as isle inaid fen.
Cumtach meic cach graid .7c 'supporting a son of each grade, etc.', i.e. a payment is given to someone by the head [i.e. legal guardian] of the son to be guarded in time of assembly, or for his being given to his father after the termination of fosterage, or payment for accompanying him which they give to the sons of the lower grades of his own place.[1255]

14.c.1.11 Sen smur cion*nadh* .i. i*ar* mbl*iad*ain .i. bl*iad*ain no ni as mo o do rin*ned* an cions*macht cair*de.
Sen smúr cinad 'old rust of crime', i.e. after a year, i.e. a year or any longer period from when the penalty fines of a treaty were established.[1256]

14.c.2.12 Fot*h*ana .i. m*edh*g.
Fothana 'curds', i.e. whey.[1257]

14.c.3.13 Ba feisi .i. fesda.
Bó feisi 'cow of spending the night', i.e. feast.[1258]

---

estimate colours by their nobleness and by their permanence', i.e. the estimation of the colour is according to the extent to which its existence is noble to one and according to its permanence."); and *The Evernew Tongue* at 110.3.

1254 The lemma is common in the legal texts concerning fosterage, e.g. *Cáin Íarraith*. For the lemma, cf. also the *Triads of Ireland* § 149. See O'Don. Suppl. *s.v. iarrath*.

1255 The entry concerns payments made for fostering sons. The entry likely comes from the fragmentary text *Cáin Íarraith*; cf. CIH 1762.5–8 which refers to supporting a son of a king. If the textual identification is correct, the tract quoted at the beginning of the entry is not attested elsewhere, and, thus, provides an otherwise lost fragment of the canonical tract.

1256 For the lemma, see *Cóic Conara Fugill* 53, § 118 H (CIH 1038.24). The translation of the last part of the gloss is tentative. The sense seems to be that any crimes committed after the treaty has been established are to be considered old crimes where no action is to be taken.

1257 See *Cáin Aicillne* 356, § 13 (CIH 483.32 and 484.3; AL 2: 254.5 and 16).

1258 The cow here in legal contexts is a payment from a defaulting debtor to his surety; the cow remains in the possession of the creditor. For the lemma, see *Di Gnímaib Gíall*

14.c.4.14 A bailiu i mbailiu
A bailiu i mbailiu 'from place to place'.[1259]

14.d.1.15 Met*h*ir .i. cert bi*us* im c*h*aoir*adh* claim*h*, uinge d'i*a*rann.
Meither 'covering', i.e. a piece of cloth which is around a mangy sheep, an ounce of iron.[1260]

14.d.3.16 Rud*h* .i. roid*h* .i. corc*air*.
Rud 'iron ore', i.e. madder, i.e. purple dye.[1261]

14.d.4.17 [Met*h*ir .i. cert bi*us* im c*h*aoir*adh* claim*h*, u]i[nge d'i*a*rann.]
Meither 'covering', i.e. a piece of cloth which is around a mangy sheep, an ounce of iron.[1262]

14.d.5.18 Rud*h* .i. ro[idh .i. corc]*air*.
Rud 'iron ore', i.e. madder, i.e. purple dye.[1263]

14.d.6.19 U*m*a (nu) [i]na cloit*h*ib*h* ⟨.i. na mianac*h*⟩ .i. on cloid*h*e .i. toc*h*ailt na tanalac*h* ⁊c .i. leaca.
Umae ina clóithib 'copper in the diggings', ⟨i.e. of the mines⟩, i.e. from *claide* 'digging', i.e. digging up the thin layers, etc., i.e. slabs of rock.[1264]

(CIH 1756.18; *AL* 2: 136.5; *CCIH* 288). The word *feis* has a range of meanings, including 'spending the night, bed, entertainment, feast'; *eDIL s.v. 2 feis(s)*, *fess*.

1259 See *Cethairṡlicht Athgabálae* (CIH 363.33; *AL* 1: 106.11) where the lemma is part of a gloss on the main text. The entry here is incomplete.

1260 The entry refers to the fine of an ounce for stealing the cloth covering off of a mangy sheep. See *Cethairṡlicht Athgabálae* (CIH 390.20–21; *AL* 1: 188.17) where the lemma is part of a gloss on the main text.

1261 As noted by Kelly (*EIF* 268, n. 150), the glossator in the source text has confused the word for 'iron ore', *rud*, with the word for 'madder', *roid.* which makes a red dye. See *Cethairṡlicht Athgabálae* (CIH 390.34–38; *AL* 1: 188.34–36, 190.1–2) where the lemma is part of a gloss on the main text. Cf. 14.d.5.18 RUDH.

1262 This is a repeat of 14.d.1.15 METHIR. The entry refers to the fine of an ounce for stealing the cloth covering off of a mangy sheep. See *Cethairṡlicht Athgabálae* (CIH 390.20–21; *AL* 1: 188.17) where the lemma is part of a gloss on the main text.

1263 This is a repeat of a previous entry in the MS. See 14.d.3.16 RUDH. As noted by Kelly (*EIF* 268, n. 150), the glossator in the source text has confused the word for 'iron ore', *rud*, with the word for 'madder', *roid.* which makes a red dye. See *Cethairṡlicht Athgabálae* (CIH 390.34–38; *AL* 1: 188.34–36, 190.1–2) where the lemma is part of a gloss on the main text.

1264 The interpretation of the entry is tentative as there could be a copying mistake in the

14.d.8.20 Inbleogain gill .i. *ara* ndleag*ur* geall do gab*ail*.
Inbleogain gill 'distraint of a pledge', i.e. so that a pledge should be taken.[1265]

14.d.9.21 Cróc*h* .i. gac n-*ard*h, g*ach* n-*air*egda.
Croch 'high', i.e. every high thing, every pre-eminent thing.[1266]

14.d.9.22 Croc*h* .i. ua*chtar*, ut [est] u*achtar* bain*ne*.
Cróch 'cream', i.e. top, *ut est* top of milk.[1267]

14.d.10.23 Brat gan lom*mus* .i. gan clúm.
Bratt cen lommus 'a covering without being threadbare', i.e. without feathers [which poke out].[1268]

14.f.1.24 Salla*ch* diollat ⟨.i. an t-edac*h* b*e*r*ar* [i]man salc*h*ar⟩ .i. brat gan lom*da*, ⁊ ion*ar* gan toll*us*, no brat dub, ⁊ ion*ar* dub*h*. ní b*e*rt*ar* do*n* oide o at[h]*air*, ⁊ o mat[h]air an lenib*h* taob amuig don *iarrath*. (bo d*h*e*ar*ba m*ar* si*n*) dana altrom go tog*h*a .i. i ccin*n* .xiiii. bl*iadna* do ing*h*in, i ccion*n* sec*h*t mbl*iadna* deg do mac .i. a ttog*h*a i cill no i ttuait*h* no a bpos⟨ad⟩ ⁊c̄.
Salach díllat 'a child's swaddling clothes', ⟨i.e. the clothes that are put on the filth [i.e. to keep the child clean]⟩, i.e. a covering without bareness, and a tunic without a hole, or a black covering, and

lemma. It is also possible that the glossator in the source text did not fully understand all of the terms in the text. The entry as it stands refers to mining copper ore. See *Cethairšlicht Athgabálae* (CIH 390.36; AL 1: 188.34–36) where the lemma is part of a gloss on the main text. Cf. 14.d.3.16 RUDH. For the use of *on* in glossing, see Breatnach 1990b.

1265 Without the larger context, it is difficult to interpret the lemma.

1266 Cf. *SC* Y.273 *Crochcuit .i. croc cach n-ard ⁊ cach n-ind. cuid aesa airegde ind sin*. Cf. 14.d.9.22 CROCH.

1267 The lemma is a later form of *croth* 'cream, curds', although here it could be a misreading of ⟨c⟩ for ⟨t⟩; *eDIL s.v. 2 cróch*. This entry in many ways is explained by the previous one; cream (lit. 'top of milk' in the gloss) rises to the top of the milk. See O'Dav 494 (*Dúilchinni*; CCIH 123 and n. 79: *Croich .i. uachtar bainne, ut est is* [*co* F] *croich no lemnacht do ughdar sóir* "*Croich*, i.e. cream (lit. top of milk), ut est 'it is with cream or new-milk to a noble author'."). Cf. 14.d.9.21 CRÓCH

1268 The lemma glosses *lommus* 'thread bareness'. See *Cáin Íarraith* (CIH 1762.19; AL 2: 160.17) where the lemma is part of a gloss. Cf. 14.f.1.24 SALLACH DIOLLAT. I should like to thank one of the anonymous readers for comments on this entry.

a black tunic. Things which are given to the foster-father from the father and the mother of the child apart from the fosterage-fee. (A milch cow for that) for the fosterage until [the age of] choice, i.e. at the end of 14 years for a girl, at the end of 17 years for a boy, i.e. their choice for the church or for the laity or for marriage, etc.[1269]

14.f.13.25 Serg, ⁊ macra .i. galra bid *ar* lenbuib*h*.
Serg, ⁊ macrae 'wasting sickness, and illness', i.e. sicknesses which children get.[1270]

14.f.16.26 Fo-fe, ⁊ fo-fi ⁊ fo-fic*h* .i. fua*cht*naig*adh* .i. ofence.
Fo-fe, ⁊ fo-fi ⁊ fo-fich 'commits an offence, and commits an offence, and commits an offence', i.e. does injury, i.e. *offence*.[1271]

14.g.1.27 Ta[lent]um Lá[tene], talenton Graeca. Talanntan [i] nGaoid[hilge].
Talentum Látene 'talent in Latin', *talenton Graeca* 'talent in Greek'. *Tallann* 'talent' in Irish.[1272]

1269 The sense of the first part of the gloss is that the swaddling clothes are given against filth, i.e. given to keep the children clean. If we interpret *ní bertar* as 'they are not given', it would contradict what is found in *Cáin Íarraith* where swaddling clothes are given to the nurse along with the fosterage-fee. For the first half of the entry, see *Cáin Íarraith* (*CIH* 1762.18–20; *AL* 2: 160.14–17; also 1764.36 and 902.7–8; *AL* 2: 170.10–11). For the age at which fosterage ends, see *GEIL* 88–89. Cf. 14.d.10.23 BRAT GAN LOMMUS.

1270 One would expect this entry to be found in *Cáin Íarraith*, but it is not in any of the surviving fragments of the text. For part of the lemma, cf. O'Dav 1247 (probably from *Bretha for Catšlechtaib*; *CCIH* 145: *Macrae .i. toirse no mifre...* "*Macrae*, i.e. sadness or dejection..."). It is possible that we should understand *macra* as *eDIL* x.v. *? 2 mac(c)rad* 'sickness, disease'.

1271 The first two parts of the lemma are presumably all forms of *fo-fich* 'commits an offence', but which forms is uncertain. The verb *fúachtnaigid* 'is aggressive or violent, makes an attack, does injury' frequently glosses *fo-fich* in the legal texts; *eDIL s.v. fo-fich*. This is one of the rare instances where Dubhaltach glosses an Irish term with an English word.

1272 The missing letters are supplied from O'Curry's transcription. The context of the entry is unknown. This is the only example of Greek in Dubhaltach's Glossary. The form *lá* seems to be derived on the analogy of *lá* 'day' from earlier *laithne*; the form *Laithne* is used as the gen. sg. of *Laiten* 'Latin' in the title of another glossary copied by Dubhaltach, *Dúil Laithne*. It is also possible that Dubhaltach left out a suspension mark. Dubhaltach made numerous annotations in Greek in his grandfather's copy of *Sanas Cormaic*; cf. TCD MS 1317 [H.2.15B], p. 163.

14.h.1.28 Foguirre, dog*h*uirre .i. fuaidr*edh*.
Foguirriud, doguirriud 'opposition', i.e. impugning.[1273]

14.h.2.29 As, los, gert .i. as na collu, los na lag*h*, gert an tu*ar* .⁊c̄.
Ás, los, gert 'growth, increase, manure', i.e. *ás* 'growth' [means] the bodies, *los* 'increase' [means] the calves, *gert* 'product' [means] the manure.[1274]

14.h.4.30 Fresgisin imsc*air* .i. saoil*acht*ain iomsg*artha*.
Frescissin imscair 'hope of separation', i.e. hope of parting mutually.[1275]

14.h.5.31 Miasl*ach* bo, no g*a*c[h] mil .i. miof*h*ocal dio*m*olta do beir duine *ar* boin e .⁊c̄.
Míaslach bó, nó cach míl 'dung of a cow, or of every animal', i.e. a bad word of excessive praise that a person calls a cow, etc.[1276]

14.h.7.32 Flait*h* cuitrid .i. an t*r*eas flait*h* do be*r* rat*h* do ceile.
Flaith cuitrid 'lord of a share', i.e. one of the three lords who gives a *rath* to a client.[1277]

14.h.8.33 At*h*c*h*ur saoire go seduib .i. an tan ata an f[*lai*]t*h*, ⁊ an cele i mbet*h*ad*h*, no ata an d*a*r*a* de ⁊ as m*a*rb*h* *ar*aile.

1273 The second word in the lemma appears to be a variant of the first; *eDIL s.v. foguir(r)iud, fogurrad*. For the gloss, see *eDIL s.v. fúaitriud*. See the first part of O'Dav 953 (*Cáin Lánamna*; CCIH 136: *Fogurradh .i. fuaidrid…* "*Fogurrad* ('proclamation, public notice'), i.e. of opposition…"); *Cáin Lánamna* § 22 and gloss 6 (CIH 512.31 and 513.4; AL 2: 382.3). In view of the fact that the remaining entries in this section of the glossary derive from *Cáin Ṡóerraith*, it is surprising that this entry does not seem to do so. That being said, it could derive from a different version of the text.

1274 See *Cáin Ṡóerraith* § 3, and discussion in Thurneysen 1925a: 241–243 (CIH 1771.9 and 1772.18–19; AL 2: 198.z and 200.1–2; CCIH 288–289). For discussion, see also EIF 230, n. 78; and Stokes 1903: 13. The combination of growth, increase, and manure (or milk because *gert* is also used of milk) is found frequently in the legal texts.

1275 The first word in the lemma and the gloss are in the acc. sg; *eDIL s.vv. frescisiu, frescsiu* and *saílechtu*. See *Cáin Ṡóerraith* § 3, and discussion in Thurneysen 1925a: 241 (CIH 1772.3; AL 2: 198.16; CCIH 288–289) where the lemma is found in commentary. See O'Don. Suppl. *s.v. fresgisin*.

1276 For the lemma, see *Cáin Ṡóerraith* § 3 (CIH 1772.19–21; AL 2: 200.3–6; CCIH 288–289).

1277 See *Cáin Ṡóerraith* § 5, and discussion in Thurneysen 1925a: 247 (CIH 1773.29; AL 2: 202.26; CCIH 288–289) where the lemma is part of a commentary.

Athchor saíre co sétaib 'returning the *saer*-stock with *séts*', i.e. when the lord and the client are both alive, or one of them is and the other is dead.[1278]

14.h.11.34 Ath*c*[h]ur saoire gan seoda .i. an tan as m*ar*b a ndís.
Athchor saíre cen séota 'returning the *saer*-stock without *séts*', i.e. when both of them are dead.[1279]

14.h.12.35 Déisde, fesd*h*ide, no esdide .i. tioru*air*si .i. fuigioll.
Deistiu, festide, nó estide 'remnant, residuary legatee, or heir', i.e. remnant, i.e. remainder.[1280]

14.h.13.36 M*a*c sg*r*ine .i. m*a*c do-[g]ni f*er* re coibdeal*ach* ⟨na riocht fen⟩ .i. cuirt*er* i sg*r*in lea*thair* e amac[h] *ar* muir in *airet* b*us* leir gelsgiat*h* .⁊c̄.
Mac scríne 'son of a shrine', i.e. a son whom the father begets on a kinswoman ⟨in her own form⟩, i.e. he is put into a leather shrine out on the sea as far as a white shield will be visible.[1281]

1278 The missing letters are supplied from O'Curry's transcription. See *Cáin Ṡóerraith* § 5, and discussion in Thurneysen 1925a: 248 (*CIH* 1775.5–7; *AL* 2: 208.15–17; *CCIH* 288–289) where the entry is part of a commentary on the main text.

1279 See *Cáin Ṡóerraith* § 5, and discussion in Thurneysen 1925a: 248 (*CIH* 1775.8; *AL* 2: 208.18; *CCIH* 288–289) where the entry is part of a commentary on the main text.

1280 The last word in the lemma is a variant of *festid* 'residuary legatee, heir'. See O'Dav 896 (*Bretha Nemed Toísech*; *CCIH* 134: *Feistidh no deisti .i. tiruairsi no comarba fil dia eis in fir mairb, amail adeir* [*Duil Roscadach* F] *ar is cach feistidh fiach frisgni marbfolta, no is é gnías tagra iman folaid agartar for in marb* "*Feistid* or *deisti*, i.e. remainder, or a successor who is after the dead man, as saith the Duil Roscadach 'for it is every successor of debts that serves dead-wealths', or it is he that brings a suit for the wealth that is claimed from the dead man.") and note that the F version attributes the entry to *Dúil Roscadach* (*CCIH* 134); cf. *Bretha Nemed Tóisech* (*CIH* 2227.30), but it is not a close match for this entry. See also *Cáin Ṡóerraith* § 6, 249 and 250 (*CIH* 1776.18 and gloss 3; *AL* 2: 212.20 and 25) for one of the lemmata. Cf. 7.a.3.4 DÉISTE and 7.a.1. FEISTE.

1281 The entry refers to putting the child begotten of incest into a leather box which was to be left on the sea as far away from land as a white shield could be visible. The phrase *na riocht fen* is problematic. It could refer to recognizing the woman as being a kinswoman, in other words, it was not a case of mistaken identity or being unaware that the woman was a relative. It is also possible, as suggested by O'Neill 2017: 3, that the woman was a kinswoman by blood and not by "marriage or adoption." See *Córus Fine* (*CIH* 744.28–29; *CCIH* 235–239; Byrne 1930: 98; and O'Neill 2017: 3). It should be noted that Dubhaltach owned the section of TCD MS 1337 [H.3.18] where *Córus Fine* is found (O'Sullivan 2000: 442).

14.h.15.37 Cíos n-*air*dbide .i. *air*debe cin*n*t*a*c[h] do b*air*gin no do l*eth*b*air*g*h*en, do tsen fine bi*us* si*n* .⁊c̄.
Cís n-airdbide 'specified rent', i.e. specified stipulation for a loaf or for half a loaf, that is for the old kin, etc.[1282]

14.h.17.38 Faer (air) se*cht*mui*n* .i. foirit*h*in im *tr*ebad*h* do b*h*eir an cele do*n* flait*h* isi*n* se*cht*mui*n*, faor buana ma*r* si*n*.
Fáer (air) sechtmain 'delay [of plowing] for a week', i.e. helping with plowing that the client gives the lord during the week, a delay of reaping is likewise.[1283]

14.h.19.39 Fuaichne fog*h*la .i. fóic*h*nín, no foic[h]enn, no mat*hair* fog*h*la, no tos*a*c[h] cointine.
Foichne fogla 'a shoot of contention', i.e. *foichnín*, or *foichenn* 'blade of young corn', or mother [i.e. beginning] of damage, or beginning of contention.[1284]

14.h.20.40 M*air*b*h*elod*h* .i. dol o dlig*adh* ⁊ se beo, beoelod*h* .i. [i]s contra.
Marbélúd 'evading due to death', i.e. escaping from what is due and he still living, *béoélúd* 'evading while living', i.e. it is the opposite.[1285]

1282 See the passage from a commentary on adoption for care of the elderly, *CIH* 161.21–22 (*CCIH* 20). As many of the other surrounding passages in Oxford MS Rawl.B.506 also concern kindred and/or derive in part from *Córus Fine*, it could well be that the ultimate source of this passage is *Córus Fine* as indicated by Dubhaltach in his glossary.

1283 The parentheses in the lemma are in the MS. For the lemma and part of the gloss, see *Cethairṡlicht Athgabálae* (*CIH* 394.16–17; *AL* 1: 200.7).

1284 The entry is problematic for a number of reasons. The context of the entry is not secure, but see *CIH* 143.14, which is from a section concerning the lord and his client (*CCIH* 18). For the first half of the lemma, see *eDIL s.v. foichne*, which suggests reading *foglas* instead of *foghla* in other examples of the phrase, thus giving 'greenish corn blades' here; cf. *Cóir Anmann* 110 (109 in Stokes 1897). This interpretation, however, does not fit well with the glosses which refer to the start of injury and strife; cf. the first part of O'Dav 1212 (no id.; *CCIH* 144: *Mathair .i. tosach*... "*Máthair*, i.e. beginning..."). Cf. 14.h.20.40 MAIRBHELODH. It is likely that the commentary in *CIH* 143.14 derives from *Cáin Aicillne*; see *CIH* 1781.14 (*AL* 2: 230.z) for the lemma which is found within a commentary. It is possible, following *AL*, that the entry refers to trespass injury; see *eDIL s.v. fúachtain*; the form *fuaichne* here might be a later derivative. See O'Don. Suppl. *s.v. fuaichne foghla*.

1285 See the commentary at *CIH* 143.1 and 14, which is from a section concerning the lord and his client (*CCIH* 18). It is likely that the commentary in *CIH* 143.14 derives from *Cáin Aicillne*. See *Cáin Aicillne* § 5, 343 (*CIH* 1780.29 and 1781.11–14; *AL* 2: 228.16 and 230.18–22) where parts of the entry are found in a commentary. The second part of the entry

14.h.20a.41 At[h]gab*ail ar* fud .i. atg*h*aba*l* sa h-anad*h* bi*us* i laim*h* biodb*adh*.
Athgabáil ar fut 'distraint after delay', i.e. distraint in respect of being delayed which is in the hand of the defendant.[1286]

14.h.21a.42 At*h*gab*ail* tulla .i. i laim fech*eman* toich*eda* bi*us* a h-and[a] tre oibne.
Athgabáil tulla 'immediate distraint', i.e. it will be in the hand of the plaintiff during the period of stay on account of suddenness.[1287]

14.h.22.43 Ces loin ⟨aisill loin⟩, no dena.
Ces lóin ⟨aisill lóin⟩, nó dena 'rump steak ⟨rump steak⟩, or make'.[1288]

14.h.23.44 Anbfolta aigilline, mailis an cele, ma*r* b*eth* biad ⟨goide⟩ do tab*air*t do*n* flait*h* ma*r* bia[d].
Anfolta aicillne, mailís in chéili, mar beth biad goide do thabairt don ḟlaith mar biad. 'misconducts of base clientship, the client's evil-doing, such as giving ⟨stolen⟩ food to the lord as food'.[1289]

---

refers to the tenant absconding with the stock advanced to him by his lord while his lord is still alive. Cf. 14.h.19.39 FUAICHNE FOGHLA.

1286 The *sa* in the gloss in unexpected; it might be an error for *as*. See *Cethairṡlicht Athgabálae* (*CIH* 396.15; *AL* 1: 208.19, z, and 210.1) where most of the entry is found in a commentary. In this form of distraint, the distrained items are given to the plaintiff when the period of delay is finished. See the discussion in Binchy 1973: 35–51 where he suggests that this stage in the distraint process happens before the stage referenced in 14.h.21a.42 ATHGABAIL TULLA below.

1287 See *Cethairṡlicht Athgabálae* (*CIH* 397.16; *AL* 1: 208.24 and 212.29) where most of the entry is found in a commentary. In this form of distraint, the commentaries state that the distrained property is brought to the plaintiff immediately upon being taken. See the discussion in Binchy 1973: 51–65 where he suggests that this stage in the distraint process happens after the stage referenced in 14.h.20a.41 AT[H]GABAIL AR FUD. He suggests that the later commentators misunderstood parts of the legal stages of distraint and that we do not have two different types of distraint but rather two different stages in the process (56).

1288 The entry is incomplete. The interpretation of the last word is uncertain as it does not appear in the version of the source text listed here. One wonders if it is not a mistake for *tona*, which would give us another term for a rump steak; cf. *ces tona* (*CIH* 1781.21). The interpretation here of *dena* as being an impv. 2 sg. form of *do-gní* is not satisfactory. See *Cáin Aicillne* § 6, 346 (*CIH* 1781.24–25; *AL* 2: 232.13–14) where the lemma and gloss are found in a commentary.

1289 The entry appears to be incomplete, but it is possible that ⟨.i.⟩ was left out after *aigillne*. See *Cáin Aicillne* § 7, 347 (*CIH* 1781.32–33; *AL* 2: 234.14) where part of the entry is found in a gloss.

14.h.24.45 Tat*hchar ar* díu*m*un*n* .i. at*h*c[h]ur *ar* dimiad*h*aig*h*e lais b*eth* aige .i. nac*h* fiu leis an cele b*eth* agan flait*h*, no leis an flait*h* an cele do b*eth* aige.

Tathchor ar diumann 'giving back on account of contempt', i.e. giving back on account of contempt that he has for him, i.e. it is not fitting for the client to be with the lord, or for the lord to have the client.[1290]

Entries in O'Curry's Transcription Which Have Not Been Found in the MS

OC.1 Elg .i. ere.

Elg 'Ireland', i.e. Ireland.[1291]

OC.2 Finne .i. fine duthaidh.

Fínné 'witness', i.e. natural kinsman.[1292]

OC.3 Fithis .i. fath uais.

Fithis 'ring', i.e. [< *fath* 'covering' + *úais* 'noble'] noble covering.[1293]

OC.4 Foir [...] .i. remheach.

Fóir [...] 'pursuing party [...]' i.e. coursing.[1294]

OC.5 Mac saoir lethe .i. mac aga mbi ceannus sealbha ⁊ maoine ara aithidh fein.

Mac saoir lethe 'a half-free son', i.e. a son who has command of property and of wealth for his own repaying.[1295]

1290 Here Dubhaltach quotes a section of the laws concerning parting from one's lord or client out of contempt. See *Cáin Aicillne* § 56 (CIH 1802.12–13; *AL* 2: 328.21 and 24).

1291 See *SC* Y.510 *Elg .i. Ere no ordricc.* Cf. 4.c.11.71 ELGE.

1292 The interpretation of the entry is tentative.

1293 The interpretation of the entry is tentative. See *eDIL s.v. fithis* 'circuit, channel, loop, ring'.

1294 The interpretation of the entry is tentative. See *eDIL s.v. 3 fóir* 'pursuing party, rescuers, crew, company'; Dinneen *s.v. réimeach* 'coursing, in full career, in the ascendant'.

1295 The sense of the entry might be that the son has command of his own wealth in order either to pay for his own debts or pay for his freedom. This category of son is not listed in *eDIL s.v. 1 mac, macc.*

Transcription

What follows is a close transcription of the manuscript. Where my reading differs from O'Curry's, I have indicated that in the notes. I have not indicated systematic differences which result from the fact that O'Curry regularly transcribes manuscript long 'e' as ⟨ea⟩, and he regularly adds glide vowels when expanding contracted syllables, such as ⟨aigh⟩ or ⟨uidh⟩. The close transcription preserves Dubhaltach's punctuation, but the edited text adds full stops to the end of every entry. Editorial insertions are in [square] brackets. Dubhaltach himself uses round brackets within his glossary, which have been reproduced in the transcription (where round brackets are otherwise not used). Expanded manuscript abbreviations are in *italics* in both the transcription and edited text. The ⟨angled brackets⟩ in the transcription and edited text are used to indicate that the enclosed material has been written above the main line of the text. Where Dubhaltach has underlined a word or phrase in the MS, that has been represented in the transcription but not in the edited text. Manuscript ⟨ꜵ⟩ and ⟨æ⟩ have been transcribed as such, but they have been changed to ⟨ao⟩ and ⟨ae⟩, respectively, in the edited text.

Where letters in the manuscript are not legible, they have been indicated by ellipses within square brackets, e.g. [...]. To the best of my ability, I have tried to indicate where there is text, even if it is not legible. There are some entries which O'Curry was able to read which I cannot. Those entries have been included in the transcription and translation as close to their conjectured original position as possible. This has been made possible by the fact that O'Curry includes the manuscript page numbers next to entries which he can only partially read. O'Curry's notes are included with his transcription in the volume (pp. 367–409). There are some entries which I have not been able to locate; these are included at the end of the transcription and edition. There are some entries which I have been able to read but were not included in O'Curry's transcription. These entries have been noted in the close transcription of the manuscript and in the notes to the edited text. The notes to the edited text are mainly concerned with the contents of the entry rather than differences between O'Curry's reading of the manuscript and my own. Differences in manuscript readings are confined to the notes in the close transcription so as to keep the notes in the edited text from becoming too unwieldly.

 | DOI:10.1163/9789004755673_006

TCD MS 1401, p. 1[1]

[a]1 [.]ara .i. [.]sa[.]dibadh.[2] [..]aforfog*h*t as .i. eig*h*em *ar*n[..]p[..] dl[..]oc*ar* as ro [..]ug no [......][3]

2 .i. [..]ur*n*[.] na cric*h*e sin fes[.]. anurr*adh* .i. fer [..]t[4] cuigid do eod[.]a [...]a .i. c[.]c [....] mi[..] .i. a[.]*ous*[..][5]

3 [..]gigd[.]. tuillem*h* an ciont*aigh* .i. a cain*achte* ⁊ [.]dib.[6] bainleab*aidh* .i. biat*had* do b*ei*r fine di *ar*oile gan oion[.....]s[7] [....]

4 [..] fo luig*h*e cána. bán .i. fíor.[8] mesioc*h* .i. cui*m*gec[9] adbo .i. toibgel*us*.[10] aig*h*e .i. og*h* æ.[11] Airecor*us* [..] .i. dui*n*e do[..][12]

5 [...]c[..]dæirib*h* biat*hus* [..] .i. duine eric anisi da[....]s ce[.]*et*an [.]r*ar* cuire cuit*h* [..]l[.][13]

6 [.]ba fiallac*h* go t*r*i nonb*ar*uib*h*. slóg*h* i*ar*mota.[14] corc[15] .i. clan*n* no cinel.[16] o[..]*ar*n [...]

7 [.]uid*h* .i. ogluc*h* bi*us* ag dol f*r*ia [..]ll[.]uib. rod*h*aid*he* .i. duine teglom*us* roid*h* .i. cinel derg[17] //)[18] t*r*iall c[..]

8 [t]uid*h*rec ⟨folu⟩ .i. do d*h*erac*h* fola doní an liaig*h* ag sgæil*adh* cuislenn.[19] fiac*h* iom*raid*h na gaide .i. a luad ag

---

1 There is a lot of scattered staining on the page. Both sides of the page are damaged and missing parts of the text.

2 The first letter could be a ⟨t⟩ or a ⟨d⟩; the second letter is uncertain.

3 None of this line is in O'Curry's transcription.

4 Perhaps for 'bert'?

5 None of this line is in O'Curry's transcription.

6 The reading is uncertain. This entry is not in O'Curry's transcription.

7 The last two words may or may not belong to the entry; the reading of the last word is tentative. They are not included in O'Curry's transcription of the entry.

8 This entry is not in O'Curry's transcription.

9 This entry is not in O'Curry's transcription.

10 The reading of this word is uncertain. This entry is not in O'Curry's transcription.

11 This entry is not in O'Curry's transcription.

12 This entry is illegible. This entry is not in O'Curry's transcription.

13 Most of this line is illegible.

14 The beginning of this entry is illegible.

15 A gloss above this word has been erased.

16 This entry is not in O'Curry's transcription.

17 It is uncertain whether this entry ends here. This entry is not in O'Curry's transcription.

18 '//)' is used to indicate a type of symbol known as a *cenn fo eite* 'head under wing' which is used by scribes to indicate that the text which follows it belongs with the text at the end of the line below it.

19 This entry is not in O'Curry's transcription.

9 [...]inges .i. do cui*mg*h*ith*i*edh* .i. conigsiod.[20] coim*h*c*h*isi .i. coi*mh*fec*h*ain. rergad*air* .i. ro reimn*ighed*ar. brot*h* .i. brat*h* doni

10 ꝏn*ar*,[21] combrot*h* .i. b*r*at*h* maille re duine eile.[22] áindlicet .i. ionglaine no neim*h*cet, licet[23] .i. cetoig[the][24]

11 [.]sreol[.]c[25] .i. lu*cht* ⟨ɫ fer⟩ f*aire*.[26] ad c*h*eat*h* .i. ad-c*h*if*eth*. p*r*oiceptai .i. sermonuig*h*.[27] coim*hg*niom*h* .i. coim*hgh*niom*agh*ad*h* cion*adh* ag daran*n* rete

12 fec*ht* ⟨[..]ad[.]⟩[28] *air*m*h*idin .i. *ar*rac*htus* do nid dꝏine ag t*ar*raing b*eth*adh*aigh* as lath*aig*. fiac*h* duineacait*he* .i. fiac*h* an c*h*ionuid*h* an c*h*a[i]

13 [th]m*he*[29] do denad*h* duine. *air*lim .i. leím *air* .i. leim do berid *air*neis *ar* g*h*ort, no *ar* fer, no *ar* clad*h*. t*air*rsce .i. t*air*iscia[30] .i. ceim

14 [n]iug*adh*[31] do nid sp*r*e t*ar* fer no gort .⁊c̄. diog*h*uin feoir.[32] eat*ham*iain[33] .i. s*ar*ug*adh* fer ferain*n* da ttig somꝏin eat*h*a .⁊c̄.

15 brec*h*tán .i. cinel annluin*n*. treoir .i. eol*us* no t*r*eóir do ní nec*h* dfogl*aigh*ib*h*.[34] cu seic*h*ill .i. cú bi*us* ag seic*h*em

16 eic*h* o s*h*ealluib*h* o suilib*h* .i. cu do cí duine aga lenm*h*ui*n* ⁊ n*ach* leis fein í. tacomul .i. cengal. foc*h*uir*adh*

17 [.i.] g*air*m no t*air*ring do ni nec*h* *ar* coin. dag do ait .i. an g*r*is gabail. duirb .i. dae do*n* rob*et* don orba .i. don ⟨im⟩[35] feran*n*

---

20 This entry is not in O'Curry's transcription.

21 There might be a long word lost with the damaged edge of the page.

22 O'Curry breaks this entry into two and omits some of the words.

23 Dubhaltach switches to roman script for this Latin word.

24 Part of the ⟨t⟩ (or a letter which starts in a similar manner) is visible at the end of the line. The remaining two letters are conjectured as the edge of the page is damaged; another potential reading is ⟨aid⟩. The second half of the entry is not in O'Curry's transcription.

25 The reading of the headword is very uncertain.

26 This entry is not in O'Curry's transcription.

27 O'Curry reads 'searmontaigh'.

28 The beginning of the line is damaged, so this reading is not secure. There is a word above this which is mostly illegible: ⟨[..]ad[.]⟩. The gloss is not included in O'Curry's transcription.

29 O'Curry reads 'caithmhe'. Both edges of the page are damaged, and it is difficult to see all the letters which O'Curry reads. The missing letters are supplied from O'Curry's transcription. At the beginning of l. 13, the letters look more like ⟨dṅe⟩.

30 O'Curry reads 'tairisciu'.

31 The missing letter is supplied from O'Curry's transcription.

32 Above the ⟨f⟩ is the abbreviation for ⟨er⟩ which has been crossed out in a lighter colored ink.

33 O'Curry reads 'eathamain'. The final syllable is difficult to read.

34 O'Curry transcribes 'dfogluighibh'.

35 The ⟨im⟩ is not in O'Curry's transcription. It is difficult to determine whether it is meant to be a correction or a gloss.

18 duibell .i. dæ da neibill an teine saig*h*nen. tap .i. oban*n*.[36] fer asa he .i. fer ler leis. tad*h*b*h*uis .i. taisbo*n*si

[b]1 fualang .i. teit*h*em*h* no a l*ethét*.[37] ceirt iomain .i. am*h*uil ro imeoc*h*aidis an *air*neis fein gan iomain

2 iomain ⟨.i. an eall*aigh*⟩ sgoric[38] an duine .i. na g*h*ort feoir no *ar*b*ha* ⁊ *ar*d urc*har* flesga[39] ⁊ t*r*i desce[im]en*na*[40] o t*h*ire a tuai*m* ⟨.i. raoi[..] om[..] *e*rad*he* ⁊ [.]acli an l*eth* ber[.] as⟩[41]

3 sec*htar* c*r*ic*h* .i. g*ach* ionad osin amac*h*.[42] iomaig*h* .i. iomain .i. tio*m*ain. andom*h*na .i. inde doia*mh*ne[43] isna[44] cuit*h*ec*h*a .⁊c̄

4 iomt*h*ac*h* .i. eimt*h*oinge. follan .i. mait*h* slan. cobran*na* gall .i. coirt*he* bi*us* a c*h*in*n* t*h*ire. foic*h*lige .i. foc*h*lœid[45] .i. to

5 c*h*ailt. ceat*h*ra .i. cœi doib*h* iot*h*ra. lias cœr*ac* .i. c*r*o cœr*ac*. eic*h*las, ⁊ bacg*h*abail .i. ait i mbid eic*h*.

6 dic*h*eall diceilt .i. ad*h*bal c*h*eilt. *cét*ciont*ach* .i.[46] bit*h*ben*ac*. direg*ar* .i. dergit*h*er. ruir*mh*id .i. ro *air*m*h*id. toig*h*len[nan][47] ⟨.i. lendan⟩[48]

7 de sec*h*tmui*ne*[49] .i. sec*ht* b*air*gen. tuat*h*gabail .i. ~~amui~~[50] gabail bi*us* *ete*r na da t*h*uait*h* amuil ataid .h. eric maig*he* la

8 mum*h*uin. aclaig*he* .i. íoc lóig*he*. acluig*h*ed*h* .i. iocuid lóg*h*. tallaid .i. tuaslaicid. gadaig*h* .i. beanuid*h*. goilid*he* .i.

9 luid*he* ég*he* mar d*er*t*er* lesi*n* g*r*ein. turlais ⟨ł tuluid⟩ .i. luaid*h*is. cic*h*siod .i. ceímn*igh*siod. fesat*ar*, fiasat*ar* .i. fuac*htn*aigter

10 ciuc*hus*t*ar* .i. ceimn*ighius*t*ar*. duin*n* .i. flait*he*. aib*h*riteod*h* .i. ab*h*ratód*h* no soad*h* .i. an tan do fuit a hab*hr*a d*ar* an súil.

---

36 O'Curry reads 'obunn'.
37 O'Curry reads 'leitheid'.
38 O'Curry reads 'sgeric'.
39 O'Curry reads 'sleigid'.
40 The letters in the middle of the word are difficult to read. I have relied on O'Curry's transcription to fill in the letters which I cannot see.
41 The gloss starts above *arbha*. O'Curry does not print the gloss.
42 O'Curry combines this entry with the previous entry.
43 O'Curry reads 'doimne'. The middle letters in the word are difficult to read, so the reading is not certain.
44 This word is omitted in O'Curry's transcription.
45 O'Curry reads 'sochlaoidh'.
46 The ⟨.i.⟩ looks similar to a ⟨⁊⟩; it is possible that Dubhaltach conflated the two.
47 The missing letters are supplied from O'Curry's transcription.
48 The gloss is squeezed in at the edge of the page above the headword.
49 The lemma is not in O'Curry's transcription.
50 This word has been crossed out.

11 seis .i. t*air*is .i. dén co*m*n*aigh*e. Seis[51] .i. ionsaigh. t*arr*ac*h*taig*h* .i. nec*h* t*arr*aig*h*t*er*. dúisi .i. di uaisi .i. mionn*a* adbal

12 [ú]aisle. ocmoda .i. tad*h*all, adall. comaitg*h*es .i. coim*h*d*eacht*. noaig*h*t*er*,[52] núit*h*er .i. ord*er*cuigt*er*. bad*h*ad*h* .i. ebl*edh*

13 ad-roille .i. do *air*illn*adh*. dob*hus*[53] .i. droic*h*bes, no deg*h*b*h*és. do[54] derlaic .i. do[55] adb*h*al log*h*. anac*h*t .i. aincist*ar*

14 tiomortain .i. cro .i. bas dia no dee tré-ág*h* .i. lait*h*e na tt*r*i nág*h* .i. ag*h ar* ec*h*uib, ág*h ar arm*uib*h*

15 ág*h* for d*h*æinib*h*. góla .i. gorta quasi gula[56] .i. c*r*aos.[57] f*r*iot*h*g*h*uin .i. gui*n* i naig*idh* gona. fosieag*ar* .i.

16 airgit*her*. in*n*tec*h* fog*h*lad*h* .i. inte dut*h*uid*h* na ffog*h*l*aighedh* .i. u*ar*bot*h*a, na coil.[58] turg*aire* .i. t*air*riach

17 .i. sg*r*e*th*emla*cht* furaile*cht*ec*h* do b*eth ar* a*m*adan mig*h*niom*h* do de*n*am*h*. fuit*h*b*h*iol .i. fois*h*iob*h*al. fuid*h*ben*n* .i.

18 foidub*h*aid. cod*ar*sna .i. co*m*sgæilt*ach* no co*mthár*sna. ion*n*lac*h*taid*h* .i. fer d*h*énta ion*n*luig*h*. ærc*h*aid*h* .i. fer dénta coire. tél

19 [a]c*h*tac*h* .i. fer do ní telac*h*. deocraid*h*tid*h* ⟨.i. sacrilegan⟩[59] .i. (fer denta toc*r*aíd*h ar* dia) .i. fer do b*hei*r luig*h*e éit*h*ig*h* agan egl*uis*, ⁊ ni tincen*n*

20 [d]lig*hedh*. dilsioc*h* .i. duine as diles do gabail no do m*ar*b*adh* uaide si*n* tig dilsiug*adh* duine indils*igh* cen [c]er[t][60]

21 geinite .i. serrac*h* no l*air*. ǽnm*h*ais .i. ænc*h*rut*h*, no ændluim*h* táid*h*c*h*it*h*er[61] .i. teg*ar* no tegt*er*

22 don-rósad .i. do rónsad.

---

51 The first ⟨s⟩ is written in roman script.
52 O'Curry reads 'no aightear' and includes it with the previous entry.
53 O'Curry reads 'tobhus'. The first letter looks very much like a ⟨t⟩.
54 The ⟨do⟩ is squeezed in above the line.
55 The ⟨do⟩ is squeezed in above the line.
56 Dubhaltach shifts to roman script for this word.
57 O'Curry reads 'traos'.
58 O'Curry suggests reading 'coillidh' for 'coill'.
59 The ⟨i⟩ is written in roman script.
60 The missing letters are supplied from O'Curry's transcription.
61 O'Curry reads 'tuidhchithear'.

Transcription, p. 2[62]

[a]1 [b].n.[63] br*i*ogac*h*[64] .i. uallac*h*. fósa[aid .i. ...]sinec[65] i*ar*doc[66] .i. i*ar* digde[67] .i. buidec*us* i*arum*. ait*h*enaig*h*[68] .i. firenaigid,

2 [...]aidig[.][69] at*h*m*h*ochta .i. at*h*moaig*h*t*h*e.[70] foichmen[71] .i. scoitad, no fodiub*adh*. forrud*h* .i. f*or* rit*h*. cæ*m*nac*ht*

3 [....]. sgeo[72] .i. iompoid*h*, no sg*edh*id*h*. 7.[73] fuit*h*rib*he* .i. gort, iom*air*, d*h*lig*h*t*h*ir b*h*i. nu*r*itor*adh*[74] .i. duilesg

4 [toisgi]d*h* .i. cait*h*em*h*.[75] im-desid*h* .i. t*ar*rus*tar*. toc*h*m*us*t*ar* .i. toib*h*ges. im-toigren .i. eim*h*t*h*oib*h*gid. for-nesa .i. [tin][76]

5 [...] tainses. r*us* .i. g*r*uaid*h*. rosa .i. g*r*uaid*he*. éo .i. édail. con-a*m*ad*hair* .i. ro coi*m*meisio*m*nag*h*est*har*. t*ur*baid .i. l*e*t*h*g[..][77]

6 [eallach]ta .i. *ar* na eallac*h*.[78] incesdnug*adh* .i. cesdnug*adh* a hin*n*e. fuasnad*h* .i. fuaid*redh*, no co*m*sgæil*edh*.

7 an*mchair*des .i. c*air*di*us* an*m*a, c*air*d*us* cic*he*, ⁊ glúine. coimrec*ht* .i. co*mair*git*er*. fuirecht .i. *áir*git*er*, no gebt*er*

8 ruid*h*bec*h* .i. ro dib*hech* .i. ro d*h*oid*h*lec*h*.[79] ainmec*h* .i. ainém*h*ioc*h*. di-ciallat*ar* .i. adbal dic*h*lit*h*er. lénaid*h* .i. lio[..]

---

62 There is a lot of scattered staining on the page. All sides of the page are damaged and missing bits of text. The mounting has covered part of the top and most of the bottom lines of the page. Shadows of the letters are visible, but not enough is visible to be able to read anything. O'Curry saw the pages before they were mounted.

63 For *Bretha Nemed*.

64 O'Curry reads 'gothach'.

65 Too much of the entry is illegible to make any sense of the reading. This entry is not in O'Curry's transcription.

66 O'Curry reads 'ardoc'.

67 O'Curry reads 'comdide'.

68 A letter is crossed out at the beginning of the word.

69 This word is not included in O'Curry's transcription.

70 O'Curry reads 'achmoaighthe'.

71 O'Curry reads 'faichmen'.

72 O'Curry reads 'sgeon'.

73 The numeral is omitted in O'Curry's transcription.

74 Dubhaltach has written an ⟨n⟩ followed by another minim. Based on the source text, the reading should be as that given in O'Curry's transcription, 'murthoradh'.

75 This entry is not in O'Curry's transcription. The missing letters have been supplied from the source text.

76 O'Curry reads 'tin'. The missing letters are supplied from O'Curry's transcription.

77 O'Curry reads 'lethsg'.

78 O'Curry combines this entry with the previous one.

79 O'Curry reads 'bidhleach'.

9 *ar*dblor caim*he* .i. *ar*dg*h*lor cáintem*h*uil. i*n*dlem*h* .i. indile éim*he*. de*ar*la .i. ad*h*bal diolait*h*er. duab*ar* .i. duai[bsech][80]

10 rélug*adh* .i. foillsiog*adh*. ind*edh*ad[81] .i. aisn*edh*id. fát*h* .i. fo f*hédh* no aoid. for cæi[82] .i. *ar* coisir o c*h*allain*n* go hinid

11 ma*r* b*hius* rí, ⁊ oll*om* *ar* cuid oidc*he* *ar* imtec*h*t *ar* a cceil*edu*ib*h*. fæsam*h* .i. eim*h* .i. didion i*ar* bfeis .i. i*ar* ffesda.

12 fæsam*h* .i. c*ar*adrad*h*. fuirir*edh* .i. fosr*eth*nug*adh*. cæi*m*cele[83] .i. giolla .t. sab .i. so ab. coccrun*n*[84] .i. ciallrun*aigid*[85]

13 con-dailid*h*[86] .i. cæinindlig*h*. banataid .i. edac*ht*ain no edáil b*h*an. bio-ram*h*na .i. mna bior*ac* b*r*iat*r*ac*h*a. meram*h*ná

14 mná m*e*ra.[87] mui*n*emná .i. mná b*hius* ag nec*h* isi*n* mui*ne*. sleit*h*em*h*ná .i. mna do c*hum* a ttiag*ar* *ar* sleit*h*. codaig*he*[88] .i. c[oim][89]

15 t*h*eig*he* on tes. giab*air* ⟨ł c⟩ .i.[90] merd*r*ec*h*. temrac*h*a .i. uaisle. ⟨con do⟩ tescm*ar*r .i. tes*ar*gain,[91] no go ro t*h*es*ar*ge. dog*h*b*h*aid*h*

16 .i. do-g*h*ab*h*áltaid*h* ní as dec*air* do gabail. fuid*h*bit*h*e .i. ni *ar* na foidi-ub*adh*. derc*h*ana .i. adb*h*alc*h*anaid*h*. sgor .[i.]

17 c*h*inn*edh*. sgot*h* .i. in*n*sge. tuilc*h*edol[92] .i. cetol toll. sguirde .i. cin*n*te. cait*h*che ⟨⁊ cæit*h*em*h*⟩[93] .i. cion*n*ta. toc*h*mag*h*ad .i. toib*h*g*h*id

18 toc*hmustar* .i. toib*h*git*h*er. mainbt*h*ec*h* .i. mait*h*t*h*oicec*h*

[b]1 d.r.[94] tomait*he* ní bia .i. tomait*h* an buille, ⁊ na tug e .i. bag*ar* is na búail. b*r*ait*h*em*h*nac .i. fer[95] do ní b*r*at*h* nei[ch]

---

80 The edge of the page is damaged; the missing letters are supplied from the gloss in O'Dav 608.

81 O'Curry reads 'rideadhad'.

82 One letter is crossed out after this word.

83 O'Curry reads 'caoimceile'.

84 O'Curry reads 'coccrunn'.

85 O'Curry reads 'ciallrun'.

86 O'Curry reads 'can-dailidh'.

87 The full stop after *mera* looks like a comma.

88 O'Curry reads 'comdaighe'.

89 O'Curry reads the gloss as 'coimtheigheadh'. The missing letters are supplied from O'Curry's transcription.

90 The gloss is written above the ⟨g⟩.

91 The ⟨g⟩ is written over one or two letters.

92 O'Curry reads 'tuilcheatol'.

93 The last two words are written above the line with an insertion mark.

94 The abbreviation might stand for *Duil roscada*, a potential source for the following entries. It should be noted that there is also a horizontal line drawn across the page separating the entries above and below it.

95 Added above the line.

2 mandrad*h* .i. sgæil*edh*. ad-cet*h* .i. ad c*h*ífe*th*. ad-suiter .i. asduig*h*ter. násad*h* .i. sasad*h*, no sosad*h*. clú[96] .i. urdcercad*h*

3 f*air*be .i. fír éibe firinn*ar*b*a*.[97] t*air*im .i. tat*h*æirim. clot*h*ach .i. ionc*h*ach. *ar*b*h*ar .i. sluag*h*. *air*b*h*re .i. slúaig*h*te

4 coitse*achtus* .i. coi*mh*eist*achtus*.[98] sionn*us* .i. se*mnaghius* no etorgn*ughius*. sec*h*moall*adh*[99] .i. sec*h*mailligh. aseic*h* seg*h*maine .i. as

5 sain an ní da seic*h*enn an menma ⁊ an tsuil. ní *ar*tha .i. ní *ar*atha. forrand*ar* .i. urrann*tar* no

6 forrua*mnaghth*er. credbaig*h*ter .i. cremnig*h*ter. cloth*ar* cloat*har* .i. clui*n*ter. forsaid*h* .i. fi*us* f*orusda* no fiors*hæ*id*he*. cota .i. cin*n*[us][100]

7 rirt*h*er .i. rof*h*iren*naghth*er. con-oat*har*[101] .i. coim*étthar*.[102] venite[103] .i. tait. mad*h* t*h*óis[104] .i. ma t*h*oinge. rud*h*rac*h* .i.

8 ro durad*h* gua. do-gó sinser .i. beirid an si*n*ser a rog*h*a. cuit*h*c*h*uire te*ch*ta .i. ogl*ach* (bi*us* ag gaba[il][105]

9 fiadh*aigh* i gcuit*ac*) ⁊ do ní cuac*hairacht* tog*arm*a *ar* an bfiad*h* do cu*m* an cuit*he*. torla[106] .i. naid*h*m. ⁊ desmer*echt*

10 *air*. cat*h* fer ferta .⁊ *araile*. coimdid*h* .i. comd*hú*th*ad* .i. áit as coitc*h*en do g*a*c æn mar ata an f*hair*rge ⁊c̄.

11 eccoimdig*h* .i. a c*h*ont*r*ar*dha* sin.[107] for ton dire .i. *ar* son dire. 1 coim*h*dig*h*[108] ⟨treib*he*⟩[109] .i. a l*ár*, a h*air*med*a*, a h[i][110]

12 [o]nada[111] soillsi, ⁊ na hion*a*da i mbí at*h*aig*h*e c*h*aic*h*.[112] eccoi*m*dig*h* t*r*ebe .i. g*a*c ionad osi*n* amac. 3 coimdig*h*[113] fait*h*c*h*e .i. a slig*h*t*h*e a

96 There is a mark above the ⟨c⟩ that I cannot interpret. The word is also underlined.
97 The first part of the word is underlined.
98 There is a line after this word.
99 The ⟨s⟩ is in roman script.
100 The missing letters are supplied from O'Curry's transcription.
101 O'Curry reads 'con-eathar'.
102 O'Curry reads 'coimeadthar'.
103 Dubhaltach wrote this word in roman script.
104 O'Curry reads 'madhthoir'.
105 The missing letters are supplied from O'Curry's transcription.
106 O'Curry reads 'torlu'.
107 This line is indented.
108 The numeral 1 is written above this word. This and the following numerals are not included in O'Curry's transcription.
109 This word is written above the line with an insertion mark.
110 The missing letter is supplied from O'Curry's transcription.
111 The missing letter is supplied from O'Curry's transcription.
112 O'Curry reads 'chaigh'.
113 There are two items above the ⟨c⟩. The first is the letter 'b', and the second is the numeral '3'. The 3 makes sense as this entry corresponds to the third item in heptad 64.

13 re*dh*e *arda*, ⁊ an tionad i mbí at*h*aig*h*e caig*h*. eccoi*m*dig*h* fait*h*ce .i. g*a*c ionad di osi*n* am*a*c. a*s* *ed* as[114] fait*h*ch*e* an*n*[115] .i. na *cethr*[e][116]

14 guirt as nesa do*n* baile .i. gort g*a*ca h*air*de ime, ⁊ cid *hé* an sliab*h* bud nesa don baile roba am*h*ail

15 fait*h*ch*e*. no así an f*h*ait*h*ch*e* an ro saig*h* guit*h* cluig. 2 coimdig[117] cat*r*ac*h* .i. a hur*lair*, a relge, a p*r*iom*h*sraide, ⁊ g*a*c

16 ionad*h* i mbí at*h*aig*h*e caig*h*. eccoi*m*dig*h* cat*r*ac*h* .i. g*a*c ion*a*d ⟨in*n*te⟩[118] osin am*a*c. 4 coimdig*h*[119] raite .i. (róid no na cu*ar*ta ing*h*elta ⟨⁊ g*a*c⟩[120]

17 idir f*h*ait*h*ch*e* ⁊ dirin*n*) .i. a slig*h*t*h*e, ⁊ a hionad a *ar*da r*édh*e ⁊r̄. 5 coi*m*dig*h*[121] s*h*leb*h*e .i. a slig*h*t*h*e .⁊rl. 6 coi*m*dig*h*[122] caill[e][123]

18 a cluaint*h*e, a g*ur*tin*adh*e,[124] ⁊ na hion*a*da i mbí at*h*ꝍig*h*e c*h*aig*h*. eccoi*m*d*igh* caille[125] .i. o si*n* am*a*c. 7 coi*m*d*igh*[126] *t*rag*h*a .i. ionad in at*h*aig*h*id

19 dꝍine ⁊ longa m*a*r*a*ꝍn, ⁊ ton*n*a go coitcen*n*. eccoi*m*d*igh* *t*rag*h*a .i. g*a*c ionad n*a*c*h* at*h*aig*h*ion*n* a*cht* longa anꝍn*ar*[127]

20 fém*edh* .i. diult*a*d. *airí*asa*cht* .i. ꝍnt[u]g*hadh*.[128] oillian, culpait .i. an léne cona hall sgóit. tum*h*ad*h* ot*r*aig*h* f*r*i nec*h*

21 giolla an c*h*aca do rad ris, no a l*ethét*. slán[129] faille .i. ag si*n* fort slán dam *ar* re cid f*h*aill iom*h*coi*mhét*a

---

114 These three words are written above the line with an insertion mark.

115 O'Curry lists this as a separate entry: '[faithche] a seadh as faithche ann'. I include it with the previous entry because it closely follows it in Oxford, Bodleian Library MS Rawl. B.487.

116 The missing letter is supplied from O'Curry's transcription.

117 There are two items above the ⟨c⟩. The first is the letter 'a', and the second is the numeral '2'. The 2 makes sense as this entry corresponds to the second item in heptad 64.

118 This word is written above the line with an insertion mark.

119 The numeral 4 is written above the ⟨c⟩ which makes sense as this entry corresponds to the fourth item in heptad 64.

120 '⁊ *gac*' is omitted from O'Curry's transcription.

121 The numeral 5 is written above the ⟨c⟩, however, this is usually the sixth item in heptad 64.

122 The numeral 6 is written above the ⟨c⟩, however, this location does not normally appear as part of the standard list of seven locations given in heptad 64; see *CIH* 56.9 where it is used in commentary.

123 O'Curry reads 'caillid' with the later dental inflection of *1 caill* 'wood, forest'.

124 O'Curry reads 'gurtinne'.

125 O'Curry reads 'caillid'.

126 The numeral 7 is written above the ⟨c⟩, and this is usually the seventh item in heptad 64.

127 O'Curry lists this entry separately from the rest under 'Eccoimdigh tragha'.

128 O'Curry reads 'aontughadh'. I follow his reading here.

129 Dubhaltach begins the word with a roman capital ⟨s⟩.

22 do neit im in sréd. slán[130] nait*h*ne .i. t*r*eb*air*e ro gaib*h* f*er* an tig*h*e andside re fi*us* daingne, no *ar* daingn[e]

23 [131][...............................] ea[b]la [....................................]

Transcription, p. 3[132]

[a]1 [..]b [.]sen[..]e[...]. [..........................]

2 [......].i. an cuid a[..]tog*h*a[...]do cia [...] [........]d[...]na gæ[....]s[......]

3 [........................] .⁊. [.......................] [Duicheat .i. cuigid [..]][133]

4 [........].i. cor éisisi .i. (eg[.]uisis .i. cor, esi*et*em*h* .i. cor[...], no eccn[e] .i. [.]osnad*h*.

5 [.....] a[..]olanuib, ⁊ [....]anuisge [..][134]

6 [..]ugille *ar* [..]osi dfi*et*b[.][135]

7 [...]fuill*em*a .i. in a[..]gi[.]⁊ urgais an an*m*æin, ⁊ an fuillem*h*. u*r*gais .i. erguid*he* [ua]is[136]

8 [urfo]g*r*aig*h* cuir ⁊ cu*nnar*t[a] .i. dæ[in]e [danach coir car]cu*nnradh* sin, ma*r* ata m*ac* mna bæit*h* .⁊c̄ [⁊ ni in]an*n* si*n* urfog*r*aig*h* leabtan*us*a [.⁊c̄.][137]

9 [Urfograigh leapandis .i. daoine danach coir leabaidh do thabhair]t[138] .i. dæine bi*us* i nag*adh* dlig*edh*, ⁊ do ní sin urfog*r*aig*h* cuir, ⁊ cun*nar*t*h*a diob*h*.

10 [......]at*h*a no .s. i. diult*adh* no c*r*osad tu*arus*tail do gabail .⁊c̄.[139] t*áir*cit*h*er .i. tat*h*aoir

---

130 Dubhaltach begins the word with a roman capital ⟨s⟩.

131 I cannot read any of this line because it is cut off with only the top third or so of the letters visible.

132 The page has a lot of scattered staining. All sides of the page are damaged and missing bits of text. The top third is almost impossible to read due to fading and staining and tears in the page. The writing reverses after the fouteenth line, i.e. turn the page 180°. There is a horizontal line across the page where the writing begins upside down.

133 This entry is in O'Curry's transcription, but I have not been able to find it on the page.

134 The rest of the line appears to be empty.

135 The rest of line is empty.

136 Other than the entry for *duicheat*, this is the first entry on this page listed in O'Curry's transcription.

137 The missing words in this line are supplied from O'Curry's transcription.

138 The missing words are supplied from O'Curry's transcription.

139 This entry is not in O'Curry's transcription.

11 [...] no fe[...] uenouidir[.][140] *ar* nec*h* .i. fecem*hnus* indlig*ht*a*c*. as é an roac*h* .i. ge no geall*a* ni a b[riathraib]

12 [nibi] cor in eg[mais athar][141] [cia sias][142] .i. cait i suideab*h*sa.[143] cia lias .i. cait i luideib*h*sa. cia er*us* .i. cait i ereoc[hadh][144]

13 [...]at[....] bec. findte fertsa*c* .i. ⟨m*ac*⟩ na had*h*alt*r*aig*h*e.[145] findte diabl*adh*e .i. an tseanor*ac*.

14 [........] Deo grát*ias* Senobia[146] go ria.[147]

[b]1 D.R. .i. m*a*d a[...] do l*eth* ibe ⁊[148] l*eth*i*a*rr[149] .i. l*eth* biadaid [......]fe[...]l*eth* .i. b[...] afaco .i. mogad*h*[.][150]

2 do bir*ar ar* an fer d*h*a ndent*er*.[151] fuic*h*ec*h*t .i. an gnio*mh* f[erdha][152] .i. coi*m*riac*ht*ain ⁊c̄. naid*m* ⁊ urnaidm*h* bi*us* id*e*r fer ⁊ mnaoi .i. naidm*h*

3 .i. coib*h*c*h*e do*n* mnæi, ⁊ urnaidm*h* ag an f*h*er uirrisi[153] =comt[us .i.] cu*m*aid*h* úais= im íoc leis da nden*ad* si[154] fogail doba n*ar* n[o] olc d*h*ó.

4 do-góad[155] .i. tog*h*aid. dog*h*óidís .i. do t*h*og*h*dæis. tuirc*hr*eic .i. cio-t*h*oir*adh* nes[156] .i. siocla .i. sort ionm*uis* ber*ar* do mnæi i gcoibc*h*e

---

140 The first part of the line is illegible; the reading of the remainder of the line is not certain. This entry is not in O'Curry's transcription.

141 This entry is not in O'Curry's transcription.

142 The missing words are supplied from O'Curry's transcription.

143 O'Curry reads 'ruideabhsa'.

144 The missing letters are supplied from O'Curry's transcription.

145 This entry is cross-referenced in O'Curry's transcription, but it is not included.

146 The reading of this word is tentative. If it is for Zenobia, whose feast day is October 30th, it would provide a date for this section of the glossary. This line is not included in O'Curry's transcription.

147 The last five words are in darker ink. There is a line under this line of text across the page. Turn the page 180° because the orientation of the writing changes.

148 There might be an insertion mark before the Tironian note, but anything above the line is illegible.

149 There is probably a suspension mark above the end of this word, but it is not legible.

150 The transcription of this line is tentative.

151 None of the foregoing is in O'Curry's transcription. The beginning of this line may or may not belong with the previous entry.

152 The missing letters are supplied from O'Curry's transcription.

153 After this the following is surrounded by a rectangle of ink "=comt[us .i.] cu*m*aid*h* úais=." O'Curry lists the following text as a separate entry.

154 This word is omitted by O'Curry.

155 O'Curry reads 'togead'.

156 O'Curry reads 'a neas'.

5 con-duic*h*et .i. cui*nngh*id.[157] aicc .i. íesg.[158] tec*h*tm*h*uig*h*e .i. sealb*h* b*h*eod*h*ile b*h*i*us* *ar* an mag*h*. tion*n*sg*r*a[159] .i. tionsgedol creice an tsiogail do be*rar* do[160] m

6 nœi *ar* t*h*oil go noige do be*th* aice. slab*h*ra tobra .i. sál b*h*ú*ar* do b[erar][161] do mnœi *ar* coi*met* a genuis di. taid*h*be .i. tœi eibe ut [..][162]

7 m*ar*bt*h*aid*h*be .i. ni ebi*us* a coib*h*ce a ttœi o m*h*naoi, ⁊ m*ar*b[163] i[164] fen, no a fer, no ce*chtar* doib*h* an*n*. beot*h*aid*h*be .i. ní ebes a c*h*oib*h*ce a ttœí o mnœi

8 ⁊ beo i fen sa fer, no as beo ne*chtar* de. cutai*m* .i. co*m*t*h*uiti*m*. l*eth*c*h*utaim .i. tuiti*m* .i.[165] coi*m*tuiti*m* do*n* d*ar*a l*eth*. iomcutai*m* .i. co*m*t*h*uiti*m*

9 doib*h* m*ar* œn .i. don lana*muin*, iolr*adh* na ffoc*ail* si .i. l*et* cutman*n* ⁊ imcut*main*n. domrúid*h* .i. reime deach*adh* .i. ruid*h* .i. ro[166] fœid

10 cob*hus* .i. coi*m*f*h*eis.[167] tog*h*luas*acht* .i. ní do be*i*r *ar* mnœi b*r*et*h* clain*ne*[168] re nionb*aidh*. clam*h*doid .i. ben ag mbí lam*h* clam*h*. cl*ár* ai*m*rid .i. ben

11 na be*i*r clan*n*. din*n*is .i.[169] mion*na*. im-rolaid*h*[170] .i. em*h* *ar* luad*h* fir ag tec*h*t no ag dul doc*hum* a m*h*ná. duit*h*in[171] .i. ceo no duit*hin*[172]

12 .i. dat*h* na[173] sine .i. g*r*ian, ⁊ esga. aig*h*néta .i. aig*h*nes no b*r*etem*hnus*. airsinsior .i. firsins*e*r. sleit*h* .i. coim*h*ria*cht*ain le*n*[174] mnœi gan

157 This entry might be for O'Curry's 'duicheat .i. cuigid [..]', an entry which I have not been able to locate anywhere on page 3.

158 O'Curry reads 'ésg'. It is possible that the ⟨e⟩ was made over an ⟨i⟩ although both letters are visible.

159 The ⟨s⟩ is made over a ⟨g⟩.

160 O'Curry reads 'don'.

161 The missing letters are supplied from O'Curry's transcription.

162 The remaining writing at the edge of the page is illegible.

163 The ⟨b⟩ was added over another letter as a correction in a different colored ink.

164 The ⟨i⟩ was added above the ⟨f⟩ in a different colored ink.

165 Two or three letters were crossed out before the '.i.'.

166 O'Curry reads 're'.

167 The suspension mark is over the ⟨o⟩.

168 The suspension mark was added later in a different colored ink.

169 There are a few letters crossed out after the '.i.'.

170 O'Curry divides the word as 'im ro laidh'.

171 O'Curry reads 'duithin'.

172 O'Curry reads 'duithin'.

173 O'Curry reads 'nu'.

174 O'Curry reads 'le'.

13 fios di.[175] fæig*he* .i. fóeig*he* óng*h*lǽid. slet*h*er .i. teigt*er* do cu*m* mná gan f*hius* di. sleit*h* t*ar* lónlaingen .i. dul do

14 cu*m* mna gan f*hius* di na deg*h*aid aní*ar*. sl*eth* d*ar* glún .i. idir a d*ha* cois. sl*eth* fo t*h*æb*h* .i. d*ha* cois na mna t*ar* an f*h*er

15 cr*ioch* mna fir i nai*m*sir a hégnigt*he*[176] re [ł la][177] f*er* oile .i. *air*m i gcluin-ter a hég*h*em*h* go a tec*h*. eatt*air* na mna .c.na .i. g*ac* ionad o

16 thá si*n* amac*h* genmót*ha* an baile a gcluin*fidha* an ég*h*em*h*. cr*ioch* na[178] contiona[179] .i. i mac*haire* si*n* ⁊ ionan*n* cr*ioc*

17 riagailt*er* aca i gcaill. foeg*h*em*h* ⟨fogra⟩[180] tasg adalt*raighe*, ⁊ t*ur*suig*he* .i. fog*ra* táisg bi*us* ag an .c. muinti*r* i na*m* a negn*igh*t*he*.

18 co*mair*r .i. do co*mh*raic. tat*h* .i. g*ruth* do ngoirt*er* mæt*h*al. mac caill*ech*[181] .i. caillec*h* dub*h*. forcort*har* .i. egn*igh*t*er* ben .i. do b*ratar*

19 fior-rec*ar* éigne. ced, no cu⟨ac⟩ad[182] .i. foills*igh*id no in*n*isid. ad-cua .i. ⟨do⟩ in*n*is. mat*h*ó .i. ma dia ttoinge

20 lam*hchomairt* .i. com-im*er*t lám*h* .i. basg*haire*. dluethad lam*h* .i. glaca diad*h*ad*h* ra c*h*ele. basc .i. baiscm*hellaib*

21 t*r*eas b*r*agad, no usg*ar*.[183] tartad*h*[184] ⟨.i. tortad*h*⟩ rig*h* .i. tornad*h* no glacad*h* do beir ríg[185] *ar* mnáoi da hegniugad*h*

22 do éc .i. do in*n*is. ben urnad*ma*[186] .i. adalt*rach* urnad*ma*.[187] cuitil .i. cæi t*h*oll .i. for orb*hasac*. meam*m* .i. pog. ban*ar*ad

23 [l]uac*h*[188] .i. ben gab*us* do laim*h* no do ní ionad mna an tig*he*. collud*h* nóig*he* .i. lot óig*he* mna, ⁊ *air* a son si*n* do b*er* an f*er* siocai[l di][189]

---

175 Dubhaltach drew a line separating these two words. It looks as if a few letters might have been erased after ⟨di⟩. There is a gap between ⟨di⟩ and the start of the following entry.

176 O'Curry reads 'héignithe'.

177 The correction is written above ⟨re⟩.

178 A letter ⟨m⟩ was crossed out before this word.

179 O'Curry reads 'crioch gan dicelt', but this is clearly a mistake for the same entry which appears on page nine. The reading of the sixth letter is tentative as there is a line drawn through this part of the MS.

180 This word is written above the line with an insertion mark.

181 The lemma is underlined. O'Curry prints 'mac cailleach' as two words, but whether he chose to interpret the lemma as two words or one is unknown.

182 One letter after ⟨u⟩ was erased, and ⟨ac⟩ was written over the line with an insertion mark.

183 O'Curry reconstructs the entry as '.i. baiscmhellad[aibh] treas [teas] braghad no asgar [uisgi]'.

184 O'Curry reads 'turtudh'.

185 The ⟨g⟩ is written over another letter.

186 O'Curry reads 'urnamda'.

187 O'Curry reads 'urnamda'.

188 The missing letter is supplied from O'Curry's transcription.

189 The missing letters are supplied from O'Curry's transcription.

24 be[190] *m*uine .i. ben dan dir b*eth* i mui*n*e. be nio*mr*ama[191] .i. ben bi*us ar* ionn*r*am*h* o ionad*h* dionad. at*h*cor i*ar* bfoltuib*h* .i. at*h*cor do nid m*air* .i. di

25 (*ar*[...]*ar*in*n* f*or* an at*air* [...]le[.]) i*ar* san mis c*h*ic*he* .i. i*ar* mb*eth* don cloin*n* re re mís *ar* c*h*ic*h*ib*h* na mna. frit*h*bert breit*he* .i. bert

26 f*r*it*h*ir do ni ben do mill*adh* na clain*n*e bi*us* na broin*n*, ⁊ fos bert a naig*idh* bre*th*e cl*ainn*e na nionb*aidh*, no na ttegmail di *ar*

27 æ̃nc*h*or. at*aid* .3. f*r*itberta b*r*et*h*a an*n* .i. [1]b*r*oc*h*an ⟨.i.⟩[192] do losuib*h*, ⁊ deolosuib*h* do c*ur* a lenib*h* as a*n* mnæi. [2]Snait*he* .i. ima b*r*agaid *co*n*a* teg*h*

28 ma lenaib*h* d*h*i. [3]sog*h*ab*h*ail duile .i. sec*h*na di coim*h*riac*ht*ana i nai*m*sir coi*m*perta. an f*r*itb*er*t .b. .s. erata[193] coi*m*p*er*ta inti .i. sed .da .s.

29 ⁊ t*r*i seoid. m*ar* so. sed do g*r*adib*h* fene. *da* .s. do g*radaib* fl*ath*a, ⁊ 3 .s. do ri*gaib cona* gco*m*g*r*adaib*h*. seoid si*n* bent*ar* (do*n* mn*æ*i) leisi*n* fer *ar* son

30 firiad*h*ta no toir*m*esg do c*h*ur *ar* an ccoi*m*p*er*t cl*ainn*e tegm*us* et*ar*ra. coi*mpert*[194] fo [co]smaili*us*[195] lac*h*ta .i. dat*h* ban do b*h*eit *ar* ad*h*b*ar* no

31 *ar* g*h*enem*h*ui*n* cl*ainn*e. lion*n* tog*h*luas*acht* .i. br*eth* na coi*m*perta an tan n*ac* bi a*cht* na lion*n* gan c[or]t*us*[196] geinem*h*na no crot*h*a dæn*n*a. tog*h*l*uasacht*

32 colla .i. br*e*t*h* leinib*h* m*air*b*h*. togl*uasacht* beocur*p*[197] .i. ambeo re nion-b*aidh* [1]b*r*ioc*h*t[198] fola, [2]fuil foll*us*, ⁊ [3]cur*p*gne .i. 1 coi*mpert eter* b*eth* na fuil ⁊ na

33 lin*n* bain i gcon*n*tab*art* et*ur*ra. 2 fuil .f. uirre fen. 3 cuirpg*h*ne .i. gne cuirp dæn*na air*. incind*h* co*m*lain*n* gan sgis a*cht* sgeo cneid .i. a*n*

34 lenab*h* i mbi inc*h*in*n* co*mlan*, n*ac* bi sgis aige *ar* na b*r*eit*h*, *acht* ag sg*eth*, ⁊ ag cned*idh*. crucrebaide .i. in geinem*h*ui*n eter* ⟨ɫ t*a*res⟩[199] b*eth* di na fuil f

---

190 The reading of this word is uncertain.
191 O'Curry reads 'niomma'.
192 The '.i.' is written above the line with an insertion mark.
193 O'Curry reads 'iarata'.
194 The ⟨c⟩ looks like it was made over another letter.
195 The missing letters are supplied from O'Curry's transcription.
196 The missing letters are supplied from O'Curry's transcription.
197 O'Curry reads 'beoc*h*cuirp'.
198 There is a gap in the line between this entry and the previous one.
199 This sequence is omitted in O'Curry's transcription.

35 ollus, ⁊ na dluim cuirpg*h*ne. ré f*h*abt*h*a .i. ai*m*sir leig*h*is. imu*rc*h*ur* upt*h*a *ar* d*h*aig*h* ser[ce fir] .i. im[ur]c*hur* piseog.[200]

36 cosg nurcuil .i. teg*us*g do ní ben *ar* an ni toir*m*isgt*e*r go millen*n* a c[ele no an leanabh bhios na][201] b*r*oin*n* fen

37 sem*edh* ala b*hu*ar .i. sem*ed* og f*or* an d*ar*a bu*ar* .i. d*r*oc*h* blat*h* f*or* læguib*h* an fir [tre connm?][202]

38 creim .i.[203] forbaig*h* .i. ben no crim a ccod*ha* do*na* læguib .⁊c̄. ion*n*ad .i. ni no soc[har tig ..][204]

39 [eimh ime .i.][205] fal na timc*h*ell. lias tuig*h*it*he* .i. c*r*o gam*h*na *ar* na t*h*uig*he*. f[.....]p[....][206]

Transcription, p. 4[207]

[a]1 [208][......]

2 [......]

3 [.....]

4 [...] g

5 [....]daigin*n* serce

6 [..]si .i. [.]*éth*uigte serce.[209]

[b]1 [210][..........] fa [.........] [meid .i. moid, on[..]][211]

2 [....]s[....]g[.......]as [.....] [taoi .i. an. (?)][212]

3 [.....]do [...]a[....]n[....]l[....]be[.....] cli [ceann] .i. ben [nach beir clann]

200 The missing letters are supplied from O'Curry's transcription.

201 The missing words are supplied from O'Curry's transcription. There is a tear in the page.

202 The missing letters are supplied from O'Curry's transcription.

203 ⟨.i.⟩ is omitted in O'Curry's transcription.

204 The missing letters are supplied from O'Curry's transcription.

205 The missing words are supplied from O'Curry's transcription.

206 The entry is illegible.

207 The page has a lot of scattered staining. All sides of the page are damaged and missing bits of text. The top third is almost impossible to read due to fading and staining and tears in the page. The writing reverses after the first third of the page like page 3, i.e. turn the page 180°.

208 This section of the page is in the upper left corner and surrounded by an ink line. The area of text is triangular in shape. Most of it is illegible.

209 Nothing from this block of text is in O'Curry's transcription.

210 I cannot read the first line. There might be one line of text partially cut off above this line.

211 O'Curry lists this entry as being found on page 4, but I cannot find it.

212 O'Curry lists this entry as being found on page 4, but I cannot find it. I print it as it is found in O'Curry's transcription.

4 [tri blia]d[h]na [fuilingidh a fear ....][213] e[...] fo[......]e .i. be[....]

5 [.............]de[.............]de[.....]

6 .i. [.....]tad*h* an og*h* ⁊ [.]a[..]*air*. [..]at[...]aig[...][214]

7 .i. ber*thar* fuil misia mna .i. as siad [......]e .i. [....][215]

8 mem naisi .i. pog da deoin do geib*h* ben. iom*airius* da rud*he* .i. [....] na [....]*th*[..][216]

9 tait*h*m*h*ett .i. iom*r*ad*h* no cui*m*niug*adh*, ⁊ u*r* ait*h*m*edh* ma*r* si*n*.[217] etla trebt*ha*[218] .i. ní goides ben [.....]

10 [..] da fer. saintuillema*r*[219] co clot*h*[220] gan iomc*h*og*ur* .i. ioen*ncadh*[221] bid*h* do tab*ar*t do mnæ[i] [..] goides [..]

11 tuill*adh* clu no cuidec*hus* di o c*ar*aid*h* no o comaigt*ach* sec*h* a fer. neim*h*iomc*h*og*ur* .i. [.i. iomchogur ⁊c̄. re a] fer [fein][222]

12 [.]o rainig. diollat lige .i. etac*h* (as fiu l*eth* coib*h*ce a mna) gaibes fer i m[naoi] [ar nei]rge as [a] [..][223]

13 rocluic*he*[224] is c*rius* .i. cluit*he* don mnæi, ⁊ lam fir na c*rius*. roc*h*luit*he* .i. sp*air*n, ⁊ l[amh fir na crios, nu a fear] [..][225]

14 f*r*iotaig*he* d*r*uis doi[..]n do*n* mnæi go hait diun*air*.[226] m*e*ra*cht* .i. d*r*uis. [golladh fuidhe .i.] faoisid[niughadh ⁊ gollta an][227]

15 [.]ag*h*tig ⟨do⟩[228] ni an ben t*ar*sna an tig*he* .i. fæisidniug*hadh* di in guilte. fe[abus ruine .i. run] do [denum do mnaoi gan] [..][229]

16 fer an ni b[udh] imdergad do. reabac*h* luirge ⟨.i. riabsad*h* an talman do ni⟩[230] .i. riabac*h* a talmaide re luirg ben si*n* [bios o] tig do tig*h* [go] [...] [fri a]

---

213 The missing letters are supplied from O'Curry's transcription.
214 The reading of this line is tentative. It is not in O'Curry's transcription.
215 The reading of this line is tentative. It is not in O'Curry's transcription.
216 This entry is not in O'Curry's transcription.
217 This entry might be the second half of the previous entry.
218 The reading of the second and third letters is uncertain.
219 O'Curry reads 'paintuilleamur'.
220 O'Curry reads 'cioth'.
221 The reading is uncertain.
222 The missing words are supplied from O'Curry's transcription.
223 The missing letters are supplied from O'Curry's transcription.
224 O'Curry reads 'cluice'.
225 The missing words are supplied from O'Curry's transcription.
226 This fragment of an entry is not in O'Curry's transcription.
227 The missing words are supplied from O'Curry's transcription.
228 This correction was added above line in darker ink with an insertion mark.
229 The missing words are supplied from O'Curry's transcription.
230 O'Curry reads 'nisi'.

17 cele, ⁊ lorg*h* ina laim*h*.[231] gu ed ⟨.i. ed br*e*cce⟩ .i. derb*adh* ⟨tre ed brege⟩ sgeoil brege *ar* a fer ga[n adhbar][232] do ni ben. [golgaire lenimh .i. bualadh, agus comhadh][233]

18 bid*h* do*n* lesmat*air* on lescl*ainn* go mbid i *ngair* guil. liud*h* sgit*h* .i. ni as sgit*h* le fer do [li]ud f*air* [cen] fer no cen g[..][234]

19 coib*h*dealac*h*[235] .i. duine ris a mbí coimfial*us*, no coi*m*dealac*hus*[236] gæil [no caradr]ad [a]g nec [i n]geall fiac*h* .i. ben [bheith][237]

20 as feic*h* ag hin*n*e sec*h* a fer. locc-bergenach .i. loc b*erath*genac*h*, no loc*h*ta salac*h* *ar ar* t*air*ismec*h* salc*har* go [s]oil[eir]

21 do cac*h*[238] loc suide, luide, tec*h*, ⁊ cuile, ⁊ iad uile, gan sguab*adh* gan glan[adh].[239] [fuarthair ... toirmis]g[ios] gniomr*adh* ⁊ lana*m*-n*us*a[dh].[240]

22 beir geoanach .i. bir bria*th*rac*h* e.[241] am*h*n*us* .i. olc. io*m*am*h*n*us* .i. co*m*olc. aid*h*c*h*e iodn*aidh*e .i. [...]

23 [.....] [.]aiccib b*hius* ai[.] [..]uir [.]e[.]nenual

[c]1 [242]b.n.[243] fer reime .i. an cainte bi*us* ag ruai*mned* a oile[244] in[245] oemas a oile.[246] f[*er*] raite .i. ap*ad* in raitig dorn na

2 brollac*h* ó æn lo amac*h*, no fer *téit* for foriod, ⁊ roba glan fon rod. f*er* fuid*h*re .i. fuid*h*ir crúi elas re dlig*hedh* a fuidre[247]

---

231 The missing words are supplied from O'Curry's transcription.

232 The missing letters are supplied from O'Curry's transcription.

233 The missing words are supplied from O'Curry's transcription.

234 The missing letters are supplied from O'Curry's transcription.

235 O'Curry reads 'coibhdeallach'.

236 O'Curry reads 'coimdalachus'.

237 The missing words are supplied from O'Curry's transcription.

238 There is a mark after this word which I cannot decipher.

239 The missing letters are supplied from O'Curry's transcription.

240 The missing text is supplied from O'Curry's transcription.

241 This entry is written in between the descenders of the writing on the line below it. This is the last line of section b on this page; the writing for section c is oriented 180° from section b.

242 This section of the page was written first.

243 For *Bretha Nemed*.

244 O'Curry reads 'oide'.

245 There is a mark after this word which I cannot interpret.

246 O'Curry reads 'oide'.

247 O'Curry queries whether something is missing at the end of this line and the beginning of the next. He reads this word as 'fuidreadh'. The numeral 4 is written in the upper right corner of the page. The page as bound in the MS is upside down to the original order in which Dubhaltach wrote it.

3 fuid*h*ir si*n* elós ria na f*h*lait*h* go sedaib*h* a f*h*lat*h*a leis. nos .i. fi*us* nua, no fi*us* naonm*ar*, ⁊ nos .i. u*r*d*ar*cug*h*ad*h*[248]

4 diog*h*uin .i. s*ar*ug*adh*. tlenam*h*ain .c. m*ui*n*ti*re neic*h* .i. do[249] et*h*lod*h* a c*h*edmui*nti*re and[250] .i. dul go a p*r*iom*h*m*h*nǽi. diam*h*ui*n* .i. gl[an][251]

5 cuin*n*test*ar* .i. cui*nn*git*h*er .i. i*arr*t*ar*. toic*h*re*ach*ta .i. toic*h*id*h*e dirge.[252] duan .i. dúinis indealt .i. æin siolla.[253] forrduain .i. reco*m*ar[c]

6 .i. da siolla ⟨on⟩[254] duna n*n*[255] .ut. iomco*m*ar*c* flat*h*a feim*h*en. ⁊ cas-b*air*dnein[256] i*ar*co*m*ar*c* .i. t*r*i siolla.[257] l*eth*m*h*io*m*asg[258] .i. droc*h* f*h*ásg isi*n* ran*n*

7 go ruige a leat*h*. uad*h* .i. egsi. aid*h*bsi .i. taisben*adh*. gign*igh*ter .i. gin-f*igh*ter. os .i. og*us*. *ar*sit*h*er .i. t*áirr*it*h*er.[259] forts*h*esid

8 .i. t*air*isid*h*. ad-bosaid .i. obuid. ad-nesa .i. do b*er* táinsíom*h*ad*h*. ad-buib .i. oibéb*h*uid*h*. miod*h*b*h*a .i. m*eth*on bet*h*a inter

9 bonu*m* et malu*m*. miod*h*b*h*a .i. toraind. uintsi .i. an*n*so. cuinni*us* .i. con-*nus* .i. con*n*ad*hus* .i. m*a*c, no[260] cui*nn*i*us* on i*arr*a*dh*. datán

10 oide. dat*h*nait .i. mui*m*e. céin .i. fén. glenuid*h* .i. lenuid. beit*h*ium .i. bid*h* dam. iorcaid*h* .i. urcoideac*h*,[261] no iut[.]

11 ainferg*a*c. ior*air* .i. *ar*guin t*r*e ferg. ainb .i. aineolac*h*. *air*b*h*e .i. esn*a*c. *air*bec*h* .i. esn*a*c.[262] elge .i. feran*n* no elg .i. ére. condag*ar* .i. i*arr*t*har*

12 boimbil, boim .i. æib*h*in*n*, no sgiat*h*, no boi*m* do b*h*ile sgeit*h*. ro nétad*h* .i. ro gonad*h*, no ro bít*h*. néth .i. dia cat*h*ad[263]

13 do*m*-ig*edh* .i. tig*edh* dam*h*. iomorran*n*[264] .i. im⟨f*h*⟩orran.[265] lia .i. comorba. lia .i. iomad. d*r*uis.i. mer*acht*. guirn .i. suirn, no ait*h*in*n*e .i.

---

248 O'Curry reads 'urtarughadh'.
249 O'Curry reads 'to'.
250 It is possible that this word was struck through.
251 The missing letters are supplied from O'Curry's transcription.
252 The ⟨g⟩ was added above the line.
253 O'Curry combines this entry with the previous one.
254 This word is added above the line with an insertion mark.
255 O'Curry reads 'duna n̄'.
256 The ⟨nei⟩ is written over ⟨em⟩ in a lighter colored ink.
257 O'Curry treats the second half of the gloss as a separate entry.
258 O'Curry reads 'leadhmhiomasg'.
259 O'Curry reads 'tairsithear'.
260 One letter was crossed out before the ⟨n⟩. This word is not in O'Curry's transcription.
261 The ⟨d⟩ was made over another letter, perhaps ⟨p⟩.
262 The ⟨e⟩ was made over another letter.
263 O'Curry reads 'catha'.
264 O'Curry reads 'iomorrán'.
265 ⟨ḟ⟩ is written above the line with a reference mark.

14 gæ ornæ .i. ga oirgne. n*ár* .i. næm*h*. derosg[266] .i. derb*hchinnedh*. fochrac*h* .i. dui*ne* do b*er* foic*h*reic celsi*ne* do neoc*h*. urla

15 ta .i. uasal læite um*h*alóide. dimsi .i. nem*h*maisi. ség*h*uin .i. fer gon*us* séig .i. ag*h* all*aidh*, no ség*h*ui*n* .i. *air*e ec*ht*a

16 buasac*h* .i. bá f*h*esac*h*. airberac*h* .i. nec*h* do b*er* oirb*h*ire *ar* nec*h* ma*r* ata cáinte. *arr*c*h*ogad*h* .i. seguinid*h*, no cú gon*us*

17 osa. *arr* .i. fiad*h* no os. deog*h*b*air*e .i. sgo*air*e. foircit*h*er .i. fior d*héch*ait*h*er. urano[267] .i. *air*e næi .i. duine *ar* nec*h* dfia

18 d*h*nu*is*e *air* no na diaig*h* c.[268] de*ar*cnuid*h* no[269] dercnuid*h* .i. anr*a*d i*ar* sa ní drec*hus* do*n* eal*adh*ain. noit*h*gern[270] .i. cli. olsone, no ollosna .i.

19 can. sæg*h*al .i. dos. sæircerdne .i. m*a*c fu*r*m*adh*. cæinc*h*erdne .i. foc*h*log. coictriall .i. d*r*isiug. taip*h*nem*idh* .i. tam*h*un. doineim*idh*[271] .i. ob

20 lóire.[272] ræd[273] .i. ro éd. ainb*h*fét*h* .i. ainéol*us*. d*r*eteall .i. torc muice. bainteoluid .i. bang*h*adoig*h*e. fur .i. úir. ta

21 .i. an[..]on[274] tai .i. an t⟨an⟩oc[275] loma no co*rm*a .i. tanog, no d*e*rbog, no ian, co*rm*a no loma. fureg .i. fl*edh*. tút*h*

22 .i. balad*h*. con-clec*h* .i. do clis. ad-cuitig*h* .i. ro eitig*h*. indbertad .i. déna*mh*. imdeall .i. b*r*uit*h* (no tab*air*t n*ethe* a hin*ne* ⟨ł in⟩) fo[r][276]

23 cludad*h*, clit*h*iug*h*ad*h*, no téig*h*ed*h*, do himdilled*h*, ⁊ do heim*h*d*h*ail*edh* (ider coire, ⁊ dab*agh*) an coi*rm*. lait*h* .i. lion*n*. tet*h*raig*h* .i. t*r*aig*h*id*h*.

24 loc*r*an*n*, ⁊ loic*het* .i. an tsoillsi. ble*mh*aid*m* .i. glemaidem*h*, no b*r*is*edh*. cnom*h*aidm, b*r*is*edh* cno.[277] tet*h*n[a]t*ar*[278] .i. tait*h*mig*h*id .i. sgæilid.

25 tud*h*c*h*aid*h* .i. do deac*h*uid. át*h* téc*ht*a .i. inad dlig*h*t*hach* no ait no baile. frecm*air*c .i. fior f*h*iafraige.[279] miodc*h*ui*ne* .i. ag leaguib*h*

266 There is a line either above this word or below the one above it, i.e. *lia*, but I cannot interpret it.
267 O'Curry reads 'uruno'.
268 I do not know how to interpret the ⟨c⟩; it is not in O'Curry's transcription.
269 O'Curry reads 'ro'.
270 O'Curry reads 'roithghearn'.
271 O'Curry reads 'toinemhidh'.
272 O'Curry reads 'dolóre'.
273 O'Curry reads 'rae'.
274 It looks like Dubhaltach started the gloss, crossed it out, and tried to correct it. The end result is quite messy, and it looks like he started the entry afresh with *tai*.
275 The ⟨an⟩ is written above line with an insertion mark. O'Curry reads 'tonach'.
276 The missing letter is supplied from O'Curry's transcription.
277 The ⟨c⟩ is written above a letter which is crossed out.
278 The missing letter is supplied from O'Curry's transcription.
279 O'Curry reads 'fhiafhraighe'.

26 coiglig*he* .i. cæi acla[ighe][280] .i. cæi iota loig*he*. mi*us*cait*h*[281] .i. malla*cht*. biolf*h*ot*h*ac*h* .i. gan fot*h*ac*h*. grec*h*[282] .i. cnu. baidsid*he* .i. fer do ni

27 baisd*h*ed, ma*r* ata oll*amh* baisdi*us* grada *ar* na fil*edh*ib*h*.[283] foirb*h*led .i. f*or* f*h*ill*edh* na fil*idachta* .i. duan, ⁊ f*or*duan .⁊c̄. tora*chta*[284] .i. do

28 ro*acht*, no do ria*cht*. uid*h*br*eth* .i. guib*h*r*eth*. oimb*h*r*eth* .i. guibr*eth* om*h*. oimblig*h* .i. blig*h*id*h* a hinn*e*. f*air*ben .i. firin*n* *ar* b*éin*[285] no firen

Transcription, p. 5[286]

[a]1 [287]e[id]g*edh* deoltæide[288] .i. gaid. tiomg*aire*[289] .i. i*ar*raid*h*. aig*he* .i. aimsir. m*air*n .i. brat*h*. midis .i. [measaid.][290]

2 [dear][291] .i. esgit*he*r. seoid gabla .i. seoid gab*hlaigh*ter isi*n* eric .i. d*air*t .i. iiii. sg*r*eab*ail* a luac*h*. d*ar*taid [.i. ...]

3 [col]p[thach][292] .i. ui. sg*r*iab*ail*. sam*us*g [.i.] da. sg*r*eb*al* dég. lulg*ach* .i. 24 sg*r*eab*ail*. eislis .i. ail siod*h* lesa. combac*h* .i. coi*m*b[riseadh][293]

4 ca[294] .i. ci*nus*. ad-bo .i. urfog*r*aid*h*. im*h*de .i. eim*h*d*h*idnig*h*.[295] manchuine .i. lu*cht* coi*m*id*heachta*, ⁊ coi*m*[eadtha][296]

---

280 I follow O'Curry's transcription of the word.

281 O'Curry reads 'mioscatih'.

282 O'Curry reads 'greth'; the MS is difficult to read due to a stain. The reading provided here is not secure.

283 The reading of the final syllable is uncertain.

284 O'Curry reads 'dorachta'.

285 O'Curry reads 'bean'.

286 There is a lot of scattered staining on the page. All sides are damaged and missing parts of the text. It is possible that the page originally had another line of text across the top of the page which has since been cut off. This is especially visible in the upper left corner of the page.

287 There might be a few words in the upper left corner of the page, but I cannot read them.

288 The reading of this word is uncertain. The first letter might be ⟨b⟩. Some of the ⟨t⟩s look like ⟨g⟩s on this page of the MS.

289 There is a mark above the ⟨t⟩ which I cannot interpret.

290 The missing word is supplied from O'Curry's transcription.

291 The missing word is supplied from O'Curry's transcription.

292 O'Curry reads 'colpach'.

293 The missing letters are supplied from O'Curry's transcription.

294 The reading of this word is tentative.

295 There is a letter erased after the second ⟨d⟩.

296 The missing letters are supplied from O'Curry's transcription.

5 [r]o-fesad[297] .i. fu*acht*n*aigh*id. for-uast*ar*[298] .i. fua*cht*n*aigh*[t]er.[299] cæi*mthe*ch*t*ad*ha*[300] .i. coi*m*ide*acht*ad*ha* .i. lu*cht* coi*m*id*acht* *ar* son bi*us*

6 dæntoisg. dérac*h* .i. lomr*ach*.[301] glin*ne* .i. daingen. treab*air*e dfirub*h*an .i. fulang. ciol*ar* .i. c[orn][302]

[b]1 [303][fer medh]on goide l*eth*e .i. f*e*r aga mbí[304] fios an gadaige. fer m*ed*-*h*ongoide láin .i. f*e*r ga mbi[305] ⟨fios⟩ an gad[aige] ⁊ [na][306]

2 goide mále. iorcha, ⟨*edgedh*⟩[307] i*ar* c*h*a .i. landæir, ca .i. tec*h* .⁊c̄.[308] mís eim*h*glet(*h*)he[309] .i. mí a ndentæi eim*h*gle .i.

3 suid*h*iug*adh* cána no c*air*de no dlig*adh* .⁊c̄. sgenman*na* .i. n*eth*e sgin*nius* do*n* in*n*eoin on ord gaba*n*

4 duil .r.[310] tret*h*nac*h* .i. trentonn*a*c. ub*ha*, ab*ha* .i. ab*h*an*n*.[311] góla .i. gúala.[312] blæid*h*is .i. béicis. Ruib*h*en[313] .i. tuillid

5 iodnac*har*, iod*h*nag*ar* .i. tiodnaict*e*r. d*e*rbana*r* .i. diuba*r*t*ar*. deolad*hacht* .i. g*r*asia .i. ní a naisgid*h*. deoin ⟨*edgedh*⟩[314] .i. corr *us*ge

6 coic, coc*air*e, fert*h*ig*h*is .i. fer do b*e*r tene ⁊ *us*ge do*na* hæideiduib*h*, ⁊ isi*n* ⟨ł agan⟩ egl*us* bios. lánc*h*at*h*aig*h*[315] .i. lánad*h*oin

7 t*r*i iomar*e*, no díre bios ag fulang na heaguilsi .i. c*é*trann, cuingeall, ⁊ ud*h*b*air*t. c*é*tran*n* .i. flesg lai*m*e

297 O'Curry reads 'feasad'.
298 O'Curry reads 'for-uartur'.
299 O'Curry reads 'fuachtnaighthear'.
300 O'curry reads 'coimtheachtadha'.
301 O'Curry reads 'lomrach'.
302 The missing letters are supplied from O'Curry's transcription.
303 There is a tear in the paper, and the beginning of the line is missing. It is possible that there is an entry completely missing or that Dubhaltach's source citation (if there was one here) is also lost.
304 O'Curry reads 'mbeadh'.
305 O'Curry reads 'mbeadh'.
306 The missing letters are supplied from O'Curry's transcription.
307 The name of the source written above the lemma is not part of the entry. It is possible that Dubhaltach added the name of his source here after the edge of the page was torn.
308 O'Curry lists *ca* as a separate entry.
309 Dubhaltach wrote an ⟨h⟩ over another letter as a correction after he had already put a *punctum* over the ⟨t⟩.
310 Perhaps the source is *Duil roscada*.
311 O'Curry reads 'abhainn'.
312 The ⟨g⟩ is made over another letter. This entry is not in O'Curry's transcription.
313 The ⟨r⟩ is capital.
314 The name of the source written above the lemma is not part of the entry.
315 O'Curry reads 'lanchothaigh'.

8 ⁊ orba laime[316] na man*ac*[h] fein do benatt*ar* as coill *ar* na t*h*iod*h*nacal da nerlam*h*[317] ó t*h*osac*h*[318]

9 cuingell[319] .i. ni geallt*ar* do*n* egl*us* isi*n* cionuid do nit*er* ria. udb*air*t .i. feran*n* iodbai*r*t[320] na huasuil

10 na mb*eth*aid*h*[321] i*ar* t[r]osg*adh*[322] do d*h*ia ⁊ dona nꜵm*h*uib*h*. ceng*ar* .i. ceimn*igh*ter. 7 cꜵgdac[323] .i. ain*m* g*r*aid

11 t*r*e ma*r* c*h*an*us*, na t*r*i *cóic*a salm, fog*h*laint*idh*, deisgibal, st*ar*uide, foirc*etlaigh* sꜵ́i canoine d*r*uimcli

12 ag si*n* na sec*h*t ng*r*aid egna. 6 fog⟨laintig*h*⟩[324] .i. f*er* ag a mbi eol*us* indeic*h* leabr*aibh* dfoc*h*oir aige, ui*m*e si*n* goirt*er*

13 de fer tiachtana foc*h*oireac*h*. 5 desgib*al* .i. f*er* ag a *m*bi eol*us* foc*h*oire uile .i. 12 leab*har* na foc*h*oirec*h*

14 4 st*ar*uide .i. fer ag a *m*bi .30. daice*acht*uib*h* nꜵ*m*ta ina f*h*ogloim. 3 f*or*c*et*l*aid* .i. f*er* ag a *m*bi g*r*amadac*h* cro

15 san ⁊ siollꜵb*ha*, ⁊ rim*he*, ⁊ ret*ha* na bl*iad*na, ⁊ ret*ha* g*r*ene, ⁊ esga. 2 sꜵi canoine .i. f*er* ag a mbi eol*us*

16 canoine, ⁊ can*us* sgela iosa .i. b*r*eit*er* nde (isi*n* inad glan i mbi) .i. ecna cadluic canoine

17 1 d*r*uimcli .i. f*er* ag a mbí eol*us* iomlan na hegna on leab*ar* as mó da ngoirt*er* cuilmen, g*us*

18 [in][325] leab*har* as lug*h*a da ngoirt*er* deic*h* b*r*et*h*ir,[326] ina ndeac*h*raigt*er* .i. i ndeg*hch*oir*igh*t*h*er an

19 tiomna mait*h* do rin*n*e día do Mꜵisi[327]

---

316 Part of the MS is damaged; it might be from an earlier repair.

317 An earlier ⟨o⟩ is corrected to an ⟨e⟩ in lighter colored ink.

318 Some letters are erased at the end of the line.

319 Part of the MS is damaged; it might be from an earlier repair.

320 O'Curry reads 'iodbrait'.

321 The ⟨d⟩ is written over a ⟨g⟩ in lighter colored ink.

322 O'Curry reads 'ttrosgad*h*'. Part of the MS is damaged; it might be from an earlier repair.

323 O'Curry reads 'caogadach', but note that he changed his mind about this reading to 'caogdach' when he published *Lectures on the Manuscript Materials of Ancient Irish History* in 1861, pp. 494–495.

324 Several letters are crossed out; the correction is added above the line with a reference mark.

325 This word is supplied from O'Curry's transcription.

326 O'Curry reads 'breithis'.

327 O'Curry reads '*ar* saoisi'. Note that he changed this reading to 'Maoisi' when he published *Lectures on the Manuscript Materials of Ancient Irish History* in 1861, pp. 494–495. The remainder of the line is empty.

20 cat*hair* ataig*h* .i. cat*hair* i naitcen*n* cac*h* a s*hoc*h*ar*, ⁊ a d*hoc*h*ar*: cat*hair* ataig*h th*all i gcion*n* cille:

21 cat*hair* ataig*h* an *airc*h*in*n*igh*: cat*hair* ataig*h* .i. cat*h*æir ep̄s[328]

22 fet*h*æl[329] .i. mion*n*, ma*r* ata, clog, c*r*os, bacc*h*all, minist*er* no soisgel .⁊c̄. minist*er* .i. mion*n*a aisdir bi*us ar*

23 aisd*er* isi*n* túait*h* le tab*air*t mion*n ar* c*h*ac*h*. ⁊c̄.[330]

[c]1 *edghedh*.[331] dírec*h*, ⁊ derac*h* .i. lomr*adh*. tairecc[332] .i. torra*cht*ain. súiltec*h* .i. f*er* sellce*acht*a .i. seallac. erent*ac* .i.

2 f*er* f*or* a nern*aigh*ter fiac*h*. díc*h*ealtac*h* .i. an f*er* cub*us* b*r*ait*h* .i. an f*er* bi*us* ag ceilt an uilc

3 tuid*h*in æsa escána .i. t*ár*gad*h* an lo*cht*a ná bí isi*n* riagail. ealgn*us* .i. eolgnais

4 com*h*raite .i. an t*urc*h*ar* do b*he*r duine t*r*e f*er*g, ⁊ *gur*ob ail leis a guin. duinet*h*aid*he* .i. táites

5 di*m*irt *ar* an dui*ne ar* na marb*adh* .i. a f*h*olac*h* an cuirp m*air*b deis a m*ar*bt*h*a.

6 fog*h*ail t*r*ebdire .i. fogail do dena*m* is na t*r*ebaib*h* i n*air*illn*aigh*ter dire. roch bi .i. ro b*hi*

7 pliun .i. t*air*isiom*h*. toit*h*fliun .i. t*air*risiom*h*, no fuillid*he*, cos*m*ail ⁊ pliun. egl*us*[333] l*eth*dire[334] .i. egl*us*

8 n*ac* bí na dlig*hedh* t*r*e ttesdan*n* l*eth*dire uait*he*. eagl*us*[335] na[336] foltmaisi .i. egl*us* i mbi óglæc*h* l[...][337]

9 na cen*n* uirre leis *ar* maisioc*h* folt *air*[338]

328 The rest of the line is left blank. The last four words are added later in a darker colored ink. They are listed as a separate entry in O'Curry's transcription.

329 O'Curry reads 'feathal'.

330 The rest of line is left blank. There is a line drawn under this section of text across the page. The following lines are in a darker colored ink.

331 In *marg. sin.* for *étged*.

332 The reading might be 'taireacc'.

333 O'Curry reads 'egluis'.

334 O'Curry reads 'leithdire'.

335 O'Curry reads 'eagluis'.

336 This word is written above the line.

337 O'Curry does not note that at least one word is missing; the edge of the page is damaged.

338 The rest of the line is empty.

Transcription p. 6[339]

[a]1 [340][forbuain] indlig[htheach] no f*or*rge[341] no forr*a*c[h] indlig[htheach] .i. ni do b[h]uain da ceilib[h] do[n] r[h]ig t*ar* an ni d[ligeas][342]

2 r[uice,] ruca .i. ruaid*h* cec*h*[343] imderg*tha*.[344] bos[345] .i. bá[346] fi*us* .i. fi*us* mait*h*. eallac*h* .i. suidiug*adh*, no or[dúghadh][347]

3 [cicht] .i. [rinnai]g*he*.[348] sg*r*ipt .i. sg*r*ibnid*h*. culma*re*[349] .i. c*air*pteoir. c*r*uitig*h* .i. c*r*uitere. cuislen*naigh*[350] .i. f*eth*ánac*h* gnæ[351] .i. oib[.]

4 [...]er[.....]nt*er*.[352] b*r*on*nus* .i. sof*hius*[353] b*r*on*n*. bert .i. b*reith*em*h*nus. *air*illn*edh* .i. dlig*edh*. ad-ren .i. iocaid*h*. ad-ealla .i. aid*h*[l]id[354]

5 breas .i. *ar*dfoll*us*. sruit*h* .i. uasal. i*ar*ngl*us* .i. i*ar* ngleof*h*esa. i*ar* soillsi[355] gl*us* .i. soillsi i*ar*ngl*us*a[356]

6 [....]ll[.] soillsi. clio*th*c*h*a clucha .i. clu*th*ma*re*[357] .i. teta. ainfig*h* .i. gan fig*he*. sging .i. iomd*ad*h.[358] imsging .i.

7 [...] iom[.]d[.] . manac*h* innerge de*th*b*h*ire .i. man*ach* img*h*es ona eagl*us* du*th*c*hus* do cu*m* egluisi oile da

---

339 There is a lot of scattered staining over the page. All sides of the page are damaged and missing parts of the text.

340 Part of the top line is illegible due to the library mounting which covers part of it.

341 This word is not included in this entry in O'Curry's transcript, but he does have a headword 'forrge' in his transcription with a note to see this entry.

342 The missing words are supplied from O'Curry's transcription. Several of the missing letters must be from expanding an abbreviation or suspension due to the amount of space in the MS.

343 There is a symbol after this word which I cannot interpret. It is not included in O'Curry's transcription.

344 O'Curry reads 'imdearga'.

345 The numeral 6 is written above this word.

346 O'Curry reads 'bo'.

347 The missing letters are supplied from O'Curry's transcription.

348 The missing letters are supplied from O'Curry's transcription.

349 O'Curry reads 'culmuire'.

350 The ⟨u⟩ is written over another letter partially crossed out.

351 O'Curry reads 'gnaei'.

352 This entry is not in O'Curry's transcription. It is possible that this entry belongs with the previous one.

353 O'Curry reads 'fofhios'.

354 The gloss is not in O'Curry's transcription.

355 ⟨.i. biad⟩ is crossed out after this.

356 The reading of the last letter is tentative. O'Curry reads 'iarnguls'.

357 O'Curry reads 'cluthmuire'.

358 The reading of the last syllable is uncertain.

8 adnacal inte, no di*arraidh* coth*aighthe* tre ria*cht*anus .i. di aitber*air* eirge[359] aisde a hin*n*e, ma*r* si*n* in*n*erge

9 cattuctatad*h* ma det*h*bir no in*n*detbir. at*air* an*n*oide .i. at*air* eglu*s*e dutc*hus* do nec*h*

10 cro rig*h*, ⁊ senaid*h* .i. cruin*n*iog*adh*, no dail an rig*h* no an tsenuid*h*. ⟨colpa⟩[360] cennait*he* .i. cen*n* snait*he* sꜵg*h*ail

11 no cen*n* aig*he* .i. aimsire[361] .i. ai*m*sir is an*n* ioc*us* an colpa cen*n*ait*he* da ngoirt*er* colpa cen*n*ad*air*te

12 se*acht* b*air*gen .i. b*air*gen ioc*us* an m*ar*b*h* i gcion*n* se*acht*m*ui*ne deis a bais. Fl*edh* croil*ighe*. i gcion*n* mis, sꜵ

13 lim g*ur*ob ionan*n* si*n* cui*m*niug*adh* miu*s*a na m*ar*b*h* re heglu*s* ioc*ar* si*n* os na m*ar*b*aibh*.

14 re com*h*loig*h*t*he* .i. ai*m*sir ⟨no⟩[362] c*air*de fa fiacaib*h* co*m*logu*is* an feicem*h* donti *ar* a mbí fiac*h* aige

15 uinge ⟨don eglu*s* teide⟩[363] diubaid*h* nuire .i. *air*ged uam*ha* no leabt*ha* .i. diub*h*aid .i. adbal eibe na huire

16 .i. i mbúain no i ndena*m* na huaig*h*e do*n*a dꜵinib*h*si. deor*aidh*, mu*r*cu*r*-t*he*, fꜵi*n*dl*edh*aig*h*, fu*r*fog*r*aig, ⁊

17 taisdeall*aigh*, si*n* uat*ha* maille se*acht* b*air*gin. lainbiath*adh* g*ach* graid*h* a fl*edh* croil*ig*e, no 7m*ad* log*h* e[nech]

18 se*acht*m*adh* loig*he* enec*h* g*ach* graid a se*acht* b*air*gen no a se*acht*m*adh* lainbiath*adh*.[364] rúsg nd*air*ti .i. r*u*sg diosg

19 <u>no *etram*</u>. fertag*ar*[365] .i. adnaict*er*. ion*n*ota*cht* .i. tosac*h* .i. tec*h*t in*n*. ion-forb*air*t .i. fas, no

20 bisioc*h*. anailge .i. sam*h*laig*h*t*he* no.[366] éit*h*em*h*lac*hus* .i. cosmúil*acht*, no

21 no t*ar*raingcolm*hacht* b*hius* eidir n*e*t*h*ib*h*, ⁊ go h*air*ide *ede*r danaib*h*, no cerduib*h* .⁊c̄.

22 [*ed*]g*edh*.[367] coinsi .i. cꜵin-gn*ú*s dia soad*h* g*a*c nda[t]h.[368] tet*h*natt*ar* .i. roten*n*sat*ar*, no rot*h*esgsat. foid*h*erc .i. foirreil[369]

---

359 A few letters before this word are crossed out.

360 This word is written above the line with an insertion mark.

361 The shape of the ⟨r⟩ here is normally used after ⟨o⟩.

362 This word is written above the line with an insertion mark.

363 The gloss is written above first two headwords. O'Curry reads 'teid'.

364 O'Curry lists this part of the entry as two separate items without glosses *s.vv. lainbiathadh*, etc. and *seachtmadh*, etc.

365 O'Curry reads 'feartatar'.

366 A letter before is crossed out, and a word after this is crossed out.

367 This form is for *étged*.

368 The missing letter is supplied from O'Curry's transcription.

369 The first ⟨i⟩ is written under the ⟨o⟩.

23 bit*h* .i. guin. cota-imtiagad .i. comaitg*h*eth*adh*.[370] taith .i. an g*r*ut*h* tait*h*. faigneoir .i. cerd cait*h*es an sdan

24 rena f*h*aingnib*h*. ceobat*h* .i. an muir nem*hair*gsion*adh* b*híus* fá c*h*éo. do roac*h*t .i. do ro ait*h*ed*h*, do roilg*edh*[371] .i. do ro log[adh][372]

25 ad ro-g*r*eim .i. ro ing*r*eim. ad-glenad .i. ad*h*a glanuid*h*, no glenoid, no t*h*eglomuid. eigceall .i. d*r*oic*h*iall. g*a*c æ .i. g*ach*

26 og*h* æ dib*h*. an*m*chaide .i. cait*h*ium*h* an*m*a go háit*h* no go had*h*a. fub-tad*h* .i. fo diub*adh* b*e*t*h*a. fuadac*h* do[373] t*a*r*r* .i.

27 ben torr*a*c fuaid*igius* fer leis. guat*h*asg .i. tasg gúa a len*n*ain, no neic*h* as ionmui*n* le do tab*air*t do[374] cu*m* na mna

28 uat*h*b*h*as .i. dub*h*aig*h*ed*h*, no an luc*h* etorra, ⁊ a léne, no an erc luac*r*a do*n*a mnaib[375] ben*us* si*n*.

29 mir méne .i. g*r*im*h* as mian leis an mnæi t*h*orr*aigh*. d*r*ut*h*lac*h* .i. læc*h*-d*r*uta .i. fer l*e*t*h*c*h*ui*nn*. næi .i. et*har*. fo-glen .i. deg*h*len.

30 do-*air*r[376] .i. t*a*rr*aigh*ter, do ecma .i. tegm*hus*. *sédrac* .i. t*r*en, nertma*r*. iomaig*h* .i. iomain. ad-rire .i. iocaid*h*. urnasg .i. ua[sal][377]

31 fonasg. taisealb*adh* .i. taisben*adh*. u*r*co*n*n .i. uas*a*l c*h*odn*a*c[h]. ni hois .i. na fæm*h*, ni hog*har*. ní fæmt*har*

32 t*air*id*h*in lin*n*e muilin*n* .i. clad*h* con*n*m*hus* an t*us*ge leisi*n* muilean.[378] clad*h* fot*h*aid*h* mona .i. gáin*n*ir mona

33 apain .i. ebiltin. *á*r*chú* lom*h*na .i. cu *a*ra mbi lomán da cengal. ruib do meal*ar* .i. ba, ⁊ cæir[e][379]

34 ruib na doi*m*eal*ar* .i. capuill, ⁊ muca. féisi .i. muc. cit*r*iug, ⁊ t*r*eteall .i. an*m*an*n*a do cæir*ibh*

35 tasc*artha* .i. an cait*h*cliat*h*. forcraid*h*, aigbele, ⁊ *ét*toll*us* .i. lo*cht*a na ndénta n*a*c dioráit*h*. coib*h*dealac

36 duine aga *m*bí coi*m*d*h*eala, no gæl re nec*h*. am*h*uis rúin, ⁊ raid*h*, ⁊ ioma-gall .i. am*h*uis ⟨bid⟩[380] ma*r* si*n* ag tigerna

370 O'Curry reads 'comaitghethach'.
371 There is a superfluous suspension mark. The ⟨g⟩ is added below the line.
372 The missing letters are supplied from O'Curry's transcription.
373 Three letters before this word are struck through.
374 The ⟨o⟩ is made over another letter.
375 The word 'mnaib*h*' is written a second time and struck through.
376 O'Curry reads 'do-arr'.
377 The missing letters are supplied from O'Curry's transcription.
378 The ⟨e⟩ is made over another letter as a correction.
379 The missing letter is supplied from O'Curry's transcription.
380 This word is inserted above the line with a reference mark.

37 ro rir .i. do ro rec. ni ria .i. na rec. ar-aid*h*e .i. *ar* son. dénm*h*ec*h* .i. dis*h*om*h*æinec*h*

[b]1 duil .r.[381] *air*benat*har*[382] .i. ion*nar*bt*ar*. friot*h*aige .i. fior-ion*n*saig*h*id*h*. sich[383] .i. ionsaig*h*id*h*. aill .i. uasal

2 em*h*ad[384] tem*r*ac*h*a .i. eblid na huaisle. fu[i]reg*ar* .i. *air*git*e*r. forb*h*ac*h* .i. forb*h*uain .i. ní ben*us* ri t*ar* dlig*h*[edh] ⟨da che[le]⟩[385]

3 conai*meacht* .i. do cæin ai*m*sig*edh*. com*h*ad*h* .i. coi*m*[eada]d*h*.[386] forcmad*h* .i. fiorcoim*h*[eadadh][387]

Transcription of p. 7[388]

Marg. sup. sin.[389]
Duil.r.[390]
Marg. sup. dext.
...lioi[391]
Marg. sup. intercol.
duil[392]
Do aitig*h*dl*us*[393] an caid*e*rne[394] si uile[395]

[a]1 feiste .i. tioru*air*si .i. i*ar*d*r*aig*h*e. bá .i. m*a*it*h*[396]

---

381 This abbreviation might be for *Duil roscada*.
382 O'Curry reads 'arrbeanathar'.
383 The ⟨s⟩ is made over another letter.
384 O'Curry reads 'eamhad'.
385 The missing letters are supplied from O'Curry's transcription.
386 The missing letters are supplied from O'Curry's transcription.
387 The missing letters are supplied from O'Curry's transcription. The page mounting obscures part of the last line.
388 The page consists of writing in two columns with notes across *marg. sup.* partially obscured by library tape.
389 There is writing across the very top of the page, but it is obscured by library tape. A hand-held UV light was able to pick up some words, but not enough so that I can read them.
390 The interpretation of the abbreviation as *dúil roscada* is tentative.
391 The beginning of this word is illegible. It appears again on page 13.
392 The top half of the letters is obscured by library tape.
393 ⟨dl⟩ is uncertain; it could be ⟨oe⟩ or something else. Cf. *eDIL s.v. áittiugad* 'establishing, proving'.
394 *eDIL s.v. caitirne* 'quaternion; tract, subject matter'.
395 'Regarding proving is the subject matter of all of this'. Just to the left of this phrase, there is a numeral 7 is later ink than the surrounding text. UV light (November 16, 2022) shows that there is writing above the numeral, but I cannot make out the words.
396 This word should end the entry, but O'Curry carries on; he misses the head word

i*m*be*d*[397] .i. ebriug*hus* bꜵisi .i. bág*h* [no][398] iom*a*d bꜵisi
déiste .i. déis as ed, tioru*air*sin béos
g*r*iot*h* .i. criot*h*nug*hadh*. gu*air*iug*hadh* .i. ⟨fuastori⟩[399]
g*air*iug*adh* .i. denam g*arrtha*[400] no éig*h*e
t*ar*gad .i. tionol. f*air*ge .i. at*htair*git*h*er[401]
aid*h*ilgn*ech* .i. dlig*h*t*h*e*ch*. aid*h*b*h*en .i. ad*h*b*ha* d*h*íona
fórm*ac*[h] ⁊ tórm*ac*[h] .i. m*é*tug*hadh*. tiug*h*ragac*h* .i.
t*airgedhach* ag*hach* .i. fer t*h*ionoilte g*h*niom*ha* t*air*
meallac*h* .i. ꜵibin*n*. dinnis .i. mionna
ioc*ht* .i. gniom*h*. siniomon .i. sen som*h*ꜵin*ac*[h][402]
s*h*eall ⁊ sell .i. am*har*c. brot*h* sguad*h* .i. brut*h*
sgeit*hius* an f*hair*rge. bérd*air*[403] .i. b*reith*emn*ag*t*er[404]
fúirest*ar* .i. *air*gid*h*ter .i. geib*h*ter. biora .i. b*reith*
em*hnaidh*. briog*h* ⁊ b*r*iog*htar* .i. fírén*aigh*t*h*er
torgaib*h* .i. do rin*ne* t*or*gabail cionad*h*
sochla .i. soc*h*lad*h*, no soc*h*lú. eisil .i. eis =
éolac*h* .i. ainéolac*h*. cám*h*[405] .i. cáinte
éirit*h*e .i. ioctha. fo-coislit*h*er .i. foxl*aight* =
er .i. sg*a*rad*h* le ní,[406] no diog*h*bal*aigh*ter
do-negaid .i. feduid. f*r*is-gab*h*aid .i. abs[407]
tinent.[408] sas*ar* .i. ionsoig*h*ter. don*n* .i. goid
do*nn*uig*h*e don*nach* .i. gaduig*h*e. líu, lia .i. liom*h*nad*h*
oillían .i. léine m*h*ór. culpait .i. coiler

---

starting on the next line and combines the two entries. It is possible that this is one long entry.

397 There is at least one letter, or some form of reference mark, in *marg. sin.* which is illegible and only partially visible. The reading of the lemma is tentative.

398 There is a gap in the text. O'Curry reads *no*, but there is nothing visible, and it looks like at least one word was erased.

399 This word is struck through and the reading is uncertain. Maybe also ⟨fuaftosi⟩?

400 O'Curry reads 'gairtha'.

401 There might be a faint length mark next to the first ⟨a⟩.

402 In O'Curry's transcription, it is difficult to determine whether he is reading *somhaomeach* or *somhaoineach* because his sequence of minims is joined together.

403 O'Curry reads 'bérdarum'. There is a mark above the ⟨ar⟩ with looks like the suspension mark for ⟨m⟩.

404 The expansion of the third syllable is uncertain.

405 The ⟨c⟩ is written over another letter. O'Curry reads 'cumh'.

406 One character, possibly a Tironian note, is struck through after 'ní'.

407 O'Curry reads 'abtinent'.

408 The ⟨i⟩ overwrites an ⟨e⟩. Here and elsewhere Dubhaltach uses different letter forms to indicate he is writing in Latin.

25 ut cail coim*hét*, ⁊ pait .i. cenn. bít*h* .i. gui*n*

26 fæt*h*, æt*h* .i. mion*n*a. iardac*h* ⟨.i. ait*h*gin⟩[409] .i. i*ar*am*h* dig*h*de

27 .i. buidec*hus* i*ar*sin enecl*ann* ber*ar* i*ar*dac*h*

28 do-maister .i. tom*hais*ter. toimdig*h*ter .i. to*mhais*ter, ⁊

29 b*ar*am*hlaigh*ter. airlít*h*ec*h* .i. fer denta uas*a*l

30 liot*h*a. tiomortain .i. on mbas raidter

31 no tiom*ar*ta.

32 ad-roig*h*est*ar* .i. ro guidest*ar*, no ro eisgest*ar*

33 urt*h*uasa*cht* .i. eist*acht*,[410] tuaisit*h*er .i. ester, no

34 leigid*h* fa na cluasuib*h*, no t*air*is ga*n* fi*ar*f*hoghidh*

35 an ni do dlig*h*fed*h* do *denam*

36 nas*ar* .i. naisgter .i. cengailter

[b]1 f*air*ben .i. fíreipt*her* .i. fírbent*ar*. cu*m*t*hus* .i. com*h*mait*hius*

2 cuindrig*h* .i. cæindrig*h*. ræ.i. feran*n*. naisi .i. cenguilsi

3 cam .i. comlan*n*. cai*m*p*er* .i. fer co*mlainn*. diam*h*ain .i. diainim

4 dim*h*ed*h* .i. toi*mh*dennis .i. b*ar*am*luigh*is. *édgedh*.[411] im*eth* .i. ni*meth* .i. egl*us*. t*r*egan

5 dit*h*ec*h* .i. séna. feraid .i. feg*air* .i. at*htair*gid*h* .i. tionol

6 roch*air* .i. ro seic*h*ig*h*ter .i. ro hion*n*saig*h*ter

7 f*r*iomall .i. mailli*d* f*r*iom, *édgedh*. læb*h* .i. l*eth*t*r*om no l*eth*taob*h*

8 no*m*ad*h* nó .i. nom*adh* nae .i. fer. fém*edh* .i. diultad*h*

9 aniu t*ar* am*ar*ac .i. tar an*air*tec*h* ⁊ do geb*air* tfiac*h*a[412]

10 re, toe, toræ .i. focail raiter re fer na bfiac*h* du*ar* .i. dui*n*e[413]

11 for-reit*h* .i. foir*igh*nig*h*. for-r*eith*er .i. foir*igh*nig*h*ter

12 ada-bon*n*. ⟨.i. obaim⟩ ad-bois .i. obais. díuirb .i. dui*n*e g*an* feran*n*

13 eítnge .i. fer d*r*oc*h* urlap*ra* .i. e g*an* teng*aid*. as-roib. ro ob

14 coib*h*che .i. com*h*oig*h*e cuir, ⁊ cu*nnar*t*h*a

15 boibre .i. bo eibert .i. geim d*r*ut do ni, ⁊ amadan eisein[414]

16 buicne .i. ceo da b*h*uaic. fer l*eth*cui*nn* e.[415]

---

409 This word is written as a gloss above *iardach* with reference marks.

410 The MS has a comma, but it should probably be a full stop.

411 It is likely that Dubhaltach names his source here.

412 This line looks like it was added in later as it is squeezed between two lines of text.

413 This entry is partially covered by a stain in *marg. dext.* It is written from the bottom upwards. There may be more written after *duine*, but it is covered by an ink stain.

414 It should be noted that the second half of the entry was added later in a slightly smaller script size and lighter colored ink.

415 Dubhaltach initially wrote both the lemma here and in the line below and left the remainder of the line empty. He later added the definitions to both entries in a lighter ink color and using a smaller script size to make everything fit the available space on the line. It is

17 boicmell .i. meall buic .i. meall congnai ima brag*h*uid .i. in reindinic[416]
18 coisid .i. teg*us*g*a*d. aille .i. alleluia. ionráit*h* .i. nec*h* as io*n* =
19 gabt*h*a i rait*high*ius. esomain .i. es som*h*æin. næill .i. luig*h*e
20 colt*r*a .i. seca[417] dion*n*ba .i. ⟨gan⟩[418] ba for dion*n* f*or* dul*ach*[419]
21 ailtl*eth*an con*are* .i. fer[420] teg*h*l*eth*an *ar* an con*air* e da rad*h* frier[421]
22 sesaid .i. ionsoig*h*id. cec*h*latt*ar* .i. do *conncattar*. ad-bela .i. ebi .i. ba[s][422]
23 conóad .i. coim*hét*uid. slatra[423] ⁊ lat*r*a ⟨.i. ambfial⟩[424] ⟨.i. anb*h*al⟩[425] .i. ⟨láidir dana⟩[426] quasi more latrom
24 eidg*edh*.[427] frepad*h* .i. leig*hius*. seg*ar* .i. ion*n*saigt*e*r. urgn*aigh*ter .i. uasal
25 f*h*og*h*aint*e*r. ruib*h*d*h*it*h*er .i. ro eidis imdib*h*t*e*r. sias .i. ion*n*saigter
26 fúac*har* .i. fúa*cht*n*aig*ter. ⟨duil⟩[428] brasul .i. fer aga *m*bí ulc*h*a bras m*ar* ulgar
27 ag d*r*ud ⁊ ag osg*h*l*adh* a beoil c*h*aintig*h*. con-amad*hair* .i. cæín, no co*m*
28 aimsig*h*t*e*r. duil.[429] eidg*edh*.[430] inm*h*uille, muill*edh* .i. gresa*cht*, no brus-dad
29 bǽidsioc*h* .i. ben b*h*æt*h* .i. sec*h* as bæt. fresán .i. im*ri*sin .i. ime
30 re son .i. fál re fog*ar* na firin*n*e. talmuidioc*h* .i. fer mire
31 no cut*h*aig*h*,[431] no gal*air* m*h*oir. terbsad .i. g*r*eamuig*h*id no sgæilid

---

quite possible that he added both of these definitions at the same time that he added the second half of the *boibre* entry.

416 See previous note.

417 There is an empty space in the line between this entry and the one that follows it.

418 This word is inserted above the line with a reference mark.

419 O'Curry lists the last two words as a separate entry *s.v. fordionn.*

420 This word is inserted above the line with a reference mark.

421 The reading ought to be *fri* given the verbal construction. It looks as if Dubhaltach initially wrote *fer* which he corrected to *fri* without crossing out the ⟨er⟩. It is possible that this copying mistake is the reason that *fer* was inserted with a reference mark earlier in the gloss.

422 The second gloss is written above the previous word. The edge of the paper is worn and letters could be missing.

423 O'Curry lists *slatra* only as the lemma.

424 This gloss is written above the first lemma.

425 This gloss is written below the first lemma.

426 These two words are inserted above the line with a reference mark.

427 This form is for OI *étged.*

428 The word 'duil' is inserted above the line. There is a dividing line between the end of the previous entry and the start of the next one.

429 Dubhaltach added a diagonal line after this word to indicate that this section of material has ended.

430 Another section of material begins here.

431 O'Curry reads 'cuthaigh'. Although the first letter looks very much like an ⟨o⟩, it is likely that it is really a ⟨c⟩ which was accidentally closed in rapid writing.

32 æib*h*ilteoir .i. *g*rad*h* egailsi bi*us* m*ar* æibil isin teoir .i. i leigen*n* crab*aidh*

33 duil.[432] seol .i. suaill. aigdig*h*t*er* .i. uga eisgit*h*er. tiog*h*baid*h* .i. deige[nach][433]

34 bas*aig*id*h*. foic*h*lit*er*[434] .i. oirc*h*illa*igh*t*er*.[435] f*ed*hid*h* .i. at*htairg*id*h*

35 cáit*h*, cát*h*aig*h*e .i. nem*h*ni, no f*o*rorbf*h*ás*ac*. f*r*esl*uig*e .i. luig*h*e f*r*is

36 ad-anna .i. adannaig*h* .i. fadoig

Transcription p. 8[436]

1 [...].i.[.]aing*h*en. cis .i. cia, no caidiad. coinin[437] l*eth* .i. cæin[....]. ceallad .i. [t]emceall*ad*, no teglom*ad*.[438] *conotar* .i. coi*m*e[d][439]

2 [d]roc*h* .i. dorc*h*a, no nem*h*sol*us*.[440] fær .i. fuirec*h*, no foir*idh*in. dít*h*ec*h*, coindircle .i. c*air*deml*acht*. læbad*h* .i. sæb*h*ad*h*. miod*h*[lach .i.][441]

3 m*ed*hon læc*hus*, no met*h*lac*hus*. do-luaisg*et* .i. tog*h*luais*et*. f*er* dit*h*re .i. f*er* *ar* doit*h* re, no *ar* dóit*h* tíre.

4 ben f*r*ia huait*h*ne .i. re niod*h*nuib*h*, ⁊ uait*h*ne cin*n* a lenib*h* uait*h*e. cimidi*h* i ræ .i. b*r*aig*h*e *ar* na gabail i rae ca[tha]

5 t*r*i b*r*iat*r*a (an egcui*nn* .i. an mic big) doni t*estus* no fiad*h*n*us*e .i. an lion ceall, an la sun*nr*adac*h*. easp*uc etir* a p[ars]

6 ⁊ a cailioc*h* .i. idir a ablai*n*, ⁊ a cailis. iuidig*h*ec*h*t .i. iudiciumm[442] .i. b*r*et*h*em*h*n*us*. com*h*ad .i. coi*mét*uid*h*. co-næ .i. c[o]*m*[443]

7 do-boing .i. toibg*h*id*h*. f*er* cuitc*h*ernsa .i. f*er* bi*us* i gcu*m*a re nec*h* hi*mon*[444] do*m*an ag cosn*am* rig*h*e no abdaine.

---

432 The source notation is written *inter col.*

433 O'Curry reads 'deigeneadh'.

434 There might be a length mark over the ⟨o⟩.

435 O'Curry reads 'oirchillltear', but there a short dash after ⟨ll⟩ suggesting a suspended syllable.

436 The top left side of the page is damaged and some writing has been worn away. The same is true of the upper right third of the page.

437 This entry is not in O'Curry's transcription.

438 This entry is not in O'Curry's transcription.

439 The end of the page is worn; I follow O'Curry's reading of the final letter.

440 I follow O'Curry's reading of the lemma; the MS is worn and part of the lemma is illegible.

441 I follow O'Curry's reading of the lemma; the MS is worn and part of the lemma is illegible.

442 The reading of the last few letters is uncertain as they consist of a row of minimns. It should be noted that Dubhaltach has shifted to roman script for this Latin legal term.

443 The missing letter is supplied from O'Curry's transcription.

444 Some of the letters are overwritten; the transcription is tentative.

8 fer fuiche .i. fer *tét* go mnæi na gnais. urg*artha* .i. c*r*osta. fris-ráilt*e*r .i. f*r*it*h*áilt*e*r, no firin*n*lit[er][445]

9 ria*cht*aig*he* .i. fer ria*cht*an*us*. mb*h*rog*hthar*[446] .i. firen*igh*te*r*. con-seic*h*it*h*er .i. tait*hnemhach* ionsaigt*e*r. fuillmec*h* .i. f*e*r ga[ch][447]

10 fuill*edh* loig*hacht ar* breig do den*am* na f*h*iadn*uis*e. foilmer .i. f*e*r b*hius* ag[448] leim *ar* nec*h* go foi[l][449]

11 ag breit*h* a s*et* uad*h*. f*air*be .i. fior eibe ut fer f*air*be .i. f*e*r fior eibe æi .i. an f*e*r bi*us* ag

12 fior ebe na cuisi i naig*idh* neic*h ar* log*h*. finem*h*n*us* .i. fine iom*h*æin uais. feiles*ac* .i. f*e*r fea[llas][450]

13 *ar* les c*h*aig*h*. eitsec*h* .i. ré gan tec*h* aige. fuireg*ar* .i. *air*gid*h*ter .i. geibt*e*r. fo-coisle .i. foxl*adh*

14 . meadb*ha* .i. mesamnuig*h*[451] .i. bret*h*em*h*.[452] mead*h* .i. bá .i. mait*h*. dána các*h* go hiat*h* .i. go mion*na*

15 églaim*m* .i. inc*h*rec*h*ad*h*. c*ar*aid clæc*h*lod*ha* .i. duine aga *m*bí clæc*h*lod*h* c*air*desa re a t*h*igerna maille

16 in[453] tab*artus* do tab*air*t do*n* tigerna .⁊c. lu*cht* codaig*h* næim*h* no firen .i. len*us* dæn næm am*h*áin, no

17 lu*acht* æn patruin. feall *ar* c*h*olb*ha* .i. faell *ar* an ti bi*us ar* colb*ha* a lebt*ha* no a ng*ar* do.

18 sruaim .i. iomud. tæi. tæiet*us* .i. tosd. derlait*h*er .i. derb diog*h*lait*h*e*r*. esges .i. im u*m*aloid[454]

19 roeach .i. ro sec*h*, no roiseic*h*em .i. ro ionsaig*adh*. clot*h* .i. uirderc. córǽi .i. ǽi cóir .i. caing*an* cóir

20 gab*h*ail la flait*h* .i. dul anaig*id* na flat*ha*. dag*h*rac*h* .i. deg*hair*ec*h*. im-tobaing .i.

---

445 I follow O'Curry's reading of this word; the MS is worn and part of the writing is illegible.

446 O'Curry reads 'inbhroghthar'.

447 O'Curry reads 'gan'; the edge of the page is missing. It should be noted that there is a line of text running sideways up *marg. sin.* for ll. 8–11. The tops of the letters are missing, but the first three might be 'ios'; I cannot read the remainder of the letters.

448 ⟨fo⟩ is written after ⟨ag⟩ and crossed out.

449 I follow O'Curry's reading of the last letter; the edge of the page is missing.

450 I follow O'Curry's reading of the last four letters; the edge of the page is missing.

451 The last four letters are a correction written over maybe ⟨*acht*ic⟩.

452 O'Curry reads 'breitheamh'.

453 O'Curry reads 're'; part of the first letter is missing due to wear at the edge of the page.

454 The ⟨l⟩ is written over another letter, perhaps a ⟨c⟩.

21 éim*h*toibg*h*it*h*er.[455] tósa .i. imden*adh*, no mion*n*aig*ad*. muireac*h* .i. moiriat*h*ac*h* .i. rig*h* moi*r* ferui[nn][456]

22 nodh .i. urd*air*c. con*ár*d*h*ata .i. com*h*aididn*igh*t*he*.[457] manda m*air*m*h*esa .i. iom*a*d moi*r* mesa

23 n*ár* .i. fíor. uircria .i. crena ⟨.i. cennach⟩, (no)[458] c*r*iona, caill*ech*, no terca. asné .i. asé. om*h* .i. indlig*thech*

24 coimpert .i. coim*h* eibt*e*r, coim*air*bertnug*adh*, ⁊ gei*n*nem*h*iun*n*. sais .i. ion*n*s*aigh*is. imitect .i. tect ui*m*[e][459]

25 coindfe .i. comad*hus*. coi*m*d*h*eilit*h*ec*h*. fiad*h*at .i. tig*e*rna. dit*h*le .i. adb*h*al élaidt*he*. ro-sgot

26 .i. ro ion*n*saig*h*t*e*r. tret*h*on*n* .i. t*r*i t*r*eoín. uais .i. uasal. ion*n*sa, no an*n*sa. lúiter .i. ti

27 onoilt*e*r. ro-ná .i. ro cengail, ut ro-nas. déis .i. f*e*ran*n*. beab*h*ais .i. ég*h*ais. bert .i.

28 b*r*it*h*em*h*nag*h*t*h*er ł is.[460] laithne .i. laitin. ion*n*sguc*h*ud*h* g*r*ad*h* no ceíme .i. árdug*adh* g*r*aid*h* .⁊c no ceim[e][461]

29 aig*h*ne f*r*isnin*n*le b*r*e*th* .i. aig*n*ne firin*n*lit*h*er do dena*m* b*r*e*th*em*h*n*us*a .i. legaid*h* cuirp an b*r*e[ith][462]

30 em*h*nuis, ⁊ berid*h* an tollam*h*an b*r*e*th*, ase si*n* aigne as onor*agh*e do*n*a haig*h*ne*d*aib*h* .⁊c.

31 cod-ródaig*h* .i. ro c*h*um*h*daig*h*. dos-nalla .i. didnig*h*. tóirsiod .i. do rósad .i. do roin*n*e. dæn .i. duin[e][463]

32 urgna*m* .i. urf*h*og*h*na*mh*. coitg*h*e .i. comtuige .i. co*m*c*h*um*h*dac*h*. túid*h*men*ar* .i. cengailt*e*r. urlata .i.

33 uasal lúite. ad-raig*h* .i. cenglaid*h*.[464] árag*ar* .i. cenguilt*e*r. fos-geallaid*h* .i.[465] fuig*h*lid*h*[466] .i. b*r*iat*r*aigig.

34 sern*ar* .i. s*r*eat*h*naig*h*t*e*r. fǽnán .i. ionan*n*. annac*h* .i. ánoig*h*e adalt*r*ais. fuada .i. eire, no fodla

---

455 The ⟨b⟩ is made over another letter(s), possibly ⟨l⟩ and/or ⟨i⟩.
456 I follow O'Curry's reading of the last two letters; the edge of the page is damaged.
457 O'Curry reads 'comhaidnighthe'.
458 The word 'no' is crossed out.
459 I follow O'Curry's reading of the last letter; the edge of the page is damaged.
460 The sense of the correction is that the last word should read 'brithemhnaghthis'.
461 I follow O'Curry's reading of the last letter; the edge of the page is damaged.
462 I follow O'Curry's reading of the last letters; the edge of the page is damaged.
463 Most of this word is lost in the damaged edge of the page. O'Curry reads 'duine'.
464 The last syllable is written over some letters which I cannot read.
465 O'Curry reads 'fos-geallaighi'.
466 The second ⟨i⟩ looks like it is written over an ⟨o⟩ or ⟨e⟩.

35 frit*h*id .i. ionan*n*. fuigeall .i. lanfuigioll. urfuigioll[467] .i. ordug*adh* suidig*h*te geall. ad-boib .i. obt*har*.

36 fodotlena .i. ḟoet*h*lás. forto-tuigidt*he*r .i. tig i ffortac*h* imden*ma*. feat*h*al .i. mion*n*, egc*us*c. ud*h*ban*ar* .i. iod*h*b*ar*[tar][468]

37 ad-uid*h*bre .i. ad*h*a iod*h*b*h*ras. slatra[469] .i. dánáu, no ainbḟiele[470]

38 aibgider crab*ad*.[471] daifenn .i. fu*ar*uige, no su*ára*g*h*e

Transcription p. 9[472]

1 IS é b.n.[473] clu .i. u*r*dercad*h*.[474] clo, cluas*ach* .i. [....]ge.[475] *ar*al*eth* iarait*h* .i. fi[...]*us*[476] si du[...........].[477] [.....] .i. se*t*ran[478]

2 [..].[479] siride .i. siort*h*oir bi*us* ag sired*h* aide no aite. forraid*h* .i. foirid*h*. cuirioc*h*[480] [.]occe .i. [t]on*n* criot*h*aig*h* no [loit][481]

3 [b]ag*h*.[482] diot*h*c*hus* .i. adb*ar* toc*hus*. d*r*inges .i. d*r*emnis. dlæi fulla .i. an draoi fullan .i. an cuid do la b*r*io*cht* for dlaoi do cur dui*ne* *ar* [.......]

467 This word is underlined twice.

468 I follow O'Curry's reading of the last letters; the edge of the page is damaged.

469 This word has two entries in Dubhaltach's Glossary (p. 7b), but only one in O'Curry's transcription, which is not the entry found here.

470 The reading of this word is uncertain.

471 Dubhaltach is referring to the text *Apgitir Chrábaid* 'The Alphabet of Piety'.

472 The writing is in one column with staining and damage on all four sides of the page.

473 The beginning of the line is mostly illegible, but there are four or five letters at the start of the line which might be an indication of Dubhaltach's source. The reading is tentative. It is not in O'Curry's transcription.

474 The reading of the last letter is tentative. This entry is included in O'Curry's transcription, and it is also found on page 2 of the MS.

475 The gloss is illegible. This entry is not included in O'Curry's transcription.

476 Perhaps this sequence is for 'firc*hus*'.

477 The remainder of the line is illegible. The entry is not in O'Curry's transcription.

478 The entry is not in O'Curry's transcription. The reading is very tentative.

479 There are one or two letters at the beginning of the line which are illegible.

480 O'Curry reads 'luirioch'. The first letter looks like a ⟨b⟩, and it is likely that Dubhaltach made the ⟨c⟩ over the ⟨b⟩.

481 Most of this entry is illegible. The missing letters are supplied from O'Curry's transcription. It is possible that there are more letters at the end of the line which are not legible.

482 The beginning of this entry likely starts on the end of the previous line and is mostly illegible. O'Curry reads the last syllable of the word as 'bog'.

4 [l]a[483] si*n* d*r*aoi si*n* do hoil*edh* nuad*h*a fullon, ⁊ uaide ain*m*n*igh*te*r* dlæoi fulla. coir an*mann* si*n*. d.r.[484] ~~d[..]~~[485] lait*h* lat*hach* .i. sraid*h* .i. uisge [na][486]

5 hu*achtar* ⁊ cec*hair* na hioc*htar*. cec*hair* .i. cec*hair* na hu*achtar* ⁊ *us*ge[487] na hioc*htar* .i. dubt*h*onn*a*c. com*m*or cuan[488] .i. ionad ina com*m*[or] a[.....][489]

6 [..] .i.[490] gaduig*hedh*. tacomal .i. acomal .i. cengal. do ec*h*ma .i. doiṡec*h*anta. in*n*tec*h*, ⁊ buaile gal*air* .i. ait imbi gal[ar][491]

7 [...]toingit .i. em*h* t*h*oinge.[492] andom*h*na .i. inde doi*m*ne. crioc*h* g*a*n dicelt .i. gan falac*h*.[493] for-tuig*h*ite*r* .i. fíort*h*uig*h*ite*r* .i. fir*m*io[nnaightear][494]

8 [..ig]igis .i. ina*edh*ris.[495] faot*h* .i. luig*h*e .i. min*n*a. aín .i. iomaig*h* .i. iomain. ruig*hledh* .i. ro fuig*hledh*. f*r*iosg*a*rt .i. f*r*eg*r*ais. foruail [....][496]

9 [..]ob*h*liugs[.][497] . *air*be[498] .i. fal. filc ⟨.i. maith⟩ .i. foill secd*h*a .i. in cuaille. ága ⟨ł ionag*h*a⟩[499] .i. iomáin amac*h*[500] o tág*h*a .i. iomáin amuic*h*.[501] eab*h*la[...][502]

---

483 The reading is supplied from O'Curry.
484 Perhaps this abbreviation is for *Dúil Roscadach*.
485 A word is crossed out after 'd.r.', but only the first letter is legible.
486 The reading is supplied from O'Curry's transcription.
487 The ⟨g⟩ is uncertain. O'Curry reads 'uisge'.
488 O'Curry reads 'fuan'.
489 The end of the line is illegible.
490 The reading of the beginning of the line is uncertain. Perhaps 'frim' is to be read. The entry is not in O'Curry's transcription.
491 The reading is supplied from O'Curry's transcription.
492 This entry is not in O'Curry's transcription. The edge of the page is badly worn, and the beginning of the lemma is illegible. The reading, however, is tentative.
493 This entry is not in O'Curry's transcription, but the lemma is.
494 The reading is supplied from O'Curry's transcription. The edge of the page is torn.
495 The reading is very uncertain. This entry is not in O'Curry's transcription.
496 The form of the ⟨r⟩ is unexpected after an ⟨o⟩. The end of the line is illegible. O'Curry reads 'fornual'.
497 It is uncertain whether this word belongs with the previous entry. Most of it is illegible; it is not in O'Curry's transcription.
498 O'Curry reads 'airle'.
499 The addition is written above the lemma.
500 O'Curry reads 'aonach'.
501 The final three words of the entry are listed as a separate entry in O'Curry's transcription *s.v. Tagha*. O'Curry reads 'aonuich'.
502 The remainder of the line is illegible. The entry is not in O'Curry's transcription.

10 [..]ac[..]e .i. iono*cht*. a[...] adeir, ⁊ an m[.] as uga doge lona menmu ac denam[503]

11 [.]c [..] eab*h*la .i. tæbuail anuig.[504] aig, taig .i. im na hec*h*uib*h*, ⁊ im na cæirib*h*. M*ar* si*n* .g.*ath* uaitug*ud*.[505] //)[506] edgaid[507]

12 timine .i. sadail nec*h* as time da fine

13 Ruib to-meal*ar* .i. ain*mnighth*e at*h*cogn*us* a ccuid m*ar* taid ba, caoir, ⁊ gob*air* ⁊c̄. Ruib ná to-meal*ar* .i. ain*mnighthe* [...][508]

14 [.]et*h*or .i. fer doni t*r*i an f*h*ail. íre .i. fera*nn*. m*ét* na nirea*nn*[509] .i. na b*h*fera*nn*. buirisg .i. bior asa eisg .i. poll b*eth*[510] na l*ar*. ce*nn*, ⁊ costa*cair* .i. [..]*ar*[..][511]

15 [..][512] ca .i. a c*h*e*nn* de fen. mæl macha .i. cuaille mæl am*h*uil mac*h*ad*h*. cátaid*h* .i. úaislétaid*h*. odh*ar*.i. oin*edh* no ointer[513] .i. tugt*ar*[514] [...]

16 [.]asa*cht*. bradaid*h* .i. foxl*adh*. lios .i. ima mbí an clad*h*. airlisi .i. ima mbí an taile an fál. Sui, sæi .i. on tsoad*h* .i. iompod*h*.

17 indorsa[515] .i. in*n*osa no anu*air*si. medla, máda, ra*cht*, sas, féis, ⁊ tuir*edh* .i. an*manna* do m*h*uic. metoll.i. fogail do ni an

18 m*h*uc mor da ngoirter medla. ruired .i. ro feraid. cec*h*laid, clasaid .i. toc*h*luid. ingelt .i. glet*h* a hin*n*e. fer iondraic [...][516]

19 [..]dic*h*e. cl*eth*e lui ⟨.i. na ngrad fene⟩ .i. se*cht* ccin*n* gan cois, no æn gas *con*a cian*n*. m*edh*ontaid*he* lui .i. se*cht* gais gan a ccen*n*a. lú lui .i. se*cht* nda[.][517]

20 [.]e no se*cht* slap*air*, ni riagailter lu lui na m*edh*ontaid*h* lui, *acht* do l*us*, do g*air*leoig, ⁊ do praisig*h*. fuirir*edh* lui .i. buin*ne* go ccen*n*

21 no se*cht* ccin*n* gan buinne. ag*h* .i. bo. ⁊ ed .i. ailbin bo. ima-dic*h*et .i. em*h*d*h*idnid. sec*h*n*us* n*air*gsin .i. do c*h*i an dui*ne* aspred*h* ar

---

503 None of this line is in O'Curry's transcription.
504 The reading is uncertain. This entry is not in O'Curry's transcription.
505 The reading of this word is tentative.
506 The *cenn fo eite* symbol is used here to indicate that Dubhaltach has ended a section of material and is moving on to another one.
507 This word is presumably for *étged*. There does not seem to be any additional writing on the remainder of the line.
508 The remainder of the line is illegible.
509 O'Curry reads 'mireann'.
510 The reading is uncertain. O'Curry reads 'bheith'.
511 The end of the line is illegible.
512 The beginning of the line is illegible.
513 O'Curry reads 'oirtear'.
514 This word is not in O'Curry's transcription.
515 O'Curry reads 'atorsa' but queries the reading.
516 The end of this line and the beginning of the next are illegible.
517 The end of this line and the beginning of the next are damaged.

22 foguil ⁊ sec*h*n*naidh* iad sa noidc*he*, ⁊ ní f*h*idir gu áit i rabatt*ar*. faill naididin. faill do [den]a*m*[518] u*m*pa i*ar* naididniug*adh*. legad do luide

23 .i. leigen do*n* spre*dh* luid*he*[519] san fer. feis ⟨i bfeis⟩[520] .i. i mbuail*idh* no i nat*h*lompu*re* coitcin*n*. feis i bfual .i. i nat*h*buail*idh* s*h*alaig

24 feis i nandom*h*ain .i. bid i lenmui*n* isi*n* tsesgin*n*, no isi*n* derg moin, no isi*n* luit*h*, ⁊ et*h*aid an fer ime. coib*h*nit*her* .i. cui*m*rig*h*ter[521]

25 gealtat*har* .i. ing*h*ilt*er*. ime .i. fal. edárb*ha* .i. ba bí*us* etorra .i. *air*b*he* no fál. fagh .i. sliab*h*. der*us*g .i. cin*nedh* d*h*ireac*h*. cutai*m* .i. t[522]

26 uiti*m*. cit .i. cǽra. cit*r*iog*ha* .i. uán .i. troig*h* .i. clan*n* cite. cetem*h*uin .i. cæra som*h*æin. uainc*h*en*n* .i. fuan b*h*i*us* mu*n* ccen*n* .i. srián

27 adbalud .i. eblid .i. bás*aigh*id. derc nát*ha* .i. toll c*airi*ol*ach* át*h*a. teingléir .i. tengaid*h* léir. lua*mh*n*acht* .i. lua*mairacht*. coslac*h* .i. luac*h*

28 cúisi .i. luac*h* do ber fer na cuisi do nec*h* oile do cion*n* a cuisi do s*h*esam*h* do, ut d*icitu*r sed*h*a gac coslac*h* .i. an ses*edh* cuid

29 do*n* c*h*úis do nti do ní *air*bert æonu*air*e i n*airecht* dá ttig tobac*h*. cad*h*na .i. caingne. tl*us* .i. tuill*edh* uais do b*erar* risi*n*

30 ní bi*us* esbad*h*ach. com*hair*sior .i. at*h*c*h*om*hair*ct*e*r. dime, ⁊ diomt*ha* .i. on didion. solam*h* .i. luat*h*. uball fab*h*aill i.i. uball bi*us*

31 *ar* fos*h*iub*h*al for a nuall f*or* an tuin*n* .i. uball tui*n*n*e*. ág*h*a fine .i. óg*h* æ b*h*í*us* *ar* an ffine. flait*h* gelf*h*ine sin. fo-c*h*erd

32 fo-c*h*eird .i. do c*h*uir. frit*h*e .i. ní do amuig*h* ag dol i mug*h*a.[523] ut frit*h*e treb*h*e .i. ní do gab*ar* isi*n* treb*h* t*h*all. frit*he*[524] catrac*h* .i. i l*ar*

33 an cille no an duine. frit*he*[525] fait*h*e .i. *ar* an f*h*ait*h*c*h*e i gcu*airt* ingelta. frit*he*[526] raite .i. do[527] gab*ar* *ar* an rod i gcu*air*t ingelta

34 idir fait*h*ce, ⁊ dirin*n*. frit*h*e roead*h*a no s*h*leb*h*e .i. ní do gab*ar* isi*n* roif*h*iod*h* no isi*n* sliab i gcu*air*t ingelta. frit*he*[528] t*rach*t*a*

35 .i. isi*n* tráig*h* gab*ar*. frit*he*[529] f*air*ige .i. isi*n* f*hair*ige imuig*h* geibt*h*er. ollob*hair* aigsi*n* .i. folab*air*t do ní nec*h* ag faig

518 The missing letters are supplied from O'Curry's transcription.

519 The ⟨d⟩ is written over a ⟨g⟩.

520 This phrase appears to be part of the lemma, but it is written over it; there is an insertion mark immediately after 'feis'.

521 O'Curry reads 'coimrightear'.

522 The word that ends this line continues onto the start of the next.

523 O'Curry reads 'a múg*h*a'.

524 O'Curry reads 'fri'.

525 O'Curry reads 'fri'.

526 O'Curry reads 'fri'.

527 O'Curry reads 'ni do'.

528 O'Curry reads 'fri'.

529 O'Curry reads 'fri'.

36 si*n* ne*the*, ⁊c̄. ocht*rach* .i. ot*rach*. oil .i. aoil no pluic. ruid*hedh* .i. imde*ar*-
g*adh*. miod*h*bac*h* .i. fer miod*h*b*adh*. s*ár*a saml*adh* .i. saml*adh*[530]

37 ad*h* as s*ár* .i. dui*ne* do sam*h*lug*adh* fri ní as mesa inas e fein .i. re coin no
re cec*hair*. deorad*hus* .i. diorat*hus* .i. nem*h*ci*n*tad*h*

38 d*arm*na .i. d*áir* mœine do nid t*air*b*h*. *air*m i tto*th* .i. inad i tt*air*i*n*g. mad
ois[531] .i. da néisgísi. oid*h*the .i. éisgid*h*si

39 dí*th* .i. dit*h*im .i. díot*h*. siasra .i. reimn*igh*t*h*e no ⟨ion⟩saig*h*t*h*e.[532] coic-
cenuid .i. rún no coccub*us* u*m* cionuid*h*. at*h*rola .i.

40 la asa hait*h*le .i. ní do t*h*iom*ar*gui *ar* nec*h*. *air*ite .i. gab*h*áil. cliad*h*ra,
cléra .i. bolg no criól, no tíag*h*

41 lob*har* .i. dui*ne* t*r*og*h*. lœch .i. an t*air*e ec*ht*a. fuag*ar*taid*h* .i. an fu*r*fo-
gr*aidh*. am*hus* ala tuait*h*e .i. deor*aidh*. direct*h*aid .i. iondraig*aidh*.[533]

42 dr*uth* .i. go rat*h*. díoc*hus*g .i. anm*her*[534] gan rat*h*. ad*h*ma .i. aid*h*me .i.
cul*adh*[535] no glés. ang*ar*[536] .i. iongor. dimeltaid .i. fe*r* ad

43 bal-cait*h*m*h*ec*h*. fœl*us* .i. fuilngnis. slab*h*ra, slaib*h*re .i. sal b*huar*.i. bu*ar*
tig t*ar* sal. tion*n*sg*r*a .i. tin*n*sg*et*al. tiasg .i. tin*n*sg*na*[537]

44 com*h*lun*n*[538] .i. coi*m*líon. fuilac*h* .i. fulang. dam*h*rad*h* .i. b*eth* *ar* dáim*h*.
cuim*h*lec*h*ta .i. comsloin*n*te. osuic .i. uga .i. tog*h*a le hos

45 .i. re bel .i. biad*h*.[539] cotuig*h*e tionc*h*uir. ní do cur fon tion .i. fontœb*h* da
coim*h*teg*h*ad*h*. cum*al* sec*h*tm*adh* m*ar*b*h*t*h*a .i. an

46 sectm*adh* cuid do*n* coirpdire. oir sec*h*t coirpdire g*ach* urr*adh* i
gcoitcin*ne* *ar* na m*ar*b*adh*. biad*h*m*hoch* .i. biad*h* go moc*h*

47 to .i. an tab*air*t. as-do .i. b*ei*reid*h* oca.[540] suier[...] an ta[..][541]

---

530 The end of this word appears on the beginning of the next line, but the word also finishes here with an abbreviation for the same final syllable.

531 O'Curry reads 'cis'.

532 ⟨ion⟩ is added above the line with an insertion mark. O'Curry reads 'ionsaighe'.

533 O'Curry reads 'iondraigach'.

534 O'Curry reads 'ainmhear'.

535 O'Curry reads 'culath'.

536 O'Curry reads 'angur'.

537 O'Curry reads 'tinn' but is unable to read the remainder of the line. The last two or three letters and the suspension mark at the end of the word are very difficult to read. The reading of the final syllable of this word is tentative.

538 O'Curry reads 'comlunn'.

539 The last gloss is omitted by O'Curry.

540 This entry is not in O'Curry's transcription. The reading of the entry is tentative.

541 This entry is not in O'Curry's transcription. The bottom of the page is worn and damaged.

Transcription, p. 10[542]

1 [543][..]e[.......]rite[.......]c[....]fot[h] nionais .i. [...]

2 [.........]eciu*m*[.]ta mil[.]s[..] indile[.] ti[..]t*er*[.]ag [.]ec*h*[.]nos .i. fot*h* nio[nais] .i. ai[d]brait*er* ag nec*h* i*ar* no[..]

3 [...]reimdilsi .i. ani[544] ⟨...⟩ fot*h*uig*h*t*er* ⟨aidbraid⟩ do dilsiug*ad* roi*m*h*e* ria*m* ag nec*h* [.]ene*tt*[.]uaid, no roi*mh*e e fein da roim*he*[545]

4 f[o]t*h*[a] c[o]m[*h*]*ar*da .i.[546]fot*h* creca go reimdilsi, no fot*h* nionais aca m*ar*aon. fot*h*a le*th*a*r*da .i. fot*h* creca go rei*m*[dilsi,]

5 [no foth][547] nionais[548] ag an d*ar*a de, no fot*h* creca nama ga aroile. tad*h*at .i. gaduig*he*. fo*r*ng*air*e .i. fo*r*[con]g*ra*

6 [... ⁊c an][549] ceimn*ugh*ad*h*. cran*n*uigid*h* .i. cuirid c*r*an*nch*or. tat*h*ad .i. ata liom. tuid*h*in .i. c*r*uin*n*iug*adh* no tuinid*h* .i. orlaim*h* no se[..][550]

7 [...]a*n*it*h* .i. is dæisæct ase as.c.giallna.[551] saoit*h*e .i. ni as sæt*h* le nec*h* m*ar* ata diub*air*t. cui*nn*dfec .i. c[..] .i. cuidb*h*ide no..[552]

8 [...] .i. sasal ionsi*nd*[553]

9 [caitheamh][554] tola mna .i. f*er* dfæid*h*ec*h*tain le .i. do dul cuigt*h*e, ma do foad*h*, ma do fæid*eth*, muna ffoa, muna f*h*o, muna ffoa[dh][555] ⟨sin uile o d*h*ul cuigt*he*⟩[556]

---

542 The page has severe staining on its upper third and on all four sides. The top third and sides of the upper third of the document are stained, worn, and parts of the text are missing. Most of the first line has been completely cut off and only the bottom of some letters is visible.

543 The first line is barely visible.

544 There is a faded gloss above this and the next word. The second gloss begins ⟨aidbraid⟩.

545 The first three lines are not in O'Curry's transcription.

546 The missing letters are supplied from O'Curry's reading 'fot*h*com*h*arda'.

547 The missing letters are supplied from the previous entry.

548 O'Curry reads the beginning of the line as 'fot lionais'.

549 The missing letters are supplied by O'Curry's transcription.

550 O'Curry divides this entry into two, *s.vv. tuidin* and *tuinidh.*

551 This entry is not in O'Curry's transcription. The reading is very uncertain.

552 The last two words are written below the line.

553 The lemma is illegible. This entry is not in O'Curry's transcription. It is possible that it belongs with the previous entry.

554 The first word is supplied from O'Curry's transcription.

555 The last two letters are supplied from O'Curry's transcription.

556 This sequence is written above ⟨fæid*eth*⟩. There is a line drawn above the phrase, but it is uncertain whether it is meant to separate the entries or divide the page into sections.

10 cullat*h* [a]ge[557] .i. edac*h* leabt*h*a do ber ben d*h*o cu*m* fir ant*a*n naisgter iad ma-le. toit*h*len .i. do étlod. torla .i. naidm

11 [...]d[..] c[.]ac*h* .i. ait*h*ec*h* .i. deglæc*h*[558] aiccit*h*er .i. uga ésgter. do-r*a*raic .i. ro t*air*gister. doit*h*c*h*en .i. dáit*h* .i. luait*h*cíonad

12 [....]*ed* .i. au*m*egaig*hed*.[559] lait*h*rec*h* laig*h*en .i. lat*hair* in ro heillg*edh* e. im-id-rub*air*t .i. do rinne miebter. dioc*h*unduil .i. coi*m*tec*h*t*us* .i.

13 [....] .i. mugugad*h*. roc*h*ma .i. ro at*h*cuma. foilmgid*h* ⟨ł n⟩ .i. cu do ni foileim *ar* nec*h*. cu *con* .i. cu na ccuilen. cu l[oirge][560]

14 .i. cu ris na gabann greim lorg. cu ot*r*aig*h* .i. (madr*ad* gerr) as iside an cu f*r*isa ngaib*h* mæit*h*f*h*lesg. cot-ris*edh* .i. do [...][561]

15 no do cengolad*h*. fes*edh* .i. fua*chtnaigh*fed*h*. con-reis .i. cui*m*rig*h*si no cuib*r*ig*h*. apt*h*a .i. ebiltin. *air*bir .i. t*air*b*h*ir. fec*h*ad .i. fec*h*[562]

16 aid. fresluide .i. p*r*eapuide. cu lomna .i. cu danad *á*rac*h* lom*h*an ima gob. conair cæimt*echt*a .i. conair tiag*ur* isi*n*

17 f[aith]c[h]e.[563] tacm*h*aisi .i. tacmainge.[564] indisi .i. buail*idh* bo. m*á*r*us* .i. mo*r* ráid*h*is. cana .i. cuilen. canan*n*a .i. cuileoin. cirde .i.

18 [ai]d[565] no tesguid. cuimnett*ar* .i. do coim*m*ion*nagh*ed*ar* .i. do at*h*cu*m*at*ar*. puibl[a]i[d][566] .i. tesgad*h*. cu na ttri ngnio*m* .i. lorg*airacht* goide gabalt[aige][567]

19 [...] legt*er*,[568] ⁊ diongbail fir fo*r*rain ide*r* da f*h*iall*ach* .i. da c*e*tern. *á*rc*h*u .i. cu bi*us* f*or* *arach* .i. cengal. abac*h* .i. cnu*m*h*us* .i. feis a[..][569]

20 [...]all*aid* iarra ní s*h*eduig*h*es t*ar* na locaib*h*.[570] doc*h*t*air* .i. coisgter .i. múi*n*ter. collúd*h* .i. collód*h* .i. soad*h* do c*h*olla. muiltt*er* .i.

---

557 The missing letter is supplied from O'Curry's transcription.

558 This entry is not in O'Curry's transcription.

559 This entry is not in O'Curry's transcription. The reading is tentative.

560 The missing letters are supplied from the source text.

561 The end of the line is illegible.

562 The end of this line and the beginning of the next are badly worn and some letters are illegible. O'Curry does not print the gloss. The reading is tentative.

563 I follow O'Curry's reading of the text; the beginning of the line is badly worn and mostly illegible.

564 The ⟨t⟩ in the gloss looks like it is made over a ⟨g⟩.

565 I follow O'Curry's reading of the text; the beginning of the line is badly worn and mostly illegible.

566 I follow O'Curry's reading of the text; the end of the word is illegible due to a hole in the paper.

567 O'Curry reads 'us'; the end of the line is badly worn and mostly illegible. See *EIF* 116.

568 There might be another word in *marg. sin.*, but it is illegible due to wearing.

569 The end of the line is illegible.

570 The beginning of the line is illegible. The material at the beginning of the line is not in O'Curry's transcription.

21 leitir,[571] no frislaig*h*ter. tóirb*h*enad .i. [to]ir*ith*nid.[572] 5 an*m*an*n*a cat su*nn* .i. bréoinde .i. breo nuall, ⁊ nia t*r*en, no breó án .i. c*r*ónan ina in[ne][573]

22 ⁊ meoinde .i. mo do g*h*ni meig*h*il .i. meoain ⟨.i. meig*h*leac*h*⟩ ina in*n*e. ringcne .i. riac*h*aid nec*h*, ⁊ riac*h*t*har* é. cruib*h*ne .i. cruib nia .i. nia tren

23 [a l]*us*[574] a cruibe. *air*cne .i. a h*airc* nœi m*i*c laim*h*iac*h*, no a b*air*cne .i. nia t*r*en tugad*h* a b*air*c bresail b*r*ic .i. cait b*r*oin*n*geala d*h*uba

24 iach .i. fiad*h* c*h*at all*aidh* gaba*r* d*h*fiad*h* .i. as fiad*h*ant*as*.[575] folam .i. cat ler mait*h* loim, ⁊ coi*metus* loim go mait*h* ionan*n* e, ⁊ an

25 cat cuile a*cht gur*ob isi*n* tsenbaile b*hius*, ⁊ folom *ar* an mbuaile. glasnen*n*ta .i. cat beg b*hius* isi*n* tsenb*h*aile isi*n* nen*n*toig g*h*la[is][576]

26 ag diotuig*adh* loc*h*ad*h*. breoin*ne* .i. cat ait*aghius* rig, ⁊ tigerna, ⁊ *air*cin*n*eac*h*, ⁊ do ní c*r*onán doib*h*. meoi*n*de, le meg*h*ile, ⁊ e coim*het* i ccuid[577] bid*h* cruib[ne][578]

27 le coi*met* muilin*n*, ⁊ sab*h*aill, ⁊ at*h*a. Ringcne le h*air*fid*edh* clan*n*a na n*ardaire*c*h*. da sg*r*iobad*h*, ⁊ iadsan da sg*r*iobad san

28 b*air*cne .i. cat ban sin[579] luc*h*[580] l[a]m*h*a[581] .i. lam*h*aid*h* luc*h*. rórdam*us* .i. ro im*r*aidm*h*is. tœsnam*h*ad*h* .i. tumad*h*, n[o][582]

29 fliuc*hadh* a*r*áin. tu*ir*enn .i. c*r*uit*h*ne*acht*. cic*h*sime .i. ceimn*igh*imne. con-et*h*a .i. coim*e*t*a*. ⟨buicne .i. ceo d*h*a buaic .i. cáinte⟩[583] ol .i. oll .i. mo*r*. lat .i. slat. du*m*h*a* .i. io[nad][584]

---

571 The reading of this word is tentative; the MS is badly worn and partially illegible.

572 The missing letters are supplied from O'Curry's transcription. O'Curry reads 'toirighnid'.

573 I follow O'Curry's reading of the final word; the MS edge is badly worn and the end of the word is illegible.

574 O'Curry reads 'bios'; the edge of the page is damaged; cf *CIH* 1550.17.

575 O'Curry reads 'fiad*h*ant*acht*'.

576 I follow O'Curry's reading of the final word; the MS edge is badly worn and the end of the word is illegible.

577 The last two words are added above the line and separated from the text above it by two lines.

578 I follow O'Curry's reading of the final word; the MS edge is badly worn and the end of the word is illegible.

579 An empty space follows this word in the MS possibly indicating that Dubhaltach is shifting to a new section of material.

580 O'Curry reads 'luc'.

581 Dubhaltach might have corrected the second letter to an ⟨a⟩ which he wrote above the line, but it is not clear in the MS. O'Curry reads 'lamha'.

582 I follow O'Curry's reading of the last letter.

583 This entry is written above *con-etha*.

584 I follow O'Curry's reading of the last word; the end of the line is missing.

30 bru*ar* .i. spuille*ch* *ar*áin. b*r*u*ar*[585] sraife .i. iomad sraib*h*. *air*gedluib .i. luib *air*gid. fot*h*b*h*la .i. fod*h*eid*h*b*h*le[586] .i. diailbe[587]

31 .i. deroile. fíí, ⁊ híí .i. d*r*ung no d*r*eam, no gibe ní *ar* chena, na mbi iol-r*adh*. cele særf*h*lat*h*a .i. sæirc*h*ele. ma[nac*h*][588]

32 riagla .i. særman*a*c. desid*h* .i. t*ar*rust*ar*. f*r*is-com*hair* .i. fiorcoi*medh*t*ur*. adsuit*e*r .i. astuig*h*t*e*r.[589] fégad*h* .i. fec*h*ain súl. im[chisin][590]

33 .i. eim*h*d*h*ec*h*sain *ar*a m*h*enmuin. secfaid*h* .i. sec*h*mallaid*h*. cor go ffi*us*[591] go ttreb*aire* .i. cun*n*r*adh* go ffi*us*

34 diub*ar*ta ag nec*h*, ⁊ t*r*eb*aire* (.i. urr*adh* aniu)[592] re co*m*all an cun*n*at*h*a. cuidig fesa ⁊ t*r*eab*aire* .i. an c*h*uid do*n* cun*n*r*adh* in*ar* fe[as][593]

35 diub*ar*t do b*eth*, ⁊ ⟨cuid⟩[594] t*r*eb*ar*e .i. an cuid le ffuil an urr*adh* i nur-r*adhus* a coi*m*líon*n*ta. gan f*hius* gan t*r*eb*air*e a c*h*ont*r*arda si*n*.

36 nec*h* dia*m*ba cu*m*a a ebirt, ⁊ a aigde .i. duine ag*ar*ob ionan*n* an ní adeir se, ⁊ an ní b*híus* na inntin,[595]

37 g*ur*ob m*ar* adeir se b*hius* an ní rec*us*, no nac*h* ccelion*n* mait*h* na olc da mbi isin sed rec*us*[596] .⁊c̄. cria[597] .i. cen*n*

38 ria .i. rec. taid*h*c*r*ia[598] .i. tait*h*cen*n*ac*h* ł aith[cennach]. iom*ar*r .i. tio*mar*-gui*n*. acht .i. cu*nn*tab*ar*t. cías*ar* .i. céimn*igh*t*e*r. tat*h*luig*h*t*e*r .i tait*h*-mig*h*t*e*r.

39 ad-road .i. do roc*hair*. cu*m*sgug*udh* .i. co*m*sgæil*edh*. fom*hus* .i. foi*me*-sum*h*n*ugh*ad*h*. tuid*h*mid*h*e .i. astuig*hth*e. ion*n*longad .i. io*m*-fuilng[et][599]

---

585 The ⟨.i.⟩ and possible an ⟨s⟩ are crossed out.

586 The meaning of the short lines over the ⟨d⟩ in this word and the ⟨o⟩ in *fothbhla* is unknown. O'Curry ignores both in his transcription.

587 The reading of this word is uncertain.

588 O'Curry reads 'manac*h*'.

589 A vertical line follows this entry.

590 The missing letters are supplied from *CIH* 1349.4.

591 The last two words are repeated and then crossed out in lighter colored ink.

592 The last word and the parentheses were added later in a different colored ink.

593 The last two letters are supplied from O'Curry's transcription; the end of the line is damaged.

594 This word is added above the line with a reference mark.

595 It is possible that there is another letter at the end of the line; the edge of the page is damaged.

596 This word is left out of O'Curry's transcription.

597 O'Curry reads 'cri'.

598 O'Curry reads 'taoithcria'.

599 O'Curry reads the last three letters as '-adh'; I supply the missing letters from *Di Astud Chor* § 23, gloss d. The edge of the page is damaged.

40 tiondain, no tiodain .i. tiod*h*naic. ni *air*b*h*e .i. ni raib*h*e. ad-roir .i. ad*h*a ro oirg. meisi. cui*m*geach.

41 tat*h*[600] .i. tait*h*mec*h*. *ar-gair* .i. u*rgair*id*h* .i. c*r*os*adh*. bailiud*h* .i. élód*h* a ba as mait*h*. ad-dai*mh*ed .i. aididn*igh*id. bret*h* .i. b*h*ret*h*ema[n][601]

42 com*ha*[602] .i. na b*h*féc*h*em*h*an. coiccert .i. na h*aire*c*h*ta. blaid*h*re .i. bal re ré. neg*har* .i. nig*h*ter. suiter, no soat*har* .i. iompóit*he*r. imced[adh][603]

43 ém*h*d*h*éc*h*ad*h*. sæit*he* .i. b*r*eg*airacht* (as sæt*h* le nec*h*) nó diub*airth*. con-derb*hara* .i. coi*md*h*i*ubra. amne .i. am*hladh* so.

44 sen*arusg* .i. seinc*h*in*nedh* óg*h*. fo-suid*h* .i. astaid*h* go t*r*e f*hius* mait*h*. do-rait*h*m*acht* .i. ro s*r*et*hnighedh*, no ro tait*h*m*ighedh* .i. ro sgæi[ledh][604]

45 roc*h*ad .i. ro ionsaig*h*id*h*. inc*h*ren*ar* .i. c*r*eac*ar* a hin*n*e. se*r*n*ar* .i. s*r*et*h*-n*aghtar*.[605] m*ac* beoat*ar* .i. m*ac* i ttesg*air*[e]. forng*aire* .i. f*orcon*g*r*a. dlig*hedh* ænd*acht*[a, no]

46 iolda*chta*[606] .i. bi*us eter* cen*n* is mem*r*u, do b*r*ig*h* g*ur*ob æn an cen*n* i l*eth* ris na mem*r*uib*h*, ⁊ g*ur*ob iol[ardha an] mem*air* i l*eth* ris [an cceann][607]

47 [na .iiii. mna][608] dligt*ha*ca .i. .c. m*uin*ter go m*a*ca ⁊ .c. m*uin*ter gæ*n* m*a*ca [⁊] adalt*r*ac*h* go m*a*ca ⁊ be cuitgernsa [⁊ in mac gor]

48 [...].i. [.]saidcer cra[...][609]

600 Dubhaltach has used a *spiritus asper* instead of his usual *punctum*.

601 The final letter is supplied from O'Curry's transcription.

602 Dubhaltach has used a *spiritus asper* instead of his usual *punctum*.

603 The last letters of the line are supplied from O'Curry's transcription.

604 O'Curry leaves out ⟨do-⟩ at the beginning of the lemma. The last letters of the line are supplied from O'Curry's transcription; the edge of the page is damaged.

605 This entry also appears on p. 8, but O'Curry lists it only once.

606 O'Curry reads 'athachta'.

607 The missing letters are supplied from O'Curry's transcription. The bottom and edge of the page are damaged.

608 This entry is not in O'Curry's transcription. The missing letters are supplied from CIH 1358.17.

609 The reading of the last line is uncertain because the bottom of the page is missing.

Transcription, p. 11[610]

[a]1 [li]b*er*.2.[611] fren .i. fr*em**h*[612] [.....................] [deoraidh aigenta .i. an deoraigh...][613]

2 *ed*ged[614] [mainch... .i. ma ... don]

3 [t]æob*h* am*ac*[h] [do ni neach][615] annoit [.i. eagluis duthchuis....

4 .i. eagluis an pharráisde i gcomhuigheann neach, no as neasa do neach ar fineachas .r.][616] [eachtrannus .i. neach

5 téid amach inn ionad eachtrann].[617] escom*h*an, iongglan .i. excomunicatus. ara-c*h*eala .i. *air*c[heallus no][618]

6 [eas no goidea]s tæidid*h* .i. tæit*h*nig*h*id*h*. eagl*us* c*h*uir .i. at*hair* .i. egl*us* cuires cuir *ar tus ar* an man*a*c andoi[d]

7 [um leit*h*]t*r*iun[619] an c*h*et*m*hanaig*h*. egl*us* coi*m**dh*idin .i. egl*us* ga mbiter na comaididin re ré desi an t[ath]*air*

8 [⁊ an mac] le*th*t*r*i[a]n[620] ma man*a*c m*a*c manaig*h*. eagl*us* con-ran*na*[621] diobad*h*. egl*us* com*h*roin*nius* diob*adh* an m*h*anaig*h*

9 [re] ré t*r*ir .i. at*air*, m*a*c ⁊ ua. ro-negam .i. riocfam.[622] dlom*h*aim .i. raid*h*im.[623] sǽrm*h*anac[h] .i. an dec*h*mad*h*

---

610 The page has dark staining on its upper third and on all four sides; there is extensive damage to this part of the page. O'Curry lists entries in his transcription for this page which I have not been able to read. I am uncertain how many lines of text are on the top of the page.

611 Dubhaltach also writes 'L[iber] 2°' across the top margin of TCD MS 1316 [H.2.15A], p. 43 along with 'Senc[h]*us*.' Dubhaltach owned that section of the MS; Ó Muraíle 1996c: 375.

612 I partially rely on O'Curry's transcription for the reading of this word. The remainder of the top line is illegible to me.

613 The entry is supplied from O'Curry's transcription; I have not been able to find it on the page.

614 The page is so badly damaged that it is difficult to tell whether this is the only word on the line.

615 The missing letters are supplied from O'Curry's transcription.

616 Most of this entry is illegible. It is supplied from O'Curry's transcription.

617 The entry is supplied from O'Curry's transcription; I have not been able to find it on the page.

618 The missing letters are supplied from O'Curry's transcription.

619 The missing letters are supplied from O'Curry's transcription.

620 The missing letters are supplied from O'Curry's transcription.

621 O'Curry reads 'con-eadranna'.

622 There is a spot of ink under the ⟨r⟩ which makes it look like ⟨p⟩.

623 O'Curry reads 'naidhim'.

10 [m]ac, no an .c. tuiste. dærm*h*anac*h* .i. man*ach* crui, gola ⟨.i. prisun⟩, gob*h*la ⟨.i. na croiche⟩,[624] gill do bas, ⁊ manac*h* nuna[625]

11 [a]*n*ma*n*na[626] breit*h*e. bret*h*, ri*ar*, coigert,[627] *et*ercert, ⁊ comha *ut dicitur* tre chom*ha* .i. t*r*e si*n* mbreit*h* d*ar*ab ain*m* comha

12 [f]echt[628] feile .i. ced oid*h*che æid*h*ig*h*echt duine (go tig*h* duine oile) mari, oll*am*, fl*aith*, no gibe cinel duine e. gnai

13 [th]les[629] .i. gac*h* æidig*h*ec*h*t on c*het* adaig*h* amac*h*. folac*h* not*h*rasa .i. iomf*h*ulaing no f*r*iteol*adh* duine b*hius* in ot*h*ras.

14 [fer][630] máma mog*h* .i. an fer gab*us* do laim*h* ma*m* ⁊ gnio*m* an d*h*uine. bi*us* loite do dena*m* *ar* a s*h*on f*edh* a luide ot*hrus*

15 [fer o]guib*h* toguib*h* .i. fer a t*h*ogbala na s*h*uide ⁊ na leab*adh*, ⁊ in a gluas*acht ar* cena f*hedh* a ot*hrus*a.[631]

16 [sl]iocht[632] aroisg .i. eol*us* b*r*at*h* b*hius* ag suil an f*h*og*h*l*aidh*e *ar* ní *air*ide do lot no do goid dergabad .i. urfog*r*a de

17 [th]nes*ac*[633] gan maill, ⁊ banabad*h*, ní ass maille inás. lán næinf*h*ir .i. láinf*h*iac*h* b*hius ar* æn duin*e* am*h*ai*n*

18 rio*th* go moirseisior, no go cuig*er* .⁊c. .i. iomlaine na ffiac*h*, no d*h*ioluid*hacht* an milltenuis do ni an cuidea*cht*[a][634]

19 do buain do buain[635] do g*ac* æn dib*h* go moirses*er*, go cuig*er*, no gibe nuim*er* adeir dlig*edh* .⁊c.

20 lán an c*h*iontaig*h* .i. lainf*h*iac*h* dleg*ar* don ciont*ac*. fæindleg*h*ac*h* .i. fer n*ac* ttig fa dlig*edh* cor*us*a fine.[636]

21 urfog*r*ac*h* .i.[637] fer b*hius* re dena*m* uilc go ffog*r*an*n* an[638] tinbleog*h*an as neasa uaid e .i. an

---

624 The interlinear glosses are very difficult to read; I rely on O'Curry's transcription for some of the letters.

625 O'Curry lists *gola* to *nuna* as a separate entry in his transcription.

626 The missing letters are supplied from O'Curry's transcription.

627 This word is omitted by O'Curry.

628 The missing letter is supplied from O'Curry's transcription.

629 The missing letters are supplied from O'Curry's transcription.

630 The first word is supplied from O'Curry's transcription.

631 O'Curry combines this entry with the previous one in his transcription. The missing letters are supplied from his transcription.

632 The missing letters are supplied from O'Curry's transcription.

633 The missing letters are supplied from O'Curry's transcription.

634 The missing letter is supplied from O'Curry's transcription.

635 Dubhaltach has repeated the phrase in what is likely a mistake.

636 This is not a reference to the text *Córus Fine* itself; *CCIH* 238.

637 A word is crossed out after ⟨.i.⟩.

638 A word is crossed out after this word.

22 lu*cht* gæil as goire d*h*ó. fuinm*h*aell, no fuinm*h*eall ⟨ƚ b⟩[639] .i. foinbleog-n*as*, teglom*as*, no tionoiles. deor*adh* freacair .i. deor[ad][640]

23 do niter do urr*adh* ma*r* so .i. fer si*n* d*h*o ní minicniug*ad* cionta ⁊ ní f*he*-*t*uid a f*h*ine a cionta dioc do gnait*h*, ⁊ as aml[aid]

24 [c]uirid ([641]a cion dib*h*, ⁊ do níd deor*adh* freac*air* de .i. do ber a f*h*ine .uii. ccu*m*ala do f*h*lait*h*, sect mbl*iad*na pén*e*[642] do egluis

25 [⁊] da c*h*umail c*hair*de do g*a*c l*eth* do na c*eithr*e l*eth*ib*h* .i. risi*n* a ffuil comcu*air*d c*air*de do*n* ciont*a*c, ⁊ sæ*r* iad ma*r* si*n* *air*a

26 [c]iont*a*b*h*,[643] ⁊ na diaig*h* si*n* da ttug*adh* nec*h* dia f*h*ine bos g*r*ain, no urg*h*a sgine,[644] no ingelt da ecuib*h* na ferann *ar* c*air*d[e]

27 [f]uill*adh*[645] a cion orra aris. faic*h*ill .i. tu*ar*u*s*tal. faill tiom*air*g*th*e ag rig*h* .i. gan an ciont*a*c*h* do t*h*iomargad*h* ré

28 *edghedh* duine *air*i*th*e. dlig*edh* cen*n*dac*h*ta .i. dlig*hedh* uac*hta*r*u*-sánac*h*ta,[646] no tigerna*m*l*a*c*ht*. ead*ar*f*h*lait*h* .i. foit*h*tigerna .⁊c̄[647]

[b]1 [ad]bar eile d*ar*ob ainm[648]

2 ⁊. ait*h*ne na mbean tet*h*a fein, *ar* sgat*h* fer ata d*r*eam diob*h* so, ⁊ ní h*edh* ata drem oile. be[649] foiclig*h*e ⟨.i. ben foiclig*h*ter a tig*h* atech⟩[650] .i. ben bi*us*

3 focholcæi .i. for clæn con*air*, *air*m i bfæi aidc*he*, ní f*h*æi *ar*oile an be niomra*m*a. be fot*h*la ⟨i.[651] dia bfoetlonn ni da s*edh*uib*h* sec*h* an p*r*iom mnæi .i. a m*ed* an airech⟩ .i. ben dia bfot[l][652]

4 enan*n* a cele a t*r*eabad sech an ben n*ar*uis .i. an airec*h*. be fæindil .i. ben fo nindile i tt*h*ig urd

---

639 The correction ⟨ƚ b⟩ is written above the ⟨m⟩ of the previous word.

640 The missing letters are supplied form O'Curry's transcription.

641 There is no closing parenthesis.

642 O'Curry reads 'féne'.

643 O'Curry was able to see ⟨c⟩.

644 OCurry reads 'sgrie'.

645 O'Curry was able to see ⟨f⟩.

646 O'Curry reads 'uachtaranachta'.

647 The abbreviation is not in O'Curry's transcription. O'Curry includes the text on line 29 with this entry. There is a horizontal line drawn under line 28 which extends for the entire width of the MS page.

648 The missing letters are supplied from O'Curry's transcription. O'Curry reads '.adbar eile darab aimn edgeadh.'

649 O'Curry reads 'bean'.

650 The gloss is written above the text. The reading of the first letter of *atech* is uncertain.

651 The gloss starts on line 31 above the headword and continues above the text onto line 32.

652 The missing letter is supplied from O'Curry's transcription.

5 [al]ta.[653] in c*ar*th*a*ch .i. dor*m*uine. be ~~niondra .i. ben bi*us* irin*n* na re ed~~[654] .i. ben teid ⟨*ar* fæindel asa tig*h*⟩[655] i ccomm*d*h*ail fir ele

6 [t]*ar*[656] cen*n* a f*h*ir fein .i. in c*a*rt*a*c .i. dor*m*uine. be nion*n*ra .i. ben bi*us* i rin*n* na ræ e an ban *air*gec*h* .i. ben

7 [b]i*us* for *air*ge ion*n*ra i gcom*us* *air*ge, ⁊ ag dena*m* trebt*h*a fo ion*n*amail mog*h*a dæíre.

8 [b]e nan*n*ra .i. ben bi*us* an*n* isi*n* re .i. mat*air* na ndilectad, bi*us* go macuib*h* ⁊ go lescl*ainn* iomd*h*a leis[657] a cele deg ⁊[658] a meic aige in iona[d][659] a fir.

9 [be] nurnuide .i. ben æntum*n*a b*hius* ag urnuide a cele go hai*m*sir n*air*c*h*en*n* .i. urnaid*m* niodnuide, no urnaid*hm*

10 ad*h*all .i. f*r*i re ima tab*air*t. be f*h*uis i ffoltaib*h* .i. ben bios i bfoisdine (go bfol*adh* toc*h*us*a* aice) *ar* cion*n*

11 [cai]c*h*[660] do coim*het* a henig .i. an p*r*im ben be c*h*a*r*na. ben b*hius* imbæisi cuigir, no nonb*air*

12 [ar]a cc*ar*nuid fir iom*dha* *triar* i nænlo no i næn oidc*h*e os *air*d, no cuig*er* fo c*h*l*eth*, no nonb*air* *ar*

13 [f]ud[661] a bet*h*a dferaib*h* taid*h*e. be cat*h*a .i. ben t*r*esa ccuirt*er* cat*h* tengann, *ar* olc*us* a teng*ann*, no do ni [...]

14 [t]eng*ann* go ccuirt*er* cat*h* ui*m*pe, no ben do b*eredh* cat*h* am*h*[ail] do b[er]*edh* [meadhbh cruachan][662]

15 [.................][663]

---

653 The missing letters are supplied from O'Curry's transcription.
654 There is a line through all of this text. See the entry on the line below.
655 This phrase is added above the line with an insertion mark.
656 The missing letter is supplied from O'Curry's transcription.
657 O'Curry reads 'deis'. I should like to thank one of the anonymous readers for comments on this reading.
658 The rest of the entry is squeezed in above the line of text at the edge of the paper.
659 The missing letter is supplied from O'Curry's transcription.
660 The missing letters are supplied from O'Curry's transcription.
661 The missing letters are supplied from O'Curry's transcription.
662 The missing letters are supplied from O'Curry's transcription.
663 There appears to be some writing below the last line of the text, but it is illegible because the bottom of the page is obscured by the mounting. It is possible that the writing belongs with the end of the previous entry.

Transcription p. 12[664]

[a]1 [....]ær [..]b[.]. be [.....] [.]c bri[.] atac*h*.[665] Be [.]n[..][.....]olc ł n[...]ac[666]

2 [....]*ar* [.]t[.] [..]bc c[..] ag [....] be nind[lightheach] .i. ben as indlig*h*t*a*c do ne[ch]

3 [do beith aige ara] fial*us*ag risi*n* fer .i. an ben coibdealac .i. ben oile f*r*is a coibdeal*aigh* no in dlig*ed* lan[amnusa][667]

4 be neccomlan[668] .i. ben nac*h* comlan do nec*h* do nec*h* aige im guin im goid, no im gal*ar* coisi no

5 [laime .i. bean nim] slan lam *ar* gaid .i. ben gat*h*ac*h* no baclam[a]c, no as eccomlan df*er* aga *m*bi [no as.......][669]

6 [...]a .i. ben coma*r*ba fo-sisith*ar* ahat*ar* indrota[..] fæisidaid an [.]a[.]es*are*[........][670]

7 [be ei]g*h*ensa .i. ben bi*us* i bfirgen*us* uais amuil bi*us* ban *air*cinn*a*c p*r*imc[aithr]e m[ar] cen*n*[....][671]

8 [...]bi*us* [..] gaibi*us* fergnioma ingen*us*, ⁊ tiomorgain a cuirp am*ail* bis ban*air*cin[...][672]

9 [..]*us* g[.]n [.]imoc*h*[...]. be da cret .i. an ben as uaisle dib*h* aga *m*bí da c*r*eit da

10 [no] ria fior ⁊ c*ar*pa[t] ep*acht*[673] no ruadi do m*a*c *cair*de. be rait .i. an ben as apad do[....]

11 [...] ceilib*h* ann ⁊ do b*ere*d*h* Med*h*b*h* cruacan, ⁊ [.....]

---

664 The page has bad staining on its upper two-thirds of the page and on all four sides. The top third and sides of the upper third of the document are stained, worn, and parts of the text are missing. The bottom is jagged, but it does not look like any text is missing.

665 There are at least two entries on the first 1.5 lines of the page which I cannot read. O'Curry does not include any of the text from these lines.

666 The reading is very tentative.

667 The missing letters are supplied from O'Curry's transcription.

668 I am uncertain whether there is another letter after the ⟨n⟩.

669 The missing letters are supplied from O'Curry's transcription. The remainder of the line was illegible for O'Curry too.

670 This entry is not included in O'Curry's transcription.

671 The missing letters are supplied from O'Curry's transcription. The remainder of the line was illegible for O'Curry too.

672 It is possible that this line of text belongs with the previous entry. Part of it seems to concern virginity.

673 O'Curry reads 'esbuig', but I cannot verify this.

12 [....] mac a brat*har* ma beg ⁊c̄. [b]1 duil .r.[674] urn*us*ta*r* .i. baoi ag urn*aide*.[675] æis toga[676] .i. æis to [...]

[b]2 *air*cennca .i. fir*chin*n*te*. toraid .i. ⟨on⟩ torra*cht*ain .i. tainig. fert*ar* .i. fertaig*h*ter .i. adnaicter. creadal ⟨.i. cre*d*m*us*⟩[677] .i. credm*he*

3 anch*ar*a de .i. ain*m* do*n* æibilteior. feadb*h* .i. baint*r*eabt*ach*. fec*h*aid .i. fua*cht*naig*h*id. ailed*h* .i. ellned*h*

4 fionn .i. cionad*h*. cæim*ht*h*ias ⟨ł es⟩[678] .i. cæi*m*tec*ht*ach*t*aig*h* .i. do ni coi*m*id*acht*. coi*m*riad .i. coi*mim*t*acht*, no coi*m*ce*m*níug*h*[adh][679]

5 fon*n* fri fon*n* .i. bon*n* fri bon*n*. utsad*ha* .i. iostad*ha* .i. aite soid*h* no ionad*h* co*mnaigh*e. sgiolla .i. dæsg*air* oba*nn*

6 i*arr*a*ir* .i. i*arradh*. t*air*fent*ar* .i. tairpent*ar*. terbad*h* .i. ion*nar*ba[680] no delug*adh*. frecur .i. fiorat*h*c*h*ur

7 doda niongaib .i. diongb*hus* no do ni a d*h*iongbail. eitsec*h* .i. duine gan tec*h*. cuidig*h* geill .i. lu

8 ac*h* tob*h*aig*h*. luig*h*e cana .i. mion*na* do tab*air*ter b*eth* umal do*n* riag*h*ail. ba na f*or*b*h*aig*h*e .i. ba an

9 luac*h* tobaig. com*h*logad ruis .i. laigsi*ne*, no com*m*ait*h*em*h* ber*ar* do*n* dui*ne* *ar* a mbi fiach

10 fiac*h* lesaig*hth*e .i. fiac biata ⁊ lesaig*hth*e na cciont*ach*. fer didin .i. fer bi*us* ag didin an c*h*int*aigh*

11 toc*h*uire*dh* ⟨.i. ciond⟩ .i. an cuire*dh* ⟨.i. ciond⟩ cugad.[681] tom*us* .i. tuair*im*. accuib*h*di*us* .i. in u*m*l*acht*, in æntu*ga*[682] do dlig*hedh*. egcuibdi*us*

12 a c*h*ontrar*dha* si*n*. diong*h*aib*h* g*ach* degen*ach* .i. gibe nec*h* aga ruib*he* an ciont*ach* ⟨da biath*ad* no da cuim*h*dac*h*⟩ fa deir*adh* diol*adh* *ar*a son

13 banapad .i. biath*adh* an ciont*aigh* re nden*am* cion*adh*. dergap*ad* .i. an biath*adh* i*ar* nden*am* cion*adh* do*n* ciontac

14 dergs*aru*g*adh* .i. dorn do buai*n* as b*r*olla*ch* a*n* ciont*aigh*, cid*h* re nde*nam*, cid i*ar* nden*am*, cion*adh*. com*air*legad .i. an

---

674 Dubhaltach indicates his source here. It is presumably for *Dúil* (*Roscadach*). He has also drawn a line separating the entries from those that are above.

675 O'Curry reads 'urnaighte'.

676 O'Curry reads 'coga'.

677 The gloss is barely visible above the lemma.

678 The alternative ending, ⟨ł es⟩, is written above the lemma.

679 The missing letters are supplied from O'Curry's transcription.

680 The ⟨a⟩ is written above the ⟨b⟩.

681 Both of the glosses are difficult to read; neither of them is in O'Curry's transcription. They could be corrections to the last two syllables of each word instead of glosses.

682 O'Curry reads 'aontumha'.

15 ciont*ach* do legad*h* fon c*h*aill. coim*h*ríom*h* in*n*sge f*air* .i. co*mh*aig*h*nes a nag*aidh* an biod*h*b*hadh* no an coint*aig*

16 gin tuillm*h*id*echt* .i. gin toi*mh*lid*echt* .i. gin toi*m*li*us* .i. it*h*es a ferann, no i bes no c*h*aites re a bele [é][683]

17 senc*h*let*h*e .i. lu*cht* lanamna b*hius* ag lenmui*n* do t*r*i g*h*lunuib a ndiaig*h* a c*h*eile, ⁊ o b*eth* ⟨ma*r* si*n*⟩[684] agan at*air* ⁊ agan

18 m*ac* ⁊ agan ua as *ete*r le slio*cht* an t*r*ir si*n* gan iadsan na a sli*cht* do leigen do gnat*h*, ⁊ eincl*eth*e na[685] da[oin]e[686] sin[687]

19 ioc cana ⟨ł congbail, no gabail⟩[688] re hainffine .i. ma*r* do rach*adh* duine ona fine fa riagail cana ⁊ fine oile ⟨.i. dlig*edh* cor*us*a fine tugt*e*r isi*n* cain sin⟩

20 gníad*h* .i. focal cuirt*e*r *ar* son an *air*ec ec*ht*a .i. an fer ris a ndent*ur* com*air*le an gnio*mh*a no an e*cht*a do

21 dena*m* ⁊ do be*i*r com*air*le do cac*h* cu*m* an gnio*mha*. bot*hach* .i. dær fuidir .i. dær bot*h*ac*h* bi*us ar* bot*achus* no

22 *ar* buailid[689] *ar* fe*dh* sam*h*ruid*h*,[690] no fog*h*m*air*. sec*h*f*us* .i. ion*n*saig*h*fes. baile ata tall .i. Senc*us* mo*r*.

23 cæm*h*sad .i. dfasad. æs c*air*de .i. an drong bi*us* fon statuid sio*th*cana dá ngoirt*e*r c*air*de. sio*th*

24 no riagail ordoig*h*id lu*cht* crice no d*ha* ⟨⁊̄c⟩[691] *et*a*r*ra fein, ⁊ bí cáin fo eirin*n* uile ⟨⁊ cac*h*⟩ ag adrad di

25 g*r*in g*r*iun .i. feran*n*. im-ruim*ethar* .i. ro reimnig*heth*ar in ioma*r*b*us*. urrad*us* ⟨.i. cionta⟩ .i. *air* arát*hus* .i. a c*h*ionta.

26 iomglan mis ⟨ano a cont*r*ar*dha*⟩ .i. neimhg*h*laine bi*us ar* nec*h ar* fe*dh* mis t*r*e biat*had* ciont*aigh* fri re deachm*aigh*e .i. cion an

27 ciont*aigh* go cen*n*[692] mi*us*a .i. do b*eth* ar tí biat*hus* e *ar* fe*dh* deic*h* la. tu*cht* .i. gne. rag*h*b*h*a .i. ro gab*h*a[693]

28 cob*hach* .i. coib*h*fiac*h*ac*h*. matbosaide .i. madia ngabasid*h*e. lias .i. do læg*h*aib*h* ⁊[694] cæirib*h*. mac*h*[695]

683 The missing letter is supplied from O'Curry's transcription.
684 The last two words are added above the line with an insertion mark.
685 The ⟨a⟩ is written subscript.
686 The missing letters are supplied from O'Curry's transcription.
687 The ⟨e⟩ and ⟨sin⟩ are written below the line and blocked off in ink.
688 The last four words are written above the first two words.
689 O'Curry has the note 'buailid*h*eac*h*t' after this word in his transcription.
690 O'Curry reads 'samhraidh'.
691 The ⟨⁊̄c⟩ is written above the line with an insertion mark.
692 The ⟨e⟩ is a correction over an original ⟨n⟩.
693 O'Curry reads 'ro gabhadh'.
694 O'Curry reads '⁊ do'.
695 Dubhaltach uses a *spiritus asper* instead of his usual *punctum*.

29 ad*h* .i. do indilib*h*, ⁊ deac*h*aib*h*. tos*ach* cána .i. i*ar* nesc*air*e .i. ffogu*r* cana.[696] andegh*adh* cána .i. i ffoirc*h*enn

30 sec*h*t mbliadan i tt*us* a hat*h*núidig*h*t*h*e.[697] éric .i. fíriac. céin m*hair*da[698] .i. an ccéin[699] m*hair*id

Transcription, p. 13[700]

[a]1 ben*nacht ar* an*main* featla ⟨ꝉ fac*ht*na⟩[701] do*m* seac*h*na *ar* an ngal*ar*

2 negcoir. a coi*m*de sa m*i*c mu*r*a na[702] ⟨leg⟩[703] inne ar ett*r*eoir[704]

3 glac*ad*[705] talm*haidhacht*[706] .i. gal*ar* mo*r* an la si*n* a*n* gab*us* a*n* rann si*n*

4 fæon fleacain .i. re re roil

5 ecan .i. fæon fo leacain

6 dub*h*aig*h*id .i. aigid fedil no *sechtea*rdub*h*áin[707]

7 *ar*a net*h*at .i. *ar*a nu*r*nuid*h*id .i. *ar*a *m*be*th*

8 inoiricill[708]

9 inbleog*an* saic*h*t*h*e no sǽoit*h*e .i. gallraig*h*teac*h*[709]

10 áb*h*ain*n* .i. cl*ár* b*hius* (ag (bual*adh* bas dǽoine) le cúrt*h*oir .i. fe*r* do ní cúrad

11 .i. gredad*h* smac*ht*aig*h*te *ar* m*a*caib do ní cion*n*ta

12 fog*h*nisse[710]

[b]1 iosa[711]

---

696 This entry is not included in O'Curry's transcription.

697 Dubhaltach uses a *spiritus asper* over the first ⟨t⟩ instead of his usual *punctum*.

698 O'Curry reads 'mharda'.

699 O'Curry reads 'cein'.

700 There is a lot of scattered staining on the page. All sides of the page are damaged and missing bits of text. The writing goes in multiple directions; see the schematic drawing. The writing was done in multiple stages. The page contains Dubhaltach's signature.

701 The correction is written above line.

702 The ⟨a⟩ is written subscript.

703 This sequence is written above the line.

704 This poem is included with the following entry in O'Curry's transcription.

705 O'Curry reads 'glicc'.

706 O'Curry reads 'talmhuigheacht'.

707 O'Curry reads 'sumdubhain'.

708 There is something in *marg. sin.* at a 90-degree angle to this text block that I cannot read: 'ios'[a]?

709 O'Curry reads 'gallraiteach'.

710 This word is not in O'Curry's transcription.

711 *Íosa* 'Jesus'. This line is not included in the edition of the glossary, but it is listed in the Sources Listed in the Manuscript and Marginalia section pp. 447–449

2 indul .i. u*air*, no óir[712]

[c]1 sea*ch*ain se*acht* ngæi gona an leigin*n*, ma dail g*ur*bad sær sen

2 c*r*uit is tiompan. pen*n* c*r*uaid*h* cen*n*dub*h*. fit*h*cioll buanf*ach*, brandub b[en][713]

[d]1 foib*h*rit*h*e .i. rat*h* fubaid*h*e .i. boim berrta .⁊c̄. ⟨.i. fo ba .i. fo mait*h* an n*eth*e do roimn*e*[714]⟩[715]

2 fiod*h* defid*h* *ar* du*n* .i. coill dee *ar* ⟨ł ag⟩ an dún ga *m*bi .i. fid*h* nim*edh*

3 ait*h*gin g*ach* fed*h*a o t*air*c*h*ell ⟨.i. timceall⟩ go diorain*n* ⟨.i. adb*al* rinn⟩ .i. ti*m*ceall na coill*idh* *ar* f*a*d

4 cl*ár* sadall .i. cl*ar* diallaid

5 fer lesac*h* .i.[716] cresion .i. c*r*eidmeac*h*. leam*h*ad*h* .i. bod m*air*b*h*e[717]

6 crela .i. c*rí*ola .i. c*r*o iall orba fertsi[718] si*n* ⁊c̄

7 no orba c*r*uib*h* no sliosda

8 toxaig*ad* on toxal no foxal dudly forbesse[719]

9 apad raitig*h* .i. ap*adh* bert*er* *ar* nec ⁊ e *ar* an rod no *ar* slig*h*e

10 iatiaig*h* ⟨.i. mealog⟩ .i. tiac*h* .i. aiteog. tigseal .i. buain

11 fo-coisle .i. foxluig*h*. reac*h*oll mbr*eth* .i. roic*h*iall na mbr*eth*

12 lug*ar*man .i. luga g*ar*man ł[720] lingua g*ar*man no an g*arm*an ce*n* buir.

13 áig*h*e fine .i. cen*n*e fine

14 aitgi*n* snomtha[721] f*ed*h*a .i. buain c*r*oin*n*[722] d[e]na c*r*annuib

15 ancharai .i. æib*h*illt*h*eoir no deor*adh* de læig*h*tec no læig*h* a lias[723] ⟨.i. laoig*h* i[724] tec no cro⟩

16 i*ar*uasaoitt ⟨ł masait⟩[725] .i. i*ar* mbr*eth* cl*ainn*e

17 cneam*h* cosaite .i. sort[726] piseog

---

712 This line is written in much smaller letters than the surrounding entries.
713 The missing letters are supplied from O'Curry's transcription.
714 O'Curry reads 'roinne'.
715 This sequence is written above the line in a different ink color.
716 Dubhaltach did not finish the entry.
717 This entry is not in O'Curry's transcription. The last word of the gloss is written under the lemma.
718 O'Curry reads 'sertri'.
719 Dubhaltach's signature here is not listed in Ó Muraíle 1996c.
720 ⟨no⟩ is crossed out before the ⟨l⟩.
721 The ⟨s⟩ is not in Dubhaltach's usual script for writing Irish.
722 There might be a letter or two after this word which I cannot read.
723 This entry has a box drawn around it.
724 The reading is uncertain. There might be more than one letter here.
725 The correction is written above the line.
726 The ⟨s⟩ is not in Dubhaltach's usual script for writing Irish.

18 cuic*h* apa nos m*ar*ba ⟨.i. piseoga⟩ tigsel ⟨.i. buain⟩ .i. i*n* guimin ⟨.i. cro-cen*n*⟩[727] ro hoige ⟨.i. fuaig*edh*⟩ ui*m*pe[728]

19 i*ar* mbr*eth* us .i. ní t*ar* éis br*eth*em*h*nuis tuill*adh* leis

20 m*ar*b-cnai .i. lomrad olla .i. ciro[729] cnu olla .i. lomrad

21 sloig*hedh* fuidr*echt*a .i. slog*h* fuidir.[730]

22 t*r*eas bunsac bon loisg[731] *ar* sgiat ngeal

23 dubaig*idh* no cert f*or* cuaille ⟨.i. oig*h*id fedil⟩

24 aire .i. trosgad*h*

25 codnac*h* t*air*gt*h*e[732]

26 turtgal .i. gail egent*ach* ⟨bi*us ar* m*h*næi re br*eth* cloin*ne*⟩[733] turtad .i. eigean ⟨.i. extorion⟩[734]

27 t*r*eas bunsac*h* ⟨bon*n*[735] *ar* sgiat*h* ngeal⟩[736] .⁊c .i. m*ar* bud*h* as[737] ⁊ sn*ath*[738] b*eth* t*r*eas an*n*[739] *acht* fallas

28 com*h*lut*h* ngusgan*n*ail

[e]1 Senc*h*as[740]

Transcription, p. 14[741]

[a]1 D[ud]ly D[742]

2 D D Dud

3 ly for

[b]1 liasrad*h* .i. déna*m* lias no cro do læguib et ceteri

---

727 The form of the long ⟨e⟩ is the same as that at the end of *cenne* in line 13.

728 O'Curry has several different readings for this entry.

729 The reading of this word is uncertain.

730 There is a suspension mark (or perhaps a stray mark) over the ⟨f⟩ which I cannot expand.

731 The ⟨g⟩ appears to have been made over the compendium for ⟨ar⟩.

732 O'Curry reads 'teighte'.

733 This part of the entry is written above the line.

734 O'Curry reads 'extortion'.

735 A word has been crossed out after this which I cannot read.

736 The phrase is written above the line with an insertion mark.

737 The reading of this word is uncertain (perhaps 'i' or 'ri'?); O'Curry reads 'eadh'.

738 It is possible that this word should be read as 'sn*ach*'.

739 This word is written above the line with an insertion mark.

740 This word is written upside down in relation to the d-block of entries.

741 There is a lot of scattered staining on the page. All sides of the page are damaged and probably missing bits of text. The writing goes in multiple directions; see the schematic drawing. The writing was done at multiple stages. Part of Dubhaltach's name appears in [a].

742 It appears that Dubhaltach did a pen test here with parts of his name.

2 acht .i. [a]chtug*adh* dlig*ed*. *air*esg, ⁊ *arus*g .i. cin*n*iod*h* dligt*ech*
3 fær .i. foirit*h*in no cob*air* g*h*eill. urcorat*har* .i. at*h*cuiriter .i. faidig*h*ter[743]
4 coic .i. de*arg*. dunn .i. róid*h*. líog*h* .i. dat*h*. i*ar*rat*h* .i. lua*ch* oilemna. cumd
5 meic g*a*c graid .⁊c .i. cen*nach* ber*ar* do nec*h* do cion*n* an m*aic*[744] do coim*hét*
6 i nai*m*sir ænaig*h*, no re a at*hcar* for a at*hair* i*ar* ndi-ailtre, no luac
7 ac coim*et*ech*t*a do b*h*erid do macaib*h* na
8 na ngrad*h* as isle inaid fen.[745]
[c]1 sensmurcion*nadh* .i. i*ar* mbl*iad*ain .i. bl*iad*ain no ni as mo o do rin*ned* an cions*macht*
2 c*air*de[746] fot*h*ana .i. m*edh*g
3 ba feisi .i. fesda
4 a bailiu i mbailiu
[d]1 [747]met*h*ir .i. c*e*rt bi*us* im c*h*æir*adh* claim*h*
2 uinge di*a*ran*n*
3 rud*h* .i. roid*h* .i. corc*air*
4 [.]i[.....][748]
5 rud*h* .i. ro[idh .i. corc]*air*[749]
6 u*m*a nu na cloit*h*ib*h* ⟨.i. na mianac*h*⟩ .i. on cloid*h*e .i. toc*h*ailt
7 na tanalac*h* ⁊c .i. leaca
8 inbleogain gill .i. *ar*a ndleag*ur* geall do gab*ail*
9 cróc*h* .i. g*a*c n*a*rd*h* g*a*c*h* n*air*egda. cro*ch* .i. ua*chtar* ut u*achtar* bain*n*e
10 brat gan lom*mus* .i. gan clúm
[e]1 dub⟨alt⟩ fir⟨bis⟩[750]
[f]1 salla*ch* diollat ⟨.i. an teda*ch* ber*ar* man salc*h*ar⟩ .i. brat gan lom*da*, ⁊ io
2 n*ar* gan toll*us*, no brat dub, ⁊

743 O'Curry reads 'fadaightear'.
744 O'Curry reads 'mac'.
745 A line is drawn under this line of text.
746 This word is followed by another word which has been crossed out that I cannot read.
747 The first three lines of [d] form a separate section. These three lines look as if they were written in their current location after the edge of the page was torn. This assessment is based on the fact that the last line of this section is visible as is part of the line above it immediately to the left on the page. The duplicate entries make sense if they were rewritten after the damage to the page.
748 This line is to the left of the previous three lines of text. The page is torn, but part of ⟨i⟩ is visible.
749 This entry appears to be a repeat of line 14d3 above. Perhaps Dubhaltach rewrote the line after the corner of the page was torn.
750 The second half of each part of Dubhaltach's signature is written above the first part. See the MS image.

3 ion*ar* dub*h*. ní bert*ar* do*n* oide
4 o at*air*, ⁊ o matair an lenib*h*
5 tæb amuig don i*arr*at*h*.
6 (bo d*hear*ba (m*ar* si*n*) dana
7 altrom go tog*h*a .i.
8 i ccin*n* .xiiii. bl*iadna* do ing*h*in.
9 i ccion*n* sec*h*t mbl*iadna* deg
10 do mac .i. a[751] ttog*h* a[752] i cill
11 no i ttuait*h* no a bpos⟨ad⟩[753]
12 ⁊c̄.
13 serg, ⁊ mac
14 ra .i. galra
15 bid *ar* lenbuib*h*.
16 fo-fe, ⁊ fo-fi
17 ⁊ fo-fic*h* .i. fua*cht*
18 naig*adh* .i. ofence[754]
[g]1 Ta[lent]um lá,[755] talenton Græca. talanntan [i] ngæid[hilge][756]
[h]1 foguirre, dog*h*uirre .i. fuaidr*edh*
2 as, los, gert .i. as na collu, los na lag*h*
3 gert an tu*ar* .⁊c̄
4 fresgisin imsc*air*[757] .i. sæil*acht*ain iomsg*arth*a[758]
5 miasl*ach*[759] bo, no g*a*c mil .i. miof*h*ocal dio*m*olta
6 do beir duine *ar* boin e .⁊c̄
7 flait*h* cuitrid .i. an t*r*eas flait*h* do be*r* rat*h* do ceile
8 at*hch*ur sæire go seduib .i. an tan ata

751 O'Curry reads 'i'.
752 ⟨a⟩ *om.* O'Curry.
753 The ⟨ad⟩ is added above the line.
754 This is one of the rare instances where Dubhaltach glosses an Irish term with an English word.
755 This word in omitted in O'Curry's transcription.
756 The missing letters are supplied from O'Curry's transcription; parts of the entry are missing due to tears in the page.
757 O'Curry reads 'imsearc'.
758 See O'Donovan's Supplement in O'Reilly, *s.v. fresgisin*. O'Donovan mentions that he got the entry from H.2.15, p. 208, loose sheets which suggests that he was working, at least in part, with the orginal document itself and not necessarily O'Curry's transcription. The page number of H2.15 given here corresponds to other sources regarding where the glossary was found. See the Introduction, pp. 1–2
759 O'Curry reads 'maslach'.

9 an f[*lai*]t*h*,[760] ⁊ an cele i mbe*th**adh*,[761] no ata an d*ar*a de

10 ⁊ as m*ar*b*h* *ar*aile

11 at*h*cur sæire gan seoda .i. an tan as m*ar*b a ndís.

12 déisde, fesd*h*ide,[762] no esdide .i. tioru*air*si .i. fuigioll

13 [c].f.[763] m*ac* sg*r*ine .i. m*ac* do ni fer re coibdeal*ach* ⟨na riocht fen⟩ .i. cuirt*er* i sg*r*in leat*hair* e amac *ar* muir

14 in *airet* b*us* leir gelsgiat*h* .⁊c̄.[764]

15 cíos n*air*dbide .i. *air*debe cin*n*t*ac* do b*air*gin no

16 do l*eth*b*air*g*h*en, do tsen fine bi*us* si*n* .⁊c̄.[765] c.f.[766]

17 fær (air) se*cht*mui*n* .i. foirit*h*in im

18 t*r*ebad*h* do b*h*eir an cele do*n* flait*h*[767] isi*n* se*cht*mui*n*, fær buana ma*r* si*n*

19 fuaichne[768] fog*h*la .i. fói*ch*nín, no foicenn, no mat*hair* fog*h*la, no tos*ac* cointine

20 m*air*b*h*elod*h* .i. dol o dlig*adh* ⁊ se beo

21 beoelod*h* .i. scontra

20a [769]atgab*ail* *ar* fud .i. atg*h*ab*al* sa hanad*h* bi*us* i laim*h* biodb*adh*

21a at*h*gab*ail* tulla .i. i laim fech*eman* toich*eda*[770] bi*us* a hand[a]

22a tre oibne

22 ces loin ⟨aisill loin⟩, no dena[771]

23 anbfolta aigilline, mailis an cele, ma*r* b*eth* biad ⟨goide⟩[772] do tab*air*t do*n* flait*h* mar bia[d]

---

760 The suspension mark is illegible; the missing letters are supplied by O'Curry.

761 The expansion of the final syllable is uncertain.

762 O'Curry reads 'feisdide'.

763 Cf. 'c.f.' for *Córus Fine* below. The entry which follows comes from this text; *CIH* 744.28–29. Dubhaltach has written the title of the text at the beginning in TCD MS 1337, p. 214a; O'Sullivan 2000: 442; *CCIH* 235.

764 Dubhaltach has drawn a rectangular shape around this entry.

765 This entry is written starting part way through the column of entries; it is partially blocked off from the rest by a few lines of ink.

766 This abbreviation is for *Córus Fine*.

767 The word ⟨fær⟩ is crossed out after this word.

768 The lemmata here and the following four lemmata (*beoelodh* is part of the entry above it although it is written as if it were a distinct lemma) in the same column in the MS are written in larger letters and darker ink than the glosses which follow them, which suggests that Dubhaltach might have added the glosses later.

769 This and the following two lines are written next to lines 20–22 and are separated by a vertical line.

770 The ⟨toich*eda*⟩ is omitted from O'Curry's transcription.

771 It is possible that Dubhaltach never completed the entry when he went back to fill in the others in this section.

772 This word is written above the line with an insertion mark.

24 tat*hchar ar*[773] díu*m*un*n* .i. at*h*cur *ar* dimiad*h*aig*h*e lais b*eth* aige .i. nac*h* fiu leis an

25 cele b*eth* ag an flait*h*,[774] no leis an flait*h* an cele do b*eth* aige

Entries in O'Curry's Transcription Which Have Not Been Found in the MS

Elg .i. ere.
Finne .i. fine duthaidh.
Fithis .i. fath uais.
Foir [...] .i. remheach.
Mac saoir lethe .i. mac aga mbi ceannus sealbha ⁊ maoine ara aithidh fein.

---

773 The ⟨ar⟩ is omitted from O'Curry's transcription.
774 After this word ⟨⁊⟩ is crossed out.

Eugene O'Curry's Transcription

What follows below is Eugene O'Curry's alphabetic transcription of Dubhaltach's Glossary listed in the order in which it is found in TCD MS 1401. The table contains a column for the headword and entry, a column with the corresponding entry reference in the edited text, and a column for the marginal notes made by O'Curry. O'Curry uses a '+' to indicate where he was unable to read all of an entry. He also underlines words and letters where his reading is uncertain. These notes have been reproduced as they are found in the manuscript. O'Curry indicates lenition by putting a *punctum* over individual letters; all of the *puncta* have been transcribed as ⟨h⟩. For further discussion about O'Curry's transcription methods, see the Introduction, pp. 6–7.

No.	Headword and entry	Entry reference	O'Curry's notes	MS fol.
			The figures in the margin refer to the pages in the old MS in which the word is to be found.	10
	.A.			10
1	Abach .i. cnumhus .i. feis.	10.19.49		10
2	Abailiu [ ] imbailiu	14.c.4.14	thus 14+	10
3	Ábhainn .i. clár bios (ag bualadh bas daoine) le cúrthoir .i. fear do ní cúradh .i. greadadh smachtaighthe ar macaibh do ní cionnta.	13.a.10.5		10
4	Accuibdios .i. in umlacht, in aontumha do dligheadh. Eccuibdios a chontrardha sin.	12.b.11.41		10
5	Ach		fec cuig anmanna cat	10
6	Acht .i. cunntabairt.	10.38.85		10
7	Acht .i. achtughadh dligheadh.	14.b.2.2	14+	10
8	Aclaige .i. ioc loighe.	1.b.7.66	fec caiglighe.	10
9	Acluighead .i. iocuid lógh.	1.b.8.67		10
10	Ad-anna .i. adannaigh .i. fadoig.	7.b.36.112		10
11	Adbalad .i. eblid .i. basaighid.	9.27.83		10
12	Ad-bela .i. ebi .i. bas.	7.b.22.88		10
13	Ad-bo .i. urfhograidh.	5.a.4.15		10
14	Ad-boib .i. obthar.	8.35.97		10
15	Ad-bois .i. obais.	7.b.12.70		10
16	Ada-bonn .i. obaim.	7.b.12.69		10
17	Ad-bosaid .i. obuid.	4.c.8.54		10
18	Ad-buib .i. oibebhuidh.	4.c.8.56		10

 | DOI:10.1163/9789004755673_007

(*cont.*)

No.	Headword and entry	Entry reference	O'Curry's notes	MS fol.
19	Ad cheath .i. ad cifeadh.	1.a.11.27		10
20	Ad-ceath .i. ad chifeadh.	2.b.2.70		11
21	Ad-cua .i. do innis.	3.b.19.66		11
22	Ad-cuitigh .i. ro eitigh.	4.c.22.113		11
23	Ad-daimheadh .i. aididnighid.	10.41.100		11
24	Ad-ealla .i.	6.a.4.16	6+	11
25	Ad-gleanad .i. ada glanuid, no gleanuid, no teaglomuid.	6.a.25.50		11
26	Adma .i. aidhme .i. culath no glés.	9.42.127		11
27	Ad-neasa .i. do bear táinsiomhadh.	4.c.8.55		11
28	Ad-raigh .i. ceanglaidh.	8.33.87		11
29	Ad-rean .i. iocaidh.	6.a.4.15		11
30	Ad-rire .i. iocaid.	6.a.30.66		11
31	Ad-road .i. do rochair.	10.39.88		11
32	Ad ro-greim .i. ro ingreim.	6.a.25.49		11
33	Ad-roigheastar .i. ro guideastar, no ro eisgeastar.	7.a.32.44		11
34	Ad-roille .i. do airillneadh.	1.b.13.85		11
35	Ad-roir .i. adha ro oirg.	10.40.95		11
36	Ad-suitear .i. astuightear.	10.32.74		11
37	Ad-suitear .i. asduightear.	2.b.2.71		11
38	Ad-uidhbre .i. adha iodhbhras.	8.37.102		11
39	Agh .i. bó.	9.21.62		11
40	Ágha fine .i. ógh ae bhíos ar an ffine. Flaith gelfine sin.	9.31.94		11
41	Aga, no ionagha .i. iomain, aonach.	9.9.31		11
42	Aibhriteodh .i. abhratodh no soadh .i. an tan do fuit a habhra dar an suil.	1.b.10.76		12
43	Aicc .i. ésg.	3.b.5.31		12
44	Aiccithear .i. uga ésgtear.	10.11.18		12
45	Aidhbhean .i. adhbha dhíona.	7.a.7.10		12
46	Aidhbsi .i. taisbea̲nadh.	4.c.7.49		12
47	Aidhche iodhnuidhe .i. [_]	4.b.22.35	4+	12
48	Aidhilgneach .i. dlightheach.	7.a.7.9		12
49	Aig, taig .i. im na heachuibh, ⁊ im na caoiribh.	9.11.35		12
50	Aigbele.		fec forcraidh.	12
51	Aigde.		fec neach diamba ⁊c̄.	12
52	Aigdightear .i. uga eisgithear.	7.b.33.106		12
53	Aige .i. aimsir.	5.a.1.3		12
54	Aighe fine .i. ceann fine.	13.d.13.23		12
55	Aighne frisninnle breath .i. aigne firinnlithear do denam breitheamnusa .i. leghaidh cuirp an bhreitheamhnuis, ⁊ beridh an tollamhan breath, ase sin aigne as onoraighe do na haigneadhaibh. ⁊c̄.	8.29.78		12
56	Aighneta .i. aighneas no breitheamhnus.	3.b.12.49		12

(*cont.*)

No.	Headword and entry	Entry reference	O'Curry's notes	MS fol.
57	Aileadh. ellneadh.	12.b.3.20	thus	12
58	Aill .i. uasal.	6.b.1.90		12
59	Aille .i. alleluia.	7.b.18.79		12
60	Ailtleathan conuire .i. fear teghleathan ar an conaire da radh fear.	7.b.21.85		13
61	Ain .i. iomaigh .i. iomain.	9.8.24		13
62	Ainb .i. aineolach.	4.c.11.68		13
63	Ainbhféth .i. aineolus.	4.c.20.105		13
64	Aindliceat .i. ionglaine no neimceat [_]	1.a.10.25	1+	13
65	Ainfigh .i. gan fighe.	6.a.6.22		13
66	Ainmeach .i. ainémhioch.	2.a.8.29		13
67	Airbhe .i. easnach.	4.c.11.69		13
68	Airbheach .i. easnach.	4.c.11.70		13
69	Airbearach . neach do beir oirbhire ar neach mar ata cáinte.	4.c.16.89		13
70	Airbir .i. tairbhir.	10.15.34		13
71	Airbhre .i. sluaighte.	2.b.3.78		13
72	Airceannca .i. fircinnte.	12.b.2.13		13
73	Aircne.		fec cuig anmanna cat	13
74	Aire .i. trosgadh.	13.d.24.36		13
75	Aireasg, ⁊ arusg .i. cinniodh dlightheach.	14.b.2.3		13
76	Airgeadluibh .i. luib airgid.	10.30.67		13
77	Airiasacht .i. aontughadh.	2.b.20.107		13
78	Airillneadh .i. dligheadh.	6.a.4.14		13
79	Airite .i. gabhail.	9.40.118		14
80	Airle .i. fál. [ ]	9.9.29	9+	14
81	Airlim .i. leim air .i. leim do beirid airneis ar ghort no ar fér no ar cladh.	1.a.13.32		14
82	Airlisi .i. ima mbi an taile an fál.	9.16.49		14
83	Airlítheach .i. fear dénta uasal líotha.	7.a.29.42		14
84	Airm i ttoth .i. inad i ttairing.	9.38.111		14
85	Airmhidin .i. arrachtus do nid daoine ag tarraing beathadhaigh as lathaig.	1.a.12.30		14
86	Airsinsior .i. firsinsear.	3.b.12.50		14
87	Aitheanaigh .i. firenaigid.	2.a.1.4	1+	14
88	Aithghin gach feadha o tairchell (.i. timceall) go diorainn (.i. adbal rinn) .i. timceall na coillidh ar fad.	13.d.3.10		14
89	Aithgin snomta feadha .i. buain croinn dena crannuibh.	13.d.14.24		14
90	Aithne na mban tetha fein, ar sgath fear ata dream dibh ⁊ ní headh ata dream oile.	11b, l. 1[1]		14

1 See Appendix 4.

(*cont.*)

No.	Headword and entry	Entry reference	O'Curry's notes	MS fol.
91	Amne .i. amlaidh so.	10.43.110		14
92	Amhnus .i. olc.	4.b.22.23		14
93	Amhuis ruin, ⁊ raidh, ⁊ iomagall .i. amhuis bid marsin ag tighearna.	6.a.36.82		14
94	Amhus ala tuaithe .i. deoraidh.	9.41.123		14
95	Anacht i. aincistur.	1.b.13.88		14
96	Anailge .i. samhlaighthe.	6.a.20.37		15
97	Anbhfolta aigillme, mailis an cele, mar beadh biadh goide do thabairt don flaith mar biadh.	14.h.23.44		15
98	Anchara de .i. ainm don aoibilteóir.	12.b.3.17		15
99	Ancharai .i. aoibillteoir no deoraidh dé.	13.d.15.25		15
100	Andeagaidh cana .i. i ffoircheann seacht mbliadhan, a ttus a hathnuidighthe.	12.b.29.68	12	15
101	Andomhna .i. inde doimne cuitheacha ⁊c̄.	1.b.3.51		15
102	Andomhna .i. inde doimne.	9.7.19	9	15
103	Angur .i. iongor.	9.42.128	9	15
104	Anmanna breithe. breath. riar. edirceart ⁊ comha. Ut dicitur tre chomha .i. tré sin mbreith darab ainm comha.	11.a.11.16	11	15
105	Anmchaide .i. caithiumh anma go haith no go hadha.	6.a.26.53	6	15
106	Anmchairdes .i. cairdius anma, cairdius ciche, ⁊ gluine.	2.a.7.25	2	15
107	Annach .i. anóighe adaltrais.	8.34.92	8	15
108	Annoit .i. eagluis duthchuis [_] .i.eagluis an pharráisde i gcomhnuigheann neach, no as neasa do neach ar fineachas .r.	11.a.3.4	11+	15
109	Ano		fec iomglan mis	15
110	Aoibhilteoir .i. gradh eagailsi bios mar aoibil isin teoir .i. leigeann crabaidh.	7.b.32.104		15–16
111	Aois coga .i. aois co [_]	12.b.1.12	12+	16
112	Aonmhais .i. aonchruth, no aon dluimh.	1.b.21.105		16
113	Aorchaidh .i. fear denta coire.	1.b.18.100		16
114	Aos cairde .i. an drong bios fon statuid siothchána dá ngoirtear cairde. Sioth nó riaghail ordoighid lucht criche no da ⁊c̄. Eatorra fein, ⁊ bi cain fo eirinn uile ⁊ cach ag adrad di.	12.b.23.56		16
115	Apadh raithigh .i. apadh bertear ar neach ⁊ é ar an ród no ar slíghe.	13.d.9.17		16
116	Apain .i. ebiltin.	6.a.33.73		16
117	Aptha .i. ebiltin.	10.15.33		16
118	Ara-cheala .i. aircheallus no [_] eas no goideas.	11.a.5.7	11+	16
119	Aragur .i. ceangailtear.	8.33.88		16
120	Ar-aidhe .i. ar son.	6.a.38.85		16
121	Ar a nethat .i. ara nurnuidhid .i. ara mbeith inoiricill.	13.a.7.3		16

(*cont.*)

No.	Headword and entry	Entry reference	O'Curry's notes	MS fol.
122	Arbhar .i. sluagh.	2.b.3.77		16
123	Archu .i. cu bhios for arach .i. ceangal.	10.19.48		16
124	Archu lomhna .i. cu ara mbi lomán da ceangal.	6.a.33.74		16
125	Ardblor caimhe .i. ardghlor cainteamhuil.	2.a.9.32		16
126	Ardoc .i. comdide .i. buideachus iarum.	2.a.1.3		16
127	Ar-gair .i. urgairidh .i. crosadh.	10.41.98		16
128	Arr .i. fiadh, no os.	4.c.17.91		17
	.Duil.r.			17
129	Arrbeanathar .i. ionnarbtar.	6.b.1.87		17
130	Arrchogadh .i. seguinidh, no cu gonus osa.	4.c.16.90		17
131	Arsithear .i. tairsithear.	4.c.7.52		17
132	As, los, geart .i. as na collu, los na lag, geart an tuar. ⁊c̄.	14.h.2.29		17
133	Aseich segmaine .i. assain an ni da seicheann an meanma ⁊ an tsuil.	2.b.4.82		17
134	Asné .i. as é.	8.23.60		17
135	As-roib .i. ro ob. [_]	7.b.13.73	7+	17
136	Atair annoide .i. atair eagluise duthchus do neach.	6.a.9.26		17
137	Athchor iar bfoltuibh .i. athchor do nid [ ] for an athair [ ] iar san mis chiche .i. iar mbeith don cloinn re ré mis ar chichibh na mna.	3.b.24.80	3+	17
138	Athchur saoire go seduibh .i. an tan ata an flaith ⁊ an cele i mbeathaidh, no ata an dara de, ⁊ as marbh araile.	14.h.8.33		17
139	Athchur saoire gan seoda .i. an tan as marbh a ndis.	14.h.11.34		17
140	Athghabail ar fud .i. athghabhail sa hanadh bios i laim biodhbhadh.	14.h.20a.41		17
141	Athghabail tulla .i. i laim fecheamh bios a handa tre oibne.	14.h.21a.42	14+	17
142	Athmhochta .i. achmoaighthe.	2.a.2.5	1+	18
143	Atorsa .i. innosa, no anuairsi.	9.17.51	9+	18
144	Athrola .i. la asa haithle .i. ni do thiomargui ar neach.	9.39.117		18
145	Ath techta .i. inad dlightheach nó ait no baile.	4.c.25.123		18
	.B.			18
146	Bá .i. maith .i. ebriughas baoisi .i. bagh no iomad baoisi.	7.a.1.2	7+	18
147	Badhadh .i. ebleadh.	1.b.12.84		18
148	Ba feisi .i. fesda.	14.c.3.13		18
149	Baidsidhe .i. fear do ní baisdedh, mar ata ollamh baisdius gradha ar na filidhibh.	4.c.26.130		18
150	Baile atatall .i. Seancus mor.	12.b.22.54	12+	18
151	Bailiudh .i. élódh aba as maith.	10.41.99		18
152	Bainleabaidh .i. biathadh do beir fine dia roile.	1.a.3.7		18
153	Bainteoluid .i. banghadoighe.	4.c.20.107		18
154	Bánabadh.		fec deargabadh.	18

(*cont.*)

No.	Headword and entry	Entry reference	O'Curry's notes	MS fol.
155	Ban airgeach.		fec be nionnra.	18
156	Ba na forbhaighe .i. ba an luach tobaigh.	12.b.8.35		18
157	Banapad .i. biathadh an chiontaigh re ndenam cionadh.	12.b.13.43		18
158	Banaradluach .i. bean gabhus do laimh, no ni ionad mna an tighe.	3.b.22.76		18
159	Banataid .i. edachtain no edail bhan.	2.a.13.47		18
160	Baoidsioch .i. bean bhaoth .i. seach as baoth.	7.b.29.100		18
161	Basc .i. baiscmhellad[aibh] treas [teas] braghad no asgar [uisgi].	3.b.20.70	3+	19
162	Be .i. bean téid ar faindel asa tigh i ccomhdhail fir ele tar ceann a fir fein .i. in cartach .i. dormuire.	11.b.5.39		19
163	Beabhais .i. egais.	8.27.74	8+	19
164	Bean foiclighe .i. bean foiclightear a tigh ateach .i. bean bios fo cholcai .i. for claon conair, airm i bhfaoi aidche ni fhaoi aroile an be niomrama.	11.b.2.35	11+	19
165	Bean fria huaithne .i. re niodhnuibh, ⁊ uaithne cinn a lenibh uaithe.	8.4.13		19
166	Beannacht ar anmain featla (no fachtna) dom seachna ar an ngalar negcoir. a coimde sa mic muire na leg inne ar ettreoir. [_] glicc talmhuigheacht .i. galar mor an la sin angabus an rann sin.	13a, l. 1[2]	13+	19
167	Bean urnamda .i. adaltrach urnamda.	3.b.22.73		19
168	Béardarum .i. breitheamnuighear.	7.a.13.19		19
169	Beart .i. breitheamnus.	6.a.4.13		19
170	Beart .i. breitheamhnaighthear, no breitheamhnaighthis.	8.27.75		19
171	Be carna. bean bhios imbaoisi cuigir no nonbair ara ccarnuid fir iomdha .i. triar i naonla no i naon oidhche os aird. no cuigear fo cleath, no nonbar ar fud a beatha dfearaibh taidhe.	11.b.11.44		19
172	Be catha .i. bean tresa ccuirtear cath teangann ar olcus a teangann, no do ni [_] teangann go ccuirtear cath uimpe, no bean do beireadh cath amhuil do beireadh meadhbh cruachan.	11.b.13.45		20
173	Be da create .i. an bean as uaisle dibh aga mbí da creit [ ] no fior ⁊ carpat esbuig no ruaidi do mac cairde [ ]	12.a.9.9	12+	20
174	Be eigeansa .i. bean bios i bhfhirgeanus uais amuil bios ban aircinneach primcaithre mar ceann [ ]	12.a.7.8	12+	20
175	Be faoindil .i. bean fo nindle i ttigh urdalta.	11.b.4.37		20

2 See Appendix 4.

(*cont.*)

No.	Headword and entry	Entry reference	O'Curry's notes	MS fol.
176	Be fothla .i. bean dia bhfotleanann a cele a treabad seach an bean naruis .i. an aireach .i. dia bfoetlonn ní da seduibh seach an priom mnaoi .i. a mead an aireach.	11.b.3.36	11+	20
177	Be fhuis i ffoltaibh .i. bean bios i bhfoisdine (go bfoladh tochusa aice) ar cionn caich do coimhead a henigh .i. an prim bean.	11.b.10.43	11+	20
178	Beir geoanach .i. bir briathrach é.	4.b.22.32		20
179	Beithíum .i. bid dam.	4.c.10.65		20
180	Be muine .i. bean dan dir bheith i muine.	3.b.24.48		20
181	Be nannra .i.bean bios ann isin re .i. mathair na ndileachtadh bhios go macaibh ⁊ go leascloinn iomda deis a ceile deg ⁊ a meic age anionad a fir.	11.b.8.41	thus	20–21
182	Be neccomlan .i. bean nac comlan do neach aige im guin im goid no im galar coisi no laime .i. bean nim slan lam ag gaid .i. bean gatach no baclamhach, no as eccomlan dfear aga mbi no as [_]	12.a.4.6	12+	21
183	Be nindlightheach .i. bean as indlightheach do neach do beith aige ara fialusag risin fear .i. an bean coibdealach .i. bean oile fris a coibdealaigh, no in dligeadh lanamnusa.	12.a.2.5	11+	21
184	Be niomma .i. bean bhios ar ionnramh o ionad dionad.	3.b.24.79		21
185	Be niomrama.		fec bean foiclige	21
186	Be nionnra .i. bean bios i rinn na rae e, an ban airgeach .i. bean bios for airge ionnra i gcomus airge, ⁊ ag denam trebtha fo ionnamail mogha daoire.	11.b.6.40		21
187	Be nurnuide .i. bean aontumna bios ag urnuidhe a cele go haimsir naircheann .i. urnaidm niodnuide, no urnaidm [_] adhall .i. fri re ima tabairt.	11.b.9.42		21
188	Beo elodh.		fec mairbh elod.	21
189	Beothaidhbe .i. ni ebeas a coibche attaoi on mnaoi ⁊ beo i fen sa fear, no as beo neachtar de.	3.b.7.37		21
190	Be rait .i. an bean as [_] do beireadh [_] Meadhb cruachan ⁊ [_] mhac a brathar ma beag [_]	12.a.10.10	12+	22
191	Biadhmhoch .i. biadh go moch.	9.46.141		22
192	Biolfhothach .i. gan fothach.	4.c.26.128		22
193	Biora .i. bretheamhnaigh.	7.a.14.21		22
194	Bioramhna .i. mna biorach briathracha.	2.a.13.48		22
195	Bith .i. guin.	6.a.23.42, 7.a.25.37		22
196	Blaidhre .i. bal re ré.	10.42.104		22
197	Blaoidhis .i. beicis.	5.b.4.33		22
198	Blemhaidmh .i. glemaideamh, no briseadh.	4.c.24.119		22

(*cont.*)

No.	Headword and entry	Entry reference	O'Curry's notes	MS fol.
199	Boibre .i. bo eibeart .i. geim druth do ní, ⁊ amadán eisein.	7.b.15.75		22
200	Boicmell .i. meall buic .i. meall congna ima braghaid .i. in reindinic.	7.b.17.77		22
201	Boimbil, boim .i. aoibhinn, no sgiath, no boim do bhile sgeith.	4.c.12.73		22
202	Bos .i. bo fios .i. fios maith.	6.a.2.3		22
203	Bothach .i. daor fuidir .i. daor bothach bios ar bothachus no ar buailidh [buailidheacht. E. Curry] ar feadh samhraidh no foghmair.	12.b.21.52		22
204	Braitheamhnach .i. fear do ní brath neich.	2.b.1.68		22
205	Brasul .i. fear aga mbi ulcha bras mar ulgar ag drud ⁊ ag osgladh a beoil caintigh.	7.b.26.97	7+	22
206	Brataidh .i. foxladh.	9.16.47		23
207	Brat gan lommus .i. gan clúmh.	14.d.10.23		23
208	Breachtán .i. cinel annluinn.	1.a.15.35		23
209	Breas .i. ardfollus.	6.a.4.17		23
210	Breath .i. bretheaman.	10.41.101	10+	23
211	Breath.		fec anmanna breithe	23
212	Breoinde.		fec cuig anmanna cat.	23
213	Briocht fola, fuil follus, ⁊ cuirpghne .i. 1. coimpeart edir bheith na fuil ⁊ na linn bain i gconntabhairt eatorra. 2. fuil follus uirri fen. 3. cuirpghne .i. gne cuirp daona air.	3.b.32.86		23
214	Briogh ⁊ brioghtar .i. fírenightear.	7.a.15.22		23
215	Bronnus .i. fofhios bronn.	6.a.4.12		23
216	Broth .i. brath.	1.a.9.24		23
217	Broth sguadh .i. bruth sgeithius an fhairrge.	7.a.12.18		23
218	Bruar .i. spuilleach arain.	10.30.65		23
219	Bruar sraife .i. iomad sraibh.	10.30.66		23
220	Buasach .i. bá fheasach.	4.c.16.88		23
221	Buicne .i. ceo da bhuaic. fear leathcuinn e.	7.b.16.76		23
222	Buicne .i. ceo dhá bhuaic .i. cainte.	10.29.61		23
223	Buirisg .i. bios as a eisg .i. poll bheith na lar.	9.14.42		23
	.C.			24
224	Ca .i. cinus.	5.a.3.14		24
225	Ca .i. teach ⁊c̄.	5.b.2.27		24
226	Cadhna .i. caingne.	9.29.88		24
227	Caimpear .i. fear comlann.	7.b.3.54		24
228	Cairde.		fec aos cairde	24
229	Cáith, cáthaighe .i. neimni no fororbhfhasach.	7.b.35.110		24
230	Caithche ⁊ caitheamh .i. cionnta.	2.a.17.63		24

(*cont.*)

No.	Headword and entry	Entry reference	O'Curry's notes	MS fol.
231	Caitheamh tola mna .i. fear dfhaoideachtain le .i. do dul cuigthe, ma do foadh, ma do faoideadh, muna ffou, muna fho, muna ffoadh, sin uile o dul cuigthe.	10.9.13		24
232	Cam .i. comlann.	7.b.3.53		24
233	Cana .i. cuilen.	10.17.42		24
234	Cananna .i. cuileoin.	10.17.43		24
235	Can-dailidh .i. caoinindligh.	2.a.13.46		24
236	Caogadach .i. ainm graidh tre mar chanus, na tri caogada salm, foghlaintidhe, deisgibal, staruide, foirceadlaidhe, saoi canoine, druimcli. ag sin na seacht ngraidh eagna. Foglaintigh .i. fear ag a mbi eolus i ndeich leabhraibh dfochoir aige, uime sin goirtear de fear tiachtana fochoireach. Desgibal .i. fear ag a mbi eolus fochoire uile .i. 12. leabhar na fochoireach. Staruidhe .i. fear aga mbi. 30. daiceachtuibh naomtha ina fhogloim. Foirceadlaidhe .i. fear aga mbi gramadac <u>crosan</u> ⁊ siollaobha, ⁊ rime, ⁊ reatha na bliadhna, ⁊ reatha grene ⁊ esga. Saoi canoine .i. fear ag a mbi eolus canoine, ⁊ canas sgela iosa .i. breithear nde (isin inad glan i mbi) .i. eacna cadluic canoine. Druimcli .i. fear ag a mbi eolus iomlan na heagna on leabhar as mo dá ngoirtear cuilmean gus in leabhar as lugha da ngoirthear deich breithis, ina ndeachraigtear .i. i ndeghchoirightear an tiomna maith do rinne dia do *ar* saoisi.	5.b.16.43	5+	24–25
237	Caoimceile .i. giolla .t.	2.a.12.43		25
238	Caoimhthias, no coimhtheis i. caoimteachtachtaigh .i.do ni coimideacht.	12.b.4.22		25
239	Caoincerdne .i. foclog.	4.c.19.100		25
240	Caomnacht .i. [_]	2.a.2.8	1+	25
241	Caomhsad .i. dfasad.	12.b.23.55		25
242	Caraid claochlodha .i. duine ag a mbi claochlodh cairdeasa re a thighearna maille re tabartus do tabhairt don tighearna ⁊c̄.	8.15.40		25
243	Cataidh .i. uaisletaidh.	9.15.45		25
244	Cathair ataigh .i. cathair easpuig.	5.b.20.44		25
245	Cathair ataigh .i. cathair i naitceann cach a shochar ⁊ a dhochar, cathair ataigh thall i gcionn cille, catair ataigh an airchinnigh.	5.b.20.44		26
246	Casbairdnein iarcomarc .i. tri siolla.	4.c.5.46		26
247	Ceachair .i. ceachair na huachtar ⁊ uisge na hiochtar .i. dubhthonnach.	9.5.12		26
248	Ceachlattar .i. do conncattar.	7.b.22.87		26
249	Cead, no cuacad .i. foillsighid, no innisid.	3.b.19.65		26

(*cont.*)

No.	Headword and entry	Entry reference	O'Curry's notes	MS fol.
250	Ceadrann.		fec tri iomuire	26
251	Ceangar .i. ceimnightear.	5.b.10.42		26
252	Ceann, ⁊ costacair [_] .i. a cheann de fen.	9.14.43	9+	26
253	Ceathra .i. caoi doibh iothra.	1.b.5.56		26
254	Cechlaidh, clasaid .i. tochluid.	9.18.55		26
255	Cedciontach .i. bithbeanach.	1.b.6.60		26
256	Céin .i. fén.	4.c.10.63		26
257	Cein mharda .i. an cein mhairid.	12.b.30.70		26
258	Ceirt iomain .i. amhuil ro imeochaidis an airneis fein gan iomain.	1.b.1.47		26
259	Cele saorfhlatha .i. saoirchele.	10.31.70		26
260	Ceobath .i. an muir neamhairgsionadh bíos fá cheo.	6.a.24.46		26
261	Ces [aisill] loin [loin] no dena.	14.h.22.43	14+	26
262	Ceteamhuin .i. caora somhaoin.	9.26.81		26
263	Ciabair.		fec giabair	27
264	Cia erus .i. cait inereochadh.	3.a.12.18		27
265	Cia lias .i. cait i luidebhsa.	3.a.12.17		27
266	Ciasar .i. ceimnightear.	10.38.86		27
267	Cia sias .i. cait i ruideabsa.	3.a.12.16		27
268	Cichsime .i. ceimnighimne.	10.29.59		27
269	Cichsiod .i. ceimnighsiod.	1.b.9.72		27
270	Cicht .i. rinnaighe.	6.a.3.5		27
271	Cimidh irae .i. braighe ar na gabail i rae catha.	8.4.14	8+	27
272	Ciolar .i. corn.	5.a.6.24		27
273	Cios nairdbide .i. airdebe cinnteach do bairgin, no do leathbairgin, do tsean fine bhios sin. ⁊c̄. c.f.	14.h.15.37		27
274	Cirde .i. [_]a̲id no teasguid.	10.17.44	10+	27
275	Cis .i. cia, no caidiad.	8.1.2		27
276	Cit .i. caora.	9.26.79		27
277	Citriogha .i. uan .i. troigh .i. clann cite.	9.26.80		27
278	Citriug, ⁊ treteall .i. anmanna do caoiribh.	6.a.34.78		27
279	Ciuchustar .i. ceimnighiustar.	1.b.10.74		27
280	Cladhfothaid mona .i. gainnir mona.	6.a.32.72		27
281	Clamhdoid .i. bean ag a mbi lamh clamh.	3.b.10.44		27
282	Clar aimrid .i. bean na beir clann.	3.b.10.45		27
283	Clar sadall .i. clar diallaid.	13.d.4.11		27
284	Cliadhra, cléra .i. bolg, no criol no tiag.	9.40.119		28
285	Clethe lui (.i. na ngradh fene) .i. seacht ccinn gan cois, no aon gas cona cionn.	9.19.58		28
286	Cli ceann .i. bean nach beir clann, tri bliadhna fuilingidh a fear [_]	4.b.3.7	4+	28
287	Cliothcha clucha .i. cluthmuire .i. teta.	6.a.6.21		28
288	Cloth .i. uirdearc.	8.19.48		28
289	Clothach .i. ionchach.	2.b.3.76		28

(*cont.*)

No.	Headword and entry	Entry reference	O'Curry's notes	MS fol.
290	Clothar cloathur .i. cluintear.	2.b.6.86		28
291	Clú .i. urdearcadh.	2.b.2.73		28
292	Cluice is crios .i. cluithe don mhnaoi, ⁊ lamh fir na crios.	4.b.13.19		28
293	Cneamh cosaite .i. sort piseog.	13.d.17.28	+	28
294	Cnomhaidhm . briseadh cno.	4.c.24.120		28
295	Cobhach .i. coibfhiacach.	12.b.28.63		28
296	Cobranna gall .i. coirthe bios a cinn tire.	1.b.4.54		28
297	Cobhus .i. coimfheis.	3.b.10.42		28
298	Coccrunn .i. ciallrun.	2.a.12.45		28
299	Codarsna .i. comsgaoilteach no comtharsna.	1.b.18.98		28
300	Codnach teighte	13.d.25.37	thus	28
301	Cod-ródaigh .i. ro cumhdaigh.	8.31.79		28
302	Coibhche .i. comhoighe cuir, ⁊ cunnartha.	7.b.14.74		28
303	Coibhdeallach .i. duine ris a mbi coimfialus no coimdalachus gaoil no caradradh ag neach i ngeall fiach .i. bean bheithas feich ag hinne seach a fear.	4.b.19.29	4+	29
304	Coibhdealach .i. duine aga mbi coimdheala no gaol re neach.	6.a.35.81		29
305	Coibhnithear . coimrightear.	9.24.71	9+	29
306	Coic, cocaire, fearthighis .i. fear do bheir tene ⁊ uisge dona haoideaduibh, ⁊ isin, no agan, eagluis bhios.	5.b.6.39		29
307	Coic .i. dearg.	14.b.4.6		29
308	Coicceanuid .i. rún coccubus um chionuidh.	9.39.116		29
309	Coicceart .i. na haireachta.	10.42.103		29
310	Coictriall .i. drisiug.	4.c.19.101		29
311	Coiglighe .i. caoi aclaighe .i. caoi iota loige.	4.c.26.126		29
312	Coimchisi .i. coimhfeachain.	1.a.9.22		29
313	Coimdidh .i. comdhuthaidh .i ait as coitcheann do gach aon mar ata an fhairrge .⁊c̄. eccoimdigh .i. a contrardha sin.	2.b.10.97		29
314	Coimdigh caillidh .i. a cluainte, a gurtinne ⁊ na hionada imbi athaighe chaigh. eccoimdigh caillidh .i. o sin amach.	2.b.17.104		29
315	Coimdigh cathrach .i. a hurlair, a relge, a priomhsraide ⁊ gach ionad imbi athaighe chaigh. eccoimdigh cathrach .i. gach ionad innte o sin amach.	2.b.15.101		29–30
316	Coimdigh faithche .i. a slighthe a hionada reidhe arda, ⁊ an tionad imbi athaighe caigh. eccoimdigh faithche .i. gach ionad di o sin amach.	2.b.12.100		30
317	Coimdigh raite .i. (roid no na cuarta inghelta idir fhaithche ⁊ dirinn) .i. a slighthe, ⁊ a hionada arda reidhe ⁊c̄.	2.b.16.102		30
318	Coimdigh shlebhe .i. a slighthe .⁊c̄.	2.b.17.103		30

(*cont.*)

No.	Headword and entry	Entry reference	O'Curry's notes	MS fol.
319	Coimdigh tragha .i. ionad in athaighid daoine ⁊ longa maraon, ⁊ tonna go coitceann.	2.b.18.105		30
320	Coimdigh treibhe .i. a lar, a hairmeada, a hionada soillsi, ⁊ na hionada imbi athaighe chaigh. eccoimdigh trebhe .i. gach ionad o sin amach.	2.b.11.99		30
321	Coimhghniomh .i. coimhghniomhughadh cionnadh ag darann rete feacht.	1.a.11.29	1+	30
322	Coimpeart .i. coimh eibtear, comhairbeartnughadh, ⁊ geneamhuinn.	8.24.62		30
323	Coimpeart fo cosmailios lachta .i. dath ban do beith ar adhbar no ar gheneamhuin na cloinne.	3.b.30.82		30
324	Coimreacht .i. comairgitear.	2.a.7.26		30
325	Coimriad .i. coimimteacht, no coimceimníughadh.	12.b.4.23		30
326	Coimhriomh innsge fair .i. comhaighneas a naghaidh an biodhbhaidh no an ciontaigh.	12.b.15.47		30–31
327	Coimtheachtadha .i. coimideachtadha .i. lucht coimideacht ar aon bios daontoisg.	5.a.5.20	5+	31
328	Coindfe .i. comhadhus, coimhdheilitheach.	8.25.65		31
329	Coinsi .i. caoin-gnús dia soadh gach ndath.	6.a.22.39		31
330	Coisid .i. teagasgaid.	7.b.18.78		31
331	Coitghe .i. comtuige .i. comchumhdach.	8.32.84		31
332	Coitseachtus .i. coimheisteachtus.	2.b.4.79		31
333	Colludh nóighe .i. lot óighe mna ⁊ air a son sin do bear an fear siocail di.	3.b.23.77		31
334	Collúdh .i. collodh .i. soadh do colla.	10.20.51		31
335	Colpach .i. sé sgreabail.	5.a.3.9		31
336	Colpa ceannaithe .i. ceann snaithe saoghail, no ceann aige .i. aimsire .i. aimsir is ann iocus an colpa ceannaithe da ngoirtear cholpa ceannadairte.	6.a.10.28		31
337	Coltra .i. seaca.	7.b.20.83		31
338	Comha .i. na bhfecheamhan.	10.42.102		31
339	Comhadh .i. coimeaduid.	8.6.18		31
340	Comhadh .i. coimheadadh.	6.b.3.95		31
341	Comairlégad .i. an ciontach do legadh fon chaill.	12.b.14.46		31
342	Comairr .i. do comraic.	3.b.18.61		31
343	Comhairsior .i. athchomhairctear.	9.30.90		31
344	Comaitgheas .i. coimhdeacht no aightear.	1.b.12.82		32
345	Combach .i. coimbriseadh.	5.a.2.13		32
346	Combroth .i. brath maille re duine eile.	1.a.9.24		32
347	Comdaighe .i. coimtheigheadh on teas.	2.a.14.52		32
348	Comha		fec anmanna breithe.	32
349	Comhlogad ruis .i. laigsine, no commaitheamh bearar don duine ar a mbi fiach.	12.b.9.36		32

(*cont.*)

No.	Headword and entry	Entry reference	O'Curry's notes	MS fol.
350	Comlunn .i. ciomlíon.	9.44.134		32
351	Commor fuan .i. ionad ina commor [_]	9.5.13	9+	32
352	Comhrainn ceidfhir air i. ar neach teid do hannoid, ⁊ a athair ⁊ a sheanathair an annoid.		fec annoid	32
353	Comraite .i. an turchar do bheir duine tre fheirg ⁊ gurab ail leis a guin.	5.c.4.54		32
354	Comtus .i. cumaid uais.	3.b.3.26	3+	32
355	Co-nae .i. com [_]	8.6.19	8+	32
356	Conaimeacht .i. do caoin aimsigeadh.	6.b.3.94		32
357	Con-amadair .i. caoin no comaimsightear.	7.b.27.98		32
358	Con-amadhair .i. ro coimmeisiomnaighestur	2.a.5.20		32
359	Conair coimteachta .i. conair tiagur isin faithche.	10.16.38	10+	32
360	Conardhata .i. comhaidnighthe.	8.22.56		32
361	Con-cleach .i. do clis.	4.c.22.112		32
362	Condagur .i. iarrthar.	4.c.11.72		32
363	Con-dearbhara .i. coimdhuibra.	10.43.109		33
364	Condo teascmarr .i. teasargain, no go ro theasairge.	2.a.15.55		33
365	Con-duicheat .i. cuinngid.	3.b.5.30		33
366	Con-eathar .i. coimeadthar.	2.b.7.90		33
367	Con-eatha .i. coimeada.[3]	10.29.60		33
368	Co-nae .i. com [_][4]	8.6.19	8+	33
369	Conoad .i. coimheaduid.	7.b.23.89		33
370	Conotar .i. coimead.	8.1.5		33
371	Coraoi .i. aoi coir .i. caingean coir.	8.19.49		33
372	Co-reis .i. cuimrighsi no cuibrigh.	10.15.32		33
373	Con-seichithear .i. taithneamhach ionsaightear.[5]	8.9.27		33
374	Cor go ffios go ttreabhaire . i. cunradh go ffios diubarta ag neach, ⁊ trebaire (.i. urradh aniu) re comall an cunnartha.	10.33.78		33
375	Cosg nurcuil .i. teagusg do ni bean ar an ni toirmisgtear go milleann a cele no an leanabh bhios na broinn fen.	3.b.36.91		33
376	Coslach .i. luach cuisi .i. luach do beir fear na cuisi do neach oile do chionn a chuisi do sheasamh do, ut dicitur Sedha gach coslach .i. an seseadh cuid don chúis don tí do ni airbeart aon uaire i naireacht da ttig tobach.	9.27.87		33
377	Cota .i. cinnus.	2.b.6.88		34

3 This lemma is out of order in the transcription.

4 This lemma is a repetition of a previous entry and is out of order.

5 This lemma is out of order in the transcription.

(*cont.*)

No.	Headword and entry	Entry reference	O'Curry's notes	MS fol.
378	Cota-imtiagad .i. comaitghethach.	6.a.23.43		34
379	Cot-riseadh .i. [_] no do ceangoladh.	10.14.30	10+	34
380	Cotuighe tionchuir . ní do chur fon tion .i. fon taobh dá coimhtheagadh.	9.45.139		34
381	Crannuighid .i. cuirid crannchor.	10.6.6		34
382	Creadal .i. credmhe .i. creadmus.	12.b.2.16		34
383	Credbaightear .i. creimnightear.	2.b.6.85		34
384	Creim forbaigh .i. bean no crim a ccoda dona laoghuib ⁊c̄.	3.b.38.93		34
385	Crela .i. críola .i. cro iall orba sertsi sin ⁊c̄. no orba cruibh no sliosda.	13.d.6.15		34
386	Cresion .i. creidmeach.	13.d.5.13		34
387	Cri .i. ceann.	10.37.81		34
388	Crioch gan dicelt .i. i machaire sin ⁊ ionann crioch riagailtear aca i gcaill.	9.7.20		34
389	Crioch mna fir i naimsir a héignithe re fear oile .i airm i gcluintear a hegheamh go a teach.	3.b.15.57		34
390	Cróch .i. gach nárd, gach naireagda.	14.d.9.21		34
391	Cróch .i. uachtar. ut. uachtar bainne.	14.d.9.22		34
392	Cro righ ⁊ seanaidh .i. cruinnioghadh no dail an righ no an tseanaidh.	6.a.10.27		34
393	Cruibne		fec cuig anmanna cat	34
394	Cruitigh .i. cruitire.	6.a.3.8		35
395	Crucrebaide .i. in geineamhuin edir beith di na fuil follus ⁊ na dluim cuirpghne	3.b.34.88		35
396	Cu con .i. cu na ccuilen.	10.13.27		35
397	Cuic apa nos marba .i. piseoga.	13.d.18.29		35
398	Cuidig feasa, ⁊ treabaire .i. an cuid don cunnradh inar feas diubart do beith, ⁊ cuid treabuire .i. an cuid le ffuil an urradh i nurradhus a coimlíonnta. gan fios gan treabaire a contrarda sin.	10.34.79		35
399	Cuidig geill .i. luach tobhaigh.	12.b.7.33		35
400	Cuig anmanna cat sunn .i. breoinde .i. breo nuall, ⁊ nia tren, no breo an .i. cronan ina inne. ⁊ meoinde .i. mo do gní meighil .i. meoain .i. meighleach ina inne. ringne .i. riachaid neach ⁊ riachtar é. cruibne .i. cruib nia .i. nia tren bios a cruibe. aircne .i. a hairc naoi mic laimhiach, no a baircne .i. nia tren tugadh a bairc breasail bric .i cait broinngeala dubha. ach .i. fiadh chat allaidh gabar dfiadh .i. as fiadhantacht. folam .i. cat ler maith loim, ⁊ coimeadus loim go maith, ionann e ⁊ an cat cuile act gurob isin seanbaile bhios. ⁊ folom ar an mbuailidh. glas-neannta .i. cat beag bhios isin	10.21.54	+	35–36

(*cont.*)

No.	Headword and entry	Entry reference	O'Curry's notes	MS fol.
	tseanbhaile isin neanntoig ghlais ag diothughadh lochadh. breoinne .i. cat aitighius righ. ⁊ tighearna, ⁊ aircinneach ⁊ do ní cronan doibh. meoinde, le meigle, ⁊ coimhead a ccuid bidh. cruibne, le coimhead muilinn, ⁊ sabhaill, ⁊ atha. Ringcne le hairfideadh clanna na nardaireach, da sgríobadh, ⁊ iadsan da sgríobadh san. bairche .i. cat ban sin.			
401	Cuimhneattur .i. do coimhmionnaigheadar .i. do athcumatur.	10.18.45		36
402	Cuimhleachta .i. comsloinnte.	9.44.137		36
403	Cuindfech .i. cuidbide, no [_]	10.7.11	10+	36
404	Cuindrigh .i. caoindirigh.	7.b.2.50		36
405	Cuingeall		fec tri iomuire.	36
406	Cuinnius .i. connus .i. connadhus .i. mac, cuinnius on iarraidh	4.c.9.60		36
407	Cuinnteastur .i. cuinngitear .i. iarrtur.	4.c.5.43		36
408	Cuirpgne		fec briocht fola.	36
409	Cuisleannaigh .i. feadanach.	6.a.3.9		36
410	Cuithchuire techta .i. oglách (bhios ag gabail fiadhaigh i gcuiteach) ⁊ do ní cuachaireacht togarma ar an bhfiadh do cum an cuithe.	2.b.8.95		36–37
411	Cuitil .i. caoi tholl .i. for orbhasach.	3.b.22.74		37
412	Cullath age .i. edach leabtha do beir bean do cum fir an tan naisgtear iad ma-le.	10.10.14		37
413	Culmuire .i. cairpteoir.	6.a.3.7		37
414	Cu lomna .i. cu danad árach lomhan ima gob.	10.16.37		37
415	Culpait .i. coiler. ut cail coimhead, ⁊ pait .i. ceann.	7.a.24.36		37
416	Culpait		fec oillian	37
417	Cu [_] .i. cu ris na gabann greimlorg.	10.13.28	10+	37
418	Cumh .i. cainte.	7.a.18.26		37
419	Cumhal seachtmadh marbtha .i. an Seachtmadh cuid don coirpdire. oir seacht coirpdire gach urradh i gcoitchinne ar na marbadh.	9.45.140		37
420	Cumd [_] meic gach graidh. ⁊c̄. .i. ceannach bearar do neach do choinn an mac do choimead i naimsir aonaigh, no re a athchar for a athair iar ndi-ailtre, no luach a coimeideachta do berid do macaibh na ngradh as isle inaid fen.	14.b.4.10	14+	37
421	Cumsgughadh .i. comsgaoileadh.	10.39.89		37
422	Cumthus .i. comhmaithius.	7.b.1.49		37
423	Cu na ttri ngníomh .i. lorgaireacht goide. gabaltus [_] legtear, ⁊ diongbail fir forrain ider da fhiallach .i. da cethearn.	10.18.47	10+	37–38

(*cont.*)

No.	Headword and entry	Entry reference	O'Curry's notes	MS fol.
424	Cu otraigh .i. (maidrdh gearr) a siside an cu fris angaibh maoithfhlesg.	10.14.29		38
425	Cu seichill .i. cu bhois ag seicheam eich o shealluibh o suilibh .i. cu do cí duine aga leanmhuin ⁊ nach leis fein i.	1.a.15.37		38
426	Cutaim .i. tuitim.	9.25.78		38
427	Cutaim .i. comthuitim.	3.b.8.38		38
	.D.			38
428	Dag do ait .i. an gris gabail.	1.a.17.40		38
429	Daghrach .i. deaghaireach.	8.20.51		38
	.aibgidir crabadh.			38
430	Daisfeann .i. fuaruige, no suaraige.	8.38.104		38
431	Dámhradh .i. beith ar dáimh.	9.44.136		38
432	Dana cách go hiath .i. go mionna.	8.14.38		38
433	Daon .i. duine.	8.31.82		38
434	Daormhanach .i. manach crui go [_][6]	11.a.10.15	11+	38
435	Darmna .i. dáir maoine do nid tairbh.	9.38.110		38
436	Dartaid .i. [_]	5.a.2.8	5+	38
437	Datán .i. oide.	4.c.9.61		38
438	Dathnait .i. muime.	4.c.10.62		38
439	Dear .i. esgithear.	5.a.2.6		38
440	Dearbanar .i. diubartar.	5.b.5.36		39
441	Dearchana .i. adbhalchanaidh.	2.a.16.58		39
442	Dearc nátha .i. tóll cairiolach átha.	9.27.84		39
443	Dearcnuidh. ro dearcnidh .i. anrad iar sa ni dreachus don ealadhain.	4.c.18.95		39
444	Deargabadh .i. urfhogra dethneasach gan maill, ⁊ banabadh, ní ass maille inás.	11.a.16.23		39
445	Deargapadh .i. an biathadh iar ndenam cionadh don ciontach.	12.b.13.44		39
446	Deargsarugadh .i. dorn do buain as brollach an ciontaigh, cidh ré ndenam, cid iar ndenam cionadh.	12.b.14.45		39
447	Dearla .i. adhbul diolaithear.	2.a.9.34		39
448	Dearlaithear .i. dearb dioghlaithear.	8.18.45		39
449	Dearosg .i. dearbhchinneadh.	4.c.14.83		39
450	Dearusg .i. cinneadh dhireach.	9.25.77		39
451	Deis .i. fearann.	8.27.73		39
452	Deisde, feisdide, no esdide .i. tioruairsi .i. fuighioll.	14.h.12.35		39
453	Déiste .i. déis as éd tioruairsin béos.	7.a.3.4		39

6 The internal cross-referencing is not always consistent. Several entries, e.g., *gola*, refer to this entry but are listed as separate entries in the transcription.

(*cont.*)

No.	Headword and entry	Entry reference	O'Curry's notes	MS fol.
454	Dénmheach .i. dishomhaoineach.	6.a.37.86		39
455	Deocraidhtidh (.i. sacrilegan) .i. (fear denta tocraidh ar dia) .i. fear do bheir luighe eithig agan eagluis, ⁊ ní tinceann dligheadh.	1.b.19.102		39–40
456	Deoghbaire .i. sgoaire.	4.c.17.92		40
457	Deoin .i. corr uisge.	5.b.5.38		40
458	Deoladhacht .i. grasia .i. ní a naisgidh.	5.b.5.37		40
459	Deoltaide .i. gaid.	5.a.1.1		40
460	Deoradhus .i. diorathus .i. nemhcintadh	9.37.109		40
461	Deoraidh aigenta .i. an deoraidh [_]	11.a.1.2	11+	40
462	Deoraidh freacair .i. deoraidh do nitear do urradh mar so .i. fear sin do ni minicniughadh cionta ⁊ ni fheaduid a fhine a cionta dioc do gnaith, ⁊ as amhlaidh cuirid a cion dibh, ⁊ do níd deoraidh freacair de .i. do beir a fhine .uii. ccumala do flaith, seacht mbliadhna féne do eagluis, ⁊ dá chumail chairde do gach leath dona ceithre leithibh .i. risin a ffuil a comcuaird cairde don ciontach, ⁊ saor iad mar sin ara ciontaibh, ⁊ na diaighsin dá ttugadh neach dia fhine bos grain no [tur]<u>uga</u> sgrie, no ingelt da eachuibh na fearann ar cairdi fuilleadh a cion orra aris.	11.a.22.30		40
463	Derach .i. lomrach.	5.a.6.21		40
464	Desidh .i. tarrustur.	10.32.72		40
465	Dia, no dee tre-agh .i. laithe na ttri nagh .i. agh ar eachuibh, agh ar armuibh agh for dhaoinibh.	1.b.14.90		40–41
466	Diamhain .i. diainimh.	7.b.3.55		41
467	Diamhuin .i. glan.	4.c.4.42		41
468	Dicheall diceilt .i. adhbal cheilt.	1.b.6.59		41
469	Dichealtach .i. an fear cubus braith .i. an fear bios ag ceilt an uilc.	5.c.2.51		41
470	Di-ciallathar .i. adbal dichlithear.	2.a.8.30		41
471	Dilsioch .i. duine as dileas do gabail no do marbad. Uaide sin tig dilsiughadh duine indilsigh <u>cen ceart</u>	1.b.20.103	11+	41
472	Dime, ⁊ diomtha .i. on didion.	9.30.91		41
473	Dimheadh .i. tiomhdennis .i. baramluigheas. [ ] .edgead.	7.b.4.56		41
474	Dimealtaid .i. fear adbal-caithmheach.	9.42.129		41
475	Dimsi .i. neamhmaisi.	4.c.15.86		41
476	Dinnis .i. mionna	3.b.11.46 and 7.a.10.14		41
477	Diochunduil .i. coimteachtus [_] .i. mugugadh.	10.12.24	10+	41
478	Díochusg .i. ainmhear gan rath.	9.42.126		41
479	Dioghuin .i. sarughadh.	4.c.4.40		41

(*cont.*)

No.	Headword and entry	Entry reference	O'Curry's notes	MS fol.
480	Dioghuin feoir. Eathamain .i. sarughadh feir fearainn da ttig somaoin eatha .⁊c̄.	1.a.14.34		41
481	Diollat lige .i. etach (as fiu leath coibhche a mna) gaibeas fear i mnaoi ar neirge as a [_]	4.b.12.18	4+	41–42
482	Diongaibh gach degeanach .i. gibe neach aga ruibhe an ciontach da biathadh no do cumdach fa deireadh díoladh ara son.	12.b.12.42		42
483	Dionnba .i. gan ba.	7.b.20.84		42
484	Diorainn.		fec aithghin	42
485	Diothchus .i. adbar tochuis. [ ] .⁊g⁊.	9.3.8		42
486	Direach, ⁊ derach .i. lomradh.	5.c.1.47		42
487	Direagur .i. deirgithear.	1.b.6.61		42
488	Directhaid .i. iondraigheach.	9.41.124	9+	42
489	Dith .i. dithim .i. dioth.	9.39.114		42
490	Ditheach. Coindircle .i. cairdeamlacht.	8.2.8		42
491	Dithle .i. adbal élaidhte	8.25.67		42
492	Diuirb .i. duine gan fearann.	7.b.12.71		42
493	Dlaoi fulla .i. an draoi fullon .i. an cuid do la briocht for dlaoi do cur duine ar [_] la sin draoi sin do hoileadh nuadha fullon, ⁊ uaide ainmnightear dlaoi fulla. coir anmann sin.	9.3.10	9+	42
494	Dligheadh aondachta, no athachta .i. bios idir ceann is meamru do brigh gurob aon an ceann i leith ris na meamruibh ⁊ gurob iolardha an meamair i leith ris an cceann.	10.45.119		42–43
495	Dligheadh ceanndachta .i. dligheadh uachtaranachta, no tighearnamlacht.	11.a.28.33		43
496	Dligheadh seachtmuine .i. seacht bairgean.	1.b.7.64		43
497	Dlomhain .i. naidhim.	11.a.9.13		43
498	Dlueathad lamh .i. glaca diadhadh ra cheile.	3.b.20.69		43
499	Do-arr .i. tarraightear.	6.a.30.62		43
500	Do-boing .i. toibhghidh.	8.7.20		43
501	Dochtair .i. coisgtear .i. múintear.	10.20.50		43
502	Doda niongaib .i. diongbus no do ni a dhiongbail.	12.b.7.31		43
503	Do dearlaic .i. do adhbal logh.	1.b.13.87		43
504	Do eachma .i. doisheachanta.	9.6.16		43
505	Do éc .i. do innis.	3.b.22.72		43
506	Do ecma .i. teagmhus.	6.a.30.63		43
507	Doghbhaidh .i. do-ghabhaltaidh, ni as deacair do gabail.	2.a.15.56		43
508	Doghoidis .i. do thoghdaois.	3.b.4.28		43
509	Do-gó sinsear .i. beirid an sinsear a rogha.	2.b.8.94		43
510	Doithcean .i. daith .i. luaithchionadh.	10.11.20		43
511	Do-luaisgeadh .i. toghluaiseadh.	8.3.11		43

(*cont.*)

No.	Headword and entry	Entry reference	O'Curry's notes	MS fol.
512	Dom-igeadh .i. tigeadh dam.	4.c.13.76		43
513	Do-maistear .i. tomhaistear.	7.a.28.40		43
514	Domruidh .i. reime deachaidh .i. ruidh .i. re faoidh.	3.b.9.41		44
515	Do-neagaid .i. feduid.	7.a.21.29		44
516	Donn .i. goid.	7.a.22.32		44
517	Donnuighe, donnach .i. gaduighe.	7.a.23.33		44
518	Dorachta .i. dorocht, no do riacht.	4.c.27.132		44
519	Do raraic .i. ro tairgistear.	10.11.19		44
520	Do roacht .i. do ro aitheadh.	6.a.24.47		44
521	Do roilgeadh .i. do ro loghadh.	6.a.24.48		44
522	Don-rosad .i. do ronsad.	1.b.22.107		44
523	Dos-nalla .i. didnigh.	8.31.80		44
524	Dreteall .i. torc muice.	4.c.20.106		44
525	Dringeas .i. dremnis.	9.3.9		44
526	Droch .i. dorcha, no neamhsolus.	8.2.6		44
527	Druis .i. mearacht.	4.c.13.80		44
528	Druth .i. go rath.	9.42.125		44
529	Druthlach .i. laochdruta .i. fear leathchuinn.	6.a.29.59		44
530	Duabar .i. duai[_]	2.a.9.35	2+	44
531	Duar .i. duine.	7.b.10.66	7+	44
532	Dubhaigid .i. aigid fedil no sumdubhain.	13.a.6.2		44
533	Dubhaigid no ceart for cuaille .i. oighid fedil.	13.d.23.35		44
534	Duibell .i. dae da neibill an teine saighnen.	1.a.18.42		44
535	Duicheat .i. cuigid [_]	3.a.3.3	3+	44
536	Duineathaidhe .i. táiteas dimirt ar an duine ar na marbadh .i. folach an cuirp mairbh deis a marbtha.	5.c.4.55		45
537	Duinn .i. flaithe.	1.b.10.75		45
538	Duirb .i. dae dono robead don orba .i. don fearann.	1.a.17.41		45
539	Duisi .i. di uaisi .i. mionna adbal [_]isle.	1.b.11.80	1+	45
540	Duithin .i. ceo, no duithin .i. dath nu sine .i. grian ⁊ easga.	3.b.11.48		45
541	Dumha .i. ionad.	10.29.64		45
542	Dunn .i. roid.	14.b.4.7		45
	.E.			45
543	Eabhla [_]	2.b.23.112 and 9.9.32	2+	45
544	Eachtrannus .i. neach téid amach inn ionad eachtrann.	11.a.4.5	11	45
545	Eadarbha .i. ba bhios eatorra .i. airbhe no fál.	9.25.74		45
546	Eadarfhlaith .i. foithighearna. [ ] . adbar eile darab aimn edgeadh.	11.a.28.34		45
547	Eadtollus.		fec forcraid	45

(*cont.*)

No.	Headword and entry	Entry reference	O'Curry's notes	MS fol.
548	Eagluis coimhdhidin .i. eagluis ga mbitear na comhaididin re ré desi an, tathair, ⁊ an mac leithtrian ma manach mac manaigh.	11.a.7.10		45
549	Eagluis con-eadranna diobhadh. eagluis comroinnios diobhadh an mhanaigh re ré trir .i. atair, mac ⁊ ua.	11.a.8.11		45
550	Eagluis chuir .i. athair .i. eagluis cuireas cuir ar tus ar an manach andoid um leithriun an cheadmhanaigh.	11.a.6.9	10+	46
551	Eagluis na foltmaisi i. eagluis i mbi oglaoch na ceann uirre leis ar maisioch folt air.	5.c.8.61		46
552	Ealgnus .i. eolgnais.	5.c.3.53		46
553	Eallach .i. suidiughadh, no ordúghadh.	6.a.2.4		46
554	Eamhad teamracha .i. eblid na huaisle.	6.b.2.91		46
555	Eascomhon, iongglan .i. excomunicatus.	11.a.5.6		46
556	Easomain . eas somhaoin.	7.b.19.81		46
557	Easpuc edir aran, ⁊ a cailioch .i. idir a ablainn ⁊ a chailis.	8.5.16		46
558	Eathor .i. fear do nitri an fhail	9.14.39	9+	46
559	Eattair na mna ceadhna .i. gach ionad o tha sin a mach genmotha an baile a gcluinfidhe an égheamh.	3.b.15.58	fec crioch mna fir ⁊c	46
560	Eccoimdigh.		fec coimdidh	46
561	Eccoimdigh caillidh.		fec coimdigh caillidh	46
562	Eccoimdigh cathrach.		fec coimdigh cathrach	46
563	Eccoimdigh faithche.		fec coimdigh faithche.	46
564	Eccoimdigh tragha .i. gach ionad nach athaighionn acht longa a naonar.	2.b.18.105		46
565	Eccoimdigh trebhe.		fec coimdigh treibhe	47
566	Eccuibdios.		fec a ccuibdios	47
567	Éd .i. ailbin bó.	9.21.63		47
568	Edirceart.		fec anmanna breithe	47
569	Eglaimm .i. inchreacadh.	8.15.39		47
570	Egluis leithdire .i. egluis nach bi na dligheadh tre tteasdann leithdire uaithe.	5.c.7.60		47
571	Eibirt.		fec neach diamba ⁊c̄.	47
572	Eichlas, ⁊ bacghabail .i. ait i mbid eich.	1.b.5.58		47
573	Eigceall .i. droichiall.	6.a.25.51		47
574	Eimh ime .i. fal na timceall.	3.b.39.95		47
575	Eirithe .i. ioctha.	7.a.19.27		47
576	Eisil .i. eiseolach .i. aineólach.	7.a.17.25		47

(*cont.*)

No.	Headword and entry	Entry reference	O'Curry's notes	MS fol.
577	Eislis .i. ail siodh leasa.	5.a.2.12		47
578	Eitheamhlachus .i. cosmuileacht, no tarraingcholmacht bios eidir neithibh, ⁊ go hairidhe eidir danaibh, no cearduibh. ⁊c̄.	6.a.20.38		47
579	Eitnge .i. fear droch urlapra .i. egan teangadh.	7.b.13.72		47
580	Eitseach .i. duine gan teach.	12.b.7.32		47
581	Eitseach .i. se gan teach aige.	8.13.33		47
582	Elg .i. ere.	OC.1		47
583	Elge .i. fearann, no elg .i. ere.	4.c.11.71		47
584	Eo .i. edail.	2.a.5.19		48
585	Ereantach .i. fear for a nernightear fiach.	5.c.1.50		48
586	Eric .i. firiac.	12.b.30.69		48
587	Esgeas .i. im umaloid.	8.18.46		48
588	Etla treabtha .i. ni goideas bean [_] da fear.	4.b.9.15	4+	48
	.F.			48
589	Faer (air) seachtmuin .i. foirithin im treabadh do beir an cele don flaith isin seachtmuin, faor buana mar sin.	14.h.17.38		48
590	Fagh .i. sliabh.	9.25.76		48
591	Faichmen .i. scothadh no fodiubadh.	2.a.2.6		48
592	Faichill .i. tuarustal.	11.a.27.31		48
593	Faigneoir .i. ceard caitheas an sdan rena fhaingnibh	6.a.23.45		48
594	Fail naididin . faill do denam umpa iar naididnighadh.	9.22.66		48
595	Faill tiomairgthe ag righ .i. gan an ciontach do tiomargadh re edhgheadh duine airithe.	11.a.27.32	11+	48
596	Fairbe .i. fir eibe, firinnarba.	2.b.3.74		48
597	Fairbe .i. fior eibe, ut fear fairbe .i. fear fior eibe aoi .i. an fear bhios ag fior ebe na cuisi i naighidh neich ar logh.	8.11.30		48
598	Fairbean .i. fireiptear .i. firbeantar.	7.b.1.48		49
599	Fairbean .i. firinn ar bean no firen.	4.c.28.136		49
600	Fairge .i athtairgithear.	7.a.6.8		49
601	[faithche.] a seadh as faithche ann .i. na ceithre guirt as neasa don bhaile .i. gort gacha hairde ime, ⁊ cidh é an sliabh budh neasa don baile roba amhail faithche, no asi an fhaithche an ro saigh guth cluig.	2.b.12.100		49
602	Faoighe i. fóéige onghlaoidh.	3.b.13.52		49
603	Faoindleaghach .i. fear nach ttig fá dligheadh corusa fine.	11.a.20.27		49
604	Faolus .i. fuilngnis.	9.43.130		49
605	Faonán .i. ionann.	8.34.91		49
606	Faon fleacain .i. re re roileacan .i. faon fo leacain.	13.a.4.1		49
607	Faor .i. foirithin no cobair gheill.	14.b.3.4		49
608	Faor .i. fuireach no foiridhin.	8.2.7		49

(*cont.*)

No.	Headword and entry	Entry reference	O'Curry's notes	MS fol.
609	Faosam .i. caradradh.	2.a.12.41		49
610	Faosamh .i. eimh .i. didion iar bhfeis .i. iar ffesda.	2.a.11.40		49
611	Faoth, aoth .i. mionna.	7.a.26.38		49
612	Faoth .i. luighe .i. mionna.	9.8.23	9+	49
613	Fath .i. fo fheadh no aoid.	2.a.10.38		49
614	Feabus ruine .i. run do denum do mnaoi gan [_] fear an ni budh imdeargadh do.	4.b.15.24	4+	49–50
615	Feachadh .i. [_]	10.15.35	10+	50
616	Feachaid .i. fuachtnaighid.	12.b.3.19		50
617	Feacht feile .i. ced oidhche aoidhigheacht duine (go tigh duine oile), mari, ollamh, flaith, no gibe cinel duine é.	11.a.12.17		50
618	Feadbh .i. baintreabhthach.	12.b.3.18		50
619	Feall ar cholbha .i. feall ar an ti bhios ar colbha a leabtha no a ngar do.	8.17.42		50
620	Fearaid .i. feagair .i. athtairgsidh .i. tionol.	7.b.5.59		50
621	Fear asa he .i. fear ler leis.	1.a.18.44		50
622	Fear cuitchearnsa .i. fear bios i gcuma re neach himon doman ag cosnamh righe no abdaine.	12.7.21	8+	50
623	Fear didin .i. fear bios ag didin an ciontaigh.	12.b.10.38		50
624	Fear dither .i. fear ar dith re, no an dith tíre.	9.3.12		50
625	Fear fuiche .i. fear teid go mnaoi na gnais.	8.8.22		50
626	Fear fuidre .i. fuidir crui elas re dligheadh a fuidreadh [ ]. [ ] fuidir sin elos ria na flaith go sedaibh a fhlatha leis.	4.c.2.38		50
627	Fear iondraic .i. [_] ice.	9.18.57	9+	50
628	Fear leasach .i.	13.d.5.12	thus	50
629	Fear máma mogh .i. an fear gabhus do laimh mam ⁊ gniomh an duine bhios loite do denam ar a shon feadh a luide othruis. fear oghuibh toguibh .i. fear a thogbala na shuide ⁊ na leabaidh, ⁊ ina ghluasacht ar cheana feadh a othrusa.	11.a.14.20		50–51
630	Fear meadhon goide lain .i. fear ga mbeadh fios an gadaighe ⁊ na goide mále. [ ] .duil .r.	5.b.1.26		51
631	Fear meadhon goide leithe .i. fear aga mbeadh fios an gadaighe.	5.b.1.25		51
632	Fear oguibh toguibh.		fec fear mama mogh	51
633	Fear raithe .i. apadh in raitigh dorn na bhrollach o aon lo amach, no fear teid for foriod, ⁊ ro ba glan fon rod.	4.c.1.37		51
634	Fear reime .i. an cainte bios ag ruaimneadh a oide oemas a oide.	4.c.1.36		51
635	Feartatar .i. adnaictear.	6.a.19.34		51
636	Fear tighis.		fec coic	51

(*cont.*)

No.	Headword and entry	Entry reference	O'Curry's notes	MS fol.
637	Feartur .i. feartaightear .i. adnaictear.	12.b.2.15		51
638	Feasad .i. fuachtnaighid.	5.15.31		51
639	Feasatar, fiasatar .i. fuachtnaightear.	1.b.9.73		51
640	Feathal .i. mionn, egcusg.	8.36.100		51
641	Feathal i. mionn, mar ata clog, cros, bachall, ministear no soisgeal ⁊c̄.	5.b.22.45		52
642	Feghadh .i. féchain sul.	10.32.75		52
643	Feileasach .i. fear feallas ar leas chaigh.	8.12.32		52
644	Féis.		fec medla	52
645	Feseadh.i. fuachtnaighfeadh.[7]	10.15.31		52
646	Feis i bhfeis .i. i mbuailidh no i nathlompuire coitcin̄.	9.23.68		52
647	Feis i bhfual .i. i nathbuailidh shalaig.	9.23.69		52
648	Feis i nandomhain .i. bid i leanmuin isin tresgin, no isin dearg moin, no isin laith, ⁊ eathaid an fer ime.	9.24.70		52
649	Féisi .i. muc.	6.a.34.77		52
650	Feiste .i. tioruairsi .i. iardraighe.	7.a.1.1		52
651	Feithidh .i. athtargadh.	7.b.34.109		52
652	Femeadh .i. diultadh aniu tar amarach .i. tar a nairteach ⁊ do geabair tfiacha.	7.b.8.64		52
653	Femhead .i. diultadh.	2.b.20.106		52
654	Fiach duineachaithe i. fiach an chionuidh an chaithmhe do denadh duine.	1.a.12.31		52
655	Fiach iomraid na gaide .i. a luad ag [_]	1.a.8.20	1+	52
656	Fiach leasaighthe .i. fiach biata ⁊ leasaighthe na cciontach.	12.b.10.37		52
657	Fiadhat .i. tighearna.	8.25.66		53
658	Fiasatar		fec feasatar	53
659	Fíí, ⁊ híí .i. drung no dream, no gibe ni ar cheana na mbi iolradh.	10.31.69		53
660	Filc .i. foillseacdha .i. maith .i. in cuaille.	9.9.30	9+	53
661	Findte diblaidhe .i. an thseanorach.	3.a.13.21	fec findte . feart-sach[8]	53
662	Fineamhnus .i. fine iomhaoin uais.	8.21.31		53
663	Finne .i. fine duthaidh.	OC.2		53
664	Fiodh de fidh ar dun .i. coill dee ar (no agan) dun ga mbí .i. fidh nimeadh.	13.d.2.9		53
665	Fionn .i. cionadh.	12.b.4.21		53
666	Fithis .i. fath uais.	OC.3		53
667	Flaith cuitrid .i. an treas flaith do beir rath do chele.	14.h.7.32		53

7 This entry is out of order in the transcription.

8 The entry cross-referenced does not exist in the transcription.

(*cont.*)

No.	Headword and entry	Entry reference	O'Curry's notes	MS fol.
668	Fleadhcroilighe . i gcionn mis. saoilim gurab ionann sin ⁊ cuimniughadh miosa na marbh, re heagluis iocar sin os na marbaibh.	6.a.12.30		53
669	Fo-cheard, fo-cheird .i. do chuir.	9.31.95		53
670	Fochrach .i. duine do beir foichreic celsine do neoch.	4.c.14.84		53
671	Fo-coisle .i. foxluigh.	13.d.11.20		53
672	Fo-coisle .i. foxladh.	8.13.35		53
673	Fo-choislithear .i. foxlaightear .i. sgaradh le ní no dio-ghbhalaightear.	7.a.19.28		54
674	Fo-chuireadh .i. gairm no tairring do ni neach ar coin.	1.a.16.39		54
675	Fodotleana .i. fhoethlás.	8.36.98		54
676	Foégheamh fogra tasg adaltraighe ⁊ tursuighe .i. fogra táisg bios ag an ceadmuinntear i nam a neg-nighthe.	3.b.17.60		54
677	Fo-fe, ⁊ fo-fi, ⁊ fo-fic .i. fuachtnaigheadh .i. ofence.	14.f.16.26		54
678	Fogail trebdire .i. foghail do denam is na trebaibh i nairillnightear dire.	5.c.6.56		54
679	Fo-glean .i. deghlea<u>n</u>. [ ]	6.a.29.61	6+	54
	.DUPALT-[ACH] FIRBIS.		thus in margin	54
680	Foguirre, doguirre .i. fuaidreadh.	14.h.1.28		54
681	Foibhrithe .i. rat fubaide .i. boim bearrta ⁊c̄ .i. fo ba .i. fo maith an nedhe do roinne.	13.d.1.8		54
682	Foichlige .i. sochlaoidh .i. tochailt.	1.b.4.55		54
683	Foichlitear .i. oirchilltear.	7.b.34.108		54
684	Foidherc .i. foirei[_]	6.a.22.41	6+	54
685	Foilmear .i. fear bhios ag leim ar neach go foil [_] ag breith a sead uadh.	8.10.29	8+	54
686	Foilmgid, no foilngid .i. cu do ni foileim ar neach.	10.13.26		54
687	Foir [_] .i. <u>re</u>mheach.	OC.4		55
688	Foirbhledh .i. for fhilleadh na filideachta .i. duan, ⁊ forduan .⁊c̄.	4.c.27.131		55
689	Foircitear .i. fior dhéchaithear.	4.c.17.93		55
690	Folach nothrasa .i. iomfhulang no fritheoladh duine bhios in othras.	11.a.13.19		55
691	Folam.		fec cuig anmanna cat	55
692	Follan .i. maith slan.	1.b.4.53		55
693	Fomhus .i. foimheasumhnugadh.	10.39.90		55
694	Fonn fri fonn .i. bonn fri bonn.	12.b.5.24		55
695	Forbhach .i. forbuain .i. ni benus ri tar dligeadh da chele.	6.b.2.93		55
696	Forbuain indlightheach, no forrach indlightheach .i. ni do bhuain da ceilibh don rhig tar an ni dligheas.	6.a.1.1		55

(*cont.*)

No.	Headword and entry	Entry reference	O'Curry's notes	MS fol.
697	For caoi .i. ar coisir o challainn go hinid mar bhios ri ⁊ ollomh ar cuid oidhche ar imtheacht ar a cceilead-huibh.	2.a.10.39		55
698	Forcmadh .i. fiorchoimheadadh	6.b.3.96		55
699	Forcorthar .i. eignightear bean .i. do bratar. fior-recar éigne.	3.b.18.64		55
700	Forcraidh, aigbele, ⁊ éadtollus .i. lochta na ndénta nach dioraith.	6.a.35.80		55
701	Fordionn . forduladh.	7.b.20.84		56
702	Formach ⁊ tormach .i. meadughadh.	7.a.8.11		56
703	For-neasa .i. tin [_] tainseas.	2.a.4.16	2+	56
704	Forngaire .i. forcongra.	10.45.118		56
705	Fornguire .i. f[_] ⁊c̄ .i. an ceimnugadh.	10.5.5	10+	56
706	Fornual	9.8.27	9+	56
707	Forrach.		fec forbuain ind-lightheach	56
708	Forraidh .i. foiridh.	9.2.6		56
709	For-randur .i. urranntur, no forruamnaightear.	2.b.5.84		56
710	Forrdhuain .i. recomarc .i. da siolla on duna n̄ .ut. iom-comarc flatha feimhen.	4.c.5.46		56
711	For-reith .i. foirighnigh.	7.b.11.67		56
712	For-reithear .i. foirighnightear.	7.b.11.68		56
713	Forrge.		fec forbuain ind-lighteach	56
714	Forrudh .i. for rith.	2.a.2.7		56
715	Forsaidh .i. fios forusda no fiorshaoidhe.	2.b.6.87		56
716	Fortach.		fec forto-tuigidht-ear.	56
717	For ton dire .i. ar son dire.	2.b.11.98		56
718	Fortshesidh .i. tairisidh.	4.c.7.53		56
719	Forto-tuigidtear .i. tig i ffortach imdenma.	8.36.99		56
720	Fortuighitear .i. fiorthuighitear .i. firmionnaightear.	9.7.21		56
721	For-uartur .i. fuachtnaighthear.	5.a.5.19		56
722	Fos-geallaidhi .i. fuighlidh .i. briathraigig.	8.33.89	8+	56
723	Fosieagar .i. airgitear.	1.b.15.93		57
724	Fo-suidh .i. astaidh go tre fhios maith.	10.44.112		57
725	Fotha leatharda i. foth creaca go [_] fot lionais ag an dara de, no fothcreaca na ma ga aroile.	10.4.3	10+	57
726	Fothana .i. meadhg.	14.c.2.12		57
727	Fothbhla .i. fodheidhble .i. diailbe .i. deroile.	10.30.68		57
728	Fothcomharda .i. foth creaca go reimdilsi, no foth nionais aca maraon.	10.4.2		57
729	Freacmairc .i. fior fhiafhraighe.	4.c.25.124		57
730	Freacur .i. fiorathchur.	12.b.6.30		57

(*cont.*)

No.	Headword and entry	Entry reference	O'Curry's notes	MS fol.
731	Freapadh .i. leighius.	7.b.24.91		57
732	Freasan .i. imrisin .i. ime re son .i. fál re fogar na firinne.	7.b.29.101		57
733	Freasluide .i. preapuide.	10.16.36		57
	.liber .2.			57
734	Fren .i. fremh.	11.a.1.1		57
735	Fresgisin imsearc .i. saoileachtain iomsgartha.	14.h.4.30	14+	57
736	Fresluighe .i. luighe fris.	7.b.35.111		57
737	Fri, cathach .i. lár na cille no an dúine.	9.32.97		57
738	Fri fairrge .i. isin fhairrge imuigh geibhthear.	9.35.102		57
739	Fri faithe .i. ar an fhaithche i gcuairt ingelta.	9.33.98		57
740	Friomall .i. mailleadh friom. [ ] .edgeadh.	7.b.7.61		57
741	Friosgairt .i. freagrais.	9.8.26		58
742	Friothaighe .i. fior-ionnsaighidh.	6.b.1.88		58
743	Friothghuin .i. guin i naighidh gona.	1.b.15.92		58
744	Fri raite .i. ni do gabar ar an rod i gcuairt ingelta idir faithche, ⁊ dirinn.	9.33.99		58
745	Frithe roeadha no shlebhe i. ni do gabar isin roifhiodh no isin sliabh i gcuairt ingelta.[9]	9.34.100		58
746	Fris-comhair i. fiorchoimeadhtur.	10.32.73		58
747	Fris-gabhaidh .i. abtinent.	7.a.21.30	7+	58
748	Fris-raitear .i. frithailtear no firinnlitear.	8.8.24	8+	58
749	Frithbheart breithe . beart frithir do ni bean do milleadh na clainne bhios na broinn, ⁊ fos beart a naighidh breithe clainne na nionbaidh no na tteagmail di ar aonchor. Ataid tri frithbearta breatha ann .i. 1. brochan .i. do losuibh, ⁊ deolosuibh do chur a lenibh as an mnaoi. 2. Snaithe .i. ima braghaid cona teagma lenab dhi. 3. soghabhail duile .i. seachna di coimriachtana i naimsir coimpearta. an frithbheart breithe. sed iarata coimpearta inti .i. sed, da sed ⁊ tri seoid. mar so. sed do gradhaibh fene. da sed do gradhaib flatha, ⁊ tri seoid do riogaibh cona gcomghradhaibh. seoid sin beantar don mnaoi leisin fear ar son firiadhta no toirmeasg do chur ar an ccoimpeart cloinne teagmus eatorra.	3.b.25.81		58–59
750	Frithe .i. ni do amuigh ag dul a múgha .ut frithe trebe .i. ní do gabar isin trebh tall.	9.32.96		59
751	Frithe roeadha no shlebhe .i. ni do gabar isin roifhiodh no isin sliabh i gcuairt ingelta.	9.34.100		59

9 This entry is out of order in the transcription and a repetition of an entry which follows below.

(*cont.*)

No.	Headword and entry	Entry reference	O'Curry's notes	MS fol.
752	Frithid .i. ionann.	8.35.94		59
753	Fri Trachta .i. isin traigh gabar.	9.34.101		59
754	Fuachar .i. fuachtnaightear.	7.b.26.96		59
755	Fuada .i. éire no fodla.	8.34.93		59
756	Fuadach do tarr .i. bean torrach fuaidighios fear leis.	6.a.26.55		59
757	Fuagartaid .i. an furfhograidh.	9.41.122		59
758	Fuaichne foghla .i. fóichnin, no foicheann, no mathair foghla, no tosach cointine.	14.h.19.39		59
759	Fualang .i. teitheamh nó a leitheid.	1.b.1.46		59
760	Fuarthair [ ] toirmisgios gniomradh ⁊ lanamnusadh.	4.b.20.31	4+	59
761	Fuasnadh .i. fuaidreadh, no comsgaoileadh.	2.a.6.24		59
762	Fubtadh .i. fo diubadh beatha.	6.a.26.54		59
763	Fuiceacht .i. an gniomh feardha .i. coimriachtain ⁊c̄.	3.b.2.24		59
764	Fuidhbheann .i. foidiubhaidh.	1.b.17.97	1+	60
765	Fuidhbithe .i. ni ar na foidiubhadh.	2.a.16.57		60
766	Fuigeall .i. lanfuigioll.	8.35.95		60
767	Fuil fhollus.		fec briocht fola.	60
768	Fuillmeach .i. fear gan̲ [ ] fuilleadh loigheacht ar breig do denam na fhiadnuise.	8.9.28	8+	60
769	Fuinmheall, no fuinbheall .i. foinbleognus, teaglomus, no tionoileas.	11.a.22.29		60
770	Fuireacht .i. airgitear no gebtear	2.a.7.27		60
771	Fuireag .i. fleadh.	4.c.21.110		60
772	Fu̲i̲reagar .i. airgitear.	6.b.2.92	6+	60
773	Fuireagur .i. airgidhtear .i. geibtear.	8.13.34		60
774	Fuireastar .i. airgidhtear .i. geibhtear.	7.a.14.20		60
775	Fuirireadh .i. fosreadnughadh.	2.a.12.42		60
776	Fuirireadh lui .i. buinne go cceann, no seacht ccin̄ gan buinne.	9.20.61		60
777	Fuithbhiol .i. foishiobhal.	1.b.17.96		60
778	Fuithribhe .i. gort, iomair, dheighthir bhi.	2.a.3.10		60
779	Fulach .i. fulang.	9.44.135		60
780	Fur .i. úir.	4.c.20.108		60
	.G.			61
781	Gabháil la flaith .i. dul a naighidh na flatha.	8.20.50		61
782	Gach ae .i. gach ógh ae dibh.	6.a.25.52		61
783	Gadaig .i. beanuid.	1.b.8.69		61
784	Gae ornae .i. ga oirgne. [ ] .edgeadh.	4.c.13.81		61
785	Gan fios gan treabaire		fec cuidig feasa	61
786	Gealtathar .i. inghiltear.	9.25.72		61
787	Geinite .i. searrach no lair.	1.b.21.104		61
788	Giabair no ciabair .i. meirdreach.	2.a.15.53		61
789	Gignightear .i. ginfightear.	4.c.7.50		61
790	Gill do bas		fec daormanach	61

(*cont.*)

No.	Headword and entry	Entry reference	O'Curry's notes	MS fol.
791	Gin tuillmhideacht .i. gin toimhlideacht .i. gin toimlius .i. gin itheas a fearann, no ibeas no chaitheas re a bele é.	12.b.16.48		61
792	Glas neannta		fec cuig anmanna cat	61
793	Gleanuidh .i. leanuid.	4.c.10.64		61
794	Glinne .i. daingean.	5.a.6.22		61
795	Gnaei .i. [_]	6.a.3.10	6+	61
796	Gnaithleas .i. gach aoidigheacht on chead adhaigh amach.		fec feacht feile	61
797	Gniadh .i. focal cuirtear ar son an aireach eachta .i. an fear ris a ndentar comairle an gniomha no an eachta do deanam ⁊ do beir comairle do cach cum an gníomha.	12.b.20.51		61–62
798	Gobhla		fec daormanach	62
799	Goilide .i. luide ege mar deirthear lesin grein.	1.b.8.70	1+	62
800	Góla .i. gorta quasi gúla .i. traos.	1.b.15.91		62
801	Gola		fec daormanach	62
802	Ǵola [.i. prisun], gobhla [.i. na croiche] . gill do bas, ⁊ manach núna.	11.a.10.15		62
803	Golgaire lenimh .i. bualadh, agus comhadh, bidh don leasmathair on leascloinn go mbid i ngair guil.	4.b.17.27	4+	62
804	Golladh fuidhe .i. faoisidniughadh ⁊ gollta an [_] agthigh do ni an bhean tarsna an tighe .i. faoisidniughadh di in guilte.	4.b.14.23	4+	62
805	Gothach .i. uallach.	2.a.1.10		62
806	Greth .i. cnu[_]	4.c.26.129	4+	62
807	Grin griun .i. fearann.	12.b.25.57		62
808	Grioth .i. criothnughadh.	7.a.4.5		62
809	Guairiughadh .i. gairiughadh .i. denam gartha no éige.	7.a.4.6		62
810	Guathasg .i. tasg gua a leannain, no neich as ionmuin le do tabairt do cum na mna.	6.a.27.56		62
811	Gu ed [.i. ed brecce] .i. dearbhadh [tre ed brege] sgeoil brege ar a fear gan adhbar do ni bean.	4.b.17.26		62
812	Guirn .i. suinn, no aithinne .i. gae ornae .i. ga oirgne.	4.c.13.81		62
813	Hìí		fec fìí	63
	.I.			63
814	Iardach .i. iaramh .i. aithghin .i. iaramh dighde .i. buidhechus iarsin eneachlonn bearar iardach.	7.a.26.39		63
815	Iar mbreith us .i. ní tar eis bhreitheamnuis, tuilleadh leis.	13.d.19.31		63
816	Iarnglus .i. iar ngleofheasa.	6.a.5.19		63
817	Iarrair .i. iarradh.	12.b.6.27		63
818	Iarrath .i. luach oileamna.	14.b.4.9		63

(*cont.*)

No.	Headword and entry	Entry reference	O'Curry's notes	MS fol.
819	Iar soillsi glus .i. soillsi iarnguls [_]	6.a.5.20	6+	63
820	Iaruasaoitt. (no masait) .i. iar mbreith cloinne.	13.d.16.27		63
821	Iatiaig i. mealog .i. tiach .i. aiteog.	13.d.10.18		63
822	Ima-dicheat .i. emhdhidnid.	9.21.64		63
823	Imcedeadh .i. emhdhechadh.	10.42.107	10+	63
824	Imhde .i. eimdhidnigh.	5.a.4.16	5+	63
825	Imdeall .i. bruith (no tabairt nethe a hinne (no inhinne) for cludadh, clithiughadh, no téigheadh. do himdilleadh, ⁊ do heimdaileadh (ider coire ⁊ dabhaigh) an coirm.	4.c.22.115		63
826	Im-desidh .i. tarrustur.	2.a.4.13		63
827	Ime .i. fál.	9.25.73		63
828	Imeadh .i. nimeadh .i. eagluis.	7.b.4.57		64
829	Im-id, rubairt .i. do rinne miebtear.	10.12.23		64
830	Imiteacht .i. teacht uime.	8.24.64		64
831	Im [_] .i. eimhdhechsain ara mheanmhuin.	10.32.76	10+	64
832	Im ro laidh .i. emh ar luadh fir ag teacht no ag dul do cum a mhna.	3.b.11.47		64
833	Im-ruimeadhar .i. ro reimnigheadar in iomurbus.	12.b.25.58		64
834	Imsging .i.	6.a.6.24	6+	64
835	Im-tobaing .i. eimhtoibhghithear.	8.20.52		64
836	Im-toigren .i. eimhthoibhgid.	2.a.4.15		64
837	Imurchur uptha ar dhaigh serce fir .i. imurchur piseog.	3.b.35.90		64
838	Inbleogain gill .i. ara ndleagar geall do gabail.	14.d.8.20		64
839	Inbleogan saichte no saoithe .i. gallraiteach.	13.a.9.4		64
840	Inbhroghthar .i. firenightear.	8.9.26		64
841	In-carthach .i. dormuine.	11.b.5.38	fec be	64
842	Inceasdnughadh .i. ceasdnughadh a hinne.	2.a.6.23		64
843	Incind comlainn gan sgis acht sgeo cneidh .i. an lenabh imbi inchinn comlan nach bi sgis aige ar na bhreith acht ag sgeith, ⁊ ag cnedhidh.	3.b.33.87		64
844	Inchreanar .i. creacar a hinne.	10.45.115		64
845	Indbeartadh .i. denamh.	4.c.22.114		64
846	Indisi .i. buailidh bó.	10.17.40		65
847	Indleamh .i. indile éimhe.	2.a.9.33		65
848	Indul .i. uair, no oir.	13.b.2.7		65
849	Ingelt .i. gleth a hinne.	9.18.56		65
850	Inmhuille, muilleadh . greasacht, no brusdadh.	7.b.28.99		65
	.Duil. eidgeadh.			65
851	Innteach, ⁊ buaile galair .i. ait i mbi galar [_]	9.6.17	9+	65
852	Inteach foghladh .i. inte duthuidh na ffoghluigheadh .i. uarbhotha, na coillidh.	1.b.16.94		65

(*cont.*)

No.	Headword and entry	Entry reference	O'Curry's notes	MS fol.
853	Ioc cana (no congbail, no gabail) re hainffine .i. mar do rachaidh duine ona fhine fa riaghail cana ⁊ fine oile .i. dligheadh corusa fine tugtear isin cain sin	12.b.19.50		65
854	Iocht .i. gniomh.	7.a.11.15		65
855	Iodnachar. Iodnagar .i. tiodnaictear.	5.b.5.35		65
856	Iomaigh .i. iomain .i. tiomain.	1.b.3.50 and 6.a.30.65		65
857	Iomain [.i. an eallaigh] sgeric an duine .i. na ghort feoir no arbha ⁊ ardurchar sleigid [_] desceimeanna a tuaim [_] seachtar crich .i. gach ionad osin amach.	1.b.2.48	1+	65
858	Iomamnus .i. comolc.	4.b.22.34		65
859	Iomarr .i. tiomarguin.	10.38.84		65
860	Iomcutaim .i. comthuitim doibh mar aon .i. don lanamuin. iolradh na ffocal si .i. leathchutmann, ⁊ iomcutmainn.	3.b.8.40		65–66
861	Iomglan mis .i. neamhghlaine bios ar neach ar feadh mis tre biathadh ciontaigh fri re de achmaighe .i. cion an ciontaigh go ceann miosa do beith ar tí biathus é ar feadh deich la. ano a contrardha.	12.b.26.60		66
862	Iomorrán .i. imfhorran.	4.c.13.77		66
863	Iomthach .i. eimthoinge.	1.b.4.52		66
864	Ionforbairt .i. fas no bisioch.	6.a.19.36		66
865	Ionnadh .i. ni no sochar tig [_]	3.b.38.94	3+	66
866	Ionnlachtaidh .i. fear dhenta ionnluigh.	1.b.18.99		66
867	Ionnlongadh .i. iomfhuilngeadh.	10.39.92	10+	66
868	Ionnotacht .i. tosach .i. teacht inn.	6.a.19.35		66
869	Ionnsguchadh gradh, no ceime .i. ardughadh graidh no ceime.	8.28.77		66
870	Ionraith .i. neach as ionghabhtha i raithighios.	7.b.18.80		66
871	Iorair .i. arguin tre feirg.	4.c.11.67		66
872	Iorcaidh .i. urcoideach, no iut ainfeargach.	4.c.10.66	4+	66
873	Iorcha, iar cha .i. landaoir.	5.b.2.27		66
874	Íre .i. fearann.	9.14.40		66
875	Iuidigheacht .i. iudicium, breitheamnus	8.6.17		67
	.L.			67
876	Lainbiathadh gach graidh a fleadh croilighe, no seachtmadh logh eneach.	6.a.15.32		67
877	Laith .i. lionn.	4.c.23.116		67
878	Laith .i. lathach .i. sraid .i. uisge na huachtar agus ceachair na hiochtar	9.4.11		67
879	Laithne .i. laitin.	8.28.76		67
880	Laithrech laighean .i. lathair in ro heillgeadh é.	10.12.22		67
881	Lamhcomairt .i. com-imirt lamh .i. basgaire.	3.b.20.68		67

(*cont.*)

No.	Headword and entry	Entry reference	O'Curry's notes	MS fol.
882	Lán an chiontaigh .i. lainfhiach dleagur don ciontach.	11.a.20.26		67
883	Lanchothaigh .i. lanadhoin [ ]	5.b.6.40	5+	67
884	Lan naoinfhir .i. lainfhiach bhios ar aon duine amhain.	11.a.17.24		67
885	Laobh .i. leathtrom, no leath taobh.	7.b.7.62		67
886	Laobadh .i. saobadh.	8.3.9		67
887	Laoch .i. an taire echta.	9.41.121		67
888	Laoigteach, no loigh a lias .i. laoigh i teach no cro.	13.d.15.26		67
889	Lat .i. slat.	10.29.63		67
890	Latra		fec slatra	67
891	Leadhmhiomasg .i. droch fhasg isin rann go ruige a leath.	4.c.6.47		67
892	Legadh do luidhe .i. leigean don sprédh luighe san fér.	9.22.67		67
893	Lenaidh .i. lio[_]	2.a.8.31	2+	68
894	Lethcutaim .i. tuitim .i. comhtuitim don dara leath	3.b.8.39		68
895	Lia .i. comorba.	4.c.13.78		68
896	Lia .i. iomad.	4.c.13.79		68
897	Lias .i. do laoghaibh ⁊ do chaoiribh.	12.b.28.65		68
898	Lias caorach .i. cro caorach.	1.b.5.57		68
899	Liasradh .i. denamh lias no cró do laoghuibh et ceteri.	14.b.1.1		68
900	Lias tuighithe .i. cro gamhna ar na thuighe.	3.b.39.96		68
901	Liogh .i. dath.	14.b.4.8		68
902	Lionn togluasacht .i. breath na coimpearta an tan nach bí acht na lionn gan corthus geineamhna no crotha daona.	3.b.31.83		68
903	Lios .i. ima mbí an cladh.	9.16.48		68
904	Liu, lia .i. liomhnadh.	7.a.23.34		68
905	Liudh sgith .i. ni as sgith le fear do liudh fair .i. cen fear no cen g[_]	4.b.18.28	4+	68
906	Lobhar .i. duine trogh.	9.41.120		68
907	Locc bergenach .i. loc berathgenach, no lochta salach ar ar tairismeach salchar go soileir do cach[_] loc suide, luide, teach ⁊ cuile ⁊ iad uile gan sguabadh gan glanadh	4.b.20.30		68
908	Lochrann, ⁊ loichead .i. an tsoillsi.	4.c.24.118		68
909	Lú lui .i. seacht nda[_] no seacht slapair, ni riaghailtear lu lui na meadhontaidh lui acht do lus, do gairleoig ⁊ do praisig.	9.20.60	9+	69
910	Luamhnacht .i. luamaireacht.	9.27.86		69
911	Luc lamha .i. lamhaidh luch.	10.28.55		69
912	Lucht codaigh naoimh no firen .i. lenus daon naomh amhain, no lucht aon patruin.	8.16.41		69
913	Lugarman .i. luga garman no lingua garman, no an garman cen buir.	13.d.12.22		69

(*cont.*)

No.	Headword and entry	Entry reference	O'Curry's notes	MS fol.
914	Luighe cana .i. mionna do tabairtear beith umhal don riaghail.	12.b.8.34		69
915	Luirioch [_] .i. tonn criothaigh no loitbog.	9.2.7	9+	69
916	Luitear .i. tionoiltear.	8.26.71		69
917	Lulgach .i. ceithre sgreabail fichiod.	5.a.2.11		69
	.M.			69
918	Macadh .i. do indilibh ⁊ deachaibh.	12.b.28.66		69
919	Mac beothar .i. mac i tteasgaire.	10.45.117		69
920	Mac cailleach .i. cailleach dubh.	3.b.18.63		69
921	Mac saoir lethe .i. mac aga mbi ceannus sealbha ⁊ maoine ara aithidh fein.	OC.5		69
9	.c.f.			69
922	Mac sgrine .i. mac do ni fear re coibdealach (na riocht fein) .i. cuirtear i sgrin leathair é amach ar an muir in airead bus léir gelsgiath .⁊c̄.	14.h.13.36		69–70
923	Mada		fec medla	70
924	Mad cis .i. da néisgísi.	9.38.112		70
925	Madhthoir .i. ma thoinge.	2.b.7.92		70
926	Mainbtheach .i. maithtoiceach.	2.a.18.66		70
927	Mainch [ ] .i. ma [_] don taobh amach do ni neach.	11.a.2.3	11+	70
928	Mairbhelodh .i. dol ó dligheadh ⁊ se beo, beoelodh .i. Scontra.	14.h.20.40		70
929	Mairn .i. brath.	5.a.1.4		70
930	Manach innerge dethbhire .i. manach imgheas ona eagluis duthchuis do cum eagluisi oile da adnacal inte, no diarraidh cothaighthe tre riachtanus .i. di aitbear-air eirge aisde a hinne, marsin innerge cattuctatadh ma dethbir no inndethbir.	6.a.7.25	6+	70
931	Manach nuna		fec daormanach	70
932	Manach riaghla .i. saormanach.	10.31.71		70
933	Manchuine .i. lucht coimideachta ⁊ coimeadtha.	5.a.4.17	5+	70
934	Manda mairmheasa .i. iomad moir measa.	8.22.57		70
935	Mandradh .i. sgaoileadh.	2.b.2.69		70
936	Maol macha .i. cuaille maol amuil machadh.	9.15.44		71
937	Marb-cnai .i. lomradh olla .i. ciro cnu olla .i. lomradh.	13.d.20.32	13+	71
938	Marbhtaidhbe i. ni ebius a coibhche a ttaoi o mhnaoi, ⁊ marbh i fen no a fear, no ceachtar diobh ann.	3.b.7.36		71
939	Marus .i. mor ráidhis.	10.17.41		71
940	Maslach bó, no gach mil .i. miofhocal diomolta do beir duine ar boin. ⁊c̄.	14.h.5.31		71
941	Matbosaide .i. madia ngabaside.	12.b.28.64		71
942	Mathó .i. ma dia ttoinge.	3.b.19.67		71
943	Meadh .i. bá .i. maith.	8.14.37		71
944	Meadh na mireann .i. na bhfearann.	9.14.41		71

(*cont.*)

No.	Headword and entry	Entry reference	O'Curry's notes	MS fol.
945	Meadbha .i. measamnuigh .i. breitheamh.	8.14.36		71
946	Meadhontaidhe lui .i. seacht gais gan a cceanna.	9.19.59		71
947	Meallach .i. aoibhinn.	7.a.10.13		71
948	Meamm .i. pog.	3.b.22.75		71
949	Meam naisi .i. pog da deoin do gheibh bean.	4.b.8.12		71
950	Mearacht .i. druis.	4.b.14.22		71
951	Mearamhna .i. mna meara.	2.a.13.49		71
952	Medla, máda, racht, sas, féis ⁊ tuireadh .i. anmanna do mhuic.	9.17.52		71
953	Meid .i. moid, on [_]	4.b.1.3	4+	71
954	Meisi .i. cuimhgeach.	10.40.96		71
955	Methir .i. ceart bios im chaoiridh chlaimh, uinge diarann.	14.d.1.15		72
956	Metoll .i. foghail do ni an mhuc mhor da ngoirtear medla.	9.17.53		72
957	Midis .i. measaid.	5.a.1.5	5+	72
958	Ministear .i. mionna aisdir bhios ar aisdear isin tuaith le tabairt mionn ar cach .⁊c̄.	5.b.22.46		72
959	Miodbha .i. toraind.	44.c.9.58		72
960	Miodhba .i. meadhon beatha inter bonum et malum.	4.c.8.57		72
961	Miodhbach .i. fear miodhbadh.	9.36.107		72
962	Miodchuine .i. ag leagúibh.	4.c.25.125		72
963	Miodhlach .i. meadhon laochuis, no meatlachus.	8.3.10	8+	72
964	Mioscaith .i. mallacht.	4.c.26.127		72
965	Mir méne .i. greim as mian leis an mnaoi thorraigh.	6.a.29.58		72
966	Mis eimhghlethe i. mí a ndentaoi eimhgle .i. suidi-ughadh cána no cairde no dligheadh .⁊c̄.	5.b.2.28		72
967	Muilltear [_] no freaslaightear.	10.20.52	10+	72
968	Muineamhna .i. mna bhios ag neach isin muine.	2.a.14.50		72
969	Muireach .i. moiriathach .i. righ moir fhearainn.	8.21.54		72
970	Murthoradh .i. duileasg.	2.a.3.11		72
	.N.			72
971	Naidhm ⁊ urnaidhm bios idir fear ⁊ mnaoi .i. naidhm .i. coibhche don mnaoi, ⁊ urnaidhm ag an fear uirrisi im ioc leis da ndenadh foghail doba nair no olc do.	3.b.2.25		72
972	Naisi .i. ceangailsi.	7.b.2.52		73
973	Naoi .i. eathar.	6.a.29.60		73
974	Naoill .i. luighe.	7.b.19.82		73
975	Nár .i. fíor.	8.23.58		73
976	Nár .i. naomh.	4.c.14.82		73
977	Násad .i. sasadh, no sosadh.	2.b.2.72		73
978	Nasar .i. naisgtear .i. ceangailtear.	7.a.36.47		73

(*cont.*)

No.	Headword and entry	Entry reference	O'Curry's notes	MS fol.
979	Neach diamba cuma a ebirt, ⁊ a aigde i. duine agarob ionann an ni a deir sé, ⁊ an ní bhios na in̄tin, gurob mar a deir sé bhíos an ni recus, no nach cceilionn maith na olc da mbí isin sed .⁊c̄.	10.36.80		73
980	Neagur .i. nightear.	10.42.105		73
981	Neimhiomcogur .i. iomchogur ⁊c̄. re a fear fein [_] rainig.	4.b.11.17	4+	73
982	Néth .i. dia catha.	4.c.12.75		73
983	Ni airbhe .i. ni raibhe.	10.40.94		73
984	Ni artha .i. ni aratha.	2.b.5.83		73
985	Ní hois .i. na faomh, ni hoghar .i. ni faomthar.	6.a.31.70		73
986	Nimheadh		fec imeadh	73
987	Ni ria .i. na reac.	6.a.37.84		73
988	Nodh .i. urdairc.	8.22.55		73
989	Nomhadh nó .i. nomhadh nae .i. fear.	7.b.8.63		74
990	Nos .i. fios nua, no fios naonmuir, ⁊ nos .i. urtarughadh.	4.c.3.39		74
991	Nuithear .i. ordearcuightear.	1.b.12.83		74
	.O.			74
992	Ochtrach .i. otrach.	9.36.104		74
993	Ocmoda .i. tadhall, adall.	1.b.12.81		74
994	Odhar .i. oineadh no oirtear.	9.15.46		74
995	Oidhthe .i. eisgidhsi.	9.38.113		74
996	Oil .i. ail no pluic.	9.36.105		74
997	Oillian .i. léine mhor.	7.a.24.35		74
998	Oillian, culpait .i. an lene cona hall sgóit.	2.b.20.108		74
999	Oimbligh .i. blighid a hinne.	4.c.28.135		74
1000	Oimbreath .i. guibreath omh.	4.c.28.134		74
1001	Ol .i. oll .i. mór.	10.29.62		74
1002	Ollobhair aigsin .i. folabairt do ni neach ag faigsin nethe. ⁊c̄.	9.35.103		74
1003	Olsona, no ollosna .i. can.	4.c.18.97		74
1004	Omh .i. indlightheach.	8.23.61		74
1005	Os .i. ogus.	4.c.7.51		74
1006	Osuic .i. uga .i. togha le hos .i. re bel.	9.44.138		74
	.P.			75
1007	Paintuilleamur co cioth gan iomchogur .i. ioeanncadh bidh do thabairt do mhnaoi [_] goideas [_] tuilleadh clu no cuideachus di o caraid no comaighteach seach a fear.	4.b.10.16	4+	75
1008	Pliun .i. tairisiomh.	5.c.7.58		75
1009	Proiceaptai .i. searmontaigh.	1.a.11.28		75
1010	Puibleadh .i. teasgadh.	10.18.46		75

(*cont.*)

No.	Headword and entry	Entry reference	O'Curry's notes	MS fol.
	.R.			75
1011	Racht		fec medla	75
1012	Rae .i. ro éd.	4.c.20.104		75
1013	Ragbha .i. ro gabhadh.	12.b.27.62		75
1014	Raitmacht .i. ro srethnigheadh, no ro taithmigheadh .i. ro sgaoileadh.	10.44.113	10+	75
1015	Reabach luirge [.i. riabsad an talman do nisi] .i. riabach an talmaidhe re luirg, bean sin bios o tig do tigh go [_] fri a cele ⁊ lorg ina laimh.	4.b.16.25	+	75
1016	Reacoll mbreath .i. roichiall na mbreath.	13.d.11.21		75
1017	Reargadair .i. ro reimnuigheadar.	1.a.9.23		75
1018	Re comloigthe .i. aimsir, no cáirde fa fiachaibh comlogus an feiceamh don ti ar ambi fiach aige.	6.a.14.31		75
1019	Re fhabtha .i. aimsir leighis.	3.b.35.89		75
1020	Relughadh .i. foillsioghadh.	2.a.10.36		76
1021	Re, toe, torae .i. focail raitear re fear na bhfiach.	7.b.10.65		76
1022	Ria .i. reac.	10.38.82		76
1023	Riachtaidhe . fear riachtanuis.	8.9.25		76
1024	Riar		fec anmanna breithe	76
1025	Rideadhad .i. aisneidhid.	2.a.10.37		76
1026	Ringcne		fec cuig anmanna cat	76
1027	Rioth go moirseisior, no go cuigear .⁊c̄. .i. iomlaine na ffiach, no dioluidheacht an mhillteanuis do ni an chuideachta do buain do gach aon dibh go moirseisear, go cuigtear, no gibe nuimhear a deir dligheadh .⁊c̄.	11.a.18.25		76
1028	Rirthear .i. rofhirenightear.	2.b.7.89		76
1029	Rochadh .i. ro ionsaighid.	10.45.114		76
1030	Rochair i. ro seichightear .i. ro hionnsaightear.	7.b.6.60		76
1031	Roch bi .i. ro bhi.	5.c.6.57		76
1032	Rochluithe .i. spairn, ⁊ lamh fir na crios, nu a fear [_]	4.b.13.20	4+	76
1033	Róchma .i. ro athcuma.	10.13.25		76
1034	Roeach .i. ro seach, no roiseicim .i. ro ionsaigheadh.	8.19.47		76
1035	Roithghearn .i. cli.	4.c.18.96		76
1036	Ro-ná .i. ro ceangail. ut ro-nas.	8.27.72		76
1037	Ro-neagam i. ro iocfam [ ] [no piocfam]	11.a.9.12		77
1038	Ro nétadh .i. ro gonadh, no ro bith.	4.c.12.74		77
1039	Rórdamus .i. ro imraidhmis.	10.28.56		77
1040	Ro rir .i. do ro reac.	6.a.37.83		77
1041	Rosa .i. gruaidhe.	2.a.5.18		77
1042	Ro-sgoth .i. ro ionnsaightear.	8.25.68		77
1043	Rudh .i. roidh .i. corcair.	14.d.3.16		77

(*cont.*)

No.	Headword and entry	Entry reference	O'Curry's notes	MS fol.
1044	Rudhrach .i. ro duradh gua.	2.b.7.93		77
1045	Ruibhdhithear .i. ro eidir imdibhtear.	7.b.25.94		77
1046	Ruib do mealar .i. ba ⁊ caoire.	6.a.33.75		77
1047	Ruibhean .i. tuillidh [_]	5.b.4.34	5+	77
1048	Ruib na doimealar .i. capuill ⁊ muca.	6.a.34.76		77
1049	Ruib na to-mealar .i. ainmthighe [_]	9.13.38	9+	77
1050	Ruib to-melar .i. ainmthighe atcognus a ccuid, mar táid ba, caoire ⁊ gobair ⁊c̄.	9.13.37	9+	77
1051	Ruice, ruca .i. ruaid. cech imdearga.	6.a.2.2		77
1052	Ruidbeach .i. ro dibheach .i. ro bidhleach.	2.a.8.28		77
1053	Ruideadh .i. imdeargadh.	9.36.106		77
1054	Ruighleadh .i. ro fuighleadh.	9.8.25		77
1055	Ruiread .i. ro fearaid.	9.18.54		77
1056	Ruirmhid .i. ro airmhid.	1.b.6.62		77
1057	Rus .i. gruaidh.	2.a.5.17		78
1058	Rusg ndairti .i. rusg diosg no eadtram.	6.a.18.33		78
	.S.			78
1059	Sab .i. so ab.	2.a.12.44		78
1060	Sais .i. ionnsaighis.	8.24.63		78
1061	Sallach diollat .i. an tedach bearar man salchar .i. brat gan lomda ⁊ ionar gan tollus, no brat dubh ⁊ ionar dubh. ní bearthar do oide o athair ⁊ o mathair an lenibh taobh a muigh don iarrath. (bo dhearba mar sin) dana altrom go togha .i. i cinn .xíííí. bliadhna do ingin. i ccionn seacht mbliadhna deg do mac .i. i ttogh i cill no i ttuaith no a bposadh ⁊c̄.	14.f.1.24		78
1062	Samusg .i. da sgreabal deg.	5.a.2.10		78
1063	Saoghal .i. dos.	4.c.19.98		78
1064	Saoircerdne .i. mac fuirmeadh.	4.c.19.99		78
1065	Saoithe .i. breagaireacht (as saoth le neac) nó diubairt.	10.43.108		78
1066	Saoithe .i. ní as saoth le neach mar ata diubairt.	10.7.10	10+	78
1067	Saormhanach .i. an deachmadh mac, no an ced tuiste.	11.a.9.14		78
1068	Sarasamhlaidh .i. samhladh as sar .i. duine do samhlughadh fri ni as measa inas e fein .i. re coin no re ceachair.	9.36.108		78
1069	Sas		fec medla	79
1070	Sasar .i. ionsoighthear.	7.a.22.31		79
1071	Seachain seacht ngaoi gona an leiginn, madail gurbad saor sean. cruith is tiompan. peann cruaidh ceanndubh. fithchioll buanfach. brandubh bean.	13c, l. 1[10]		79
1072	Seacfaidh .i. seachmallaidh.	10.33.77		79

10 See Appendix 4.

(*cont.*)

No.	Headword and entry	Entry reference	O'Curry's notes	MS fol.
1073	Seachfus .i. ionnsaighfeas.	12.b.22.53		79
1074	Seachmoallaigh .i. seachmailligh.	2.b.4.81		79
1075	Seachnus nairgsin .i. do ci an duine aspredh ar faghail ⁊ seachnaidh iad sa noidhche, ⁊ ní fhidir ga áit i rabattar.	9.21.65		79
1076	Seachtar crich		fec iomain sgeric	79
1077	Seacht bairgean .i. bairgean iocus an marbh i gcionn seachtmuine deis a bhais.	6.a.12.29		79
1078	Seachtmadh loighe eneach gach graidh a seacht bairgean, no a seachtmadh lainbiathadh.	6.a.15.32		79
1079	Seadrach .i. tren, neartmhar.	6.a.30.64		79
1080	Seagur .i. ionnsaightear.	7.b.24.92		79
1081	Seall ⁊ sell .i. amharc.	7.a.12.17		79
1082	Seanarusg .i. seinchinneadh ógh.	10.44.111		79
1083	Seansmurcionadh .i. iar mbliadhain .i. bliadhain, nó ní as mo ó do rinneadh an cionsmacht cairde.	14.c.1.11		79–80
1084	Searg ⁊ macra .i. galra bid ar lenbuibh.	14.f.13.25		80
1085	Searnar .i. sreathnaightear.	8.34.90 and 10.45.116		80
1086	Seasaid .i. sreathnaightear.	7.b.22.86		80
1087	Sedha gach coslach		fec coslach	80
1088	Seghuin .i. fear gonus séig .i. ag allaidh, no seguin .i. aire echta.	4.c.15.87		80
1089	Seis .i. ionsaigh.	1.b.11.78		80
1090	Seis .i. tairis .i. den comnuighe.	1.b.11.77		80
1091	Semead ala bhuar .i. semead og for an dara buar .i. droch blath for laoguibh an fhir tre connm[_]	3.b.37.92	3+	80
1092	Senchlethe .i. lucht leanamna bhios ag leanmuin do tri glunuibh a ndiaigh a cheile, ⁊ o bheadh mar sin agan athair ⁊ agan mac, ⁊ agan ua, as eidir le sliocht an trir sin gan iadsan na a sliocht do leigeann do gnath, ⁊ einclethe na daoine sin.	12.b.17.49		80
1093	Seoid gabhla .i. seoid gabhlaighthear isin eric .i. dairt .i. ceithre sgreabail a luach.	5.a.2.7		80
1094	Seoil .i. suaill.	7.b.33.105		80
1095	Sgeanmanna .i. nethe sginnius don in̄eoin on ord gabhan̄.	5.b.3.29		80
1096	Sgeon .i. iompoidh no sgeidhidh.	2.a.3.9		81
1097	Sgerig		fec iomainsgerig	81
1098	Sging .i. iomdhadh[ ]	6.a.6.23	6+	81
1099	Sgiolla .i. daosgair oban.	12.b.5.26		81
1100	Sgor .i. cinneadh.	2.a.16.59		81
1101	Sgoth .i. innsge.	2.a.17.60		81
1102	Sgript .i. sgribnidh.	6.a.3.6		81

(*cont.*)

No.	Headword and entry	Entry reference	O'Curry's notes	MS fol.
1103	Sguirde .i. cinnte.	2.a.17.62		81
1104	Sias .i. ionnsaightear.	7.b.25.95		81
1105	Siasra .i. reimnighthe, no ionsaighe.	9.39.115		81
1106	Sich .i. ionnsaighidh.	6.b.1.89		81
1107	Siniomon .i. sean somhaomeach.	7.a.11.16		81
1108	Sionnus .i. semnuighius no eatorgnuighius.	2.b.4.80		81
1109	Siride .i. siorthoir bios ag sireadh aide no aite.	9.2.5		81
1110	Slabhra, slaibhre .i. sal bhuar .i. buar tig tar sal.	9.43.131		81
1111	Slabhra tobru .i. sal bhuar do bearar do mhnaoi ar choimhead a geanuis di.	3.b.6.34		81
1112	Slán-faille .i. ag sin fort slan dam ar ré cid faill iomchoimheada do neith im in <u>sred</u>.	2.b.21.110	see this again	81
1113	Slan naithne .i. trebaire ro gab fear in tighe andside re fios daingne, no ar daingne.	2.b.22.111		81
1114	Slatra .i. ainbfial .i. anbal, ⁊ latra .i. laidir dána quasi more latrum.	7.b.23.9		81
1115	Sleith .i. coimriachtain le mnaoi gan fios di.	3.b.12.51		82
1116	Sleith dar glún .i. idir a dhá cois.	3.b.14.55		82
1117	Sleitheamhna .i. mna do cum a ttiagur ar sleith.	2.a.14.51		82
1118	Sleith fo thaobh .i. da chois na mná tar an fhear.	3.b.14.56		82
1119	Sleith tar lónlaingen .i. dul do cum na mna gan fhios di na deaghaidh a niar.	3.b.13.54		82
1120	Slethear .i. teigtear do cum mna gan fhios di.	3.b.13.53		82
1121	Sliocht aroisg .i. eolus ⁊ brath bhios ag suil an fhoghluidhe ar ní airide do lot, no do ghoid.	11.a.16.22		82
1122	Sloigeadh fuidreachta .i. slogh fuidir.	13.d.21.33		82
1123	Sochla .i. sochlodh, no sochlu.	7.a.17.24		82
1124	Solamh .i. luath.	9.30.92		82
1125	Somairius da ruidhe .i. [_]	4.b.8.13	4+	82
1126	Sruaim .i. iomad.	8.18.43		82
1127	Sruith .i. uasal.	6.a.15.18		82
1128	Sui, saoi .i. on tsoadh .i. iompodh.	9.16.50		82
1129	Súilteach .i. fear sellceachta .i. seallac.	5.c.1.49		82
1130	Suitear, no soathur .i. iompoithear.	10.42.106		82
	.T.			82
1131	Tacmhaisi .i. tacmainge.	10.17.39		82
1132	Tacomal .i. acomal .i. ceangal.	9.6.15		82
1133	Tacomul .i. ceangal.	1.a.16.38		82
1134	Tadhat .i. gaduighe.	10.5.4		83
1135	Tadhbhuis .i. <u>taisbonsi.</u>	1.a.18.45	1+	83
1136	Tagha .i. iomain amuich.	9.9.31		83
1137	Tai .i. an tonach loma no corma .i. tanog, no dearbog, no i an corma, no loma.	4.c.20.109		83
1138	Taidbhe .i. taoi eibe .ut. [_]	3.b.6.35	3+	83

(*cont.*)

No.	Headword and entry	Entry reference	O'Curry's notes	MS fol.
1139	Taipnemhidh .i. tamhun.	4.c.19.102		83
1140	Taircell		fec aithghin ⁊c̄	83
1141	Taircithear .i. tathaoir.	3.a.10.13		83
1142	Tairecc .i. torrachtain.	5.c.1.48		83
1143	Tairfentur .i. tairpentur.	12.b.6.28		83
1144	Tairidhin linne muilinn .i. cladh connmhus an tuisce leisin muileann.	6.a.32.71		83
1145	Tairim .i. tathaoirim.	2.b.3.75		83
1146	Tairrsce .i. tairisciu .i. céimníughadh do nid spre tar fér no gort .⁊c̄.	1.a.13.33		83
1147	Taisealbadh .i. taisbenadh.	6.a.31.68		83
1148	Taith .i. an gruth taith.	6.a.23.44		83
1149	Taithmeatt .i. iomradh no cuimniughadh, ⁊ ur aith-meadh mar sin.	4.b.9.14		83
1150	Talentum, talenton. Graece. talanntan i ngaoidhilge.	14.g.1.27		83
1151	Tallaidh .i. tuaslaicid.	1.b.8.68		83
1152	Talmuidioch .i. fear mire, no cuthaigh, no galair mhoir.	7.b.30.102		84
1153	Taoi .i. an . (?)	4.b.2.5	4+	84
1154	Taoi, taoieatus .i. tosd.	8.18.44		84
1155	Taoidhidh .i. taoithnighidh.	11.a.6.8		84
1156	Taoithcria .i. taitceannach, no aithcheannach.	10.38.83		84
1157	Taosnamhadh .i. tumadh no fliuchadh arain.	10.28.57		84
1158	Tap .i. obunn.	1.a.18.43		84
1159	Targadh .i. tinol.	7.a.6.7		84
1160	Tarrachtaigh .i. neach tarraightear.	1.b.11.79		84
1161	Tascartha .i. an caithcliath.	6.a.35.79		84
1162	Tath .i. gruth da ngoirthear maothal.	3.b.18.62		84
1163	Tath .i. taithmeach.	10.41.97		84
1164	Táthad .i. atá liom.	10.6.7		84
1165	Tathchar diúmunn .i. athcur, ar dimiadhaighe lais beith aige .i. nach fiú lais an cele beith agan flaith, no leis an flaith an cele do beith aige.	14.h.24.45		84
1166	Tathluightear .i. taithmightear.	10.38.87		84
1167	Teachtmhuighe .i. sealbh beodhile bhios ar an magh.	3.b.5.32		84
1168	Teamracha .i. uaisle.	2.a.15.54		84
1169	Tearbadh .i. ionnarba no dealughadh.	12.b.6.29		84
1170	Tearbsad .i. greamuighid no sgaoilid.	7.b.31.103		84
1171	Teathnattur .i. ro teannsatur no rotheasgsat.	6.a.22.40		85
1172	Teathnatur .i. taithmighid .i. sgaoilid.	4.c.24.121		85
1173	Teathraigh .i. traighidh.	4.c.23.117		85
1174	Teingleir .i. teangaidh leir.	9.27.85		85
1175	Telachtach .i. fear do ni telach.	1.b.19.101		85
1176	Tiasg .i. tinn [_]	9.43.133	9+	85
1177	Tigseal .i. buain.	13.d.10.19		85

(*cont.*)

No.	Headword and entry	Entry reference	O'Curry's notes	MS fol.
1178	Tigsel .i. buain .i. ī g[?] uimin [.i. c[r]ocs̄] ro hoige [.i. fuaig ⁊̇] uimpe.	13.d.18.30	thus	85
1179	Timine .i. sadail neach as time da fhine.	9.12.36		85
1180	Tiodain		fec tiondain	85
1181	Tioghbaidh .i. deigeanach bhásaighid.	7.b.33.107	7+	85
1182	Tiomgaire .i. iarraidh.	5.a.1.2		85
1183	Tiomortain .i. cro .i. bas.	1.b.14.89		85
1184	Tiomortain .i. on mbás raidtear no tiomarta.	7.a.30.43		85
1185	Tiondain, no tiodain .i. tiodhnaic.	10.40.93		85
1186	Tionnsgra .i. tinsgeadal.	9.43.132		85
1187	Tionnsgra .i. tionsgeadol creice an tsiogail do bearar don mnaoi ar thoil go noige do bheith aice.	3.b.5.33		85
1188	Tiughragach .i. tairgeadhach agach .i. fear thionoilte gníomha táir.	7.a.8.12		85
1189	Tleanamhain. ced muinntire neich .i. to ethlodha chedmhuinntire and .i. dúl go a priomhmnaoi.	4.c.4.41		85–86
1190	Tlus .i. tuilleadh uais do bearar risin ní bhios easbhad-hach.	9.29.89		86
1191	To .i. an tabairt [_]	9.47.142	9+	86
1192	Tobhus .i. droichbes no deghbhes.	1.b.13.86		86
1193	Tochmaghadh .i. toibhghid.	2.a.17.64		86
1194	Tochmustur .i. toibhgeas.	2a.4.14		86
1195	Tochmhustur .i. toibhgithear.	2.a.18.65		86
1196	Tocuireadh .i. an cuireadh cugad.	12.b.11.39		86
1197	Toe		fec re	86
1198	Togead .i. toghaid.	3.b.4.27		86
1199	Toghluasacht .i. ni do bear ar mhnaoi breith clainne ré nionbaidh.	3.b.10.43		86
1200	Toghluasacht beochuirp .i. ambeo re nionbaidh.	3.b.32.85		86
1201	Toghluasacht r̲olla .i. breath leinibh mairbh.	3.b.31.84	+	86
1202	Toichreachta .i. toichidhe dirge duan .i. dúinis indealt .i. aoin siolla.	4.c.5.44		86
1203	Toighleannan .i. leandan.	1.b.6.63		86
1204	Toimdightear .i. tomhaistear, ⁊ baramhlaightear.	7.a.28.41		86
1205	Toinemhidh .i. dolóre.	4.c.19.103		86
1206	Toirbheanad .i. toirighnid.	10.21.53		86
1207	Toirsiod .i. do rósad .i. do roinne.	8.31.81		86
1208	Toithfliun .i. tairisiomh, no fuillide, cosmail ⁊ pliun.	5.c.7.59		87
1209	Toithlean .i. do étlodh.	10.10.15		87
	.D.R.			87
1210	Tomaithe ni bia .i. tomaith an buille ⁊ na tug é .i. bagur is na buail.	2.b.1.67		87
1211	Tomus .i. tuairim.	12.b.11.40		87
1212	Torae		fec re	87

(*cont.*)

No.	Headword and entry	Entry reference	O'Curry's notes	MS fol.
1213	Toraidh .i. on torrachtain .i. tainig.	12.b.2.14		87
1214	Torgaibh .i. do rinne turgabail cionadh.	7.a.16.23		87
1215	Torla .i. naid[_]	10.10.16	10+	87
1216	Torlu .i. naidhm. ⁊ desmearacht air. cath fear fearta. ⁊ araile.	2.b.8.96	2+	87
1217	Tormac		fec formac	87
1218	Tósa .i. imdenadh, no mionnaighidh.	8.21.53		87
1219	Toxaigheadh on toxal no foxal.[11]	13.d.8.16		87
	.Dudly Forbesse.			87
1220	Treabaire dfirubhan .i. fulang.	5.a.6.23		87
1221	Treas bunsach bon loisg ar sgiath ngeal.	13.d.22.34		87
1222	Treas bunsach bonn ar sgiath ngeal ⁊c̄ i. mar budh eadh ⁊ sn beiread treas ann acht fallas comluth ngusgannail.	13.d.27.40	13+	88
	.Duil .r.			88
1223	Treathnach .i. trentonnach.	5.b.4.30		88
1224	Treathonn .i. tri treoin.	8.26.69		88
1225	Tregean, ditheach .i. séna.	7.b.4.58		88
1226	Treoir .i. eolus, no treoir do ni neach dfogluighibh.	1.a.15.36		88
1227	Tri briathra (an egcuinn .i. an mic big) do ni teastus no fiadhnuisi .i. an lion ceall, an la runradhach.	8.5.15		88
1228	Tri iomuire, no dire bios ag fulang na heaguilsi .i. céadrann, cuingeall, ⁊ udhbairt. céadrann .i. fleasg laimhe, ⁊ orba laimhe na manach fein do beanattar as coill ar na thiodhnacal da nerlamh o thosach. cuingeall .i. ni gealltar don eaglais isin cionuid do nithear ria. udbairt .i. fearann iodbrait na huasail na mbeathaidh iar ttrosgadh do dhia ⁊ dona naomhaibh.	5.b.13.41		88
1229	Tuaisitear .i. eistear, no leigidh fa na cluasaibh, no tairis gan fiarfhaidhe an ni do dhlighfeadh do denamh.	7.a.33.46		88
1230	Tuathgabail .i. gabail bios edir na da thuaith amhuil ataid hua eirc maighe la mumhuin.	1.b.7.65		88
1231	Tucht .i. gne.	12.b.27.61		88
1232	Tudhchaidh .i. do deachuidh.	4.c.25.122		89
1233	Tuidhchithear .i. teagar no tigtear.	1.b.21.106		89
1234	Tuidhin aosa eascána .i. targadh an lochta ná bí isin riagail	5.c.3.52		89
1235	Tuidin .i. cruinniughadh.	10.6.8		89
1236	Túidmeanar .i. ceangailtear.	8.32.85		89
1237	Tuidhmidhe .i. astuighthe.	10.39.91		89

11 This is how O'Curry transcribes the entry.

(*cont.*)

No.	Headword and entry	Entry reference	O'Curry's notes	MS fol.
1238	Tuilcheatol .i. ceatol toll.	2.a.17.61		89
1239	Tuinidh .i. orlaimh no [_]	10.6.8	10+	89
1240	Tuirchreic .i. ciothoiridh a neas .i. siochla .i. sort ion-muis bearar do mhnaoi i gcoibhche [_]	3.b.4.29	3+	89
1241	Tuireadh		fec medla	89
1242	Tuireann .i. cruithneacht.	10.29.58		89
1243	Tumhadh otraigh fri neach .i. giolla an chaca do radh ris, no a lethéid.	2.b.20.109		89
1244	Turbaid .i. leathsg[_] .i. ar na eallach.	2.a.5.21	2+	89
1245	Turgaire .i. tairriach .i. sgredheamlacht furailteach do beith ar amadan mighniomh do do denumh.	1.b.16.95		89
1246	Turlais [no tuluid] .i. luaidhis.	1.b.9.71		89
1247	Turtadh .i. egean .i. extortion.	13.d.26.39		89
1248	Turtgal .i. gail eigeantach bios ar mhnaoi re breith cloinne.	13.d.26.38		90
1249	Turtudh [.i. torthadh] righ .i. tornadh no glacadh do bheir righ ar mnaoi dá heigniughadh.	3.b.21.71		90
1250	Tuth .i. baladh.	4.c.21.111		90
	.U.			90
1251	Uadh .i. egsi.	4.c.7.48		90
1252	Uaincheann .i. fuan bhios mun cceann .i. srian.	9.26.82		90
1253	Uais .i. uasal, ionnsa, no annsa.	8.26.70		90
1254	Uathbhas .i. dubhaighead, no an luch eatorra, ⁊ a lene, no an earc luachra dona mnaibh beanus sin.	6.a.28.57		90
1255	Ubha, abha .i. abhainn.	5.b.4.31		90
1256	Uball fabhaill i. uball bios ar foishiubhal for a nuall for an tuinn .i. uball tuinne.	9.30.93		90
1257	Udbairt		fec tri iomuire	90
1258	Udbanar .i. iodhbartar.	8.36.101		90
1259	Uenite .i. tait.	2.b.7.91		90
1260	Uidhbreadh .i. guibhreath.	4.c.28.133		90
1261	Uinge [don egluis teid] diubaidh nuire .i. airgead uamha no leabtha .i. diubhaidh .i. adbal eibe na huire .i. i mbuain, no i ndenam na huaighe dona daoinibsi. deoraidh, murchuirte, faoindleadhaigh, furfograig, ⁊ taisdeallaigh, sin uatha maille seacht bairgin.	6.a.15.32		90–91
1262	Uintsi .i. annso.	4.c.9.59		91
1263	Uircria .i. creana .i. ceannach, criona, cailleach, no tearcá.	8.23.59		91
1264	Uma nu na cloithibh i. na mianach .i. on cloidhe .i. tochailt na tanalach .⁊c̄. .i. leaca.	14.d.6.19	14+	91
1265	Urconn .i. uasal chodnach.	6.a.31.69		91
1266	Urcorathar .i. athcuiritear .i. fadaightear.	14.b.3.5		91

(*cont.*)

No.	Headword and entry	Entry reference	O'Curry's notes	MS fol.
1267	Urfograch .i. fear bhios re denam uilc go ffogrann an tinbleoghan as neasa uaidh é .i. an lucht gaoil as goire dho.	11.a.21.28		91
1268	Urfograigh cuir ⁊ cunnarta .i. daoine danach coir car cunnradh sin, mar ata mac mna baith .⁊c̄. ⁊ ni inann sin ⁊ urfograigh leabtanusa .⁊c̄.	3.a.8.10		91
1269	Urfograigh leapandis .i. daoine danach coir leabaidh do thabhairt .i. daoine bhios i naghaidh dligheadh, ⁊ do ni sin urfograigh cuir ⁊ cunnartha diobh.	3.a.9.11		91
1270	Urfuigioll .i. ordughadh suidighte geall.	8.35.96		91
1271	Urgais .i. erguidhe uais.	3.a.7.9		92
1272	Urgartha .i. crosta.	8.8.23		92
1273	Urgnaightear .i. uasal fhoghaintear.	7.b.24.93		92
1274	Urgnam .i. urfhoghnam.	8.32.83		92
1275	Urlata .i. uasal laoite umhalóide.	4.c.14.85		92
1276	Urlata .i. uasal lúite.	8.32.86		92
1277	Urnasg .i. uasal fonasg. .Duil.r.	6.a.30.67		92
1278	Urnustur .i. baoi ag urnaighte.	12.b.1.11		92
1279	Urradus .i. cionta .i. air arátus .i. a chionta.	12.b.25.29		92
1280	Urthuasacht .i. eisteacht.	7.a.33.45		92
1281	Uruno .i. aire naoi .i. duine ar neach dfiadhnuise air no na diaigh.	4.c.17.94		92
1282	Utsadha .i. iostadha .i. aite soid no ionad comnuighe.	12.b.5.25		92

APPENDIX 1

Table of Correspondences across Glossaries

The following table lists the correspondences between the entries in Dubhaltach's Glossary and other glossaries cited in this volume. Some of the correspondences are just that and only bear a loose resemblance to the material in Dubhaltach's Glossary; some of the correspondences are exact. The point of the table is to provide readers with an overall sense of the number of entries which correspond to entries in other known glossaries and where there is overlap (or not) amongst them. Totals for each column can be found at the end of the table. For the abbreviations used in the table, see the list of abbreviations, pp. XII–XIII. For discussion of the individual glossaries, see the Introduction, pp. 32–40.

 | DOI:10.1163/9789004755673_008

MS ref.	Headword	O'Dav	O'Cl	DDC	SC	Lec. Gl.	Stowe Gl.	Metr. Gl.	MG	OM
1.a.4.9	Bán		×			×	×			
1.a.4.10	Mesio*ch*	×								
1.a.6.15	Corc		×			×		×		
1.a.7.18	Rod*h*aid*he*	×								
1.a.10.25	Áindlicet	×								
1.a.12.30	*Air*m*h*idin		×							
1.a.13.33	T*air*rsce	×								
1.a.15.35	Brec*h*tán		×							
1.a.18.42	Duibell	×	×	×						
1.a.18.43	Tap		×		×			×		
1.a.18.45	Tad*h*b*h*uis		×							
1.b.3.51	Andom*h*na	×								
1.b.4.54	Cobran*n*a gall		×		×					
1.b.5.56	Ceat*h*ra	×								
1.b.5.57	Lias caor*a*c[h]		×							
1.b.5.58	Eic*h*las, ⁊ bacg*h*abail	×								
1.b.7.66	Aclaig*he*	×								
1.b.8.67	Acluig*h*ed*h*	×								
1.b.8.68	Tallaid		×							
1.b.10.75	Duin*n*	×								
1.b.10.76	Aib*h*riteod*h*		×							
1.b.11.80	Dúisi	×	×							
1.b.12.81	Ocmoda	×								
1.b.12.84	Bad*h*ad*h*	×								
1.b.15.91	Góla									
1.b.21.105	Áonm*h*ais		×							
2.a.1.1	Br*i*ogac*h*	×								
2.a.1.3	I*ar*doc[h]	×	×							
2.a.2.6	Foichmen	×								
2.a.2.8	Ca*om*nac*ht*	×								
2.a.3.10	*Secht*[mad] fuit*h*rib*h*e									
2.a.3.11	Mu*r*t[h]or*adh*		×							
2.a.4.12	[Toisgi]d*h*									
2.a.4.14	Toc*h*m*ustar*	×								
2.a.4.15	Im-toigren[n]	×								
2.a.4.16	For-nesa	×								
2.a.5.17	R*us*	×	×	×						
2.a.5.18	Rosa	×								
2.a.5.20	Con-a*m*ad*hair*									
2.a.6.22	[Eallach]ta	×								
2.a.6.24	Fuasnad*h*	×								
2.a.7.25	An*mchair*des									
2.a.8.28	Ruid*h*bec*h*	×								
2.a.8.30	Di-ciallat[h]*ar*	×								

Ir. Gl.	BND *Gl.*	*Cotaimside Gl.*	*Ni Tulach Gl.*	*Breth Gl.*	*Arra Gl.*	*Adhmad Gl.*	*Dúil Laithne*	*Fonnaidh Gl.*	*Egerton 158*	*Mat Gl.*
×										
	×									
	×									
	×									
	×									
	×									
	×									
		×								
	×									
	×									

(*cont.*)

MS ref.	Headword	O'Dav	O'Cl	DDC	SC	*Lec. Gl.*	*Stowe Gl.*	*Metr. Gl.*	MG	OM
2.a.8.31	Lénaid*h*	×								
2.a.9.32	*Ar*dblor caim*h*e	×								
2.a.9.33	I*n*dlem*h*	×								
2.a.9.34	De*ar*la	×								
2.a.9.35	Duab*ar*	×								
2.a.10.36	Rélug*adh*		×							
2.a.10.37	Ind*edh*ad		×							
2.a.11.40	Faosam*h*	×	×							
2.a.12.41	Faosam*h*	×	×							
2.a.14.52	Codaig*h*e	×								
2.a.15.53	Giab*air* ł ciabair	×	×		×					
2.a.15.55	⟨Condo⟩ tescm*ar*r	×								
2.a.16.59	Sgor	×								
2.a.17.60	Sgot*h*	×	×			×				
2.a.17.64	To*ch*mag*h*ad	×								
2.a.18.65	To*ch*m*ustar*	×								
2.a.18.66	Mainbt*h*ec*h*	×								
2.b.2.69	Mandrad*h*	×	×							
2.b.2.72	Násad*h*	×	×							
2.b.2.73	Clú	×								
2.b.3.74	F*air*be									
2.b.3.75	T*air*im	×								
2.b.3.76	Clot*h*a*ch*	×								
2.b.3.77	*Ar*b*har*	×								
2.b.3.78	*Air*b*h*re		×							
2.b.5.84	For-randa*r*	×								
2.b.6.86	Cloth*ar* cloat*har*		×							
2.b.7.93	Rud*h*ra*ch*	×	×		×					
2.b.8.95	Cuit*hch*uire te*chta*	×								
2.b.8.96	Torla	×								
2.b.10.97	Coimdid*h*	×								
2.b.11.98	For ton dire		×							
2.b.16.102	4 Coimdig*h* raite	×								
2.b.20.107	*Air*íasa*cht*	×								
3.a.7.9	U*r*gais	×								
3.b.5.33	Tion*n*sgra		×							
3.b.6.34	Slab*h*ra tobra		×							
3.b.8.38	Cutai*m*	×								
3.b.11.46	Din*n*is	×	×					×		
3.b.11.48	Dait*h*in	×								×
3.b.13.54	Sleit*h tar* lónlaingen	×								
3.b.18.63	Maccaille*ch*	×								
3.b.20.68	Lam*h*c*h*om*air*t	×								

Ir. Gl.	BND *Gl.*	*Cotaimside Gl.*	*Ni Tulach Gl.*	*Breth Gl.*	*Arra Gl.*	*Adhmad Gl.*	*Dúil Laithne*	*Fonnaidh Gl.*	*Egerton 158*	*Mat Gl.*
			×	×						
			×		×					

(*cont.*)

MS ref.	Headword	O'Dav	O'Cl	DDC	SC	*Lec. Gl.*	*Stowe Gl.*	*Metr. Gl.*	MG	OM
3.b.20.70	Basc		×							
3.b.21.71	Tartadh ⟨.i. tortadh⟩ righ	×	×							×
3.b.22.74	Cuitil	×								
3.b.22.75	Meam*m*	×	×		×					×
3.b.25.81	Frit*h*bert breit*he*...	×	×							
3.b.36.91	Cosg n-urcuil					×				
4.b.8.12	Mem n-aisi		×		×					×
4.b.14.22	Mera*cht*	×								
4.b.22.33	Am*hnus*		×							
4.b.22.35	Aid*hche* iodn*aidh*e		×							
4.c.1.36	Fer reime		×							
4.c.3.39	Nos	×	×	×	×					
4.c.4.40	Diog*h*uin	×								
4.c.4.41	Tlenam*h*ain *cét*m*uint*ire neic*h*	×								
4.c.4.42	Dia*mh*ui*n*	×	×			×				
4.c.6.47	L*eth*m*h*io*m*asg	×								
4.c.8.55	Ad-nesa	×								
4.c.8.57	Miod*h*b*h*a	×		×						×
4.c.9.58	Miod*h*b*h*a	×		×						×
4.c.9.59	Uintsi	×								
4.c.9.60	Cuinni*us*	×								
4.c.9.61	Datán	×	×					×		
4.c.10.62	Dat*h*nait	×						×		
4.c.10.66	Iorcaid*h*	×								
4.c.11.71	Elge		×							
4.c.12.73	Boimbil, boim	×								
4.c.12.75	Néth	×	×		×					
4.c.13.77	Iomorran*n*		×							
4.c.13.78	Lia	×								
4.c.13.79	Lia	×								
4.c.13.80	D*r*uis	×								
4.c.13.81	Guirn		×		×					
4.c.14.82	N*ár*		×							
4.c.14.83	D*e*rosg	×								
4.c.14.84	Fochrac*h*	×								
4.c.14.85	Urlata	×	×							
4.c.15.86	Dimsi				×					
4.c.16.88	Buasac*h*	×								
4.c.17.93	Foircit*h*er	×								
4.c.20.105	Ainb*h*fét*h*	×								
4.c.20.106	D*r*eteall	×								
4.c.20.107	Bainteoluid	×	×							
4.c.20.108	Fur	×								

Ir. Gl.	BND *Gl.*	*Cotaimside Gl.*	*Ni Tulach Gl.*	*Breth Gl.*	*Arra Gl.*	*Adhmad Gl.*	*Dúil Laithne*	*Fonnaidh Gl.*	*Egerton 158*	*Mat Gl.*
						×				
						×				

(*cont.*)

MS ref.	Headword	O'Dav	O'Cl	*DDC*	SC	*Lec. Gl.*	*Stowe Gl.*	*Metr. Gl.*	*MG*	OM
4.c.20.109	Tai	×								
4.c.21.110	Fu*r*eg	×								
4.c.22.112	Con-cle*ch*	×								
4.c.22.113	Ad-cuitig*h*	×								
4.c.23.116	Lait*h*		×							
4.c.23.117	Tet*h*raig*h*	×								
4.c.24.118	Loc[h]*rann* ⁊ loic*het*	×								
4.c.26.127	Mi*us*cait*h*	×	×		×	×				
4.c.26.128	Biolf*h*ot*h*a*ch*	×								
4.c.26.129	Gre*ch*				×					
4.c.28.135	[In]oimblig*h*	×								
5.a.1.4	M*ai*rn		×							
5.a.2.12	Eislis									
5.a.2.13	Combac*h*		×							
5.a.4.15	Ad-bo	×								
5.a.6.21	Dérac*h*									
5.a.6.22	Glin*ne*									
5.b.2.27	Iorcha, i*ar* c*h*a	×	×	×	×					
5.b.4.30	Tret*h*nac*h*									
5.b.4.34	Ruib*h*en	×								
5.b.5.38	Deoin	×								
5.b.6.39	Coic, coc*aire*, fert*h*ig*h*is		×							
5.b.13.41	T*r*i iomar*e*…									
5.b.16.43	7 Caogdac[h]	×								
5.b.22.45	Fet*h*aol	×								
5.c.1.47	Díre*ch*, ⁊ dera*ch*	×								
5.c.3.53	Ealgn*us*	×								
6.a.2.2	R[uice,] ruca	×			×	×				
6.a.2.3	Bos		×							
6.a.2.4	Eallac*h*		×							
6.a.3.5	[Cicht]	×		×	×					
6.a.3.7	Culma[i]*re*		×		×	×	×	×		
6.a.3.10	Gnae	×	×							
6.a.4.13	Bert	×								
6.a.4.17	Breas	×								
6.a.5.19	I*ar*ngl*us*	×								
6.a.6.23	Sging		×		×	×				
6.a.6.24	Imsging				×					
6.a.9.26	At[h]*air* an*n*oide		×							
6.a.22.39	Coinsi		×							
6.a.22.40	Tet*h*natt*ar*									
6.a.23.42	Bit*h*		×			×				
6.a.24.46	Ceobat*h*	×								

Ir. Gl.	BND *Gl.*	*Cotaimside Gl.*	*Ni Tulach Gl.*	*Breth Gl.*	*Arra Gl.*	*Adhmad Gl.*	*Dúil Laithne*	*Fonnaidh Gl.*	*Egerton 158*	*Mat Gl.*
								×		
			×		×					
								×		
				×						
			×							
			×							
			×		×					
			×		×					
							×			
								×		
								×		
									×	

(*cont.*)

MS ref.	Headword	O'Dav	O'Cl	*DDC*	SC	*Lec. Gl.*	*Stowe Gl.*	*Metr. Gl.*	*MG*	OM
6.a.26.53	An*m*chaide	×								
6.a.26.54	Fubtad*h*	×	×							
6.a.31.68	Taisealb*adh*		×							
6.a.33.74	*Árchú* lom*h*na		×							
6.a.33.75	Ruib do-meal*ar*									
6.a.34.76	Ruib na doi*m*eal*ar*									
6.a.34.77	Féisi	×								
6.b.1.90	Aill	×				×				
6.b.2.91	Tem*h*ad temr*a*c*h*a	×								
7.a.1.1	Feiste	×								
7.a.1.2	Bá		×							
7.a.2.3	I*m*be*d*	×							×	
7.a.3.4	Déiste	×								
7.a.4.6	Gu*ai*riug*hadh*									
7.a.6.7	T*ar*gad		×							
7.a.6.8	F*air*ge	×								
7.a.7.9	Aid*h*ilgn*ech*									
7.a.7.10	Aid*h*b*h*en	×	×						×	
7.a.8.11	Fórm*a*c[h] ⁊ tórm*a*c[h]		×							
7.a.10.13	Meallac*h*		×							
7.a.10.14	Dinnis	×	×					×		
7.a.11.15	Ioc*h*t				×					
7.a.12.18	Brot*h*sguad*h*	×								×
7.a.14.20	Fúirest*ar*	×								
7.a.14.21	Biora									
7.a.15.22	Briog*h* ⁊ briog*h*t[h]*ar*	×								
7.a.17.24	Sochla	×	×							
7.a.17.25	Eisil		×							
7.a.18.26	Cám*h*			×						
7.a.22.31	Sas*ar*	×								
7.a.22.32	Don*n*	×								
7.a.23.33	Do*nn*uig*h*e, don*nach*	×								
7.a.24.36	Culpait			×	×					
7.a.25.37	Bít*h*		×			×				
7.a.26.38	Faot*h*, aot*h*		×					×		
7.a.33.45	Urt*h*uasac*ht*					×				
7.b.2.51	Rae		×							
7.b.2.52	Naisi		×							
7.b.3.53	Cam		×		×					
7.b.3.54	Cai*mper*	×	×		×					
7.b.3.55	Diam*h*ain	×	×		×					
7.b.4.57	Ime*dh*				×					×
7.b.4.58	Tregan, dit*h*e*ch*		×							

Ir. Gl.	BND *Gl.*	*Cotaimside Gl.*	*Ni Tulach Gl.*	*Breth Gl.*	*Arra Gl.*	*Adhmad Gl.*	*Dúil Laithne*	*Fonnaidh Gl.*	*Egerton 158*	*Mat Gl.*
										×
										×
						×				
			×		×					
			×		×					
			×		×					
									×	
			×		×					
									×	

(*cont.*)

MS ref.	Headword	O'Dav	O'Cl	DDC	SC	*Lec. Gl.*	*Stowe Gl.*	*Metr. Gl.*	MG	OM
7.b.5.59	Feraid	×								
7.b.6.60	Roch*air*	×								
7.b.7.62	Laob*h*	×	×							
7.b.8.63	No*m*ad*h* nó		×							
7.b.8.64	Fém*edh*		×							
7.b.10.65	Re toe torae		×							
7.b.10.66	Du*ar*	×	×		×					
7.b.12.69	Ada-bon*n*	×								
7.b.12.70	Ad-bois	×								
7.b.12.71	Díuirb	×								
7.b.13.72	Eítnge		×							×
7.b.13.73	As-roib	×								
7.b.15.75	Boibre	×								
7.b.16.76	Buicne	×								
7.b.17.77	Boicmell	×								
7.b.18.79	Aille		×							
7.b.19.81	Esomain	×								
7.b.19.82	Naoill	×								
7.b.20.83	Colt*ra*	×								
7.b.20.84	Dion*n*ba	×								
7.b.21.85	Ailtl*eth*an con*ar*e		×							
7.b.22.86	Sesaid	×								
7.b.22.87	Cec*h*latt*ar*	×								
7.b.23.89	Conóad		×							
7.b.23.90	Slatra ⁊ lat*ra*		×							
7.b.24.91	Frepad*h*	×	×							
7.b.24.92	Seg*ar*	×								
7.b.25.95	Sias									
7.b.26.96	Fúac*har*									
7.b.27.98	Con-amad*hair*									
7.b.28.99	Inm*h*uille, muill*edh*		×							
7.b.29.100	Báoidsioc*h*	×								
7.b.30.102	Talmuidioc*h*	×								
7.b.31.103	Terbsad	×								
7.b.32.104	Aoib*h*ilteoir	×								
7.b.33.105	Seol		×							
7.b.34.109	F*edh*id*h*									
7.b.35.111	Fresl*uig*e	×								
8.2.6	[D]roc*h*		×							
8.2.7	Faor	×								
8.12.32	Feiles*a*c[h]	×								
8.13.35	Fo-coisle	×								
8.14.36	Meadb*ha*	×								

Ir. Gl.	BND *Gl.*	*Cotaimside Gl.*	*Ni Tulach Gl.*	*Breth Gl.*	*Arra Gl.*	*Adhmad Gl.*	*Dúil Laithne*	*Fonnaidh Gl.*	*Egerton 158*	*Mat Gl.*
			×	×	×					
			×		×					
								×		
								×		
								×		
		×								
		×	×							
			×		×					

(*cont.*)

MS ref.	Headword	O'Dav	O'Cl	DDC	SC	*Lec. Gl.*	*Stowe Gl.*	*Metr. Gl.*	MG	OM
8.14.37	Mead*h*		×					×		
8.14.38	Dána các*h* go h-iat*h*							×		
8.18.43	Sruaim	×				×				
8.18.44	Taoi, taoiet*us*		×							
8.18.45	Derlait*h*er	×								
8.18.46	Esges		×							
8.19.47	Roeach	×								
8.19.48	Clot*h*		×				×			
8.21.54	Muire[dh]ac*h*	×								
8.22.55	Nodh	×	×							
8.22.56	Con*á*rd*h*ata	×								
8.22.57	Manda m*air*m*h*esa	×	×							
8.23.58	N*á*r	×	×							
8.23.59	Uircria		×							
8.24.64	Imitec[h]t	×								
8.25.65	Coindfe	×	×	×						
8.25.66	Fiad*h*at		×							
8.25.68	Ro-sgot[h]		×		×	×				
8.26.69	Tret*h*o*nn*	×	×							
8.26.70	Uais		×							
8.27.72	Ro-ná	×								
8.27.73	Déis		×							
8.27.74	Beab*h*ais		×							
8.27.75	Bert	×								
8.31.82	Daon	×								
8.32.83	Urgna*m*		×							
8.32.86	Urlata	×	×							
8.34.90	Sern*ar*	×								
8.34.91	Fáonán	×	×							
8.34.92	Annac*h*	×	×							
8.34.93	Fuada	×								
8.35.95	Fuigeall		×							
8.36.100	Feat*h*al	×	×		×					
8.37.103	Slatra					×				
9.1.1	Clu	×								
9.2.5	Siride	×								
9.2.7	Cuirioc*h* [.]occe	×								
9.4.11	Lait*h*, lat*hach*	×	×							
9.5.12	Cec*hair*	×	×							
9.6.15	Tacomal	×	×						×	
9.7.18	[Im]toi*n*git	×								
9.7.19	Andom*h*na	×								
9.8.24	Áin	×	×							

Ir. Gl.	BND *Gl.*	*Cotaimside Gl.*	*Ni Tulach Gl.*	*Breth Gl.*	*Arra Gl.*	*Adhmad Gl.*	*Dúil Laithne*	*Fonnaidh Gl.*	*Egerton 158*	*Mat Gl.*
								×		
			×		×					

(*cont.*)

MS ref.	Headword	O'Dav	O'Cl	DDC	SC	*Lec. Gl.*	*Stowe Gl.*	*Metr. Gl.*	MG	OM
9.8.26	Friosg*ar*t		×							
9.9.30	Filc	×								
9.9.31	Ága ⟨ł ionag*h*a⟩	×								
9.11.35	Aig, taig	×								
9.13.37	Ruib do-meal*ar*									
9.13.38	Ruib ná to-meal*ar*									
9.14.40	Íre	×	×							
9.14.41	M*é*t na n-irean*n*	×	×							
9.14.42	Buirisg	×								
9.15.45	Cátaid*h*		×							
9.15.46	Odh*ar*	×								
9.16.47	Bradaid*h*	×								
9.16.48	Lios		×							
9.17.51	Indorsa	×								
9.17.52	Medla, máda, rac*ht*, sas, féis, ⁊ tuir*edh*	×	×							
9.18.56	Ingelt		×							
9.19.58	Cl*ethe* lui	×	×							
9.19.59	Me*dh*ontaid*h*e lui	×	×							
9.20.60	Lú lui	×	×							
9.20.61	Fuirir*edh* lui	×	×							
9.21.62	Ag*h*		×							
9.21.63	*Et*, ed		×							
9.21.64	Ima-dic*h*et	×								
9.23.68	Feis ⟨i bfeis⟩	×								
9.25.74	Ed*á*rb*h*a	×								
9.25.76	Fagh	×								
9.25.77	Der*us*g	×								
9.25.78	Cutai*m*	×								
9.26.79	Cit									×
9.26.80	Cit*r*iog*h*a		×							
9.29.89	Tl*us*	×								
9.30.92	Solam*h*		×							
9.33.99	F*r*i*the* raite	×								
9.34.100	Fri*th*e roead*h*a no s*h*leb*h*e	×								
9.35.103	Ollob*hair* aigsi*n*	×								
9.36.107	Miod*h*bac*h*	×								
9.38.110	Da*rm*na	×								
9.38.111	*Air*m i ttot*h*	×								
9.38.112	Mad ois	×								
9.39.116	Coiccenuid	×	×		×					
9.39.117	At*h*rola	×								
9.42.127	Ad*h*ma		×							

Ir. Gl.	BND *Gl.*	*Cotaimside Gl.*	*Ni Tulach Gl.*	*Breth Gl.*	*Arra Gl.*	*Adhmad Gl.*	*Dúil Laithne*	*Fonnaidh Gl.*	*Egerton 158*	*Mat Gl.*
										×
										×

(*cont.*)

MS ref.	Headword	O'Dav	O'Cl	DDC	SC	*Lec. Gl.*	*Stowe Gl.*	*Metr. Gl.*	MG	OM
9.43.132	Tion*n*sg*ra*		×							
9.43.133	Tiasg	×								
9.44.134	Com*h*lun*n*	×								
9.44.137	Cuim*h*lec*h*ta	×								
10.5.5	Fo*r*ng*aire*		×							
10.6.7	Tat*h*ad									
10.7.11	Cui*nn*dfec[h]	×			×					
10.10.16	Torla	×								
10.12.22	Lait*hrech* laig*h*en	×								
10.13.26	Foilngid*h*	×								
10.14.30	Cot-ris*edh*	×								
10.15.32	Con-reis	×								
10.17.40	Indisi						×			
10.17.42	Cana	×	×							
10.17.44	Cirde	×								
10.20.50	Doc*htair*	×								
10.20.52	Muiltt*er*	×								
10.21.54	5 An*manna* cat su*nn*	×			×					
10.29.61	⟨Buicne⟩	×								
10.29.64	Du*mh*a	×								
10.38.83	Taid*hc*ria	×								
10.38.84	Iom*arr*	×								
10.38.85	Acht	×								
10.38.86	Cías*ar*	×								
10.39.91	Tuid*h*mid*he*	×								
10.40.96	Meisi	×			×					
10.42.104	Blaid*h*re	×								
10.44.111	Sen*arus*g		×							
10.45.116	Sern*ar*	×								
10.45.118	Forng*ai*re		×							
11.a.3.4	Annoit		×							
11.a.5.6	Escom*h*an, iongglan	×								
11.a.9.12	Ro-negam	×								
11.a.10.15	Daorm*h*anac*h*	×								
11.a.22.30	Deor*adh* freacair	×								
11.a.27.31	Faic*h*ill		×							
11.b.11.44	Be c(*h*)*ar*na	×								
12.b.2.13	*Air*c[h]ennc[h]a		×							
12.b.2.15	Fert*ar*	×								
12.b.2.16	Creadal	×	×				×			
12.b.3.19	Fec*h*aid		×							
12.b.3.20	Ailed*h*		×							
12.b.4.21	Fionn		×							

Ir. Gl.	BND *Gl.*	*Cotaimside Gl.*	*Ni Tulach Gl.*	*Breth Gl.*	*Arra Gl.*	*Adhmad Gl.*	*Dúil Laithne*	*Fonnaidh Gl.*	*Egerton 158*	*Mat Gl.*
								×		
			×		×					

(*cont.*)

MS ref.	Headword	O'Dav	O'Cl	*DDC*	*SC*	*Lec. Gl.*	*Stowe Gl.*	*Metr. Gl.*	*MG*	OM
12.b.4.22	Caoim*hth*ias *nó* caoim*hth*es		×							
12.b.5.24	Fon*n* fri fon*n*	×								
12.b.5.26	Sgiolla	×	×			×		×		
12.b.6.29	Terbad*h*		×							
12.b.6.30	Frecur	×								
12.b.8.34	Luig*h*e cana		×							
12.b.20.51	Gníad*h*		×							
12.b.25.57	G*r*in, g*r*iun		×							
12.b.25.58	Im-ruim*ethar*	×								
12.b.26.60	Iomglan mis…		×							
12.b.27.61	Tu*cht*							×		
12.b.28.65	Lias		×							
13.b.2.7	Indul	×								
13.d.5.13	Cresion	×								
13.d.5.14	Leam*h*ad*h*	×								
13.d.10.18	Iatiaig*h*	×								
13.d.10.19	Tigseal	×								
13.d.11.20	Fo-coisle	×								
13.d.11.21	Reac*h*oll mBr*eth*	×								
13.d.18.29	Cuic*h* apa nos m*ar*ba									
13.d.26.39	Turtad	×								×
14.b.4.6	Coic[h]	×								
14.b.4.7	Dunn	×								
14.b.4.8	Líog*h*	×								
14.d.9.21	Cróc*h*				×					
14.d.9.22	Croc*h*	×								
14.f.13.25	Serg, ⁊ macra	×								
14.h.1.28	Foguirre, dog*h*uirre	×								
14.h.12.35	Déisde, fesd*h*ide, no esdide	×								
14.h.19.39	Fuaichne fog*h*la	×								
OC.1	Elg				×					
Total		**276**	**158**	**10**	**33**	**17**	**5**	**12**	**3**	**11**

Ir. Gl.	BND *Gl.*	*Cotaimside Gl.*	*Ni Tulach Gl.*	*Breth Gl.*	*Arra Gl.*	*Adhmad Gl.*	*Dúil Laithne*	*Fonnaidh Gl.*	*Egerton 158*	*Mat Gl.*
							×			
1	8	3	17	3	13	3	2	9	3	4

APPENDIX 2

Table of Textual Blocks and Entry Numbers

Below is a table indicating the major textual blocks found within Dubhaltach's Glossary. The table has columns for any of the sources named in the glossary, where the source appears in the MS (see also Appendix 4, pp. 447–449), the glossary entry groups, and whether those entries have correspondences with material found in *CIH* and/or other textual sources. Many of the cells in the 'Text' column are empty because Dubhaltach was using texts which are no longer extant or for which the source could not be found. When a cell has been left empty, it indicates that there is no information for that particular category. *CIH* ranges provided are estimates; some of the entries skip around within the textual blocks and jump back and forth between extant versions of some of the legal texts. There are also textual gaps within some of the runs, i.e. some of the material is not found within the surrounding text as printed in *CIH*. The sources listed on the table are only those which have significant blocks within the glossary or whose source is named in the glossary itself. See the edited text for full details. The source abbreviations are expanded in Appendix 4. It should be noted that it is not always clear how far an identification can be applied to a block of entries; this is especially true with material following the abbreviation for *Dúil* (*Roscadach*) because so little of that text survives.

Source named in DG	MS location	Entry Run	*CIH* correspondence	Text
		1.a.1.1–1.a.12.30		
		1.a.12.31–1.a.15.36	78.14, 66.37, 75.15, 67.11, 73.36, 579.16, and 198.19	*Bretha Comaithchesa*
		1.a.15.37–1.a.18.45		
		1.b.1.46–1.b.22.107		
[b].n.	2a, l. 1	2.a.1.1–2.a.18.66	1111.1–1114.11	*Bretha Nemed Dédenach*
d.r.	2b, l. 1	2.b.1.67–2.b.23.112		*Dúil* (*Roscadach*)
		2.b.11.99–2.b.18.105	56.30–58.33	*Heptad 64*[1]
			314.21	

1 The entries overlap with material also found in Heptad 64.

 | DOI:10.1163/9789004755673_009

(*cont.*)

Source named in DG	MS location	Entry Run	*CIH* correspondence	Text
		2.b.20.106–2.b.20.107		*Muirbretha/Bretha Éitgid*[2]
		3.a.1.1–3.a.14.22		
D.R.	3b, l. 1	3.b.1.23–3.b.39.97		*Dúil* (*Roscadach*)
		4.a.1.1		
		4.b.1.2–4.b.22.35	145.33–146.40	*Tract on Marriage and Divorce*
b.n.	4c, l. 1	4.c.1.36–4.c.28.136	1114.20–1117.35 1118.2–1120.11	*Bretha Nemed Dédenach*
e[id]*gedh*	5a, l. 1	5.a.1.1–5.a.6.24		*Bretha Éitgid*
⟨*edgedh*⟩	5b, l. 2	5.b.1.25–5.b.3.29	265.14 and 267.28	*Bretha Éitgid*
Duil .r.	5b, l. 4	5.b.4.30–5.b.5.37		*Dúil* (*Roscadach*)
⟨*edgedh*⟩	5b, l. 5	5.b.5.38–5.b.22.46	864.25	*Bretha Éitgid*
edghedh	5c, l. 1	5.c.1.47–5.c.8.61	1175.9, 275.4, 322.34	*Bretha Éitgid*
		6.a.1.1–6.a.2.3		
		6.a.2.4–6.a.4.13	1117.37–1117.42	*Bretha Nemed Dédenach*
		6.a.4.14–6.a.4.16		
		6.a.4.17–6.a.6.24	2213.38–2214.3	*Bretha Nemed Toísech*
		6.a.7.25–6.a.20.38		
[*ed*]*gedh*	6a, l. 22	6.a.22.39–6.a.37.84	937.22	*Bretha Éitgid*
duil .r.	6b, l. 1	6.b.1.87–6.b.3.96		*Dúil* (*Roscadach*)
		7.a.1.1–7.b.4.56		
édgedh	7b, l. 4	7.b.4.57–7.b.7.61		*Bretha Éitgid*
édgedh	7b, l. 7[3]	7.b.7.62–7.b.8.64		*Bretha Éitgid*
		7.b.10.65–7.b.18.79	1121.39–1122.16	*Bretha Nemed Dédenach*
		7.b.12.69–7.b.21.85[4]	1381.4–1382.3	*Digest B* (*56*)
		7.b.22.86–7.b.23.90		
eid*gedh*	7b, l. 24	7.b.24.91–7.b.26.96	1163.13, 1163.17–19, 325.23 ff., 1212.35 ff., and 2283.1 ff.	*Bretha Éitgid*
duil	7b, l. 26	7.b.26.97–7.b.27.98		*Dúil* (*Roscadach*)
duil	7b, l. 28[5]			
eid*gedh*	7b, l. 28	7.b.28.99–7.b.32.104	1177.9, 1180.23	*Bretha Éitgid*

2 The entries overlap with material also found in *Muirbretha/Bretha Éitgid*.

3 This word seems to bookend the previous block of entries.

4 Note that entry 7.b.18.80 has not been traced to the surrounding source text.

5 This word seems to bookend the previous block of entries.

(*cont.*)

Source named in DG	MS location	Entry Run	*CIH* correspondence	Text
duil	7b, *intercol.*, l. 33	7.b.33.105–7.b.36.112[6]		*Dúil* (*Roscadach*)
		8.1.1–8.7.20		
		8.7.21–8.8.23	45.3–45.4	*Heptad 49*
		8.8.23–8.12.33	1421.18–1422.2	*Citations on those who cannot act as a witness*
		8.13.34–8.37.103		
aibgider crab*ad*	8, l. 38	8.38.104		*Apgitir Chrábaid*
IS é b.n	9, l. 1	9.1.1–9.1.2	1130.11, 1129.24	*Bretha Nemed Dédenach*
		9.1.3–9.3.9		
coir an*mann* si*n*	9, l. 4	9.3.10		*Cóir Anmann*
d.r.	9, l. 4	9.4.11–9.11.35		*Dúil* (*Roscadach*)
edgaid	9, l. 11	9.12.36–9.47.144	276.3	*Bretha Éitgid*
		9.17.53–9.25.76	75.17, 578.1[7]	*Bretha Comaithchesa*
		9.32.96–9.35.103	55.18, 906.35, 1211.22, and 1853.21–22	*Heptad 64*
		10.1.1–10.5.4	2168.28, 2169.4–6, 712.13	*Aidbred*
		10.5.5–10.13.25		
		10.13.26–10.21.53	312.35–37	*Bretha Éitgid*
			111.22, 1389.27, 1390.25	*Bretha for Conṡlechtaib*
		10.21.54	See edited text and pp. 50–55	*Bretha for Catṡlechtaib*
		10.28.55–10.31.69		
		10.31.70–10.48.121	995.15, 1348.24–1357.1, 1196.36–1198.8, 1358.17–38	*Di Astud Chor*
[li]b*er*.2.	11a, l. 1			
		11.a.1.1		

6 Due to the placement of the word *dúil*, it is impossible to determine how many of these entries should be associated with that text.

7 See the edited text for details; the citations skip around.

(*cont.*)

Source named in DG	MS location	Entry Run	*CIH* correspondence	Text
*ed*ged	11a, l. 2	11.a.1.2–11.a.28.34	1156. 37, 1399. 17, 1156.39, 1399.22–35, 1157.6, 1399.28, 1157.14–15, 1399.36–37, 1157.15–16, 1399.36–37, 307.12–19, 1629.30–1630.3, 1639.12–23, 1400.21–32, 307.33, 1630.23, 1639.41, 1401.15, 307.35, 1630.25, 1640.1, 1401.18	*Bretha Éitgid*
		11.b.2.35–12.a.10.10		*Categories of Women*
duil .r.	12b, l. 1	12.b.1.11–12.b.30.70		*Dúil* (*Roscadach*)
	13.a.1–13.a.3			*Poem and entry on epilepsy*
		13.a.4.1–13.a.12.6		
		13.b.2.7		
	13.c.1			*Seven things which distance one from learning*
Sen*chas*	13e, l. 1	13.d.1.8–13.d.27.40	370.22–387.5	*Cethairṡlicht Athgabálae*
[Dubhaltach's name]	14a, ll. 1–3			
		14.b.1.1–14.b.4.10		
		14.c.1.11–14.c.3.13		
		14.c.4.14–14.d.6.19	363.33, 390.20–36	*Cethairṡlicht Athgabálae*
		14.d.8.20–14.d.10.23		
[Dubhaltach's name]	14e, l. 1			
		14.f.1.24–14.f.16.26		
		14.g.1.27		
		14.h.1.28		
		14.h.2.29–14.h.12.35	1772.18–1776.18	*Cáin Ṡóerraith*
[c].f.	14h, l. 13	14.h.13.36	744.28–29	*Córus Fine*
c.f.	14h, l. 16	14.h.15.37	161.21–22[8]	*Córus Fine*
		14.h.17.38–14.h.24.45		

8 This passage in *CIH* has not been identified as coming from *Córus Fine*.

APPENDIX 3

List of Glossary Doublets

There are a number of entries in Dubhaltach's Glossary which appear to be doublets. It is worth gathering them together in one place as it can help lend further understanding of the overall structure of the glossary. Considering the amount of overlap in legal vocabulary across the texts, we should not be surprised to find at least some repeated entries, especially considering the fact that some of the headwords are accompanied by what appear to be the standard glosses for them.[1]

(a) Some of the entries are true doublets, such as 1.a.4.11 *Adbo*/5.a.4.15 *Adbo*; 1.b.3.51 *Andomhna*/9.7.19 *Andomhna*; 6.a.23.42 *Bith*/7.a.25.37 *Bíth*; 9.1.1 *Clu*/2.b.2.73 *Clú*; 6.a.35.81 *Coibhdealac*[*h*]/ 4.b.19.29 *Coibhdealach*; 8.6.18 *Comhad*/6.b.3.95 *Comhadh*; 3.b.8.38 *Cutaim*/9.25.78 *Cutaim*; 3.b.11.46 *Dinnis*/7.a.10.14 *Dinnis*; 8.13.33 *Eitsech*/12.b.7.32 *Eitsech*; 2.b.3.74 *Fairbe*/8.11.30 *Fairbe*; 9.8.23 *Faoth*/7.a.26.38 *Faoth, aoth*; 8.13.35 *Fo-coisle*/13.d.11.20 *Fo-coisle*; 10.5.5 *Forngaire*/10.45.118 *Forngaire*; 1.b.3.50 *Iomaigh*/6.a.30.65 *Iomaigh*; 7.a.24.35 *Oillían*/2.b.20.108 *Oillian, culpait*; 8.34.90 *Sernar*/10.45.116 *Sernar*; 4.b.2.5 [*Taoi*]/ 8.18.44 *Taoi, taoietus*; 4.c.24.121 *Tethn*[*a*]*tar*/6.a.22.40 *Tethnattar*; 3.b.5.33 *Tionnsgra*/9.43.132 *Tionnsgra*; 2.a.4.14 *Tochmustar*/2.a.18.65 *Tochmustar*; 10.10.16 *Torla*/2.b.8.96 *Torla*; 4.c.14.85 *Urlata*/8.32.86 *Urlata*.

(b) Some entries only appear to be so because they are homophones, e.g. 6.a.4.13 *Bert*/8.27.75 *Bert*.

(c) In some of the instances where pairs are found consecutively in the MS, it is a case of earlier glossators trying to differentiate homonyms, e.gg., 4.c.13.78 *Lia*/4.c.13.79 *Lia*; 1.b.11.77 *Seis*/1.b.11.78 *Seis*.

(d) In some cases, the doublets are really two different words entirely, e.gg., 1.a.4.12 *Aighe*/5.a.1.3 *Aighe*; 4.c.23.116 *Laith*/9.4.11 *Laith, lathach*.

(e) Sometimes we find the same headword, but the gloss assigns a different meaning within the headword's semantic range, e.gg., 10.38.85 *Acht*/14.b.2.2 *Acht*; 2.a.5.20 *Con-amadhair*/7.b.27.98 *Con-amadhair*; 7.b.3.55 *Diamhain*/4.c.4.42 *Diamhuin*; 8.36.100 *Feathal*/5.b.22.45 *Fethaol*; 1.b.15.91 *Góla*/5.b.4.32 *Góla*; 4.c.8.57 *Miodhbha*/4.c.9.58 *Miodhbha*; 4.c.14.82 *Nár*/8.23.58 *Nár*; 3.b.6.34 *Slabhra tobra*/9.43.131 *Slabhra, slaibhre*; 8.37.103 *Slatra*/7.b.23.

1 See the edition for textual notes.

 | DOI:10.1163/9789004755673_010

90 *Slatra* 7 *latra*; 6.a.23.44 *Taith*/10.41.97 *Tath*. In those instances, the translation reflects the difference in meaning assigned by the gloss. In other words, the translation of a word found in multiple entries might not be the same in every case.

(f) In a few instances, the doublets seem to come from the same ultimate source text, even if the slightly different spellings suggest Dubhaltach had access to different versions of the text or a secondary text, e.gg., 6.a.33.75 *Ruib do-mealar*/9.13.37 *Ruib do-mealar*; 6.a.34.76 *Ruib na doimealar*/ 9.13.38 *Ruib ná to-mealar*.

(g) In other instances, the issue is that the lemma is found in different forms in the source texts, and the entries themselves reflect that difference, e.gg., 9.31.94 *Ágha fine*/13.d.13.23 *Áighe fine*; 14.h.12.35 *Déisde, fesdhide, no esdide*/7.a.3.4 *Déiste*; 11.a.16.23 *Dergabad*/12.b.13.44 *Dergapad*; 4.c.14.83 *Derosg*/9.25.77 *Derusg*; 7.a.26.39 *Iardach*/2.a.1.3 *Iardoc*[*h*]; 9.6.15 *Tacomal*/ 1.a.16.38 *Tacomul*.

(h) Sometimes the lemma is the same, but is found in a different case, e.gg., 10.15.33 *Aptha*/6.a.33.73 *Ap*[*th*]*ain*; OC.1 *Elg*/4.c.11.71 *Elge*.[2]

(i) Finally, there are also a few doublets which arise due to the fact that Dubhaltach rewrote them after part of the MS was damaged, egg., 14.d.1.15 *Methir*/14.d.4.17 [*Methir*]; 14.d.3.16 *Rudh*/14.d.5.18 *Rudh*.

The list of doublets below does not take into account entries such as DG 2.a.7.27 *Fuirecht*, DG 8.13.34 *Fuiregar*, and DG 7.a.14.20 *Fúirestar* where, despite the difference in form of the headword, the gloss in all three entries is almost identical. These entries are cross-referenced to each other within the edited text. The list also does not include the series of entries which begin with the same word as part of a phrase, such as the series of entries beginning with *bé* 'woman', nor does it include runs of entries all from the same verb, such as those from *ad-boind* 'proclaims, gives notice'; these can be found in the alphabetical list of entries.

10.38.85 Acht .i. cu*nn*tab*a*rt.
Acht 'exception', i.e. doubt.

14.b.2.2 Acht .i. [a]chtug*adh* dlig*ed*.
Acht 'stipulation', i.e. a stipulation of law.

2 For the designation OC, see p. 68. The difference in case suggests that the entries derive from different sources.

1.a.4.11 Adbo .i. toibgel*us*.
Ad-bo 'may proclaim', i.e. [...]

5.a.4.15 Ad-bo .i. urfog*r*aid*h*.
Ad-bo 'may proclaim', i.e. proclaims.

9.31.94 Ág*h*a fine .i. óg*h* ae b*h*íus *ar* an ffine. Flait*h* gelf*h*ine sin.
Ágae fine 'head of a kindred', i.e. [< *óg* 'whole, complete, perfect' + *áe* 'of them'] complete one of them who is before the kindred. That is chief of the *gelḟine* 'kindred'.

13.d.13.23 Áig*h*e fine .i. cen*n*e fine.
Áige fine 'head of a kindred', i.e. heads of the kindred.

1.a.4.12 Aig*h*e .i. og*h* ae.
Áige 'head (of the family)', i.e. [< *óg* 'whole, complete, perfect' + *áe* 'of them'] complete one of them.

5.a.1.3 Aig*h*e .i. aimsir.
Áige 'time', i.e. point of time.

6.a.36.82 Am*h*uis rúin, ⁊ raid*h*, ⁊ iomagall[ma] .i. am*h*uis ⟨bid⟩ ma*r* si*n* ag tigerna.
Amuis ruin, ⁊ raid, ⁊ imacallma 'confidential, and conversational, and council attendants', i.e. attendants like that whom a lord has.

9.41.123 Am*hus* ala tuait*he* .i. deor*aidh*.
Amus ala túaithe 'hireling of another territory', i.e. an outsider.

1.b.3.51 Andom*h*na .i. inde doia*mh*ne isna cuit*h*ec*h*a .⁊c̄.
Andomna 'marshes', i.e. [< *1 inne* 'middle, center' + *domne* 'depth, depths'] center of depth in the pits, etc.

9.7.19 Andom*h*na .i. inde doi*m*ne.
Andomna 'marshes', i.e. [< *inne* 'center' + *domain* 'deep, depths'] middle of depth.

10.15.33 Apt*h*a .i. ebiltin.
Apthu 'death', i.e. death.

6.a.33.73 Ap[th]ain .i. ebiltin.
Apthain 'death', i.e. death.

6.a.4.13 Bert .i. br*eith*em*h*nus.
Bert 'judgement', i.e. judgement.

8.27.75 Bert .i. bri*th*em*hnaghth*is.
Bert 'he judged', i.e. he judged.

6.a.23.42 Bit*h* .i. guin.
Bíth 'wound', i.e. wound.

7.a.25.37 Bít*h* .i. gui*n*.
Bíth 'wound', i.e. wound.

9.1.1 Clu .i. u*r*dercad*h*.
Clú 'fame', i.e. making known.

2.b.2.73 Clú .i. urdc*e*rcad*h*.
Clú 'fame', i.e. making known.

6.a.35.81 Coib*h*dealac[h] [.i.] duine aga *m*bí coi*m*d*h*eala, no gaol re nec*h*.
Coibdelach 'relative', i.e. a person with whom there may be kinship, or a relationship with someone.

4.b.19.29 Coib*h*dealac*h* .i. duine ris a mbí coimfial*us*, no coi*m*dealac*hus* gaoil [no caradr]ad [a]g nec[h] [i n]geall fiac*h* .i. ben [bheith]as feic*h* ag h-in*n*e sec*h* a fer.
Coibdelach 'relative', i.e. a person with whom there may be kinship or relationship of kinship or alliance with someone for surety of fines, i.e. a woman will be an obligation by [this] reason in addition to her husband.

8.6.18 Com*h*ad .i. coi*mét*uid*h*.
Comad 'guarding', i.e. guarding.

6.b.3.95 Com*h*ad*h* .i. coi*m*[eada]d*h*.
Comad 'guarding', i.e. guarding.

2.a.5.20 Con-a*m*ad*hair* .i. ro coi*m*meisio*mnagh*est*har*.
Con-amadair 'has estimated', i.e. has jointly-estimated.

7.b.27.98 Con-amad*hair* .i. caoín no co*m*aimsig*h*ter.
Con-amadair 'had judged', i.e. [< *caín* 'well'] well or it is obtained.

3.b.8.38 Cutai*m* .i. co*m*t*h*uiti*m*.
Cutaim 'falling down', i.e. falling down.

9.25.78 Cutai*m* .i. tuiti*m*.
Cutaim 'falling down', i.e. falling.

14.h.12.35 Déisde, fesd*h*ide, no esdide .i. tioru*air*si .i. fuigioll.
Deistiu, festide, nó estide 'remnant, residuary legatee, or heir', i.e. remnant, i.e. remainder.

7.a.3.4 Déiste .i. déis as ed tioru*air*sin béos.
Deistiu 'remnant', i.e. a tenant who is still a remainder.

11.a.16.23 Dergabad .i. urfog*r*a de[th]nes*ac*[h] gan maill, ⁊ banabad*h*, ní ass maille inás.
Dergapaid 'harboring a person after they have committed a crime, lit. red harboring', i.e. proclaiming hastily without delay, and *bánapaid* 'harboring a person before they have committed a crime, lit. white harboring', it is not as urgent.

12.b.13.44 Dergap*ad* .i. an biath*adh iar* nden*am* cion*adh* do*n* ciontac[h].
Dergapaid 'red harboring', i.e. the feeding after a crime has been committed by the guilty party.

4.c.14.83 Derosg .i. derb*h*c*h*in*nedh*.
Derosc 'verdict', i.e. exact determination.

9.25.77 Der*usg* .i. cin*nedh* d*h*ireac*h*.
Derosc 'verdict', i.e. just penalty.

7.b.3.55 Diam*h*ain .i. diainim.
Diamuin 'unblemished', i.e. [< *dí-* negative prefix + *ainim* 'blemish, defect'] unblemished.

4.c.4.42 Dia*m*h*uin* .i. gl[an].
Diamuin 'spotless', i.e. clean.

3.b.11.46 Din*n*is .i. mion*n*a.
Dindis 'denial by oath', i.e. oaths.

7.a.10.14 Dinnis .i. mionna.
Dindis 'denial by oath', i.e. oaths.

8.13.33 Eitsec*h* .i. ré gan tec*h* aige.
Eistech 'houseless', i.e. anyone who does not have a house.

12.b.7.32 Eitsec*h* .i. duine gan tec*h*.
Eistech 'houseless', i.e. a person without a house.

OC.1 Elg .i. ere.
Elg 'Ireland', i.e. Ireland.

4.c.11.71 Elge .i. feran*n* no Elg .i. Ére.
Elge '[In] Ireland', i.e. land or *Elg*, i.e. *Ére* 'Ireland'.

2.b.3.74 F*air*be .i. fír éibe firin*narba*.
Fairbe 'a paid advocate', i.e. [< *fír* 'true' + *eipe* 'cutting'] faithful cutting [< *fír* 'true' + *indarba* 'expulsion, banishment, rejection'] of true-expelling.

8.11.30 F*air*be .i. fior eibe ut [est] fer f*air*be .i. fer fior eibe aoi .i. an fer bi*us* ag fior-ebe na cuisi i n-aig*idh* neic*h ar* log*h*.
Fairbe 'a paid advocate', i.e. [< *fír* 'true' + *eipe* 'selecting, cutting'] faithful cutting, *ut est* a person who advocates, i.e. a person who faithfully advocates a lawsuit, i.e. the person who faithfully advocates the case against someone for a fee.

9.8.23 Faot*h* .i. luig*h*e .i. min*n*a.
Fáeth 'oath', i.e. oath, i.e. oaths.

7.a.26.38 Faot*h*, aot*h* .i. mion*n*a.
Fáeth 'oath', *óeth* 'oath', i.e. oaths.

8.36.100 Feat*h*al .i. mion*n*, egc*us*c.
Fethal 'appearance', i.e. distinguishing characteristic, appearance.

5.b.22.45 Fet*h*aol .i. mion*n*, ma*r* ata, clog, c*r*os, bacc*h*all, ministe*r* no soisgel .⁊c̄.

Fethal 'halidom', i.e. venerated object, namely bell, cross, crozier, service-set or gospel, etc.

8.13.35 Fo-coisle .i. foxl*adh*.
Fo-coisle 'takes away', i.e. taking away.

13.d.11.20 Fo-coisle .i. foxluig*h*.
Fo-coisle 'takes away', i.e. takes away.

10.5.5 F*or*ng*aire* .i. f*or*[con]g*ra* [... ⁊c an] ceimn*ughadh*.
Forngaire 'direction', i.e. command [...] etc., the progression.

10.45.118 Forng*aire* .i. f*orcon*gra.
Forngaire 'direction', i.e. command.

1.b.15.91 Góla .i. gorta quasi gula .i. c*r*aos.
Góla 'abyss', i.e. hunger; *quasi* 'as if' *gula* 'opening of the mouth, throat, gluttony', i.e. mouth.

5.b.4.32 Góla .i. gúala.
Góla 'prison', i.e. prison.

7.a.26.39 Iardac*h* ⟨.i. ait*h*gin⟩ .i. i*a*ram*h* dig*h*de .i. buidec*hus* i*ar*sin enecl*ann* ber*ar* i*ar*dac*h*.
Íartach 'restitution', ⟨i.e. restitution⟩, i.e. [< *íaram* 'afterwards' + *dígde* 'asking pardon'] afterwards pardon, i.e. good-will after the honor-price which is taken as restituion.

2.a.1.3 I*ar*doc[h] .i. i*ar* digde .i. buidec[h]*us* i*arum*.
Íartach 'restitution', i.e. [< 1 *íar* 'after' + *dígde* 'beseeching, asking pardon'] after beseeching, i.e. gratitude afterwards.

1.b.3.50 Iomaig*h* .i. iomain .i. tio*m*ain.
Imm-aig 'drives', i.e. driving, i.e. driving.

6.a.30.65 Iomaig*h* .i. iomain.
Imm-aig 'drives', i.e. driving.

4.c.23.116 Lait*h* .i. lion*n*.
Laith 'ale', i.e. ale.

9.4.11 Lait*h*, lat*hach* .i. sraid*h* .i. uisge [na] h-u*achtar* ⁊ cec*hair* na h-io*chtar*.
Laith 'puddle', *lathach* 'mire', i.e. way, i.e. the water of the upper part and the mud of the lower part.

4.c.13.78 Lia .i. comorba.
Lía 'successor', i.e. successor.

4.c.13.79 Lia .i. iomad.
Lía 'flood', i.e. abundance.

14.d.1.15 Met*h*ir .i. cert bi*us* im c*haoiradh* claim*h*, uinge d'i*ar*an*n*.
Meither 'covering', i.e. a piece of cloth which is around a mangy sheep, an ounce of iron.

14.d.4.17 [Met*h*ir .i. cert bi*us* im c*haoiradh* claim*h*, u]i[nge d'i*ar*an*n*.]
Meither 'covering', i.e. a piece of cloth which is around a mangy sheep, an ounce of iron.

4.c.8.57 Miod*h*b*h*a .i. m*eth*on bet*h*a inter bonu*m* et malu*m*.
Midba 'average', i.e. [< *medón* 'middle, center' + *betha* 'life, existence'] a middle life *inter bonum et malum* 'between good and evil'.

4.c.9.58 Miod*h*b*h*a .i. toraind.
Midba 'average', i.e. division.

4.c.14.82 N*ár* .i. naom*h*.
Nár 'honorable', i.e. holy.

8.23.58 N*ár* .i. fíor.
Nár 'honorable', i.e. true.

7.a.24.35 Oillían .i. léine m*h*ór.
Ollín 'item of clothing', i.e. large linen cloth.

2.b.20.108 Oillian, culpait .i. an léne cona h-all sgóit.
Ollín, *culpait* 'large linen cloth, hood', i.e. [< *oll* 'great, large' + *lín* 'linen, cloth'] the tunic with its large sheet.

14.d.3.16 Rud*h* .i. roid*h* .i. corc*air*.
Rud 'iron ore', i.e. madder, i.e. purple dye.

14.d.5.18 Rud*h* .i. ro[idh .i. corc]*air*.
Rud 'iron ore', i.e. madder, i.e. purple dye.

6.a.33.75 Ruib do-meal*ar* .i. ba, ⁊ caoir[e].
Rop do-melar 'an animal which is eaten', i.e. cows and sheep.

9.13.37 Ruib do-meal*ar* .i. ain*mnighth*e at*h*cogn*us* a ccuid m*ar* taid ba, caoir[e], ⁊ gob*air* ⁊c̄.
Ruip do-melar 'animals which are eaten', i.e. so named for chewing their share again such as cows, sheep, and goats, etc.

6.a.34.76 Ruib na doi*m*eal*ar* .i. capuill, ⁊ muca.
Rop ná tomelar 'an animal which is not eaten', i.e. horses and pigs.

9.13.38 Ruib ná to-meal*ar* .i. ain*mnighth*e [...]
Ruip ná to-melar 'animals which are not eaten', i.e. so named [....]

1.b.11.77 Seis .i. t*air*is .i. dén co*mnaigh*e.
Seiss 'you should sit', i.e. remain, i.e. do a staying.

1.b.11.78 Seis .i. ionsaigh.
Seis 'you should claim', i.e. claim.

8.34.90 Sern*ar* .i. s*r*eat*h*naig*h*t[h]*e*r.
Sernar 'is arranged', i.e. is arranged.

10.45.116 Sern*ar* .i. s*r*et*h*n*agh*t*ar*.
Sernar 'is arranged', i.e. is arranged.

3.b.6.34 Slab*h*ra tobra .i. sál b*húar* do-b[erar] do mnaoi *ar* coi*met* a genuis di.
Slabrae torbae 'marriage portion of profit', i.e. [< *sál* 'sea' + *búar* 'cattle'] sea of cattle which is given to a woman for preserving her chastity.

9.43.131 Slab*h*ra, slaib*h*re .i. sal b*huar* .i. bu*ar* tig t*ar* sal.
Slabrae, slaibre 'livestock', i.e. [< *sál* 'the sea' + 1 *búar* 'cows, cattle'] a sea of cows, i.e. cows which come across the sea.

8.37.103 Slatra.i. dánáu, no ainbḟiele.
Slatra 'bold', i.e. bold, or shamelessness.

7.b.23.90 Slatra ⁊ lat*r*a ⟨.i. ambfial⟩ ⟨.i. anb*h*al⟩ .i. ⟨láidir, dana⟩ *quasi more latrom*.
Slatra 'strong' and *latra* 'mighty', ⟨i.e. shameless⟩, ⟨i.e. shameless⟩, i.e. ⟨strong, bold⟩ *as if more latronum* 'in the manner of thieves'.

9.6.15 Tacomal .i. acomal .i. cengal.
Taccomol 'joining', i.e. joining, i.e. binding.

1.a.16.38 Tacomul .i. cengal.
Taccomol 'joining', i.e. binding.

4.b.2.5 [Taoi .i. an...]
Tóe 'silence', i.e. the [...]

8.18.44 Taoi, taoiet*us* .i. tosd.
Tóe 'silence', *taitius* 'stealth', i.e. silence.

6.a.23.44 Taith .i. an gru*th* tai*th*.
Táth 'a kind of cheese', i.e. the pressed curds.

10.41.97 Ta*th* .i. tai*th*mec.
Táth 'joining', i.e. dissolving.

4.c.24.121 Te*th*n[a]t*ar* .i. tai*th*mig*h*id .i. sgaoilid.
Tethnatar 'they will have broken', i.e. releases, i.e. bursts.

6.a.22.40 Te*th*natt*ar* .i. rotenn*s*at*ar*, no ro*th*esgsat.
Tethnatar 'they have cut', i.e. they broke, or they destroyed.

3.b.5.33 Tion*n*sgra .i. tionsgedol creice an tsiogail do b*erar* do mnaoi *ar th*oil go n-oige do b*eth* aice.
Tinnscra 'bride-price', i.e. beginning payment of the *sical*s which is given to a woman for the desire for her to be a virgin.

9.43.132 Tion*n*sg*r*a .i. tin*n*sg*et*al.
Tinnscra 'bride-price', i.e. beginning.

2.a.4.14 Toc*h*m*u*st*ar* .i. toib*h*ges.
Tochmastar 'which may be levied', i.e. which he levies.

2.a.18.65 Toc*h*m*ustar* .i. toib*h*git*h*er.
Tochmastar 'which may be levied', i.e. which is levied.

10.10.16 Torla .i. naidm.
Torla 'bond', i.e. a bond.

2.b.8.96 Torla .i. naid*h*m, ⁊ desm*erecht air*: cat*h* fer ferta, ⁊ *ara*i*le*.
Torla 'bond', i.e. a bond, and an example of it: battle of men of a boundary, etc.

4.c.14.85 Urlata .i. uasal laoite um*h*alóide.
Aurlatu 'obedience', i.e. [< *úasal* 'high, noble, honorable' + *lúaite* 'going'] honorable going of humility.

8.32.86 Urlata .i. uasal lúite.
Aurlatu 'obedience', i.e. [< *úasal* 'high, noble, honorable' + *lúaite* 'going'] honorable going.

APPENDIX 4

Sources Listed in TCD MS 1401 [H.5.30] and Marginalia

What follows is a list of the marginalia and their location within TCD MS 1401 [H.5.30]. For the marginalia which indicate Dubhaltach's source, the full name of the source text has been provided. The source abbreviations indicate the start of textual blocks of entries. For textual blocks of material, see the discussion on pp. 40–59 and Appendix 2. For discussion of some of the longer marginalia, see the Introduction, pp. 60–62.

p. 2a, l. 1, [b].n.: *Bretha Nemed.*
p. 2b, l. 1, d.r.: *Dúil* (*Roscadach*).
p. 3a, l. 14, Deo grát*ias* Senobia go ria. 'Thanks be to God, Zenobia thus far'.
p. 3b, l. 1, D.R.: *Dúil* (*Roscadach*).
p. 4c, l. 1, b.n.: *Bretha Nemed.*
p. 5a, l. 1, e[id]g*edh*: *Bretha Éitgid.*
p. 5b, l. 2, ⟨*edgedh*⟩: *Bretha Éitgid.*
p. 5b, l. 4, Duil .r.: *Dúil* (*Roscadach*).
P. 5b, l. 5, ⟨*edgedh*⟩: *Bretha Éitgid.*
p. 5c, l. 1, *edghedh*: *Bretha Éitgid.*
p. 6a, l. 22, [*ed*]g*edh*: *Bretha Éitgid.*
p. 6b, l. 1, duil .r.: *Dúil* (*Roscadach*).
p. 7, *marg. sup. intercol.* Do aitig*h*dl*us* an caide*r*ne si uile 'About proving is the subject matter of all of this'.
marg. sup. intercol. duil
marg. sup. sin. Duil.r.
marg. sup. dext. ...lioi
p. 7b, l. 4 *édgedh*: *Bretha Éitgid.*
p. 7b, l. 7 *édgedh*: This word seems to bookend the previous block of entries.
p. 7b, l. 24 eidg*edh*: *Bretha Éitgid.*
p. 7b, l. 26 duil: *Dúil* (*Roscadach*).
p. 7b, l. 28 duil: This word seems to bookend the previous block of entries.
p. 7b, l. 28 eidg*edh*: *Bretha Éitgid.*
p. 7b, *intercol.*, l. 33 duil: This word likely refers to the text *Dúil* (*Roscadach*).
p. 8, *marg. sin.* illegible note
p. 8, l. 38 aibgider c*r*ab*ad*: The one entry so marked is from *Apgitir Chrábaid* 'Alphabet of Piety'.

 | DOI:10.1163/9789004755673_011

p. 9, l. 1 IS é b.n: The reading is tentative. 'This is *Bretha Nemed*'.
p. 9, l. 4 coir an*mann* si*n*.: The one entry so marked is from *Cóir Anmann* 'Fitness of Names'.
p. 9, l. 4 d.r.: *Dúil* (*Roscadach*).
p. 9, l. 11 edgaid: *Bretha Éitgid*.
p. 11a, l. 1 [li]ber.2. Dubhaltach also writes 'L[iber] 2°' across the top margin of TCD MS 1316 [H.2.15A], p. 43 along with 'Senc[h]*us*.' Dubhaltach owned that section of the MS (Ó Muraíle 1996c: 375).
p. 11a, l. 2 *edged*: *Bretha Éitgid*.
p. 11b, l. 1 [Ad]bar eile d*a*rob ainm ⁊ ait*h*ne na mbean tet(*h*)a fein *ar* sgat*h* fer; ata d*r*eam diob*h* so, ⁊ ní h-*edh* ata drem oile. 'Other material for which there is the name and characteristic of the women who themselves go under the protection of men; some of these are here, and others are not'.[1]
p. 12b, l. 1 duil .r.: *Dúil* (*Roscadach*).
p. 13a, l. 1 Ben*nacht ar* an*main* Fac*ht*na/ do*m* seac*h*na *ar* an ngal*ar* n-egcoir.
A coi*m*de sa, M*ic* Mu[i]*r*a,/ na ⟨leg⟩ inne ar ett*r*eoir.
'A blessing on the soul of Fachtna/ to protect me from the unjust illness.
Oh, Lord, Son of Mary,/ do not abandon sense on account of weakness'![2]
p. 13a, l. 3 Glac*ad* talm*haidhacht* .i. gal*ar* mo*r* an la si*n* a*n* gab*us* a*n* rann si*n*.
Glacad talmaidechta 'epilepsy seized', i.e. a great illness on the day in which I recited that poem.[3]
p. 13b, l. 1 iosa
p. 13c, l. 1 Seac*h*ain se*acht* ngaoi gona an leigin*n* [.i.] ma dail g*ur*bad saor, sen, c*r*uit[h] is tiompan, pen*n* c*r*uaid*h* cen*n*dub*h*, fit*h*c[h]ioll, buanf*ach*, brandub[h], b[en].
Sechain secht ngae gona in léiginn 'avoid seven spears which wound learning', i.e. if someone pours [drink] though it may be free, song, harp and timbrel, a black-tipped rough pen, *fidchell*, *búanbach*, *brandub*, a woman.[4]
p. 13d, l. 8 Dudly Forbesse (This is the English version of Dubhaltach's name.)
p. 13e, l. 1 Senc*h*as: The block of entries above this word in the MS derives from *Cethairślicht Athgabálae* (*SM* 2).
p. 14a, ll. 1–3 D[ud]ly D
D D Dud
ly for

1 See the discussion in the Introduction on pp. 58–59
2 See the discussion in the Introduction on p. 60
3 See the discussion in the Introduction on p. 60
4 See the discussion in the Introduction on p. 61

p. 14e, l. 1 dub⟨alt⟩ fir⟨bis⟩
p. 14h, l. 13 [c].f.: The one entry so marked is from *Córus Fine*.
p. 14h, l. 16 c.f.: The entry likely derives from *Córus Fine*.

Bibliography

Manuscripts

Dublin, National Library of Ireland MS G.11
Dublin, Royal Irish Academy MS C.i.2 [1234]
Dublin, Trinity College MS 1287 [H.1.13]
Dublin, Trinity College MS 1315 [H.2.13]
Dublin, Trinity College MS 1316 [H.2.15A]
Dublin, Trinity College MS 1317 [H.2.15B]
Dublin, Trinity College MS 1336 [H.3.17]
Dublin, Trinity College MS 1337 [H.3.18]
Dublin, Trinity College MS 1363 [H.4.22]
Dublin, Trinity College MS 1387 [H.5.15]
Dublin, Trinity College MS 1401 [H.5.30]
London, British Library MS Egerton 83
London, British Library MS Egerton 88
London, British Library MS Egerton 158
London, British Library MS Egerton 1782
London, British Library MS Harley 432
Maynooth, Russell Library MS 79
Oxford, University of Oxford, Bodleian Library MS Rawlinson B.487
Oxford, University of Oxford, Bodleian Library MS Rawlinson B.506

Printed and Digital Primary Sources

Adhmad Glossary, ed. and trans. Alice Rebecca Taylor-Griffiths. In *Studies in Medieval Irish Legal Ancillary Material.* 2 vols. Unpublished Ph.D. dissertation: Department of Anglo-Saxon, Norse and Celtic, University of Cambridge (2020), 2: 40–64.

"The Advice to Doidin," ed. and trans. Roland M. Smith, *Ériu* 11 (1932): 66–85.

Aidbred, ed. and trans. Charlene M. Eska. In *Lost and Found in Early Irish Law: Aidbred, Heptad 64, and Muirbretha.* Medieval Law and Its Practice 36, 82–234. Leiden: Brill, 2022.

Aidbriugh Glossary: see *Bretha Nemed Dédenach* [glossary].

Aided Con Culainn, ed. A.G. Van Hamel. In *Compert Con Culainn and Other Stories.* Medieval and Modern Irish Series 3, 69–133. Dublin: The Stationery Office, 1933.

"Aithirne's Mother," ed. and trans. E.J. Gwynn. *Zeitschrift für celtische Philologie* 17 (1928): 153–156.

Ancient Laws and Institutes of Ireland, eds. and trans. W.N. Hancock et al., 6 vols. Dublin: His Majesty's Stationery Office, 1865–1901.

Annals of the Four Masters, ed. and trans. John O'Donovan. In *Annala rioghachta Eireann: Annals of the Kingdom of Ireland, by the Four Masters, from the earliest period to the year 1616*, 7 vols. 2nd ed. Dublin: Hodges, Smith & Co., 1856.

Apgitir Chrábaid, ed. and trans. Vernam Hull, in "*Apgitir Chrábaid*: The Alphabet of Piety." *Celtica* 8 (1968): 44–89.

Auraicept na n-Éces: The scholars' primer; being the texts of the Ogham tract from the Book of Ballymote and the Yellow book of Lecan, and the text of the Trefhocul from the Book of Leinster; ed. from eight manuscripts, with introduction, translation of the Ballymote text, notes, and indices, ed. George Calder. Edinburgh: John Grant, 1917.

Bechbretha: An Old Irish law-tract on bee-keeping, ed. and trans. Thomas Charles-Edwards and Fergus Kelly. Early Irish Law Series 1. Dublin: Dublin Institute for Advnaced Studies, 1983.

Bretha Comaithchesa, ed. and trans. W.N. Hancock et al. In *Ancient Laws and Institutes of Ireland*, 4: 68–159. Dublin: His Majesty's Stationery Office, 1865–1901.

Bretha Comaithcheso, ed. and trans. Thomas Charles-Edwards. Early Irish Law Series 9. Dublin: School of Celtic Studies, Dublin Institute for Advanced Studies, 2022.

"*Bretha Crólige*," ed. and trans. D.A. Binchy, *Ériu* 12 (1938): 1–77.

"*Bretha Déin Chécht*," ed. and trans. D.A. Binchy, *Ériu* 20 (1966): 1–66.

Bretha Éitgid, ed. and trans. W.N. Hancock et al. In *Ancient Laws and Institutes of Ireland*, 3: 82–547. Dublin: His Majesty's Stationery Office, 1865–1901.

Bretha for Catṡlechtaib, ed. and trans. Kevin Murray, in "*Catṡlechta* and Other Medieval Legal Material Relating to Cats." *Celtica* 25 (2007): 143–159.

Bretha Nemed Dédenach, ed. E.J. Gwynn, in "An Old-Irish Tract on the Privileges and Responsibilities of Poets." *Ériu* 13 (1942): 1–44, 57–60, 220–231.

Bretha Nemed Dédenach glossary, ed. E.J. Gwynn, in "An Old-Irish Tract on the Privileges and Responsibilities of Poets." *Ériu* 13 (1942): 54–56; *Aidbriugh* glossary, ed. and trans., Alice Rebecca Taylor-Griffiths. In *Studies in Medieval Irish Legal Ancillary Material*. 2 vols. Unpublished Ph.D. dissertation: Department of Anglo-Saxon, Norse, and Celtic, University of Cambridge (2020), 2: 13–39.

Bretha Nemed Toísech, ed. E.J. Gwynn, in "An Old-Irish Tract on the Privileges and Responsibilities of Poets." *Ériu* 13 (1942): 44–53, 232; for the first third of the text, see Liam Breatnach. 1989. "The First Third of *Bretha Nemed Toísech*." *Ériu* 40: 1–40.

"The Burning of Finn's House," ed. and trans. E.J. Gwynn and J.H. Lloyd. *Ériu* 1 (1904): 13–37.

Cáin Aicillne, ed. and trans. [into German] Rudolf Thurneysen, in "Aus dem irischen Recht I [1. Das Unfrei-Lehen]." *Zeitschrift für celtische Philologie* 14 (1923): 335–394.

"*Cáin Domnaig*," ed. and trans. Vernam Hull, *Ériu* 20 (1966): 151–177.

Cáin Ḟuithirbe, ed. and trans. Liam Breatnach, in "The Ecclesiastical Element in the Old-Irish Legal Tract *Cáin Fhuithirbe*." *Peritia* 5 (1986): 36–52.

Cáin Lánamna: An Old Irish Tract on Marriage and Divorce Law, ed. and trans. Charlene M. Eska. Medieval Law and Its Practice 5. Leiden: Brill, 2010.

Cáin Ṡóerraith, ed. and trans. [into German] Rudolf Thurneysen, in "Aus dem irischen Recht II [2. Das Frei-Lehen]." *Zeitschrift für celtische Philologie* 15 (1925): 238–260. Addenda and corrigenda in Rudolf Thurneysen, "Aus dem irischen Recht IV." *Zeitschrift für celtische Philologie* 16 (1927): 211–213.

Cethairṡlicht Athgabálae, ed. and trans. W.N. Hancock et al. In *Ancient Laws and Institutes of Ireland*, 1: 64–305. Dublin: His Majesty's Stationery Office, 1865–1901.

Coibnes Uisci Thairidne, ed. and trans. D.A. Binchy, in "Irish Law Tracts Re-edited: I. *Coibnes uisci thairidne*." *Ériu* 17 (1955): 52–85.

Cóic Conara Fugill: Die fünf Wege zum Urteil, ed. and trans. [into German] Rudolf Thurneysen. Abhandlungen der Preussischen Akademie der Wissenschaften. Jahrgang 1925. Philosophische-Historische Klasse. Nr. 7, Berlin: Der Akademie der Wissenschaften, 1926.

Cóir Anmann, ed. and trans. Whitley Stokes, in "*Cóir anmann* (Fitness of Names)". In *Irische Texte mit Wörterbuch*, ed. Ernst Windisch and Whitley Stokes 3, 285–444, 557. Leipzig: S. Hirzel, 1897.

Cóir Anmann: A late Middle Irish treatise on personal names, ed. and trans. Sharon Arbuthnot, 2 vols, Irish Texts Society 59 and 60. London: Irish Texts Society, 2005–2007.

Corpus Iuris Hibernici, ed. D.A. Binchy. 6 vols. Baile Átha Cliath: Institiúid Árd-Léinn Bhaile Átha Cliath, 1978.

Corpus genealogiarum Hiberniae, ed. M.A. O'Brien. Dublin: Dublin Institute for Advanced Studies, 1962.

Córus Bésgnai: An Old Irish tract on the church and society, ed. and trans. Liam Breatnach. Early Irish Law Series 7. Dublin: School of Celtic Studies, Dublin Institute for Advanced Studies, 2017.

Críth Gablach, ed. D.A. Binchy. Dublin: Stationery Office, 1941. 1970 reprint with addenda: Medieval and Modern Irish Series 11. Dublin: Dublin Institute for Advanced Studies.

Di Astud Chor, ed. and trans. Neil Mcleod, in *Early Irish Contract Law*. Sydney Series in Celtic Studies 1. Sydney: Centre for Celtic Studies, University of Sydney, 1991.

Dictionary of Irish Biography https://www.dib.ie/ Accessed July 31, 2024.

Díre-tract, ed. and trans. Rudolf Thurneysen. In *Irisches Recht.* [*I. Dīre. Ein altirischer Rechtstext. II. Zu den unteren Ständen in Irland*]. Abhandlungen der preussischen Akademie der Wissenschaften, Philosophisch-historische Klasse, Jahrgang 1931, nr. 2., 1–26. Berlin: Der Akademie der Wissenschaften, 1931, pp. 3–60.

Dúil Dromma Cetta https://www.asnc.cam.ac.uk/irishglossaries Accessed July 6, 2024. See also Whitley Stokes "Irish Glosses, edited by a member of the Council from a manuscript in the library of Trinity College, Dublin [H. 3. 18, p. 61, col. 1]." *Transactions of the Philological Society* 6 (1859 [*issued* 1860]): 168–215.

Dúil Laithne, ed. Whitley Stokes. In *Goidelica: Old and Early-Middle-Irish glosses, prose and verse*. 2nd ed. London: Trübner and Co., 1872, pp. 71–83.

Early Irish Glossaries Database, ed. Paul Russell, Sharon Arbuthnot, and Pádraic Moran. 2nd ed. Cambridge: Department of Anglo-Saxon, Norse and Celtic, 2009. http://www.asnc.cam.ac.uk/irishglossaries Accessed July 31, 2024.

Early Modern Letters Online http://emlo.bodleian.ox.ac.uk/home Accessed July 31, 2024.

eDIL 2019: *An electronic dictionary of the Irish language*, based on the Contributions to a Dictionary of the Irish Language. Dublin: Royal Irish Academy, 1913–1976. http://www.dil.ie 2019 Accessed July 17, 2024.

"*The Evernew Tongue*," ed. and trans. Whitley Stokes, *Ériu* 2 (1905): 96–162.

Félire Óengusso Céli Dé: The Martyrology of Oengus the Culdee, ed. and trans. Whitley Stokes. London: Henry Bradshaw Society, 1905.

Fidbretha, ed. and trans. Charlene M. Eska, in "The Early Irish Law Tract *Fidbretha* 'Tree-Judgments'." *North American Journal of Celtic Studies* 9 (2025): 38–53.

Findṡruth Fíthail, ed. and trans. Roland M. Smith, in "Fithal and Flann Fína." *Revue celtique* 47 (1930): 30–38.

Foclóir Gaeḋilge agus Béarla: An Irish-English dictionary, comp. and ed. Patrick S. Dinneen. Dublin: Irish Texts Society, 1927.

Foclóir Gaeilge-Béarla, ed. Niall Ó Dónaill. Baile Átha Cliath: Oifig an tSoláthair, 1977.

Foclóir nó Sanasán Nua: A new vocabulary or glossary, ed. Mícheál Ó Cléirigh. Louvain, 1643.

Fuidir-tract, ed. and trans. [into German] Rudolf Thurneysen. In *Irisches Recht.* [*I. Dīre. Ein altirischer Rechtstext. II. Zu den unteren Ständen in Irland*]. Abhandlungen der preussischen Akademie der Wissenschaften, Philosophisch-historische Klasse, Jahrgang 1931, nr. 2., 1–26. Berlin: Der Akademie der Wissenschaften, 1931, pp. 61–83.

Giolla na Naomh Mac Aodhagáin. *The MacEgan Legal Treatise*, ed. and trans. Fergus Kelly. In *The MacEgan Legal Treatise: An Early Modern Irish law-text by Giolla na Naomh Mac Aodhagáin (†1309)*. Early Irish Law Series 8. Dublin: School of Celtic Studies, Dublin Institute for Advanced Studies, 2020.

"The Glossary in Egerton 158," ed. Whitley Stokes. In *Archiv für celtische Lexikographie*, ed. Whitley Stokes and Kuno Meyer, 3, 145–214, 247–248, 290. Halle: Max Niemeyer, 1907.

Gormac glossary, ed. and trans. Alice Taylor-Griffiths, in "A Tale of Two Gormacs. A case-study in Reading Medieval Irish *glossae collectae*." *North American Journal of Celtic Studies* 6 (2022): 15–77.

Gúbretha Caratniad, ed. and trans. [into German] Rudolf Thurneysen, in "Aus dem irischen Recht III [4. Die falschen Urteilssprüche Caratnia's]". *Zeitschrift für celtische Philologie* 15 (1925): 302–370. Addenda and corrigenda in Rudolf Thurnseysen. "Aus dem irischen Recht IV." *Zeitschrift für celtische Philologie* 16 (1927): 214–229 and

Rudolf Thurnseysen. "Aus dem irischen Recht v." *Zeitschrift für celtische Philologie* 18 (1930): 353–356.

"Handbook of Gynaecology and Midwifery," ed. Winifed Wulff. In *Irish Texts 5*, ed. J. Fraser, P. Grosjean, S.J. and J.G. O'Keeffe. London: Sheed and Ward, 1934.

Heptad 64, ed. and trans. Charlene M. Eska. In *Lost and Found in Early Irish Law: Aidbred, Heptad 64, and Muirbretha.* Medieval Law and Its Practice 36, 238–317. Leiden: Brill, 2022.

Irish Glosses: A mediaeval tract on Latin declension, with examples explained in Irish, to which are added The Lorica of Gildas with the gloss thereon, and a selection of glosses from the Book of Armagh, ed. Whitley Stokes. Dublin: The Archaeological and Celtic Society, 1860.

"An Irish Penitential," ed. E.J. Gwynn, *Ériu* 7 (1914): 121–195.

Irish Script on Screen http://www.isos.dias.ie Accessed July 18, 2024.

An Irish-English Dictionary, ed. Edward O'Reilly. Edition with John O'Donovan's supplement. Dublin: James Duffy, 1864.

Irsan, ed. and trans. Pádraic Moran. In *De Origine Scoticae Linguae* (*O'Mulconry's Glossary*). Corpus Christianorum 7, 247–271. Turnhout: Brepols Publishers, 2019.

Isidore of Seville, *Etymologiae*, ed. W.M. Lindsay. In *Isidori Hispalensis Episcopi etymologiarum sive originum libri XX*, 2 vols. Oxford: Oxford University Press, 1911.

Keating, Geoffrey. *Trí Bior-Ghaoithe an Bháis*, ed. Osborn Bergin. Dublin: Dublin Institute for Advanced Studies, 1931.

"The Lecan Glossary," ed. Whitley Stokes. In *Archiv für celtische Lexikographie*, ed. Whitley Stokes and Kuno Meyer, 1, 50–100. Halle: Max Niemeyer, 1900.

Lexique étymologique de l'irlandais ancient, ed. J. Vendryes, E. Bachellery, and P.-Y. Lambert. Dublin: Dublin Institute for Advanced Studies / Paris: Centre National de la Recherche Scientifique, 1959–.

Llyfr Blegwryd, ed. Stephen J. Williams and J. Enoch Powell. 2nd ed. Caerdydd: Gwasg Prifysgol Cymru, 1961.

Llyfr Iorwerth, ed. Aled Rhys Wiliam. Cardiff: University of Wales Press, 1960.

Mac Fhirbhisigh, Dubhaltach. *Leabhar mór na ngenealach: The great book of Irish genealogies, compiled (1645–1666) by Dubhaltach Mac Fhirbhisigh.* 5 vols., ed. and trans. Nollaig Ó Muraíle. Dublin: De Búrca Books, 2003.

"A Medieval Glossary," ed. A.I. Pearson, *Ériu* 13 (1942): 61–87.

The Metrical Glossaries, ed. and trans. Whitley Stokes, in "On the Metrical Glossaries of the Mediaeval Irish." *Beiträge zur Kunde der indogermanischen Sprachen* 29 (1893): 1–120. Also published in *Transactions of the Philological Society* 22 (1894): 1–103.

The Metrical Dindsenchas, 5 vols., ed. and trans. E.J. Gwynn. Todd Lecture Series 8–12. Dublin: Hodges, Figges, & Co., 1903–1935.

Muirbretha, ed. and trans. Charlene M. Eska. In *Lost and Found in Early Irish Law: Aid-*

bred, Heptad 64, and Muirbretha. Medieval Law and Its Practice 36, 320–351. Leiden: Brill, 2022.

Ó Cléirigh, Mícheál. 1643. *Foclóir nó Sanasán nua: A New Vocabulary or Glossary*, Louvain.

"O'Clery's Irish Glossary," ed. and trans. Arthur W.K. Miller, *Revue celtique* 4 (1879–1880): 349–428, 479–480 and *Revue celtique* 5 (1881–1883): 1–69.

"O'Davoren's Glossary," ed. and trans. Whitley Stokes. In *Archiv für celtische Lexikographie*, ed. Whitley Stokes and Kuno Meyer, 2, 197–504. Halle: Max Niemeyer, 1904; and Whitley Stokes. *Three Irish Glossaries*. London: Williams & Norgate, 1862.

O'Mulconry's Glossary, ed. and trans. Pádraic Moran. In *De Origine Scoticae Linguae (O'Mulconry's Glossary)*. Corpus Christianorum 7, 125–245. Turnhout: Brepols Publishers, 2019.

The Passions and Homilies from Leabhar Breac: Text, translation and glossary, ed. and trans. Robert Atkinson. Dublin: Royal Irish Academy, 1887.

"A Poem on the Airgialla," ed. and trans. Máirín O Daly, *Ériu* 16 (1952): 179–188.

The Poems of Blathmac, ed. and trans. James Carney. In *The Poems of Blathmac Son of Cú Brettan: Together with the Irish Gospel of Thomas and a poem on the Virgin Mary*. Irish Texts Society 47, 2–88. Dublin: Irish Texts Society, 1964.

Pseudo-Historical Prologue to the Senchas Már, ed. and trans. John Carey, in "An Edition of the Pseudo-Historical Prologue to the *Senchas Már*." *Ériu* 45 (1994): 1–32.

Róa, cis lir-side?, ed. and trans. Fergus Kelly. In *Early Irish Farming*, Early Irish Law Series 4, 537–544. Dublin: School of Celtic Studies, Dublin Institute for Advanced Studies, 1997.

Sanas Cormaic https://www.asnc.cam.ac.uk/irishglossaries/ Accessed July 12, 2024. See also Whitley Stokes. *Three Irish Glossaries*. London: Williams and Norgate, 1862; Whitley Stokes and John O'Donovan. *Sanas Chormaic: Cormac's Glossary*. Irish Archaeological and Celtic Society, Calcutta: O.T. Cutter, 1868; and Kuno Meyer. "Sanas Cormaic. An Old-Irish glossary compiled by Cormac úa Cuilennáin, king-bishop of Cashel in the tenth century." In *Anecdota from Irish Manuscripts*, ed. Osborn Bergin, R.I. Best, Kuno Meyer, and J.G. O'Keeffe, 4, i–xix and 1–128. Halle: Niemeyer.

Slicht Othrusa, ed. and trans. D.A., in "Sick-Maintenance in Irish Law." *Ériu* 12: 78–134.

Stowe Glossaries, ed. and trans. Whitley Stokes, in "The Stowe Glossaries." In *Archiv für celtische Lexikographie*, ed. Whitley Stokes and Kuno Meyer, 3, 268–289. Halle: Max Niemeyer, 1907.

"Supplement to O'Reilly's Irish-English Dictionary", ed. John O'Donovan. In Edward O'Reilly, *An Irish-English Dictionary*, rev. ed., 557–725. Dublin: James Duffy, 1864.

Tecosca Cormaic, ed. and trans. Kuno Meyer. In *The Instructions of King Cormac Mac Airt*. Todd Lecture Series 15. Dublin: Hodges, Figgis, & Co., 1909.

Tochmarc Étáine, ed. Ludwig Christian Stern, in "Das Märchen von Étáin." *Zeitschrift für celtische Philologie* 5 (1905): 522–534.

Tract on Marriage and Divorce, ed. and trans. Fergus Kelly. In *Marriage Disputes: A fragmentary Old Irish law-text.* Early Irish Law Series 6. Dublin: School of Celtic Studies, Dublin Institute for Advanced Studies, 2014.

The Triads of Ireland, ed. and trans. Kuno Meyer. Todd Lecture Series 13. Dublin: Royal Irish Academy, 1906; Fergus Kelly. 2025. *The Triads of Ireland: An Old Irish wisdom text.* Dublin: School of Celtic Studies, Dublin Institute for Advanced Studies.

Tromdámh Guaire, ed. Joynt, Maud. Medieval and Modern Irish Series 2. Dublin: Stationery Office, 1941.

The Trotula, trans. Monica H. Green. Philadelphia: University of Pennsylvania Press, 2001.

Uraicecht na Ríar, ed. and trans. Liam Breatnach. In *Uraicecht na Ríar: The poetic grades in early Irish law.* Early Irish Law Series 2. Dublin: Dublin Institute for Advanced Studies, 1987.

"Urchuillti Bretheman," ed. Roland M. Smith. In *Irish Texts*, ed. J. Fraser, Paul Grosjean, and J.G. O'Keeffe, 4, 24–27. London: Sheed and Ward, 1934; Rudolf Thurneysen. 1930. "Aus den irischen Recht v." *Zeitschrift für celtische Philologie* 18: 362–364.

Secondary Sources

Abbott, T.K., and E.J. Gwynn. 1921. *Catalogue of the Irish Manuscripts in the Library of Trinity College, Dublin.* Dublin: Hodges, Figgis, & Co.

Ahlqvist, Anders. 1980. "Old Irish *bé, ben* 'Woman'." *Ériu* 31: 156–163.

Arbuthnot, Sharon. 2005–2007. *Cóir Anmann*: *A late Middle Irish treatise on personal names*, 2 vols, Irish Texts Society 59 and 60. London: Irish Texts Society.

Arbuthnot, Sharon. 2012. "Finn, Ferchess and the *rincne*: versions compared." In *The Gaelic Finn Tradition*, ed. Sharon J. Arbuthnot and Geraldine Parsons, 62–80. Dublin: Four Courts Press.

Arbuthnot, Sharon. 2019. "The Explanatory and Etymological Glosses in the Dictionary of the Irish Language." In *From Glosses to Dictionaries: The beginnings of lexicography*, ed. Chiara Benati and Claudia Händl, 123–144. Newcastle upon Tyne: Cambridge Scholars Publishing.

Arbuthnot, Sharon. 2021. "The Medieval Irish Vocabulary of Sex and Reproduction: Insights from the Trotula and other medical texts." *Kelten* 89: np. https://kelten.vanhamel.nl/k89-2021-arbuthnot-irish-literature-medieval-medicine Accessed July 2, 2024.

Arbuthnot, Sharon, Pádraic Moran, and Paul Russell. 2023. "The Celtic Tradition." In *Medieval Glossaries from North-Western Europe: Tradition and innovation*, ed. Annina Seiler, Chiara Benati, and Sara M. Pons-Sanz, 351–371. Turnhout: Brepols Publishers.

Barney, Stephen A., et al. trans. 2006. *The Etymologies of Isidore of Seville*. Cambridge: Cambridge University Press.

Binchy, D.A. 1938. "Sick-Maintenance in Irish Law." *Ériu* 12: 78–134.

Binchy, D.A. 1943. "The Linguistic and Historical Value of the Irish Law Tracts." *Proceedings of the British Academy* 29: 195–227, also separately paginated 3–35. In *Celtic Law Papers: Introductory to Welsh medieval law and government*, ed. Dafydd Jenkins. Studies Presented to the International Commission for the History of Representation and Parliamentary Institutions 42. Bruxelles: Les Editions de la Librairie Encyclopédique, 1973.

Binchy, D.A. 1952. "The Saga of Fergus mac Léti." *Ériu* 16: 33–48.

Binchy, D.A. 1960. "IE. *$Q^{u}E$* in Irish." *Celtica* 5: 77–94.

Binchy, D.A. 1966a. "*Bretha Déin Chécht*." *Ériu* 20: 1–66.

Binchy, D.A. 1966b. "Varia III [1. The Old Negative Form of *dia* 'if'; 2. (*bó*) *trelaeg*; 3. *Atromriug*; 4. The Date of the So-Called 'Hymn of Patrick']." *Ériu* 20: 229–237.

Binchy, D.A. 1973. "Distraint in Irish Law." *Celtica* 10: 22–71.

Binchy, D.A. 1981. "Brewing in Eighth-Century Ireland." In *Studies on Early Ireland: Essays in honour of M.V. Duignan*, ed. B.G. Scott, 3–6. Belfast: Association of Young Irish Archaeologists.

Binchy, D.A. 1984. "The Original Meaning of *co nómad náu* (*nó*); Linguists v. Historians?" *Celtica* 16: 1–12.

Blom, Alderick. 2024. "The Irish Glossary Tradition." In *Wörter—Texte—Schreiberhände/Words—Texts—Scribal Hands*, ed. Brigitte Bulitta and Stephen Pelle, 189–214. Berlin: De Gruyter.

Borsje, Jacqueline. 2010. "Rules & Legislation on Love Charms in Early Medieval Ireland." *Peritia* 21: 172–190.

Borsje, Jacqueline. 2012. "Love Magic in Medieval Irish Penitentials, Law and Literature: A dynamic perspective." *Studia Neophilologica* 84: 6–23.

Borsje, Jacqueline, and Fergus Kelly. 2003. "'The Evil Eye' in Early Irish Literature and Law." *Celtica* 24: 1–39.

Breatnach, Liam. 1981. "The Caldron of Poesy." *Ériu* 32: 45–93.

Breatnach, Liam. 1984. "Canon Law and Secular Law in Early Ireland: The significance of *Bretha Nemed*." *Peritia* 3: 439–459.

Breatnach, Liam. 1987. *Uraicecht na Ríar: The poetic grades in early Irish law*. Early Irish Law Series 2. Dublin: Dublin Institute for Advanced Studies.

Breatnach, Liam. 1989. "The First Third of *Bretha Nemed Toísech*." *Ériu* 40: 1–40.

Breatnach, Liam. 1990a. "Lawyers in Early Ireland." In *Brehons, Serjeants and Attorneys: Studies in the history of the Irish legal profession*, ed. Daire Hogan and W.N. Osborough, 1–13. Dublin: Irish Academic Press.

Breatnach, Liam. 1990b. "On the Citation of Words and a Use of the Neuter Article in Old Irish." *Ériu* 41: 95–101.

Breatnach, Liam. 1996a. "On the Glossing of the Early Irish Law-Texts, Fragmentary Texts, and Some Aspects of the Laws Relating to Dogs." In *Celtica Helsingiensia. Proceedings from a Symposium on Celtic Studies*, ed. Anders Ahlqvist, Tom Sjöblom, Glyn Welden Banks, and Harri Nyberg, 11–20. Helsinki: Societas Scientiarum Fennica.

Breatnach, Liam. 1996b. "On the Original Extant of the *Senchas Már*." *Ériu* 47: 1–43.

Breatnach, Liam. 2005a. *A Companion to the Corpus Iuris Hibernici*. Early Irish Law Series 5. Dublin: School of Celtic Studies, Dublin Institute for Advanced Studies.

Breatnach, Liam. 2005b. "Miscellanea Hibernica." In *A Companion to Linguistics: A festschrift for Anders Ahlqvist on the occasion of his sixtieth birthday*, ed. Bernadette Smelik, Rijcklof Hofman, Camiel Hamans, and David Cram, 141–151. Nijmegen: Stichting Uitgeverij de Keltische Draak.

Breatnach, Liam. 2006. "Satire, Praise and the Early Irish Poet." *Ériu* 56: 63–84.

Breatnach, Liam. 2011. *The Early Irish Law Text Senchas Már and the Question of its Date*. E.C. Quiggin Memorial Lecture 13. Cambridge: Department of Anglo-Saxon, Norse and Celtic, University of Cambridge.

Breatnach, Liam. 2016. "The Glossing of the Early Irish Law Tracts." In *Grammatica, Gramadach and Gramadeg: Venacular grammar and grammarians in medieval Ireland and Wales*, ed. Deborah Hayden and Paul Russell, 113–132. Studies in the History of the Language Sciences 125. Amsterdam: John Benjamins.

Buckley-Coogan, Jody. 2019. "Dlíthe Luath-Ghaeilge: Staidéar ar theanga agus ar dhátú gluaiseanna agus tráchtanna." Unpublished Ph.D. dissertation: School of Arts, English and Languages, Queen's University, Belfast.

Butler, Sara M. 2105. *Forensic Medicine and Death Investigation in Medieval England*. London: Routledge.

Byrne, Mary E. 1930. "On the Punishment of Setting Adrift." *Ériu* 11: 97–102.

Carey, John. 1990a. "The Two Laws in Dubhthach's Judgment." *Cambridge Medieval Celtic Studies* 19: 1–18.

Carey, John. 1990b. "Vernacular Irish Learning: Three notes: 2 *compóit mérda*." *Éigse* 24: 39–41.

Carey, John. 1992. "The Testimony of the Dead." *Éigse* 26: 1–12.

Carey, John. 2003. "An Anecdote about Aithirne in *Bretha Nemed*." In *The Celtic Heroic Age*, 4th, ed. John T. Koch and John Carey, 63–64. Aberystwyth: Celtic Studies Publications.

Carney, James. 1964. *The Poems of Blathmac Son of Cú Brettan: Together with the Irish Gospel of Thomas and a poem on the Virgin Mary*. Irish Texts Society 47. Dublin: Irish Texts Society.

Charles-Edwards, Thomas. 1993. *Early Irish and Welsh Kinship*. Oxford: Oxford University Press.

Charles-Edwards, Thomas. 2000. *Early Christian Ireland*. Cambridge: Cambridge University Press.

Charles-Edwards, Thomas. 2021. "Early Irish Law, St Patrick, and the Date of the *Senchas Már*." *Ériu* 71: 19–59.

Charles-Edwards, Thomas. 2022. *Bretha Comaithcheso*. Early Irish Law Series 9. Dublin: School of Celtic Studies, Dublin Institute for Advanced Studies, 2023.

Clancy, Thomas Owen. 2007. "Spaghetti Junction: OI *rót*, *rout*, ScG *ròd*, *rathad*, Scots *rod*, *rode*, English *road*, and some other minor by-ways." In *Fil súil nglais: A festschrift in honour of Colm Ó Baoill*, ed. Sharon Arbuthnot and Kaarina Hollo, 17–28. Tigh a' Mhaide, Brig o'Turk, Perthshire: Clann Tuirc.

Corthals, Johan. 2007. "Stimme, Atem und Dichtung: Aus einem altirischen Lehrbuch für die Dichterschüler (*Uraicept na Mac Sésa*)." In *Kelten-Einfälla an der Donau: Akten des Vierten Symposiums deutschsprachiger Keltologinnen und Keltologen (Linz/Donau, 17.–21. Juli 2005)*, ed. Helmut Birkhan and Hannes Tauber, 127–147. Vienna: Verlag der Österreichischen Akademie der Wissenschaften.

Corthals, Johan. 2010. "The *Áiliu* Poems in *Bretha Nemed Dédenach*." *Éigse* 37: 59–91.

Corthals, Johan. 2022. "*Coire Érmae*, the *Áiliu* Poems, and Virgilius Maro Grammaticus." *Cambrian Medieval Celtic Studies* 84: 1–11.

D'Arbois de Jubainville, Henri. 1895. *Études sur le droit celtique*, 2 vols, Cours de littérature celtique, 7, 8, Paris: Thorin et fils.

Dedio, Stefan. [In preparation] "On the Value of Cats in Medieval Welsh Law."

Eska, Charlene M. 2016. "*Recholl Breth*: Why it is a 'Shroud of Judgments'." In *Ollam: Studies in Gaelic and related traditions in honor of Tomás Ó Cathasaigh*, ed. Matthieu Boyd, 173–184. Madison: Fairleigh Dickinson University Press.

Eska, Charlene M. 2022. *Lost and Found in Early Irish Law: Aidbred, Heptad 64, and Muirbretha*. Medieval Law and Its Practice 36. Leiden: Brill.

Eska, Charlene M. 2025. "The Early Irish Law Tract *Fidbretha* 'Tree-Judgments'." *North American Journal of Celtic Studies* 9: 38–53.

Etchingham, Colmán. 1999. *Church Organisation in Ireland AD 650 to 1000*. Maynooth: Laigen Publications.

Flower, Robin. 1926. *Catalogue of Irish Manuscripts in the British Museum*, vol. 2. London: The British Museum.

Green, Monica H. (trans.). 2001. *The Trotula*. Philadelphia: University of Pennsylvania Press.

Green, Monica. 2005. "Flowers, Poisons and Men: Menstruation in medieval western Europe." In *Menstruation: A cultural history*, ed. A. Shail and G. Howie, 51–64. London: Palgrave Macmillan.

Griffith, Aaron, David Stifter, and Gregory Toner. 2018. "Early Irish Lexicography—A Research Survey." *Kratylos* 63: 1–28.

Gwynn, E.J. 1907. "On a Source of O'Clery's Glossary." *Hermathena* 14: 464–480.

Gwynn, E.J. 1909. "O'Clery's Glossary II [On a Source of O'Clery's Glossary]." *Hermathena* 15: 389–396.

Gwynn, E.J. 1928. "Aithirne's Mother." *Zeitschrift für celtische Philologie* 17: 153–156.

Gwynn, E.J. 1942 "An Old-Irish Tract on the Privileges and Responsibilities of Poets." *Ériu* 13: 1–60, 220–232.

Hallinan, Maria. 2019. "The Transmission of Irish Law in the Fourteenth and Sixteenth Centuries: Exploring the social and historical contexts." *Studia Celtica Posnaniensia* 4: 27–43.

Hindley, Katherine Storm. 2023. *Textual Magic: Charms and written amulets in medieval England*. Chicago: The University of Chicago Press.

Hull, Vernam, 1968. "*Apgitir Chrábaid*: The Alphabet of Piety." *Celtica* 8: 44–89.

Jasanoff, Jay. 1989. "Old Irish *bé* 'Woman'." *Ériu* 40: 135–141.

Jenkins, Dafydd. 1986. *The Law of Hywell Dda: Law texts from medieval Wales*. Llandysul, Dyfed: Gomer Press.

Karras, Ruth Mazo. 2012. *Unmarraiges: Women, men, and sexual unions in the Middle Ages*. Philadelphia: University of Pennsylvania Press.

Kelly, Fergus. 1976. "The Old Irish Tree-List." *Celtica* 11: 107–124.

Kelly, Fergus. 1988. *A Guide to Early Irish Law*. Early Irish Law Series 3. Dublin: Dublin Institute for Advanced Studies (2009 reprint with updated bibliography).

Kelly, Fergus. 1999. "Trees in Early Ireland." *Irish Forestry* 56: 39–57.

Kelly, Fergus. 2007. "Onomatopeic Interjections in Early Irish." *Celtica* 25: 88–107.

Kelly, Fergus. 2011. "The Recovery of Stolen Property: Notes on legal procedure in Gaelic Ireland, Scotland and the Isle of Man." In *Tome: Studies in medieval Celtic history and law in honour of Thomas Charles-Edwards*, ed. Fiona Edmonds and Paul Russell, 165–171. Woodbridge, Suffolk: The Boydell Press.

Kelly, Fergus. 2014. *Marriage Disputes: A fragmentary Old Irish law-text*. Early Irish Law Series 6. Dublin: School of Celtic Studies, Dublin Institute for Advanced Studies.

Kelly, Fergus. 2020. *The MacEgan Legal Treatise: An Early Modern Irish law-text by Giolla na Naomh Mac Aodhagáin (†1309)*. Early Irish Law Series 8. Dublin: School of Celtic Studies, Dublin Institute for Advanced Studies.

Kelly, Matthew (trans.). 1848–1854. *Cambrensis Eversus*. 3 vols. Dublin: The Celtic Society.

Kenny, Gillian. 2007. *Anglo-Irish and Gaelic Women in Ireland c. 1170–1540*. Dublin: Four Courts Press.

Knott, Eleanor. 1944. "O'Clery's Glossary and its Forerunners. A Note on Glossary-Making in Medieval Ireland." In *Measgra i gcuimhne Mhichíl Uí Chléirigh .i. Miscellany of historical and linguistic studies in honour of Brother Michael Ó Cléirigh, O.F.M., Chief of the Four Masters, 1643–1943*, ed. Sylvester O'Brien, 65–65. Dublin: Assisi Press.

Lynch, John. 1662. *Cambrensis Eversus*. Saint Malo.

Mac Airt, Seán. 1956. "Lexicographical Notes." *Celtica* 3: 262–271.

Mac Eoin, Gearóid. 1981. "The Early Irish Vocabulary of Mills and Milling." In *Studies on*

Early Ireland: Essays in honour of M.V. Duignan, ed. B.G. Scott, 13–19. Belfast: Association of Young Irish Archaeologists.

Mac Giolla Easpaig, Dónall. 2005. "The Significance and Etymology of the Placename *Temair*." In *The Kingship and Landscape of Tara*, ed. Edel Bhreathnach, 423–448. Dublin: Four Courts Press.

MacMathuna, Liam. 1976. "Some Words for '(Man-made) Ridge' in Irish: *fu(i)th(a)irbe; immaire, indra, indrad*." *Bulletin of the Board of Celtic Studies* 26: 445–449.

Mahon, William John. 1987. *Contributions to the Study of Early Irish Lexicography*. Unpublished Ph.D. dissertation: Department of Celtic Languages and Literatures, Harvard University.

McCone, Kim. 1986a. "Werewolves, Cyclopes, *Díberga*, and *Fíanna*: Juvenile delinquency in early Ireland." *Cambridge Medieval Celtic Studies* 12: 1–22.

McCone, Kim. 1986b. "Dubthach maccu Lugair and a Matter of Life and Death in the Pseudo-Historical Prologue to the *Senchas Már*." *Peritia* 5: 1–35.

McCone, Kim. 1997. *The Early Irish Verb*, 2nd ed. Maynooth Monographs 1. Maynooth: An Sagart.

McLaughlin, Roisin. 2008. *Early Irish Satire*. Dublin: School of Celtic Studies, Dublin Institute for Advanced Studies.

McLeod, Neil. 1987. "Interpreting Early Irish Law: Status and currency (part 2)." *Zeitschrift für celtische Philologie* 42 (1987): 41–115.

McLeod, Neil. 1991. *Early Irish Contract Law*. Sydney Series in Celtic Studies 1. Sydney: Centre for Celtic Studies, University of Sydney.

McLeod, Neil, 1996. "Property and Honour-Price in the Brehon Law Glosses and Commentaries." *The Irish Jurist* 31: 280–295.

McLeod, Neil. 1999. *Bloodshed and Compensation in Ancient Ireland*. Perth: Centre for Irish Studies, Murdoch University.

McLeod, Neil. 2002. "Compensation for Fingers and Teeth in Early Irish Law." *Peritia* 16: 344–359.

McLeod, Neil. 2004. "The Blood-Feud in Medieval Ireland." In *Between Intrusions: Britain and Ireland between the Romans and the Normans*. Sydney Series in Celtic Studies 7. Edited by Pamela O'Neill, 114–133. Sydney: University of Sydney.

McLeod, Neil, 2013. "The Lord of Slaughter." In *The Land beneath the Sea: Essays in honour of Anders Ahlqvists' contribution to Celtic studies in Australia*. Sydney Series in Celtic Studies 14. Edited by Pamela O'Neill, 101–114. Sydney: University of Sydney.

McManus, Damian. 1988. "Irish Letter Names and their Kennings." *Ériu* 39: 127–168.

Meyer, Kuno. 1901. "Mitteilungen aus irischen Handschriften." *Zeitschrift für celtische Philologie* 3: 17–39, 226–263, 447–466.

Meyer, Kuno (ed.). 1905. "Three Poems in *bérla na filed*." *Zeitschrift für celtische Philologie* 5: 482–494.

Meyer, Kuno. 1909. *A Primer of Irish Metrics*. Dublin: School of Irish Learning, Hodges, Figgis, & Co., Ltd.

Meyer, Kuno. 1910. "Mitteilungen aus irischen Handschriften." *Zeitschrift für celtische Philologie* 7: 297–312.

Meyer, Kuno 1918. "Mitteilungen aus irischen Handschriften (*Fortsetzung*)." *Zeitschrift für celtische Philologie* 12: 358–397.

Miller, Arthur W.K. 1879–1880. "O'Clery's Irish Glossary." Part 1. *Revue celtique* 4: 349–428, 479–480.

Mistry, Zubin. 2015. *Abortion in the Early Middle Ages c. 500–900*. York: York University Press.

Moran, Pádraic. 2019. *De Origine Scoticae Linguae* (*O'Mulconry's Glossary*). Corpus Christianorum 7. Turnhout: Brepols Publishers.

Murphy, Gerard. 1961. *Early Irish Metrics*. Dublin: Royal Irish Academy.

Murray, Kevin. 2007. "*Catślechta* and Other Medieval Legal Material Relating to Cats." *Celtica* 25: 143–159.

Ní Dhonnchadha, Máirín. 1994–1995. "*Caillech* and Other Terms for Veiled Women in Medieval Irish Texts." *Éigse* 28: 71–96.

Ní Mhaonaigh, Máire. 2022. "International Vernacularisation, c. 1390 CE: The 'Book of Ballymote'." In *Medieval Multilingual Manuscripts: Case studies from Ireland to Japan*. Studies in Manuscript Cultures 24. Ed. Michael Clarke and Máire Ní Mhaonaigh, 209–229. Berlin. De Gruyter.

O'Brien, M.A. 1932. "Varia IV: 7. Old Irish, etc. *uindse, ondar*." *Ériu* 11: 162–163.

Ó Corráin, Donnchadh. 2002. "Pica." In *The Field Day Anthology of Irish Writing*, vol. 4. Ed. Angela Bourke et al., 33–34. Cork: Cork University Press.

Ó Corráin, Donnchadh, Liam Breatnach, and Aidan Breen. 1984. "The Laws of the Irish." *Peritia* 3: 382–438.

Ó Cuív, Brian (ed. and trans.). 1975. "Three Middle Irish Poems." *Éigse* 16: 1–17.

O'Curry, Eugene. 1861. *Lectures on the Manuscript Materials of Ancient Irish History*. Dublin: James Duffy.

O'Curry, Eugene. 1873. *On the Manners and Customs of the Ancient Irish: A series of lectures*, 3 vols. London: Williams and Norgate.

Ó Fionnáin, Mark. 2023. *Colour Terminology in Modern Irish*. Leiden: Brill.

O'Grady, Standish Hayes. 1926. *Catalogue of Irish Manuscripts in the British Museum*, vol. 1. London: The British Museum.

Oliver, Lisi. 1993. "Forced and Unforced Rape in Early Irish Law." *Proceedings of the Harvard Celtic Colloquium* 13: 93–106.

Ó Muraíle, Nollaig. 1987. "The Gaelic Personal Name (An) Dubhaltach." *Ainm* 2: 1–26.

Ó Muraíle, Nollaig. 1996a. "'Aimsir an chogaidh chreidmhigh': An Dubhaltach Mac Fhirbhisigh, a lucht aitheantais agus polaitíocht an seachtú haois déag." In *Nua-*

léamha: gnéithe de chultúr, stair agus polaitíocht na hÉireann, c. 1600–c. 1900, ed. Máirín Ní Dhonnchadha, 89–117. Baile Átha Clíath: An Clóchomhar.

Ó Muraíle, Nollaig. 1996b. "Aspects of Intellectual Life in Seventeenth-Century Galway." In *Galway: History and society; interdisciplinary essays on the history of an Irish county*, ed. Gerard Moran and Raymond Gillespie, 149–211. Dublin: Geography Publications.

Ó Muraíle, Nollaig. 1996c. *The Celebrated Antiquary Dubhaltach Mac Fhirbhisigh (c. 1600–1671): His lineage, life, and learning.* (Revised ed. 2002). Maynooth Monographs 6. Maynooth: An Sagart.

Ó Muraíle, Nollaig. 1997. "Dubhaltach Mac Fhirbhisigh and County Galway." *Journal of the Galway Archaeological and Historical Society* 49: 22–35.

Ó Muraíle, Nollaig. 2003. *Leabhar mór na ngenealach: The great book of Irish genealogies, compiled (1645–1666) by Dubhaltach Mac Fhirbhisigh.* 5 vols. Dublin: De Búrca Books.

Ó Muraíle, Nollaig. 2004. "Linking Clann Aodhagáin with Mac Fhirbhisigh." *The Irish Genealogist* 11: 179–185.

Ó Muraíle, Nollaig. 2005. "Temair/Tara and other Place of the Name." In *The Kingship and Landscape of Tara*, ed. Edel Bhreathnach, 449–477. Dublin: Four Courts Press.

Ó Muraíle, Nollaig. 2012. "Dubhaltach Mac Fhirbhisigh: His life and significance." In *Pathfinders to the past: The antiquarian road to Irish historical writing, 1640–1960*, ed. Próinséas Ní Chatháin and Siobhán Fitzpatrick with Howard Clarke, 1–13. Dublin: Four Courts Press.

O'Neill, Pamela. 2017. "Old Irish *muirchrech* 'sea-boundary'." *Ériu* 67: 1–9.

O'Rahillly, Thomas F. 1913. "On the Terminations *-áiste, -iste*, etc." *Gadelica* 1: 283–292.

O'Sullivan, Anne, and William O'Sullivan. 1962. "Edward Lhuyd's Collection of Irish Manuscripts." *Transactions of the Honourable Society of Cymmrodoroin*: 57–76.

O'Sullivan, William. 1999. "The Book of Domhnall Ó Duibhdábhoireann, Provenance and Codicology." *Celtica* 23: 276–299.

O'Sullivan, William. 2000. "The Manuscript Collection of Dubhaltach Mac Firbhisigh." In *Seanchas: Studies in early and medieval Irish archaeology, history and literature in honour of Francis J. Byrne*, ed. Alfred P. Smyth, 439–447. Dublin: Four Courts Press.

Petrie, George. 1839. "Remarks on the Book of Mac Firbis, an Irish Manuscript Lately Transcribed for the Academy." *Transactions of the Royal Irish Academy* 18: 3–13.

Petrie, George. 1845. *The Ecclesiastical Architecture of Ireland, Anterior to the Anglo-Norman Invasion; Comprising an Essay on the Origen and Use of the Round Towers of Ireland.* Dublin: Hodges and Smith.

Plummer, Charles. 1916. "Notes on Some Passages of the Brehon Laws." *Ériu* 8: 127–132.

Plummer, Charles. 1926–1928. "Notes on Some Passages of the Brehon Laws. IV." *Ériu* 10: 113–129.

Power, Nancy. 1936. "Classes of Women Described in the *Senchas Már*." In *Studies in Early Irish Law*, ed. R. Thurneysen et al., 81–108. Dublin: Hodges Figgis & Co.

Richards, Melville (trans.). 1954. *The Laws of Hywel Dda (The Book of Blegywryd)*. Liverpool: University Press of Liverpool.

Riddle, John M. 1992. *Contraception and Abortion from the Ancient World to the Renaissance*. Cambridge, MA: Harvard University Press.

Riddle, John M. 1997. *Eve's Herbs: A history of contraception and abortion in the West*. Cambridge, MA: Harvard University Press.

Roberts, Brynley F. 2022. *Edward Lhwyd c. 1660–1709, Naturalist, Antiquary, Philologist*. Cardiff: University of Wales Press.

Russell, Paul. 1988a. "The Celtic Preverb **uss* and Related Matters." *Ériu* 39: 95–126.

Russell, Paul. 1988b. "The Sounds of a Silence: The Growth of Cormac's Glossary." *Cambridge Medieval Celtic Studies* 15: 1–30.

Russell, Paul. 1996. "*Dúil Dromma Cetta* and Cormac's Glossary," *Études celtiques* 32: 147–174.

Russell, Paul. 1999a. "Laws, Glossaries and Legal Glossaries in Early Ireland." *Zeitschrift für celtische Philologie* 51: 85–115.

Russell, Paul. 1999b. "*Moth, toth, traeth*: Sex, gender and the early Irish grammarian." In *History of linguistics 1996: selected papers from the Seventh International Conference on the History of the Language Sciences (ICHoLS VII), Oxford, 12–17 September, 1996. Volume I: Traditions in linguistics worldwide*, ed. David Cram, Andrew Linn, and Elke Nowak, 203–213. Amsterdam: John Benjamins.

Russell, Paul. 2005. "*Quasi*: Bridging the etymological gap in early Irish glossaries." In *A Companion to Linguistics: A festschrift for Anders Ahlqvist on the occasion of his sixtieth birthday*, ed. Bernadette Smelik, Rijcklof Hofman, Camiel Hamans, and David Cram, 49–62. Nijmegen: Stichting Uitgeverij de Keltische Draak.

Russell, Paul. 2008. *'Read it in a Glossary': Glossaries and learned discourse in medieval Ireland*. Kathleen Hughes Memorial Lectures 6. Cambridge: Department of Anglo-Saxon, Norse and Celtic, University of Cambridge.

Russell, Paul. 2017. "'Mistakes of all Kinds': The glossography of medieval Irish literary texts." *Proceedings of the Harvard Celtic Colloquium* 37: 1–32.

Russell, Paul. 2023. "*Do Dhubhfhoclaibh*: Word-Lists and glossaries in the Book of Uí Mhaine." In *Book of Uí Mhaine*. Codices Hibernenses Eximii III, ed. Elizabeth Boyle and Ruairí Ó hUiginn, 191–228. Dublin: Royal Irish Academy.

Sayers, William. "'Rincne Quasi Quinque' (*Sanas Cormaic*): Quantification, simile, and word-play." *Eolas* 8 (2015): 2–11.

Scott, B.G. 1983. "An Early Irish Law Tract on the Blacksmith's Forge." *The Journal of Irish Archaeology* 1: 59–62.

Sharpe, Richard. 2013. *Roderick O'Flaherty's Letters to William Molyneux, Edward Lhwyd, and Samuel Molyneux, 1696–1709*. Dublin: Royal Irish Academy.

Simms, Katharine. 1998. "The Contents of the Later Commentaries on the Brehon Law Tracts." *Ériu* 49: 23–40.

Skemer, Don. C. 2006. *Binding Words: Textual amulets in the Middle Ages*. University Park, PA: Pennsylvania State University Press.

Smith, Roland M. 1932. "The Advice to Doidin." *Ériu* 11: 66–85.

Stacey, Robin Chapman. 1994. *The Road to Judgment: From custom to court in medieval Ireland and Wales*. Philadelphia: University of Pennsylvania Press.

Stokes, Whitley. 1900. "A Collation of the Second Edition of O'Clery's Irish Glossary." In *Archiv für celtische Lexikographie*, ed. Whitley Stokes and Kuno Meyer, 1, 348–359. Halle: Max Niemeyer.

Stokes, Whitley, 1903. "On Dr Atkinson's *Glossary to vols. I–V* of the *Ancient Laws of Ireland*." *Revue celtique* 24: 404–407.

Stokes, Whitley. 1907. "The Stowe Glossaries." In *Archiv für celtische Lexikographie*, ed. Whitley Stokes and Kuno Meyer, 3, 268–289. Halle: Max Niemeyer.

Stüber, Karin. 2010. "Mit *cen* 'ohne' negierte Komplemente im Altirischen." *Zeitschrift für celtische Philologie* 57: 124–140.

Taylor-Griffiths, Alice Rebecca. 2020. *Studies in Medieval Irish Legal Ancillary Material*. 2 vols. Unpublished Ph.D. dissertation: Department of Anglo-Saxon, Norse and Celtic, University of Cambridge.

Taylor-Griffiths, Alice. 2022. "A Tale of Two Gormacs. A Case-Study of Reading Medieval Irish *glossae collectae*." *North American Journal of Celtic Studies* 6: 15–77.

Theuerkauf, Marie-Luise. 2024a. "The Irish Jerusalem: Etymological politics and the study of Greek in medieval Ireland." *Celtica* 36: 70–86.

Theuerkauf, Marie-Luise. 2024b. "*Dindshenchas Érenn* 'Knowledge of Ireland's Notable Places': The Theban origins of Tara." In *Classical Antiquity and Medieval Ireland: An anthology of medieval Irish texts and interpretations*, ed. Michael Clarke, Erich Poppe, and Isabelle Torrance, 353–366. London: Bloomsbury.

Thurneysen, Rudolf. 1923. "Irisches und Gallisches. 4. Der Nominativ zu air. *Roída*." *Zeitschrift für celtische Philologie* 14: 5.

Thurneysen, Rudolf. 1925a. "Aus dem irischen Recht II [2. Das Frei-Lehen; 3. Das Fasten beim Pfändungsverfahren]." *Zeitschrift für celtische Philologie* 15 (1925): 238–276.

Thurneysen, Rudolf. 1925b. "Aus dem irischen Recht III [4. Dia falschen Urteilssprüche Caratnia's; 5. Zur Überlieferung und zur Ausgabe der Texte úber das Unfrei-Lehen und das Frei-Lehen]." *Zeitschrift für celtische Philologie* 15 (1925): 302–376.

Thurneysen, Rudolf. 1928. *Die Bürgschaft im irischen Recht*. Abhandlungen der preussischen Akademie der Wissenschaften. Jahrgang 1928. Philosophisch-Historische Klasse. Nr. 2, Berlin: Der Akademie der Wissenschaften.

Thurneysen, Rudolf. 1933. "Allerlei Nachträge." *Zeitschrift für celtische Philologie* 19: 125–233.

Thurneysen, Rudolf. 1936. "*Cáin Lánamna*." In *Studies in Early Irish Law*, ed. R. Thurneysen, Nancy Power, Myles Dillon, Kathleen Mulchrone, D.A. Binchy, August Knoch, John Ryan, S.J., 1–80. Dublin: Royal Irish Academy.

Thurneysen, Rudolf. 1946. *A Grammar of Old Irish*, rev. ed. and trans. D.A. Binchy and Osborn Bergin. Dublin: Dublin Institute for Advanced Studies.

Tranter, Stephen J. 1997. "*Ut dixit Cicero*: A note on *De Dlighedh Gotha*." *Studia Celtica Japonica* 9: 11–17.

UC Davis Veterinary Medicine Center for Equine Health https://ceh.vetmed.ucdavis.edu/health-topics/glanders. Accessed July 4, 2024.

Valante, Mary. 1998. "Taxation, Tolls and Tribute: The language of economics and trade in Viking-Age Ireland." *Proceedings of the Harvard Celtic Colloquium* 18: 242–258.

Wycherley, Niamh. 2015. *The Cult of Relics in Early Medieval Ireland*. Turnhout: Brepols Publishers.

Alphabetical List of Entries

Subject Index

The topics in the index are referenced by page when they do not appear within the glossary itself and by glossary entry number when they appear within the glossary. When a topic is referenced in one of the notes associated with a glossary entry, it is referenced by the appropriate glossary entry number. When a topic appears in both, the pages numbers are given before the glossary entry numbers.